J.A. Parks

Principles & Practice of Valuation

Kolkata
Eastern Law House Private Ltd.
54 Ganesh Chunder Avenue
Kolkata (Calcutta) 700 013

New Delhi
Eastern Law House Private Ltd.
36 Netaji Subhash Marg, Daryaganj
New Delhi 110 002

J.A. Parks

Principles & Practice of Valuation

SIXTH EDITION

by

D.N. Banerjee
Former Chairman
Central Valuation Board
West Bengal

ASSISTED BY

Basudev Dey
Chartered Surveyor (UK)
Former Chairman, Institution of Valuers
West Bengal

Kolkata New Delhi
EASTERN LAW HOUSE

Published and processed by
EASTERN LAW HOUSE PRIVATE LTD.
54 Ganesh Chunder Avenue
Kolkata (Calcutta) 700 013
Tel: (033) 2215-1989/2301 Fax: (033) 2215-0491
Email: mail@elh.co.in • elh.cal@gmail.com
www.elh.co.in

First Edition 1942
Second Edition 1960
Third Edition 1965
Fourth Edition 1970
Fifth Edition 1998
Sixth Edition 2015

ISBN 978-81-7177-294-0

Printed at
Dey's Offset, Kolkata

Preface to the Sixth Edition

John A. Parks brought in the concept of valuation, particularly in the field of compulsory acquisition, because in 1942 when the book had come out with its maiden appearance, perhaps this was the only book relating to valuation of land & buildings. The process of industrialization agitated the field of valuation elsewhere in the West. But in spite of being late, John A. Parks was the figure who enriched this country with the techniques of valuation ahead of many countries of the world.

The concept of valuation pervades as an offshoot of the subject of economics in the various fields. Price and value are distinctly different since the days of Adam Smith who in 1776 wrote it in his famous book *Wealth of Nations.* Now it is covered by the techniques of valuation as a subject on a 'Cost Approach' basis with 'Market Approach' and 'Income Approach' to which I have chosen to bring in it another approach which is 'Benefit Approach', as because the practice of infrastructure development is now privatized like 'Build, Operate and Transfer (BOT)' and also other form like 'Build, Operate and Own (BOO)'. Since then privatization is mostly a feature that concerns Planning Commission of India for allocation of resources on priority basis. If a Highway is to be assessed with the establishment of township or a bridge on a river or a land on the opposite side to be connected by a underpass then allocation of resources which generally occupy as an advantage for the nation requires a series of discussions on the comparative advantage, reason being, it is neither 'Cost Approach' nor 'Market Approach' can do it, not even the 'Income Approach' out of investment made, it is difficult to ascertain at the stage of funding as to how development of such nature may evolve in future, if it facilitates new area to spill over like Hudson underpass linking New York with New Jersey, or Hong Kong underpass linking Kowloon with 'new territory' it becomes difficult to estimate as a method of development, particularly in case of privatization. When a bridge linking Kolkata with Howrah or a bridge over the river Tames in London is placed for valuation it has become somewhat possible today with the infiltration of computerized forms of comparison.

With the 'benefit method' as a devise in such emerging situation even possible now to be privatized which means some parties will bid for it and invest big amount in order to find out which one will be a proper estimate. Thus, the above consideration not to be prevalent techniques and usual practices of 'Cost Approach', 'Income Approach' and 'Market Approach' are inadequate. On all this consideration, the book is an exhaustive study in land acquisition method under the law of compulsory acquisition gliding over other fields of valuation like cost approach, income approach, and market approach including this emergence of benefit approach which has become the main thrust of the day. Now the book in which I have attempted a detailed study of the subject with as usual treatment as fiscal and non-fiscal both immovable and movable assets, it is treated as a unique contribution by the expert valuer for the purpose he deals with. This motive which impels me for this great job and if it proves as of similar benefits to the academic circle as well as an adjunct to the Faculty of Economics, I shall be amply rewarded.

Kolkata
14th February 2015 D.N. BANERJEE

Preface to the First Edition

In India today there must be thousands of so-called Valuation Experts and during the few years I have been in this country, I have heard many of them give evidence in valuation cases. The point which has most impressed me is the lack of the knowledge possessed by these "experts" of the principles governing a simple straightforward valuation. The English Valuation Text Books, which are numerous in number, do not assist the valuer in this country to any appreciable extent. They deal mainly with compulsory purchase under Special Acts of Parliament and which are not applicable to this country, and whilst the principles in many cases are the same, the method of application varies considerably.

This lack of knowledge is not confined to the expert, the following is an extract from a recent judgment in a Land Acquisition Court.

> "While an expert may give valuable evidence as regards the value of structures, I have often found it difficult to understand how the opinion of an expert as regards the value of the land itself can be of much assistance to the Court. If the opinion of the expert is based on materials like recent sales of land in the neighbourhood or the income yielding capacity and the state of the money market which justifies capitalisation at a certain rate, I do not see why these materials should not themselves be placed before the Court, so that the Court can make its own decision from the materials."

If these materials are placed before the Court without a witness giving evidence regarding the relative values of one site with another, how can the Court come to a fair decision in a particular case.

To assist students, valuers, pleaders, advocates and those gentlemen whose duty it is to decide valuation matters I have written this book. I have attempted to set out in a simple manner the principle and application of making a valuation of land and buildings. I have dealt with many aspects which have not been discussed before and if by the use of this book valuers and their legal advisers obtain "fair values" for their clients, the time taken in preparing this book will have been worth while.

In compiling this book I was assisted by a paper on the Valuation of Leasehold Interests and the effects of Income-Tax thereon written by W.R. Jenkins, Esq., B.Sc (Lond.), F.S.I, published in the Surveyor's Institution Journal, dated April 1942, a paper on the Valuation of Life Interests in Real Property and Reversions written by F.L. Collins, Esq., F.I.A., and published in the Surveyors' Institution Journal, dated April 1937, and for the two English Cases *"Colls v Home & Colonial Stores"* and *"Jolly v Kine"* I had to rely on "Curtis on the Valuation of Land and Houses". The Valuation Tables used for all the examples have been taken from Parry, third edition, and where logarithms have been used, they have been taken from Chambers Mathematical Tables.

Throughout this book I have been considerably assisted by the criticisms and advice of Mr. K.P. Chatterjee, M.A., B.L., Advocate of the Calcutta High Court and it is his legal knowledge and enlightenment of the case law on the subject that has made this book possible. Many thanks are also due to Ahmed Subhan, B.A. and Satya Charan Dutta, B.Sc., for the work they did after office hours typing the manuscript and I must acknowledge the invaluable help given to me by my Head Clerk, Monmotho Nath Banerjee, who corrected the proofs and supervised the printing.

Calcutta
20 December 1942 JOHN A. PARKS

Contents

CHAPTER PAGE

Table of Cases

Bibliography

The Appraisal of Real Estate, 9th Ed. (1987) by American Institute of Real Estate Appraisers, USA.

Aspects of Land Economics by W. Lean & B. Goodall (1966), London.

The A–Z of General Insurance by Paul Frankland, Singapore.

Basic Real Estate Appraisal by Richard M. Betts & Silas J. Ely, 2nd Ed. (1990), New Jersey.

The Concept of Private Property by Percy E. Wagner, Chicago.

Corporate Mergers Amalgamations & Takeovers by J.C. Verma, 3rd Ed. (1997), New Delhi.

Evolution of the Income Approach by James H. Burton, American Institute of Real Estate Appraisers, Chicago.

A Guide to the Depreciation and Valuation of Plant and Machinery (1989) by Australian Institute of Valuers and Land Administrators.

Guidance Notes by The Royal Institute of Chartered Surveyors, London.

Guidance Notes on the Valuation of Fixed Assets by The European Group of Valuers of Fixed Assets (TEGOVOFA), 2nd Ed. (1988), London.

Guidance notes with background paper on The Valuation of Fixed Assets by The International Assets Valuation Standards Committee, London.

Insurance Valuation by B.P. Holland (1987), Centre for Advanced Land Use Studies, College of Estate Management, White Knights, Reading.

International Valuation Standards by The International Assets Valuation Standards Committee, London.

Jems and Jewelry Appraising by Anna M. Miller (1988), New York.

Law of Acquisition of Land in India by P.K. Sarkar (1998), Eastern Law House, Calcutta.

Mahoney's Urban Land Economics by W.K.S. Christiansen, New Zealand Institute of Valuers, Wellington.

Modern Methods of Valuation by Britton, Davies & Johnson, 8th Ed. (1989), London.

Paper on Obsolescence in Valuation by Kirit P., Budhbhatti at Continuing Education Programme, Sardar Patel University, Gujarat.

Professional Practice Estimating & Valuation by Roshan Namavati, Mumbai.

Property Appraisal and Assessment Administration, Improving Real Property Assessment: A reference manual, Assessment Digest by International Association of Assessing Officers, Chicago.

Standard on the Valuation of Property affected by Environmental Contamination by International Association of Assessing Officers, Chicago.

Standard on Urban Land Valuation by International Association of Assessing Officers, Chicago.

The Real Estate Handbook edited by Maury Seldin & James H. Baykin, 2nd Ed. (1989), Illinois.

Theory & Practice of Valuation by Roshan Namavati (1987), Mumbai.

Theory and Practice of Valuation by A.K. Mitra, 2nd Ed. (1986), Eastern Law House, Calcutta.

The Valuation and Sale of Residential Property by David Mackmin (1989), London.

Valuation in Court (Immovable Properties) by Roshan Namavati (1984), Mumbai.

Valuation under Central Excise by R. Krishnan & R. Parthasarathy (1995), Delhi.

The Valuation of Real Property by A.E. Mirams (1938), Calcutta.

CHAPTER

1

Concepts and Theories of Value

VALUE is a word of many meanings. Value of any thing means its worth or utility as also the qualities inherent in the thing on which its utility or worth depends. Value can be defined as the power of one goods to command other goods in a transaction which is not vitiated with fraud, duress or ignorance. If a farmer is able to exchange a plough for five baskets of potato, we have a measurement of the comparative value of these two commodities. That is how the concept of value dawned on the society. The essential characteristics that a commodity must have in order to command value are the elements of utility, scarcity and transferability. Sunshine possesses utility but is not scarce in an open space. Rotten eggs may be scarce but possess no utility. A tiny island in the midst of an ocean may obtain the character of scarcity and utility but is hardly transferable. That is how the ultimate quality of value evaporates from these things. But this is just a general comment. Value can be added to each of these items in changed circumstances. Artificial sunshine can be brought inside a closed compartment and thus a value added to the original substance. Similarly, rotten eggs can be processed for useful utilisation provided a technology is evolved. Likewise, an island in the deep ocean may be brought under communication in course of time so as to lend it the colour of transferability. But till then all these things do not attract value in the sense the concept of value is generally understood.

Goods and services

So long we have been talking about tangible assets or goods meant for transactions or exchange. But we pay not only for goods we need but also for services we avail ourselves of. In this sense, "service" means an activity or performance that provides the need that people are willing to pay for, such need not being identical with that of tangible commodities or goods. Thus, we pay for education, health care, transport and communication, accounting, recreation, legal aid, financial support including banking and insurance, domestic help and the like. Rendering of service is often inter-twined with delivery of goods like after-sale services, repairs, etc. Services may be organised by the Government or a public agency, or by a private company or individual. As a matter of fact, service sector of the economy makes the major contribution in the advanced countries in building up their Gross National Product (GNP), that is, the value of the finished goods and services. This share may be more than one-half, because service industries depend more on performance by people than on machinery for their output. The volume of output rises as more of human resources are trained in different fields of economic activity. On the other hand raw materials for feeding industries are gradually becoming more scarce. As a result, dependence on research for better utilisation of existing tangible resources is gaining ground. That is how the service sector or the tertiary sector of the economy is gradually growing. The computer application in recent decades together with tourism industry have provided a strong stimulus to the growth of this tertiary sector, following agriculture and manufacturing industries in the primary and secondary sectors of the economy aided by intellectual property of human resources. All these services account for value.

Definition of valuation

Let us now look into some of the definitions of value or valuation as expressed in different dictionaries each different from the other in language, but essentially meaning the same. This will give an idea as to how the concept of value is conveyed in common parlance before we embark on its treatment on the technical sense it assumes in the discipline of valuation studies. In Webster's *New Twentieth Century Dictionary*, the word 'value' has been defined to mean—

"1. Worth, that property or those properties of a thing which render it useful or estimable: the degree of that property or of such properties, utility, power or capacity of procuring or producing good.
2. Price, the rate of worth set upon a commodity the amount for which a thing is sold: as, the value of a thing is what it will bring on the market.
3. Estimate of the intrinsic worth of a thing, appreciation: esteem.
4. Import: precise signification; as, the value of a word or phrase.
5. In music, the relative duration of a tone as signified by the note.
6. In political economy, worth, as estimated by the power of purchasing or being exchanged for other commodities, the quantity of labour or of the product of labour which will exchange for a given quantity of labour or of some other product thereof.
7. In the arts, the relation of the subjects or elements to each other; as, the values of colouring."

In some other everyday dictionaries, 'valuation' has been defined as the "act of determining the value or price of anything" or as an "estimation of a thing's worth specially by a professional valuer"; or as "the awareness or acknowledgement of the quality, nature, excellence or the like of something."

The Oxford Advanced Learner's Dictionary (8th Ed.), gives the following definition of "value":

"1. how much something is worth in money or other goods for which it can be exchanged;
2. how much something is worth compared with its price;
3. the quality of being useful or important;
4. beliefs about what is right and wrong and what is important in life; moral values;
5. the amount represented by a letter or symbol (as in mathematics)".

Likewise, the word "valuation" has been defined there as:

"1. a professional judgment about how much money something is worth, its estimated value;

2. a judgment about how useful or important something is; its estimated importance."

It would appear that the value of a thing is usually measured with reference to its price, but when we speak of the price of anything we do not necessarily mean the value or the market value of the thing. Again, value or valuation of anything and its price cannot be the same except by coincidence. Hadley has stated "a price is a fact and a value is an estimate of what the price ought to be". We shall, however, deal with it more elaborately in the next chapter.

Science and art of valuation

In India, the science and art of valuation began with assessment of compensation in compulsory acquisition of land under the Land Acquisition Act of 1894 which is repealed and replaced by the Right to Fair Compensation and Transparency in Land Acquisition, Rehabilitation and Resettlement Act 2013. That is why valuation has taken the colour of estimating the market value of land and building on the basis of which compensation is assessed. But the very idea of compensation payable under a law of acquisition suggests that such compensation is in the nature of an indemnity or compensatory damage which results in limiting recovery to the market value of the condemned property even when the property was worth to the owner much more than the market value. Thus, valuation for compulsory acquisition is a typical valuation relevant in the field of exercise of the power of eminent domain by the State.

But valuation is now practised in multiple other contexts. Any single definition of value hardly satisfies the multiplicity of uses to which the term is put under modern practices. The same property may simultaneously have different value for different purposes or under different situations. In other words, when we come across the expression 'value of the property' in diverse contexts, the sense that it carries for one purpose or in one situation may be quite different from that in which it is used for another. The diverse purposes for which valuation becomes necessary may include the contingencies of sale, mortgage, rent-fixation, land acquisition, levy of betterment charges, municipal taxation, levy of stamp duty on transfer of property, auction reserve, court fees and probate, loss recovery on insurance, preparation of financial statement of companies and also fiscal requirements for wealth tax, income tax, gift tax, capital gains etc. In this way, valuation finds different basis for different purposes and also assumes different meaning in different situations.

Value-in-use and value-in-exchange

At the first instance, distinction has to be made between VALUE-IN-USE and VALUE-IN-EXCHANGE. If a commodity is capable of being used and providing satisfaction, it has VALUE-IN-USE. Thus VALUE-IN-USE means utility although the commodity may or may not have any value in the exchange market. Air has a VALUE-IN-USE but it has no market value. The elements of scarcity and transferability convert a commodity of VALUE-IN-USE into a commodity having VALUE-IN-EXCHANGE. Thus the same air bottled in a cylinder may become a commodity of VALUE-IN-EXCHANGE to patients or hill-climbers. VALUE-IN-USE is essentially non-market related. In the field of valuation, the expression is used to denote the value that a specific property has for a specific use to a specific user, although such value may not be translated in monetary terms in the exchange market. As we have already seen, value is an estimate of price and pricing always takes place under conditions of marketing dependent on the forces of supply and demand. A commodity obtains VALUE-IN-EXCHANGE only in a situation where marketing takes place, although it is not synonymous with price.

Different kinds of value

The expression 'MARKET VALUE' has been a subject-matter of decision in the courts of law in connection with proceedings of land acquisition, wealth tax or income tax. It has been looked at from various angles focussing light on its various facets. But essentialy, 'MARKET-VALUE' has been defined as the estimated amount for which a property should exchange on the date of valuation between a willing buyer and a willing seller in an arm's-length transaction after proper marketing. The matter has been discussed in detail in a subsequent chapter.

The expression 'MARKET VALUE' has been further chiselled as 'OPEN MARKET VALUE' to mean value of the property offered for sale in a market in such manner that every person who desires to purchase can make an offer and due publicity of the sale has been made to induce conditions of marketing appropriate to the commodity under the most favourable conditions. Thus a precious diamond when put on sale in the immediate market may not find a buyer, but that does not mean that it has no value. In order to provide for an open market condition for its sale, due publicity has to be given in an appropriate manner to bring the proposed sale to the notice of the class of intending purchasers to whom the diamond has value and also the time necessary to make a decision on marketing.

FAIR VALUE means the amount that will fairly compensate an owner who was involuntarily deprived of the economic enjoyment of a property where there is neither a willing buyer nor a willing seller. It is not necessarily intended to reflect a likely market transaction price for the subject property, because the owner did not initiate a market transaction. FAIR VALUE is thus primarily a legal concept specific to particular jurisdictional statutes involving expropriations, condemnations, infringements etc. in exercise of the power of the eminent domain.

'LIQUIDATION OR FORCED SALE VALUE' means the amount which may reasonably be expected to be obtained from the sale of a property within a time-frame too short to obtain a value under open market conditions. The seller may be an unwilling seller and the buyer may be motivated by the knowledge of the disadvantage the seller suffers from.

POTENTIAL VALUE is estimated in a situation when a property has got an inherent value which may enhance with the passage of time or in some alternative use within sight. It often happens that some planning proposals in the offing or some developmental project in contemplation of an appropriate authority offers a better prospect for beneficial user of a property in forseeable future. The inherent quality of the property itself might create condition for its particular suitability for such better use. The evaluation of potenial value becomes relevant in such situation.

SPECIAL VALUE arises when a property offered for sale is of a specialised nature and has a utility restricted to particular use or user. Property specially designed or meant for special purposes account for special value, particularly those which have a unique feature or location. It may also arise on account of a premium that a purchaser is too willing to pay for having a special interest in the property.

SALVAGE VALUE is attached to a property which has already run its useful span of life but has not become absolutely useless inasmuch as the materials it contains may be disposed of for value. SALVAGE VALUE may also be obtained for a property the useful life of which has been brought to an abrupt end owing to any accident or natural calamity. The concept of SALVAGE VALUE is that the property is valued for salvage disposal rather than the purpose it was originally intended for. In accounting terminology it is also termed as the net realisable amount for an asset with no further use to an enterprise. Though SALVAGE VALUE refers to a property which has outlived its useful span of existence, it does not necessarily imply that the property has no further utility. It is possible that the property could be rebuilt or converted to a similar or different use with renovation. When that is also not possible it yields place to SCRAP VALUE or DEMOLITION VALUE.

REPLACEMENT VALUE is obtained by working out the present cost of equivalent property as distinguished from identical property. When referred to portions of such property, it means the cost of replacement of such portions at current market rates to provide equivalent benefits. When a property is to be substituted by an identical property, both qualitatively and quantitatively in all respects, we get REPRODUCTION VALUE instead of REPLACEMENT VALUE. But substitution by an identical property proves often a myth in view of the fact that each property is somewhat unique when the subject matter is land and building. But all properties, no matter how varied they are in physical attributes or geographical locations, are economically substitutable in terms of service utility or income productivity. Therein lies the significance of the concept of REPLACEMENT VALUE.

The Replacement Value is often computed on the basis of DEPRECIATED REPLACEMENT COST which is a method of valuation based on an estimate of the current market value of the land for its existing use to which is added the current gross replacement costs of improvements less allowances for physical deterioration and obsolescences. Because of land's unique characteristics, when land is valued separately from improvements to or upon the land, economic principles require that improvements to or on the land be valued as they contribute to the total value of the property.

EXISTING USE VALUE of a property contemplates its continued use for the same application as of the date of valuation having regard to the capacity of the property to continue to maintain the same service utility or income productivity, but not considering alternative or more probable uses, if sold. Such use has to be distinguished from HIGHEST AND BEST USE which means that use of the property, from among all reasonably probable or alternative uses, which is found to be physically possible, financially feasible, legally permissible and economically desirable.

RATEABLE VALUE of a property means the value as are entered in the assessment book of the concerned local body or municipality which forms the basis of levy of tax on the land and building comprised in the property. Such RATEABLE VALUE is generally the gross annual rent at which the property, *i.e.* land and building may reasonably be expected to let from year to year, less in the case of building, a statutory allowance towards repairs and maintenance to enable the building to command the rent. In case of property which are not usually let out or the rental value of which cannot be easily estimated, such rateable value is reckoned as a specified percentage of the capital value thereof.

INVESTMENT VALUE is the value of a property to a particular investor, or a class of investors for specified investment objectives. INVESTMENT VALUE should be distinguished from the market value of an investment property inasmuch as investment value is subjective in nature being the value referable to specific investor or group of investors and that too, for the purpose of investment with identified objectives which includes guidelines for investment. Such guidelines may prescribe a specified percentage of income after tax deduction, internal rate of return in cash or in commercial use of the asset for a specified number of years etc.

INSURABLE VALUE means the value of a property as ascertained on the basis of definitions or methodology contained in the terms of contract of the insurance policy.

DEPRIVAL VALUE of a property is applicable only to the present owner to whom the property has a special utility value from which he is deprived on account of the asset's exit from use or its disposal. The valuation of a DEPRIVAL VALUE is on the basis of non-market concept of VALUE-IN-USE which often overrides the VALUE-IN-EXCHANGE.

BOOK VALUE is known as the value of a property as entered in the books of accounts of a company or organisation representing its original or historical cost of acquisition as diminished by cumulative depreciation till the year when accounting is made. The market value of the property may remain constant over the period or may also increase depending on market situation, but the BOOK VALUE will gradually go downwards commensurate with the rate of depreciation.

COLLATERAL VALUE means the amount that the creditor will be willing to loan upon the subject property offered as security for repayment. It is often (but not always) deemed as a percentage of its fair market value or its market value on a stand-alone basis. This is reasonable because the lender is really interested in how much he can recover out of an eventual sale if the borrower fails to meet the loan obligations and the lender has to foreclose on the collateral property according to the provisions of law.

SENTIMENTAL VALUE occurs owing to any particular sentiment motivating the vendor or the purchaser in the transaction of the property that may not reflect its actual market price. The owner may be very much attached to the property to demand a fancy price and on the contrary, the purchaser may find the property ideally suited for his purpose and hence prepared to pay a fancy price. Sometimes, purchasers compete with each other in obtaining a property with higher price than what the market commands in a bid to satisfy their sentiment of predominance accounting for sentimental value of the property.

RESIDUAL VALUE is the net realisable value of the asset at the end of its useful economic life based on prices prevailing at the date of valuation. Net realisable value is the realisable value less the estimated cost of realisation.

REVERSIONARY VALUE is computed when a property given on lease reverts back to the owner on the expiry of a specified period of lease. It is calculated as the present worth of the future benefit of such reversion.

GOING CONCERN VALUE is an important concept in the realm of valuation. It is expressed in terms of value ascribed to an established business, not to its constituent parts. There is often a fallacy in the popular assumption that the value of an organic whole is equal to the sum of the values of its parts. This is particularly true about going concerns. Sometimes, an enterprise possesses special production rights, extraordinary contracts, unique patents and licences, know-how or expertise of specialised nature, special goodwill and other intangible properties which may not be transferable to another owner even if the enterprise passes on to another hand. In such situation the value allocated or apportioned to the individual components of the business property based upon their respective contribution to the whole, may not reflect the actual value of the business itself. The actual value may be much more as the concern smoothly goes on. This approach to value is particularly relevant in the field of valuation for the purpose of financial reporting. The individual assets in such case have no GOING CONCERN VALUE but the total business has as it comprises the net value of all tangible and intangible assets of an enterprise measured after consideration of all liabilities. The underlying assumption is that value is created by a proven business operation and also that the business will continue and the enterprise will carry on its operation for the forseeable future.

CHAPTER

2

Value, Price and Cost

Value, in economics, means the power of a commodity to command other commodities in exchange. Value relates to the terms upon which one commodity exchanges for others.

Early theories of value were theories of what governs prices in the long run. As a matter of fact, the theory of prices is sometimes spoken of as a theory of value. The late Victorian School stressed the psychological aspect of value, but failed to draw any distinction between it and price. According to Professor Alexander, amalgamation of the object with human appreciation of it is implied in value. In other words, economic value is not inherent in material objects, but is attached to them by human appreciation. This is a philosophic theory which is not essentially different from a psychological concept of the Victorian School. But the difficulty arises how to measure the philosophic value when the question is to compensate a person for the loss of a house built by his ancestors. To such a person, the psychological attachment may be immense but it may not reflect the economic value. When it boils down to the question of measurement of economic value in the market context, psychological or philosophic value do not act as the sole guide.

It is interesting to look into the definition given by John Ruskin. He says: 'Value is the life-giving power of anything, cost the quality of labour required to produce it, price the quantity of labour which the producer will take in exchange'. This is perhaps more of a literary conception. But for generations, it was held that the value of an object ought always to equal the sacrifice required for its production. Adam Smith harped on this aspect when he stated that 'The real price of everything, and what everything really costs to the man who wants to acquire it, is the toil and trouble of acquiring it'. Ricardo says: 'the value of a commodity or the quantity of any other commodity, for which it will exchange, depends on the relative quantity of labour which is necessary for its production'. Thus, land and labour were considered the two natural denominators of value. In a different vein, according to J.S. Mill: 'Value is a relative term, the value of a thing means the quantity of some other thing or things in general which it exchanges for'. But this definition do not carry us any further as there is no ratio between the two objects so exchanged except in a mind which measures them both. As pointed out by Professor Dibblee, the well-known Oxford economist, the study of the mind in such case becomes as essential to the determination as is a study of the objects. We are thus inevitably made to fall back on the relative prices. He says: 'Obviously, the quantity of some one thing for which the quantity of some other thing will exchange is the price of the latter, expressed in terms of the former and *vice versa*. But value is not necessarily the price of a thing'.

Value and price

Value must not be confused with price. A commodity's price means its exchange power reckoned in terms of money, while value means its exchange power determined or estimated in terms of other commodities.

Price is essentially the worth of a commodity measured in terms of standard monetary unit as determined in the market and it must never be assumed that the terms are synonymous for all purposes. If value can be defined as the power of one commodity to command other commodities in transactions it must be in a situation uninfluenced by extraneous circumstances that bear upon the price in a market. The extraneous circumstances may be of various kinds. The passing of a rent control law may be the means of causing a slump in land values. The lowering of interest in government securities may have the effect of making more money available for investment in property. The collapse of share market may also have the same effect of rush towards alternative investments.

Abnormal conditions like war may tend to increase land values, but the general public always look upon investment in land as a safe security, even if the return in many instances may be very low. On the other hand, serious upheaval like communal riots or extremist activities may cause prices to drop to an appreciable level for some years, although there may not be any possibility of further trouble. Thus, rise and fall can occur in a very short space of time. In this context, the long run trend of prices enter into the process of valuation. But the science and art of valuation has gone beyond it. As a reasonable estimate of price, it ought to take into account the sedimentation of price level after the dust and storm of transient events settle down. It is essential to study how prices are, or should be, fixed against the background of a given organisation or society in a given context of social institutions.

The obvious distinction between price and value can be further explained with reference to the price level. If, according to the prevailing purchasing power of currency within a country, a house is valued as worth three motor cars, five refrigerators, and six computers taken together, then the respective value may remain unchanged even when the price of each of the commodities uniformly undergoes manifold rise as a result of havoc in the general price level caused by sudden inflation, as happened in the erstwhile Soviet Union after its collapse. In this case, the price of each of the commodities has changed but not the value. If, however, the price of a single commodity out of the bundle undergoes revision, it becomes a matter for estimating the value.

Since value is an estimate of price as it ought to be, we are faced with two distinct set of problems—first, we have to analyse how pricing does in fact takes place; and secondly, we have to find out how ideally it ought to work in the context of prevalent situation undergoing changes in the foreseeable future. The function of price is actually to ration a limited supply of goods amongst the consumers. In balancing supply and demand, prices perform an important social function on being projected at the point of intersection of the supply curve and demand curve on a geometric diagram. On the one side, it reflects how much things are worth to the consumers; on the other, it represents the scarcity of things and the cost of making them available to the consumer. Even then pricing is not always an accurate index. The higher bidders for whom the goods have great utility are able to buy what they want so intensely. But high prices mean less to a rich man than to a poor man, so that those who buy goods are not necessarily those for whom the goods have the most utility. On the other hand, the person having the highest utility may not be able to opt for the goods simply because the marginal value of limited money at his disposal is much too high for the price payable for the goods. If the import of price is thus often person-specific, value is all the more so. For instance, the value of wines in a society of teetotallers may hardly be anything, but in a society of hardened drinkers, it may assume considerable value. The rise in air-fare may have no value to a common poor villager while he is hard hit when the bus fare in the rural route rises. Likewise, a landlord constrained by the Rent Control Act finds no change in the value of his property even amidst a boom in the market prices of real estate as because his income is fixed by way of rent from a tenant whom he cannot evict. Thus, in valuation you have always to ask as to whom the valuation should be made for. Being person-specific valuation is not a uniform exercise for all.

Value and utility

In order to possess value an article must have utility, that is, it must have the want-satisfying power. Thus, food has value and so has clothing, as because, those who consume or use the said commodities derive some satisfaction from such consumption or use. Hence, they desire them because of the utility they possess. That is why these products have a demand and consequently find a market. But the demand in order to be effective in economics must be backed by purchasing power. No article will account for value if those who want it have no monetary means or commodities in possession to offer in exchange.

Value and scarcity

In order to possess value, an article must be scarce, that is, it must be so limited in supply as to exclude free availability and those who opt for it must be ready to part with something in exchange, be it in the form of money or some other goods or services. Because, none will supply such limited resources unless he gets something else in exchange for it. Air or sunshine has great utility but seldom any value. There is so much of it that ordinarily everyone can have any quantity without paying for it. But under certain circumstances, air or sunshine can also be scarce. For example, compressed air is bought and sold.

Value and transferability

Transferability in economics means marketability. Unless an article is capable of being passed on from one hand to another, it does not obtain a market for transaction and consequently is of no value in exchange. The transferability has several aspects to be considered. First of all, traditional economy withholds many items from marketability. For example, a mother out of love, cooks for the family, a grandfather offers free tuition to his grandchildren, a sister offers free nursing to her brother. These services lie imbedded in the non-monetary sector and are not generally brought out for transfer in the market. Let us look at transferability in another profile. A person who transfers by way of sale any property, has in the back of his mind the dominating consideration that the value of the money transaction fetches has a preference to him to the property transacted. Correspondingly, the person who buys has a preference for the property than the money parted with by way of price. That is how a transaction is motivated. Now, there are various issues as regards the item of transfer as well. In ancient days, even human beings were bought and sold for slavery. Now, whether it still exists in some form or other is a debatable issue. Bonded labour is a glaring example in some countries and so is traffic in women. But the fact remains that human skill or efficiency, by and large, is something that is inseparable from the owner and hence non-marketable, but the services out of it or the intellectual property it may yield is a commodity that accounts for value in market and that now in a big way. So, a cassette, of a musician sells in the market and not his musical skill as such. It however, remains to be seen how brain drain has to be treated since it results in transportation of the human capital or human resources capable of yielding intellectual property of value from one country to another.

In the ultimate analysis, we may say, we arrive at price by translating goods or services in terms of the prevailing currency at the existing market and assess the relative worth of other goods or services by re-translating them again the other way. In valuation, the screen of price is taken away though such valuation is also expressed in the same monetary terms. The worth of other goods or services are estimated against the goods or services exchanged for. There is enough socio-economic reasons for this exercise. Because, one single currency operates when the market nexus is confined within the same country. But in an era of globalisation, we are confronted quite often with the regime of intervening multiple currencies whose mutual exchange ratio are determined in a money market that is not often perfect, rather quiet often imperfect and in some situations, monopolistic. This leads us to assess the purchasing power parity of different currencies in an objective manner for the purpose of valuation. The absence of direct transferability is thus an inhibiting factor for assessing purchasing power parity for the purpose of estimating value.

Value and cost

The cost of production theory of value simply looks at the matter from the side of supply. Cost is not certainly the same as value. It only conditions the supply curve of a commodity. Indeed cost, inasmuch as it is applied to anything capable of being constructed or reproduced, is nothing more than the usual bedrock price acceptable to a seller. It is only in so far as the seller is able to impose his estimate of his contribution in production on the buyer, that he succeeds in satisfying his equation of price and value. Cost may exceed both price and value in various situations. A common illustration is that of a high class residence around which has sprung up a slum or blighted area or incongeneal environment. On the contrary, a tiny shop-room involving insignificant cost of construction in the busy centre of the city may attract a selling price in multiples of capital cost. But it is usual to find old Maharaja palaces standing in majestic ornateness amidst rural settings but sprouting banyan trees for sheer loss of value or price, not even capable of attracting dwellers to pay for its bare maintenance. The difference in cost and value is often considerable, so much so that in many countries, the gain in capital value is taxed as an unearned increment. It has aptly been observed by Jevons in his "Principles of Economics", that 'value means not an object, but the circumstances of an object'.

Purpose of valuation

Next comes the purpose for which valuation is made. The valuation for the purpose of land acquisition is not the same as that for bank mortgage. Again, valuation for the purpose of municipal taxation is not the same as that for imposition of stamp duty on transfer of immovable property. These issues are discussed in detail in the relevant chapters hereafter.

Since valuation is an essential exercise for assessing the present worth of future benefits accruing to a property, certain macro-economic factors cannot be lost sight of. Thus, the trend of inflation, the influence of parallel economy, the fiscal laws at work, probable governmental monetary policy in the foreseeable future, state of institutional finances, inflow of foreign money—all have their due weightage in shaping the valuation process.

The ever-increasing spheres of State activity witnessed in recent times have brought in a spurt of legislation affecting valuation of land and building. The law imposing ceiling on rent realisable on urban real property emaciates the market potentiality of such property. So also the ceiling prescribed for landholdings in urban or rural areas. Again, planning laws defining use-pattern of lands and buildings through zoning restrictions together with municipal building codes provide for permissible vertical and horizontal development of real estate and thus put a check and balance to the exercise of ownership rights which has its inevitable bearing on valuation. The juristic concept of easement has undergone vast expansion in the form of right to light, air, access and support. Environmental considerations and pollution hazards arising out of noise, odour, vibrations and the like are posing inviolable compulsion to further entrench the rights in the laws of easement. The theories of valuation of real property cannot but take account of the multi-facet impact in the wake of multi-pronged legislation in the field of property development, because development now means not merely value addition to land and building but also conformity to legal provisions in force.

A man may have a premises to sell for ₹10,00,000 but that may not be the value of the property. The situation and class of the building may suit a prospective purchaser. It may be ideal for his purpose and may have a special value to him prompting him to opt for that transaction; whereas, another purchaser may not have any special reason, other than speculation, for purchasing the property and the value to him would be less than the man who wanted the premises for a specific purpose. If a property was for sale and two prospective purchasers were determined to outbid each other, the selling price would definitely not be the value of the property. On the other hand, there may be a dearth of purchasers for a property at a sale, and if the sale is in pursuance of a decree of the High Court, then the selling price may be less than the true market value. Thus, the purpose of valuation is a guiding factor in the field of valuation.

Value to the individual

We must be careful not to be confused with the value to the individual and be conscious of the value to the market. A German economist, Menger has said that the value of a commodity is the 'importance which actual goods receive from us, from the fact, that we are conscious of being dependant on our disposal of them, for the satisfaction of our wants'. This seems rather like a statement of the value to the individual, and omits any reference to the market. According to Professor Cassel, an economist of wide repute, whenever value means anything more than price, it refers to psychological processes, and though these processes are undoubtedly real, they are not capable of objective measurement. We cannot, however, allow the matter to rest here, for it is the duty of the valuer to discover value and to measure it. The fact is that although price and value are not considered as interchangeable terms, in the case of a buyer and a seller, price is of value to both, but they are viewing the subject from completely different angles of vision. A seller is obsessed with his sacrifice which is subjective, Ricardo even thought that the cost included in property was the same as value. But modern thinking do not accept it. For the individual, the value of one thing may be estimated by the effort which he is prepared to make to obtain it, or to put it in another way, by the number of other values he is prepared to exchange for it. But before he thinks of attaching any value to the thing from a personal point of view, a desire to possess it must be present. But such desire differs from mere impulse. The salient feature of desire is the adoption of a line of action to secure this object. The sale and purchase of an article is the transfer between individuals of commodities less strongly desired, for those considered more essential. In fact, the individual's valuation of an article always behaves in quantum. It ranges between the highest price at which under any condition he would buy and the lowest at which he would consider the article just its worth. Such a complex behaviourism is hardly to be found reflected for transactional purposes except on the canvas of the market which is a mirror that reflects the value not to the individual but to the community with which we are concerned.

Cost of reproduction

The "cost of reproduction" has a much greater bearing on value than the "cost of production". For example, if a house costs ₹ 20,00,000 to build in 1980 and in 1995 the depreciation was estimated at 15%, the owner may say the value is ₹ 20,00,000 less 15% or ₹ 17,00,000. But if this same house could in 1995 be built for ₹ 15,00,000 due to improvement in building technology, no one would pay ₹ 17,00,000 for it, although the actual cost of building the house in 1980 was ₹ 20,00,000.

Pricing and time-element

The function of price is to ration a limited supply of goods amongst consumers. The consumer's preference has to be matched in terms of price against the seller's willingness to sell primarily covering the cost of production.

The principle that value depends on supply and demand simply means that in the case of nearly every commodity more will be bought if the price is lowered and less will be bought if the price is raised but the selling price may not fall if the supply could be controlled. In the same way, the selling price may be pegged up if there is a sudden spurt in demand owing to influx of population and consequent rush of buyers. An understanding of the mechanism by which supply and demand are balanced, therefore, is fundamental in economics. This mechanism is generally referred to as 'pricing'; for it is the movements in prices that tend to restore the balance between supply and demand. In balancing supply and demand, prices perform an important social function. On the one hand, they reflect on 'values', *i.e.* our estimate of how much things are worth; on the other hand, they reflect on the cost of making them available to the consumers. Thus, prices preserve a balance between value and cost. The rise and fall in prices occur in the canvas of time. Thus, the short-run and long-run determination of price is a relevant consideration in the field of valuation in the same way as whether the market is perfect or imperfect or in a state of monopoly. It follows therefore that all valuations must clearly state the date to which the valuation relates and time is the essence of all valuations.

CHAPTER

3

Value Considerations in Variety of Property

The long history of human civilization centres around the idea of property and ownership. From the days when semi-civilized man began to claim possession over his tools and hunting instruments up to the modern times when the quest for profit, dividend, interest drives a man to activities, the idea of property is a supreme factor in the process of evolution. Modern civilization would fall to pieces if the idea of property is banished. According to Hobbes, "take away the civil law and no man knows what is his own, and what is another man's". His view is that private property is part of the political order, and maintenance of this order is essential to human happiness; therefore, the law of property is as binding upon men, both morally and legally, as other essential laws of the state. In the same vein the utilitarian philosopher, Bentham holds that "property and law—are born together. Before laws were made there was no property, take away law, and property ceases".

In evaluating this theory of property, as applicable in modern times it may be said that while law confers upon property-owners a secure sense of possession, it does not afford any clue as to the absolute justification of property. Because property lies at the root of economic, legal and political power and law tends to protect only those who have domain over property and the propertyless are practically excluded from the meaning of such protection. As Rousseau observes, "under bad Governments, law serves only to maintain the poor in misery and the rich in usurpation." While the Constitution of India eloquently champions the values that State should uphold, the governance in actual practice depends upon the nature and quality of how those are implemented. The same is true about the laws of property that governs the society under the canopy of the Constitution.

A historical background

The concept of property arose out of the exclusive right of acquiring, possessing, enjoying and disposing of anything. It may be a right unlimited in point of duration and unrestricted in point of disposition in which case it is viewed as ownership. Ownership is very often subjected to control or diminution whether by contractual obligation or by operation of law of the land. Property as a broad term includes movables, immovables and intangibles which are held under such a right of ownership as well as rights falling short of ownership.

The primitive man in his battle for food and shelter acquired for himself the right to his dwelling and cultivable field. He protected this right jealously against all forms of intrusion. Thus he had possession of the complete bundle of rights which we now call ownership. With the increase of population the primitive man discovered the formula of living in clusters which needed common defence for the common good. There was a surrender of some of the rights out of total ownership as a process of living together under the community Government as then existed. In course of time when monarchy was established by and large, the concept of land being owned by the emperors, kings and other rulers came to be accepted. The lands were held by families on payment of royalty to the king. The historic man released a few sticks out of the bundle of rights in exchange for protection, but he retained the right of his possession as well as the right to pass on the land to his progeny including the authority to transfer the land to others or let others make limited use of the land without owning it. With the rise of feudalism, the concept of proprietary ownership of land underwent further changes lending newer shades of complexion with growing complexities of life.

The story was however different where the law governing property developed from customary practices nurtured through centuries in ancient time. The authority of the kind was substituted by the mandate of the community whether guided by religious precepts or early tribal laws. Under such system, land was considered as vested in the supreme sovereign power of God. The individual enjoyed the right of possession and use but with restrictions on transfer. Thus, we find the earliest documented evidence of granting the use of land to tillers in the Bible. In Genesis 12:7, God promises to grant the use of land to Abraham, the patriarchal head of the Hebrew people. In Genesis 13:17, Lot, nephew of Abraham, was asked to inspect his land by walking through it. Genesis 13:15 says, "For all the land which thou seest, to thee I give it, and to thy seed forever".

With the rise of modern Government, we find that the ownership of land is affected by three categories of rights specifically retained by Government. The Government enjoys the taxing power with the right to impose compulsory exaction on any property. With police power, it has the right to regulate the enjoyment, user or possession of property. And the power of eminent domain vests the Government with the authority to acquire any property on payment of compensation. Escheat is a right which reverts to Government any land forfeited on account of absence of any legitimate inheritance to it. The Mahomedan law even recognises the State as the successor to any property which do not find inheritance in sharers, distant kindreds or residuaries. We shall see later that restrictions on land use and development through zoning regulations, environmental requirements and other constraints imposed by Government in exercise of police power have substantially eroded the concept of property as well as rights or interests arising out of property.

Rights and interests in property

The rights and interests in property spread out in a wide spectrum. From simple ownership it ranges up to license which does not confer any right but only permissive possession. The following list give a catenated domain over property or asset:

- Fee simple which means full ownership over the property, subject only to the power of eminent domain of the Government.
- Lease-holds of various descriptions and tenures.

- Joint ownership.
- Individual ownership of apartments and flats in a co-operative society.
- Individual ownership of flats or apartments in a condominium under the Apartment Ownership Act.
- Life-estate.
- Possession as trustee.
- Mortgagee-in-possession.
- Hire-purchase.
- Lien or charge including assignment, temporary custody in bailment, pawn etc.
- License or permissive possession.

Correspondingly, transfers by person competent to do so admit of diverse forms as follows:

- Sale.
- Leases or tenancies of various descriptions including sub-lease or sub-tenancy.
- Mortgage including reverse mortgage.
- Gift.
- Agency.
- Trust.
- Buy-Back.
- Will or Testament.
- Leave and License.

Acquisition of property including rights or interests therein also abides by various ways that are increasing in form as days go by and newer transactions are practised. The following forms of acquisition are in vogue:

- Compulsory acquisition by competent authorities.
- Purchase by contemporaneous payments or exchange.
- Purchase by deferred payments through credit card, hire-purchase etc.
- Reversion on termination of lease, forfeiture etc.
- Tenancy or sub-tenancy.
- Acquisition through mortgages of appropriate kind.

- Power-of-Attorney.
- Trustee.
- Easement.
- License, franchise, etc.
- Intestate succession by way of inheritance.
- Testamentary succession by Will.
- Donee of gift.
- Adverse possession.

A valuer has to acquaint himself with the incidence of each form of transaction, the varied nature of rights or interests in property as well as diverse ways of acquisition of such rights or interests. Because, in the process of valuation, we rarely value the property itself excepting some personal movables. What we actually value are the rights or interests that vest in persons having such rights or interests. The differences in forms thereof quite often account for differences in valuation.

Asset and property

The word 'asset' is very often now used in the valuation parlour along with the term 'property'. The two are not exactly synonymous. The word 'asset' according to *Oxford Advanced Learner's Dictionary*, 8th Ed. means—

(1) a person or thing that is valuable or useful to something;

(2) a thing of value, especially property that a person or company owns, which can be used or sold to pay debts.

'Property' on the other hand is intended to mean things (*i*) owned, (*ii*) possessed and (*iii*) capable of being disposed of. In valuation parlour, we can make a distinction between the two terms 'Asset' includes human qualities like industry, perseverance, integrity, devotion, aptitude etc. which also ultimately count for monetary value in turning out goods and services by exalting human labour. But these qualities cannot be parted with and are personal in character. These are, therefore, non-transferable assets of an individual and hence cannot be termed as 'property'. Because, property essentially is characterized by the elements of acquisition, possession and transfer whether in market transactions or otherwise. Better performances in production are achieved quite often by research and development on intellectual property. Since Research and Development (R&D) plays a pivotal role in the realm of creating newer and newer assets, the term 'asset' is preferred in valuation parlour.

'Asset' is a much wider term than the word 'property'. All properties are assets but all assets are not properties. Assets includes anything which is of value to mankind, ultimately capable of being translated in monetary worth for marketisation in future. On the other hand, transferability is a necessary incidence with property. This narrows the realm of property as asset includes also areas that are not readily marketable. For example, gifts of nature like ambient air, sunshine, climate etc. which have value-in-use are also considered as assets, but these are not property in the sense that they have no value-in-exchange being natural resources available in abundance. As we shall see later, much of assets can also ultimately be converted into property by the application of technology or human labour, as for example, an oxygen cylinder or a bottled water etc. But that is a different question and does not obliterate the distinction between a property and an asset. In substance, property is a sub-set of asset.

Assets are of different kinds. These may be classed as—

- Tangible asset,
- Intangible asset, and
- Financial asset.

Tangible asset. Tangible assets are those, which can be perceived by sense organs. Fixed tangible properties like lands and building, plant and machinery, fixture and building services, mines and forests come under this definition. Also movables like a car or a refrigerator or a furniture also falls under this category. The field of tangible assets is fuelled by newer and newer ways of encroachment on the areas of value-in-use or non-monetised economy. While ambient air has only value-in-use, it obtains value-in-exchange when filled in cylinder for medical use. Similarly water becomes a tangible assets when bottled up as drinking water. Similar instance can be quoted in the newly developed industry of tourism. A place of scenic beauty is entertaining as an excellence of nature having only value-in-use. But as soon as the place is brought under commercial communication for the purpose of promotion of tourism, the same obtains a value-in-exchange and is raised to the arena of a property or asset. Since tourism is a service industry that primarily satisfies the visual sense, it may legitimately come under tangible asset.

Intangible asset. All kinds of services of marketable value are intangible assets. A class of intangible assets is new entrant in the realm of property. As for example, while aptitude or skill or talent is personal in nature, some of the end-results thereof in the form of 'product' or 'process' are marketable assets. The development of industrial product or process or agricultural seeds has been made possible by human research based on scientific knowledge and technology of production. The Patent Act ensures the monopoly of enjoyment for a limited a period of the fruits of one's research and developments through licenses issued. Thus a patent of such product or process under the law becomes an intangible asset for the limited period it enjoys monopoly. It can be marketed through licenses issued apart from being owned and possessed. The scientific discoveries or inventions do not, however, fall under this category unless technologically translated as marketable product or process.

Similarly, legislations like Copyright Act, Designs Act, or the Trade Marks Act have also brought in intangible assets ensuring intellectual property rights for a limited period.

The modern commercial world has identified rights, interests, lien, etc. in property unaccompanied by possession at all. Thus, the rights of lease or mortgage have created situation in which it is possible to own a property without possession or possess a property without ownership. This gives right to intangible assets arising out of tangible property in the form of rent-receiving interest or right to enter upon a property in accordance with the terms of lease or mortgage. But now even movables have been brought under this category. The factories very often hire the service of machineries or spares on payment of monthly rent, subject to a lien of the lending organization on agreed terms. This forms an intangible asset in movables. Buy-back is another innovation in sales. Person obstensibly sales a car to another without any desire to part with it for ever. He accordingly comes to a contractual agreement with the other that he reserves the right to buy-back the car on making payments as agreed to. An intangible asset now comes into existence by creating a non-possessory interest in the car. Thus the field of intangible assets gets ramified day by day. We can get a fair picture only as on the date.

Financial asset. All actionable claims fall in this category. The stock, shares and debentures of different companies can be termed as financial assets as because these are acquired, possessed and are also transferable freely in the market. These assets are different in kind from those, which are tangible or intangible. The process of production nowadays has become more and more capital-intensive and requires a huge investment that an individual proprietor can hardly afford. He has to borrow from the market and distribute fragmented ownership of the company amongst large number of small investors. They are the persons who are admitted as partners to the company by issuance of shares or debentures. Like guests to the team of promoting investors they are even given the liberty to freely step in and step out. This is to ensure transaction of stock, shares and debentures in the financial market giving rise to a new kind of asset which now go by the name of financial asset.

Non-monetised sector

A reference in this context is relevant to the non-monetised sector of the economy having value-in-use because this sector harbours the potential for different forms of property in the sense we understand it for valuation considerations. The vast non-monetised sector characterised by the gifts of nature like air, sunshine, river, ocean, space, electromagnetic waves, light waves, etc. on the one hand and human instinct for free services arising out of love, affection, duty, etc. on the other hand are gradually being encroached upon by the monetised economy dominated by market transactions. More concretely, the developed economies of the world are gradually exploring specialisation in various fields and sharper division of labour in practices which are generally integrated in the non-monetary sector of the traditional economies. The market nexus is being extended thereby. For example, the grandmothers are being replaced by babysitters, motherly care by nursing services, household cooking by home delivery services, and even mothering of a child by surrogate mother. On the other hand, inventive mankind is ever on the march to bring within the market nexus products to harness and sustainably exploit the free gifts in our environment. Newer regions hitherto unexplored in the waves of light or in the electromagnetic field are being exploited in developing communication, photography, computer appliances; tourist spots are being established in distant recesses which had hitherto been virgin; oxygen is being bottled for extended commercial use; atoms are being subjected to fission and fusion. The list can be expanded by numerous instances. Thus, a view of the hinterland of property is relevant before we proceed for a discussion on the valuation considerations in variety of property.

Viewed from this angle, the gradual growth of the monetised sector marked by the attribute of marketability is not at all a recent phenomenon. It has been a distinct trend throughout. The proprietary right over land has matured from an era when it was really a free gift to be exploited for possession by anyone who had the might or access. The survey and delineation giving legal right to land came much later in history. Today it is inconceivable to view any domain over land without any legal right thereto.

Real estate and real property

Property is anything that is capable of being owned. The term 'Real Property' is not, however, susceptible of such simple definition. Generally, it may be said that things which are specifically recoverable and may pass on to the heir are 'Real Estate'. In its popular sense, the term refers to lands and building also commonly known as 'Realty'. But the expression 'real property' includes all forms of rights and interests arising out of land and building.

To trace the origin of the terms, it may be said that the English Common Law recognised land held freely and in 'fee' as that which passes on death to the heir, *i.e.* to the blood relation appointed by law as the successor. The highest form of estate or title to land known to the English law is 'fee simple' in possession free from restriction and encumbrance. 'Freehold' is the another name for such 'fee simple' and came later on to be known as the 'real estate'. The terminology of 'fee simple' is derived from the principle tenure of land called 'free holding' which dates back from about the time of William the Conqueror when three important tenancies were in vogue in England, *i.e.* (*i*) a freeholding; (*ii*) a holding in villeinage, or (*iii*) a lease for a term of years. The first was held of the Crown by free service, *i.e.* by service free from the more menial services, but always subject to military or knightly service. As time elapsed, freehold land came to be practically equivalent to absolute property, but nevertheless always subject as has already been mentioned, to certain rights of acquisition by the Crown for a public purpose. In America, this right is termed as 'the right of eminent domain'. In the Indian context, land and building held in absolute ownership in the sense as above has come to be known as 'Real Estate'. But quite a number of rights or interests less than ownership can also be carved out of it whether by way of limited possession, leasehold tenure, reversion, right to receive rent, or expectancy of possession, each of which is a property. Thus the expression 'real property' has been coined to include all forms of rights and interests arising out of land and building.

There are certain things, however, which cannot be owned by anyone and are, therefore, not property in the legal sense. These things are called *'res nullius'*, i.e. things which belong to no one, and in their natural state, they include ambient air, river, mountain, wild creatures, etc.

Movable and immovable

It is customary to classify property into movables and immovables. The distinction between movable and immovable property had been nicely explained in the case of *Sukry Kurdepa* v *Goondakull*[1] in the following manner:

> "Moveability may be defined to be a capacity in a thing of suffering alteration of the relation of place, immoveability incapacity for such alteration. If, however, a thing cannot change its place without injury to the quality by virtue of which it is what it is, it is immovable. Certain things such as a piece of land are in all circumstances immovable. Other such as trees attached to the ground are, so long as they

1 (1872)6 Mad HC 71.

are so attached, immovable; when the severance has been effected they become movable."

It is difficult to draw a clear-cut line of demarcation between a movable property and an immovable property. Generally speaking, land, building and anything imbedded in land is considered as immovable. On the other hand, anything which can be moved or carried from one place to another is a movable property. But an exhaustive definition is not possible. The General Clauses Act in s. 3(26) defines immovable property as follows:

"Immovable property shall include land, benefits to arise out of land, and things attached to the earth, or permanently fastened to anything attached to the earth."

The Transfer of Property Act gives no positive definition of immovable property except stating in s. 3 that "immovable property does not include standing timber, growing crops or grass". The said Act, however, defines the expression "attached to the earth" to mean the following—

"(*a*) rooted in the earth, as in the case of trees and shrubs;

(*b*) imbedded in the earth, as in the case of walls or buildings; or

(*c*) attached to what is so imbedded for the permanent beneficial enjoyment of that to which it is attached."

The line of distinction between a movable and immovable property becomes all the more thin as we follow the Transfer of Property Act. Standing timber is not an immovable property but a growing timber is, because standing timber are trees meant to be cut down as they are fit for use for building or repairing houses. If the tree is growing, it draws sustenance from the soil and hence, it is immovable. But when a tree has already grown to its full stature and stands as mere timber to be immediately withdrawn from the land, the function of the land in relation to the trees is that of a mere warehouse.[2] On this test, standing timber is a movable property as viewed in the case of *Shantabai* v *State of Bombay.*[3] A

2 *Marshall* v *Green* [1875]1 CPD 35 (39).

3 1959 SCR 265; 1958 SCJ 1078; 1958 SCA 727.

fruit-bearing tree would not be standing timber and would be classed as immovable property.[4] But if according to custom of a particular locality a fruit bearing tree is used as building or for repairing houses it can be treated as standing timber.[5] If all the factors go to show that the parties intended to deal with the tree as timber, then again it would be called standing timber and not growing trees.[6] The American as well as the English law courts have taken the similar view.

Plant and machinery are generally considered as movable property.[7] But there are certain items of plant and machinery which add to the convenience of user like lifts, pumps etc. and accordingly taken as real property. So also fixtures which are articles that have the primary characteristics of personal property but may become so much part of the land or building to which they are affixed that they assume the characteristics of real property. Here again, the intention of the parties provide the key to the solution of any dispute arising. The mode of annexation is also an important element for consideration. If the plant or fixture cannot be removed without great damage, it affords a strong ground for thinking that it was intended to be annexed in perpetuity.

The list of movable property is too big to be listed exhaustively. It is necessary, however, to mention the consumable items of durable nature like aircraft, computer, television, washing machine and the like which are prone to obsolescence and abide by the estimate of price peculiar to each item. The aspect of depreciation, however, is an important feature for consideration.

Ownership—meaning thereof

The highest form of right with regard to real estate go by the name of 'ownership' which is also known as 'fee simple estate'

4 *Suresh Chand* v *Kundan* (2001)10 SCC 221; (2001)7 SCALE 612; *Ali Saheb* v *Mohidin* (1911)13 Bom LR 874; (1912)10 All LG 516; *Moti Singh* v *Deoki Singh* AIR 1936 Pat 66.

5 *Badan* v *Suraj* 3 All LJ 20; *Krishna Rao* v *Babaji* 24 Bom 31.

6 *State of Himachal Pradesh* v *Motilal Pratap Singh & Co.* AIR 1981 HP 8.

7 *Perumal Naicker* v *Ramaswami Kone* AIR 1969 Med 346; *Meghraj* v *Krishna Chandra* AIR 1924 All 365.

or 'freehold estate'. Such owner is entitled to (1) use the property in any manner he thinks fit, (2) abuse the property so long as it does not result in a nuisance, (3) enjoy the property by exclusive possession, (4) derive benefits, income or profit from the property, and (5) dispose of the property during his lifetime by sale, gift or other approved methods. He is vested with and has control over what is called the 'bundle of rights' in the property. His right is superior to all other rights and often identified as the real estate itself from which other lesser estates in the property flow. Thus he may grant lease of the property, create mortgage, induct licence, impose charge and so on.

Life estate

Short of ownership, there may be life estate in which the duration of interest is limited to the life of the owner. A life estate is a useful mechanism for providing someone with the use of property during his lifetime after which it terminates. If the grantor has retained the future interest to himself, the property will go back to him on 'reversion' after termination of the life estate. If, however, the grantor has given the estate for life to one person on the termination of which it is desired to pass on to another person, the interest of the latter is that of a 'remainder'. An interest in property restricted in its enjoyment to the owner personally cannot be transferred by him as provided under s. 6(*d*) of the Transfer of Property Act.

Leasehold interest

Land or building may be leased. A leasehold interest in the property is the right to occupy and use that property for a fixed term or in perpetuity subject to payment of rent or premium and to the observance of covenants contained in the lease. The person who grants the lease is called the 'lessor' and the person who takes it the 'lessee'. The term of lease may be from month to month, or year to year or for any term running into any number of years or even in perpetuity. When a price is paid it is called premium and the periodic recurrent consideration is called rent which usually takes the form of cash payment and sometimes, sharing of crops or rendering of service periodically or on specified occasions. Thus, leasehold interests are primarily titles to income either in cash or occupation benefits for a given period of time. On termination of lease, the lessor gets back the property as reversioner. If the covenant so permits, he may exercise the right of re-entry for violation of the terms of lease agreement by the lessee. Lessee can create a sub-lease if the agreement so provides. Thus a transaction of lease may give rise to a plethora of interests which are transferable and hence relevant for valuation purposes.

In the urban areas, lease of premises is generally regulated by the rent control law of the State. Such legislation aimed at offering protection to tenants against economic exploitation by the landlords or owners, provides for fixation of fair rent or standard rent, security of the continuance of tenancy against unjust eviction and other ameliorative measures. The impact of such legislation on valuation of real property is fully discussed in a subsequent chapter.

Interests in property

As absolute ownership consists of an aggregate of rights, a wide variety of rights can be carved out of ownership. These subordinate rights are called interests in property. Thus, there may be interests arising out of mortgage as between a mortgagor and a mortgagee. There may be an interest accuring to the beneficiary of a trust as endowed under the Indian Trusts Act 1882. An annual allowance charged on land is also an interest, so also a right to collect dues at a fair held on a plot of land or from a *haat* or market; a right to enter upon land and remove trees; or a right to graze over the land of another person; or to carry away fish from the lake or marshy land. The rights enjoyed in another's land by way of easement including sharing of profit on land belonging to someone else amounting to *profits a prendre* are all immovable property as benefits arising out of land.

Co-ownership

So far we have discussed real property taken in the name of a single juristic person. When ownership of property is vested in co-owners or co-tenants, a different species comes into existence. The usual type of co-ownership are joint tenancy or tenancy in common. There are also concurrent ownerships in the form of condominiums and housing co-operatives.

A typical example of joint tenancy is the coparcenary property of an undivided family governed by the Mitakshara School of Hindu law. The essential element in the nexus of a coparcenary property is succession by survivorship and not by inheritance. That is to say, each newly born son in the family obtains a proportionate interest in the ancestral property upon his birth and likewise, upon the death of any co-owner, the interests of the surviving co-owners get correspondingly enhanced. There is unity of interest and unity of possession amongst the co-owners in the sense that all the co-owners have exactly the same legal interest and same right of possession over the joint property. The Hindu Succession Act has preserved the joint tenancy system of Mitakshara School for those governed by it, although the Act recognises tenancy in common as a general rule for undivided possession.

Tenancy in common is the co-ownership of real property in which two or more owners hold separate title to the same property with each co-owner having a right of full use and possession and each separate estate being inheritable. Upon the death of a tenant, his interest passes on to his heirs and not to the surviving co-owners as in a joint tenancy. The right of each co-owner extends to the whole of the property until there is a partition and each co-owner may dispose of his interest by deed or will.

Concurrent ownership

Co-operatives and condominiums are a form of concurrent ownership in multi-unit building complexes in urban areas. With the growth of population and rising costs of land in urban centres, it is becoming increasingly difficult for people to find exclusive land and building for dwelling purposes. Also land resources are becoming more and more scarce. This had led to co-operatives and condominiums in high-rise structures or what are commonly known as vertical sub-division developments. Gradually, such form of concurrent ownership is also being extended to commercial uses of property and horizontal sub-division development. In co-operatives, the entire land and building comprising the common property belongs to the housing co-operatives society which administers the areas of common uses and facilities. The individual flat-owner as a member thereof enjoys title to and exclusive right of possession over his own flat together with proportionate share in the areas of common uses and facilities since inception. In case of any transfer, the co-operative society has generally a right of pre-emption in order to regulate its membership pattern under the State Co-operative Societies Act. In the case of other condominiums, most of the States in India have passed Apartment Ownership Acts to enable construction of building complexes designed for concurrent ownership by group of flat-owners not falling below a minimum number. As occupancy begins, the flat-owners together with the original promoter, if necessary, form an association which is entrusted to administer the areas of common uses and facilities. The transfer of ownership of individual flats is generally not subjected to any constraint of pre-emption in such cases.

Intangible assets including goodwill

Property is not only the 'thing' subjected to ownership but includes also dominion or right that do not have physical substance since such rights or privileges nevertheless generate income to the owner. Hence the distinction between tangible and intangible property which is also expressed as corporeal and incorporeal rights. Intangible property includes rights such as trade marks, copyrights, patents, designs and personal rights capable of transfer. The best example is the goodwill of a company. All assets of the company taken together may not indicate the total value. Aggregation may have a synergic effect. This synergic result is reflected in goodwill. Goodwill may attach to personal reputation and qualities or to the brand names. The term 'goodwill' has been defined in the Webster's *New Twentieth Century Dictionary* as "the commercial advantage possessed by any business, due to its established popularity, reputation, patronage, advertising, location, etc. over and beyond its mere stock or capital". It is the influence exerted with the view of transfering the custom of any shop or trade to any successor. It is the benefit and advantage of the goodname, reputation in connection of a business.[8] The *Oxford Advanced Learner's Dictionary* defines the goodwill as "(1) friendly or helpful feelings towards other people or countries (2) the good relationship between a business and its

8 Narayanan, *Intellectual Property Law,* 3rd Ed., p. 209.

customers that is calculated as part of its value when it is sold". The goodwill of the business is not capable of being transferred independently of the concerned property even though the value of the goodwill may be substantially diminished thereby. But it must be remembered that when goodwill attaches to land and/or building, it does not form a separate element in the saleable value of the property but gets included in the open market value or special value arising out of the trading potential of the property. In this view, goodwill is peculiar to business concerns. Like goodwill, intellectual property is also a specimen of intangible asset. The intellectual property may include copyrights, patents, trade marks, trade secrets, designs, products of individualised talent or creativity which are usually protected by law from unauthorised use by others.

Power-of-Attorney

It is now-a-days not uncommon to find an agent in possession of a property on behalf of the principal. An 'agent' is defined in s. 182 of the Indian Contract Act 1872. The relationship of a principal and an agent may arise under multiple situations the statutory form of which is mostly governed by the Powers-of-Attorney Act 1882. There is, however, a difference between an agent and a person acting under the authority of a power-of-attorney. In the case of agency, the agent himself may execute the instrument of the principal but in case of power-of-attorney, it is the name of principal which is used in the instrument. The power-of-attorney may be general or special. On the authority of a general power-of-attorney the agent may manage, buy or sell real or personal property, borrow money by mortgage or otherwise, lease out the property, sue or be sued etc. Special power-of-attorney is usually executed for a particular purpose like presenting a document for registration, or initiate execution proceedings and the like.

Licensee in possession

It is possible that a person permits another to look after his property and possess the same as a care-taker performing entrusted jobs. A licensee is not an agent for the licensor. He can be asked to leave any time the licensor deems it necessary. If, however, there is any contract to the contrary, such contract has to be honoured. Contract may be express or implied.

Adverse possession

Adverse possession for twelve years ripens into ownerships in case of a private immovable property. So adverse possession has also some potential value. The law of adverse possession is itself a subject of legal study. A possession is said to be in adverse, only after the owner thereof is made aware of such intention. Mere possession is not enough.

Valuation consideration in uses of property of immovable nature

From the above discussion, it would appear that the process of valuation should invariably be accompanied by an attempt to view the asset in proper light so that the utility of an asset or property may be measured with due consideration of its existing use, probable alternative uses or expected future use in the foreseeable future. The urban lands are transacted mostly for residence, services and investment. Dealings in real estate for speculation are also common. When developed with building, land imbibes potential for multiple uses, viz., residential, commercial, mercantile, industrial, institutional, storage, congregational and the like. Each kind of use has its own implication and impact on valuation. An outline of valuation considerations relevant in the context of occupational uses of a few types of land and building is given hereinafter. It may be added that the variety of uses of urban land and buildings has received a terrible spurt with the increasing need made to be felt in the society with innovative devises as well as newer advertising techniques. An analysis of the property may be of help to a valuer in adopting the proper approach to valuation. Hence this exercise, the list of property discussed below is illustration and not exhaustive.

(1) *Residential property*

Residential houses are problems in themselves because no fixed percentage could possibly be laid down which would cover the diverse types of property which come under this heading.

When estimating the security of rent of a house, enquiries and an inspection of the district must be made, to see if that type of house is suitable for the neighourhood. You may have a large mansion type house which 50 years ago was surrounded by open spaces, now, the district having deteriorated, it may be surrounded by very small and poor class houses. The security of rent for this house will not be the same as a similar house situated in an excellent residential district although the rent of the former will be much less than the rent of the latter.

Lower and middle class people invariably use the bus, tram, train or other rapid/mass transit system for getting from their homes to their places of business or work; therefore, it stands to reason that rents from small dwelling houses situated near bus and tram routes, will be better secured than rents from small dwelling houses in districts which are not served by any modern transport facilities. The same applies, but to a lesser extent, to large residential houses in good residential localities. The owners and tenants may not require the bus or other transit system; they will invariably travel to their places of business by car. The cook, however, who has to visit the bazar each morning, may have to walk several miles to the market with the result that a little dissatisfaction in the mind of the tenant occurs. Again the car may refuse to start, and the tenant himself may be put to considerable trouble owing to the lack of transport facilities. All these little items, each in themselves very trifling, must be taken into account, because good rents from large houses, can only be considered well secured, if there is available modern transport facilities within a reasonable distance.

Generally it is found that the smaller the property, the more are the outgoings in proportion to the rent and the stability of the tenant is less than found in large houses. The large residential houses are usually let on lease, with the result, that the lessee has usually been approved by a responsible person and is found to be a man of substance. He will look after the property well and will not get involved in litigation due to non-payment of rent. The costs of collection and management will be considerably less than the small property, and although these items will be thoroughly considered and accounted for when making deductions for outgoings, they have a direct bearing on the security of the rent and, therefore, the year's purchase becomes involved.

Another factor, which must be carefully considered, when valuing new houses, is that the initial rents are likely to be on the high side, and not maintainable over a period of years.

The general public seem to have a fascination for a new house. It is probably due to the fact that all the fittings and fixtures are new and give a much better appearance than after a few years when the polish has worn off. A careful comparison with rents of older houses is essential and a valuation must be based on the fair rent or the security will vary considerably. If the rent of a new house is taken as the fair rent without any check being made, then the investment becomes a speculation, and the year's purchase must be considerably less than the fair figure which would be applied for the capitalisation of a proved fair rental.

The security for residential houses is usually better than for business premises and shops. Shopping districts decline very rapidly for very little reason, and prudent shopkeepers will move into more popular districts. The same applies to business premises. The uncertainty of trade and commerce often results in changes of address with the result that capitalisation of income from shops and business premises is more a speculation than from residential houses. Many tenants live the whole of their lives in one house, and even if they change, it is usually to move to another house in the same district.

As regards small residential property, the fact that adequate provision may have been made in the valuation for all outgoings does not mean that the net rent can be capitalised at the same year's purchase as large residential houses. The very fact that large deductions have been made for vacancies and bad debts (owing to the instability of the tenants), makes this an undesirable form of investment. If a valuation is made on the Land and Building method as a check to a rental valuation, many of these small houses would not be valued as standard structures. The security would have to be ridiculously low if the two valuations were to coincide. The reason is, in cases where land values becomes excessive, these small houses do not develop the land. The correct method would undoubtedly be to check the valuation by the rental method with a valuation by the land and building method, and the buildings would in most cases have to be valued as old materials. Every case must of course be treated on its merits.

The Municipal Corporation building by-laws and rules and regulations have a great bearing on the valuation of houses in residential districts. In the major towns, particularly metropolitan cities in India, a substantial portion of the site must be left as an open space. In most cases this means that the value of the land is equal to, or in excess of, the cost of construction of the buildings erected thereon. In these very good residential districts, the class of the tenants is high, and there is a reasonable degree of certainty, that, not only will the rents be paid but are likely to be maintained. This type of property cannot always be valued on the rental basis, especially where there is much open land left.

The rent a person would pay for a house whose grounds required a lot of upkeep, would naturally be less in proportion to the rent of a good house with small grounds, because any prudent tenant when taking a house of this description, would take into account the cost of keeping the gardens in repair, and the only fair method of valuation may be by the land and building method. This will be discussed in detail in a later chapter.

Flats are a totally different proposition. The main factor to be considered is the gross rent and its relationship to the outgoings. In flats, the outgoings are usually considerable, owing to the cost of maintenance of lifts, passages and staircases, lighting, upkeep of roads and gardens; the cost of decorating the premises for each new tenant and the general upkeep of the building; there are great risks of vacancies and bad debts. All these factors, together with other points, such as the desirability of the site and the total amount involved, must be considered before fixing a percentage to represent security.

(2) *Condominiums and co-operatives*

Co-operative housing has become an emerging phenomenon in big cities ever since land price had been soaring too high to be within the reach of purchasing power of common city-dwellers. The aftermath of World War II has witnessed an incessant migration of people to the metropolitan cities and big towns in India. As a result, acute dearth of dwelling space in the cities and big towns have compelled people to think in terms of common ownership of high priced land for dwelling purposes instead of the age-old concept of exclusive ownership of premises comprising both land and building. Thus, multi-storeyed buildings sprang up in the residential areas one by one which came to be occupied by a number of flat-owners with corporate ownership of the land comprised in the premises together with areas of common uses and facilities. At first, the intending flat-owners organise themselves into a registered co-operative housing society with membership limited to a homogeneous group or class and then under the banner of such society purchase the land, construct the building, make allotment of individual flats amongst the members and undertake the administration of the total unit. Each State in India gave a statutory foundation to such co-operative housing activities by making adequate provisions in the respective co-operative enactments. The municipal law of each State has extended recognition to such dwelling as unit of separate assessment for imposition of property tax, so that no one owner's default could threaten another owner's unit. Co-operative ownership took root in Bombay where housing scarcity was all the more pronounced and later on, engulfed the other cities of the country.

Side by side, another form of concurrent ownership came into existence through the initiative of promoters or developers who planned the construction of condominiums with the object of inducting owners to each constituent flat and reserving areas of common uses and facilities to be administered in a corporate manner. In this case too, legal sanction for regulation of construction and management became necessary and each State passed apartment ownership laws however different the nomenclature thereof might have been.

From the point of view of valuation, these co-operatives and condominiums constitute a different category from others. First of all, the entire multi-storeyed building comprising so many individual flat-owners is not a marketable property although each flat therein is transferable at the option of the owner or by operation of law. The most dramatic aspect of this phenomenon of conversion of dwelling apartments into co-operatives or condominiums has in recent years been that the market price at which the individual units could be sold would together far exceed the amount that the entire building would command from a single buyer. This is a particular point to note for valuation purposes. There are other considerations too. The housing co-operatives rest on the foundation of collective ownership of the entire property. That is to say, the flat-occupiers do not enjoy full ownership in the matter of disposition to outsiders. While there is full liberty to exclusive possession and use and also inheritance by operation of law, the co-operative laws generally stand in the way of transfer of individual property to outsiders for valuable consideration except with the consent of the co-operative society who may exercise the right of pre-emption. This clog certainly diminishes the value of constituent flats within a co-operative housing complex. The condominiums governed by apartment ownership laws do, however, stand on a different footing. While the restriction on transfers exists in co-operatives with an obvious purpose of maintaining the homogeneity of membership group or such other identity of the co-operative body as are contained in the relevent memorandum of association, the association of dwellers in a condominium do not suffer from any such inhibition. The flat-owners inducted generally after construction of the multi-storeyed building complex combine themselves in a registered association whose sole task is to administer the areas reserved for common uses and facilities. The flat-owners are generally free to possess, use and dispose of their individual property which acts as a factor ensuring full market value of such property. The existing condominums which are converted subsequently as property subject to apartment ownership as per law do also enjoy the same privilege. The flat-owners of both co-operatives and condominiums are entitled to separate assessment under the municipal laws which give them an edge in valuation in computation of market value as compared to other big mansions or multi-storeyed buildings held under single ownership.

(3) *Time-shared property*

The idea of concurrent ownership as nourished in the system of condominiums and co-operatives has been further fine-tuned with the ushering of time-shared property units. With unique nature of occupancy, such property has made appearance in posh hill stations or sea resorts by way of arrangement amongst co-owners who entitle themselves to occupation for weeks or months or seasons as scheduled in the terms of agreement. The rich people used to maintain their own lodge in hill stations or sea resorts. But this became an uneconomic proposition in course of time. Hence the idea of concurrent ownership evolved. The standard warranty deeds generally provide that the person who buys a time-sharing unit in a resort is an owner with full rights of ownership. He can lend his property, sell it, rent it, or give it away during the weeks he owns it. Or he may keep it forever. Such property being transferable items pose valuation considerations unique to itself. The market value is the guide.

(4) *Co-ownership buildings*

Along with condominiums and co-operatives there are multi-storied buildings with co-ownership or joint ownership as the nature of occupancy right. These buildings belong to a different category in the matter of such rights. Administrated on the principles of joint ownership, each occupant family has common right over every inch of the property and municipal property tax is levied on treating the entire property as a single unit and thereafter apportioned amongst the co-owners in accordance with their respective shares. These buildings mostly belonged originally to an ancestor, developed in phases, and eventually occupied by a group of shareholders on inheritance or purchasers stepping in. It is difficult for any shareholder occupant to transfer his interest without according a right of pre-emption to the other co-sharers.

(5) *Stratum tithes*

In recent time, the building technology has undergone a fast development. In the Western countries as well as in some of the countries of the Eastern region, the major cities have undergone a vast change in the sky line by ushering in tall buildings with number of floors ranging from 25 to 100 and even beyond. These high-rise buildings are mostly located in the commercial hubs or within the Central Business Districts, or in the densely populated residential areas, having building uses altogether different. The buildings accommodate residential flats, commercial complexes, shopping malls, hotels with swimming pools, amusement centres, warehouses or godowns in the basement offices of different kinds and even consular missions—all being subjected to a particular type of professional administration for maintenance of the areas of common uses and facilities with diverse occupancy rights.

Known popularly as Stratum Tithes or Stratum Titles, the buildings are unique in character as to constitute a different category altogether for valuation purposes.

(6) *Shops and business premises*

(I) LOCATION OF THE PREMISES. Shops in popular trading localities will give better security for the rent than shops situated in areas which are partly commercial and partly residential. The best test of the popularity of the district is the make a thorough inspection of the neighbourhood and see how many vacant shops there are. There are exceptions to this rule. A bus or transport terminal may be in a residential district. There may be ample scope for a restaurant in the immediate vicinity, but invariably the upper floors will be residential only. The shopping district must be well served with bus and other transpost services. Care must be taken to note how long the locality has been a shopping centre. Is the district becoming more popular from year to year or is the popularity of the district declining? Shops situated near a market which is of long standing and increasing in popularity will be a comparatively good and better security for the rent than shops situated in a district miles away from a bazar or market. It follows, therefore, the shops in main thoroughfares offer better security than shops situated in subsidiary streets.

The location of one Bank in a district will not denote that this is a good commercial region. But the location of several scheduled Banks in a locality will invariably denote that this is the centre of the business locality.

(II) TYPE OF PREMISES. Multi-storied buildings in a business locality will usually be occupied on the ground floor by shops and Banks, and on the first and second floors by offices which will yield larger rents in proportion than for residential purposes. If the upper floors beyond the second floor are occupied as residential quarters for the tenants of the shops, then the rent from the premises would be considered well secured for this type of property. Modern buildings erected solely for office blocks would perhaps not be less secured, but generally shops with living quarters attached and occupied are better security than lock-up shops.

The rents from multi-storeyed buildings in business localities are better secured if the floors are served by an ample number of lifts. While employees of a concern may not object to walking up to the 3rd to 4th floor twice a day, clients will certainly object, and although the outgoings in a modern building will be more when taking into account the service of the lifts, the security of the rent will be better than an antiquated block lacking modern facilities.

(III) CONTINUITY OF THE RENT. The continuity of the rent is one of the most important factors to be considered when applying a security for the capitalisation of the net rent of business premises. This is the most difficult part of a valuation of this description. The estimate for deductions to be made from the gross rent can mostly be made from actual figures and data available, but estimating the year's purchase can only be done by the expert who has studied this part of property and after he has made an exhaustive enquiry. Districts change very rapidly and one crisis can overnight change a prosperous business into a losing concern. The security of rents yielded by properties in a commercial area is inferior to that of rents of houses in a residential area. The reason is not far to seek. Fortunes of trade and commerce fluctuate greatly. In periods of slump and depression following a boom in business, it is found that there is a sharp decline in the level of rents.

Apart from periodic fluctuations to which trade is subject, a particular line of business that has been carried on in a locality for many years may remove from one place to another district, owing to the growth and development of the city in different directions, where better facilities for business are offered.

(IV) AMOUNT OF THE RENT. Modern rents must be treated with great caution. A modern rent must be tested before it can be accepted as a fair rent upon which a valuation may be based. In fact all rents must be checked before they can be accepted as fair rents, because it is on the fair rent of a property that the security depends. Rents which are below the fair level of rents are a much better security than rents which are higher than the fair level. There is every reason to expect that the low rent will not only be maintained in the future, but by better management may be increased, whilst there cannot be much prospect of maintaining a high rent, and less chance of increasing it. Whereas at the slightest scare the high rent payers will be the first to go, and the long-established low rent tenants will stay and weather the storm, and still have their trade, custom and place of business, when the depression or scare has passed.

The gross amount of the rent has a direct bearing on the security. The purchase of a property of this description is undoubtedly a speculation, and the greater the risk, the larger return is expected on the capital invested. The man who invests the largest amount is liable to lose the most. The fall and decline of a once prosperous district will probably ruin an owner of a large premises, especially if he has sunk all his capital in one venture. Every prudent business man will look to this aspect of the question when he decides how much he will pay for a premises.

The same answer applies when looking at the question from another point of view. In a large city there may be too many people who could invest in property of lower value but only very few who could invest in property worth high valuation. The higher the value the less the number of purchasers and if these numbers of prospective purchasers and values were plotted on a graph, one would find that the higher the value the more rapid would be the fall in the number of prospective purchasers. This is very true. For every 10 purchasers for a property of ₹10 lakhs there would only be 5 for a property of ₹20 lakhs and probably only 3 for a property of ₹40 lakhs. The proposition that the higher the value the less the year's purchase, has been borne out by pragmative experiences.

(7) *Commercial complexes*

Commercial Complexes have almost appeared from nowhere over the past 30 years or so to dominate the retailing trade through individual shops and establishments. The metropolitan cities of India and most of the other cities or big towns are marked by a prolific growth of informal sector in retail business. The sheer force of unemployment and accompanied by continuous migration from rural to urban areas have accentuated the process of unauthorised occupation of public streets and places by enterprises in small trade and business. But this informal pattern of business attract only a specific clientele group mostly drawn from the lower and middle income brackets. The elites have opted for a more sophisticated climate for marketing. This is the impulse behind the appearance of high-valued commercial complexes and huge departmental stores where leisure hours can comfortably be spent in a congenial marketing atmosphere.

The valuation considerations of the commercial complexes are entirely different from that of individual shops and establishments discussed earlier. In valuing the individual shops and establishments catering mostly to retail trades, the rental approach to valuation is the appropriate method. The valuer has to make a reasonable estimate of the current rental value of particular retail properties for specific types of retailing. But commercial complexes are viewed mainly as an investment proposition by the promoters. The capital value of such investment property is determined by the current and expected future net income it will produce or in other words, the diagram of cashflow from investment. In recent years, commercial complexes have emerged as very attractive investments by many investors and are in general keenly sought when offered for sale because they are looked upon as safe long term investments. It is here that the expertise of a valuer is called for as sound valuation depends upon a reasonable estimate. The valuer will discount those future cashflows at an appropriate discount rate to reflect the level of risk involved in the investment. If there is an error in computing the discount rate, it may result in an accumulative deviation from the appropriate valuation of the property. The commercial complexes have an income arising from a large number of lessees paying rent at varying rates depending on the date of occupation. As inflationary spiral dominates the economic scenario, the later occupants can expect lease only at an exorbitant rate both in premium and rent. At the best of times, the valuation of such large investments is not easy as the methods by which rental income is estimated may inevitably result in over-estimation. The main question is whether the investment property has the ability to continue producing income well into the future with regular increases in the income produced by which the capital value will be enhanced. But it often happens that the quest for ever higher rental income may, in reality, result in under-occupation and the vulnerable centres may pose debatable long-term investment value. There will always be a limited number of organisations able to raise the substantial sums required for obtaining lease of commercial tenements within the complex. Again the geographical location may also be an important factor influencing the number of potential purchasers who will always seek security of income for the present and the future. Once the commercial complex suffers the blight of under-occupation and under-trading, it may be under a threat as long-term investment. The appearance of vacant shops in a centre is highly likely to adversely affect its chances of recovery even when economic conditions improve. That is why it is a wise management policy to keep a commercial complex or shopping centre fully occupied even at a reduced income flow with a good tenant mix which guarantees a steady income flow from long-term investments. As a matter of fact, there cannot be an assured sunshine for all time to come. It should not be forgotten that today's asset can rapidly become tomorrow's liability, sometimes due to factors outside the control of an investor. It is in this perspective that considerations of valuation are to be addressed by a valuer.

Investment valuations involve the capitalisation of ancipated, future income flows which may be done either through the capitalisation method of valuation or by using a discounted cashflow format which is particularly appropriate for the valuation of investments where the income arises from an agglomeration of a large number of lessees in occupation at varying dates.

(8) *Shopping mall*

The cities of this age have witnessed the appearance of a peculiar type of commercial complexes known variously as shopping mall or Big Bazar, Departmental Store or City Centre, etc. Basically commercial complexes of diverse retail trade, these buildings replace the traditional markets both in purchases or sales of consumer items of a vast variety. People coming for purchases can combine their leisure hours with the pleasure of marketing, while the sellers can cater to the need for transactions of a wide variety of customers.

The buildings occupied by a firm or company or held on franchise conform to a unique pattern of construction so that the customers may find it convenient to walk in and pick up different consumer items sold on retail trade at fixed prices and make payment in cash or through credit cards at the exit point with the advantage of marketing pleasure that replaces the usual market place where multiple sellers have to be accosted with vexatious higgling. Being under common ownership, the multiple retail trade carried on under a single umbrella finds the opportunity of effecting economy of scale in selling devices and payment facilities. The valuation of such assets has to take note of all aspects that legitimately arise for consideration.

(9) *Hotels & restaurants—holiday homes and club houses*

There are certain types of property which are designed or adopted for particular uses. Hotels and restaurants come under this category. Such properties are normally valued having regard to trading potential. The income approach to valuation is applicable in such cases. The income approach provides valuation estimates by capitalising the projected income stream of the subject property. The exercise begins with collecting and processing income and expense data. The expenses comprising outgoings have to be carefully elaborated. In case of hotel, the income data should be expressed on an appropriate per unit basis, *e.g.* rent per room or bed, rate of catering for itemwise food etc. The vacancy data or occupancy rate is also important. The averaging of income is another consideration. A part of profit may be due to goodwill which should also be properly reflected in the rate of return. If such businesses are sold as going concerns, the value of aggregate asset as going concern may far exceed the total value of all tangible assets comprised in the physical property including land, building and fixtures, if the concern has earned a goodwill. The reverse may occur if the reputation of the concern is otherwise operating on the negative way.

A class of property has grown up in recent times which is akin to hotels and restaurants. While hotels are meant for short stay creating interest of the boarders for user only for the days he has paid for, some assets of a different kind also create occupancy right of the same nature in holiday homes or club houses which offers a right consequent on membership of the organisation which owns or runs the holiday homes or the club. While hotels are meant for any one who pays for short stay. The same facility of occupancy is available only to the members who belong to the organisation or the club by way of membership.

(10) *Cinema halls and amusement centres*

Cinema halls fall under the category of licenced premises for investment purposes with a view to earning profit. Thus its valuation depends upon its capacity to generate income. There is another speciality. Apart from the main hall where cinema shows are held for amusement of public who obtain the right of entry on purchase of tickets, there are in most cases a lobby for restaurant and bar comprised in the same premises where entry is open. The owner either carries on the business himself or lets it out to others for business purposes. Thus, a cinema building admits of dual methods of valuation, the hall according to income method and the business portion according to rental method.

So far as the income method is concerned, the usual practice for rating purposes, according to the municipal law in a number of States in India, consists in calculating the gross annual receipts from sale of tickets for cinema shows or theatrical performances, to which are added all receipts from rents and advertisements; and the net receipt is obtained by deducting the taxes on the sale of tickets therefrom. A number of judicial decisions in the field of valuation for rating purposes are relevant in this context. In *Bengal Properties Pvt. Ltd.* v *L.N. Bal*[9] it was held that in assessing a cinema house a municipal authority is not permitted to take resort to two modes of assessment for a single premises even though a portion of the cinema building is let out as shops or stalls. In *Kalipada Dawn* v *Commissioners of the Vishnupur Municipality,*[10] the Court observed that where the premises being a cinema house are being used for earning profit, the authority may take into consideration not only comparable premises, the rent actually paid by the occupier, but also what an intending lessee of the cinema house might be expected to offer for the assessable premises. But this cannot be done by simply guessing the profits that may be derived by a maximum sale of tickets for

9 67 CWN 382.
10 68 CWN 949.

the seats available in the cinema house. The assessee being the cinema-owners cannot be called upon to disclose their profits or to produce their account books, because the tax authorised is a tax on the holding and not on its profits. In *Globe Theatre* v *Chief Judge, SCC Bombay,*[11] the mode of assessment of a cinema under the Bombay Municipal Corporation Act on the basis of a percentage of a rate upon sitting accommodation was recognised as a valid principle. In *Darshan Lal Mehra* v *Union of India*[12] the Supreme Court held valid the mode of computation of annual rental value of amusement centres like cinema halls on the basis of U.P. Nagar Mahapalika Adhiniyam 1959 which indicates the extent of the accommodation, its quality, the locality and other factors relating to enjoyment of the building as the considerations for valuation.

But it must be remembered that rating is not the only purpose for which cinema halls or amusement centres are valued. As a marketable property, cinema hall as a business may change hands where all the considerations of valuation relevant in an income approach or profit approach would be applicable. But the judicial decisions above provide a guide as regards the items of income and outgoings that would pertinently arise for assessing profit or income. Of course, a dual method of valuation; income approach for the cinema hall and rental approach for the business establishments in the premises, together with considerations of goodwill as an intangible asset would be legitimately attracted.

(11) *Office buildings*

Office buildings let out on rent are considered as investment and in course of investment, a direct comparison is always made with the yield obtainable in other opportunities. Another feature is that the rent payable in the immediate present is not always the same for the future. Generally, a higher rent is obtainable on revision and in filling up of vacancies that may occur in future. Accordingly, office buildings are invariably valued according to the investment method which is the

11 AIR 1947 Bom 108.
12 AIR 1992 SC 1848.

determination of the present value of the right to receive a future sum or a series of future sums by discounting them at an appropriate compound rate. In other words, it consists in capitalisation of rental income. While computing income, adequate attention has to be paid to the outgoings that constitute a liability. The outgoings in an office building is generally much more than that in residential building and also ramified under various heads. Thus the following approaches are relevant in valuation of office buildings:

First, the method of valuation may be based on the assumption that the rent immediately payable will prevail throughout the life of the investment and can, therefore, safely be capitalised for the whole term, although the basis of valuation may be at a lower rate than the additional income receivable after revision.

Secondly, the capitalisation of rental income may admit of two stages. At the first instance, the initial rent may be capitalised at a lower rate as it is more secured than the later rent and thereafter, capitalisation may be made on the basis of open market rent for the remainder of the term beginning from the period the rental income is revisable whether as per terms of agreement or under the law or practices.

Thirdly, an approach to valuation may be made on the basis of an equivalent yield in which a single remunerative rate may be applied to the rent currently receivable and also the rent receivable upon reversion. It is the weighted average yield of an investment representing the overall rate of return. The capital value is thus ascertained after taking into account both the initial rent and the reversionary yield.

(12) *Government and semi-Government property*

There are quite a large number of properties that belong to the Central or State Governments as well as public undertakings including Railways. Premises accommodating Posts and Telegraphs, Doordarshan, Akashvani, Courts, Government administrative headquarters, Legislatures, Airports are some of the examples that can be cited. The characteristics of such buildings are also that they are not transacted in market sales and, therefore, ought to be valued by an appropriate method as discussed in subsequent chapters.

The specialities that these buildings attract particularly in the field of municipal taxation and valuation need be mentioned. Properties of the Union Government are exempted from payment of all taxes imposed by a State or local authority under Art. 285(1) of the Constitution of India. Such Union property includes the properties belonging to the Railway Administration as well. But the Central Government have agreed to pay service charges in lieu of taxes to the local authorities for the purpose of which a pattern of valuation is laid down in the Government circulars from time to time. The properties of the Port Trusts are governed by the Major Port Trusts Act 1963 in the matter of valuation for the purpose of municipal assessment.

The question arose as to what constitutes the property of the Union for exemption of rates. It was laid down in *Turf Properties Ltd.* v *Corporation of Calcutta,*[13] that what constitutes property of the Union will be a question of fact and will not depend upon the way in which the municipality may choose to impose its rates and taxes. In *International Airport Authority* v *Municipal Corporation of Delhi,*[14] it has been laid down that the property vested in the Airport Authority cannot be held to be an Union property and cannot, therefore, be exempted from the levy of the municipal tax by virtue of Art. 285 of the Constitution. Then, in *Food Corporation of India* v *Angamali Municipality,*[15] the Kerala High Court has held that the Food Corporation of India is a statutory corporation, distinct and different from Union or Government. It is not a department of the Central Government and hence, not immune from tax under Art. 285(1) of the Constitution of India.

While the Central Government properties are exempted from tax under Constitutional provisions, the properties belonging to the State Government are not. There is, however, a Central legislation being the Municipal Taxation Act 1881 which in its s. 3A empowers the State Government to prohibit by an order in writing the levy by a Municipal Committee of any specified tax by the State Government in

13 61 CWN 912.
14 AIR 1991 Del 302.
15 AIR 1995 Ker 94.

which case the State Government shall pay a sum in lieu of tax to be determined by an officer appointed in this behalf.

But, it must be borne in mind that there may be necessities for valuation of Government or semi-government properties for purposes other than taxation. In such cases, these are to be taken as non-marketable properties which have no investment value. The appropriate method of valuation based on the current price of land together with cost of construction of the buildings less depreciation applicable in such cases is discussed in the subsequent chapter.

Cantonments are administered by an authority under the Cantonments Act 1924. The Cantonments accommodate the quarters or places required for the services like the Army, Navy or Airforce of the country and are held beyond the rich of municipal administration of any kind. That being so, the properties therein do not arise for municipal valuation or valuation for any other purpose not recognised by the Cantonment Act.

(13) *Institutional buildings*

School, hospital, townhall, polytechnic, university, college, sports stadium, crematorium, cemetery, abattoir, chapel, temple, club house, mosque, public library, museum, exhibition hall,—these are all examples of institutional property. They all have one element in common that they are not marketable items and, therefore, not open to sale transactions. Most of these classes of buildings have to be valued by the contractor's method or the land and building method which is discussed in details in subsequent chapters. The problem arises in determining the initial cost of the building on the date of commencement of construction and deciding the factors affecting obsolescence for deduction purposes.

(14) *Godowns and warehouses*

Many godowns and warehouses are let; it is therefore necessary to consider what security, rents for these premises offer to the owner. Many shopkeepers, especially those dealing in the piece-goods trade, have shops in the main shopping districts and generally where lands are of a very high price. Rents are consequently high and it is the exception rather than the rule for the godowns to be located in the same building. These godowns are usually situated on subsidiary streets and lanes, but it is necessary for them to be within easy reach of the shop or business premises.

The main factors to be considered when determining the security of the rent of a godown are:

1. The situation of the godown,
2. The demand for godowns in that locality,
3. The distance to the nearest shopping district,
4. The type of building and the condition of the structure. It is essential that godowns should be wind and watertight and for many types of articles damp-proof,
5. The suitability of the godowns for the types of article that will be stored there,
6. Provision for ample water-supply on the premises for fire-fighting purposes, and
7. Working height of the building.

The rents of godowns depend almost entirely on the condition of trade and this class of property can be considered mainly a speculative concern. In some instances the security will be higher and the buildings will invariably be valued at salvage value. This will usually happen when districts have changed their character and buildings erected as godowns are no longer in demand in that locality.

(15) *Cold storage*

The purpose of a cold storage is to enable trading in the distances of time. While goods are transported from one geographical place to another for the purpose of trading in response to market demand, commodities are preseved in cold storage in order to make abundant production in a season available at a future market when supply will become scarce. Thus it is a commercial coveyance in time in which the cold storage acts as a giant refrigerator. When the owner of a cold storage allows a space within it to be used by a customer, the space is not let out. The relationship is that of a hirer and a licensee (as all cold storages are to be licensed to an owner under the regulatory legal provision). The cold storage receipt given to a hirer of space against storage of commodities, is transferable by endorsement. It was observed in the case of

Bangashree Ice and Cold Storage Ltd. v *Corporation of Calcutta,*[16] that out of the two methods of valuation, *i.e.* the rental method or the land and building method, it should not be the consideration of the authorities as to which would fetch more taxes to the municipal corporation, but the consideration should be as to which of the two methods would be more easily applied in the facts and circumstances to each case.

The major considerations in a cold storage should be the purpose for which valuation is made and for whom it is made. An appropriate method shall have to be followed depending upon the circumstances of each case. If the storage space has to be valued, the rental method would be proper, while for the sale or other form of transfer of the entire cold storage, the capital value thereof has to be estimated and cross-checked with the income-producing capacity of the entire investment. Before approaching on income or profit basis, enquiries must be made to find out whether the existing business enterprise can be put to more beneficial use whereby it will yield a higher income or if that be not possible, what the next best alternative use is.

(16) *Racecourse, stadium, golf course*

Racecourse is a highly specialised property and such properties are not open to sales comparison. The cost approach may provide a clue to valuation. But racecourses are also meant for profit. It was laid down in the case of *Municipal Corporation, Bombay* v *R.W.I. Turf Club*[17] that the yardstick to assess the rateable value of a racecourse would depend on the amount of profits earned from race meetings held on the racecourse including all expenses reasonably or properly incurred which go to making of the receipts. But this is relevant particularly for valuation in the context of rating. Other purposes of valuation may attract a different method depending upon the object of valuation.

Like racecourse a golf course or a stadium shall also be recognised as a specialised property, not open to sales comparison. Valuation of such property generally abide by the cost approach.

16 1977 CLJ 522.
17 AIR 1968 SC 425.

(17) *Industrial properties and industrial estates*

Buildings erected for factory purposes have usually been erected and designed to suit a particular purpose having regard to the present and future prospects of the industry. In the same way sites are selected which will give the greatest facilities for transport and in localities where there is an ample supply of skilled semi-skilled labour. A valuer very rarely will have the opportunity of making a valuation on the rental basis owing to the lack of available data. Very few premises of this type are let, and where they are, the rent may not have any relationship to the value of the land and building. For instance, a jute press will be let to a baler who will pay a royalty rent on all the bales he presses. In these cases the rent is dependent upon the industry and not on the value of the buildings. The buildings simply restrict the baler from pressing more than the capacity of the plant and machinery.

If premises built for a special purpose become vacant and to let, it is very seldom that a tenant can be found who will pay a rent based on the cost of construction. Tenants usually pay a rent which represents the usefulness of the premises for the particular purpose to which it will be put. This is particularly true about industrial uses of premises because industries are of various types and each lay-out is purpose-specific. The lay-out of premises for one purpose may not suit the other.

There may be primary industries concerned with extracting materials direct from the land, sea, mountains or forests. These items may not involve any processing or fabrication of a finished product, viz., mining, quarrying, logging of wood etc. The secondary industries include the vast bulk of manufacturing industries that adds value to primary products. In the next stage, comes the tertiary industries which are basically service-oriented, viz., construction, transport, communication, etc. The fourth category constitutes the quaternary industries comprising activities like research, information service, know-how development. The valuation parameters are different in each case as discussed later.

In recent years, a new category of property have come up as Industrial Estates. The land of the industrial estates is generally developed by the Government and different types of structures are built up thereon with a view to creating appropriate infrastructure for industrialisation. These areas are known as Industrial Estates. It is a property of different kind from a particular factory or industry as such. Such infrastructure is served by water supply, electricity, weigh-bridge etc. to facilitate industrial activities. Since these industrial estates are virtually processed land for industrial growth, a valuation process has to evolue taking into consideration the imputes provided for development. If the structure is built by the industrial unit who occupies the same and not by the Government, the valuation abides by a different methods. Any way, the industrial estates being different in character from an individual factory or industry it is a real estate of different kind for valuation purposes.

(18) *Petrol-filling stations*

The valuation of petrol-filling stations is an exercise of much experience and knowledge of the commercial operation. The properties are somewhat akin to licensed premises often owned and sometimes let out on tied tenancies. When the oil companies own a petrol-filling station, it does not have so much of the character of an investment but is primarily an outlet for product produced on a quasi-monopoly basis. Their petrol-profits arise from the refining and wholesaling process and to some extent from rents derived from tied outlets. On the other hand, when petrol-filling stations are owned by the dealers, the profit arises mainly from retailing. The properties of a petrol-filling station includes the underground storage tank, forecourt, pumps, sales-kiosks and all items above ground connected with the sale of petrol etc. The estimated gross profit out of actual sales figure provide the basis of valuation. If in addition, there are ancilliary buildings for the repair or servicing of vehicles, these are valued in the normal way by the rental comparison method; usually rental evidence can be found from other similar workshops and like properties in the locality. In a case under the Bombay Municipal Corporation Act, the question arose if a petroleum storage tank is a 'structure' and come within the definition of 'land and building' so as to be exigible to property tax. The Supreme Court in *Municipal Corporation of Greater Bombay* v *Indian Oil Corporation Ltd.*[18] observed that the definition of the word

18 AIR 1991 SC 686.

'building' is an inclusive definition bringing within its ambit amongst others every other such structure. The structure must be an entity in itself although not necessarily a building in itself, adapted to the particular purpose it serves. Method of construction by itself is not conclusive. Considering from the angle, the Supreme Court opined that the petroleum storage tanks are 'structures' or 'things attached to the land' and are exigible to property tax.

The special aspect of the valuation of such property is that it involves projections in an imperfect and uncertain market. Direct comparable evidence is hardly available as difference in location means total variance of profitability. A station on a busy stretch of road or situated on a communicational junction offers no comparison at all to a far-off station where accessibility, visibility and lay-out cuts down the sale to a fraction. Thus it is probably more true to say that the value of a property like petrol-filling station is what it will fetch.

Storage tanks used for supply of gas or for storage of valuable liquid are assets similar to a petrol-filling station. The valuation of the same shall also abide by the same considerations that pertinently arise in the context of a petrol-filling station.

(19) *Damaged properties*

Properties that stand in a damaged state due to fire, storm or any impact of like nature are required to be valued on a different footing. The extent of damage might range from superficial to total loss and at the date of valuation, works of restoration may or may not have been undertaken. The assumption is that the property, though damaged, has a marketable value if a sale takes place at the valuation date. The vendor may have retained the benefit of any direct claim against insurance and he may pass on the benefit of such claim to a purchaser. In that event, the valuation might be prepared on that basis. It may be noted that the insurance amount does not reflect the ultimate value of reinstatement as the extent of accidental damage cannot be foretold. The insured person only indicates a notional amount acceptable to the insurance company on which he pays the premium. The value of the damaged property shall take into account various other factors.

If the landlord of the damaged property has a right to claim or enforce reinstatement against a lessee, the benefit of such claim can also be passed on to the purchaser and the property valued accordingly. If the damaged property is tenanted and the leases or sub-leases are not determinable, there may be no alternative but to reinstate the original building, regardless of the extent of the damage. Such burden of obligation would reduce the value of the property to the extent of the estimated expenditure of current cost to complete the development.

If the damage is superficial the market value would take into account the expenses to carry out the reinstatement works. In case of total loss of the building, the site value after allowing the cost to demolish any remaining structure or foundation would be appropriate. In computing the site value, the potential for development of the land for a different use ought to be taken into account. The valuer has to address himself to all such considerations.

(20) *Transport terminal*

The transport terminals of various types of conveyances including aircrafts have become items of valuation of special nature. The terminals reflect a pattern of land-use of different kind from the others of real estate. The aerodromes, the truck terminals or bus terminus call for a method of valuation different from others. These assets are not generally marketable and hence the market approach is inapplicable. The investments are generally made by public exchequer as infrastructural development. So, the income generated by such land-uses hardly measures the value thereof. The Governments or local bodies incur the necessary expenditure for public benefit. The cost approach to valuation of such specialised assets are often applied. That too is not scientific. Because, the infrastructural development of such nature leads to multi-facet benefits. Being an asset where large number of people assemble for waiting purposes, such terminals do have a rich potential for commercial exploitation. The hotels and restaurant inevitably grow up in the vicinity for short stay and refreshment. Commercial growths are also to be found. In an era of privatization, the value ultimately added to the land and building of such growth potentiality cannot be ignored. The public benefit in ultimate shape enters into the valuation process as an ingredient of valuation. The estimation of value thus enters into a complex system which are to take into consideration the possible benefits of such land-use quantified in monetary terms. A new approach of valuation to be designated as 'benefit approach' may come as an aid to the valuers. Such benefit approach, new to the system generally practised, takes into account the fall-out of the improvements, in short-run or in long-run, accordingly as applicable in varying circumstances. The nature of such fall-out again determines the return on investments. Since privatization of public services is coming as the trend for facilitating the participation of private funds refuelling public expenditure on infrastructure on the formulae of 'Build Operate and Transfer (BOT)' or 'Build Operate Own and Transfer (BOOT)' it is perhaps relevant to consider 'benefit approach' in the context of valuation coming nearer to reality.

(21) *Special Economic Zone (SEZ)*

The Special Economic Zones have emerged as a unique type of land-use regulated by the Act, namely, The Special Economic Zone Act 2005. It is with a view to providing an internationally competitive environment for exports that has led to the creation of the Special Economic Zone (SEZ). Any person who intents to set up such zone can make a proposal to the State Government concerned for setting up the SEZ which virtually means a free trade and warehousing zone. The State Government examines such proposals and forward the same to a Board of Approval constituted for the purpose. The applicant is usually called a 'Developer'. If sanctioned, the areas falling within the SEZs may be demarcated by the Central Government as the processing area for setting up manufacturing units and carrying on services exclusively for export-oriented trading and warehousing purpose that enjoyed exemption from taxes, duties and cess as incentives for export. The areas under SEZ is provided with facilities of minimum regulatory control, off-shore banking services, unique fiscal regime for the developers and a single-window clearance mechanism to facilitate the export activities. The packages of incentives are calculated to attract foreign and domestic investments for promoting export-led growth for commodities as well as services of Indian origin. At the time the relevant

Act was passed, there had already been in existence eleven functioning SEZs, out of which seven was set up by the Central Government and four by the private or joint sectors. In addition, approvals were given for setting up another thirty-five new SEZs in the private or joint sector. Thus areas under SEZ have also come up as a land-use pattern where valuation for the purpose of transfer in any contingency whatsoever is likely to be different from than what is practiced to day. Under s. 53 of the above Act, a Special Economic Zone shall be deemed to be a territory outside the customs jurisdiction and shall be deemed to be a port, airport, inland container depot, land station and land customs stations, as the case may be, under s. 7 of the Customs Act 1962. Accordingly, fourteen such SEZs have already been recognized as deemed ports under a notification of the Central Government dated the 14th March 2006. The disputes arising in the SEZ shall be adjudicated upon by special court and single enforcement agency to ensure speedy trial and investigation of notified offences.

(22) *Transferable Developmental Rights (TDR)*

This is a right of development that has very recently appeared in the metropolitan scenario to compensate people who are affected by controls of development in specific regions imposed under planning laws or municipal building code. Land holdings in municipal areas are subject to control of development through the prescribed Floor Area Ratio (FAR) or Floor Space Index (FSI). In the city of Bombay, the Development Control Regulations for Greater Bombay, 1991 enables a land owner who holds unexploited FSI in his land in a particular zone due to developmental control or expropriation owing to road-widening etc., to utilise it in some other designated zone characterised by low density. For this purpose he is given a Certificate under the regulations which is negotiable in transactions. Thus, FSI is converted into Floating FSI. In an unreported case of *Shiv Kumar Gupta* v *State of Maharashtra and the Municipal Corporation of Greater Bombay* in Writ petition No. 1615 of 1995, Mr. Justice Dhanuka in his judgment dated 11.10.1995 observed that Regulation 14 of the above Regulations provides that development rights Certificates may be used on one or more plots of land whether vacant or already developed or by erection of additional storey or any other manner consistent with the Regulations but not so as to exceed in any plot a total built-up FSI higher than that prescribed in Regulations 14 in the Appendix. The valuation of this emerging species of property right poses considerable complexity which is appropriately discussed later in this book.

CHAPTER

4

Methodology of Valuation

It would appear from the foregoing discussion that properties can be divided into two broad groups—marketable and non-marketable. When we talk of property in the context of this book, we mean immovable property or in more precise terms, lands and buildings, because there are other forms of immovable property the valuation of which is outside the scope of this book. Of course, an introductory treatment on valuation of other kinds of property or assets has been the subject-matter of an exclusive chapter in this book. For example, agricultural land; plantations of coffee, tea or rubber; mines and quarries; forest lands are discussed in this book for the purpose of valuation by way of passing reference. Each of these items of immovable property call for specialised expertise for valuation. Likewise, certain items of movables are valued only by skilled experts in the field. Stocks, shares, debentures, securities, partnership and business assets including goodwill, constitute one such specialist field; so also plant and machinery. The gems and jewelleries are precious items and are wealth in congealed form much more valuable than any other form of movable assets. Their valuation is a task confined to a few who have developed a sense of appreciation through many years of acquaintances and experiences; so is work of art and artefacts that might be sold in millions of dollars to a select class of wealthy acquirers. The later chapter touches on all these topics.

The present book is confined primarily to land and building held under different titles and in different uses and valuation considerations associated with them. There are three approaches including methods traditionally used in real property valuation:

(*i*) The market approach—sales comparison method.

(*ii*) The income approach—rental method—capitalisation method.

(*iii*) The cost approach—land and building method.

But this is not exhaustive. As we shall see later, the purpose of valuation demands valuation methodology adapted suitably to the particular purpose for which valuation is meant. But for the present, let us analyse the broad approaches to valuation as categorised above.

Market approach

The sales comparison method in a market approach is applicable to all property which is capable of being bought and sold in the market. A comparison is made for the purpose of valuation with similar properties that have recently been sold in the market and has thus acquired a market value, but the important questions are the availability of adequate sales data and data for sale of identical properties and that for sales during contemporaneous period. No two lands or buildings are exactly alike. There is always a difference in location or amenities provided in lands or buildings compared, if not also in age, occupational use or neighbourhood. Again, the market is different for different classes of buildings. A very high valued building would find only a few purchasers and the sale thereof do not take place too often. The same can be said about the specialised properties. Thus, the task of collection, verification and screening of sales data are important prerequisites to valuation according to sales comparison methodology. The real estate properties are often stratified into groups in which they can meaningfully be compared for valuation. The grouping need sufficient experiences about variety of transactions. The date of the sale is again an important factor as because prices do not remain static. Thus, valuation is often expressed in terms of a range under the sales comparison method. The expression 'market value' has been conceptually expanded and delineated by a series of judicial decisions as discussed in the subsequent chapters, but it must be understood that the judicial decisions are pronounced in the context of different purposes of valuation.

Hence, there is no absolute standard in the connotation of 'market value' as evolved by judicial decisions, but all these decisions are quite relevant from the angle of perceiving the different colour of lights in which the expression has been viewed.

Income approach

The income approach of valuation is applicable to properties which are in the nature of investment. All investments are intended to generate income or so to say, profit. The valuation consists in ascertaining the present worth of future benefits. The income approach should begin with an analysis of the present income and the series of projected income in future. When a property is let out, a reasonable expectation of yield by way of rent shall be considered as income. The primary factors that decide the yield of lands and buildings by way of rent are the location, amenities provided in the building, occupational use, age of the building and the considerations of neighbourhood. In urban scenario *situs* or location plays the key role. But in case of rented properties in urban areas, the rental value may be substantially affected by the rent control laws in operation. Hence, rental method of valuation is separately discussed in an exclusive chapter as an income approach.

The concept of income capitalisation which lies at the core of income approach involves the calculation of year's purchase on a sound basis. Again, it also leads to the assessment of interest which is a payment made for the use of capital in production. Then there is a question of ensuring the security of the capital. All these issues are discussed in a separate chapter.

Cost approach

While marketable properties are valued under the sales comparison method and investment properties with the income approach, there are properties in land and building which are meant neither for investment nor for sale in the open market because of their specialised nature. The valuation of such property is done by the method of costing which involves the following steps:

(*i*) estimate the current construction cost of the improvements including building and development, (*ii*) subtract the accrued depreciation, and

(*iii*) add the value of the land.

Each item is a subject-matter of discussion. This practice of valuing a property on the basis of aggregate of separate costs of land, structures or improvements is known also as the Land and Building method of valulation or the Contractor's method of valuation. But it must be said that the Land and Building method of valuation does not exhaust all that is to be discussed about cost approach to valuation. That is why in discussing the cost approach the Land and Building method of valuation has been separately dealt with as a chapter reflecting on land characteristics and issues arising out of buildings and other assets. Land has uniqueness of its own due to location, nature and use. As regards buildings, the estimate of accrued depreciation constitutes the most difficult aspect of the cost approach, especially for the older properties. Buildings again are susceptible to obsolescence, functional, economic or technological. All these aspects are required to be reflected in the valuation process. The Land and Building method is, however, inadequate to estimate the value to the business of properties which fall within the category of those which are rarely, if ever, sold in the open market. The oil refineries or chemical works, power stations, dock installations etc. are the typical examples where the cost approach would involve the estimation of the depreciated replacement cost. So the cost approach of valuation remains to be elaborated even after a chapter dwells on Land and Building Method of Valuation.

Benefit approach

We are next coming to valuation of infrastructure investments. The public works of the Government mean construction of roads, bridges, culverts, railways, communication lines etc. These are not meant for profit although a huge sum of money is sunk by way of investment. The advancement of public utilities is the goal of such public expenditure. These properties are never marketable, nor the cost approach to valuation gives an exact idea of the benefit that accrues to the society. As products of investment with huge expenditure, they have immense VALUE-IN-USE which is often required to be measured with great care. Again, historical monuments like Taj Mahal cannot be valued, if at all, by any cost approach. Even from MUNDANE economic viewpoint, it has generated huge income stream in tourism industry of the country. The proper approach to evaluate them is the estimation of benefits which constitutes another approach to the valuation process. This also is discussed in details in a subsequent chapter.

Valuation for specific purpose—fiscal as well as non-fiscal

The method of valuation follows the purpose for which valuation is sought for. Thus valuation may be intended for various fiscal purposes of levying taxes, by the Central Government or the State Government or the Local Government, as the case may be. The necessity for valuation may arise for non-fiscal purposes too. The fiscal authorities generally lay down their own method as embodied in the relevant statute itself. Thus for levy of municipal property tax, the concept of annual valuation of the asset is followed which is a departure from the methods spelt out in this chapter. The annual valuation is an estimate of 'gross annual rent' at which the property may reasonably be expected to let from year to year. The concept of 'reasonable expectation' has been equated by judicial decisions with the legal expectation as determined by 'fair rent' or the 'standard rent' under the rent control law in force. We know, every State in India has its own rent control law to guide the fixation of fair rent or standard rent in the urban region. The issue is further complicated by the recent trend of amending the fiscal provision that brings into existence a different kind of valuation for rating purposes popularly known as the 'unit area assessment' system. The idea is to ensure that the municipal governance do not suffer from a stagnating source of finance created by annual valuation being tethered to the 'fair rent' concept. The 'unit area' method of valuation too does not abide by the usual approaches of valuation known as market approach, income approach or cost approach. In this way the municipal valuation for property taxation makes a departure from the approaches or methodology generally followed in the valuation parlour. The significance of the departure is that the Supreme Court of India has accorded judicial recognition to this 'unit area' method of valuation for the purpose of municipal taxation provided the municipal law lays down a complete code for determination of valuation in this behalf.[1]

Other fiscal fields

The levy of stamp duty on transfer of property again follows a method of working out the market value as per guidance of a 'ready reckoner' prepared by the relevant authority or department. The authorities of Income Tax including Capital Gains follow the municipal valuation method for its own purpose. The Wealth Tax Act follows the process of determination of 'net maintainable rent' for levying the burden of taxation. The levy of court fees follows a different pattern of valuation of property involved in the suits for partition, specific performance, grant of probate, etc.

Movables

To come to the field of movables, the fiscal law for levy of excise duty conceives the valuation from a different angle. The levy of duty for the fiscal purpose works out the 'normal price' that assume a specialized character within the meaning of the Act. Similarly, levy of custom duty follow its own systems of working out the 'transaction value' as elaborated in the Act itself.

Non-fiscal field

Laws of valuation for other statutory non-fiscal purposes carve out unique methods for determination of compensation as laid down in the relevant Act. Thus, Land Acquisition Act (now the Right to Fair Compensation and Transparency in Land Acquisition, Rehabilitation and Resettlement Act 2013), Railways Act, Betterment levy under the planning law etc. have unique method of property valuation for assessing compensation for losses. The bank obtain collateral security against advances the 'realizable value' of which has to be worked out at the time of recovery of dues. Those collateral securities are mostly immovable property mortgaged by deposit of title deeds or movable assets hypothetical to the bank. These assets in huge number turned out to be 'non-performing assets'

1 *Hyderabad Municipal Corporation* v *Grita Yasamanula Samkhya* AIR 2001 SC 2046; *Kamala Mills* v *Mumbai Municipal Corporation* AIR 2003 SC 2998.

for recovery. Hence arise the need for working out the 'realizable value' thereof. After the passing of the Secrutisation Act, the duty devolves on another financial institution for recovery of the bad debts. Hence, the growing fields are demanding the system of valuation to assume newer forms for application. Valuation for insurance purpose again views the exercise of valuation from the angle of indemnification and reinstatement as discussed later in this book.

There are some other Acts that touch the field of valuation while traversing their own course. As for example, the field of auction-reserve follows its own definition in assessing valuation as reserve price. The other fields of valuation where the method of valuation is purpose-specific, are also punctuated by the methodology spelt out in the statute itself like the Electricity Act, Motor Vehicles Act, West Bengal Apartment Ownership Act, West Bengal Government Land (Regulation of Transfer) Act 1993, Workmen's Compensation Act, West Bengal (Regulation of Promotion of Construction and Transfer by Promoters) Act 1993.

Globalization and its effect

The realm of valuation is ever increasing as human civilization advances towards globalization. The role of valuation for company assets is becoming very much pronounced with activities like merger, amalgamation or take-over of companies. The valuation of stock, share and debenture are surfacing in the front seats of valuation. The valuation of Intellectual Property Rights (IPR) like patent, copyright, trademark, design etc. are assuming terrific importance that calls for valuation exercise at a high skilled level. More so, when goodwill has to be valued as well as the synergic effect of the combined productive activities. The functions of plant and machinery as fixed assets depend very much in the valuation context on the value added by intellectual property rights enriching their performance. The wave of privatization of different Governmental activities where the public sector has dominated so long calls for a valuation process as disinvestments of public sector undertakings are on the increase. The requirement of preparation of financial statement is generally relevant in the matter of drawing up the prospectus of companies. This exercise in the realm of business valuation is another area where the expertise of valuers of plant and machinery are loudly pronounced.

Ever widening field of valuation

The field of valuation does not exhaust with what has been stated above. Valuation of real estate or plant and machinery are quite often targeted to the rights and interests incidental to possession thereof. There are also cases of constructive possession or lesser interests unaccompanied by actual physical possession. Thus a freehold property means an exclusive domain over the property together with absolute right subjected only to the power of eminent domain of the State. Lesser interests in leasehold property, mortgage property, easement rights, hire purchase and buy backs, non-owning rights, such as, life estate, lien, trust etc. call for specialized issues in valuation. Even property held as licensee with powers of attorney or unauthorized in adverse possession may account for value. The exercise of valuation is also needed in the field of computation of national income or assessment of GDP (Gross Domestic Product). In the West, the insurance of human limbs significance in the world of sports or games or in any risky venture has already made its way for valuation for insurance purpose. May be, one day the systems of work prevalent in the public field whether in the sphere of education or public health or skilled development may invite the exercise of valuation for determining economic viability. In this way valuation as a vast field of study is gradually grown and snowballing as an inter-disciplinary course, highly specialized for specific purposes, deeply concerned with the laws of markets in economics, in compassed as all the system of valuation in vogue under myriads of past legislation but responding to the modem methods that marches ahead with time.

Different methods for valuation of same property under different statutes

This aspect have been dealt with in *CIT* v *Vimlaben Bhagwandas Patel*;[2] and in *Commissioner of Succession Duties* v *Executor*

2 (1979)118 ITR 134 (Guj).

Trustee and Agency Company of South Australia Ltd.[3] It will be useful to bear in mind what Dixon, J., said in 74 CLR 358:

> "I should like, however, to add for myself that there is some difference of purpose in valuing property for revenue cases and in compensation cases. In the second, the purpose is to ensure that the person to be compensated is given a full money equivalent of his loss, while in the first it is to ascertain what money value is plainly contained in the asset so as to afford a proper measure of liability to tax. While the difference cannot change the test of value, it is not without effect upon a court's attitude in the application of the test. In a case of compensation, doubts are resolved in favour of a more liberal estimate, in a revenue case, of a more conservative estimate".

The Gujarat High Court in *CIT* v *Vimlaben Bhagwandas Patel*[4] held that the competent authority should resort to checks and counter-checks by applying the various methods relevant to the valuation process. Normally in such a case the minimum valuation should be taken unless there were special facts and circumstances in the particular case where higher valuation would be justified. This was an acquisition case where the Hon'ble Court observed: "It would be too hazardous to prefer one of the recognized methods of valuation which may be advantageous to the cause of the revenue."

There is no wooden or mechanical rule that can be applied to determine the value of an asset or property in all situations whatever be the nature of the statute under which the valuation has to be fixed.

The approach to valuation for determination of the fair market value of the same property thus can differ having regard to the nature of the statutes. The permissible extent of differentiation has been set out in the observations of Paripoorman, J. in *CWT* v *Mrs. Sara Varghese*[5] where it is observed:

3 74 Commonwealth Law Reports 358 (373).
4 (1979)118 ITR 134.
5 (1991)187 ITR 450 (Ker).

"Regarding valuation, what we are concerned is the market value of the property. It is the price which a willing buyer will pay to a willing seller. It will vary from case to case. Valuation is not an exact science. Mathematical calculation is not possible. Money value attributable to the asset should be decided and estimated by the concerned statutory authority in a reasonable and judicial manner on the basis of the facts and circumstances available before him. Valuation should be made objectively and should be based on some material. Even in cases where the asset to be valued has no real market, it is for the assessing authority to fix a notional market value. A hypothetical market is contemplated. 'Imponderables' are involved in the matter of valuation. Some of the principles to be borne in mind in that direction have been stated in the Bench decision of this court in *CIT* v *P.I. George*.[6] Decisions are legion dealing various aspects regarding valuation. The qualitative and quantitative analysis in the matter of valuation will differ from asset to asset, place to place, and also considering the particular statute for which the valuation and price of the property has to be determined. It cannot be a wooden rule. Different methods and approaches necessary in the context of different statutes, under which the market value of an asset has got to be determined, pose difficult problems. The market value has got to be fixed with reference to the particular statute. The approach will differ, according to the nature of the statute, fiscal statutes and non-fiscal statutes. Land Acquisition Act is an important legislation. Among the fiscal statutes, IT Act, WT Act, GT Act, Municipalities Act, etc., are important. In fixing the market value of a particular asset or property, the approach and the analysis is likely to vary according to the subject matter of legislation. The principles that are ordinarily applied in the case of non-fiscal statutes like Land Acquisition Act cannot be applied mechanically in the cases arising under fiscal statutes."

6 (1988)69 CTR 174 (Ker); (1988)171 ITR 620 (Ker).

Two or more methods of valuation may be resorted to in valuing a property

In some cases it may be necessary to adopt even two or more methods to arrive at a correct value. In *Tribeni Devi* v *Collector of Ranchi,*[7] the Supreme Court observed:

> "In arriving at a reasonable correct market value, it may be necessary to take even two or all of those methods into account inasmuch as the exact valuation is not always possible as no two lands may be the same either in respect of the situation or the extent of the potentiality nor is it possible in all cases to have reliable material from which that valuation can be accurately determined."

Averaging of values arrived at by different methods is unscientific

In *Smt. S. Neelaveni* v *CWT,*[8] it was held that where there was a wide disparity in the value obtained by two equally valid different methods averaging could be resorted to.

In *Prodyut Kumar Dutt* v *IT Competent Authority*[9] the Calcutta High Court has held that where tenants had certain rights, the combination of Rental Method and Land & Building Method of valuation was correct.

There is however a school of thought which holds that averaging is a very bad method and should not be adopted as was held in *CWT* v *Mahadeo Jalan.*[10] Such a view probably should be understood in the context of a case where the method adopted is unimpeachable, and to invoke an alternative method is only to dispute the value returned. In cases where to obtain the correct value, valuation by different methods are attempted, an appropriate approach would be, instead of striking a mathematical average, to make adjustments for plus and minus factors by way of appropriate enhancements or discounts to

7 AIR 1972 SC 1417 (1420).
8 (1980)125 ITR 665 (Kar).
9 IAC reported in (1982)134 ITR 42 (Cal).
10 (1972)86 ITR 621 (SC).

the values obtained by the different methods and arrive at the best estimated value.

Whether the minimum or maximum valuation be adopted

The Punjab and Haryana High Court in *Jaswant Rai* v *CWT*[11] did hold that value by the method most beneficial to the assessee can be taken, but other High Courts are of the view that where there is more than one valuation that which is nearest to the correct market value, taking into account all circumstances should be the value to be adopted. In *Smt. S. Neelvani* v *CWT*[12] and *V.C. Ramachandran* v *CWT,*[13] it has been held that it is permissible even to take an average of the values arrived at by different methods. Such was also the view taken in *U.N.V. Pratap* v *CWT.*[14] But, as we have already seen, striking a mathematical average is an unscientific approach.

In determining the fair market value it would be in order to adopt the valuation which conforms to the principles enunciated in *CWT* v *Mrs. Sara Varghese*[15] which also refers to the decision of the Gujarat High Court[16] which held that in acquisition proceedings generally the minimum valuation amongst these arrived at by different relevant methods and tests should be applied unless these are special facts and circumstances to apply only one of two methods giving a valuation higher than the minimum one.

In *Jaswant Rai* v *CWT, Patiala,*[17] Hon'ble Punjab & Haryana High Court held that it was proper that the method to be adopted should be left to the assessee and the method most favourable to him adopted.

Again in *Smt. Sair Rami* v *IAC*[18] the Hon'ble Income Tax Appellate Tribunal, Jaipur Bench held that valuation by one

11 (1977)107 ITR 477.
12 (1980)125 ITR 665 (Kar).
13 (1980)126 ITR 157 (Kar).
14 (1988)170 ITR 461 (MP).
15 (1991)187 ITR 450 (Ker).
16 *CIT* v *Vimlaben Bhagwandas Patel* (1979)118 ITR 134.
17 (1977)107 ITR 477.
18 (1980)9 ITJ 568 (Jai).

method may vary with valuation by another method and it would be fair to adopt a method favourable to the assessee and allow him the choice of the method to be adopted.

Again in *CIT* v *New India Construction Co.*[19] it was held that the assessee was not bound by the method adopted by his valuer. In the instant case, the assessee's valuer valued the property by the Land & Building Method but the property was let out and subject to the Rent Control Act. In this case it was held that the Rent Capitalization Method should be adopted.

The Hon'ble Income Tax Appellate Tribunal, Jaipur Bench held in *Smt. Shanti Devi* v *IAC*[20] that the "Competent Authority shall apply land and building method, contractors method, rental or yield basis method and comparable sales method and work out each estimation of the market value on application of all the four methods and for the purpose of counter-check compare it with Municipal valuation for purpose of property tax assessment and adopt generally the minimum valuation unless there are special facts and circumstances where he may be constrained to apply one or two methods only and/or to adopt the higher valuation rather than the minimum one for reasons to be recorded by him".

The methods of valuation of market value may be (*i*) opinion of experts, (*ii*) prices paid within a reasonable time in *bona fide* sale transactions of purchase or sale of the lands acquired or of the adjacent lands possessing similar advantages, and (*iii*) a number of years' purchase of the actual or immediately prospective profits of the acquired lands. Normally, if there is evidence of comparable sales or other evidence for computation of market value capitalisation should not be adopted. However, in adopting capitalisation method, there is no rule as to the number of years' purchase. It depends upon the economic condition or factors such as prevailing rates of interests in money investments, security of the income, fluctuation, chances of increase, cost of collection, rate of return which could be reasonably expected and other relevant factors. The rate of capitalisation is normally the percentage of return on

19 (1980)17 CTR 223 (Del).
20 (1980)9 TTJ 242 (Jai).

investment that an investor would expect during the relevant period.[21]

The court can always take into account any special circumstances, apart from the methods of valuation traditionally adopted, in order to arrive, as nearly as may be, at an estimate of the market value. In some situations, the estimation of market value depends largely on evaluation of many imponderables and may involve to some extent a matter of guesswork.[22]

21 *State of Kerala* v *Lucy Kochuvareed* 1987(1) Ker LT 578.

22 *Hindusthan Oil Co. Ltd.* v *Damoderan Namboodri* 1986 Ker LT 1013.

CHAPTER

5

Market and Real Estate Market

The transactions of property take place in the market. Hence the sales comparison method, or so to say, the market approach to valuation, is necessarily prefaced by a discussion on market and market value.

Market

The term 'market' needs elaboration as it has a different meaning in economics from what is commonly understood. It is usual to describe a market as a place or locality where buyers and sellers congregate for the purpose of trading and fixing prices by bargains. Commodities are already there in view for the intending purchasers. But 'market' as an economic term does not refer to any particular market place but only to a group of buyers and a group of sellers who are in free communication with one another in the matter of transaction by fixing the price of any commodity on the basis of which they are ready to buy or sell. The purchaser opts for buying because the commodity has utility to him and is ready to pay the price he considers affordable commensurate with the utility he derives. On the other hand, the seller must cover his cost of production and earn a reasonable profit. They may be geographically apart by thousands of miles. Thus the market system is a pricing network that directs production and allocates resources. Market determination of price again is a feature determined by the conditions of the market. There are three important economic operations that describe the way the market works:

(*i*) The schedule of demand;

(*ii*) The schedule of supply;

(*iii*) The equilibrium price.

The schedule of demand describes the quantities of a commodity consumers are able and willing to buy on alternative prices, while supply schedule lays down the quantities of commodities that producers will offer on different product prices. As a general rule, at higher price, more of a product is produced and offered in the market; the lower the price, the lower the quantity supplied. Demand behaves in the reverse manner. The forces of demand and supply pinpoint the price at which a product is marketed as well as the quantity transacted at a particular market price. In other words, the price acts as a resource allocation device. The link between resource consumption and goods produced gives a price signal that is transmitted from the product market to the markets for factors of production. Thus, when the price of cloth is high, it sends immediate signal of high wage to the weavers engaged in production; or the rising return in plumbing services ensures a higher wage to the plumbers.

The pursuit of profit in a market system do not go unchecked. Competition amongst buyers and sellers acts as a control mechanism. Pure competition prevails in a market if there are a large number of independently acting buyers and sellers none of whom can influence price by their individual decisions to enter the market or withdraw from it. The product is treated as a homogeneous commodity and there is widespread diffusion of economic powers among sellers and buyers in the marketplace. Under conditions of imperfect competition, individual buyer or seller is able to influence the product price by his individual decision of marketing. A seller may also reserve a segments of market either by way of product differentiation, or sales promotion through advertisement, brand-naming, packaging or the like. Consequently, the price then loses much of its resource allocation influence to the extent the buyer or the seller is able to exert his own. When imperfect competition gives rise to monopoly through concentration of market power into a single hand of supplier, he is free to exercise absolute control over the market subject to the limit of any excess inviting threats from potential substitute or intervention by the government. The competition through demand and supply, therefore, provides a check and balance system to the concentration of economic power, thereby monitoring the prices, profits, incomes and ultimately the allocation of resources in a society where free enterprise plays a major role in the economy. The same approach has to be borne in mind as we deal with the real estate market.

Real estate market

The real estate market is subject to severe imperfections, because each individual estate has an unique interest. Besides, prices are usually negotiable and there is no one method of arriving at a transaction. The nexus of the market is built up by communication channels quite different from other forms of transactions. There are other characteristics too. The market do not really relate to real estate as such. What is being marketed are the legal rights, or interests, or the real estate. Since the supply of land is absolutely inelastic and fixed, the only element of elasticity relevant for market composition is the potential for divergent use and creation of new rights or interests. Whereas the total supply of land on earth can hardly be enhanced, the availability of land for any particular use can be augmented by diversion of land from one use to another. This diversion is the result of interaction between the forces of supply and demand leading to the fixation of price in each use. Again, rights can be created in the real estate through lease, sub-lease, charge, licence, easement etc. Each segment of rights or interests has its own market giving the shape of a collection of many markets or sub-markets within the real estate market where buying, selling, renting and other activities take place between transferors and transferees.

A thorough understanding of the structure of the market and its working is therefore essential if the market data are to be collected and applied for valuation purpose. As has already been stated, the communication of market information in the real estate market has its own unique style. Communication is effected by the words of mouth in a local market and through advertisements in newspapers and other media for a wider market. But a very important role is played by the real estate agents who act as the broker as well as the source of information. For professionals in land dealings, there are magazines and journals. The records of the registration office where landed property transactions are registered provide a storage of information that may be retrieved by property professionals.

It is also necessary to have an idea about the participants of the market. The people who buy real estates are guided primarily by three motives—purchase for use, acquisition for investment to obtain income or investment for capital gains by way of speculation. Thus, there are persons who want to own a house or place of business; and there are persons who build house for letting out to tenants for rent; and there are again others who seek only for a resale value. In practice, buyers can be motivated by a combination of all three of the above. A knowledge of all these characteristics of a real estate market as well as market trends is a requirement for the valuer advising on real estate. The real estate market is in effect of the amalgam of the transactions of buying, selling, leasing, renting, mortgaging etc. and includes the consideration of the impact of demand and supply that influence the market price and the forces that accelerate or decelerate the volume of transactions. But the responsibility of a valuer demands much more. He does not go merely by the catalogue of prices obtainable in the market since value is not always the price but an 'estimate of price as it ought to be'. Thus the nature, direction and futurity of the market price are the major concern of a valuer. That is why an understanding of the concept of 'market value' is of vital importance. The market price may act as the major indicator of market value, but it is not always equal to the market value. The price prevailing in the market may be due to transient situation that has dominated the forces that make the price what it is. But a valuer has to look beyond the smoke-screen of the present. That is how a detailed treatment of 'market value' becomes imperative.

CHAPTER

6

Market Value

Market value

Market value is usually defined as an estimated amount for which a property may exchange on the date of valuation between a willing buyer and a willing seller in an arm's-length transaction after due observance of the practices of marketing which means that the parties to the transaction had each acted with fair knowledge of the market condition and due prudence without any compulsion or external pressure.

In a break-up of the above concept of market value into its logical ingredients, the following elaboration unfolds:

First of all, market value is an estimated amount which refers to a price expressed in monetary terms. This estimate specifically excludes any special set of circumstances which may have the effect of inflating or deflating the price. Thus a price may be fixed in a typical circumstances of financing assistance, lease-back arrangements or special considerations or concessions extended to anyone associated with the same. Such special considerations should not enter into an estimate as conceived in market value.

In the second place, it arises for consideration as to whether the market price to be estimated is the best price obtainable or the most probable price of the property. The ideal consideration is the reasonable price. It may happen that the best price may not conform to a reasonable estimate. In that case it may not be the surest guide. The most probable price reasonably obtainable in the market may in such situation provide the best clue for estimation.

Thirdly, the estimate of market value should refer to the date of valuation. In other words, the estimate is time specific as on a given date because, markets and market conditions may change and the estimated amount cannot be taken as predetermined. A market value correct at one time may appear inappropriate at another time. Thus the effective valuation date should not be either a past one or a future one. It should essentially be contemporaneous.

Fourthly, the transactions should be between a 'willing buyer' and a 'willing seller'. A 'willing buyer' is one who is motivated but not compelled to buy. Likewise, a willing seller is not a forced seller, nor one prepared to hold out for a price to his absolute choice. But nevertheless he ought to be motivated to sell at the best price attainable in the market. Neither the buyer nor the seller should appear to be overeager for the transaction but should at the same time respond to the current market expectations rather than imaginary or hypothetical market that cannot be demonstrated or anticipated to exist.

Fifthly, there must be an 'arm's-length transaction' between the parties who are not influenced by any special relationship viz., creditor and debtor, landlord and tenant, husband and wife, parent company and its subsidiary company etc. That is to say, each party to the transaction should be presumed to be acting independently of each other as person to person.

Sixthly, the parties to the transaction should act with proper knowledge of the market and with such prudence as an ordinary man under ordinary circumstances is expected to possess. Every prudent person, it is supposed, shall act for his self-interest; thus the primary motivation of a buyer is to buy at the cheapest price and that of the seller to sell at the highest price. Then again it must be an open market where access to information as regards price is not hindered or obstructed. There is also an element of publicity which makes the knowledge about the market price available to all without restriction. In other words, there is no secrecy in dealing and the willing buyer and the willing seller are in a position to come freely in contact with each other and are free either to withdraw from the negotiation or to strike a bargain without any compulsion. The length of exposure time may vary with marketing condition but must be sufficient to allow the property to be brought to the attention of an adequate number of potential buyers and sellers. Moreover, the parties must act without any pressure or coercion to bring them to the transaction.

To put it briefly, "Market Value" may be said to be:

> "The price that a willing purchaser would pay to a willing seller for a property, having due regard to its existing condition, with all its existing advantages, and its potential possibilities when laid out in its most advantageous manner, excluding any advantage due to the carrying out of the scheme for the purposes for which the property is compulsorily acquired."

The various methods of assessing the market value are all designed to find out what a willing buyer will pay to a willing seller, there being no other factors like urgent need of money or urgent need of the land for a special purpose which might depress or augment the price. In the determination of this compensation the ability of a particular party or his lack of ability to develop the land and to realise its potential, is not a relevant circumstance.[1]

Judicial decisions on market value

The term "market value" has acquired definite connotation by judicial decisions. Any addition to the value of the land to the owner which is the result of such factors as are unrelated to the open market cannot be regarded as a part of the market value.[2]

Much time has been given by the courts in determining what is meant by market value and it is worthwhile to study some of the findings of Their Lordships. Let us take up the judicial decisions pronounced in the context of land acquisition

1 *Tek Chand* v *Union of India* (1991) All CJ 80 (SC); (1990)4 SCC 495; (1991)43 DLT 82.

2 *Union of India* v *Shri Ram Mehar* AIR 1973 SC 305; (1973)1 SCC 109.

which have shaped the concept since early days of valuation of real estates.

The judgment of the case *Sm. Swaranamunjury Dassi* v *Secretary of State for India-in-Council,*[3] states *inter alia:*

> "I should like to point out the principle of valuation of lands acquired, which has been laid down authoritatively in a number of cases. Mr. James refers to the case of *Kailash Chandra Mitra* v *Secretary of State for India*[4] where Sir Lawrence Jenkins observes that the market value of the land acquired is the price that the owner willing, and not obliged, to sell might reasonably expect from a willing purchaser with whom he was bargaining for the sale of the property. That proposition cannot be disputed. Again, it has been decided in the case of *Government of Bombay* v *Morwanji Muncherji Cama*[5] that there is no difference between the term 'value to the owner' as used in the Land Clauses Act in England and the expresssion 'market value' as used in s. 23 of the Land Acquisition Act (now s. 26 of the Right to Fair Compensation and Transparency in Land Acquisition, Rehabilitation and Resettlement Act 2013). Therefore, in arriving at the market value of the property, it must be considered what the owner was actually receiving from the property and what would be the amount of loss to him by the acquisition. The same thing was said in the case of *Secretary of State* v *Shanmugaraya Mudaliar*[6] where Their Lordships observed that the District Judge was right in estimating a rent for the whole of the land instead of taking the rent actually received for a part by the owner in coming to his conclusion as to the valuation of the property acquired. It was, Their Lordships stated, the best, if not the only, method he had for getting at the 'market value of the ownership'. Lastly, I should refer to the case of *Rai Bahadur Lala Narsingdas* v *Secretary of State,*[7] where Their Lordships of the Privy Council observe:

3 (1927)32 CWN 421.
4 (1910)17 CLJ 34.
5 (1908)10 Bom LR 907.
6 (1893) LR 20 IA 80 (88).
7 (1924)29 CWN 822 (824) (PC).

'Now the principle upon which the valuation of the property compulsorily acquired should be measured has been repeatedly laid down by this Board and by the House of Lords. To use the words to be found in *Fraser* v *City of Fraserville*[8] it is the value to the seller of the property in its actual condition at the time of its expropriation with all its existing advantages and with all its possibilities excluding any advantage due to the carrying out of the scheme for the purposes for which the property is compulsorily acquired'."

The decision in *Fraser's* case was that of the Judicial Committee and it was pronounced by Lord Buckmaster himself who also delivered the judgment in the case of *Narsingdas* v *Secretary of State.*[9] It has therefore been laid down by the highest authority which we are bound to follow that the value to the seller of the property in its actual condition at the time of the sale should be taken into consideration in arriving at the market value.

An extract from the judgment of Mr. Justice Mookerjee in *Alaul Haq* v *Secretary of State for India-in-Council*[10] is also to the point.

"There can be no question that in valuing land, which has been taken for public purposes under the Land Acquisition Act, the fairest and most favourable principle of compensation is to enquire what is the market value of the property, not according to its present disposition but laid out in the most lucrative and advantageous way in which the owner could dispose of it. This principle was recognised by this Court so far back as 1876 in the case of *Prem Chand Burral* v *Collector of Calcutta.*[11] With reference to this decision it may be pointed out that the most lucrative and advantageous way in which the owner can dispose of the land is to be determined with reference to its future utility, but it must not be entirely conjectural. As was observed in the case of *Rajendra Nath Banerjee* v *Secretary of State*[12]

8 [1917] AC 187 (194).
9 (1924)29 CWN 822 (PC).
10 (1910)11 CLJ 393.
11 (1876)2 Cal 103 (106).
12 (1904)32 Cal 343.

future utility is a thing that people have an eye to in buying land and the market price of the land is affected by it: such future utility must, however, be estimated by prudent business calculations and not by mere speculation and impractical imagination. See also *Fink* v *Secretary of State for India.*[13] The same principle has also been adopted by the Bombay High Court.[14] In the last case it was pointed out that in the neighbourhood of a town where building was going on, it would be unfair to assess the value of land upon its present income if there is a fair probability of the owner being able, owing to its situation, to sell or lease the land for building purposes. Substantially the same principle was recognised by the Judicial Committee in *Secretary of State for Foreign Affairs* v *Charlesworth Pilling.*"[15]

An extract from pages 174 and 182 of Cripps on *Compensation*, 8th Edition is pertinent and to the point.

"The principle of compensation is indemnity to the owner and the basis on which all compensation for lands required or taken should be assessed is their value to the owner as at the date of notice to treat and not their value when taken to the promoters. The question is not what the persons who take the land will gain by taking it but what the person from whom it is taken will lose by having it taken from him. The application of this principle must depend upon the special circumstances in each case."

Again "in assessing the amount of compensation payable when land is taken the probable use to which such land may be put is necessarily an element to be taken into consideration. Land which may probably be used for building purposes cannot be valued on the same basis as merely agricultural land."

As has already been stated, the basis on which compensation for lands taken is to be assessed is the value of the lands to the owner as it existed at the date of the notice to treat and

13 (1907)34 Cal 599.

14 In re *Dorabji Cursetji Shroff* (1907)10 Bom LR 675; *Trustees of Bombay* v *Karsondas* 33 Bom 28; In re *Dhanjibhoy Bomanji* (1907)10 Bom LR 701; *Collector of Poona* v *Kashinath* (1886)10 Bom 585 and in *Munji Khetsey* (1890)15 Bom 279.

15 (1901)28 IA 121; 26 Bom 1 (PC).

not their value, when taken, to the promoters. The propositions which follow are set out in a slightly different form by Eve, J, in *South Eastern Rail Co.*v *L.C.C.*[16]

> "All advantages which the land possesses, present or future in the hands of the owner may be taken into consideration *Cedar Rapids Manufacturing & Power Co.*v *Lacoste;*[17]*Re Lucas & Chesterfield Gas and Water Board;*[18] *Fraser* v *City of Fraserville*[19] and the owner is entitled to have the price assessed with reference to those advantages which will give the land the greatest value. The value of an owner's interest is not properly compensated by assessing the amount of pecuniary benefits obtained by past user in disregard of possible benefits in the future.[20] The probability of a more profitable future use is one such advantage which may be taken into consideration. Thus land which may be probably used for building purposes must not be valued on the same basis as purely agricultural land.[1] But although prospective value is a necessary element in the assessment of compensation, such value must be entirely excluded where it would arise from the construction of the particular works authorised by the Act which gives compulsory powers.[2] It is a recognised principle to exclude from the assessment of compensation any enhancement or diminution in value consequent on the construction of works authorized by the special Act under which the assessment is made, unless there is a special provision in the private or public Act authorizing the compulsory acquisition. There may be a special provision allowing the acquiring party to set off a claim for improvement or betterment."

16 [1915]2 Ch 252 (258).
17 [1914] AC 569.
18 [1909]1 KB 16.
19 [1917] AC 187.
20 *Trent Stoughton* v *Barbados Water Supply Co.* [1893] AC 502; but see *Eldon (Earl)* v *North Eastern Rail Co.* [1890]80 LT 723.
1 *R.* v *Brown* [1867] LR 2 QB 630; *South Eastern Railway* v *Cooper* [1924]1 Ch 211.
2 In re *Lucas & Chesterfield Gas and Water Board* [1909]1 KB 16; *Cedar Rapids Manufacturing & Power Co.* v *Lacoste* [1914] AC 569; *Fraser* v *City of Fraserville* [1917] AC 187.

In assessing the value of any probable future advantages, it is the present value alone of such advantages which falls to be determined.[3]

The general principles applicable to compensation cases were summed up by Mr. Justice Eve in the case of the *South Eastern Rail Co.* v *L.C.C.*,[4] as follows:

"(*a*) The value to be ascertained is the value to the vendor, not its value to the purchaser.

(*b*) In fixing the value to the vendor all restrictions imposed on the user and enjoyment of the land in his hand are to be taken into account, possibility of such restriction being modified or removed for his benefit is not to be overlooked.

(*c*) Market price is not a conclusive test of real value.

(*d*) Increase in value consequent on the execution of the undertaking for or in connection with which the purchase is made must be disregarded.

(*e*) The value to be ascertained is the price to be paid for the land with all its potentialities, and with all the use made of it by the vendor.

(*f*) The true contractual relation of the parties that of purchaser and vendor is not to be obscured by endeavouring to construe it as another contractual relation altogether that of indemnifier and indemnified."

Eve, J, also epitomised his judgment in the following terms, which are of general application:

"Where an owner of two contiguous pieces of land forming an area suited, and it may be best suited, for development, and use as one building site, sells under compulsion a part of one piece, as a part of that piece, and without any reference to his interest in the other piece, the purchase price of the land so contracted to be sold must be ascertained without reference to the vendor's interest in the other piece, and is not to be ascertained by deducting the value of what

3 *Cedar Rapids Manufacturing & Power Co.* v *Lacoste* [1914] AC 569 (576).

4 [1915]2 Ch 252.

is left to the vendor of the two pieces after the sale from their aggregate value immediately prior to the sale."

The general principles for determination of market value of land under the Land Acquisition Act (since repealed and replaced by the Right to Fair Compensation and Transparency in Land Acquisition, Rehabilitation and Resettlement Act 2013) were laid down with great lucidity by the Privy Council in the case of *V. Narayan* v *Revenue Divisional Officer.*[5] This judgment is of special importance as it explains how far the potentiality of a land should be considered in determining its value. Prior to this case, it was generally understood that where a piece of land possessed a potentiality which was of special value to a particular purchaser who was acquiring it for utilising that potentiality, there being no other possible purchaser in the field, that potentiality should be disregarded. In re *Lucas* v *Chesterfield Gas & Water Board,*[6] Fletcher Moulton, LJ had said that "the decided cases to his mind laid down the principle that when the special value exists only for a particular purchaser who had obtained powers of compulsory purchase, it cannot be taken into consideration in fixing the price because to do otherwise would be to allow the costs of the Scheme to enhance the value of the land to be purchased under it". The Privy Council after an elaborate examination of the authorities negatived this dictum of Fletcher Moulton, LJ and held that "Even when the only possible purchaser of the land's potentiality is the authority that has obtained the compulsory powers, the arbitrator in awarding compensation must ascertain to the best of his ability the price that would be paid by a willing vendor of the land with its potentiality in the same way that he would ascertain it in a case where there are several purchasers. Potentialities to be taken into consideration are, however, not realised potentialities, that is to say, land is not to be valued as if it had already been developed and put to the possible use."

The Privy Council in its judgment referred to *Inland Revenue Commissioners* v *Clay,*[7] as an instance: "There was a

5 66 IA 104; 43 CWN 557.
6 [1909]1 KB 16.
7 [1914]3 KB 466.

house of which the value to anyone excepting certain Trustees was no more than £ 750. Those Trustees were the owners of a Nurses' Home which adjoined the house and they were desirous of extending their premises. They accordingly purchased the house for £ 1,000, the owner thus receiving £ 250 for the potentiality his house possessed by reason of its position adjoining the Nurses' Home. It was held by the Court of Appeal that £ 1,000 was the value of the house to a willing seller.

> "* * * Had the house in that case been acquired by a Railway Company or a Local Authority under the provisions of the Land Clauses Consolidation Act 1845, before the purchase by the Trustees, the house ought, in their Lordships' opinion and for the reasons already given, to have been valued at £ 1,000 and not merely at £ 750."

It is not, however, easy to assess the addition in value on account of the potentiality of a plot of land. As was said by Lord Romer in that case the expert will have to "value the potentiality on such materials as are available to him without indulging in any feats of imagination". It must, however, be borne in mind that the land has to be valued as it stood at the material time by taking into consideration that the potentialities are not realised potentialities, as will be seen from the judgment. The learned Collector in this case had valued the land at ₹ 17,745-1/3 inclusive of Statutory Allowance. The land possessed natural advantage for water supply from a spring. The acquiring authority, *e.g.* Vijagpatam Harbour Authority badly needed this water and the acquisition was made for that purpose. On a reference under s. 18 of the Land Acquisition Act (now s. 33 of the Right to Fair Compensation and Transparency in Land Acquisition, Rehabilitation and Resettlement Act 2013) the learned Subordinate Judge valued the land at ₹ 1,05,000 on the basis of the income that the owner would get from the spring by the supply of water to the Harbour Authority after construction of elaborate and difficult engineering works. In effect the learned Judge took the potentiality as a realised potentiality. The High Court set aside the award of the learned Subordinate Judge taking the view that fifthly of s. 24 of the L.A. Act 1894 applied to the facts of this case as the value of the spring as a source of drinking water arose entirely from the requirements of the Harbour Authority. The Privy Council as stated above, held that the potentiality of the land must be taken into consideration, but as it was not a realised potentiality, the Judicial Committee determined the value at ₹46,000 inclusive of statutory allowance.The value of the potentiality was thus assessed at a little over ₹28,000. In *Clay's* case cited by the Privy Council, the addition on account of potentiality or special adaptability that was furnished by the sale figure of the property works at 33$^{1}/_{3}$%. The Privy Council case was approved by the Supreme Court in *H.M.E. Haq* v *State of West Bengal.*[8] The Supreme Court upheld an additional award of 10% "in view of the potential value or special value of the building which was situated in an important commercial locality and in the neighbourhood of the building where another Government office was located". This was a case of assessment of compensation for the requisition of premises No. 9, Chittaranjan Avenue, Calcutta under the Defence of India Act 1939.

Dealing with the doctrine of potential value of this Court in *N.B. Jeejabhoy* v *District Collector, Thana,* Civil Appeal Nos. 313-315 of 1963 decided on 30.8.1965, observed as follows:

> "A vendor willing to sell his land at the market value will take into consideration a particular potentiality or special adaptability of the land in fixing the price. It is not the fancy or the obsession of the vendor that enters the market value but the objective factor, namely, whether the said potentiality can be turned into account within a reasonably near future...... The question therefore turns upon the facts of each case. In the context of building potentiality many questions will have to be asked and answered: whether there is pressure on the land for building activity, whether the acquired land is suitable for building purposes, whether the extension of the said activity is towards the land acquired, what is the pace of progress and how far the said activity has extended and within what time, whether buildings have been put up or lands purchased for building purposes, what is the distance between the built-in-land and the land acquired and similar other questions will have to be answered.

8 (1959)1 SCA 477.

It is the overall picture drawn on the said relevant circumstances that affords the solution."[9]

The opinion of experts in valuation of properties was recognised by the Supreme Court in *Special L.A. Officer* v *T.A. Setty.*[10] In that case the Supreme Court laid down that the methods of valuation may be:

(1) Opinion of experts.
(2) Price paid within a reasonable time in a *bona fide* transactions of purchase of the lands.
(3) Number of years purchased and the actual or immediately prospective profits of the land.

What is fair and reasonable compensation is always a question of fact depending on the nature of the evidence, circumstances and probabilities in each case. The guiding star would be the conduct of a hypothetical willing vendor who would offer the lands and a willing purchaser in normal human conduct would be willing to buy as a prudent man in normal market conditions as on the date of notification under s. 4(1) of the Land Acquisition Act 1894,[11] but not an anxious buyer dealing at arm's length, nor facade of sale or fictitious sales brought about in quick succession or otherwise, to inflate the market value. When the court is called upon to fix the market value of the land in compulsory acquisition the best evidence of the value of the property is the sale of land acquired to which the claimant himself is a party, in its absence, the sales of the neighbouring lands. The transactions relating to the acquired land of recent dates in the neighbourhood lands that possessed of similar potentiality or fertility or other advantageous features are relevant pieces of evidence. In proof of the sale transactions, the relationship of the parties to the transactions, the market conditions, the terms of the sale and the date of the sale are to be looked into. These features would be established by examining either the vendor or vendee and

9 *Raghubans Narayan Singh* v *State of Uttar Pradesh* AIR 1967 SC 465.
10 AIR 1959 SC 429.
11 Now s. 11(1) of the Right to Fair Compensation and Transparency in Land Acquisition, Rehabilitation and Resettlement Act 2013.

if they are not available, the attesting witnesses who have personal knowledge of the transactions.[12]

In the determination of market of acquired land the court requires to consider the relative values of the lands in the neighbourhood, the soil condition and same or similar advantageous features on comparable sale prices.[13]

Concept to evolve rather than be predetermined

The basic concept in respect of 'fair market value' is that of the price which property would ordinarily fetch on sale in the open market on the date of the transfer. Market value is a very generalised concept. What any particular purchaser pays for land whether at public auction, or by private treaty, is not of itself market value.

The Law Commission of India 1958 which considered the question of defining the expression 'market value' in the context of ss. 23 and 24 of the Land Acquisition Act 1894 (now s. 28 and ss. 28 & 69 of the Right to Fair Compensation and Transparency in Land Acquisition, Rehabilitation and Resettlement Act 2013 respectively) made the following observations in their report:

> "A considerable volume of case-law has, however, been built up on the interpretation of the expression 'market value'. It is not possible to define the expression, nor is it possible to lay down any uniform set of rules for the determination of market value of the land applicable to all cases. In the nature of things, therefore, it must be left to the Courts to evolve the principles for the determination of the compensation in different classes of cases having regard to the nature of the property, its situation and other relevant considerations. Though the Bill of 1893 which was subsequently enacted into Act 1 of 1894 contained a definition of market value, it was dropped by the Select Committee which preferred to leave the term undefined. The Committee observed:

12 *Periyar and Pareekanni Rubbers Ltd.* v *State of Kerala* AIR 1990 SC 2192; (1991)4 SCC 195.

13 *Gurlingappa* v *Assistant Commissioner and L.A.O., Gulbarg* (1997)3 SCC 627.

> "No material difficulty has arisen in the interpretation of it; the decisions of several High Courts are at one in giving it the reasonable meaning of the price a willing buyer would give a willing seller; but the introduction of a specific definition would sow the field for a fresh harvest of decisions, and no definition could lay down for universal guidance in the widely divergent conditions of India, any further rule by which the price should be ascertained.' We agree with this view."

Some Judges have attempted a definition but we feel that no useful purpose will be served by a critical examination of these views expressed by them.

The principles for determining the market value have been fully expounded by the Privy Council in *Raja Vyricherla Narayana Gajapatraju Bahadur Garu* v *Revenue Divisional Officer, Vizianagaram.*[14]

> "The first principle established by the *Chemudu* case is that, in the case of compulsory acquisition 'the land is not to be valued merely by reference to the use to which it is being put at the time at which its value has to be determined .... but also by reference to the uses to which it is reasonably capable of being put in the future'. This proposition was treated by the Judicial Committee as axiomatic. The second principle laid down by this decision is that when the land has unusual or unique features or potentialities, the valuing officer must ascertain, as best as he can from the materials before him the price a willing purchaser would pay for the land with these features or potentialities. It is further laid down that the value of potentialities is to be taken into account even where the only possible purchaser for the potentialities is the acquiring authority. The 'market value' is defined by the Judicial Committee as "the price which a willing vendor might reasonably expect to obtain from a willing purchaser. The disinclination of the vendor to part with his land and the urgent necessity of the purchaser to buy must alike be disregarded and both must be treated as persons dealing in

14 AIR 1939 PC 98 (now known as the *Chemudu* case).

the matter at arm's length and without compulsion. The principle of awarding compensation is based on the right of the owner to be indemnified by the community for whose benefit he is deprived of the property against his will."

The Law Commission was, therefore, disinclined to lay down any uniform set of rules for determination of 'market value' and considered it advisable to leave it to the courts to evolve the principles for the determination of the same, having regard to the nature of the property, its situation and other relevant considerations.

Market price as test of value

'Market value' has been defined as the price the property may fetch in the open market if sold by a willing seller unaffected by the special needs of a particular purchase.[15]

Market value means the price which a purchaser willing to pay for similar land to a willing seller. An offer of sale of land to industrialists on concessional rate with a view to induce them to set up their industries in a particular area does not reflect the prevailing market value of the land. The industrialists are not willing purchasers in the case.[16]

In *Collector of Jabalpur* v *Babulal,*[17] the following principles were laid down in the matter of determination of market value when the question of compensation for compulsory acquisition came up for decision:

1. Compensation must be determined by reference to the price which a willing vendor might reasonably expect to obtain from a willing purchaser.

2. The value to be ascertained is the value to the vendor and not its value to the purchaser.

3. In fixing the value to the vendor all restrictions imposed on the user and enjoyment of land in his hands are to be taken into account but the possibility of such restrictions being modified or removed for his benefit is not to be overlooked.

15 *Special LAO, Davangere* v *P. Veerabhadrappa* AIR 1984 SC 774; (1984)2 SCC 120.
16 *Mahabir Prasad Santuka* v *Collector, Cuttack* AIR 1987 SC 720.
17 (1961) Jab LJ 1088; 1961 MPLJ 1219.

4. Market price is not a conclusive test of real value.

5. Increase in value consequent on the execution of the undertaking for, or in connection with which the purchase is made must be disregarded.

6. The value to be ascertained is the price to be paid for the land with all potentialities and by reference not merely to the use to which it is being put at the time at which its value has to be determined but also to the uses to which it is reasonably capable of being put in the future.

7. The true contractual relation of the parties–that of purchaser and vendor–is not to be observed by endeavouring to construe it as another contractual relation altogether that of indemnifier and indemnified.

8. The value of the land in general can also be measured by a consideration of the prices that have been obtained in the past for land of similar quality and in similar positions. But a sale of a plot situated in a locality far removed from the locality in question can furnish no guide for determination of the market value.

In *Government of Bombay* v *Morwanji Mancherji,*[18] the Bombay High Court held that 'market value' means the price which at the given time and place the land would fetch on sale according to the then existing rates of the market which depended on general pre-existing conditions apart from the individual projects of a particular purchaser. It is price offered by a willing and not forced seller to a willing purchaser.

The method of ascertaining market value with reference to market price has been particularly focussed upon in the case of *State of West Bengal* v *North Brook Jute Mills Co.*[19] and the following principles were laid down:

1. The market price has to be fixed by reference to date of declaration under s. 6 of the Land Acquisition Act.[1]

18 10 Bom LR 907.

19 (1971)75 CWN 985.

1 Now s. 19 of the Right to Fair Compensation and Transparency in Land Acquisition, Rehabilitation and Resettlement Act 2013.

2. The market value of the land is its value to the owner when he is willing to sell and what he may expect to get from a willing purchaser.

3. The value to be ascertained is the value to the seller of the property in its actual condition at the time of exploitation with all its advantages and with all its possibilities.

4. The value of the potentialities must be ascertained with such materials as are available without indulging in feats of imagination.

5. In the context of building potentiality many questions will have to be asked and answered, like,—

(*a*) whether there is pressure on the land for building activity;

(*b*) whether the acquired land is suitable for building purposes;

(*c*) whether the extension of the said activity is towards the land acquired;

(*d*) what is the pace of progress and how far the said activity has extended and within what time;

(*e*) whether buildings have been put up on lands purchased for building purposes;

(*f*) what is the distance between the built-in land and the land acquired;

It is the overall picture on the said relevant circumstances that affords the solution.

6. For ascertaining market value, the value to the owner may also be ascertained by capitalising the rent as one of the methods, though not the only method; but the method of valuation by annual crop value is not always adequate.

7. Methods of valuation may be:

(*a*) opinion of experts;

(*b*) price paid within a reasonable time in *bona fide* transaction of purchase of lands acquired and possessing similar advantages; and

(*c*) a number of year's purchase of the actual or immediately prospective profits of the lands acquired.

* * * *

8. The market value of the land on the relevant date may also be assessed on the basis of the rate shown by *bona fide* transactions of sale and purchase of land which are comparable units. It is also settled law that for such comparison certain definite kinds of elements have to exist, for example:

(*a*) the lands must be:

(*i*) of similar character as far as may be,

(*ii*) reasonably proximate to acquired land, and

(*iii*) having similar amenities and advantages; and

(*b*) there should be transactions in time reasonably proximate to the date of acquisition.

9. For capitalising the annual income, it is the probable income per year of the owner expropriated by acquisition that has to be taken into account.

The next significant case on this matter is that of *Udayan Girija Prasad* v *Special Land Acquisition Officer*[2] in which the Gujarat High Court laid down the following principles:

1. Market value is that value which is not affected by any special need of a particular purchase.

2. Where the market value of a built-up structure is to be assessed, one method which could be adopted is to find out the expenditure likely to be incurred for the construction of a similar house as reduced by depreciation.

3. The property in question should ordinarily be valued as a whole composite unit; aggregate of valuation of its different components such as land and structure would normally not give an idea of the market value.

4. The fact that the purchaser or the acquirer of property does not intend to use the property for the same purpose for which it is used or that he desires to demolish it, is irrelevant in determining its market value.

5. The market price is that price which a normal and prudent buyer, would pay after evaluating the prices prevailing in the round about area and which a normal and prudent seller is willing to accept. It is, therefore, the consensus between

2 (1976)17 GLR 668.

the buyer and the seller which would decide the price at which a particular property is bought or sold.

When a person is deprived of his property by compulsory acquisition, he must be paid compensation therefor by determining the value of the property to him, but that does not mean that in calculating the market price, the value to the seller alone must be taken into account even in the case of a voluntary sale. Market value can only be properly ascertained by finding out what a willing purchaser would pay and what a willing seller would accept.[3]

Market value as on date

The crucial date of determination of the market value would be the date of the publication of the notification under s. 4(1) of the Land Acquisition Act 1894, now s. 11(1) of the Right to Fair Compensation and Transparency in Land Acquisition, Rehabilitation and Resettlement Act 2013.[4]

The date of notification under s. 4(1) alone is relevant for computation of market value. The declaration under s. 6 now, s. 19 of the Act of 2013 only provides conclusiveness to the public purpose specified in s. 4(1) notification, now s. 11 of the Act of 2013.[5]

What has to be determined under s. 23(1) now, s. 28 of the Act of 2013 is the market value prevailing as on the date of notification under s. 4(1) now, s. 11(1) of the Act of 2013 but not what was claimed by the parties.[6]

In *Dollar Co.* v *Collector,*[7] the Supreme Court observed that the best evidence of the value of property is the sale value of the very property to which the claimant is a party. Proximity of highway or ports and many industrial and social imponderables enter the verdict of evaluation. It was also decided *inter alia* that compensation for compulsory acquisition as governed by s. 23 of the Land Acquisition Act gives high priority to market value of the land as on the date of notification

3 *State of U.P.* v *Ram Swarup* (1971)3 SCC 857.

4 *Mehtar* v *Collector, Durg* AIR 1975 MP 46; *Nursing Das* v *Secretary of State* AIR 1925 PC 91; 29 CWN 822 (PC).

5 *N. Narasimhaiah* v *State of Karnataka* (1996)3 SCC 88.

6 *Basant Kumar* v *Union of India* (1996)11 SCC 542.

7 AIR 1975 SC 1670.

under s. 4 (now s. 11). The main criterion for this is what a willing purchaser would pay a willing vendor.

An actual transaction with respect to the specific land of recent date is a guidebook that courts may not neglect when called upon to fix the precise compensation. The best evidence is the very sale that is made recently. All that need normally be proved, is that the sale was between a willing purchaser and a willing seller, that there has not been any appreciable rise or fall in value.

Market value envisaged in s. 23(1) of the L.A. Act (now s. 28 of the Act of 2013) is designed to award just and fair compensation for the land acquired and postulates price of the land prevailing on the date of publication of the notification under s. 4(1) [now s. 11(1)]. The acid test for determining market value of the land is the price which a willing vendor might reasonably expect to obtain from a willing purchaser and which would form the basis to fix the market value. The price paid in sale or purchase of the land acquired within a reasonable time from the date of acquisition of the land in question would be the best piece of evidence. A land possessing similar advantages to the land in the neighbourhood of the land acquired in or about the time of notification would supply the data to assess the market value. But exclusion of *bona fide* and genuine sale transactions in respect of the same land under acquisition and to place reliance on the award of some other land is obviously illegal.[8]

In determining market value of agricultural lands, the appellants produced two sale transactions in respect of land acquired in 1961 at ₹ 3,250 per bigha and another acquired in 1958 at ₹ 5,000 per bigha. The appellants have not produced any evidence to show that the lands were developed and fit for construction of houses and the reference court wrongly put reliance on the sale transactions of 1958 sale deeds at ₹ 5,000 per bigha. Since the lands as on the date of notification were agricultural lands, the value of the land has been rightly determined on the bigha basis instead of yard basis. The

8 *Special Tahsildar, Land Acquisition* v *Mangala Gowri* AIR 1992 SC 666 (DB).

appellants have produced sale deeds indicating the maximum which was secured viz. ₹3,250 per bigha and so entitled to the enhanced compensation at the rate of ₹3,250 per bigha, *solatium* at 15% and interest at 6% on the enhanced compensation.[9]

Market value should be determined according to the use to which the land was put on the date of notification under s. 4 of the L.A. Act (now s. 11 of the Act of 2013).[10]

For the purpose of determination of market value sale instance executed after a lapse of two years of notification under s. 4 (now s. 11 of the Act of 2013) for acquiring land in question cannot be relied on.[11]

Relevance of potentiality to market value

Potentiality means 'future utility'. It is the probable use of the property in a more lucrative manner. It is synonymously called 'special adaptability'. The relevancy of potentiality for valuation of land was considered in *Chemudu's* case.[12] The facts of this case are:

Certain lands were acquired by the harbour authorities who were constructing a harbour in Vizagapatnam. They allotted some land in the south of the harbour area to certain oil companies and other industrial concerns. There lands were said to be malarial. The appellant's land was to the south of this land and contained a spring which yielded a constant and abundant supply of good drinking water. The latter could be made available for the oil companies and the people engaged in the harbour works. The land of the appellant was acquired for execution of anti-malarial works and the appellant claimed compensation for the area as a building site. The Land Acquisition Officer disallowed this claim of potential value as a building site. Compensation was awarded as partly waste and partly cultivated land taking into consideration also an allowance for some building and trees. The appellant moved

9 *Basant Kumar* v *Union of India* (1996)11 SCC 542.
10 *Saraswati Devi (Smt.)* v *U.P. Government* AIR 1992 SC 1620 (DB).
11 *Bhikhubhai Kedarbhai Patel* v *Deputy Collector, Modasa* AIR 1996 Guj 16.
12 AIR 1939 PC 98.

for a reference to the subordinate Judge urging a further claim of potential value of the land as a source of water supply.

The court approved of his claim as a source of water supply but dismissed the claim as a building site. The potential value as a water source was real, the water could be sold to the oil companies and others at a profit. Such compensation could be allowed even where the only possible buyers could be the oil companies and the harbour authorities.

In appeal the High Court was of the opinion that supply of drinking water had no value apart from the scheme for which the acquisition was made. The harbour authorities were the only possible purchasers and the land could not be considered as a building site.

The matter was further taken up to the Privy Council. Lord Romer delivering the judgment stated:

"The compensation must be determined, therefore, by reference to the price which a willing vendor might reasonably expect to obtain from a willing purchaser. The disinclination of the vendor to part with his land and the urgent necessity of the purchaser to buy must also be disregarded. Neither must be considered as acting under compulsion ...... The value of the land is not to be estimated at its value to the purchaser. But this does not mean that the fact that some particular purchaser might desire the land more than others is to be disregarded. The wish of the particular purchaser though not his compulsion, may always be taken into consideration for what it is worth ...... It is often said that it is the value of the land to the vendor that has to be estimated. This is not in strictness accurate. The land, for instance, may have for the vendor a sentimental value far in excess of its 'market value'. But the compensation must not be increased by reason of any such consideration. The vendor is to be treated as a vendor willing to sell at 'market value' to use the words of s. 23 of the Indian Act .... There is not in general any market for land in the sense in which one speaks of a market for shares or a market for sugar or any like commodity. The value of any such article at any particular time can readily be ascertained by the prices being obtained for similar articles in the market. In the case of land, its value in general can also be measured by a consideration of the prices that have been obtained in the past for land of similar quality and in similar positions, and is what must be meant in general by the 'market value' in s. 23. But sometimes it happens that the land to be valued possesses some unusual, and it may be, unique features as regards its position or its potentialities. In such a case, the arbitrator in determining its value will have no market value to guide him and he will have to ascertain, as best as he may, from the materials before him what a willing vendor might reasonably expect to obtain from a willing purchaser for the land in that particular position and with those particular potentialities ...... The land is not to be valued merely by reference to the use to which it is being put at the time at which its value has to be determined ..... but also by reference to the use to which it reasonably capable of being put in the future ...... No one can suppose in the case of land which is certain, or even likely, to be used in the immediate or reasonably near future for building purposes but which at the valuation date is waste land, or is being used for agricultural purposes, that the owner however willing a vendor will be content to sell the land for its value as waste or agricultural land as the case may be. It is plain that in ascertaining its value, the possibility of its being used for building purposes will have to be taken into account. It is equally plain, however, that land must not be valued as though it had already been built upon, a proposition that is embodied in s. 24(5) of the Act and is sometimes expressed by saying that it is the possibilities of the land and not its realised possibilities that must be taken into consideration. But how is the increase in the value of the land by reason of its potentialities or possibilities to be measured? In the case instanced above of land possessing the possibilities of being used for building purposes, the arbitrator ..... would probably have before him evidence of the prices paid in the neighbourhood for land immediately required for such purposes. He would then have to deduct from the value thus ascertained such sum as he would think proper by reason of the degree of possibility that the land might never be so required or might not be so required for a considerable time. In the case, however, of land possessing potentialities of such an unusual nature that the arbitrator has no similar case to guide him, the value of the land must be ascertained in some other way. If the owner of the land is the only person who can do, the value to him must be ascertained by reference to what profit he might thereby have been able to derive from the land in the future. Take as example the case of an owner of vacant land that adjoins his factory. The land possesses the potentiality of being profitably used for an extension of the factory. But the owner is the only person who can turn the potentiality to account. In valuing the land, however, as between him and a willing purchaser the value to him of the potentiality would necessarily have to be included.

"The same consideration would apply to cases where the owner is not the only person but merely one of the persons able to turn the potentiality to account. The value to him of the potentiality will not be less than the profit that would accrue to him, by making use of it had he retained it in his own possession ...... But .... where the owner is himself unable to turn the potentiality to account ..... in such a case, there may be several other persons who would be able to do so or there may be only one. If there are more than one ..... the owner is entitled to be paid the value to him of the potentiality, though the ascertainment of its value may, in some cases, be a matter of considerable difficulty ..... The value of the potentiality must be ascertained by the arbitrator on such materials as are available to him and without indulging in feats of imagination ..... Upon the question of the value of the potentiality where there is only one possible purchaser .... the value should be the sum which the arbitrator estimates a willing purchaser will pay and not what a purchaser will pay under compulsion."

The Privy Council finally concluded that the special adaptability of the land for the supply of drinking water had no value apart from the scheme for which the acquisition was made. The only really possible purchaser of the special adaptability of the appellant's spring as a water supply was the harbour authority. In such circumstances the possibility of the appellant's water being made available for the harbour by any one other than the harbour authority was altogether negligible and the only enhancement in value to the appellant of his land by reason of its special adaptability as a water supply was the sum that the harbour authority as a willing purchaser would have been willing to give in excess of the land's 'poromboke' value. Their Lordships added:

> "In the present case the land must be valued not at the sum it would be worth after it had been acquired by the Harbour Authority and used for anti-malarial purposes but at the sum that the authority in a friendly negotiation .... would be willing to pay ..... in order to acquire it for these purposes ...... It is plain, therefore, that in view of the fact that the water could not be exploited by the appellant himself and that it would necessary be some years before the water could become a profit earning asset in their hands, the harbour authority, however willing purchasers they might be, would not have agreed to pay anything like that sum (claimed)."

Their Lordships in the end awarded compensation to the tune of ₹ 40,000 as against ₹ 1,05,000 awarded by the subordinate Judge.

In *Chemudu's* case market value was considered to be the value to the owner in its actual condition at the date of the notification under s. 4 with all its then existing advantages and disadvantages and defects and with all its future possibilities. It is not permissible to take into consideration any advantage due to the carrying out of the scheme for the purpose for which the property is acquired. But the value of the potentialities may be taken into account, even where the only purchaser is the authority purchasing under powers of the eminent domain.

In *Mirza Nausherwan Khan* v *Collector,*[13] the Supreme Court laid down the following principles as to potential value in a case under the Hyderabad Land Acquisition Act (9 of 1309 Fasli):

1. The determination of potential value is quite within the ken of the Appellate Judge.

13 AIR 1974 SC 2247; (1975)1 SCC 238.

2. As to the principle of belting, no general principle can be laid down. Local circumstances guide the court. It is however clear that in dealing with the value of an extensive plot of land in a city, the strip that adjoins an important road will have a higher value than what is in the rear, for obvious reasons of potential user or commercial exploitation.
3. The compensation paid for the value of a tiny plot is no measure when a large area is acquired.
4. The story of potential user disbelieved by the courts below would not be reopened by the Supreme Court.

In *Raghubans Narain Singh* v *State of Uttar Pradesh,*[14] the Supreme Court held that the potential market value is the value that a willing purchaser would pay to a willing seller for a property, having due regard to its existing condition with all its advantages and its potential possibility when laid out in its most advantageous manner excluding advantages due to carrying out any scheme for which the property is compulsorily acquired.

In *Gulzara Singh* v *State of Punjab*[15] the Supreme Court accepted the potential value as a basis to determine the market value for the purpose of compulsory acquisition. The same view was taken in the case of *Inder Singh* v *Union of India*[16] in which the Supreme Court found that *abadi* land fetching ₹ 33,600 per acre had potential value for development, such as for building houses etc. as in the immediate neighbourhood, and accordingly redetermined the market value of such *abadi* lands at ₹ 42,000 per acre, after recording the finding that the land possessed of potential value. But in the case of *Land Acquisition Officer, Eluru* v *Jasti Rohini (Smt.),*[17] the Supreme Court rejected the plea for fixation of compensation on the basis of potential value and made the following observations in the particular circumstances of the case: "In fixing the market value on the basis of its potentiality for use for building purposes, it must be established by evidence *aliunde* that the

14 AIR 1967 SC 465.
15 (1993)4 SCC 245.
16 (1993)3 SCC 240.
17 (1995)1 SCC 717.

potential purpose must exist as on the date of acquisition by other possible purchasers in the market conditions, prevailing as on the date of the notification. Existence of constructed house or construction activity in other similar lands in the locality for the purpose contended for or of purchase for such purposes as on the date of proposed acquisition *prima facie* indicates that there is demand for and the possibility of the immediate user of the land and it is a reasonable possibility to infer that the acquired lands also are possessed of potential value. Therefore, the existence of a demand for and market at the time of acquisition for potential use must be established as a fact from reliable and acceptable evidence to show that if the acquired land has been thrown into the market, others would have bought it for the special purposes or for building activity which would show the demand for and a market to purchase the land possessed of potential value for the purpose of building activity at that time. On proof thereof the land must not be valued as though it has already been built up but the possibility to use for building purpose existing as on the date of the notification must be taken into consideration. The question whether the land has potential value as a building site or not is primarily one of fact depending upon diverse factors as to its conditions, the use to which it is put or is reasonably capable of being put and its suitability for building purpose. Its proximity to residential, commercial or industrial area, existence of educational, cultural, industrial or commercial institutions, existence of amenities like water, electricity, drainage and the possibility of future extension in that area, the existence of or prospects of development schemes, the existence or absence of building activities towards the acquired land or in the neighbourhood thereof are the relevant facts to be taken into consideration in evaluating the market value on the basis of potential use of the land. It is true that an element of guess, in an estimate, would have a play in determining the market value. But the present value alone falls to be determined and feats of imagination should not run riot or travel beyond its manifest limits nor be an arbitrary or whim of the court in determining the compensation or the fixation of the market value. The existing conditions, the demand for the land in the neighbourhood and other related and relevant facts should be taken into consideration in determining the compensation on the basis of potential value of the land."

The court must consider the suitability of the acquired land for putting up the buildings for residential, commercial or industrial buildings which have already come up in the neighbourhood and also the possibility to obtain amenities like water, drainage, electricity supply etc. Absence of statutory impediments like obtaining sanction for layout would be yet another relevant circumstance. It must be established that the land is possessed of potential value as above as on the date of notification under s. 4(1) (now s. 11(1) of the Act of 2013). The determination of compensation under those circumstances must be just and adequate.[18]

Agricultural land acquired for staff quarters of the Damodar Valley Corporation was in the vicinity of important schools, offices, court and residential buildings. There was continuous rise in the valuation of immovable property which was required to be considered in assessing the market value of the land.[19]

For the purpose of determining the market value of the acquired land the future potentiality of the land and nearness to the capital city have to be taken into consideration.[20]

In the case all the plots of the acquired land are situated adjacent to national highway and the relevant factors of each plot are similar keeping in view the purpose of construction of Barog bypass road for which lands were acquired. The main factor is potentiality which was indisputably the same in respect of all the plots of acquired land as all of them could be used for the establishment of commercial units, guest-houses and residential houses. *Held,* assessment of market value of all plots at flat rates proper.[21]

18 *G. Narayan Rao* v *L.A.O.* (1996)10 SCC 607; cases referred *L.A.O.* v *Jasti Rohini* (1995)1 SCC 717; *P. Ram Reddy* v *L.A.O., Hyderabad Urban Development Authority* (1995)2 SCC 305; see also *Union of India* v *A. Ajit Singh* (1997)6 SCC 50; AIR 1997 SC 2669.

19 *Ram Narain Gope* v *Deputy Commissioner* AIR 1990 Pat 108.

20 *State of Punjab* v *Surjan Singh* AIR 1990 P&H 312.

21 *L.A. Collector* v *Sukhdev Singh* AIR 1995 HP 150; *Mangalagiri Venkata Seetaramyya* v *Special Tahsildar L.A., Vishakapatnam* AIR 1994 NOC 74 (AP).

The best method of determination of market price to the plots of land under the acquisition appears to be to rely on instances of sale of the same land or portion of it near about the date of notification under s. 4(1) of the Land Acquisition Act 1894 (now s. 11(1) of the Right to Fair Compensation and Transparency in Land Acquisition, Rehabilitation and Resettlement Act 2013). The next best method is to take into consideration the instances of sale of adjacent lands made shortly before and after the notification. When market value is to be determined on the basis of sale instances in the neighbouring locality, the potential value of the land need not be separately awarded because such sales cover the potential value.[22]

Potential value is to be distinguished from the present value, and varies with passage of time, when fresh factors come into play. The Privy Council in *Vallabhdas Naranji* v *Collector*[1] when considering the value of an irregularly shaped land near the seashore stated as under:

> "This land is absolutely worthless in itself, but has no doubt a potentiality for being used for salt works and therefore the owner is entitled to the market value of that potentiality."

Since it was necessary to expend large sums of money to set up salt works, it was considered there was no present value for the potentiality, and the value of the land to be taken was that of wasteland.

Where except for a small portion of land, the land in dispute has no value as a building site because demand for building was limited, the value of the land should be assessed on the basis of what was its worth as an agricultural land. Remote potentialities should not be taken into account.[2]

When potential value is considered, it is necessary to exclude advantages due to the carrying out of the purpose of acquisition.[3] The *Chemudu's* case discussed earlier throws further light on this issue.

22 *Jogendra Nath Chatterjee* v *State of West Bengal* AIR 1971 Cal 458; 75 CWN 737.

1 AIR 1929 PC 112.

2 *Tara Singh* v *Secretary of State* AIR 1933 Lah 503; 34 PLR 997.

3 *Bijay Kanta Lahiri* v *Secretary of State* AIR 1934 Cal 97; 58 CLJ 38.

The recognition of potential value, may be found for a variety of reasons—(*i*) potential value of agricultural land for building purposes, (*ii*) fitness of land as a base for water supply, (*iii*) contiguity of land to a lake making it specifically adaptable for use as a reservoir, (*iv*) fitness of land for reservoir, (*v*) future profitable working for mines, (*vi*) adaptability of land for railway purposes, (*vii*) contiguity of land to a reservoir making it suitable for building a mill, (*viii*) suitability for development of hydro-electric power, (*ix*) land though not itself adaptable for a reservoir, but is so adaptable in conjunction with other adjacent lands belonging to other owner. Examples of recognition of the doctrine of potential value and special adaptability may be found in many an English case decision.[4]

Fair market value nurtured as a concept

It has already been stated earlier that valuation for acquisition purposes arises not only in the context of Land Acquisition Act (now repealed and replaced by the Right to Fair Compensation and Transparency in Land Acquisition, Rehabilitation and Resettlement Act 2013) but for other fiscal purposes as well. In particular, the Wealth-tax Act and the Income-tax Act contain provisions for determination of market value. Under the Wealth-tax Act, the value of an asset is to be taken at the market price on valuation date. Therefore, the admission made by the claimants with regard to the market value of the acquired property under the Wealth-tax Act, can be taken as a substantive piece of evidence for valuation under s. 23 of the Land Acquisition Act (now s. 28 of the Act of 2013).[5]

The provisions for acquisition contained in Chapter XXA of the Income-tax Act 1961 have given rise to a number of decisions of the High Courts which shed light on the principles and methods of valuation of immovable properties. It is, therefore, worthwhile to consider the facts and the decisions given by the various High Courts in the cases directly dealing with the provisions of Chapter XXA in order to have an idea as to how the courts have viewed problems of valuation. These decisions were found relevant also for Chapter XXC as the

4 *Hughly Mills* v *Secretary of State* 12 CLJ 489; 8 IC 800.

5 *Udayan Girija Prasad* v *Spl. Land Acquisition Officer* (1976)17 GLR 668.

appropriate authority had to give hearing to the parties concerned and thereafter pass the order. It is primarily in this context that the concept of 'fair market value' evolved.

A just market value concept generally require: (1) the property to be exposed for sale in the open market allowing a reasonable time to find a purchaser who buys with knowledge of all the uses to which it can be adapted, (2) neither the willing seller nor the willing buyer being under abnormal pressure, and (3) both the seller and buyer being fully informed.

The Supreme Court in *C.B. Gautam* case[6] has indicated some of the situations where the seller may be induced to sell his immovable property at less than what might be the fair market value. He might be in immediate need of money and unable to wait; some dispute as to the title might force him to sell at a lower price; there may be a subsisting lease in favour of the intending purchaser or there might be genuine reasons for the seller agreeing to sell at a lower price to a particular person who might not be his relative etc.

In *CIT* v *Smt. Vimalaben Bhagwandas Patel,*[7] certain industrial sheds with *pucca* structures and temporary structures were sold to two persons on the condition that the transferee would abide by the terms and conditions prescribed under the ownership scheme of Baroda Industrial Development Corporation (BIDCO) since the transferor had originally purchased the said sheds under that scheme. It was also established that any purchaser under the ownership scheme was bound to pay, besides the price of the shed, a sum of ₹18,600 being the value of shares of BIDCO. The transferees let out the sheds on rent and the net annual yield which was realised by them was about ₹24,996 each. Without affording any opportunity to the transferor of being heard, the competent authority initiated acquisition proceedings. The competent authority did not disclose the report of the agent, Bank of Boroda, indicating the value of the property which the bank had estimated for purposes of advancing loans and also the particulars about the land rates prevalent in neighbouring areas. An order was passed and an appeal was filed before the

6 199 ITR 530.
7 (1979)118 ITR 134 (Guj).

Tribunal. The Tribunal allowed the appeal of the transferors and set aside the order of acquisition.

On appeal by the revenue, the Gujarat High Court held that the competent authority had acted in violation of the principles of natural justice in relying on material without disclosing it to the transferors and affording them an opportunity of being heard in the matter.

While commenting on the determination of the fair market value of property, the High Court observed that it would not be safe to wholly import the principles enunciated by the courts in ascertaining the market value while determining the amount of compensation for acquisition of a property or land since the perspective of acquisition under the Land Acquisition Act (now replaced by the Right to Fair Compensation and Transparency in Land Acquisition, Rehabilitation and Resettlement Act 2013) and that under Chapter XXA of the Income-tax Act 1961 are slightly different. In the perspective of the acquisition proceedings having far-reaching repercussions, the competent authority must be satisfied and assured by cogent, reliable and relevant evidence that the fair market value of the property in question exceeds the apparent consideration by a prescribed margin. It would be too hazardous to prefer one of the recognised methods of valuation which may be advantageous to the cause of the revenue and arrive at an estimation of fair market value of the property on that basis. Such a lopsided approach on the part of the competent authority would not be in consonance with the burden of proof required to be discharged in such quasi-criminal proceedings. It would be virtually acting on too slender a material since the decision of the competent authority to acquire would expose not only the transferee to the consequences of being deprived of the property but also the transferor to the liability of capital gains under s. 52 (since repealed w.e.f. 1.4.1988) and in a given case may affect also the persons interested in the said property having tenancy rights or any encumbrances thereon. The competent authority shall, therefore, as far as possible, collect all the relevant material and evidence by applying the well-known and recognised methods, viz., land and building method, contractor's method, rental or yield basis method and comparable sales method, and work out such estimation of the market value on application of all the four methods and for purposes of counter-check compare it with the municipal valuation for rateble purposes wherever it is possible.

It was held in the case of *Smt. Lalita Todi* v *CIT*,[8] and *Vimal Agarwal* v *Appropriate Authority*,[9] that if all the germane considerations are not taken into account the determination made of fair market value would become vitiated in law.

In *CIT* v *Ganesh Builders*,[10] the respondents executed a conveyance deed whereby plot of land measuring 4,550 sq. yds. was sold to one *M* or his nominees at a price of ₹ 65 per sq. yd. On the ground that the apparent consideration was *prima facie* very much less than the fair market value the competent authority issued a notice under s. 269D of the Income-tax Act 1961. According to purchaser's valuer, the fair market value would be ₹ 140 per sq. yd. since the plot was a developed one. Taking the view that it would be more appropriate to take into consideration the value of the plot as if it were a developed plot and permit certain deductions, the competent authority allowed certain outgoings towards road construction, encroachments, etc., as claimed by the transferor, but claim for stamp duty, brokerage and solicitors' fees was not allowed.

Adopting the fair market value at ₹ 150 per sq. yd. and allowing the aforesaid deductions, the competent authority still found that the provisions of s. 269C(2)(*a*) and (*b*) were satisfied and passed an order for acquisition. The Tribunal held that the fair market value of a developed plot in that locality would be ₹ 140 per sq. yd. and that deduction must be allowed for brokerage, solicitors' fees, stamp duty etc. On this basis, the Tribunal found that the margin between the apparent consideration paid under the document and the fair market value so determined was a little less than 15 per cent. Hence, the appeals were allowed and the orders directing the acquisition were set aside. The department appealed against this order and urged *inter alia* that the

8 (1980)123 ITR 40 (Pat).
9 (1994)210 ITR 16 (Bom).
10 (1979)116 ITR 911 (Bom).

deduction for stamp duty, brokerage and solicitors' fees had been wrongly allowed. The Bombay High Court held that when a buyer becomes willing to buy immovable property at a particular rate he knows that the documents require expenses which in law he must fully bear unless there is a contract to the contrary where the expenses are shared. Incidental expenses like stamp duty, brokerage and legal expenses may form part of the mental process of the buyer for the purpose of making an offer, but they do not form part of the price and cannot be deducted therefrom. The court, however, remanded the case back to the Tribunal so as to decide whether acquisition should be permitted even if the difference between apparent consideration and the fair market price exceeded 15 per cent.

Determination of compensation for compulsory acquisition involves consideration of the price which a hypothetical willing purchaser can be expected to pay for the lands in the existing use as well as relatable potentialities. The acid test is in the armchair of the willing vendor and a prudent willing buyer, taking all relevant prevailing conditions of the normal market. Fertility of the land, location, suitability of the purpose it was purchased, the nature of the land, the crops raised and the nature of the income likely to be derived from the lands, the expenditure to be incurred for raising the crops and the net profits etc. would be the relevant factors in arriving at the net market value and, if evidence is produced in that behalf, on its basis applying suitable 10 years multiplier, the market value need to be determined. In the case of acquisition of large tracts of lands for projects situated in several villages, stray sale deeds of small extent here and there would not form the basis to determine the compensation. The reference court should be circumspect, pragmatic and careful in analysing the evidence and arriving at just and fair market value of the lands under acquisition which could be fetched on the date of the notification. The owner or claimant should not be put to loss by undervaluation. But, at the same time public exchequer should not be put to undue burden by excess valuation. It is the statutory duty of the court to maintain the balance between diverse interests. In the instant case the court failed to apply armchair test of prudent purchaser and willing vendor or test of realised income on crops. So, the determination of compensation, was held, illegal.[11]

Market value according to present disposition

The potential value of an acquired land has brought in questions of possibilities to be considered. Such considerations are not confined only to realised potentialities or possibilities. Again, it does not extend to distant possibilities but limited to market value according to present disposition. Thus, open market considerations have started creeping in the domain of valuation for compulsory acquisition. As an intermediate step to open market value, the concept of present disposition has been nurtured by judicial decisions in our country. To trace the origin of the concept, we need to give a hind look at some of the amendments of local Acts *vis-a-vis* laws for compulsory acquisition.

For lands acquired by the Kolkata Municipal Corporation some provisions of the Land Acquisition Act were modified regarding the determination of the market value under s. 23(1) (now s. 28 of the Right to Fair Compensation and Transparency in Land Acquisition, Rehabilitation and Resettlement Act 2013) first. The provision regarding land acquired by the Kolkata Municipal Corporation Act is in s. 537(3), which runs as follows:

> Section 537(3). For the purpose of acquisition of immovable property under this section, the Land Acquisition Act, 1894, shall be subject to the amendment that the market-value of any land or building to be acquired shall be deemed, for the purpose of sub-section (1) of section 23 of that Act, to be the market-value determined according to the disposition of such immovable property at the date of declaration under sub-section (1) of section 4 thereof in respect of such immovable property.

The Howrah Improvement Act also contains the same modifications.

Similar provision in the Madras City Improvement Trust Act 1950 omitting s. 23(2) of the Land Acquisition Act 1894 has been struck down by the Supreme Court as violating Art. 14 of the Constitution in *Balammal* v *State of Madras.*[12]

11 *K. Posayya* v *Special Tahsildar* AIR 1995 SC 1641. See also *Union of India* v *Mangatu Ram* (1997)6 SCC 59; AIR 1997 SC 2704.

12 AIR 1968 SC 1425.

As origin of the rule of present disposition, some administrative steps seem to have acted as step in aid. It appears that the Government of West Bengal appointed a Commission called "Calcutta Building Commission" on 6.4.1897 to consider what amendments were required in the law relating to buildings and streets in Calcutta. The Calcutta Building Commission in its report in paragraph 139, clause (*d*) made the following observations:

> "The extravagant prices which the Corporation has been made to pay for property acquired by it have arisen from the interpretation put by the courts upon the decision of the High Court of Calcutta in the case of *Prem Chand Boral* v *Collector of Calcutta.*[13] The words, "Market Value" occasionally lead to difficulties. It is the price which a willing vendor might be expected to obtain in the open market from a willing purchaser. In the case to which we have referred, it was held that the fairest and most valuable principle of compensation to the owners was to enquire, 'what is the market value of the property, not according to its present disposition but laid out in the most lucrative and advantageous way in which the owners could dispose of it'. This expression of opinion had induced the courts to assess lands at a price in excess of what the owners would ordinarily have obtained for them in the market. We think, it is not unfair for the purpose of Land Acquisition Act that land should be valued according to its disposition at the time the declaration is made.
>
> "In the opinion of the majority, if it is shown that before the declaration is made, the owner had taken active steps towards the more favourable disposition of the land and he spent money for that purpose, further compensation might be given to him, such compensation being based on his actual loss.
>
> "The value which ought to be paid is the value of the land to the owner and nothing more."

The Commission also recommended the introduction of the clause as to valuation at 25 times the municipal valuation.

13 ILR 2 Cal 103.

It appears from the speech of the Hon'ble Mr. Risley in introducing the Calcutta Municipal Bill in 1898 before the Council that the modifications of the Land Acquisition Act had been made in the Bill in accordance with the recommendations of the Calcutta Building Commission.

Now the principles enunciated in *Prem Chand Boral's* case are well-established principles for finding out the market value of the lands acquired under compulsory powers. Indeed those very principles regulate the price of lands in the open market. "Under the Land Clauses Act, Tribunal in assessing compensation may take into account not only the present purpose to which land is applied, but also any other more beneficial purpose to which in course of events, it might within reasonable period be applied just as an owner might do if he were bargaining with a purchaser in the market."[14]

These fundamental principles of assessment of market value have been expressed in varied language by the learned Judges both in England and in this country, all pointing to the basic principle that the owner must be paid the price which he could obtain in the open market for his land.

It would also appear from the extract of the recommendations of the Calcutta Building Commission quoted above that Legislature did not intend to lay down any different principle. All that was intended, was to guard against the assessment of compensation at a price in excess of what owners could get in the open market and the 'disposition clause' was introduced as a matter of abundant caution having regard to the relatively high value of land in the city of Calcutta. But the intention of the Legislature as expressed in the amending clause appears to be that all potentialities of the land must be ruled out in assessing market value.

The interpretation of this clause as to 'valuation according to present disposition' has been the subject of various decisions by the Calcutta High Court. In the case of *Harish Chandra Neogy* v *Secretary of State*,[15] the subject to be valued was a 'bustee land' acquired by the Calcutta Municipality. Their Lordships valued the acquired land on the basis of two sales

14 Halsbury: *Compulsory Purchase*, 3rd Ed., vol. 10.
15 11 CWN 875.

and thereafter supported that valuation on the basis of 25 years' purchase of the ground rent and in doing so, observed as follows:

> "Our decision is strengthened by consideration of the rentals and disposition of the two pieces of land at the date of declaration. Section 557 of the Calcutta Municipal Act precludes any valuation based on the most advantageous disposition of the land e.g., the valuation of a bustee land on its supposition for its adaptability for use as building land to carry expensive structures which is the most advantageous use to which the land can be put in Calcutta. The Act, however, contemplates 25 years' purchase on rental or annual valuation as made by the Corporation. *The two rules must go together*."

The interpretation of s. 557 (now s. 537 of the Kolkata Municipal Corporation Act 1980) made in *Harish Chandra Neogy's* case was expressly approved in the case of *Manindra Chandra Nandy* v *Secretary of State for India*,[16] where in valuing bustee land acquired for the Calcutta Municipality, evidence of building sites was excluded from consideration.

In *Madan Mohun Barman* v *Secretary of State*,[17] the subject-matter was the valuation of bustee land acquired by the Calcutta Improvement Trust. The learned President of the Calcutta Improvement Tribunal refused to admit in evidence a sale relating to a land with building. On appeal the High Court set aside the judgment holding that such a transaction was admissible in evidence. The question of disposition does not appear to have been raised in the case.

In *Hindusthan Co-operative Insurance Society Ltd.* v *Secretary of State for India*,[18] the question was the valuation of land acquired by the Calcutta Improvement Trust. The Society had made a development scheme for a large block of land for selling out in plots by driving roadways. On coming to know that the Calcutta Improvement Trust was going to frame a scheme for making a 100 ft. roadway across the land, the Society left that 100 ft. strip open and sold plots abutting

16 ILR 41 Cal 987.
17 AIR 1925 Cal 481.
18 ILR 56 Cal 989.

on that proposed 100 ft. roadway. When the scheme was framed later on and this strip of land, 100' × 1600' was acquired by the Calcutta Improvement Trust, the Collector treated it as a road and awarded value at the rate of ₹ 150 per kottah. The Tribunal confirmed the award of the Collector on the view that at the date of the declaration, the Society had conferred rights of way over this 100 ft. roadway to the owners of the plots adjoining the same. On appeal the High Court held that the real 'disposition' of the land was that it was a part of a scheme for the purpose of selling out in different small plots to purchasers as building sites by driving roads to the areas in order to give access to the various plots and on the evidence of case, the disposition of the acquired land cannot be considered as a road. Their Lordships valued the land at ₹94,330 after deducting the value of land for a 40 ft. road which was originally in the scheme of the Society and the cost of making that roadway on the evidence of the respondent's Valuer. It may be noted here that nothing was said in this case as to whether valuation by the development method was not permitted by the amendment of s. 23 by the Calcutta Improvement Act and as a matter of fact, the valuation that was ultimately made, was made on the development method.

In *Shrosbree* v *Secretary of State,*[19] 76 bighas of land comprising solid land, low land, tank and 'Beel' was acquired by the Calcutta Municipality for the purpose of Christian Burial Ground in Tollygunj. The block of land was accessible by a roadway issuing out from Russa Road and terminating in the land. The learned Collector (Rai Bahadur M.N. Gupta) gave detailed reasons under s. 19(*i*)(*d*) of the Land Acquisition Act. It appears from the reasons that he valued the solid land by the development method and made the following deductions from the value of building sites—

Road Lands	...	...	... 20%
Largeness of Enterprise		...	... 25%
Road Making	...	...	... 7%
		Total	52%

19 A.O.D. 192 of 1933 (unreported).

Mr. Shrosbree who examined himself as an Expert witness showed by a layout plan prepared by him that the deduction for road land would not be more than 7.5% of the total area of solid land. As regards the cost of road making he agreed with the Collector's figure of 7.5%. But on the question of largeness of enterprise and time involved he explained that the deduction should not be more than 15%, making thereby a total deduction of 30% in the place of the Collector's total of 52.5%. The learned Land Acquisition Judge accepted Mr. Shrosbree's deduction of 7.5% for the road lands. But he thought that deduction for largeness of enterprise as given by Mr. Shrosbree to be too low as there would be 17 building plots of an average area of 2 bighas, and accepted the Collector's estimate on that point. On appeal the High Court accepted the evidence of Mr. Shrosbree in view of his great experience and valued the solid land by deducting 30% from the price of building sites as derived from the transactions.

A deduction of ₹ 750 per bigha was made in respect of the low lands and the tanks were valued at half the value of solid lands.

It would appear from the above that for valuing undeveloped lands under s. 23 of the Land Acquisition Act (now s. 28 of the Right to Fair Compensation and Transparency in Land Acquisition, Rehabilitation and Resettlement Act 2013) as amended by s. 475 of the Calcutta Municipal Act 1923, the development method of valuation was adopted by the High Court, though the point of present disposition was taken. It was contended by the Government that the acquired land could not be valued on the basis of developed building sites having regard to its present disposition. Their Lordships negatived that contention and observed as follows:

> "We are unable to agree with the extreme contention for, if the evidence of market value of such land be not available, then the market value of such land could be ascertained from the value of the lands of developed areas in the neighbourhood by making such deductions as would be necessary for the purpose of bringing up the undeveloped area into developed state. It is true that the land under acquisition does not enjoy the same amenity, the same convenience and the same advantages as the lands in the

residential quarters in respect of which transactions have been put in evidence. But, we see that the town is extending towards the south. There are residential quarters and sites on the south and on the north of the land under acquisition; it is no wonder that the lands to the south might some day be converted into building sites."

In *Province of Bengal* v *Uma Charan Law*,[20] 'bustee land' acquired by the Calcutta Improvement Trust was valued by Roopendra K. Mitra, J sitting with Akram, J on the basis of the sale price of a land with a three-storyed building after deducting the estimated cost of the building. The point of present disposition was not mooted in this case.

In the case of *Province of Bengal* v *Amulyadhan Auddy*,[1] the subject to be valued was a block of land abutting on a roadway with another blind lane touching at its side. The claimant's expert valued it by the development method, that is to say, by producing the blind lane across the land and dividing the land into two blocks abutting on that imaginary roadway. Roopendra K. Mitra, J sitting with P.N. Mitra, J held that the development method, as adopted by the claimant's expert, was not permissible in the case of lands acquired by the Calcutta Improvement Trust by reason of the rule as to present disposition. In course of the judgment in commenting upon the method adopted by the claimant's expert, His Lordships observed as follows:

> "Market value is what an owner, not obliged to sell, would have got from a free buyer. Certainly a free buyer in estimating the price would have taken into consideration the fact that he would be able to develop the land—to have the best user—by dividing it into 3 blocks by constructing a road across the land at the place suggested by Sarkar (Claimant's expert), but the question is whether such a method is allowable in view of the provisions of the Calcutta Improvement Act.
>
> * * * * *
>
> "The land has to be valued according to its disposition at the date of declaration. It cannot be imagined to be in

20 48 CWN 609.
1 54 CWN 297.

a different state than what it actual was at that point of time nor can be valued with reference to its possible future user by proposing a physical change of the land."

In support of the proposition that the development method is not permissible in cases of compulsory acquisition of land for the Board of Trustees for the Improvement of Calcutta, his Lordship cited the case of *Hindusthan Co-operative Insurance Society* v *Secretary of State*.[2] It is submitted with the greatest respect that there is nothing in the judgment in that case in support of that proposition. His Lordship also referred to the case of *Shrosbree* v *Secretary of State*.[3] It is submitted that as has already been stated above, in that case, Their Lordships valued the undeveloped land by the development method.

The question of present disposition came up for consideration before the Calcutta High Court in Apportionment proceedings of *Sitanath Pal* v *K.C. Basu*.[4] It was contended by Mr. Atul Chandra Gupta, Advocate, that there is no real difference between the words, 'as it then stood', which according to the Privy Council are implicit in s. 23(1) of the Land Acquisition Act (now s. 28 of the new Act of 2013) and the words, 'according to the disposition of the land' at the material time. According to him, these words really added nothing to the Land Acquisition Act. K.C. Das Gupta, J (as he then was), in the course of the judgment observed, "In any judgment, there is considerable force in this contention". But, as it was not necessary to decide that question, His Lordship pronounced no decision on the point. The Privy Council case referred to, is the *Vizagapatam Harbour* case[5] which has since found a place in English Textbooks.

In another apportionment appeal which went up to High Court regarding compensation money awarded for land acquired by the Calcutta Improvement Trust, this question was considered, vide *Santosh Kumar Dhur* v *Nanda Kishore Mullick*.[6] In that case P.N. Mukherjee, J held as follows:

2 56 Cal 989.
3 A.O.D. 192 of 1933 (unreported).
4 A.O.D. 80 of 1948.
5 43 CWN 557.
6 AIR 1958 Cal 56.

"The Legislature in amending the section 23 of the Land Acquisition Act for the purpose of the Calcutta Improvement Act did not really intend any change in the law so as to exclude from consideration all potentialities of an acquired property and not merely the remote possibilities or potentialities in cases of acquisition under the Calcutta Improvement Act. Remote possibilities must no doubt be disregarded and possibilities only and not realised possibilities should be taken into consideration. But, subject to these restrictions, the possibilities of the acquired property, that is their present value should be normally taken into account in assessing compensation and *prima facie* at least the law does not seem to be otherwise under the Calcutta Improvement Act."

This pronouncement made by P.N. Mukherjee, J should now be taken to have finally settled the meaning of the vexed clause. A literal interpretation of the clause as was made in the case of *Amulya Dhone Auddy*,[7] would render it well nigh unworkable. The necessary corollary of such a literal interpretation would be that sales in the open market must be ruled out as the sale prices must be taken to be inclusive of the potentiality of the lands sold. Vide *Raghubans N. Singh* v *State of U.P.*[8] a vendor willing to sell his land at the market value will take into consideration a particular potentiality or special adaptability of the land in fixing the price.

The expression "market value according to the disposition of the land" came up for analysis in the case of *Mathura Prasad* v *State of West Bengal.*[9] The above expression constitutes an ingredient of s. 23 (now s. 28 of Act of 2013) of the Land Acquisition Act (since repealed and replaced by the Right to Fair Compensation and Transparency in Land Acquisition, Rehabilitation and Resettlement Act 2013) as inserted by way of local amendment under provision of s. 71(*b*) of the Calcutta Improvement Act 1911 in the matter of acquisition of land under the latter Act. It was held that such market value apparently means the value of the land in a hypothetical

7 54 CWN 297.
8 AIR 1967 SC 465.
9 (1970)3 SCC 730; AIR 1971 SC 465.

market which a willing purchaser may in the prevailing conditions pay for the land to a willing vendor taking into consideration its situation and advantages. In determining the "disposition" the purchaser would normally take into consideration the advantages of the situation and the potentialities of the land. Because, the market value of land especially in urban areas depends upon its situation, special adaptability, advantages and inherent potentiality in the light of demand for land.

Estimate of market value—uncertainties and guesswork

The science and art of estimation lie at the core of valuation. It was held by the Supreme Court of British Columbia (Canada) in the case of *Rowan* v *City of Vancouver* that "a recent market price is not the best test of actual value. The whole evidence surrounding the transaction, the condition of market and other factors have to be weighed carefully". The question now arises as to what are the other factors that are to be weighed.

In *Velayudam Chettiar* v *Special Tahsildar*[10] and also in *Chand Kiran Tyagi* v *State of U.P.*,[11] it was observed that valuation of immovable property is not an exact science. It is an inquiry relating to a subject abounding in uncertainties, where there is more than ordinary guesswork and where it would be very unfair to require an exact exposition of reasons for the conclusions arrived at. It has been held repeatedly that in all valuations, judicial or otherwise, there must be room for interference and inclinations of opinion which being more or less conjectural are difficult to reduce to exact reasoning or to explain to others and it is not fair to require an exact exposition of reason for the conclusions arrived at. In short the question of fair compensation is not an algebraic problem which would be solved by an abstract formula.

The same view was echoed in *Raja S.S. Kumara Krishna Yachandra Bachadurvaru* v *Spl. L.A.O., Bangalore*[12] followed by *Administrator-General, W.B.* v *Collector*[13] in which Bhagwati, J made the following observation:

10 (1959)1 MLJ 348; AIR 1959 Mad 462.
11 (1994)24 ALR 196.
12 (1979)4 SCC 356 (358).
13 (1988)2 SCC 150.

"We are conscious that this process of determination of market value adopted by us may savour of conjecture or guess, but the estimation of market value in many cases must depend largely on evaluation of many imponderables and hence it must necessarily be to some extent a matter of conjecture or guess. We do not, therefore, think that we would be unjustified in taking the market value of the land acquired under the notifications, dated 30.10.1951 and 28.1.1954 at Rupees 9 per square yard".

We may on this point quote from another significant judgment which runs as follows: "In all valuations, judicial or otherwise, there must be room for inference and indications of opinion, which being more or less conjectural are difficult to reduce to exact reasoning, or to explain to others. Everyone who has gone through the process is aware of this lack of demonstrative proof in his own mind, and know that every expert witness called before him has had his own set of conjectures of more or less weight according to the experience or personal sagacity."[14]

A valuer ought to envision the effect of trends and critical situations in his estimate of value. Abnormal increase of land value particularly in urban areas where financial tycoons with huge resources are always ready to offer fancy price for building sites or for commercial or industrial estates, ought to enter into estimation of value. So also when there is incessant inflow of fund from the parallel economy of the country. Extra-ordinary situations and political upheavals often bear an impact on valuation of real estates. As for example, in 1956 the value of immovable properties in Bombay had gone down considerably because of the Samyukta Maharashtra Movement demanding merger of Bombay City in Maharashtra. Similarly, the values of immovable properties in Calcutta had gone down in 1970-71 because of the Naxalite Movement. The market values of immovable properties had gone down considerably in Assam owing to the continuous agitation on foreign nationals issue. Emerging economic phenomenon like huge deficit financing or inflow of foreign fund do affect valuation. Market values of immovable properties have of late gone up in Gujarat or

14 *Secretary of State* v *Charlesworth Piling & Co.* LR 28 IA 121 (PC).

Bombay or Kerala due to foreign exchange remittances from non-resident Indians; the insertion of s. 54E in the Capital Gains-tax provisions of I.T. Act has encouraged property owners to sell their properties. Many people prefer speculative investment in immovable properties in a situation of galloping rate of inflation. The relative security for the value of money offered by real estate enhances the demand for properties and their values. Thus, various political and economic conditions play their part in influencing the market values of immovable properties. A prudent valuer should analyse all these factors while making an intelligent and rational estimate of the value of property.

The expression 'market value' has been further explained by the Supreme Court in the case of *Prithvi Raj Taneja* v *State of M.P.*[15] and the court made the following momentous observation on the issue:

> "The market value means the price that a willing purchaser would pay to a willing seller for the property, having due regard to its existing condition with all its existing advantages and its potential possibilities when laid down in the most advantageous manner excluding any advantage due to the carrying out of the scheme for which the property is compulsorily acquired. In considering market value, the disinclination of the vendor to part with, his land and the urgent necessity of the purchaser to buy should be disregarded. There is an element of guesswork inherent in most cases involving determination of the market value of the acquired land. But this in the very nature of things cannot be helped. The essential thing is to keep in view the relevant factors prescribed by the Act."

On the basis of ss. 18 and 23 of the Land Acquisition Act 1894 (since repealed and replaced by the Right to Fair Compensation and Transparency in Land Acquisition, Rehabilitation and Resettlement Act 2013), the Supreme Court awarded the mean rates of compensation for land acquired under two notifications of 1951 and 1954 from the same area and held as such. "We are conscious that this process of

15 (1977)1 SCC 684.

determination of market value adopted by us may savour of conjecture or guess, but the estimation of market value in many cases must depend largely on evaluation of many imponderables and hence it must necessarily be to some extent a matter of conjecture or guess. We do not, therefore, think that we would be unjustified in taking the market value of the land acquired under notifications dt. 30th October 1951 and 28th January 1954 at ₹ 9.00 per sq. yd."[16]

In fixing the value of the land an element of guesswork is inevitable and compensation in respect of the land under acquisition cannot be arrived at with any mathematical accuracy. Nevertheless there must be some material before the court on the basis of which alone compensation should be fixed.[17] The High Court should not base its decision wholly on the basis of L.A. Officer's award in cases involving a lot of guesswork.[18]

The court can always take into account any special circumstances, apart from the methods of valuation traditionally adopted, in order to arrive, as nearly as may be, at an estimate of the market value. In some situations, the estimation of market value depends largely on evaluation of many imponderables and may involve to some extent a matter of guesswork.[19]

Open market value—how far compensation is a guide

At this stage it is necessary to recall what 'market value' actually means. The expression 'market value' is the estimated amount for which a property should exchange on the date of valuation between a willing buyer and a willing seller in an arm's length transaction alter proper marketing wherein the parties has each acted with full knowledge of the market and without compulsion but with due prudence. The art and science of estimation lie at the core of valuation. Such estimation is desired to be made in an open market situation. The necessary question that arises is what is meant by an open market. An

16 *Raja S.S. Kumara Krishna Yachandra Bachadurvaru* v *Special L.A.O., Bangalore* (1979)4 SCC 356.

17 *State of Madras* v *M.G. Varadarajulu* AIR 1976 Mad 164.

18 *Ahmad Yar Jung* v *Collector, L.A., Hyderabad* (1974)2 SCC 67.

19 *Hindusthan Oil Co. Ltd.* v *Damoderan Namboodri* 1986 Ker LT 1013.

open market is the opposite of a closed market or a market where dealings are held in secrecy behind the screen. In an open market anyone who desires to enter into the transaction should be in a position to make an offer whether for purchase or for sale. It is a market where a willing buyer and a willing seller can freely come into contact with each other and are at liberty either to withdraw from negotiation or to strike a bargain without any compulsion. The parties to the transaction act as free agents and deal with each other at arm's length. Again, all necessary publicity has been given of the proposed sale prior to such sale so that the parties have the knowledge of the market and necessary details regarding the property to be sold.

The concept of market value developed on the cradle of compulsory acquisition suffers from some inherent constraints. The very term, 'compensation' payable under the due process of law for compulsory acquisition suggests the idea of 'indemnity', although it speaks of compensation. The legal provisions bespeak of compensatory damages to distinguish them from penal damages or from awards based on the doctrine of unjust enrichment. As a matter of doctrine, the Supreme Courts in USA have construed 'compensation' in its stricter sense and have held that 'just compensation' means indemnity to the owner for the loss of the property. 'Value to the taker' is not the measure of the award. Justice Holmes have aptly remarked in *Boston Chamber of Commerce* v *Boston*[20] that "the question is what has the owner lost not what has the taker gained". The Indian Judiciary have also taken the same view that the owner of acquired property should not be permitted to profit by the acquisition. Thus the result is limiting the market value of the condemned property even when the property is worth to the owner much more than the market value in an estimation of potential worth and on the other hand, a big gain to the Government as the taker. In an open or free market for transactions of private property, the forces of competition and bargaining would have struck a different market price from the one constrained by the power of eminent domain residing with the Government for compulsory acquisition.

20 [1910]217 US 189 (195).

There is another aspect of the matter. The valuation under the law of eminent domain prescribes a money payment equal to the market value of the property at the 'time of taking' or 'at the date of publication of the notification under s. 4, sub-sec. (1)' (now s. 11 of the new Act of 2013) as enjoined in s. 23(1) of the Land Acquisition Act 1894 (now s. 28 of the new Act of 2013). Thus the market value of the property is a regulated one. Instead of actual value or real value, the valuation should be based strictly on market conditions prevailing at the time of taking, however abnormal they might have been. It is well known that in periods of depression, price fetched is too low but in booms, the market awards an unearned profit. But these factors are to be utterly disregarded in an award of compensation, however might have been the relevance of such consideration in an estimation of market value in an open market situation.

It would, however, be wrong to assume that the Indian Judiciary has not given due recognition to the inadequacies that market value suffers at the altar of the power of eminent domain. On the contrary, there is a landmark judgment of the Supreme Court of India in *Land Acquisition Officer, Eluru* v *Jasti Rohini* (*Smt.*)[1] in which the paradox of fixation of market value on the basis of the law of compulsory purchase of land has been succinctly exposed and the concept of open market value outlined. The question arose as to what would be the market value prevailing as on the respective dates of notification. The reference court relied upon the basic valuation register maintained by the municipalities on the basis of the notification issued by the Government under s. 47A of the Stamp Act. In fact, the reference court mainly relied upon that document and awarded compensation on its basis. The admissibility and evidentiary value of such entries in the basic value register was previously considered by the Supreme Court also in *Jawajee Nagnatham* v *Revenue Division Officer.*[2] After an elaborate consideration the court had in that case held that the basic value register is maintained only for fiscal purpose of collecting stamp duty and registration charges. The market value mentioned therein cannot form a foundation to determine

1 (1995)1 SCC 717.
2 (1994)4 SCC 595.

the compensation under s. 23(1) of the Land Acquisition Act 1894 (since repealed). In the same vein, the Supreme Court in the above *Justi Rohini's* case observed:

> "It is settled law that the market value should be determined on the hypothesis of the price fetched in the *bona fide* sale by a willing vendor who would agree to sell the lands to a willing vendee of the acquired land or the land in the neighbourhood possessed of similar features. The notification under section 47A which is meant to be a guide for collection of revenue cannot form the basis for determination of market value of the land under section 23(1) of the Act. The question of fixation of market value is a paradox which lies at the heart of the law of compulsory purchase of land. The paradox lies in the facts that the market value concept is purely a phenomenon evolved by the courts to fix the price of land arrived between the hypothetical willing buyer and willing seller bargaining as prudent persons without a medium (*sic* modicum) of constraints or without any extraordinary circumstances. But the condition of free market is the very opposite of the condition of the compulsory purchase which is *ex hypothesi* a situation of constraints. Therefore, to say that for compulsory purchase compensation is to be assessed and market value is to be determined in that state of affairs, has to be visualised in terms by its direct opposite."

The Land Acquisition Act lays down in s. 23 [now s. 69(2) of the new Act of 2013] the principles for determining compensation on the basis of market value of land acquired. Section 24 of the Act (now s. 40 of the new Act of 2013) puts an embargo on the court that it shall not take into consideration "the degree of urgency for the acquisition; disinclination of the person interested to part with possession of the acquired land; any increase in the value of the land acquired likely to accrue from the use to which it will be put when acquired; any increase to the value of the other land of the person interested likely to accrue from the use to which the land acquired will be put to; any layout or improvements on or disposal of the land acquired etc. without the sanction of the Collector or after s. 4(1) notification was published; special suitability or adaptability of the land for any purpose or any increase in the value of the land on account of its being put to any use which is forbidden by law or opposed to public policy." Therefore, in determining the market value of fixation of the compensation, it was held in the above case that "the courts should be alive to these factors and keep them at the back of the mind and should not be influenced by the future or later development in the locality or neighbourhood and should not get influenced by the prevailing situation as on the date of the determination of the compensation. Its consideration should alone be confined to the market value prevailing as on the date of the notification under s. 4(1)".

To solve the riddle, the Supreme Court in the above case further held that "Courts have consistently evolved the principle that the present value as on the date of the compulsory acquisition comprised of all utility reached in a competitive field as on the date of the notification and the price on which a prudent and willing vendor and a similar purchaser would agree. The value of the land shall be taken to be amount that the land if sold in the open market by a willing seller might be expected to realise from a willing purchaser. A willing seller is a person who is a free agent to offer his land for sale with all its existing advantages and potentialities as on the date of the sale and willing purchaser taking all factors into consideration would offer to purchase the land as on the date of the sale. Future suitability or adaptability of the land for any purpose shall not be taken into account. The compensation must, therefore, be determined by reference to the price which a willing vendor might reasonably expect to obtain from a willing purchaser as on the date of the notification published under s. 4(1). The disinclination of the seller to part with his land and the urgent necessity of the vendee to purchase the land must, alike, be disregarded and neither of them must be considered as acting under compulsion".

Open market value—consideration of future possibilities

There are other judicial decisions which reflect on the concept of open market value. In *R.C. Cooper* v *Union of India*[3] it was held that it is the price the property may fetch in the open market if sold by a willing seller unaffected by the special

3 AIR 1970 SC 564.

needs of a particular purchaser. The fact that the acquirer does not intend to use the property for which it is used at the time of acquisition and desires to demolish it or use it for other purposes is irrelevant.

The Supreme Court in *Special Land Acquisition Officer* v *Veerabhadrappa*[4] in elucidating the concept has stated:

> "In *Vyricherla Narayana Gajapathiraju* v *Revenue Division Officer, Vizagapatnam,*[5] the Privy Council adopted the traditional legal definition of value as the price at which the property would sell as between a willing buyer and a willing seller. In its narrowest sense, it is designed to preclude a valuation based on an assumed forced sale; the property must be appraised at what it would probably bring if the owner allowed a reasonable opportunity for negotiations. But the courts have invoked a mythical willing buyer to justify a valuation higher than any attainable sale price. According to the Privy Council, 'market value' of the land within the meaning of s. 23 of the Act is the price the property may fetch in the open market, if sold by a willing vendor unaffected by the special needs of a particular purpose. The owner is entitled to the value of the property in its actual condition at the time of expropriation, with all its advantages and with all its possibilities, excluding any advantage due to the carrying out of the scheme for the purpose for which the property is acquired. It is not only realised possibilities but also the future possibilities that must be taken into consideration.
>
> "The Privy Council further observed that there is not in general any market for land in the sense that one speaks of market for shares or commercial goods. The value of any such article at any particular time can readily be ascertained by the prices being obtained for similar articles in the market. In the case of land, its value can also be measured by a consideration of the prices that have been obtained in the past for lands of similar quality and in similar positions, and that is what must be meant in general by the 'market value' in section 23".

4 (1985)154 ITR 190 (194 and 195).
5 (1939) LR 66 IA 104.

It is also worth taking into account the observations on the concept of open market value as nicely explained in *Smt. Lalita Todi* v *CIT*,[6] and *Vimla Agarwal* v *Appropriate Authority*,[7] "it is the price which a prudent purchaser would be willing to pay taking into account the extent and the quality of title as well as all the factors which tend to push up the value or depress it. It is the price to be deduced by loading the price, reflected in the instance taken as norm, for plus factors, and unloading it for minus factors".

In case of acquisition of undeveloped lands court has to assess the market value of the lands in their the then state. Further possibilities should not be considered as realised possibilities. It should be noted that further expenditure and trouble have to be incurred to make the land acquire the status and value of developed lands. This will consume more time to dispose of the whole land. The element of speculation in such adventures has to be borne in mind.[8]

Future utility is a thing that people have an eye in buying land and the market price of the land is affected by it. Such future utility must be estimated by prudent business calculations and not by mere speculative and impractical imagination.[9]

Future utility or the likely opportunity of utilising the land for some more profitable purpose assumes relevance when there are impending prospects of development and improvement of the area of an appreciable nature in the near future. The price of lands in the locality or in the vicinity may shoot up within a short time due to such impending prospects of development. In such circumstances, it can be said that such land has potential value which should not be lost sight of at the time of assessing valuation. The assessment of the potential value on the basis of its expected user in the near future of such profitable purposes can only be done when the expected user for such purposes is almost a certainty or a proximate possibility and is so obvious that its value can be ascertained

6 (1980)123 ITR 40 (Pat).
7 (1994)210 ITR 16 (Bom).
8 *Rajah of Vijianagram* v *R.D.O.* AIR 1954 AP 12.
9 *Fink* v *Secretary of State* ILR 34 Cal 599; *Dorabji Cursetji Shroff*, in re 10 Bom LR 675.

on a reasonable consideration of the realities of the situation. But where such possibilities are too remote or non-existent, the court should not take into consideration the potentiality of the land, as in that case one would himself in speculations and conjectures as to the price the land is likely to fetch in the distant future for something which is uncertain and is yet to be a reality.[10] The land sought to be acquired is of tourist importance, so the potential value of the land must be taken into account in fixing compensation.[11]

Whether open market includes black market

A question may arise as to whether the open market for purposes of valuation means the black market price as well. The Calcutta High Court in *CED* v *Radha Devi Jalan*[12] held that an open market cannot include a black market. The existence of a parallel economy is well known, but documented figures cannot by its very nature be had. In such circumstances it would be dangerous to introduce a factor based on mere hearsay evidence.

The decisions of the Madras High Court in *S. Abdul Rahman* v *CWT*[13] and of the Gujarat High Court in *CWT* v *Sadiquali Samsuddin*[14] are also relevant in the context. In that case, valuation of money held in Ceylon at a market rate lower than the official exchange rate was upheld, having regard to the restrictions on remittances. But it was held that such consideration does not go counter to the proposition that the element of values obtaining in the black market should not weigh, in making a valuation; because, the existence of restrictions on remittance from foreign countries is the result of statutory enactments, and it is settled law that for restrictions in transfer of property an appropriate discount should be given.

In *A.S. Sivan Pillai* v *CIT*,[15] the Assessing Officer had estimated the income from export of onion on the basis of

10 *State of Orissa* v *Nityananda Majhi* AIR 1975 Ori 28.
11 *Kausalya Devi* v *L.A.O., Aurangabad* AIR 1984 SC 892; (1984)2 SCC 324.
12 (1968)67 ITR 761.
13 (1979)117 ITR 570.
14 (1985)152 ITR 190.
15 (1958)34 ITR 328 (Mad).

black market profits earned by competitors by selling the goods at higher than the controlled rates. There is no presumption, it was held, that the assessee would have similarly indulged in similar activities and that there was no case for estimate. In *State of Kerala* v *Annama,*[16] the High Court held that dealings with racketeers and other anti-social elements cannot afford a standard for governmental action or judicial consideration. Both the above decisions were quoted with approval in the case of *Commissioner of Agri. Income-tax* v *M.J. Cherian*[17] where it was held that the fact that one would be able to sell the controlled commodity at a higher price in violation of regulations does not necessarily imply that the assessee would have broken the law. It pointed out that there is no presumption in favour of any illegality about a transaction. There is no authority that any departure from this sound principle of law is justified in valuation.

Whether open market is affected by land ceiling

Does open market mean restrictions like land ceiling law have to be ignored? This was answered in the negative in successive judicial decisions. It must be understood that valuation is generally intended for a particular purpose and such purpose is regulated by legal provisions in the relevant field. So conformity to law is essential for the purpose of valuation. In that sense, where the land is saleable but subject to approval it cannot be said that it is a closed market. But it is not open in the conventional sense. Such statutory restrictions cannot be ignored in evaluation of market value. It was so held in *Corporation of Calcutta* v *Smt. Padma Debi*[18] where it was pointed out in connection with the market rent under rent control law that the law of the land must necessarily be taken as one of the circumstances obtaining in the open market placing an upper limit on the rate of rent.

Where land ceiling laws are applicable the restrictive conditions have to be given due weight though the value necessarily does not have to be identical as held in *CWT* v

16 AIR 1969 Ker 38.
17 (1979)117 ITR 37 (Ker).
18 AIR 1962 SC 151.

Rajkumari Bhuvaneshwari.[19] There are other cases also. One such decision pertaining to pre-emptive purchase of property under Chapter XX-C of the Income-tax Act was rendered by the Gujarat High Court in *Gordhandas Purshottamdas Patel* v *Appropriate Authority,*[20] where fact that land ceiling law was not taken into consideration in evaluating the apparent consideration vitiated the purchase.

Open market—effect of inflation—judicial notice

In *State of Bihar* v *S.K. Thacker*[1] the court held that judicial notice can and should be taken of the fact of continuous inflation and rising land values. That was a case where land values rose since 1957 to 1961, the latter being the year of acquisition. The court held, "Phenomenal increase of land values have been witnessed from 1975 to 1985. The value in 1975 has been trebled in 1985. If it is a case of house structures, the capital value of these structures will be the annual income multiplied twenty times. The spurt in value have naturally a bearing on the annual income".

In *Tribeni Devi* v *Collector of Ranchi*[2] the Supreme Court observed:

> "It is a well-known fact and can be taken judicial notice of, that after the termination of the Second World War in 1945, there was a rise in land values due to the increased demand of homestead lands for building purposes. The general principles for determining compensation have been set out in sections 23 and 24 of the Act ....."
>
> "The methods of valuation to be adopted in ascertaining the market value of the land on the date of the notification under section 4(1) are—(*i*) the opinion of experts; (*ii*) the price paid within a reasonable time in *bona fide* transactions of purchase of the lands acquired or the lands adjacent to the lands acquired possessing similar advantages; and (*iii*) the number of years' purchase of actual or immediately prospective profits of the lands acquired."

19 (1995)215 ITR 198 (Raj).
20 (1996)217 ITR 62 (Guj).
1 AIR 1981 Pat 81.
2 AIR 1972 SC 1417.

"These methods do not, however, preclude the court from taking any other special circumstances into consideration, the requirement being always to arrive as near as possible, at an estimate of the market value. In arriving at a reasonably correct market value, it may be necessary to take even two or all of these methods into account inasmuch as the exact valuation is not always possible as no two lands may be the same either in respect of the situation or the extent or the potentiality, nor is it possible in all cases to have reliable material from which that valuation can be accurately determined."

The High Court determined the market value of the acquired land under a notification. Subsequent notification was issued after one year of the previous notification for acquisition of similar land. Higher market value should be given to those acquired under subsequent notification, keeping in view of the general increase in price of land during that period.[3]

In *Dewan Anand Kumar* v *Union of India*,[4] it was found that after the notifications of 1959 and 1961 there was no private transactions of sale, but during the year 1959 to 1963 the prices of plots in developed colonies showed a tremendous upward trend and that had its effect on the undeveloped land under acquisition in the neighbourhood of developed colonies. *Held*, the Government as the only buyer could not take advantage of its position. It had to pay the proper market value and if prices have been rising since 1957 to 1959 onwards there is no reason why they would not have risen further. So, Government has to be put in the position of a willing purchaser and it must pay market value on that basis.

Speculation in land prices

The relevancy of the rise in price of land due to speculation in the fixation of market value was considered by the Bombay High Court in *Dhusabhai Polabhai* v *Spl. Land Acquisition Officer*.[5] The Court held:

"If a person desires to acquire land or settle down in a place which is full of promise for development, the desire

3 *Ranjit Singh* v *Union Territory of Chandigarh* AIR 1993 SC 227; (1992)4 SCC 659.
4 AIR 1973 Del 102; AIR 1984 Del 208.
5 AIR 1959 Bom 520.

could not be condemned as a mere speculative desire. There could be nothing unreal or undesirable about it. If the knowledge that acquisition by the Government is imminent raises the tone of the market and gives impetus to the market, a new market rate would be created and the transaction would be governed by that rate. It would be too dangerous a proposition to lay down and too unfair a comment on human impulses to generalise and stigmatise every transaction of sale entered into after the market had risen as a speculative transaction or demonstration of a profiteering tendency of a human mind. A speculation on the effect of establishing an educational centre in an area sought to be acquired upon prices is permissible up to a certain extent. It is permissible to the extent where it is shown that it had actually entered into the market value of the land on the date of the notification. It may be unfortunate that for launching a welfare scheme of acquisition in the interests of public education a higher compensation may have to be paid on account of the market value of the land going up as the result of speculation arising out of the prospective acquisition of the lands. But so long as section 23 stands as it is on the statute book, it is inevitable that the material rate is the market rate at the date of notification."

Expert opinion on market value

The opinion of experts as to the market value of a land is to be regarded as evidence, but its evidential value is not great, inasmuch as the value of the experts' opinion depends upon the facts on which it rests and the validity of the process by which the conclusion is reached.[6]

The real function of an expert is to put before the court all the materials together with reasons which induced him to come to a certain conclusion. Though the court is not an expert, may form its own judgment by its own observation of the materials before it.[7]

6 *L.A.O.* v *Fakir Mohomed* AIR 1933 Sind 124; 143 IC 699.

7 *State (Delhi Administration)* v *Pali Ram* AIR 1979 SC 14; (1979)2 SCC 158.

The court can be guided by opinion of surveyors. A surveyor's opinion by itself is good evidence. What value the court will put to it depends entirely on the effect of cross-examination. It will save the time of the court if a surveyor prepares a concise description of the property to be valued and add nothing more except his opinion of its value. But if he gives his reason that must be based on facts and not on hypothesis.[8]

An expert knows what factors should be considered, what information he should seek for, where he should seek it and how he should test it and apply it. But experience does not enable one to dispense with enquiry and an honest and useful valuation cannot be made simply by visiting the land and picking up orally some casual and untested information or gossip which may be interested or one-sided. These conditions apply specially to land in or near large towns.[9]

The value of expert evidence is directly proportional to the accuracy of facts which is supported by and is dependent upon the cogency of reasons. The criterion adopted by the expert must be susceptible to and admit of objective verification.[10]

Where expert witness as to value of the land gives no data in support of their opinions, their evidence should be rejected.[11]

In an ultimate analysis, the market value of an acquired land must be the near estimate of the price which a person by voluntarily selling the awarded land would have got from a willing purchaser. What could be regarded as the near estimate of the acquired land is often a matter of expert opinion. All valuations are estimates and carry with them a degree of uncertainty. The range of this uncertainty may vary in different market conditions. But reliability is crucial to the credibility of valuation. The users of valuation would accept such uncertainty as inevitable, provided it is kept within reasonable bounds and the results held within the range of reliability. Sometimes the degree of uncertainty will be abnormal because

8 *Matter of Govt. of Bombay* and *Karim Tar Mohaomed*, in re 33 Bom 325; 10 Bom LR 660; 3 IC 690.

9 *Rajendra Nath Banerjee* v *Secretary of State* 32 Cal 343.

10 *Special L.A.O., Devangiri* v *Katraiah* AIR 1977 Kant 33.

11 *Pirbhu Diyal* v *Secretary of State* 135 IC 183; AIR 1931 Lah 364.

of the exceptional market conditions or because of physical circumstances or legal constraints surrounding the property. But the valuer need to be able enough to steer through the smoke-screen of such situation and develop appropriate techniques for expressing the degrees of uncertainty and striking an appropriate approach. There is an apt remark by the Supreme Court of British Columbia in the case of *Kitsul Bros. Gravel Sales Ltd.* v *Barry Humbart and Country Squire Ltd.* in a matter where the property could not be said to have a market value in the conventional sense owing to non-existence of a market for sales comparison. The said court opined "there was no comparable property, and a price a developer would pay, for the property would depend entirely on the perception of the individual developer as to the economy of the enterprise. One developer might see the property as having no value: another might see a very large profit". The range of purposes for which a valuation may be required is substantial and includes sale, purchase, letting, obtaining finance, accounting, rating, compulsory purchase and fiscal requirements. Even apparently minor differences in the purpose for which a valuation is to be used may produce significantly different figures. In such situation, valuation is largely a matter of expert opinion. But there are also principles for employing the expertise.

The valuation of both land and building made by the Commissioner appointed by the court was his opinion as an expert. For the purpose of correct assessment of valuation the court can go into such opinion for effective determination of real question in controversy between the parties.[12]

Competence of experts

According to *Black's Law Dictionary* an expert means "A person who, through education or experience, has developed skill or knowledge in a particular subject, so that he or she may form an opinion that will assist the fact-finder."[13]

An expert, in order to be competent as a witness, need not have acquired his knowledge professionally. It is sufficient so far

12 *State of West Bengal* v *Phanindra Kumar Kundu* AIR 1973 Cal 441.
13 Black's *Law Dictionary,* 9th Ed., p. 660.

as the admissibility of the evidence goes, if he has acquired a special experience therein. In his capacity as Commissioner and Administrator of the Municipal Corporation he appears to have gained knowledge pertaining to the value of land situated in different parts of the city as also of the house properties and the said knowledge entitles him to be considered an expert so far as to render his opinion founded on such knowledge admissible in evidence.[14]

The evidence of expert witnesses is generally of assistance to the court, but it has its limitations. Every expert witness has his own set of conjectures of more or less weight according to his experience and personal sagacity with the result that the enquiry abounds with uncertainty and gives more than ordinary room for guesswork. Further, the expert witness sometimes begins with a predetermined conclusion, and tries to adjust his figures, his answers and his conjectures to that conclusion.[15]

In *Secretary of State* v *Smt. Sarala Devi Chaudhurani*,[16] it was held that an expert evidence produced consisted of the opinions of certain brokers and on examination it was revealed that those were worthless. None of them produced any account book or registers that they had been selling similar plots in the vicinity, at or near the time the notification was issued and had given no real data in support of opinions. Thus the evidence of experts produced was rightly excluded from consideration as affording no assistance in arriving at the correct value of the site in question.

An expert ought to possess special knowledge on the subject of valuation and he should have had adequate practical experience. He must be in a position to express an independent opinion of his own as an expert. Mere experience is no expertise. An experienced farmer who has enough acquaintance with land transactions and land valuation may be a pertinent witness but he is not necessarily to be cited as an expert. As against

14 *Collector, Jubbalpore* v *Nowab Ahmad Yar Jahangir Khan* AIR 1971 MP 32.
15 *Govt. of Bombay* v *Century Spinning and Manufacturing Co. Ltd.* AIR 1942 Bom 105.
16 AIR 1924 Lah 548.

his evidence and that of an expert valuer the latter has to be preferred.[17] Before an expert can give an opinion, he must be given sufficient opportunity to form an opinion. In *Jowett* v *Federal Commissioner of Taxation*[18] it was held that departmental experts if they are tied down to a formula and have no practical knowledge cannot be relied upon.

In *Government of Bombay* v *Morwanji Mancherji*[19] it was held:

> "The opinion of an expert witness is admissible in evidence not only when it rests on the personal observation and inquiry of the witness himself or on facts within his own knowledge, but also when it is founded on the case as proved by other witnesses at the trial; and under section 51 of the Evidence Act, when the opinion is admissible, the grounds upon which it is based are also admissible. But we understand it to be settled law that an expert may not be asked purely speculative, hypothetical questions having no foundation in the evidence. In other words, before the expert witness is entitled to give evidence on the hypothesis, a sufficient foundation for it must be laid by evidence ..... of the facts assumed."

In re *Stuart Russel*[20] it was observed that an expert must be given sufficient opportunity to form an opinion before he is called upon to give an opinion. His oral evidence before the Tribunal is more essential than his opinion in writing.

Whether a valuer can use his local knowledge in valuing property

A valuer can use his local knowledge, *i.e.* knowledge derived as a person in the locality having an intelligent concern with local affairs. But the valuer cannot use his "personal" knowledge or "specialised" knowledge which he has acquired by being intimately connected with that particular property or by being engaged in a particular business or transaction when gave

17 In re *Didailler* (1940)19 LVR 7.
18 (1926)38 CLR 325.
19 10 Bom LR 907.
20 (1908)3 CLR 193; 17 Ausir Digest 1080.

him specific knowledge about that particular property.[21] The judgment catalogues English cases touching on the point. In this case, the Tribunal had, *inter alia* mentioned that it is well known that during 1954 to 1962, there was considerable increase in land values. This was claimed to be a misdirection which vitiated the finding. An extract from the English judgment cited by the High Court reads as under:

> "Those statements have been severely criticised, and I have been referred to an Irish case, *Regina* v *Justices of Co. Antrim,*[22] in which a very famous law Lord was held by the Irish Court to have made a mistake in acting as a Magistrate upon his own local and particular knowledge. It seems to me that a fair criticism is that the Commissioners were not entitled to use any specialised knowledge which they had about the flats or maisonettes at a particular time. It may be that that particular sentence must be dismissed as a misdirection, and it may be that no attention should be paid to it."

It further concluded as below:

> "From the above illuminating observations of Lord Evershed M.R., it is patent that a clear and firm distinction is being drawn between matters which may be said to be a matter of local knowledge for Judges or tribunals having a local jurisdiction. This is a knowledge which is derived by such Judges or members of the tribunals as having come to their possession as persons in the locality or to quote the words of Lord Evershed "of persons who were intelligently concerned in the relevant local affairs". This "local knowledge" is, however, quite distinct from what has been described as "specialised knowledge" or "personal specialised knowledge" which is an individual knowledge of the person himself and which may have been derived by him as a result of some association of a specialised nature with that particular branch of human affairs. The above decision is a clear authority for the proposition that if a particular finding is based on "local knowledge" it is not vitiated as having

21 *Mahmudabad Properties (P) Ltd.* v *CIT* (1972)85 ITR 500 (Cal).
22 [1985]2 Ir Rep 603.

> taken into consideration something which is inadmissible. If the finding is, however, based on specialised personal or individual knowledge it would be taking into account something which is not admissible."

Whether confidential information should enter into valuation

This question arose for consideration by the House of Lords in *Lynall* v *Inland Revenue Commissioners.*[23] In that case if the confidential information was not available then the value of each share would have been £ 3 10s otherwise it would have been £ 4 10s. Each of the five law Lords, in their separate speeches, came to the same conclusion, namely that information which was of a confidential nature and which would not be disclosed by the directors to ordinary shareholders had to be ignored in arriving at the value of the share, even if the shareholder happened to be a director. Thus the value of £3 10s. was considered to be the proper value. In the course of his speech Lord Reid observed:

> "We must decide what the highest bidder would have offered in the hypothetical sale in the open market, which the Act requires us to imagine took place at the time of Mr. Lynall's death. The sum which any bidder will offer must depend on what he knows (or thinks he knows) about the property for which he bids. The decision of this case turns on the question what knowledge the hypothetical bidders must be supposed to have had about the affairs of Linread. One solution would be that they must be in fact have been omniscient. But we have to consider what would in fact have happened if this imaginary sale had taken place, or at least if we are looking for a general rule what would happen in the event of a sale of this kind taking place. One thing which would not happen would be that the bidders would be omniscient. They would derive their knowledge from facts made available to them by the shareholder exposing the shares for sale. We must suppose that, being a willing seller and an honest man, he would give as much information which he could get as a shareholder. If he was a director and had confidential information, he could not disclose that information without the consent of the board of directors."

23 (1972)83 ITR 563.

CHAPTER

7

Market Approach and Sales Comparison Method

The sales comparison method estimates the value of a property by analysing the sales prices of similar properties. The fact that valuation is an estimate of probable value regardless of the method employed, market prices in many real estate markets appear to be a better and more consistent measure of market value than hypothetical market value estimates arrived at by other approaches to value. For comparison of sales, the primary essential is an organised market where the transactions of sales take place or are recorded for knowledge of the intending buyers and sellers. It is also necessary that the sales must be genuine and provide dependable clue to what a willing owner will be able to obtain from a willing purchaser. The best way to determine the market value is to consider the prices obtained by contemporaneous sale deeds whether of the same land or of the lands in the vicinity. Where, however, no contemporaneous sale deed is available on record, resort can be taken to cases of similar lands or property in respect of which reliable evidence of sales data are forthcoming. The further prerequisite is the correct sale-price. If all such requirements are assured, instances of normal sales of like property in the locality or executed in reasonable distances of time, enjoying the same or similar advantages, can provide good evidence for ascertainment of the market value of the subject property. But these are often wishful expectations and belied in actual experiences. Other factors ramaining the same, the sales comparison approach is the most reliable valuation approach where good sales data are available.

The application of the sales comparison method generally involves the use of automated statistical techniques with multiple regression analysis being the primary one. The technique seeks to relate variations in sales prices to variations in property characteristics, and produces an equation used to estimate the value of a property based on its characteristics. If desired, the equation can be converted to tabular form for use by non-statisticians. Multiple regression analysis is a statistical technique for estimating unknown data on the basis of known and available data. It can provide valuable assistance to the valuer in eliminating the need to adjust too many percentages of comparable sales with large number of variables. First of all, it helps in identifying the variables that are statistically significant and rank them in order of importance. The technique identifies an estimated price, a range and an estimate of probabilities of variation in the prices about that range. In fact, multiple regression analysis is an aid to, rather than a substitute for judgment in the valuation process. Successful application of the technique depends upon the quantity and quality of the data employed. Additional data generally improve the reliability of the results, particularly among heterogeneous properties.

An alternative to multiple regression analysis is adaptive estimation procedure which is often called "feedback system". This technique constructs a valuation equation that is initially specified by the user although the specification may have little to do with the final result, and then continually refined as each new sale is processed by the system. Both techniques may produce accurate results if properly used and supported by reliable data.

An automated comparable sales analysis system will find a predetermined number of sales that are most comparable to the subject land based on user-defined criteria. The system will then adjust the sales prices of the comparable instances for physical and location differences in relation to the subject land. By computer application, the estimated value of the subject land can be arrived at as the median or mean of the values of the adjusted comparables. The technique has the major advantage of being self-documenting and easily supported when good comparables are available. But there is distinct disadvantage when the number of sale instances are relatively small and too heterogeneous. As already stated, the limitation of this approach lies in the difficulties in obtaining correct sale information and data consequent on market imperfection. The under-valuation in the consideration money in the sales document for various evasions may frustrate the approach unless a method in the evasion can be well established.

Evidence of sales offers

There are various methods of arriving at a valuation of a property, but whatever method is adopted, it should be supported by evidence regarding other similar premises. There are various ways of supporting at valuation, the most common of which is to give evidence of sales of similarly situated properties in the same area.

The best evidence of the value of a property is the sale of the property itself. If the sale is of recent date then all that has to be proved is that the sale was between a willing purchaser and seller, that there had not been any appreciable rise or fall, and that the level of value had remained constant since that date. If the sale took place several years ago, then that may not be the best available evidence. There may be more recent sales of land which are comparable and if the latter sale when analysed gives a greater land value than the former sale then the evidence would prove that there had been a rise in land values since the property previously changed hands. The case of *Secretary of State* v *Manmatha Nath Dey*[1] supports the contention that the sale which takes place nearest to the *Date of Declaration* or *Date of Notification*, as the case may be, is the best evidence of value. Ross, J said:

> "The real argument on behalf of the respondents is that of the two documents which the learned District Judge has taken into consideration, namely, Exts. 2 and 3; Ex. 3 gives the better criterion of the two. Ex. 2 is a sale deed of 1918

1 AIR 1925 Pat 129.

by which the very land covered by case No. 50, that is appeal No. 243 was conveyed. The rate was Rs. 441 a kottah. The evidence shows that the land was sold cheap because it was inauspicious. The other document Ex. 3 gives the rate at Rs. 600 a kottah and the learned District Judge has taken the mean roughly between these two and has arrived at the figure of Rs. 500. Now Ex. 3 is nearest in date to the acquisition itself and is therefore in my opinion the best criterion of the market value at the time of the acquisition. The land was acquired in March 1920 and this sale deed was executed on the 28th of January of that year. The land is directly opposite the land acquired in case No. 50 and I can see no reason why the rate shown in that deed, namely, Rs. 600 should not be taken as the standard of these cases. It is the best evidence on the record."

The courts have all along supported the view that market value can be determined by sales of similar lands in the neighbourhood. In *Government of Bombay* v *Karim Tar Mohamed*[2] Mr. Justice MacLeod said:

> "The valuation cannot be based on what the property was producing at the time of the notice, nor have there been any recent sales of the land to guide the court. The market value must, therefore, be determined by sales of similar land in the neighbourhood."

Evidence of other transactions relating to land may be a good guide to assessing the value of a piece of land. Judgments of the courts in cases where the value of land was determined may be good evidence if the circumstances of the case are understood and the situation similar. Accepted awards of the Land Acquisition Collector are also very good evidence when the acceptance is for property in the immediate vicinity and a comparison can be made on the merits of each plot. The condition of the party accepting must be investigated but in ninety-nine per cent of acceptances the parties are really satisfied that they have been given a fair sum representing the market value. They know that if the offer is too low, they need not accept the offer of the Land Acquisition Collector,

2 ILR (1909)33 Bom 325.

and the Collector will then make an award and they will receive that amount. They can then file a reference and any enhancement, *plus* interest, will be paid to them at a future date when the case is finally settled by the courts. The case of *Madan Mohan Burman* v *Secretary of State*[3] clearly sets out that previous decisions in Land Acquisition cases are relevant and the following extract from the judgment is worth noting:

> "In assessing the market value of a piece of land the price paid in other transactions relating to land in the neighbourhood must be of some value. What its value is, it is for the court or fact to determine; but we hold that it cannot be rejected as inadmissible on the ground given in the judgment of the learned President. For the view we take we have the authority of the Judicial Committee of the Privy Council in the case of *Secretary of State* v *Indian General Steam Navigation and Railway Co.*[4] In that case certain judgments of the High Court in other proceedings were relied on by the claimant. It was argued on behalf of the appellant to the Judicial Committee that these judgments were not evidence of the value of the land in dispute. Their Lordships, after stating in their judgment that the High Court in a very careful judgment has revised the earlier awards, dismissed the appeal, holding that no question of principle was involved in it. There cannot be a clearer authority that previous decisions in land acquisition cases are relevant in a subsequent case where the market value of lands in the same neighbourhood is in issue."

The importance of previous decisions in land acquisition cases in assessing the value of land in the same neighbourhood was emphasized by the Calcutta High Court in the later case of *Naresh Chandra Bose* v *Province of Bengal*[5] decided by G.N. Das and N.C. Chatterjee, JJ. That was also an appeal from the judgment of the Calcutta Improvement Tribunal. Before the Tribunal the claimant tendered in evidence a previous judgment of the Tribunal regarding another plot of land in the neighbourhood. That Tribunal, however, in valuing the land

3 AIR 1925 Cal 481.
4 (1907)36 Cal 967.
5 A.O.D. No. 355 of 1944 (unreported).

in dispute did not rely upon it. The High Court held that the Tribunal was in error. G.N. Das, J observed that "in our opinion the decision of the Tribunal on the question of valuation of lands which are comparable to the lands which are now under acquisition is of much greater weight than the effect of accepted awards."

The Allahabad High Court in the case of *Maharaj Kumar Arfan Rasul Khan* v *Uttar Pradesh Government*,[6] expressed the same view that decisions and awards are relevant for the purpose of ascertaining the market value of land in subsequent cases.

The Bombay High Court, however, speaks in a different voice. Judgments and awards not being interparties are not relevant for the purpose of valuing lands in subsequent cases.[7]

If a person purchased a plot of land similar to one under acquisition and he laid it out in an advantageous manner and obtained a high price for the land, that would be good evidence and should be proved to support a case. This principle is laid down in *Fink* v *Secretary of State of India*,[8] a part of the judgment being as follows:

> "If it is shown that a person has paid a certain price for a block of neighbouring land similarly situated and possessing similar advantages with a view to some profitable disposal thereof, there is no reason why another block of land the subject of acquisition should not be similarly valued. The probability of a person purchasing the land for a similar purpose is an element for consideration if the probability is not so remote that it ought to be held purely speculative, so that other things being equal, of two blocks of land, the block under acquisition should be taken to be of equal market value with the other block. The general principle cannot be denied."

If a valuer analyses a sale to prove the value of a plot of land under acquisition, the best evidence is the sale of a similarly situated vacant plot of the same size. If there are no

6 ILR (1960) All 71 (102).

7 *Government of Bombay* v *Karim Tar Mohamed* ILR 33 Bom 325; AIR 1960 Bom 78.

8 ILR (1907)34 Cal 604.

vacant lands to which a comparison can be made, then an analysis of the sale of land and buildings should be made. The correct value of the building, if deducted from the total price, will give a value for the land. If the plot is fully developed and this is proved by the rent, then the depreciated value of the building would be the correct deduction to make. If on the other hand the existing buildings do not develop the land and by an expenditure of money could not be made or adapted to develop the land then the old material value of the structures should be deducted from the total value to give the value of the land. There are, of course, two sides to each question. In *Government of Bombay* v *Karim Tar Mohamed*[9] their Lordships said:

> "With reference to the purchase of the property facing the claimant's land on the south side of Valpakhadi Road from Karmali Pirbhoy, I agree with Mr. Robertson that it cannot be relied upon, as it is a purchase of land and buildings, and the purchase price must have been fixed by what the property was producing. This cannot be taken as an instance of sale of land, though it may turn out that the balance of the purchase money after calculating the value of the building may approximate what a witness considers to be the value of the land. That would be a coincidence and not evidence. It cannot be too clearly laid down that under ordinary circumstances the value of an income producing property depends on its income irrespective of its cost, and that capital when once invested in land and buildings cannot be apportioned between them so as to give the market value of each."

This is not sound reasoning and very little reliance has been placed on this judgment in later cases. In *Madan Mohan Burman* v *Secretary of State*[10] their Lordships found that it may be difficult to determine the value of the land apart from the building, but it is not necessarily so. The extract from the judgment, quoted below, is conclusive and should be followed in all cases—

> "Another piece of evidence which we hold has been wrongly rejected is Ex. 13; that relates to the sale of a piece of land

9 ILR 33 Bom 325.
10 AIR 1925 Cal 481.

in the neighbourhood in which there was a *pucca* building. We are unable to understand why this should not be relevant. It may be difficult to determine the value of the land apart from the building but it is not necessarily so, and the claimant is entitled to put this evidence before the court and ask the Tribunal, on a consideration of the evidence, to decide what portion of the purchase price represented the value of the whole land then sold. In rejecting the evidence the learned President referred to a decision of this court. The case was not cited by him but we understand it to be the judgment of a Division Bench of this court in the case of *Manindra Chandra Nandi* v *Secretary of State.*[11] But an examination of the judgment in that case shows that no such principle was laid down as that in valuing wast land the evidence as to the sale of land with a building thereon was inadmissible. What was held in that case was that certain questions set out in the report were rightly disallowed. None of these questions related to a sale of land with buildings thereon. So far as that ruling asserts any principle, it follows the case of *Haris Chandra Neogy* v *Secretary of State,*[12] and there also we find nothing to support the decision of the learned President."

In the case of *Province of Bengal* v *Uma Charan Law,*[13] Mitter, J valued the land in question (which was bustee land) on the basis of a sale of a land with a pucca four-storeyed building by deducting the estimated value of the building from the sale price.

I do not propose to discuss in detail the value of an "offer" as evidence of market value. This is much too unreliable to be of any material value to the expert when making his valuation. A quotation from the judgment in *Government of Bombay* v *Merwanji Mancherji Cama*[14] is the best advice I can give:

"It appear to us that in ascertaining the market value under the Act too much importance must not be attached to

11 18 CWN 884.
12 11 CWN 875.
13 48 CWN 609.
14 (1908)10 Bom LR 907.

evidence of offers. An offer does not come within the category of sales and purchases. If an offer for the whole or a portion of the land under acquisition is proved, it amounts merely to an expression of opinion on the part of the offerer. But this can only be proved by the evidence of the offerer himself and is then relevant. The evidence of offers made by irresponsible brokers on behalf of undisclosed principals, or perhaps for their own purposes without any principal behind them is in our opinion useless, even supposing it is relevant, which he doubts. The evidence that the owner refused an offer so made through a broker is only evidence that in his opinion his land was worth more than the figure of value named or that the offer was for some other reason of a nature which he was unwilling to accept. Evidence of such offers by brokers for the neighbouring land is still less effective. If the offerer himself gives evidence, it is evidence that in his opinion such neighbouring land was of a certain value, and such evidence would only be relevant if he had formed an opinion by comparison of the land under acquisition."

The courts have all along adopted this principle and in *T. Kathissabi* v *Revenue Divisional Officer, Calicut*[15] it was stated:

"The argument that Government was prepared to pay Rs. 40,000 for purchase of the land by private sale is untenable as any such agreement cannot determine the real and precise market value of the land, and can only be useful in furnishing an approximate figure."

It can now be summarised that it is the duty of the valuer to collect evidence regarding sales of comparable properties. This can be done either by attending all advertised sales and noting the bidding, or by having a search made in the Government Registration Department. Any person can make this search by making payment of the requisite fees. All sales should be noted not only for use in a particular case but for use in future cases as well. It is essential that regard should always be had to the date of the sale, so that any rise or fall

15 AIR 1923 Mad 31.

in the value may be adjusted when having regard to the value at a particular date.

Any sales that are used in evidence should be dated prior to the date of declaration, because there are many factors which might influence values after the date of declaration and which cannot accurately be measured. It was noted in the *Government of Bombay* v *Karim Tar Mohamed* case[16] that:

> "Sales after the date of notification must be discarded when it is proved that values have been affected one way or the other by circumstances which have arisen that date."

On the question of evidence of market value from sales the following statement of the principles given in Cripps on *Compulsory Acquisition of Land*,[17] should be kept in view:

> "The prices paid for comparable property in the neighbourhood are the usual evidence as to the market value. Comparable sales are also plainly the best evidence of market value and are to be preferred to a value deduced from rents of comparable properties. The sales, however, must be of comparable properties such that the sales are capable of comparison by making adjustment for differences; and there would appear to be no objection to comparing sales after the date of the 'notice to treat' if they can be related back in the same way that sales well in advance of that date require to be related forward. The comparison must, therefore, take into account not only what is to be valued, i.e., the values to be disregarded and those to be taken into account, but also the qualities of the land or buildings and all the intrinsic circumstances.
>
> "The sales must also be sales on a free market and sales by agreement to an acquiring authority having compulsory powers, are not reliable evidence of value in the open market, since they would not generally satisfy the assumption of a willing seller derived from the statutory requirements of market value; and more especially would this be so if such sales were of unoccupied premises at the mercy of weather and trespassers.

16 ILR 33 Bom 325.

17 11th Ed., p. 899.

"Comparable sales must also be supplemented by the known wants of a particular purchaser and accordingly, a *bona fide* offer for the land taken may be admissible; as the vendor is notionally in the market, the price paid by him for the land, if recent enough, may be some evidence of the value and so also may be the cost of a lease."

The effect of an agreement regulating the amount of purchase price of a particular land between the owner and the requiring authority after proceedings for compulsory acquisition have been set on foot was considered by the Privy Council in the case of the *Fort Press Company Ltd.* v *Municipal Corporation of the City of Bombay.*[18] It was held that such an agreement was capable of being enforced in the ordinary way, but the power of the Collector to determine what in his view the price should be, after he has evidence of a complete contract on the point, remains notwithstanding such an agreement.

See also *Ananta Ram Banerjee* v *Secretary of State,*[19] where the Privy Council decision was considered.

Reference can be made to the judgment of the Gujarat High Court in *Collector of Baroda* v *Haridas Maganlal,*[20] where it was held that an agreement for sale can be relied upon in fixing a market value provided it was confirmed that the transaction referred to was genuine between the willing purchaser and the willing vendor.

In another Gujarat High Court judgment in *Sumatilal Chimanlal Shah* v *C.E.D.*,[21] the valuation of land taken on the basis of a sale agreement was held valid.

Burden of proof in evidence

The burden is always on the claimant to prove by adducing reliable evidence that the compensation offered by the L.A.O. is inadequate and the lands are capable of fetching higher market value. It is the duty of the court to closely scrutinise the evidence, apply the test of prudent and willing purchaser, *i.e.* whether he would be willing to purchase in open and normal

18 27 CWN 418.
19 41 CWN 1291.
20 AIR 1970 Guj 21.
21 (1982)138 ITR 143 (Guj).

market conditions of the acquired lands and then determine just and adequate compensation.[1]

It is the duty of the claimant to prove sale deeds by adducing evidence either of vendor or vendee or attesting witness of passing of the consideration under the sale deed and that the sale transactions are genuine transactions. The burden is always on the claimant and where the claimant did not make any effort in this regard to discharge the burden, rejection of the sale deeds produced by him in support of his claim for compensation would be proper.[2]

Documents produced in the court in support of the market value should not be accepted *ipso facto* without subjecting the evidence to closer and critical scrutiny. Burden lies on the claimant to prove the prevailing market value as on the date of s. 4(1) notification.[3]

The claimants were afforded full opportunity before the trial court to produce and examine witnesses and they have chosen not to examine witnesses. It was held that no useful purpose would be served by remanding the matters as the sale instances relied upon by the claimant could not be the basis for fixation of market value.[4]

It is the duty of the court to scrutinise the evidence and determine just and adequate compensation but future user of land cannot be taken into consideration as per s. 24 *fifthly* of the Land Acquisition Act 1894. The burden of proof of market value prevailing as on the date of notification under s. 4(1) is always on the claimants. The court must sit in the armchair of a prudent purchaser in open market and to put a question to itself whether as a prudent purchaser it would offer the same price in the open market as is to be determined. This should be the acid test.[5]

1 *Ahmedabad Municipal Corporation* v *Shardaben* (1996)8 SCC 93; AIR 1996 SC 3346.

2 *Parameshwari (dead) by LRs* v *Punjab State Electricity Board* AIR 1994 SC 1142; 1994 Supp (1) SCC 564.

3 *M.V.K. Gundarao* v *Revenue Divisional Officer* (1996)3 SCC 129.

4 *Bikhubhai Kedarbhai Patel* v *Deputy Collector, Modasa* AIR 1996 Guj 16.

5 *Hookiyar Singh* v *Special L.A.O., Moradabad* (1996)3 SCC 766.

Valuation of yield not a guide when better evidence available

An interesting case of valuation of a piece of land situated outside the town of Nehtaur District, Bijnor, U.P., came up before the Supreme Court in *Raghubans Narayan Singh* v *Uttar Pradesh Government*.[6] The land had an area of 6 *pucca* bighas and was grove land having in all 123 trees, a number of which were mango and naspati trees. This land was acquired under a notification under s. 4 published on 22nd December 1945, for the construction of a hostel of S.N. High School. The Collector awarded ₹ 1,164 and 4 annas as compensation for the trees and ₹ 1,050 and 12 annas as compensation for the land and of course added 15% to these amounts. On a reference to the District Judge both the appellant and the Government adduced evidence of certain sales. The appellant relied on two sales dated 20th March 1926 and 5th January 1934. He also led the evidence of one S.N. Haidar Zaidi, a Deputy Collector, who had just retired and who prior to his retirement had written two letters to the appellant dated 14th October 1945 and 20th November 1945 expressing his desire to purchase a land with a view to building a residential house for himself so that he could live therein after his retirement. In these letters he had offered ₹ 18,000 but that offer was not accepted by the appellant as he wanted ₹ 24,000 as the price of the land. The evidence disclosed that the land acquired was at a distance of about two furlongs from the town. The land abutted on the main road from Moradabad to Bijnor and is next to this school. Nearby there was a fairly large size pond. There was some evidence that some houses were constructed in the grove lands nearby. But there was no evidence to show that there was any building activity nearby of any substantial nature or that there was any definite trend of development in the direction of the acquired land. As regards income from the land there was evidence that the fruit trees grown in the land yielded approximately an annual income of ₹ 500, about 49 mango and naspati trees being fruit-bearing at that time. It appeared that the grove had been laid only about 2/3 years ago and there was evidence of the village Patwari that the grove would yield about ₹ 1,000 a year when all the trees started bearing

6 AIR 1967 SC 465.

fruits. The District Judge discarded the evidence of sales as being of no assistance. He was, however, impressed with the evidence of witness Zaidi and accepting his offer as genuine and *bona fide* held that the value of the land can be safely assessed at ₹ 18,000 and made his award accordingly. On appeal by the Government, the High Court of Allahabad took the view that even if the offer can be taken as a genuine and *bona fide* offer, "there can be no doubt that the price he was going to offer was a price which he fixed because of the peculiar circumstances in which he was placed, the circumstances having been that he was upon retirement desirous of going back to his native place to take up residence there and to build a house outside the populated area. The price which such an exceptional purchaser is going to offer will not afford a true taste about the value of the property". Holding that view the High Court rejected the evidence of the offer and fell back on the net annual income from the land which it estimated at ₹ 650 and multiplying it by 20 fixed the value of land at ₹ 13,000. On appeal against the judgment of the High Court, Supreme Court held that the evidence of the witness who had made offer to purchase grove was not only relevant but also acceptable, and valuation arrived at on the basis of it after all rested on a better footing and ought to be accepted. In the course of their judgment, Their Lordships observed as follows:

> "The evidence of witness Zaidi being the evidence of offer made by him cannot of course be equated in importance with the evidence of proper specimen sales of properties in the neighbourhood. Obviously an offer does not come within the category of sales and purchases but none the less if a person who has made an offer himself gives evidence, such evidence is relevant in that it is evidence, that in his opinion that land was of a certain value. But the evidence that the owner refused an offer so made amounts to this only that in his opinion his land was worth more than the figure of value named or that the offer was for some other reason such that he was not willing to accept—c.f. *Government of Bombay* v *Merwanji Mancherji Cama*.[7] It has also been held that an agreement to sale is a relevant matter and can be

7 (1908)10 Bom LR 907.

used in relation to fixing the value of the acquired land—c.f. *Governor General-in-Council* v *Ghiasuddin*.[8] There can, however, be no doubt that apart from Zaidia's offer being relevant it was not an offer similar to an offer made by an irresponsible broker as commented in (1908)10 Bom LR 907." Their Lordships then discussed the facts as disclosed by the evidence and held that it is difficult to see how the High Court came to the conclusion that he made the said offer in special circumstances agreeing to purchase the land under compulsion or stress of circumstances. ...... "There was no valid reason why the High Court should have refused to accept the appreciation of his evidence by the District Judge and resort to a method of valuation not always adequate, viz. the annual crop value. Such a method of valuation is not adequate at least for two reasons: (1) that the owner may not have so far put his property to its best use or in the most lucrative manner and (2) in a case like the present the grove had not yet started giving the maximum yield. Such a method of valuation by ascertaining the annual value of the produce can and should be resorted to only when no other alternative method is available."

On oral and documentary evidences

Court has a duty to subject the oral evidence to great scrutiny and evaluate the evidence objectively and dispassionately to reach a finding on compensation.[9]

In determining market value the court must act on legal evidence and not bound to accept oral evidence because the witnesses to the deed have not been effectively cross-examined or because there is no evidence in rebuttal.[10]

Paper cutting as to the publication of the price in the local newspapers is not evidence and the court committed clear error in relying on those transactions and in proof of documents of sale deed executed by the vendor.[11]

8 (1929)30 Punj LR 212.

9 *State of Gujarat* v *Rama Rana* (1997)2 SCC 693.

10 *P.R. Modi* v *Collector, Durg* AIR 1975 MP 57.

11 *Ratan Kumar Tandon* v *State of U.P.* AIR 1996 SC 2710; (1997)2 SCC 161.

Where no sale deed was produced and there was no hike in the value of the land in the locality, but only oral evidence that the market value ranged from ₹ 4 to ₹ 5 per sq. ft. was given, it was held the evidence is not acceptable.[12]

It is not open to look into and rely on documents not properly proved and brought in evidence by giving the other side opportunity to produce evidence in rebuttal. If use is made of inadmissible evidence or unproved documents, appeal court will exclude them under s. 167, Evidence Act.[13]

In comparable sale transactions, the claimant is required to prove generally (*i*) that the sale must have taken place within a reasonable time from the date of publication of notification; (*ii*) it should be a *bona fide* transaction; (*iii*) it should be a sale of the land acquired or land adjacent to the acquired land; (*iv*) the land sold and the acquired land should possess similar advantages. The claimant is required to establish the above factors by adducing material evidence and by examining the parties to the sale or persons having personal knowledge of the sale transactions and as to the authenticity of the transaction.[14]

No reliance can be placed on a transaction when no person concerned with the transaction has been examined.[15] When a claimant relies upon a sale consideration of a sale deed filed in another case which is not connected with the acquisition of his own land, he has to examine the persons concerned with that sale deed.[16]

For the purpose of determination of market value certified copy of sale deed admissible in evidence though, other factors *aliunde* have to be established that the sale deed offer comparable value for determining the compensation.[17]

12 *Pitambar Hemlal Badgujar* v *Sub-Divisional Officer* (1996)7 SCC 554.
13 *Chaturbhuj Panda* v *Collector, Raigarh* AIR 1969 SC 255.
14 *Periyar and Paree Kanni Rubbers Ltd.* v *State of Kerala* AIR 1990 SC 2192; (1991)4 SCC 195.
15 *Special Deputy Collector* v *P. Basareswara Rao* (1992)2 Andh LT 475.
16 *Special Deputy Collector* v *B. Chandra Reddy* (1992)2 Andh LT 453.
17 *State of Bihar* v *Madheshwar Prasad* (1996)6 SCC 197, case followed *P. Ram Reddy* v *L.A.O., Hyderabad Urban Development Authority* (1995)2 SCC 305.

Certified copies of documents made acceptable under s. 51A as evidence of transaction recorded therein. *Held* that does not dispense with need of examining witnesses to prove the transaction as genuine and also the extent of consideration paid and relative nature of value of land.[18]

Neither the sale deed nor the certified copies thereof exhibited in the court. *Held*, documents are inadmissible though the witnesses had been examined to speak on those transactions.[19]

Evidence of L.A.O. regarding sale of certain lands to a public Authority was only given, but the documents neither made part of the record nor was anyone examined in proof of the circumstances in which the sale came to be made. *Held*, High Court rightly did not accept that part of evidence to determine compensation.[20]

The sale deeds produced for the determination of market value was executed about one year prior to the date of acquisition and the persons connected with the sale deeds were not examined. There was no proof of passing of the consideration or circumstances in which the documents came to be executed. So, document was brought into existence to inflate the rate of market value. *Held* in the circumstances, sale deeds are inadmissible in evidence and the High Court rightly placed reliance upon the judgment in respect of land situated in the neighbouring village and acquired for the same purpose. Award of the Collector restored with some modifications.[1]

The High Court was not right in looking into documents which were not a part of the records of the case and the opposite party had not been given any opportunity to rebut the conclusions reached therein. If the High Court wanted to take into consideration any fresh evidence, it should have admitted the same in accordance with law. In that event the opposite party would have got opportunity to rebut that evidence. That

18 *Indore Development Authority* v *Satyabhama Bai* (1996)10 SCC 751.
19 *Chintaman* v *State of Maharashtra* (1996)10 SCC 36; AIR 1997 SC 448.
20 *G. Narayan Rao* v *L.A.O.* (1996)10 SCC 607.
1 *Baldev Singh* v *State of Punjab* (1996)10 SCC 37.

having not been done those documents were excluded from consideration. For considering oral evidence, court is not bound to accept the statements of witnesses only because they have not been effectively cross-examined or evidence in rebuttal has not been adduced. Judges are not computers, they are bound to call into aid their experience of life and test the evidence on the basis of probabilities.[2]

In the circumstances of non-examination of vendor or vendee to prove passing of consideration, nature of lands involved and genuineness of the documents, it was held that no reliance can be placed on such unattested documents.[3]

It is the duty of the claimant to prove sale deeds by adducing evidence either of vendor or vendee or attesting witness of passing of the consideration under the sale deed, to prove that the sale transactions are genuine transactions between the willing vendor and willing vendee; that the consideration had in fact been passed under the document duly registered, represent the prevailing market value; and also the lands under acquisition and the lands concerning the sale are similarly situated and possessed of same or similar nature, advantages etc. The burden is always on the claimant and where the claimant did not make any effort in the said regard to discharge the burden, rejection of the sale deeds produced by him in support of his claim of compensation would be proper.[4]

Sale transactions are not in evidence unless the vendor or the vendee has been examined in the court. The claimant must further establish that lands relating to the sale transactions and the lands under acquisition are possessed of the same value and also the nature of the lands are the same. The court should carefully evaluate the evidence and determine market value avoiding needless burden on the exchequer.[5]

Market value can be determined on the basis of comparable sale deeds of the relevant period. Genuineness of the sale deeds

2 *Chaturbhuj Panda* v *Collector, Raigarh* AIR 1969 SC 255; (1969)1 SCR 412.

3 *G. Narayan Rao* v *L.A.O.* (1996)10 SCC 607 case followed *Collector* v *Dr. Harisingh Thakur* AIR 1979 SC 472; (1979)1 SCC 236.

4 *Parameshwari Devi (dead) by L.R.* v *Punjab State Electricity Board* AIR 1994 SC 1142.

5 *State of U.P.* v *Rajendra Singh* (1996)7 SCC 347.

must be proved by examining vendor, vendee or in their absence by attesting witnesses. In absence of such evidence sale deeds cannot be relied on.[6]

Principle of taking judicial notice cannot be extended to escalation of market price of land every year instead the claimant must prove it by adducing evidence as per s. 57 of the Evidence Act.

The sale deed produced is for a freehold small piece of land compared to the encumbered leasehold land of 4 acres under acquisition. The vendor of the sale deed was not examined. *Held* the sale deed cannot be relied upon as proof of valuation prevailing in the area.[7]

On oral and documentary evidences adduced, the court has ultimately the responsibility of assessing the value of such evidences. It was held, "It is true that the witnesses examined on behalf of the appellants have not been effectively cross-examined. It is also true that the Collector had not adduced any evidence in rebuttal; but that does not mean that the court is bound to accept their evidence. The Judges are not computers. In assessing the value to be attached to the oral evidence, they are bound to call into aid their experience of life. As Judges of fact it was open to the appellate Judges to test the evidence placed before them on the basis of probabilities".[8]

If the courts were to accept such statements of witnesses as true merely because they are not subjected to cross-examination or effective cross-examination or because evidence in rebuttal thereof has not been adduced, it would amount to doling out public money to the claimants far in excess of their legitimate entitlement for just compensation payable for their lands. Hence no court which tests the oral evidence of the claimants on the touchstone of probabilities calling into aid, its experience of life, men and matters and finds such evidence to be untrustworthy, the same cannot be found fault with.[9]

6 *Special L.A.O. (7), Bombay Suburban District Municipal Corporation* v *Vishanji Mepani* AIR 1996 Bom 366.

7 *Ratan Kumar Tandon* v *State of U.P.* AIR 1996 SC 2710; (1997)2 SCC 161.

8 *Chaturbhuj Pande* v *Collector, Raigarh* AIR 1969 SC 255.

9 *P. Ram Reddy* v *L.A.O.* (1995)2 SCC 305.

Circumstances held relevant for comparison

The courts in different States of India have scrutinised some of the transactions entered under certain modalities and circumstances. One argument that an autonomous body would pay a higher price was shot down by the Gujarat High Court in *C.I.T., Gujarat-III* v *S.C. Shah*[10] by holding: 'the conclusion that the L.I.C. had interest in securing the land by paying a higher price was entirely conjectural'. The Allahabad High Court in *CIT* v *Jumramal Son*[11] held that auction signified public sale of property and should be taken into consideration. The Gujarat High Court in the case of *Gurudutt Villa Association*[12] held emphatically that the instance of property which belongs to a public trust and was sold in accordance with the provisions of Bombay Public Trust Act after obtaining the sanction of the Charity Commissioner, where there was no chance of underhand dealing, would be a reliable sale instance and could not be rejected. The same Court also held in the case of *H. Jamnagarwalal*[13] that sale instances of the same society could not be ignored even if those instances were of below ₹10 lakhs (relevant ceiling limit at the time for the pre-emption purpose of I.T. Act). In respect of the market rates notified by the Sub-Registrar for the purpose of registration of an immovable property, however, it has been held in *K.K. Rawat* v *Union of India*[14] by the Rajasthan High Court that these rates can have no application for determining market value and the same were limited only for payment of stamp duty.

It is the duty of the court to consider the evidence in proper perspective and to determine the compensation. Once a project was inaugurated and the lands were acquired, no prudent person would come forward and purchase land at a higher price. It may rather be distressed sale in case of acute necessity and urgency of the seller for money. But the documents produced in the case were brought up for inflating the market value. *Held,* it was unusual for land prices to go up once the

10 (1980)124 ITR 862.
11 (1985)154 ITR 689.
12 (1996)217 ITR 522.
13 (1996)217 ITR 676.
14 (1995)214 ITR 610.

acquisition was notified. So, the sale deeds were brought up sales and the enhancement was not justified.[15]

It is also the duty of the court to assess reasonable compensation which a prudent purchaser in the open market would offer. In the instant case, the High Court and the District Judge erred in accepting the sale deeds brought into existence to inflate value on coming to know of the proposed acquisition. *Held,* the market value fixed at the rate of ₹30,000 per acre as agreed to by the appellant State was proper and the claimants were also entitled to solatium, interest and additional amount as per ss. 23(2), 28 and 23(1A) of the Land Acquisition Act 1894 respectively,[16] but the Land Acquisition Act 1894 has already been repealed and replaced by the Right to Fair Compensation and Transparency in Land Acquisition, Rehabilitation and Resettlement Act 2013.

While assessing the market value of the land, situated in the interior, the sale deeds in respect of lands abutting the main road are to be ignored.[17]

Sale deeds pertaining to same lands under acquisition brought into existence after having knowledge of the proposed acquisition to inflate the market value cannot be relied upon.[18]

For the purpose of determination of compensation for the acquired land, which is dry, reliance on sale deeds relating to sales of small parcels of lands is not safe. However, it cannot be lost sight of that the acquired land was situated close to the Medical College in the heart of city with potentiality for utilisation in various commercial purposes.[19]

In the case of *Govindbhai Dajibhai (by his heirs)* v *Special L.A.O.*[20] the document relied upon is, *inter alia*, a mortgage deed. On cross-examination of the vendee by the claimants the former admitted that, when he took over possession of the land, he was aware that the land which is a small piece of land was going to be acquired. He also admitted that he was

15 *P. Venkataraju* v *Special Tehsildar, L.A.* (1996)8 SCC 614.
16 *State of U.P.* v *Smt. Ram Kumari Devi* (1996)8 SCC 577.
17 *Mir Singh* v *Union of India* (1978)1 Del LT 121.
18 *M.V.K. Gundarao* v *Revenue Divisional Officer* (1996)3 SCC 129.
19 *L.A.O.* v *Smt. Mahalakshmi Panda* AIR 1996 Ori 96.
20 AIR 1995 Guj 200.

the owner of the adjoining land and he was knowing that a power station was going to be established on the land in question and land was being measured for the purpose of acquisition. He further admitted that the land owned by him is mortgaged with some one and he did not redeem it even though its term has expired. *Held*, no reliance can be placed upon the mortgage deed for fixing the market value of land under acquisition.[1]

If a sale deed is accepted as a guide, it is necessary to see how reliable it is and should not be followed blindfolded. It may be untrustworthy and may mislead. So all sale deeds should be carefully scrutinised. All elements of value inherent in the property should be considered. All restrictions in users and enjoyment must be taken into account.[2]

Prices fetched for similar lands with similar advantages and potentialities under *bona fide* transactions of sale at or about the time of the preliminary notification are the usual and, indeed the best, evidence of market value.[3]

The Rajasthan High Court in *K.K. Rawat* v *Union of India*[4] and the Bombay High Court (W.P. No. 1106 of 1995: Prima Realty) have held that even when there was no other comparable case available, a single solitary comparable instance could be taken into consideration. As regards reliance on a different class of property, the Bombay High Court has held in the case of *Shri Chand Raheja*[5] that sale instances with built-up area rate indicate the potential of the property and can be considered for the purpose of finding out the F.S.I. rate. However, in *Mani Singh Avatar Singh* v *IAC of IT*[6] the Punjab and Haryana High Court had observed that a plot built upon cannot be compared with an unbuilt plot on which the purchaser had the opportunity of exercising a wide choice of building.

1 *Govindbhai Dajibhai (by his heirs)* v *Special L.A.O.* AIR 1995 Guj 200.
2 *Sabha Rai* v *Union of India* (1979)16 Del LT 11.
3 *Mehta Ravindrarai Ajitrai* v *State of Gujarat* AIR 1989 SC 2051; *Administrator General of West Bengal* v *Collector, Varanasi* AIR 1988 SC 943.
4 214 ITR 610.
5 213 ITR 33.
6 (1985)151 ITR 233.

Building potentiality claimed to be possessed by the acquired land has no significance when comparable sales method is resorted to and the land is comparable in its essential features with lands in respect of which comparable sale deeds are produced.[7]

The prime difficulty, of course, is in assigning monetary importance to the differences observed. Is a property with a beautiful view worth 110% of one lacking such a view or is it worth 150%? Or, if a plot of land is sloping, is the effect on relative cost (*vis-a-vis* a levelled plot) proportional to the increased structural costs or do some other factors come into play? How to quantify the differences in amenities available in the neighbourhood? These are some of the practical questions often posed.

No hard and fast rule can be laid down. But nevertheless a rational judgment on comparable circumstances is called for in each case.

In *Chimanlal Hargovinddas* v *Special L.A.O., Poona*[8] *inter alia* the following guidelines for determining market value on comparable sale transactions were laid down.

(1) The market value of land under acquisition has to be determined as on the crucial date of notification under s. 4 of the L.A. Act (dates of ss. 6 and 9 are irrelevant).

(2) As if the valuer is a hypothetical buyer willing to purchase land from the open market at a reasonable price assuming the vendor is willing to sell at a reasonable price.

(3) The court has to correlate the market value reflected in the most comparable instance which provides the index of market value.

(4) Only genuine instances have to be taken into account, ignoring got up sales.

(5) Even post-notification instances can be taken into account (*a*) if they are very proximate, (*b*) genuine, and (*c*) the acquisition has not motivated the purchaser to pay a higher price on account of development prospects.

7 *Rao Narain Singh* v *Union of India* (1993)3 SCC 60.
8 AIR 1988 SC 1652; (1988)3 SCC 751.

(6) The most comparable instances out of the genuine instances have to be identified on following considerations:

(*i*) proximity from time angle;

(*ii*) proximity from situation angle.

(7) Having identified the instances, the market value of the land under acquisition may be deduced by making suitable adjustments for the plus and minus factors *vis-a-vis* land under acquisition by placing the two in juxtaposition.

(8) The relevant factors may be evaluated in a balance sheet of plus and minus factors in terms of price variation as a prudent purchaser would do. The market value has thereafter to be deduced by loading the price reflected in the instance taken as norm for plus factors and unloading it for minus factors.

Plus factors. (1) Smallness of size, (2) proximity to a road, (3) frontage in a road, (4) nearness to developed area, (5) regular shape, (6) level *vis-a-vis* land under acquisition, and (7) special value for an owner on an adjoining property to whom it may have some very special advantage.

The Supreme Court further held that evaluation of these factors depends upon the facts of each case and there cannot be any hard and fast or rigid rule. Common sense is the best and most reliable guide.

In fact, elaborate techniques have been devised for determining comparability etc. of real estate. These are generally adaptations of the so-called grid techniques, where different attributes of the land and building in the sale instances are given percentage ratings in comparison with the subject property. The valuer also must reach a decision as to the relative significance of recent sales *vis-a-vis* sales more distant in time, as also to the adjustment because of the time-difference.

Time factor is important for comparison

Time factor is an important aspect when considering comparative sale values. If the comparative sale is far too remote from the sale value required then the sale should be appropriately screened.

Different opinions have been expressed regarding sales distanced by time. In *Government of Bombay* v *Karim Tarmahomed,*[9] it was held that sales after the date of notification (in this case acquisition of property) must not be taken into account if circumstances had changed after the date. Post-notification sale instances are to be rejected.[10] But post-notification sales can be taken into account for the purpose of arriving at the conclusion whether the prices are stable or whether they are on the increase.[11]

The Courts have always maintained that transactions in general must be relevant and they should afford a fair criteria of the value of the property on the date of valuation. If the sales have been affected when considerable time has elapsed, then the court will naturally ignore these sales. In *M.S. Naniappa* v *S.L.A.O., City Improvement Trust, Bangalore,*[12] sales within four months after the notification was duly considered. In *the State of Maharashtra* v *Waman Kalil Paniole,*[13] purchase of the remaining land at a higher price 1/2 years after notification was discarded. In another case, the Gujarat High Court thought it relevant to consider comparable sale at remote point of time from the relevant valuation date in the matter of *C.I.T. Gujarat I-II* v *Sumantilal Chotalal Shah.*[14]

The same principle has been enunciated in *Govt. of Bombay* v *Merwan,*[15] when a sale was made of a mosque at a nominal price out of religious sentiments, which should not be the guide for assessing another plot in the vicinity on the basis of its lucrative disposition.

The Bombay High Court in the case of *Vimal Agarwal*[16] clarified that the proximity from time angle and proximity from situation angle are relevant considerations for ascertaining the most comparable instances and having identified the most

9 33 BLR 325.

10 *V.G. Kulkarni* v *Special L.A.O.* (1996)8 SCC 301.

11 *R.D.O.* v *Thota Bharathudu* (1992)2 Andh WR 4.

12 AIR 1966 Mys 66.

13 AIR 1974 Bom 99.

14 (1980)124 ITR 862.

15 (1923)48 Bom 190; AIR 1924 Bom 161.

16 210 ITR 16.

comparable instances (which provides index for market value), the price therein may be taken as norm and market value of the subject property deduced by making suitable adjustments by 'plus' or 'minus' factors and working out a balance sheet of these '+' or '–' factors in terms of price valuation as a prudent purchaser would do. The actual valuation of these factors would depend upon the facts of each case. Though the court in this case suggested such adjustments on the most comparable case, yet every comparable case could also be similarly analysed and the overall results tabulated.

Experts inspected the acquired property in 1990 while the material year for determination of market value was 1972. It was held evidence by experts in such a case cannot be taken into consideration, Evidence Act, s. 45 was also referred.[17]

The word "market value" would postulate the price of the land prevailing on the date of notification under s. 4(1) of the L.A. Act. The transaction of 1984 while the notification of acquisition was made in 1982, *i.e.* after a span of more than two years the date of notification under s. 4 of the Act cannot furnish any guide to determine the market value of the acquired land.[18]

Normally, subsequent sale deeds which are not proximate in point of time of the acquisition should not be taken into consideration. However, where the market is stable and there is no fluctuation in the prices between the date of notification under s. 4 of the L.A. Act and the subsequent transactions, the same can be relied upon as held in the case *State of U.P.* v *Major Jitendra Kumar*.[19]

In determining the market value of the land, price paid in sale or purchase of the land within a reasonable time from the date of the acquisition of the land would be best piece of evidence. Where there were *bona fide* and genuine sale transactions in respect of the same land under acquisition, the High Court would not be justified in *excluding* such

17 *Special L.A.O. (7), Bombay Suburban District Municipal Corporation* v *Vishanji Mepani* AIR 1996 Bom 366.

18 *Osman Khan S/o Abdul Majid Khan* v *State of Maharashtra* AIR 1994 Bom 271; *Mumtaz Ali Khan* v *Collector, Rampur* AIR 1996 All 71.

19 AIR 1982 SC 876; 1982 All LJ 361.

transactions and placing reliance on award of some other land for awarding compensation at a higher rate within a time lag of nine months from the genuine transaction by the seller. In its absence the price paid for a land possessing similar advantages to the land in the neighbourhood of the land acquired in or about the time of the notification would supply the date to assess the market value.[20]

In considering the price fetched in comparative sales proximity of time of sale with date of notification under s. 4, L.A. Act, (now s. 11 of the new Act of 2013) closeness between the lands sold and the lands acquired, comparative size of the land, potential value of the acquired land having regard to the location and surroundings have to be kept in mind.[21]

It would be an error to discard a sale instance, when it is near to the date of publication of notification under s. 4 of the L.A. Act (now s. 11 of the new Act of 2013) either immediately before the date of publication or immediately thereafter.[22]

Sale instances produced in the case related to a period three years before the date of notification. In those instances ₹ 4,000 per *bigha* was awarded by the reference court. Another sale instance relied upon by the appellant was a small piece of land which the High Court held does not properly represent the market value of the land under acquisition. On the other hand it is held that sale instances put up relating to a period of three years before the present notification of ₹ 4,000 per *bigha* and the appellants' claim of ₹ 6,000 per bigha is not unrealistic.[23]

Where owner himself had admittedly purchased the acquired land a few years earlier the same would form the basis to determine market value. So, in determining market value, market value of adjacent lands cannot then be taken into account.[24]

20 *Special Tehsildar, L.A., Vishakhapatnam* v *A. Mangala Gowri (Smt.)* (1991)4 SCC 218; AIR 1992 SC 666.

21 *Food Corporation of India* v *Makhan Singh* AIR 1992 SC 1406; (1992)3 SCC 67.

22 *Raval Maneklal Motiram* v *State of Gujarat* AIR 1991 Guj 137.

23 *M/s. Bhatra* v *Union of India* AIR 1991 Del 284 (DB).

24 *Shakuntalabai* v *State of Maharashtra* (1996)2 SCC 152.

The sale deed relied upon by the High Court is of a date three years later than the notification under s. 4, L.A. Act (now s. 11 of the new Act of 2013) but no material was produced before the court to suggest that there was any fluctuation in the market rate. In the absence of any material showing any fluctuation in the market rate, the High Court thought it fit to rely upon sale deed and thus committed no error in relying upon that sale deed.[25] Averages of successive sales of the same property though different can be considered.[26]

Weightage on factors differentiating comparable sales

In comparable sales method of valuation of land if any of the factors, such as, location, shape, size, potentiality or tenure of one plot of acquired land widely differs from other plots of acquired lands, then the market value of each plot of land acquired has to be determined independently of the others even if all of them had been acquired pursuant to the same preliminary notification. The differential factors relating to different acquired plots greatly affect their value and if any salient factor of different acquired plot of land, which greatly affects their value is ignored or is not taken into consideration by court while determining the market value of acquired lands, it will have failed to apply the correct principle of valuation adoptable in valuation of different types of acquired lands. When the evidence in the case clearly established that different plots of lands of different claimants acquired, varied greatly as to their sizes, shapes and location (situation) they could not have fetched uniform rate, if the same had been sold in the open market by each of the claimants. Therefore, determination of the market value at a uniform rate on the wrong assumption that all the plots of the acquired lands would have fetched the same rate if sold in open market, would not be proper.[27]

A few judicial decisions reflecting on weightage given on different factors in the realm of valuation are tabulated below:

(i) *On size*: The Andhra Pradesh High Court has held *I.E. Vittal* v *A.A.*[28] that consideration for sale of small

25 *State of U.P.* v *Major Jitendra Kumar* AIR 1982 SC 876.

26 *Karachi Municipality* v *Naraindas* AIR 1933 Sind 57.

27 *Printers' House (P) Ltd.* v *Mst. Saiyadan (dead) by L.R.* AIR 1994 SC 1160.

28 221 ITR 760.

extents of lands is always more than the corresponding consideration for large extents of lands.

(ii) *On shape*: The Gujarat High Court *Surya Kiran Association* v *A.A.*[1] held that not allowing deduction because of old shape was not the right approach to valuation.

(iii) *On frontage*: The Gujarat High Court in *Surya Kiran Association's* case[2] remarked that ordinarily wide frontage should be considered as beneficial to the property than narrow frontage.

(iv) *On location*: The Andhra Pradesh High Court in *I.E. Vittal's* case[3] held that reliance on a sale instance in another locality, which was about 10 kms. away, was not right. The refusal to consider a sale instance in the same locality on the ground that it was of lower middle class, was also incorrect.

The Gujarat High Court in the case of *Surya Kiran Association* v *A.A.*[1] points out that the present stage of commercial development around the property located in commercial zone is an important point. The same court in the case of *Natwarlal D. Patel*[4] also points out that in valuing the commercial properties, the location in a residential zone and not in commercial zone, is a relevant factor to be taken into account.

(v) *On transport facilities and other amenities*: These are also relevant considerations as listed by the Rajasthan High Court in *K.K. Rawat's* case.[5]

(vi) *On time factor*: The Gujarat High Court held in *CIT* v *S.C. Shah*[6] that not only the sale instance remote in point of time could be considered but also a general presumption about the all round rise in the prices including that of realty could be raised—though it could be rebutted by evidence to the contrary.

1 218 ITR 29.
2 218 ITR 29.
3 221 ITR 760.
4 218 ITR 226.
5 214 ITR 610.
6 124 ITR 862.

The Bombay High Court took into consideration in the case of *Smt. Vimla Devi Maheshwari*[7] the purchase prices in respect of the sale instance of flats relied upon by the appropriate authority—though they were sold much earlier in point of time.

In *C.B. Gautam's* case,[8] the Supreme Court took judicial cognizance of the fact that the immovable properties in urban areas had gone up steeply in value during the preceding few years.

(vii) *On social factors*: The Gujarat High Court noted in *Smt. Varshanben B. Shah* v *A.A.*[9] that during the school hours, the place where the transacted property is situated becomes too noisy. It was also noted that because of activities in Ashram and Temple, the place could not be said to be 'peaceful' and in view of all these factors one would not pay the price for the property which it could otherwise fetch.

(viii) *On legal constraint*: The Madras High Court in the case of *S.S. Samnudhanath*[10] held that in case of distress sales, the market value can be presumed only at a lower figure. The Patna High Court in the case of *Smt. Lalita Ghode*[11] pointed out that normal values cannot be adopted in respect of property having a disputed title. This was also observed by the Supreme Court in *C.B. Gautam's* case (supra).

The Delhi High Court indicated in *CIT* v *Keshrichand*[12] that the differences exists between the valuation in freehold and leasehold lands (based on the facts of that case, freehold land was directed to be valued at 120% of leasehold land).

(ix) *On co-ownership*: Various courts have held that there are inherent disadvantages and difficulties in enjoying a co-owner's share if sold in open market. The purchaser cannot enjoy the property in the same way as other co-owner and it would require partition of

7 208 ITR 734.
8 199 ITR 530.
9 221 ITR 819.
10 120 ITR 80.
11 123 ITR 4.
12 118 ITR 692.

the property, whether by consent or suit in court. The Karnataka High Court in *CWT* v *K.N. Nagabhushana Sethy, HUF*[13] upheld 10% deduction on that account. The Kerala High Court in *CIT* v *George*[14] also justified discount of account of the incidence of co-ownership. So also the Calcutta High Court in the case of *Lalit Jabber.*[15] The Calcutta High Court in *P.K. Dutta's* case[16] upheld 10% deduction in respect of valuation of one-third share of an undivided property.

Comparable sales as the sound basis of valuation

If the claimants produce evidence of sales relating to the acquired land in the vicinity of the acquired land and requires the court to determine the compensation for the acquired land on that basis, it is known as the "comparable sales method" of valuation of land. "Comparable sales method furnishes a healthy criterion for determining the market value of the acquired land". But the sales must be genuine and is what a willing seller will be able to obtain from hypothetical willing buyer. Where the acquired land is agricultural land and compensation is claimed on the basis of agricultural land including its potentialities, the nature of the land should be considered.[17]

The Supreme Court in *Special Land Acquisition Officer* v *Veerabhadrappa*[18] after review of earlier precedents on this method in the matter of determination of compensation for compulsory acquisition held as follows:

"The function of the court in awarding compensation under the Act is to ascertain the market value of the land at the date of the notification under section 4(1) of the Act and the methods of valuation may be—(1) opinion of experts, (2) the prices paid within a reasonable time in *bona fide* transactions of purchase or sale of the lands acquired or of

13 156 ITR 484.
14 171 ITR 620.
15 113 ITR 389.
16 134 ITR 42.
17 *Atmaram* v *Collector of Nagpur* AIR 1929 PC 92; 33 CWN 458; *Rao Narain Singh* v *Union of India* (1993)3 SCC 60.
18 (1985)154 ITR 190.

the lands adjacent to those acquired and possessing similar advantages, and (3) a number of years' purchase of the actual or immediately prospective profits of the lands acquired. Normally, the method of capitalising the actual or immediately prospective profits or the rent of a number of years' purchase should not be resorted to if there is evidence of comparable sales or other evidence for computation of the market value. It can be resorted to only when no other method is available.

"It is axiomatic that the best evidence to prove what a willing purchaser would offer for purchase of the property put to sale is the evidence of sales of comparable properties, proximate of time to the date of acquisition, similarly situate and possessing the same or similar advantages and subject to the same or similar disadvantages. Market value is the price the property may fetch in the open market if sold by a willing seller unaffected by the special needs of a particular purchaser. Where definite material is not forthcoming either in the shape of sales of similar lands in the neighbourhood at or about the date of notification under section 4(1) or otherwise, the court has no other alternative but to fall back upon the method of valuation by capitalisation."

The above passage was quoted with approval in the case of *A. Premchand* v *IAC*[19] in a compulsory acquisition case.

Choice of comparable sale instances

Comparable sales should be of such lands as are—(*a*) Similar in character as far as may be; (*b*) reasonably *proximus* to the acquired lands; (*c*) should have similar amenities and advantages; and (*d*) these should be transactions of time reasonably *proximus* to the date of the acquisition.[20]

If the land involved in the award is comparable land in reasonable proximity of the land the rates found would be reliable material. The land involved in the present case is comparable possessing the same advantages and potential value in the same village and categorised in the same block

19 (1985)153 ITR 774 (Kar).
20 *Mehtar* v *Collector, Durg* AIR 1975 MP 46.

and acquired under the same notification, so cannot be awarded compensation therefor at different rates.[21]

In *Subbas Malharirao Kachure* v *IAC*,[1] the principles to be observed in considering comparable sales was made clear in the following words:

> "We find from the pleadings, the evidence, the orders and the report of the departmental valuer that Lamington Road area in Hubli City is one of the very important commercial and residential areas of the city and the locality where the property was situated, namely, Bhuspet area, was not as important as Lamington Road area. We need hardly say that transactions of sales recorded in Lamington Road area at or about the time of sale, would be relevant and had to be taken into consideration in determining the fair market value of the property. From this it follows that the valuation report of the Departmental valuer on the sale transactions of Lamington Road area at or about the time of the transfer of property, was relevant to determine the fair market value of the property. But still the Tribunal and the Inspecting Assistant Commissioner have ignored the same on the sole ground that the sales effected in the very locality of the city were not available. We are of the view that this was hardly a legal ground to ignore the sale transactions of Lamington Road area and evaluate the same. We are of the view that the sale transactions in a more important and prominent locality of the very city would undoubtedly be relevant and cannot be ignored at all in determining the fair market value of the property.
>
> "Admittedly the property sold, with irregular dimensions and very odd features of its own, was a small property adjoining another house property of the transferees commanding certain advantages and having disadvantages of its own. On the other hand, the sale of a larger piece of land on the other side of the road though situated in front of the very property with its own special advantages and disadvantages cannot be the sole criteria or basis for

21 *Union of India* v *Shri Harkishan* AIR 1996 Del 101; case followed *State of Madras* v *A.M. Nanjan* AIR 1976 SC 651.

1 (1986)159 ITR 726 (Kar).

determining the fair market value of the property in dispute. Even here the Tribunal and the Inspecting Assistant Commissioner ignoring this relevant aspect or principle has determined the fair market value of the property. We are of the view that this was an error in principle and calls for our interference."

Hence, it follows that sales in the same locality may not be the sole criterion, where there are other relevant materials of comparable sales in adjacent localities.

Further the care that should be taken in choice of comparable sales is highlighted in *Vimal Agarwal* v *Appropriate Authority,*[2] where it was observed:

"The sale instances referred to by the aggrieved persons assume more importance if they have already undergone scrutiny in the hands of the appropriate authority and a no-objection certificate has been issued in regard thereto. The instances furnished by the aggrieved parties cannot be brushed aside. No order can be passed without carefully considering the same and stating the reasons for not treating the same as comparable cases. If that is allowed to be done, the hearing given to the aggrieved parties will turn out to be a mere formality. In the instant case, it is clear from the affidavit of the Deputy Commissioner of Income-tax in the office of the appropriate authority that the sale instances referred to by the petitioner were not even considered as the records in that connection could not be located. The grievance of the respondents appears to be that the case numbers of the acquisition proceedings in these cases were not furnished by the petitioner. We fail to understand how an aggrieved party can furnish the case numbers of the acquisition proceedings to the appropriate authority the records of which are with the appropriate authority itself. All the relevant particulars on the basis of which the appropriate authority could have located the properties in question had been furnished by the petitioner. An order passed merely on the basis of the sale instances given by the appropriate authority without considering the sale instances referred to by the aggrieved parties and setting

2 (1994)210 ITR 16 (Bom).

out cogent reasons for not acting upon them, cannot be a proper and valid order."

After referring to the decision of the Supreme Court in *Dollar Co.* v *Collector of Madras*[3] where sale price prevailing in 1949-50 was made the basis of compensation for acquisition in 1959 after suitable adjustments, it was further observed as under:

> "This decision of the Supreme Court indicates that not only the sale instances remote in point of time from the date of acquisition can be considered but a general presumption about the all-round rise in the prices including that of realty can be raised which can be rebutted by evidence to the contrary that the prices had become stagnant in the locality for some valid reasons."

Comparable sales of large sized lands vis-a-vis small plots

In acquisition of large extent of land, sale deed in respect of small plot and post-notification sales, held, not relevant.[4] It has been held in *Rao Narain Singh* v *Union of India*[5] that the prices fetched under sale deeds of small bits of land ought not to, ordinarily be made the basis for determining the value of large extents of acquired land. In the same vein, sale transaction of small plots of land were held totally irrelevant for determining the price of a large tract of land in *Tarlochan Singh* v *State of Punjab*.[6] Sale instances of small extent of lands was held to be not relevant and accordingly not to be relied upon in determining compensation of a large extent of land.[7] The views of the Supreme Court in this behalf were duly echoed in the decisions of the High Court of different States. In *Mumtaz Ali Khan* v *Collector, Rampur, U.P.*[8] the Allahabad High Court held that transactions of small pieces

3 AIR 1975 SC 1670.

4 *K. Padmaraju* v *Senior Regional Manager, F.C.I., Hyderabad* (1996)10 SCC 613.

5 (1993)3 SCC 60.

6 (1995)2 SCC 424.

7 *Saunu* v *Collector, Land Acquisition* (1996)11 SCC 163; *Pehlad Singh* v *Union of India* (1996)1 SCC 310; *Special L.A.O.* v *Tagar Hanifabi* (1996)10 SCC 627.

8 AIR 1996 All 71.

of land are not valid exemplars for bigger lands. The same approach was taken by the Gujarat High Court in the case of *Raval Maneklal Motiram* v *State of Gujarat.*[9] In the case of *Bhikhubhai Kedarbhai Patel* v *Deputy Collector, Modasa,*[10] it was held, for the purpose of fixing market value of a large area of land, sale instance of an absolutely small piece of land and that too divided into various plots cannot be relied upon. For the determination of market value of vast extent of acquired land, it was held in the case of *L.A.O., Hyderabad* v *Male Pullamma*[11] that sale instances of small area of 198 sq. yard cannot form the sole basis for determination of compensation.

But it must be understood that there cannot be any absolute proposition about not taking into account the price fetched by small plots for determination of valuation of bigger extent of lands. It may sometimes happen that the bigger plot of land offer much better element of comparability than similar small plots situated in the locality. In fact, there had been a number of cases where the prices fetched by the large area of land have been considered in the determination of market value of small land in view of the presence of comparability as regards the rate per unit of land.

Sale of large area of land cannot possibly fetch price at the rate at which small plots are sold is not an absolute proposition and in a given case and circumstances it would be permissible to take into account price fetched by small plots and judicial notice can be taken thereof. In the case, price of large area of homestead land sold two-and-half years back was taken as the basis for determination of value of small area of homestead land acquired as judicial notice was taken that price of homestead land would have increased and not come down.[12]

In *Bhagwathula* v *Special Tahsildar, L.A.O.*[13] the Supreme Court held the proposition that large area of land cannot

9 AIR 1991 Guj 137.
10 AIR 1996 Guj 16.
11 (1996)8 SCC 247.
12 *Collector, Cuttack* v *Hari Behera* AIR 1996 Ori 215; case followed *Bhagwathula Samanna* v *Special Tahsildar L.A.O., Vishakhapatnam* AIR 1992 SC 2298.
13 AIR 1992 SC 2298; (1991)4 SCC 506.

possibly fetch a price at the same rate at which small plots are sold is not absolute proposition and in given circumstances it would be permissible to take into account the price fetched by small plots of land. A fully developed small plot of land in an important locality may fetch a higher value than a larger area in an undeveloped condition and situated in a remote locality. If the larger tract of land, because of advantageous position is capable of being used for the purpose for which the smaller plots are used and is also situated in a developed area with little or no requirement of further development, the principle of deduction of the value for the purpose of comparison is not unwarranted.[14]

Where the extent of land sold is insignificant compared with the large extent of land acquired, the market value of large extent of acquired lands shall not be determined on the basis of the value fetched by sale of infinitesimally small extent of land. But, in exceptional cases, when the value fetched by small extents is of building plots in a building layout formed of a large plot, it has to be seen whether the large acquired land, if it is laid out into small building plots and sold, whether they could fetch the price fetched by sale of small building plots in the already formed building layout. Then, the market value of the acquired land has to be determined with reference to the value fetched by sale of small plots by making allowances for various factors, such as loss of land required out of the acquired land to be used for roads, drains, parks, the expenditure involved informing the layout, waiting involved in the sale of plots and several other factors which will necessarily reduce the wholesale price of the acquired land. Thus, how far the value fetched by the sale of small extents of lands could form the basis for determining the market value of the acquired land has to inevitably depend upon the allowances to be made for factors which distinguish the acquired land from the plots of land sold and the sale value of which is relied upon as the basis for determining the market value of the acquired land.[15]

14 *State of Maharashtra* v *Abdul Sattar* AIR 1995 Bom 85.
15 *P. Ram Reddy* v *L.A.O.* (1995)2 SCC 305.

Adjustment to be made for large size when compared with the instance of sale of small plot

The Supreme Court in *Bhagwathula Sumanna* v *Special Tahsildar Land Acquisition Officer, Vishakapatnam Municipality*[16] stated:

> "In awarding compensation in acquisition proceedings, the court has necessarily to determine the market value of the land as on the date of the relevant notification. It is useful to consider the value paid for similar land at the material time under genuine transactions. The market value envisages the price which a willing purchaser may pay under *bona fide* transfer to a willing seller. The land value can differ depending upon the extent and nature of the land sold. A fully developed small plot in an important locality may fetch a higher value than a larger area in an undeveloped condition and situated in a remote locality. By comparing the price shown in the transactions all variables have to be taken into consideration. The transaction in regard to smaller property cannot, therefore, be taken as a real basis for fixing the compensation for larger tracts of property. In fixing the market value of a large property on the basis of a sale transaction for smaller property generally a deduction is given taking into consideration the expenses required for development of the larger tract to make smaller plots within that area in order to compare with the small plots dealt with in other sale transactions. This principle has been stated by this court in *Tribeni Devi* case."[17]

In *Kaushalya Devi Bogra* v *Land Acquisition Officer*,[18] the Supreme Court stated as under:

> "When large tracts are acquired, the transaction in respect of small properties do not offer a proper guideline ...... In certain other cases this court indicated that for determining the market value of large property on the basis of a sale transaction for smaller property a deduction should be given."

16 AIR 1992 SC 2298; (1991)4 SCC 506.
17 (1972)1 SCC 480.
18 (1984)2 SCC 324 (SCC pp. 335-36, para 13).

We may also refer to the observations of the Supreme Court in *Administrator General of W.B.* v *Collector, Varanasi,*[19] which run as follows:

"The principle that evidence of market value of sales of small, developed plots is not a safe guide in valuing large extents of land has to be understood in its proper perspective. The principle requires that prices fetched for small developed plots cannot directly be adopted in valuing large extents. However, if it is shown that the large extent to be valued does admit of and is ripe for use for building purposes; that building lots that could be laid out on the land would be good selling propositions and that valuation on the basis of the method of a hypothetical layout could with justification be adopted, then in valuing such small sites in the area at or about the time of the notification would be relevant. In such a case, necessary deductions for the extent of land required for the formation of roads and other civil amenities; expenses of development of the sites by laying out roads, drains, sewers, water and electricity lines, and the interest on the outlays for the period of deferment of the realisation of the price; the profits on the venture etc. are to be made.

"The proposition that large area of land cannot possibly fetch a price at the same rate at which small plots are sold is not absolute proposition and in given circumstances it would be permissible to take into account the price fetched by the small plots of land. If the larger tract of land because of advantageous position is capable of being used for the purpose for which the smaller plots are used and is also situated in a developed area with little or no requirement of further development, the principle of deduction of the value for purpose of comparison is not warranted."

In a Supreme Court decision in *Special LAO* v *Sri Siddappa Omanna Tumari*[1] it was observed as under:

"The market value of the acquired land must be the near estimate of the price which the claimant by voluntarily selling the awarded land would have got from a willing

19 (1988)2 SCC 150 (SCC p. 157, para 12).
1 JT 1994(7) SC 257; AIR 1995 SC 840.

purchaser. What could be regarded as the near estimate of the acquired land has to be ascertained, be it the Collector or be it the court on the basis of authenticated transactions of sales or agreements to sell relating to the same land or a portion of it wherever possible because such transactions of sale or agreements to sell are always regarded as the best evidence available for the purpose.

"It is well known as is held by this court in *Collector of Lakhimpur* v *Bhuban Chandra Dutta,*[2] that when a large area of land under acquisition is the subject-matter, it cannot fetch the price of the rate at which smaller plot or plots are sold. One aspect which, however, should weigh is that determination of the value of large extents of acquired lands on the basis of the prices fetched by smaller plots must be a matter of last resort and should be adopted when there is no possibility of determining the market value of acquired lands on the basis of comparable transactions of larger extents. Therefore, where a sale deed or an agreement to sell relating to a small extent of land is produced by the claimant, in the enquiry held for determination of compensation payable for his large extent of land, the court is not always bound to determine the market price of such large extent of acquired land on the basis of the price fetched or to that fetched by small extent of land covered by such sale deed or agreement to sell."

In general, prices fetched for small plots cannot form a safe basis for valuation of large tracts of land as the two are not comparable properties and as a matter of principle sale prices of small plots of land cannot directly be adopted in valuing large extent. The sale price of small plots of land as such cannot be accepted in fixing the market value of much larger plot of land acquired. If large extent to be valued is ripe for use for building purposes, that building lots that could be laid out on the land would be good selling propositions and that valuation on the basis of the method of hypothetical layout could be adopted, then in valuing such small, laid out sites, the valuation indicated by sale of comparable small sites in the area at or about the time of notification would be relevant.

2 (1972)4 SCC 236.

The market value of a piece of property with potentiality of urban use for the purpose of s. 23 of the L.A. Act (now s. 28 of the Right to Fair Compensation and Transparency in Land Acquisition, Rehabilitation and Resettlement Act 2013) is stated to be price at which the property changes hands from a willing seller to a not too eager a buyer. The determination of market value is the production of an economic event, that is to say, the price outcome of a hypothetical sale transaction expressed in terms of probabilities. In other words, the price fetched for similar lands with similar advantages and potentialities under *bona fide* transaction of sale at or about the time of preliminary notification are instances of the usual and indeed the best evidence of market value. So, for the purpose of valuation of large plots or extent with potentialities for urban development can be valued with reference to small but developed plots. Again, a sale deed executed subsequent to preliminary notification in respect of land under acquisition can be relied upon if it can be shown that the price was more or less stable between the date of preliminary notification and subsequent sale transaction. But necessary deductions for the extent of land required for the formation of roads and other civic amenities; expenses of development of sites by laying out roads, drains, sewers, water and electricity lines, and interest in "outlays" for the period of deferment of the realisation of the price; the profits on the venture etc. are to be made. But a very simple method of valuing land wholesale for retail prices is to take anything between one and half or one-third, according to circumstances of the expected gross valuation as the wholesale prices. Other method or valuation are resorted to if evidence of similar land are not available.[3]

Sale instance of small extent is not relevant in determining value of large track of land. Land situated in an undeveloped area though adjacent to the road, required further development. Hence the price of developed area cannot be adopted as the basis to determine compensation to the land in question. High Court deducted 78.45% land which required for building

3 *Administrator General of West Bengal* v *Collector, Varanashi* AIR 1988 SC 943; *Tehsildar (L.A.O.), Huzurnagar* v *Venkatappa Rao* AIR 1994 NOC 385 (AP); *State of Gujarat* v *Shree Devji Beehar (through L.R.)* AIR 1991 Guj 187.

purposes fixing market value at ₹ 40 per sq. yd. *Held* in such cases proper market value would be ₹ 50 per sq. yd. and the claimants are also entitled to interest @ 6% and solatium @ ₹ 15 on the enhanced compensation.[4]

There were sale instances of considerably large plots at or nearabout the acquired plots of lands on acreage basis, so the High Court had no other option than to determine market value of acquired plots comprised of several acres on acreage basis. The High Court should have found out price on wholesale basis of the larger areas in open market, because no purchaser of large extent would even think of purchasing such land by paying its price on square foot basis as was claimed by the owner of the acquired lands of comparatively smaller plots.[5]

Lands acquired were not in a developed condition in 1973 and were near the submerged area to set up pump station to drain out flood water. In course of time the area was developed in 1992. As per s. 24 subsequent development is irrelevant for determination of compensation. When a larger area is acquired then unlike a smaller area it should be determined only on the basis of yardage and not on square foot and at least 1/3rd of the acquired land to be taken for deduction for providing roads, electricity, drains and other developments. The land was valued at ₹ 60,000 in 1987 and it was held that the same should be the basis for determination of market value.[6]

Sources for obtaining comparative sales data

In respect of vacant land, the Office of the Reigstrar is a source for obtaining comparable data of sales. In *CIT* v *Dr. V.K. Bhaskaran Nair,*[7] it has been held that the value taken for registration purposes by the Registering Authority who was empowered to make a valuation for purposes of determining stamp duty would be relevant evidence. It is needless to add that this method is not conclusive and it is always possible to distinguish the same where the facts warrant it. Other sources are real estate agents, auction sales

4 *Ratan Lal Gupta* v *Union of India* (1996)7 SCC 3.
5 *State of Maharashtra* v *Gurappa Hirojirao* (1994)2 SCC 331.
6 *U.P. Jal Nigam, Lucknow* v *Kalra Properties (P.) Ltd.* AIR 1996 SC 1170.
7 (1979)116 ITR 873 (Mad).

especially where conducted by the Appropriate Authority, if available, may offer a basis.

This was pointed out in *Guran Dass* v *CIT*,[8] for reasons which may not apply on all forms of sale other than court sales, but it is an accepted fact that auction sale by Appropriate Authority often fetch very high prices and would provide reliable data.

Comparable sales for just valuation for compensation purposes

It is settled law that claimant is entitled to just and reasonable compensation and under s. 23 of the L.A. Act (now s. 28 of the new Act of 2013) to determine the market value of the lands at the prevailing prices as on the date of publication of the notification under s. 4(1) of the L.A. Act (s. 11(1) of the new Act of 2013), the sale transactions of the same lands or sales of lands situated in the neighbourhood would furnish as evidence of comparable sales. The price which a hypothetical willing vendor might reasonably expect to obtain from a willing purchaser would form the basis to fix the market value. It would be possible to have reliable evidence when sale transactions are proved by either the vendor or the vendee and if either of them was not available, the attesting witness who had personal knowledge of the transaction is to be examined by producing either the original sale deed or certified copies thereof as evidence. Under s. 51A of the L.A. Act as inserted in 1984 (now s. 97 of the new Act of 2013) the certified copies have been permitted to be brought on record as evidence of sale transaction recorded therein. The examination of the witnesses is to find that the sale transactions are *bona fide* and genuine transactions between willing vendor and willing vendee as reasonable prudent men and the price mentioned is not throw-away price at arm's length or distressed sales or brought into existence to inflate market value of lands under acquisition and the sales are accommodating ones. Equally, it must be brought on record the comparative nature of the lands covered under the sale deed and the acquired lands whether adjacent or actual distance or possessed of similar advantages and whether transactions themselves are genuine and *bona fide* transactions.[9]

8 (1984)148 ITR 770 (Punj).

9 *Inder Singh* v *Union of India* (1993)3 SCC 240; *Gulzara Singh* v *State of Punjab* (1993)4 SCC 245.

The Supreme Court, in *Dollar Co.* v *Collector*,[10] observed that the best evidence of the value of property is the sale value of the very property to which the claimant is a party. Proximity of highway or ports and many industrial and social imponderables enter the verdict of evaluation, so much so it cannot be automatically asserted with reference to a piece of land a mile and half away, that it serves as a guide for fixing the price of the plot. In the instant case, the appellant himself purchased the land in question just 10 months before the notification under s. 4 of the L.A. Act 1894 at a price of ₹ 310 per ground and spent out a little more money to fill up a pond in it and he had been awarded ₹ 1,800 per ground by the High Court. Can an owner who bought the land at ₹ 410 per ground and laid out a little more money on it, grouse on the score of inadequate or unjust recompense if within a year after his own purchase he is paid by the State 400 per cent of what he spent for the identical land? The Supreme Court pointed out that it was but fair that compulsory land acquisition while assuring a just equivalent should not be converted into an avaricious windfall. Finally, the Supreme Court laid down the following propositions:

(1) Compensation for compulsory acquisition as governed by s. 23 of the Land Acquisition Act (now s. 28) gives high priority to market value of the land as on the date of s. 4(1) (now s. 11) notification. The main criterion for this is what a willing purchaser would pay a willing vendor.

(2) The price paid by the owner recently represents an expression of market value as *bona fide* evidence of value, subject to such matters as (*a*) the relationship of parties; (*b*) the market conditions and the terms of the sale; and (*c*) the date of sale. The enquiry may not end there, but it goes a long way to solve the problem.

(3) An actual transaction with respect to the specific land of recent date is a guide-book that courts may not neglect when called upon to fix the precise compensation. The best evidence is the very sale that is made recently. All that need normally be proved, is

10 AIR 1975 SC 1670.

> that the sale was between a willing purchaser and a willing seller, that there has not been any appreciable rise or fall in value.

In *Collector of Baroda* v *Haridas Maganlal*,[11] it was held that though an agreement of sale is not a sale, and creates no interest in the property as contemplated under s. 54 of the Transfer of Property Act, it can be relied upon as good evidence for fixation of market value provided it is a *bona fide* transaction between a willing purchaser and willing vendor.

In *Special Land Acquisition Officer* v *Adinarayana Chetty*,[12] the Supreme Court held that the purpose for which the land was acquired, the reports of certain authorities as to the suitability of the land for the purpose for which it was acquired, and the delay in putting the land to use for which it was acquired were extraneous considerations which had no bearing on the question of valuation and the lower court misdirected itself as to the scope of enquiry before it when it imported those considerations into the question of valuation. The function of the court in awarding compensation under the L.A. Act is to ascertain the market value of the land at the date of the notification under s. 4(1) of the L.A. Act (now s. 11) and methods of valuation may be—(*i*) opinion of experts; (*ii*) the price paid within a reasonable time in *bona fide* transactions of purchase of the lands acquired or the lands adjacent to those acquired and possessing similar advantages; and (*iii*) a number of years' purchase of the actual or immediately prospective profits of the land acquired. The Supreme Court has further pointed out that where the courts adopts the second method but takes only four out of six transactions of alienation made by the claimant, during a particular period without giving sufficient reason why two transactions were let out, the court commits an error of principle by adopting a wrong method in ascertaining the market value of the land at the relevant time and the arbitrary selection of four transactions only out of six vitiates the finding of the lower court in the instant case. Further, the lower court committed another error arriving at an average from the four transactions. It took a second average

11 AIR 1970 Guj 21.
12 AIR 1959 SC 429.

between the maximum price obtained by the claimant and the first average already arrived at.

The Madras High Court in an appeal as to the determination of the market value held that the average of the prices fetched under the sales relied on by the Government shall be the market value and the betterment levy payable under s. 25 of the Town Planning Act has to be provided for. On appeal, the Supreme Court held in the case of *S.R.M.V. Rao Bahadur Ranee of Vuyyur* v *Collector of Madras*:[13]

> "It seems to be only fair that the highest value shown in the sale deeds relied on by Government should be preferred to the rest, unless there are strong circumstances justifying a different course. There is no reason why an average of the sale deeds should have been taken in the instant case. Betterment levy is a charge on the land under section 25 of the Town Planning Act, and deductions have to be made on that account in fixing compensation payable."

The best evidence for fixing compensation is the authentic sale of the very acquired land and of sales of adjacent land near about the time of the acquisition.[14]

Comparative sale instances—parameters for valuation

In comparable sales method a comparison is made between the subject property and other similar properties that have been sold. After ascertaining the sale prices of the properties actually sold, an adjustment for differences due to date of sale, size of the property, condition and location is made to reflect the estimated fair market value of the subject property. Comparability depends on various factors, such as, (*i*) location, (*ii*) proximity in time, (*iii*) type of construction, (*iv*) other advantages or disadvantages, (*v*) genuineness of sale, (*vi*) mode of payment etc.

The comparable sale price is compiled from sales of comparative properties in the neighbourhood or adjacent area. The time factor is important as in recent times prices have been shooting up almost every month.

13 (1968)2 SCJ 869.

14 *Bangaru Narasingha Rao Naidu* v *R.D.O.* AIR 1982 SC 63. See also *Special Deputy Collector* v *Kurra Sambasiva Rao* (1997)6 SCC 41; AIR 1997 SC 2625.

Supreme Court has focussed on relevant comparable features and upheld the efforts of the High Court in evaluating them. It was held that the High Court has taken into consideration all the relevant facts like the size of the plot, location, potential value of the land and also a few relevant sale deeds and no error of law has been committed by the High Court. So, order of High Court under appeal does not call for interference, merely on the ground that higher compensation was given for lands situated in the neighbouring village.[15]

Decisions of the courts throw further light on the paramaters for comparison and valuation on the basis of the same. The various aspects that such decisions encompass need be recounted even at the cost of some repetition.

Sales comparison is the best guide

The definition of fair market value in s. 269A(*d*) of I.T. Act brings to fore the concept of comparable sales method or the sales analysis approach or a mythical willing seller who is under no compulsion to sell and a willing buyer who is under no compulsion to buy. In many a case, it becomes difficult to resort to this method and determine the market value and, therefore, the courts and valuers have adopted other modes or methods called "capitalisation method" and "rental value method" etc. But, the other methods must be resorted to only when the fair market value cannot be determined applying comparable sales method or sales analysis approach and not otherwise.[16]

Importance of locality

In determining the fair market value of a property, the importance of locality cannot be ignored and must always be kept in view. After all, valuation is not and cannot be made in a vacuum.[17]

The fact that acquisition proceedings were not taken with regard to other properties in the same locality, is not relevant. A crime does not cease to be a crime on the ground that another crime has not been detected or punished.

15 *Jai Prakash* v *Union of India* AIR 1997 SC 2237.
16 *A. Premchand* v *IAC* (1985)153 ITR 774 (Kar).
17 *IAC* v *Laxmichand* (1986)159 ITR 730 (Kar).

Peculiar advantages not the criteria

The sale of a larger piece of land on the other side of the road, though situated in front of the very property with its own special advantages and disadvantages, cannot be the sole criteria or basis for determining the fair market value of the property in dispute.[18]

Later sales not comparable

It was held that in order to determine the price of the land, the instances of sales that had taken place later than the impugned sales, were not valid.[19]

'Plus' or 'minus' factors

The various methods of valuation considered above cannot be followed in a rigid way. Moreover, no particular method is sacrosanct. Each valuation case presents its own unique characteristics and often a combination of methods may have to be applied. For example, where land and building method is applicable for valuing the land, comparable sales instances will have to be obtained; while applying rent capitalisation method, one may have to take into consideration development potential if the present structure is quite old and dilapidated and capable of being demolished. Even in the case of a fully rented building, mechanical application of capitalisation of net rent @ 10% or so may give ridiculous or even negative value if the rent is very low and outgoings substantial. In a place like Bombay City where premium or *pugree* of rented premises, though illegal, is openly advertised in newspapers, one cannot overlook the owner's share even if such illegal or cash consideration go by the name of so-called transfer charges. Thus a valuer has to take a comprehensive view of peculiar facts and circumstances prevailing in each case and thereafter proceed to apply a method of valuation or a combination of different methods. He has further to take into consideration several other factors while giving additional weightage or discount to the primary value arrived at in the first instance. These are called 'plus' or 'minus' factors as already discussed in *Vimal Agarwal* v *Appropriate Authority*.[20]

18 *Subbas Malharirao Kachure* v *IAC* (1986)159 ITR 726 (Kar).

19 *CIT* v *Leatherite Ind. Ltd.* (1984)147 ITR 655 (P&H).

20 (1994)210 ITR 16 (Bom).

On the basis of the decisions, the following 'plus' and 'minus' factors can be identified. The evaluation of these factors would, however, depend upon the facts of each case.

Plus factors	Minus factors
(*i*) smallness of size (*ii*) proximity to a road (*iii*) frontage on a road (*iv*) nearness to developed area (*v*) regular shape (*vi*) level *vis-a-vis* land under acquisition (*vii*) special value for an owner of an adjoining property to whom it may have some very special advantage.	(*i*) largeness of area (*ii*) situation in the interior at a distance from the road (*iii*) narrow strip of land with very small frontage compared to depth (*iv*) lower level requiring the depressed portion to be filled up (*v*) remoteness from developed locality (*vi*) some special disadvantageous factors which would deter a purchaser.

The sale must be genuine for comparison

The tests for a *bona fide* sale are: whether it is sold in open market, whether there was sufficient publicity and bargaining, whether the transaction was purely on business lines, whether prior enquiry was made, and the matter gone through with due care and caution. The mere fact that parcel of land is bought by a speculator with the object of reselling it at a profit is no ground for disregarding the sale. The boom in land prices all of a sudden at a given time, should also be taken into consideration. The test of the market value is the test of the sale being in open market, the seller being a willing seller and the purchaser a prudent one, who makes his offer after making the necessary enquiries. But once the market gets normal, the former speculative boom in price should be appropriately discounted. Such speculation as had actually entered into the market price at the date of notification may be considered when fixing the value.

Unregistered sales to be disregarded

Unregistered sales for sums over ₹ 100 being invalid, they cannot be considered as proper for comparison in values. But genuine offers and agreements to sale can be considered in relation to the fixing of value of the land. But offers made by irresponsible brokers on behalf of undisclosed principals even if relevant, are often useless.[1]

Oral offers to be ignored

Oral offers unsupported by any documentary evidence do not carry any weight or afford any assistance. The court is entitled not to act on oral evidence of witnesses prior to negotiations to purchase the property acquired unless its truth was guaranteed by other evidence of surer character.[2] Similarly, evidence of a house-broker as to the value cannot be given much weight.

Price fetched in auction sale—not always comparable

In *Guram Das* v *CIT*,[3] acquisition proceedings were initiated and in fixing the fair market value, sales by auction in terms of rules known as Chandigarh (Sale of Sites and Building) Rules 1960, were taken into consideration. It was held by the High Court that the provision of the Chandigarh rules showed that a purchaser merely had to pay 25% of the sale price at the time of auction and the rest in three equated instalments and the balance amount carried interest at 6% p.a. Hence the price paid in such auction sale could not be considered as reflecting the current market value of a comparable plot sold privately.

The Allahabad High Court in *CIT* v *Jumrmal Son,*[4] however, pointed out that the auction sales should have been considered and taken into account by the Tribunal.

Auction sale by appropriate authority if considered—a discount be made

The appropriate authority has been auctioning the properties purchased by the Central Government under Chapter XX-C of I.T. Act. An interesting question arises as to what extent the price fetched in such auction would be a guide for estimating

1 *Government of Bombay* v *Morwanji Mancherji* 10 Bom LR 907.
2 *Chhogola* v *Municipal Commissioner* 1955 MBLJ 1631.
3 (1984)148 ITR 770 (P&H).
4 (1985)154 ITR 698 (All).

the market value of similarly situated properties. It is observed that in theses auctions the price fetched is generally very high. One factor could be that the buyer gets the property which is clear of encumbrances. The title of such property is clean and the buyer does not have to go through anxious period of waiting for clearance form appropriate authority. In such conditions a property auctioned by the appropriate authority should normally fetch a price higher by 10% to 20% as compared with the price prevailing in the open market. The valuer should therefore make appropriate discount while camparing the subject property with any property sold in auction by the appropriate authority.

Previous judgments of courts

Previous judgments cannot be relied on when it relates to a far off land and the former abuts a highway when the latter does not.[5]

Compensation awarded by the High Court on the basis of an earlier decision in respect of land notified on 13th July 1959. But the appellant in the case is not entitled to higher compensation merely because his land was notified two years later on 19th October 1961.[6]

Compensation determined by the High Court on the basis of judgments in similar cases. *Held* no interference by the Supreme Court is called for in the case.[7]

The court is entitled to consider evidence of what are called instances, that is to say, evidence of judgments of the court determining the market value of the land in the revenue estate.[8]

An earlier judgment of a Division Bench of the same High Court determining the market value of lands similarly situated and compulsorily acquired for the self-same purpose can be relied upon when there was no evidence to distinguish the lands involved.[9]

5 *Union of India* v *H.R. Katyal* (1979)15 Del LT 247 (SN).
6 *Mir Singh* v *Union of India* (1996)1 SCC 295.
7 *Mangat Ram* v *State of Haryana* (1996)8 SCC 664.
8 *Jai Ram Singh* v *Union of India* AIR 1989 Del 110.
9 *Collector of Cuttack* v *Smt. Jayasri Devi* AIR 1988 Ori 163.

Previous decisions of the High Court in land acquisition cases are relevant to a subsequent case where the market value of the land in the neighbourhood is in issue and date of acquisition is almost the same.[10]

In *Khwaja Fizauddin* v *State of A.P.* (CA No. 176 of 1962 decided on 10.4.1963) followed in *Land Acquisition Officer* v *H. Narayanaiah*,[11] the Supreme Court laid down that judgments are relevant if they relate to similarly situated properties and contain determinations of value on dates fairly proximate to the relevant date in a case.

The High Court reduced the compensation relying upon another judgment wherein the High Court had relied upon a sale deed in respect of land covered by the common notification. In the absence of an appeal by the State, the Supreme Court cannot go into the correctness of the High Court's relying upon a single sale deed. So, the compensation fixed by the High Court was held just and adequate.[12]

Previous awards

When several sale deeds or previous awards are produced in court as evidence of comparable sales, court has to necessarily examine every sale or award to find out as to what is the land which is the subject of sale or award and what is the price fetched by its sale or by the award made therefor. If the sale is found to be a genuine one or the award is an accepted one, and the sale or the award pertains to land which was sold or acquired at about the time of publication of preliminary notification under the Act, the court has to mark the location and the features (advantages or disadvantages) of the land covered by the sale or the award. This process involves the marking by court of the size, shape, tenure, potentiality etc. of the land. Keeping in view the various factors marked or noticed, the market value of the land has to be determined. If it is found that the land covered by the sale or the award is *identical* with the acquired land under consideration, the land

10 *Collector, Durg* v *Saroj Kumari* AIR 1975 MP 65.

11 AIR 1976 SC 2403.

12 *M.B. Gopala Krishna* v *Special Deputy Collector, L.A.* (1996)3 SCC 594.

under the sale or the market value determined for the land in the award could be taken by the court as the "price basis" for determining the market value of the acquired land under consideration. But difficulty arises when the comparable sales or awards are not of the same kind and when each of them furnishes a different "price basis". This difficulty cannot be overcome by *averaging* the prices fetched by all comparable sales or awards for getting the "price basis" as such "price basis" may vary largely depending even on comparable sales or awards and cannot be a correct reflection of the price which the willing seller would have got from the willing buyer, if acquired land had been sold in the open market. The court is to choose that sale or award relating to a land which closely or nearly compares with the plot of land the market value of which it has to determine, and to take the price of land of such sale or award as the basis for determining the market value of the land under consideration.[13]

The award virtually means a valuation made by the State itself, and is in the nature of admission on behalf of the State with regard to the value of the land in question. Awards made by the Collector are certainly material *in rem* of ascertaining the land value of comparable properties. The rates of such previous awards are dependable, unhazardous to afford a stereobate to work upon for determination of compensation.[14] Previous awards have also evidentiary value to consider the question of market value.[15]

If the land involved in the awards is comparable land in the reasonable proximity of the acquired land, the rates found in the said documents would be reliable material to afford a basis to work upon for determination of the compensation on a later date.[16]

13 *Printers' House (Pvt.) Ltd.* v *Mst. Saiyadan (dead) by L.R.* AIR 1994 SC 1160.
14 *State of Kerala* v *Valliyamma Ponnamma* AIR 1985 Ker 2.
15 *State of U.P.* v *Babua Ram (dead) by L.Rs.* AIR 1995 All 2; *Printers' House (P.) Ltd.* v *Saiyadan (Mst.) (dead) by L.Rs.* AIR 1994 SC 1160.
16 *State of Madras* v *A.M. Nanjan* AIR 1976 SC 651.

Where no contemporaneous sale deed is available on record, the court can take into consideration the award in earlier cases for similar lands provided the similarity is established through oral evidence. There should be evidence on record from which a court could be in a position to compare the nature, situation and potentiality of the land acquired with those other lands covered by the previous award.[17]

Previous awards of Collector which are, in fact, only offers cannot be of high evidentiary value. But, such award can be taken as correct valuation of neighbouring land when their owners have accepted that award.[18]

In determining market value reference court relied upon an earlier award in respect of a neighbouring village determining compensation @ ₹ 10,000 per acre. There is no material on record or any discussion in the judgment of courts below regarding basis for such reliance. *Held* reliance on such earlier award *per se* not correct and appropriate market value in the case should be ₹ 6,000 per acre. Award of the Collector being of a date prior to the introduction of the Amendment Bill of Act 68 of 1984, grant of additional amount under s. 23(1A) of the L.A. Act (now s. 69(2) of the new Act of 2013) was held illegal.[19]

A previous decision in a land acquisition case is relevant in a subsequent land acquisition case where the lands involved are in the neighbourhood.[20] The award in a land acquisition case is essentially on a question of fact depending on the facts and circumstances of each case unless a question of law or principle has been settled therein. Whenever such a judgment is sought to be used as a piece of evidence, it must satisfy the usual test of relevancy and application to the facts and circumstances of the case in which it is relied on.[1]

Value of incomplete building will be actual investment

In respect of any incomplete construction, normally there cannot be any market value as on successive valuation dates on the

17 *L.A.O.* v *A. Krishna Murthy* AIR 1984 Ori 6.
18 *Collector of Nagpur* v *Atmaram Bhagwant* AIR 1925 Nag 292.
19 *State of Bihar* v *Ratan Lal Sahu* (1996)10 SCC 635.
20 *Mehtar* v *Collector, Durg* AIR 1975 MP 46.
1 *Additional Special L.A.O.* v *P. Anantha Bhat* AIR 1972 Mys 313.

basis of the progress in the construction work and the only manner in which the value of such incomplete construction as on different valuation dates could be arrived at will be by finding out the actual amount spent on the construction as on the different valuation dates.[2]

Deduction must be made for property with defective title

At times title to the property is defective. The valuer cannot ignore the defects in the title; he has to make a proper deduction for such defects. It was held in *V.S. Nayak* v *CWT*[3] that a deduction of 33% in value was called for because of the defective title.

Valuation on the basis of comparable sales—a few peculiar instances

In *Joseph Valloran* v *CIT*[4] a large piece of land which was sold for ₹ 48,500 was valued at ₹ 94,300 by the Valuation Officer on the basis of comparable sales and competent authority initiated acquisition proceedings. The Tribunal sustained the acquisition order, though it reduced the value to ₹ 65,000. The assessee contended that sale deeds produced by the revenue offered no guidance since the lands did not have similar advantages, and the sales were in respect of very small areas, the price of which would offer no guidance for determining the price of a larger plot.

The High Court held that the revenue had not discharged its burden of proving that the value adopted in the sale deed fell short of the fair market value by more than 15% especially when the materials on record showed that the transaction had been entered into in the ordinary course of business and a fair market value had been adopted.

In *CIT* v *Mohan Singh*,[5] two commercial plots situated in Chandigarh were transferred for an apparent consideration of ₹ 1,25,000. The competent authority initiated proceedings for the acquisition and after considering the objections of the

2 *CWT* v *S. Venugopala Konar* (1977)109 ITR 52 (Mad).
3 (1968)68 ITR 171 (Mys).
4 (1977)108 ITR 544 (Ori).
5 (1978)112 ITR 430 (P&H).

parties passed an order for acquisition of the said plots. The Tribunal found that the prices per square yard in two different areas were ₹ 463 and ₹ 684, respectively, but it refused to strike a mean between the two rates on the grounds that plots in different areas were not sold at the same rate and that the difference between the rates of two plots was very large. It calculated the fair market value of the plots in dispute at the lower rate of ₹ 463 per square yard and rejected the other rate without recording any reason. The High Court set aside the order of the Tribunal by holding that the computation of the fair market value by the Tribunal was based on irrelevant consideration and was liable to be set aside. The case was remanded to the competent authority for fresh determination of the fair market value of the plots.

In *CIT* v *Sumatilal Chotalal Shah*,[6] two immovable properties comprising building and lands were sold on 11th April 1974. On the basis of the report of the District Valuation Officer in which he had relied upon two transactions, one between the Municipal Corporation and Mira & Co., and another between the Municipal Corporation and Mira & Co., and another between the Municipal Corporation and Hari Om Enterprises. The competent authority found that the estimated fair market value of the two properties exceeded the apparent consideration stated in the respective instruments of transfer by the prescribed margin. When the proceedings were initiated by issue of necessary statutory notices, the transferors objected, *inter alia*, to the two sale instances relied on by the District Valuation Officer. However, the competent authority came across two other instances of sales of contiguous immovable properties in favour of the LIC on 1967. The transferors not only objected to the consideration of the sale instances in favour of the LIC since they were not relied upon earlier for initiation of the acquisition proçeedings, but also prayed for issuance of summons to the LIC for explaining the salient and significant features of the two sale instances so as to consider whether they were comparable sale instances. The competent authority did not comply with this request

6 (1980)124 ITR 862 (Guj).

but passed an order on 31st March 1976 that the conditions of section 269C had been fulfilled. At this stage, the competent authority gave up reliance on the transaction between the Municipal Corporation and Mira & Co.

The Tribunal rejected the transaction between the Municipal Corporation and Hari Om Enterprises because it was not a sale but was an offer made to the Corporation, and the competent authority had neither investigated nor disclosed the conditions on which this offer was made. The Tribunal also found that the two sales to the LIC were stale instances which could not be considered to be comparable, that the property sold to the LIC had, better advantages in its situation and that the LIC had interest in securing the lands even by paying a price higher than the market value because their office building was adjoining the lands. The Tribunal set aside the acquisition order on the ground that there was no cogent material before the competent authority to reach the conclusion that the fair market value of the properties exceeded the apparent consideration by the prescribed margin. On appeal by the revenue, the Gujarat High Court held as under:

1. The Tribunal was justified in rejecting the transaction between the Municipal Corporation and Mira & Co.

2. The Tribunal erred in rejecting the two sales to the LIC as stale transactions. Further, the conclusion that the LIC had interest in securing the lands by paying a higher price was entirely conjectural.

3. Not only the sale instances, remote in point of time form the date of acquisition, could be considered but a general presumption about the all round rise in the prices including that of realty could be raised. Such presumption could be rebutted by evidence to the contrary that the prices had become stagnant in the locality for some valid reasons.

4. The failure of the competent authority to call witnesses at the request of the parties in connection with the sales to the LIC was because of the then prevailing opinion that the competent authority was not bound by the rules of evidence and merely on this ground the Tribunal ought not to have

concluded that the acquisition proceedings were themselves bad in law because the necessary evidence to substantiate the ultimate view of the competent authority was not there on the record. The Tribunal ought to have given an opportunity to the competent authority to record evidence as prayed for by the parties.

The High Court accordingly set aside the orders of the Tribunal and the competent authority and remanded the matter to the competent authority for completing the enquiry after recording the evidence of the necessary witness in connection with the two sale instances in favour of the LIC.

In *Hemanta Kumar Mallick* v *State of West Bengal,*[7] it was held that a judgment of a court in a land acquisition case determining the market value of land in the vicinity of the acquired land, even though not *inter partes*, could be admitted in evidence either as an instance or one from which market value of the acquired land could be deduced or inferred. The above decision was based on a case *Secretary of State* v *India General Steam Navigation and Rly. Co.*,[8] the Judicial Committee did refuse to interfere with High Court judgment in a land acquisition case. For a judgment relating to the value of land to be admitted in evidence either as an instance or as one from•which the market value of the acquired land could be inferred or deduced, must have been a previous judgment of court and as an instance. It must be proved by the person relying upon such judgment by adducing evidence *aliunde* that due regard being given to all antecedent facts and circumstances. In the case, the claimants have not produced the judgment of the High Court on which reliance has been placed for the reason that it was not a judgment then available to them relating to the market value of the land in the vicinity. There is no evidence *aliunde* adduced by them in the cases on hand to show that due regard being given to all attendant facts and circumstances. But the claimant cited a subsequent judgment of the High Court from

7 (1975)79 CWN 379.

8 ILR (1909)36 Cal 967; 10 CLJ 281; 36 IA 200; 19 MLJ 645; 11 Bom LR 1197.

a Law Report. It was also held, when judgment is rendered by a court determining the market value of lands acquired under the L.A. Act, by agreement of parties, such judgment becomes final and it would not be open to any of the parties thereto to appeal against that judgment. Hence the special leave petition dismissed.[9]

9 *Pal Singh* v *Union Territory of Chandigarh* AIR 1993 SC 225 (DB); *Hans Raj* v *Union Territory of Chandigarh* AIR 1993 SC 191 (DB).

CHAPTER

8

Rental Method of Valuation

The method of valuation to be adopted depends upon the character of the property. If the property is in the nature of investment, the appropriate method of valuation would abide by the income approach. It is true that the invested property can be both marketable as well as non-marketable. If it is marketable, the sales comparison method as discussed earlier would offer an appropriate strategy for ascertaining the value. But even in that case, the income approach to valuation will provide an alternative to iron out the uncertainties that are inherent in the valuation process. No doubt that the non-marketable investment property can be valued only in adherence to the income approach. The income approach is the preferred valuation approach when reliable income and expenses data are available along with well-supported income multipliers, overall rates and required rate of return on investment. The essential characteristics of an investment is its value with a capital sum in return or an income to be received over time. Sometimes, the income is received by way of periodic payments and often it is allowed to accumulate and taken back as a capital sum. When income is to be received from investment, it is customary to estimate the present worth of all future benefits derivable from the investment. The investor generally discounts back to its present value each instalment of income which he expects to receive in a series from the investment. The sum of the present value of such income will constitute the capital value for him. But the choice of alternatives in an investment situation is not confined to the real property market alone. When the user borrows money to purchase real estate, he will compare the interest payable on the loan with the rent he would have to pay had he not made an outright purchase. It must be borne in mind that real properties are acquired for user as well as for investment purposes. The purchaser for investment purpose may find that an alternative comparable investment will give him a better return for his money while the essential consideration for the purchaser for occupation and use is whether it would be better to rent the property he requires and utilise his capital money for an alternative investment. If he finds that the alternative investment would cover the probable rent and still leave a surplus, he will undoubtedly be motivated to opt for the alternative investment. In any case, the consideration of the alternative investments enters into the arena of choice. In this way, we are led into the bigger field of rate of interest, security of income and the notion of years' purchase.

The income approach is also deployed as a profit approach to valuation in which case the yield as well as capitalisation rate is an important element to be taken into account. All these are discussed in details in a subsequent chapter and we are concerned here with the rental method of valuation as a species of the income approach.

When a person decides to purchase a residential property by way of investment, he is virtually giving up a capital sum which will save him paying rent in the future. His income is in a non-monetary form arising out of such saving which can be said to be equivalent to the rent he would have to pay for use of the property had he not made a capital investment.

Real property is acquired, apart from investment or speculation purposes, commonly for user. The essential nature of real property is its durability and its capability to provide the user over long period of time. As an object could be used over time, payment also could be made for its use as it is used. In this way, the potential income stream of a real property investment is spread over in the future.

There is another aspect in the field of user of real property. There can be a separation of ownership and the right of use. The owner can lease out or alienate the right to use to another person in return for a periodic payment and the transferee is obliged to pay the rent for the right to use. Thus, there is a choice open to the owner. He can part with the ownership in return for capital sum, or he may retain it to himself and receive an income over time by parting with only the right to use. This provides three distinct segments of the real property marketed in the field of investment:

(*i*) person owning and using the property

(*ii*) person owning but not using the property

(*iii*) person using but not owning the property

The relative attraction of income from each of these alternatives will determine the size and content of the particular segment of real property market. The decision of both the potential users and investors based on the consideration of alternatives will be the major factor in constituting the segment market.

The rental method of valuation brings in another important issue for consideration in the context of the present day. Before the introduction of protective legislation for tenancies, a residential property was a very popular form of investment for residential builders, families and individuals. Until the Second World War the developers of large residential estates frequently developed properties for letting out in tenancies. But the rent control laws as they operate in different States of India have substantially freezed rental income of properties and entrenched the security of tenure of occupancy rights with rigid grounds for eviction so as almost to take away the proprietary rights of owners as reversioners. Hence, a different chapter hereafter has been devoted to rent and ground rent. We shall now discuss below some of the important judicial decisions which have dwelt upon the rental method of valuation as such.

Rental method—principles for determination

When land is fully developed by buildings erected thereon; when the property is let at a rent from which the fair rent can be ascertained; and when the rent has been proved and is likely to be maintained for years to come, then the rental method of valuation should be applied to determine the market value of the premises.

The rental method of valuation has been commented upon and approved in a number of High Court cases, and, before the method is further dwelt upon, the principles laid down by the Courts should be noted.

Penny v *Penny*[1] and *Earl of Eldon* v *North-Eastern Railway Co.*[2] are authorities for the proposition that if the land which has been taken is likely to continue to produce rent which is being paid for it, the rent does offer the basis on which the value will be calculated.

When a property is let on lease, the rent reserved must be taken into account. The principle laid down in In re *Athlone Rifle Range* case[3] and *Earl of Eldon* v *North-Eastern Railway Co.*[4] were followed in *Swarna Manjuri Dassi* v *Secretary of State.*[5] In awarding compensation based on rent actually received, regard has to be had to the question whether the lease was one for a considerable period, and the rent received was an amount which was likely to be received for a lengthy period. At page 433 quoting from the Irish case it is stated—

> "That the circumstances are to be considered as they existed at the date of the notice, that is immediately before its service."

In *Earl of Eldon* v *North-Eastern Railway Co.*[6] the defendants had erected buildings on the land, and the umpire took the actual rent received by the plaintiff at the time of the notice to treat, as the basis of the value of the land to him. His Lordship held (p. 724):

> "If that were a rent which could be regarded as a mere accidental figure, and as not likely to be maintained for any long period, he might well disregard it as affording no true index of the value which the plaintiff could obtain for the land if he sold it. But if the rent had been paid ever since 1839 and was likely to continue to be paid because the defendants had expended so large a sum of money on

1 [1867] LR 5 Eq 227.
2 [1899]80 LT (NS) 723.
3 [1902]1 Ir 433.
4 [1899]80 LT (NS) 723.
5 32 CWN 421.
6 [1899]80 LT (NS) 723.

the land that they were never likely to determine their tenancy, then it seems to me that the arbitrator was justified in coming to the conclusion that, having regard to the state of things existing at the time of the notice to treat, there was a reasonable prospect of the plaintiff continuing to receive the same rent, and that the rent was in the circumstances an index of the value of the land to the plaintiff. If the plaintiff had immediately before the notice to treat offered the land for sale, he would not have been able to obtain a price for the land based upon the rent he received in respect of it. If he could establish, as I think he could, that the rent was a rent which the land was likely to continue to command, the rent would afford a fair index of the value of the land to him."

When a property is valued on the rental basis, the result is the value of the land and buildings taken together and cannot afterwards be apportioned. This was the view taken in *T. Kathissabi* v *Revenue Divisional Officer, Calicut.*[7] The following is an extract from the judgment:

"Apart from this we think that when a building and its appurtenant land cannot be valued separately—and no attempt has been made to do so in these proceedings—the market value must be determined on the net rental value and when that is done the building cannot be separated from the land, for it is impossible to say what proportion of the rent is fixed on the building and what on the land. This is in accordance with the view taken in re: Land Acquisition Act (I of 1894) case in the matter of *Government of Bombay* v *Karim Tar Mohamed,*[8] and in the matter of the Land Acquisition Act (X of 1870); *Premchand Burral* v *Collector of Calcutta.*"[9]

This does not mean the land and building method cannot be employed to check a valuation done by the rental method. It simply states that after capitalisation of the rent you cannot deduct the depreciated value of the buildings on the land, and say that the result is the definite value of the land.

7 AIR 1923 Mad 31.
8 ILR 33 Bom 325.
9 ILR 2 Cal 103.

If a rent had been paid for many years and the lease had a long period to run, the solvency of the lessee must be investigated when deciding how much reliance should be given to the actual rent reserved in the lease. In *Sm. Swarna Manjuri Dassi* v *Secretary of State for India*[10] states:

> "There is the undoubted fact that the property at the time of acquisition yielded a monthly rent of Rs. 2,000 clear to the first claimant and this rent was reserved to the claimant for a period close upon a century. This matter could not be left out of consideration by any person seeking to purchase the land as an investment, because there would be a ready return for his money for a number of years. This of course assumes that the tenant is a solvent person—a question which has also to be gone into in deciding how far the lease should be taken into consideration in calculating the present market value of the land."

The judgment in the case *Rathnamasari* v *Secretary of State*[11] actually sets out a valuation on the Rental Method, so it is quoted hereunder:

> "The applicant's next contention is that the $8^1/_2$ acres of land on which the buildings stand should be valued separately and that the buildings should also be valued separately and the two added together to get the total market value of the plots with the buildings standing thereon. That is hardly the way in which property consisting of a house and garden is valued in the market. We think that a plot consisting of a house and garden is much more satisfactorily valued in the manner in which the District Judge has done, by capitalising the rental, in the absence of other evidence which would give a more satisfactory value. Taking the annual rental in this case, *viz.*, Rs. 750 and making allowance for the municipal tax payable on the land of Rs. 20 a year, charged upon this land, and deducting also what one of the claimants who gave evidence in the case says he spent for the repairs and upkeep of this building, *viz.*, Rs. 50 we get a net annual rent of Rs. 680. The learned District Judge has taken a month's rental as

10 32 CWN 421.
11 AIR 1923 Mad 332.

the cost of repairs. That will ordinarily be so, but here we have special evidence and there is nothing to contradict it, that Rs. 40 or Rs. 50 were spent for repairs. Taking therefore Rs. 680 as the net annual rental and taking twenty years' purchase, which we think is a fair figure to adopt and a figure which is ordinarily adopted in most cases, the value of these two plots with the buildings on them will come to Rs. 13,600. This we think may well be accepted as the total value of these two plots."

Their Lordships in this same case had to decide the value of several plots of land. They did not adopt the rental method in dealing with all the land; in one instance when they had to value a garden, they stated:

> "The method of capitalisation of the rental value is not a proper method to use for ascertaining the value of such a land. We think it is better to take the value of the land in the neighbourhood as proved by Government itself as the value of this land."

The rental method of valuation may be stated to be:

> "From the Gross Rent of a property deduct all the required outgoings necessary to maintain that property in a state to command that rent and then capitalise the net rent by a figure known as the Year's Purchase which represents the security of the rent. The result will be the market value of the premises in accordance with the rental method of valuation."

The gross rents are ascertained from local enquiry, admissions and statement of parties and rental receipts. In case of requisition compensation is also assessed under s. 23 of the L.A. Act now s. 28 of the Right to Fair Compensation and Transparency in Land Acquisition, Rehabilitation and Resettlement Act 2013 on the basis of fair market value of such interests in the land. Notional fair rent of a hypothetical buyer is a good criterion to assess the market value of possessory interest and the rent is to be assessed as if it were a new house to be let out for the first time.[12]

12 *Haji Mohd. Ekramal Haque* v *Province of Bengal* AIR 1950 Cal 83.

The annual value comprises the "letting value" or the "rental profit". The net annual value is the criterion and not the "gross annual value".[13] In case of buildings the net rent after deducting all charges should be the basis.[14]

Valuation of vacant plot adjunct to tenanted property

In *CIT* v *Smt. Ashima Sinha*[15] premises in Calcutta was sold in equal undivided shares to two ladies for ₹ 40,000 each. The extent of the property was 4,547 sq. ft. out of which 1,264 sq. ft. was left open. The premises were fully tenanted and the tenants could neither be evicted nor could their rents be enhanced by reason of restrictive legislation. The Valuation Officer adopted the 'yield or rental' method and calculated the total value at ₹ 59,513 and added to it the land value on reversion estimated at ₹ 56,648. On this basis, the fair market value of the property exceeded the apparent consideration by more than 25 per cent and acquisition proceedings were initiated and an order for acquisition was passed. The Tribunal held that the only proper method of valuation was by application of a multiple which the Tribunal determined to be 12½ times the net yield of the property. The Tribunal further held that since the said property was sold in two undivided shares a further deduction of 10 per cent would have to be made. On this basis, the fair market value of the property on the date of the transfer was found to be less than the value mentioned in the instrument of transfer. Revenue contended before the High Court that there was vacant land in the property sold amounting to 1,264 sq. ft. and cited the price of another vacant land situated nearby which had been sold. Dismissing the appeal, the High Court held that out of a total area of 4,547 sq. ft. only 1,264 sq. ft. had been left open. No evidence was led to show if this 1,264 sq. ft. was one regular plot or aggregations of open spaces unconnected with each other. The property had been sold to two persons in undivided equal shares. The vacant land in each share would not exceed 634 sq. ft.; *i.e.* an area less than one cottah. The requirement of the Corporation of Calcutta is

13 *Sub-Collector, Rajahmundry* v *Pillarisetti* AIR 1942 Mad 739: ILR (1943) Mad 127.

14 *State of Trav-Co.* v *Ram Krishan Iyer Narayana Iyer* AIR 1955 Trav-Co 132.

15 (1979)116 ITR 26 (Cal).

that one-third of the total of an area should be left vacant and, therefore, the available area for development in the instant case would be only 400 sq. ft. in each undivided share which is negligible for the future development of the said property.

It is humbly submitted that the High Court took the correct decision in dismissing the appeal but the reason given for such dismissal does not appeal to reason. No doubt, that in case of further construction on the subject land left vacant, one-third of the area has to be left vacant by way of statutory compliance. But that is not the only option in respect of the subject land left vacant. There was no effort to estimate the value in an alternative use of it, nor any attempt made to value the buildable portion of 800 square feet, out of 1,264 square feet on the assumption that the property will not remain undivided after the sale. The proper reason to ignore the value of the remaining vacant land should have been the patent fact that it has been left undisclosed in evidence as to whether the 1,264 square feet of land was comprised in one regular plot or was scattered in open spaces unconnected with each other. The burden of proof in this behalf lies on the Revenue who did not discharge it before the court. Thus, the conclusion the court arrived at, has nothing to dispute with but the reasons for the same lies elsewhere than what was relied upon.

Where rental method was held as proper and fair

In *CIT* v *Panchanan Das*[16] certain property, comprising land with buildings, was purchased by the respondent for ₹ 41,000. The competent authority got the property valued by the official valuer who determined the fair market value of the property under land and building method as on the date of sale at ₹ 71,400. After initiating the acquisition proceedings and hearing the objections raised, the competent authority passed an order under s. 269F(6) of I.T. Act. The Tribunal held that the fair market value of the property under the rental method on the date of the transfer was not more than the consideration disclosed in the sale deed and that the conditions necessary for the acquisition of the property were not satisfied and cancelled the order. The revenue contended before the High Court that the Tribunal erred in holding that the fair method

16 (1979)116 ITR 272 (Cal).

of valuation was the rental method and not the land and building method, that the Tribunal itself had given the go-by to the rental method, inasmuch as the valuation according to the rental method was ₹ 28,500 whereas the respondent had paid ₹ 41,000. Relying on the views of the Supreme Court in *Smt. Tribeni Devi* v *Collector*[17] that there is no infallible method and that the method of valuation to be adopted would depend on the facts and circumstances of each case and ultimately on the property itself and the surrounding circumstances, advantages and disadvantages which would govern the factor in the determination of the case, the High Court pointed out that the fact that the respondent paid more than the amount which could be arrived at by valuing according to the rental method was a relevant consideration, but could not determine the matter finally one way or the other. Hence, the court upheld the rental method followed by the Tribunal.

In *Subhakaran Chowdhury* v *IAC*,[18] the petitioners got registered a deed of conveyance in respect of property for a consideration of ₹ 1,35,000 and obtained possession from the vendors. Earlier, a valuer had valued the said property at ₹ 1,32,000 on the rental method. The said property was fully tenanted. The notice issued by the competent authority for the purpose of acquisition of the property was challenged in writ by the petitioners on the ground that there was no material for the fulfilment of the conditions precedent required. The Calcutta High Court noticed from the affidavit filed in the petition by the competent authority that he had proceeded on the basis of valuation under the land and building method. The court held that if the premises in question is let out to tenants, then according to the prevalent law, the premises in question has to be valued not on the basis of the value of the land but on the rental method.

In *CIT* v *Shri Radhye Mohan*[19] a building consisting of $2\frac{1}{2}$ storeys was sold for ₹ 1,10,000. This first floor of the building was in occupation of the owner and the ground floor had been

17 AIR 1972 SC 1417.
18 (1979)118 ITR 777 (Cal).
19 (1985)153 ITR 399 (P&H).

leased for a monthly rent of ₹ 480. The Valuation Officer applying land and building method, valued the property at ₹ 1,75,000. The competent authority took the fair market value at ₹ 1,99,300 and ordered its acquisition. In appeal, the Tribunal held that the most appropriate method to determine the value of the property was the rent capitalisation method and applying that principle, the value came to ₹ 1,08,000 only. Consequently, the Tribunal reversed the order of the competent authority. On further appeal by the Commissioner, the High Court held:

> "It is well settled that the fair market price of a property can be determined either by land and building method or by rent capitalisation method. In case a part of the building is on rent, it cannot be held that the determination of the valuation of the building by rent capitalisation method is not correct. Even that method has been recognized by the Legislature under the W.T. Rules. It has been provided in rule 1BB of the said Rules that the value of house which is used for residential purposes can be determined by multiplying the net maintainable rent by the fraction 100/8. The method is also recognized by judicial decisions. The Supreme Court in *State of Kerala* v *Hassan Koya,*[20] observed:
>
> "When the property sold is land with building, it is often difficult to secure reliable evidence of instances of sale of similar lands with buildings proximate in time to the date of the notification under section 4. Therefore, the method which is generally resorted to in determining the value of the land with buildings, especially those used for business purposes, is the method of capitalisation of return actually received or which might reasonably be received from the land and the buildings." .... The fact that a part of the building is occupied by a landlord does not make any difference. The rent of that part can be determined by the competent authority on the basis of the rent paid by the tenants in the same building or other buildings situated in the same locality. It is not necessary that the rent capitalisation method is applicable only to that property

20 AIR 1968 SC 1201.

which is on rent. We get support in the above observations from *Dewan Daulat Rai Kapoor* v *New Delhi Municipal Committee.*[21] It is evident from the above observations that for determining the annual value of the property whether it is occupied by a tenant or by the landlord, the principle applicable is as to what rent the landlord is entitled to charge from the tenant. Similarly, for finding out the fair market value of the property in the possession of an owner himself, its hypothetical rent, taking into consideration the rents prevailing in the locality, can be determined."

The Karnataka High Court in the case of *Premchand* v *IAC*[1] preferred comparative sale method even in the case of fully tenanted property and observed that rent-capitalisation method had to be resorted to only when the determination cannot be made by applying the comparative sales method and not otherwise.

Valuation of tenanted property subject to rent control legislation

In *CIT* v *New India Construction Co.*,[2] the transferor sold the first floor of a building situated in the heart of a commercial locality to the transferee for the sum of ₹ 2,20,000. The floor covered an area of 7,200 sq. ft. The transferee was given the right to effect construction above the first floor and was also made a co-lessee of the 400 sq. yds. of land held by the transferor on perpetual lease for which he was to pay ₹ 300 as ground rent. The property sold was in the occupation of three tenants on a total rent of ₹ 328 per month for residential purposes. Eviction proceedings were pending against them and the transferee was given the right to pursue them for its benefit. After the sale the transferee obtained vacant possession by paying each of the tenants ₹ 35,000. A further sum of ₹ 75,000 was spent by the transferee to convert the property from residential to commercial nature. Thereafter the transferee spent a sum of ₹ 2,75,000 for renovation and conversion of the property into commercial premises and sold the property to 20 different parties for a total consideration of

21 (1980)122 ITR 700 (SC).
1 (1985)153 ITR 774 (Kar).
2 (1980)123 ITR 68 (Del).

₹ 9,16,980. The competent authority called for a report from the Valuation Officer who determined its fair market value at ₹ 11,41,900 on the development method. The competent authority felt that the fair market value of the property exceeded the apparent consideration and initiated acquisition proceedings and passed an order for acquisition of the property. On appeal, the Tribunal quashed the acquisition order after observing that a building with vacant possession and a building with tenants especially in an area where rent control statutes prevailed were two different things altogether. Dismissing the appeal filed by the revenue the Delhi High Court held that the potential user of the property could not be ignored in determining the market value. Since there were three old tenants residing in the property and it was also subject to rent control restrictions against ejectment, the value of the property could not be measured by the value of those which are self-occupied.

It was further observed that the method of capitalisation of rental value by multiplying a number of years' yield was adopted, the value of the property at the time of sale would be even less than ₹ 1 lakh and instances of property in similar circumstances which has been let out, which were more relevant, indicated that it could not be said that the sale consideration of ₹ 2,20,000 did not represent a fair value.

In *CIT* v *Anup Kumar Kapoor,*[3] a property was sold for ₹ 1,80,000. The extent of the property was 1 bigha, 5 cottahs, 3 chittack and 4 sq. ft. out of which about 7 cottahs and 3 chittacks were left open. The buildings were occupied by tenants who were protected under the rent control legislations. The Valuation Officer adopted the yield or rental method and added thereto the reversionary value of the land and arrived at a figure of ₹ 2,73,000. The acquisition proceedings were started and an order for acquisition of property was passed.

On appeal, the Tribunal held that the property being fully tenanted, the appropriate method of valuation would be to capitalise only the rent by a certain number of years of purchase. The Tribunal found that the sale instance cited on behalf of the transferee made it apparent that the property

3 (1980)125 ITR 684 (Cal).

could not have been sold for a consideration of more than what was stated in the deed of conveyance, which also compared favourably with the value adopted in the income-tax and wealth-tax assessments of the transferor. On these facts the Tribunal held that the acquisition proceedings could not be taken in respect of the property. Here again, the department pleaded before the High Court that the competent authority was justified in valuing the vacant land on the basis of prices obtained on sale of vacant land in contiguous areas. Dismissing the appeal, the Calcutta High Court held that there was no evidence to show that the vacant land in the property was one contiguous plot or divided into several plots unconnected with each other. Further, under the prevailing building regulations of the Corporation of Calcutta, in the area where the transferred property was situate, 50 per cent of the total land had to be left open in constructing a building. Thus, at least over 12 cottahs of lands had to be left open but the land left open was only 7 cottahs and 3 chittacks. There was, therefore, no scope for development of the property. As the property was fully developed and let out to tenants in its entirety and there was no dispute as to the quantum of rent realised, the court held that the Tribunal had rightly applied the yield or rental method and that acquisition proceedings were not validly initiated.

Capitalisation of rent

The method of capitalising the rent of a number of years' purchase though one of the methods of valuation of property, can be resorted to when no other method is available.[4]

In *CIT* v *Prem Narain Tandon*[5], 3/4th of the house was let out to a tenant. The Tribunal valued the entire property on the basis of rent capitalisation. This was challenged by the Commissioner. The High Court of Allahabad held:

> "The Appellate Tribunal held that the competent authority was not justified in discarding the capitalisation method of determining the market price of the house in dispute on the basis of its annual rental value. The appellate authority

4 *Governor-General-in-Council* v *Bhola* 50 PLR 318; *Governor-General-in-Council* v *Hafiz Ghiasuddin* AIR 1949 East Punj 160.

5 (1984)145 ITR 359 (All).

observed that since 3/4th portion of the house was let out to a tenant on rent, the market value of the property could be determined on its annual rental value. Since 3/4th of the property was let out on a rent of Rs. 3,000 per annum, the Tribunal determined the rent of the entire property at Rs. 4,000 and after making an allowance to the extent of 25% for the rate, taxes etc., it determined the net rental value on the basis of Rs. 3,000 per annum. The Tribunal applied a multiple of 16 to the annual rental value and thereby determined the fair market value of the property at Rs. 48,000. The Tribunal further added 30% to the value, as the sale transaction had taken place in August 1973, whereas the house in dispute was constructed in 1968, and thus the value of the property was determined at Rs. 60,000. We find no error in the approach of the Tribunal in determining the value of the property on annual rental value. The mode of determining the value of the building on the basis of annual rental value is well recognised. Even the legislature has prescribed this method under the W.T. Rules, r. 1BB, which permits the valuation of building on the basis of the annual income by applying a multiple of 10. The Tribunal, in our opinion, did not commit any error or transgress its jurisdiction in determining the market value of the property on the basis of the annual rental value."

Where the tenanted property has been sub-let by the tenant the owner is entitled to collect only the rent payable by the tenants and has no right over the higher rent paid by the sub-tenants to the tenants. Only if the tenant is evicted under due process of law the question can arise of the sub-tenant becoming a direct tenant of the owner. The purchaser of tenanted property would be in the same position as the owner and the rent to be collected would be restricted to that rent receivable from the direct tenants. Therefore only the rent receivable from the direct tenants can be capitalised.[6]

The position should not differ even if the computation is made under the Rules. In a case where certain amount had to be paid to lessees as monthly rent to enable lessor to let out

6 *CIT* v *Smt. Asha Devi Agarwal* (1988)169 ITR 400 (Cal).

property at higher rent to Government from the gross rental received from Government, the rent paid to the lessees has to be deducted to arrive at maintainable rent.[7]

Where the property is subjected to Rent Control Act the standard rent payable under the Rent Control Act in operation can be taken to be the rent for capitalisation purpose.[8]

Capitalisation rate to vary according to situation

It is not possible to be dogmatic regarding the number of years. It varies with conditions, nature of property and the like. The number of years may be different for ground rent and unsecured ground rent. In the instant case 16 years' purchase was considered good.[9]

Rack rent may be the basis of valuation which is determination of the full letting value and deduct from it the cost of cultivation. It is not the value of estimated annual yield or value. It will leave margin of profit to the tenant. In L.A. cases the existing rent is taken as the gross annual value to the landlord. The number of years' purchase is then varied according to the rights of the tenants and prospects of future increase in the rent.[10]

Where a house and a licensed liquor shop therein were mortgaged for ₹ 60 out of which ₹ 40 was in lieu of the right to work in the shop. On acquisition of the house, it was held that the rent of the house should be taken at ₹ 60 and compensation was to be awarded accordingly by deducting $\frac{1}{4}$th from the annual rent and capitalising at $33\frac{1}{3}$ years' purchase.[11]

The usual method is to take the existing rent or profit as the gross annual value of the land and then vary the number of years' purchase according to the rights of the tenants and

7 *CWT* v *Champa Properties Ltd.* (1994)120 CTR 104 (Cal).

8 *Balbir Singh (Dr.)* v *Municipal Corporation of Delhi* (1985)152 ITR 388 (SC).

9 *Heysham* v *Bholanath Mullick* 11 BLR 230; (1871)17 WR 221; *Government of Bombay* v *Merwanji Muncherji* 10 Bom LR 907.

10 *Lakshmi Narasimha Devaru (Sri)* v *R.D.O. Mangalore, L.A.O.* AIR 1949 Mad 902.

11 *Government of Hyderabad* v *Govinda Bal* AIR 1959 Hyd 70; ILR (1951) Hyd 216.

prospects of future increase in the rent or profit. From the gross rental value deductions are to be made on account of land revenue payable by the landlord and the cost of collection.[12]

Fancy rent to be ignored

Normally the rent actually received would be an indicative factor but fancy rents paid in any exceptional circumstances would have to be ignored. In determining standard rent due consideration has to be given to the relevant factors prescribed under the Rent Control Acts.[13]

Where the property is partly rented and partly self-occupied it is not necessary that the rent capitalisation method is restricted only to that property let out on rent. For the residential portion also the probable rent can be determined on the basis of rent paid by the other tenants.[14]

Reversionary value of land

A question may arise in valuing a property by the capitalisation of rental method if the reversionary value of land ought to be added. Normally, where valuation is made by the capitalisation of income method, the yield is considered as representing the income receivable from the entire property. Hence the question of making a separate addition for reversionary value of land does not arise.[15]

12 *Rama Chandraiah* v *L.A.O., Sagar* AIR 1973 SC 701.

13 *Dewan Daulatrai Kapoor* v *New Delhi Municipal Committee* (1980)122 ITR 700 (SC) and *Sheila Kaushish* v *CIT* (1981)131 ITR 435 (SC).

14 *CIT* v *Radhey Mohan* (1985)153 ITR 399 (P&H) referring to *Dewan Daulatrai Kapoor* v *New Delhi Municipal Committee* (1980)122 ITR 700 (SC).

15 *CIT* v *Ashima Sinha* (1979)116 ITR 26 (Cal); *CIT* v *Anup Kumar Kapoor* (1980)125 ITR 684 (Cal); *CWT* v *R.S. Tandon* (1992)195 ITR 397 (Del).

CHAPTER

9

Rent and Ground Rent

Rent is a certain periodical profit in money, provisions or labour, issuing out of lands and tenements. It is a stipulated sum paid by a tenant annually, quarterly, monthly, weekly or daily for the temporary use and possession of lands, moors, houses, rooms, etc. Rent is not always pure rent for the site, it may include interest on capital expended in erecting houses, buildings, machinery; it may include allowances for profits, a sinking fund to repay capital at the end of a given period, and a sum for labour, enterprise and risks.

Rent as technically defined

Rent may be technically defined as the income which accrues from the ownership of land, or an interest in land or of other free gifts of nature. The term has been used by the economists to mean any payment which is made for the use of the primary factor in all production, *i.e.* land or natural resources. Capital which may have been so sunk in the soil as to be no longer distinguishable as capital is also merged in the concept of land.

Ricardian theory of rent

David Ricardo, the celebrated economist, conceived rent as a payment for the original and indestructible power of the soil. He started his premises on the theory of rent with the assumption that an uncultivated tract of land comes into possession of a small colony of men and so long as there is plenty of good land available, no payment will be made for any of it and no rent will, therefore, arise. Only the best land will be appropriated to use, and the return from the sale of produce will tend to just cover the expense of cultivation, including normal wages and normal profit. As population increases, there will naturally be an increased demand for produce which would compel some of the population to resort to the inferior category of land. Other things remaining the same, the inferior land will yield a lesser quantity of produce or, a lower quality of produce than the better category of land. Now, the produce of all the land must sell at the same price and that price must cover the cost of production on the poorer category of land being the marginal land which otherwise cannot continue in cultivation. In this situation, the owner of the superior land enjoys a surplus being an excess over normal price. This surplus is called 'rent' according to the Ricardian theory. Rent thus is a result of price and do not enter into price as a determinant. Rent is high because price is high but not *vice versa*.

Ricardo takes land as a factor of production or as an agent for productive activities. But land, particularly urban land in the form we find is more a product itself than a factor of production. A lot of capital and human labour is employed by an entrepreneur to make it usable as a buildable plot in conformity with the municipal building code. Even when a bare land acquires locational value, it means a spurt of economic activities as well as investments in the surrounding areas which creates locational value. Ricardo was somewhat right as regards ordinary rural land and long years of experience have proved the truth of his statement in this regard but it is quite inappropriate in the context of urban landed property. As one moves towards a town or city, or towards the central business district within a city, the proportion of the value of the land as against the value of the building gets more and more pronounced. May be, in the heart of the city, the rental value of the whole property will only be twice the rent of the land as a bare site, and the ground rent would be said to be twice covered. This proportion, however, would vary from place to place or situation to situation.

Rent as now popularly understood

In its popular sense, the term 'rent' is variously applied to the payment made by tenant for the use of a house and the land appertaining thereto; to the periodical payment made to the landlord in respect of a farm or estate; to the revenue received by the Government or some lesser owner of a forest, fishery or mine, in return for the right to extract therefrom timber, fish, or minerals, as the case may be. It is well to observe that in the application of the term 'rent' in most of these cases, other elements besides pure rent as known to the classical economists are included, such as, interest on capital invested in houses, buildings, improvements, infrastructure, etc., as well as allowances for profits and depreciation of fixed capital. For example, in the payment for a tenancy of a house, there is generally a far larger proportion of such elements as interest and depreciation, than of pure rent for the site. The payment for the latter may, as a matter of fact, be made separately in the form of ground rent in which case the whole of the balance payable to the house owner, consists of income on the capital invested therein, such income including not only interest, but allowances for depreciation, compensation for risk, and also a certain proportion of profit for enterprise and management.

The actual rent paid or the rent a property is capable of producing, in practically all cases, forms the basis of valuations. The value of land is determined by the rent which it yields; it therefore follows that the greater the rent, the greater is the value both to the owner of the property and to the general public. Value of land is the capitalized value of its rental since the value of land depends essentially upon its rental and any future change in the rental will have a corresponding reflection in the value.

Before a valuation of land can, however, be made, another factor has to be considered, that is the security of the rent and the possibility of its being maintained, therefore the actual value will depend upon the relation of the annual rent to the prevailing rate of interest.

Variations in rent

Rents in the suburbs of a large town are considerably higher than the rents in the surrounding agricultural lands, and the rent increases as the centre of the town is approached. The supply of land in a town is naturally restricted and the dictates of fashion and commercial interests usually create a keen demand for sites which have advantages from a fashionable point of view or from the commercial side. Building sites in fashionable areas have a relatively high value because of the high standard of customer they can attract and the high prices which the shopkeepers consequently charge. Tenants of shops in fashionable areas are usually charged high rents because it is known that they can charge high prices and obtain large profits. The high prices are not due to the high rents, the high prices would be charged, even if the rents were low, because in a fashionable area some people will gladly pay high prices for the privilege of shopping in an exclusive fashionable area. Owners are aware of these fashionable areas and districts, and in order to obtain as much of the profit as possible they charge high rentals. Prospective tenants will bid amongst themselves to obtain a site in these areas with the result that the majority of the surplus profit from the site finds its way into the owners' pocket. The rent of a building site is payment for differential advantages of situation.

In making valuations by the rental method it is necessary to know the full rental value of the property. The actual rental paid is always a guide but unless it is proved very little reliance can be placed upon it. Not only must it be proved that the rent is actually paid, but it must be proved that the rent is the fair rent. Proving of rents can only be done by ascertaining the actual rents paid for any adjacent and similar properties. A schedule of adjoining properties of, say, all the ground floor shops will usually show large variations. These must be carefully studied and abnormally high or low rents should be disregarded. For instance, a shop may be let to a relative and the rent would probably be low, whilst another man may offer an abnormally high rent to get in. This tenant will invariably give trouble, as his rent is much higher than other similarly situated tenants and he will either start advocating for a reduction in rent or fall into arrears of rent. Some shops may have slight advantages over others and these advantages must be discounted if the rent is to be used for comparison purposes. The best method is to reduce the actual rents paid to units of first belt at so many rupees per sq. ft. By first belt is meant the average depth of the shopping area. A shop 10' × 10' may be let for ₹ 1,500 per month, whilst another with 10 ft. frontage and 20 ft. depth may be let for ₹ 2,250 per month. By careful comparison with other shops it may be found that shops having a depth of 10 ft. have a rental value of ₹ 15 per sq. ft. and that shops having a greater depth with the same frontage may have a rental value of ₹ 15 per sq. ft. for the first 10 ft. and then the rear portion has a rental value of half the front portion. No definite formula can be laid down giving the comparative values of front and back portions, but in shops it is usually found that the portion accessible to the public has the greatest value and the portion used for storage of goods has a value much less than the front portion used by the public. In such cases a valuation by rental method would have to be checked by other methods before accuracy could be obtained.

Again actual rents paid are not always the true rack rent. A lessee on entering a premises may pay a premium or *salami* and the rental equivalent of the premium of *salami* would have to be ascertained and added to the rent paid to find the actual rent of the sitting tenant. In all cases of valuations by the rental method, it is necessary to know, the rack rent of the property. If you are valuing the lessors' interest, you want to know what is the reversionary value at the termination of the lease and the reversionary value can only be calculated when you know what is the rack rent. If you are valuing the lessee's interest, then you must ascertain the profit rental, and this can only be done by deducting the actual rent paid *plus* the rental equivalent to the premium or *salami* from the rack rent of the property. In this latter case if the rental equivalent of the premium or *salami* plus the rent paid in accordance with the lease is equal to the rack rental, then the lessee's interest will consist solely of the capitalisation of the rental equivalent to the premium for the unexpired portion of the lease.

Rents will vary according to the situation, class of premises and size of premises. If a large premises were let to a single tenant, the rent would be less than if let in severalty. The value of the premises would be the same; the deductions, however, would be considerably less in the case of the single tenant than if let to many tenants.

Actual rent as a guide ought to be fair

The actual rents paid are a guide to a valuation, but must not be adopted for the purpose unless they have been checked by rents of similar premises in the locality. Actual rents also must be carefully scrutinised to see what services they include. Some rents are inclusive of taxes, others include occupier's taxes only, whilst some are exclusive of all taxes.

For the purposes of valuation, gross rent must be the fair rent, because it is on the basis of fair rent that market value is estimated, and fair rent may be defined as the prevailing rent which is capable of being maintained, not for one or two years but at a particular date and for some time to come.

An important point on the rental method of valuation was decided in the case of *Province of Bengal* v *Uma Charan Law*.[1] The acquired premises which was a *bustee* land at No. 70, Nimtollaghat Street was yielding a very high rent, namely, ₹ 356 per month as ground rent which was proved by the owner. The Calcutta Improvement Tribunal capitalised the net rent at a little over 22.5 years' purchase and valued the land at ₹ 94,000. On appeal by the Government, the rental method of valuation was rejected as in Their Lordships' opinion, the rent which the premises was said to be yielding was fancy rent which should not be taken as the basis for capitalisation. It was held that—

> "Evidence conclusively shows that the rents which the owner was actually receiving from the tenants were far above what other tenants were paying as ground rents for properties belonging to others which were similarly situated as the acquired land ..... The rents which the owners of the acquired land were receiving were fancy rents and that introduces an element of unstability."

It was contended on behalf of the owner that the market value of a land under s. 23(1) of the Land Acquisition Act now s. 28 of the Right to Fair Compensation and Transparency in Land Acquisition & Rehabilitation and Resettlement Act 2013 means the same thing as the phrase 'value to owner' used in Land Clauses Consolidation Act of England. Their Lordships after review of the authorities laid down the following propositions:

> "The basis for determination of the market value of the land within section 23(1) of the Land Acquisition Act is the

1 48 CWN 609.

value of land to the owner. The value to the owner must be judged by an objective and not a subjective standard. If the land is likely to produce the same rent which is being paid for it, that rent does offer the basis on which the value is to be capitalised. It is necessary that one should be certain that the rent is likely to continue undiminished. One of the tests would be whether the rent that is being paid is a fair rent at the time and not a fancy rent."

Deductions from gross rent

(1) ***Municipal taxes.*** The actual rates paid on a property must not be accepted unless the Valuer has checked the assessment and ascertained that the annual value assessed by the municipality is fair. In this case we are dealing with a fair rent and, therefore, the taxes to be deducted are the actual taxes that would be paid if the assessment was based on the same fair rent. The case of *Raghunathdas Gopaldas* v *Secretary of State*[2] established this point; an extract from the judgment is as follows:

> "But I feel that this is essentially a point not to be determined by *a priori* considerations, and when we find Mr. Morris, an experienced surveyor and valuer, called by the claimants saying, 'In advising a purchaser I would deduct the full amount which the Municipality is entitled to charge under their Act even though the last bill, or the previous bills have been for small amounts', and Mr. Stevens deposing 'From the point of view of the purchaser I should advise him to deduct the full amount that the Commissioner could charge', we are unable to say the Tribunal erred in following the Collector and deducting 4 per cent from the rentals in respect of water-tax."

The amount to be deducted for municipal taxes will vary from place to place in accordance with the laws in force at that particular place.

EXAMPLE 1. To give an illustration, suppose a building was let out for ₹ 16,850 per month inclusive of property tax, service charges etc., then the annual value (A.V.) would be as follows.

2 ILR 29 Bom 514.

SOLUTION

Monthly rent (including property tax & service charges etc., if any)	=	₹ 16,850.00
Gross Annual Rent (inclusive of service charges etc.) ₹ 16,850.00 × 12	=	₹ 2,02,200.00
Less: deduction @ 10% towards repairs & maintenance	=	₹ 20,220.00
Annual value of the premises (A.V.) = ₹ 2,02,200.00 – ₹ 20,220.00	=	₹ 1,81,980.00

Assumptions:

(*a*) The incidence of the property tax is primarily on the owner;

(*b*) Deduction @ 10% is reckoned for repairs, maintenance etc. to keep the property in a state to command the assumed rent.

(2) ***Repairs and maintenance of the premises.*** There are various methods of estimating the allowance to be made for repairs and maintenance of a building and probably the most unreliable method is to take the actual cost of repairs or the average amount expended on repairs over the past few years. Many owners spend as little as possible on repairs with the result that many dilapidated buildings can be seen throughout almost every city in India, and these buildings will be bringing in rents less than the value they are capable of producing if kept in a reasonable state of repair. If they are let at present at the full rack rent, then they cannot hope to be maintained, because the buildings will become totally unsuitable in a few more years unless much capital is spent in making them serviceable and up-to-date.

A valuer must always bear in mind that he must estimate the amount necessary to be spent each year on the building to keep the premises in a state to command that rent, not for one year only but for many years to come. For instance, a new building will require very little for repairs except periodical painting of all the woodwork and pointing of the brick-work, but although he can take into account the fact that the building is new, he must also keep in mind what will be the average expenditure over, say, the next 20 years to keep that building in a first class condition, and it is for this reason along with the other reasons mentioned that actual expenditure for repairs on buildings should be disregarded as too unreliable to be of any practical assistance.

Another method which is sometimes advocated by experts who want to make the net rent as high as possible is to take a percentage on the actual cost of the building. The figures vary from 10 to 15 per cent. The cost of a building cannot possibly have a direct bearing on the amount to be annually expended to maintain the premises in a state to command the fair rent. If a person spends a considerable amount on a building making it sound, the repairs will be less, but repairs do not fluctuate according to the cost of the building but according to the gross rent.

The fairest and most accurate method of estimating repair is to take a percentage on the gross rent of the premises. If a person is receiving a large rent from a property, he will be quite content to spend a fair amount on repairs so that the rent can be maintained. If he only receives a low rent, he will only spend a little on repairs, there being not the same incentive to keep the premises in a first class condition.

In average cases a fair deduction to make would be 10 per cent of the gross rent for internal repairs and 5 per cent for external repairs. From experience this may approximate very closely to the correct figures. In exceptional circumstances these figures may vary very slightly, but for all practical purposes in average cases they may be taken as correct.

If a building is let in severalty, it may be a condition of the terms of tenancy that the cost of cleaning and lighting of the staircase is borne by the owner. If there is a lift, then the annual cost of maintenance must be estimated and the annual cost of the person required to work the lift. An electric motor having a limited life, a prudent landlord may wish to set aside a sum each year to replace the motor when necessary. All these facts must be taken into account. No definite rules can be laid down; each case must be carefully considered in accordance with the facts and figures supplied to a valuer and from his own personal observations and notes.

(3) *Collection charges and management.* The normal procedure is for an agent to collect rents and if the estate is large, he will also manage the estate. Charges vary according to the class of property and the number of tenants. If the rents are small, an agent will charge 5% for collection, as it is much more difficult and troublesome in collecting small rentals than large rentals. The general charge for collection amongst house agents is 2 per cent on the gross amount of collection and if the estate is also managed by the rent collecting agency, the charges will be from 4 to 5 per cent. This will include investigation of petty complaints and supervising petty repairs. If large repairs have to be done, then the agent would be justified in charging an additional percentage on the cost of the work to be done.

In many cases the owner collects the rents himself. A valuer, however, must include cost of collection in the deductions to be made from the gross rent; because, if the owner does the work himself, he is entitled to receive something for his labour. The cost of collection and management will vary from 2 to 5 per cent of the gross rental in accordance with the special circumstances of each case.

(4) *Vacancies and bad debts.* Vacancies and bad debts are not often estimated, the figures adopted by a valuer are usually based on actual facts. If the vacancies fluctuate each year up and down, then the average of the past 3 or 5 years may be the best guide. If the vacancies were increasing each year, then the last year's figure would be the minimum that could be taken. It may, however, be better to take a figure slightly in excess of the previous year's figures. If the vacancies were decreasing each year, then the previous year's amount would be the correct one to take. Bad debts are best estimated on an average. In a block of flats or a premises in a business area let to many tenants, there are bound to be a considerable number of bad debts. If the figures are high, then the management will probably require changing. An average of the past 5 years is the best guide. If these figures are not available, then the average of the past 3 years should be taken.

(5) *Insurance.* Many valuers ignore making provision for insurance in deductions from gross rent, because the owner may have failed to take out a policy. This is wrong, because a prudent businessman will always insure against fire and if the existing owner has failed to take this precaution, a valuer should do so, otherwise an incorrect figure will be found which cannot be said to be equivalent to the fair market value.

You cannot insure land against fire, it is the buildings erected on the land that are insured. Insurance depends on two things—

(1) the construction of the building; and

(2) the nature of occupancy of the building.

Insurance rates for premises vary according to different circumstances. The adequacy of the water supply, the pressure of the water mains and facilities for fire-fighting are some of the factors which will govern the premium to be paid and no special rates can be given which will govern property situated upcountry.

(6) *Sinking fund.* Buildings will in time become useless and if they have been allowed to get in a very bad state of repair it may be possible to estimate to a fair degree of accuracy the remaining effective life of the building. If a valuer in such a case was advising his client on the present value of premises consisting of land and buildings and the building, though very old was well let, he would make an allowance for a sinking fund. This is an annual payment which will during the life of the building accumulate to a sum required for rebuilding the premises and for one year's rent which will be lost whilst the premises are being rebuilt. Now-a-days Sinking Funds cannot be invested at more than 3% and the following is a typical example.

EXAMPLE 2. A property is producing a net rent of ₹ 1,20,000.00 per month which is likely to be maintained. The building is in a bad state of repair and cannot be expected to last more than 12 years which is taken as the remaining life for economic use of the building. What allowance should be made for sinking fund for the building?

SOLUTION

Estimated cost of rebuilding the existing structure as on the date of valuation	= ₹ 37,00,000
One year's rent will be lost during reconstruction and hence amount earmarked towards loss of business @ ₹ 1,20,000 p.m. x 12	= ₹ 14,40,000

Amount required in 12 years' time

= ₹ 37,00,000 + ₹ 14,40,000 = ₹ 51,40,000

Annual Sinking Fund (A.S.F.) to redeem Re. 1 in 12 years @ 3.5%

$$= \frac{r}{(1+r)^n - 1} = \frac{0.035}{(1+0.035)^{12} - 1} = \frac{0.035}{(1.035)^{12} - 1} = 0.068483949$$

Annual Sinking Fund (A.S.F.)

= ₹ 51,40,000 x 0.068483949 = ₹ 3,52,008

A sum of ₹ 3,52,008 invested annually in a sinking fund @ 3.5% will amount to ₹ 51,40,000 in 12 years' time.

Cross-verification:

$$\frac{(1+r)^n - 1}{r} \times ₹\,3{,}52{,}008 = \frac{(1+0.035)^{12} - 1}{0.035} \times ₹\,3{,}52{,}008$$

$$= \frac{(1.035)^{12} - 1}{0.035} \times ₹\,3{,}52{,}008$$

$$= 14.60196164 \times ₹\,3{,}52{,}008$$

= ₹ 51,40,000 (Approx.)

[Here, r = rate of interest, n = number of years]

An investor will be prudent, if out of the present rent, he accumulates a sum in 15 years through sinking fund which will completely rebuild his property without any loss in rent.

If a building is in a good state of repair and modern in design and layout, then the premises should be kept in a good state of repair by good management of the estate. The constant renovating and repairing of defective parts will give a soundly constructed building an indefinite life and provided ample allowance is made for annual repairs, then there is no necessity to provide for a sinking fund.

If the life of a building is so short, say, only 10 years, then in all probability the premises will be in a bad state of repair and only producing a fraction of the fair rent. In such cases it is better to estimate the cost of erecting a new building and the return that can be expected, as well as the capitalisation of the existing rental for 10 years and the rebuilding programme to be commenced after that period.

No fixed percentage deduction from the gross rent can be given for sinking fund. When it must be provided for, a separate calculation will be made, and deducted from the net rent before it is capitalised.

Rent of different types—rent control law

At this stage, let us look into the various types of rents that have come into vogue with practices over the time. These practices differ from region to region. We can categorise the regional differences under the following headings as we take up the topic of rent:

(*i*) Rural areas,

(*ii*) Non-municipal urban areas, and

(*iii*) Municipal areas.

The lease of property for rental purposes in the rural areas as well as non-municipal urban areas in India are governed by the provisions of lease as contained in Chapter V of the Transfer of Property Act 1882. In terms of s. 105 thereof, a lease of immovable property is a transfer of right to enjoy such property made for a certain time in consideration of a price paid called as the premium or in consideration of a periodic payment called as rent which may take the form of money or share of crop or rendering of any services. Such rent, under s. 107 of the Act, can be paid from year to year or for a term exceeding one year in which case it can be effected only by a registered instrument and in all other cases by an oral agreement accompanied by delivery of possession. There is no embargo on the amount to be negotiated whether as premium or rent which is left to be determined by the market forces of demand and supply. Section 111 of the said Act lays down the provisions as to how the lease could be terminated which generally follows the terms of agreement as are consistent with the provisions of the Act.

But the situation is entirely different in cities and towns governed by municipal administration where the rent control law of the respective State overrides the provisions of the Transfer of Property Act. It is only the matters that are not provided in the rent control law which attract the Transfer of Property Act for applicability in the cities and towns. The rent control laws in different States of India generally provide for fixation of fair rent/standard rent which is lawfully recoverable by the landlords from the tenants since the purpose of such legislation is to provide for the control of rent for the benefit of tenants, and also to secure the tenants against unreasonable eviction. Rent once fixed can be revised or increased only in conformity with the provisions of rent control law. The tenants once inducted cannot be evicted except on the ground as permissible under the said law. The result is a highly imperfect market in respect of leasehold properties for residential and commercial use. The intervention of the rent control laws on the real estate market is of preponderant impact. Consequently, various dubious bypasses to avoid the legal restrictions have cropped up particularly in a situation of soft law administration. All these features have emerged as factors to be taken into consideration in the valuation process of residential or commercial property encumbered with tenancies in the major urban centres.

With the above background held in view, we can define the following types of rents which in a general way are conceptualised in the field of valuation.

(1) ***Lease rent.*** The rent reserved in a lease document is known as the lease rent. It can also be termed as a Contractual Rent. It is the rent payable by a lessee to the lessor on the stipulated periodical intervals and the lessor has a right to realise the rent during the period of lease and hold the reversionary title to the property which entitles him to get back the property on the expiry of the term of lease. The lessee has a right of occupation and use in accordance with the terms of lease.

Strictly speaking, all leases are lettings, and all lettings are leases, within the meaning of the word, but not at law. A 'lease' requires to be stamped, and delivered under seal, and when duly executed is legally known as a Deed of Lease, and is binding on the parties thereto. A lease may be either of land, or of land and building. A lease of land again, may be merely an agricultural lease, or it may be a building lease. If the latter, lessee covenants with the grantor or lessor as he is called, to erect a building or buildings on the land—usually within a specified period. The object of the covenant is to improve the security of the lease rent, for after the buildings have been erected, the rent is then said to be secured, for a breach of the covenant to pay the rent usually carries with it the right of the lessor to entry, and the taking of the rents and profits of the whole property. Conversely, before the buildings were erected, the rent would be said to be unsecured and would be known as an unsecured *ground rent.*

(2) ***Rack rent.*** It is the full rental value of a leasehold property unaffected by any legal restriction when put to the highest and best use. In other words, it is the maximum rent which the property is expected to fetch under normal market situation.

The term orginated with the idea that rent was in the nature of a forced payment, due to the particular circumstances of the payee, the landlord being likened to one of the extortioners in the Spanish 'Inquisition'—here the victim, the tenant, is supposed to be on the "rack"—the well-known instrument of torture—and the exorbitant rent extorted, under the necessity of the tenant, thus came to be known as a 'Rack Rent', but during late years a gradual change has taken place in the use of the term, and the meaning is now generally accepted as representing the maximum annual rent, and no opprobrium attaches to the title.

(3) ***Head rent.*** The question of head rent arises when a leasehold property is subjected to sub-lease permissible under the lease agreement. The rent reserved in the initial lease is known as the Head Rent which is payable by the lessee of the first category to the original lessor. When the lessee further sub-lets the property, the right acquired by the sub-lessee cannot go beyond the right acquired by the lessor in his capacity as the lessee of the first category.

(4) ***Improved rent.*** When a property is subject to sub-lease, the rent recoverable by way of sub-lease is usually in excess of the Head Rent and is known as the Improved Rent. When the Improved Rent represents the full rental value of the property, it amounts to Rack Rent. The difference between the Improved Rent and the Head Rent is known as the Profit Rent. It is measured by the amount the Improved Rent exceeds the Head Rent.

(5) ***Nominal rent.*** Sometimes the lease agreement provides for a token rent with the sole purpose of establishing the

relationship of lessor and lessee as between the transferor and the transferee. This transaction is resorted to by taking a Nominal Rent, say one rupee, payable by way of rent monthly or yearly, so that any other right of occupancy may be excluded by implication. It is often known as the *Acknowledgment Rent* as the purpose of the transaction is merely to acknowledge a nexus of tenancy.

(6) ***Virtual rent.*** The lessee sometimes carries on improvement of the leasehold property with the consent of the lessor, expressed or implied. The rental equivalent of such an improvement is added to the lease rent and constitutes the virtual rent. The contractual rent is thus virtually enhanced by the investment made by the lessee which otherwise could have earned him a monetary return.

The concept of virtual rent is more pronounced when a lump amount has been paid in advance by way of premium towards the consideration of the lease. In the cities and towns governed by rent control laws such advance payments are usually not permissible. But underhand payments are made that go by the name of '*salami*' or '*pugree*' which is now hardly a concealed fact as evident from the leasehold transactions documented at much less than the prevailing market rent in many dealings. The Virtual Rent in such cases comprises the actual rent as inflated by the interest which the *salami* or *pugree* would have otherwise carried with it.

(7) ***Standard rent.*** It is the rent fixed by the Rent Controller in accordance with the principles for determination of fair or standard rent as embodied in rent control law in operation in a particular State. It is also regarded as the *Fair Rent*. It sets a limit to the reasonable expectation of rent by the landlord or lessor and equates it to his legal expectation.

(8) ***Economic rent.*** It is the rent which would have been fixed as between the willing lessor and willing lessee for a leasehold property under market situation unhindered by any restrictions whatsoever and determined by the interplay of the free forces of demand and supply it sometimes approximates *Rack Rent*.

(9) ***Gross rent.*** It is the rent which includes all the outgoings like municipal taxes, expenses of repairs and maintenance, collection charges and management, allowance for vacancies

and bad debts, insurance etc. After payment of all the outgoings, the gross rent dwindles down to the *Net Rent*.

(10) ***Situation rent***. This is a rent which is obtainable, largely as the result of an exclusive situation of the property, such as, a prominent corner site, nearness to a railway station, or a central market and the like.

(11) ***Monopoly rent.*** This is a payment for the right to use land or building, or both, which are so situated as to have a value peculiarly inherent to that particular property, and is usually something considerably in excess of the true rental value.

(12) ***Intangible rent***. This rent is an equated instalment paid for elements of value, other than those of a physical nature, *e.g.* 'goodwill' of a business, sporting rights, etc. There is another such form which is represented by the rent paid for a property in excess of the sum equivalent to a reasonable interest on land and buildings individually. This intangible rent is sometimes called the 'builder's profit. It is a value which is put into the property, but which is not actually represented by the expenditure of any form of capital. A value due to the marriage of land and building.

(13) ***Charge rent.*** When a land is encumbered with rental dues which runs with the land, as for example, land charged with a distress, the same is known as charge rent which the owner can secure by issue of distraint on the land in the event of non-payment.

(14) ***Sitting rent.*** This is a rent reserved and paid *qua rent*, or it may be this rent plus the annual equivalent of a capital sum paid by way of premium; or again it may be the decapitalized value of a sum agreed to be spent by the lessee for repairs or improvements, plus the rent reserved under the lease.

The concept of reasonable rent

For the purpose of valuation, the rent must be reckoned as the reasonable rent which is maintainable over a considerable period of duration with no threat of being reduced in future. Sometimes we come across a chance rent at a very high rate or a grabbing rent when a person is too eager to take possession of a property. But such rent is not certainly reasonable rent.

The criteria of 'reasonableness' has been succinctly explained by the Supreme Court of India in the case of the *Corporation of Calcutta* v *Smt. Padma Devi.*[3] It was observed: "Whether a particular act is reasonable or not depends on the circumstances in a given situation. A bargain between a willing lessor and a willing lessee uninfluenced by any extraneous circumstances may afford a guiding test of reasonableness. An inflated or deflated rate of rent based upon fraud, emergency, relationship and such other considerations may take it out of bounds of reasonableness. Equally, it would be incongruous to consider fixation of rent beyond the limits fixed by a penal legislation as reasonable".

Outgoings in urban property

In calculating the net rent as stated above, the outgoings as already discussed shall have to be deducted. In case of valuation of urban rented properties, such outgoings may comprise the appropriate items out of the following:

(*i*) Municipal taxes;

(*ii*) expenses on repairs and maintenance to keep the rented property in a position to command the rent as fixed;

(*iii*) charges incurred for collection of rent and management of the property when the property let out is in the nature of an estate;

(*iv*) cost of services and amenities provided to the occupier like maintenance of security, lift, water-pump, fire extinguishing services, garage etc;

(*v*) allowances for vacancy and bad debts;

(*vi*) payment for insurances;

(*vii*) ground rent in case of leasehold properties;

(*viii*) service charges for furniture, fixture etc., if any.

The above list may not be exhaustive.

Principle of Communibus Annis

The concept of reasonable rent refers to a rent that prevails in an average year in accordance with the principle of

3 AIR 1962 SC 151.

Communibus Annis. It should not be taken as the rent for a particular year as it is not unlikely that in the relevant year, the rent might have been low due to war, riots, epidemic etc. or it might have been high when the owner had carried out structural repairs or the tenant might have agreed to pay increased rent for a short duration of stay for one or two years.

In case of properties which are valued on profit basis the exceptionally good profit received during a particular year should not be the basis for valuation, but the profit of an average year should be adopted.

Principle of Rebus Sic Stantibus

The concept of reasonable rent requires that a property should be valued in its existing condition without any attempt to speculate its future potentiality or contemplated improvements or a future change in user. A plot of land used for agricultural purpose cannot be valued on the basis of its possibility of being used for building purposes. Similarly, a mill or a factory which is closed down with no future possibility of regaining functioning should be valued not on the basis of a 'working mill', but as a warehouse for storage of machinery.

Ground rent

In all the above definitions of rent, we have presumed that the land has been built upon, or so to say, rent is for the land and building. But, there is also a parallel practice of leasing out the vacant land in which a person obtains the privilege of building on another man's land. Ground rent is the rent paid for the use of the bare land usually with a view to enable construction of building or structure by the lessee as an avenue of investment. When ground rents are realised by granting of lease of vacant land, they are normally a relatively small proportion of the full rental value thereof. The person owning the leasehold is entitled to the reversion of the property if the ground rent is not paid properly. To the lessor, it is thus in the nature of a secured income. It is an usual practice that ground rents are created for a very long term of years, for example, 99 years or even 999 years. This means that, unless there is a rent revision clause, the income is fixed in monetary terms for that period of time. So, the essential feature of a leasehold creating ground rent is a secured income for a long period of time. The transaction stands in close comparison with the essential characteristics of an investment in Government Security without a final date of repayment or with a final date of repayment of years ahead. Both these transactions entitle the holder to a fixed income for many years and both are secured in the sense that the Government is never expected to default nor the lessee for ground rent in view of the fact that the ground rent is much below the full rental value and nobody would like to risk a reversion by defaulting in payment. For this reason, secured ground rents and long-term Government securities are close substitutes for one another, and the yield on leasehold for ground rent would generally follow the yield on long-term Government securities.

If land is let on lease without any stipulation that the lessee shall erect a building on the land within a certain time, then the rent would be unsecured and there would not be any additional value to revert to the lessor at the termination of the lease. A typical example of this is land in towns and cities let for *bustee*-dwellers, here the owner will let on lease the land to a tenant who will erect huts on the land and then sublet the buildings room by room. The buildings being only of a temporary character and usually the property of the lessee, they offer very little security to the owner. In such cases the owner will charge the full rental value of the land, as the reversionary value is the same as the present value, other factors being constant.

The most common form of ground rent is for the lease to contain provisions that the lessee shall erect a building on the land within a stipulated period and costing not less than a certain sum of money. At the termination of the lease, the lessor will have the full ownership of the land and all buildings erected thereon. The fact that the reversionary value will contain something more than land value and the fact that if at any time during the period of the lease the lessee gets in arrears of rent, the lessor may obtain possession of the whole, gives security to the ground rent and is most commonly referred to as a secured ground rent. A secured ground rent is therefore rent from land secured by land and buildings.

Ground rent as income from investment

If the rent that is received by the lessee for land and buildings is the full annual value of the property, it is the rack rent. The security of a ground rent is usually known as a ground rent so many times secured. If the ground rent of a site is ₹ 250 per annum and the rack rent is ₹ 1,000 per annum, then the ground rent would be known as four times secured. It is very obvious that secured ground rents are one of the most attractive forms of investment.

It has already been explained that the nearest to gilt-edged securities is the return from secured ground rents. This form of investment is very popular, owing to the fact that investors with limited capital, can build a house without having to make any outlay for land. This form of investment is, therefore, very secure to the freeholder with the result that the return by way of rent is very low. If open land is let on lease with the usual building clauses then the rack rent is usually several times that of the ground rent and the amount to be forfeited in the event of a non-payment of rent, is so great that a lessee will make every effort to see that the ground rent is paid on the due date. This form of investment possesses most of the characteristics of the ideal investment; and there is little wonder that the yield by way of rent is only slightly higher than Government securities. Government securities are secured by the country's assets, whilst the ground rent is secured by the buildings erected on the land, and the reversionary value at the termination of the lease. It cannot be said that these two forms of investment are similarly secured, and a difference of one per cent is usually well justified.

The proposition cited above received judicial approval in the case of *Province of Bengal* v *Trustees for the Improvement of Calcutta.*[4] At page 836 of the Report Mr. Justice Mitter made the following observations:

> "The first item of evidence which is also supported by authoritative textbooks is that the best security is Government Security; the next best is the secured ground rent and the third best is the unsecured ground rent; that the fair return in the case of secured ground rent should be half to one above the return from Government Securities."

Unsecured ground rents are a very different proposition, there is no security of a building and the reversionary value

4 50 CWN 828.

at the termination of the lease will probably not be more than the present value whilst many factors may result in a diminution of the value. This form of investment usually yields about one per cent more than secured ground rents. In the case of *Government of Bombay* v *Merwanji Muncherji Cama,*[5] His Lordship observed:

> "In valuing ground by the capitalization of a ground rent, we do not think that in any case more than twenty years purchase should be allowed, and in the case of an unsecured rent we doubt whether more than 16⅔ years' purchase should be allowed."

This, of course, is a fact, and you cannot rely on facts in one case to support another. But it is interesting to note that Their Lordships took 5% for a secured ground rent, and 6% for an unsecured one, thereby making a difference of one per cent between the two forms of security. A well-secured ground rent in Calcutta would usually yield about 4.5% during the relevant time. Before any figure less than 4.5% is taken, the ground rent would have to be very well secured by a rack rent which in its turn if well secured, then the absolute maximum security may be as low as 4%. *Bustee* ground rents should never be valued at more than 20 years' purchase, and in most cases 16⅔ years' purchase would be fair. The class of tenant who will take land on lease for the erection of *bustee*-dwellings, is not usually a man of substance. His outlay on buildings is very small and his sub-tenants are of the lowest class. Non-payment of rent is a common occurrence, and the cost of eviction and the lengthy process which has to be followed to obtain vacant possession, makes unsecured ground rents in *bustee* land not a very desirable proposition, and it is for this reason 6% or 16⅔ years' purchase is considered as fair.

In the case of *Province of Bengal* v *Trustees for the Improvement of Calcutta,*[6] Their Lordships after considering the evidence as to rents of other lands and values thereof were of opinion that these rents could not be taken as basis as they were not fair rents and were also erratic. Their Lordships thereupon fell back upon principles enunciated by them and

5 (1908)10 Bom LR 10.
6 50 CWN 825.

held that the fair return from land at the relevant time would be 5% of its capital value. "At the relevant date the return from Government Securities was 3.64 per cent. Even if the cases before us are to be considered to be cases of secured ground rent, the fair percentage of return would be from 4.14 to 4.64 and with the owner's share of Municipal taxes added the percentage would be about 4.64 to 5.14. On this evidence the percentage given by the learned Arbitrator which is 5 per cent, the owner's share being included, does not seem to be excessive".

Ground rents generally when well secured, should be valued between 4.5% and 5% or from 23 to 20 years' purchase. Unsecured ground rents should never be valued at more than 20 years' purchase, and can be (according to the circumstances of the case), valued at 16⅔ years' purchase. Unsecured ground rents will, therefore, vary from 5 to 6%.

Legislative interventions affecting ground rent

It must be understood that there is no sacrosanct principle of valuation in this behalf. There are always circumstances particularly legislations which alter the situation in a big way. The related laws and circumstances must be taken into account in arriving at a just value of ground rent. As for example, The Calcutta Thika Tenancy (Acquisition and Regulation) Act 1981 has changed the scenario of tenancy rights arising out of lease of vacant land for earning ground rent. Before the passing of said Act, there were three parties to a *thika* tenancy—*viz.*, the landlord, the *thika* tenant and the *bharatia*. The landlord was the owner of the vacant land, which was leased out to the *thika* tenant on ground rent. The *thika* tenant constructed hut or structure thereon and became its owner while the *bharatia* was the occupant of the hut on payment of rent to the *thika* tenant. But in the wake of passing of the above Act in 1981, all rights comprised in a *thika* tenancy that belonged to the landlord, are now vested in the State Government and the *thika* tenant has become the virtual owner of the house property and the *bharatia,* a tenant under him within the meaning of the rent control law. There may be similar legislative interventions in other States too. All these factors have to be taken into consideration in the case of a valuation of a property qualified by a ground rent.

CHAPTER

10

Income Approach to Valuation—Capitalisation Techniques

Real property market forms part of the general investment market and as such it has to compete for its capital requirement with other avenues of investment. Other things being equal, an investor will usually employ his capital sum in such form of investment as will earn him the maximum return by way of income, whether such income is derivable as rent or as interest on capital or profit from the user of the premises by way of yield. Every investment means parting with liquidity which has to be compensated by way of return or income. Formerly, we had two major forms of investment, namely, Government securities and real estates; and as such, comparison was made only between the two in case of an investment proposition. Now the advancement of economic and the societal intercourse have thrown open multiple channels of investment; and newer forms of financial instruments as well as commercial papers come within the arena of consideration in the general investment market. Thus, it becomes necessary to compare property investment not only with the return obtainable from Government securities but also with the yield out of other sound investments. The purchaser of an interest in real property shall consider the alternatives open to him not only in the real property market but in the investment market in general. The yield an investor estimates will depend partly on his subjective valuation and partly on the objective factors in the market. Having made his subjective valuation, he will look to the market particularly in different alternatives to make a choice as to where to invest and how much to invest.

Criteria for investment

In income approach to valuation, it is inevitable to make a comparison of the return on investment with other available alternatives so that a just valuation can be arrived at. For the purpose of comparison it is necessary to understand the investment criteria that motivate an investor. Sometimes a few of such criteria may favour investment in real estate while a number of others may have the result of making an investor fugitive from it. But an overall estimation is the responsibility of the valuer. It is, therefore, necessary to look into the investment criteria that have developed over the time touching upon different aspects inherent in investment. The edifice of an income approach to valuation can be built up only upon these considerations detailed as follows:

(1) SECURITY OR SAFETY. It means reliability on the expectation of a net income during the investment period and also an assurance of getting back the original invested amount without loss or hazard.

(2) YIELD. It means return on the investment as distinguished from return of the investment. Usually the yield takes the form of interest on capital, or rent if the property is leased out, or profit if the investment is in the nature of a business. Other things remaining the same, it is the highest yield which is the most desirable expectation of an investment.

(3) LIQUIDITY. It means the ease with which an investment can be converted into liquid money. This is a factor in value. Common stocks and bonds are considered more desirable than real estate, as they can be bought and sold more readily and at less expense. Real estate demands huge sum of money to be sunk in block capital while stocks and shares enables disintegration of any block investment into small parcels of ownership for easy transfer from one hand to another.

(4) FREEDOM FROM MANAGEMENT BURDEN. Investments that require the least attention and minimum

supervision are usually the more attractive ones. Real estate generally requires considerably more management effort than financial investments like securities and are consequently less preferred from this angle of consideration.

(5) PROSPECTS FOR APPRECIATION. When purchasers of either corporate stocks or real estate can anticipate an increase in the value of investment, they are satisfied with lower current earnings. The real estate is often preferred for its prospect of capital appreciation despite low return as compared to other investments.

(6) BURDEN OF PROPERTY TAX. It reduces in attractiveness of real estate as compared to other investments that evade the tax net.

(7) SHELTER FROM INCOME TAXES. Appreciation of real estate is subject to tax on capital gains while many investments are sheltered from income tax and hence preferred.

(8) HYPOTHECATION. Using of investments as a security for a loan provides a practical substitute for investment liquidity. The relative stability of real estate makes in superior to many other investments in this respect.

(9) LEVERAGE. Return on investments can often be increased by what is known as 'trading upon the equity'. Advantage in equity results when property yield is higher than the cost of loan money. A similar leverage occurs when low equity is held on a highly depreciable property or property experiencing rapid market appreciation.

(10) CURRENT AND FUTURE RETURNS. Current earnings available to the owner are often reduced by the loan repayments and the situation often calls for determination of cash flow. In the typical real estate investment, the reversionary returns are the proceeds from the sale of the property. With financed property, in owner's reversion consists of the selling price less any amount owing on the loan. If any loan principal has been paid off, the owner's reversion will be a greater portion of the sales price. This increase is sometimes called *equity build up*. The owner reversion is also

increased by any value appreciation that occurs during the holding period. Tax on capital gains is another consideration that reduces the value of real estate.

(11) YIELD VERSUS RECAPTURE. Return on investment may take the form of interest, yield or capital gain. Return of investment may be viewed as recapture, recovery or amortization.

In real estate equity investments, recapture of investment capital is not always clearly defined as it is with loans. In loans, the portion of the payment that goes for repayment of the loan principal is reckoned as loan amortization. It is the return of the lenders investment capital. In real estate, recapture of the land value is usually unnecessary. Because, land is a permanent asset; when one land use is no longer in demand, another use usually takes its place. But what about improvements? Since they are subject to physical deterioration and obsolescence, it is argued that whatever part of the invested capital went for buildings and structures must be recaptured during their productive life. In the calculation of the investor, the recapture of such funds invested in assets with limited life can come out of the annual net operating income or the proceeds of a future sale. When investment recovery comes from the net income, recapture can be thought of either as an expense or as a surcharge on the capitalization rate for the investment. When capital recovery is to come from future sale proceeds then recapture is a part of the reversion.

How recapture is handled in valuation is a matter of capitalization technique used. It may be provided out of annual income or earmarked to be recovered from net resale proceeds. The capitalization rate is the connecting link between an income estimate and a value estimate. Therefore, selecting the appropriate rate is a critical part of the income approach.

Rates in vogue

Four distinct types of rates are accordingly in vogue in the investment market:

(i) INTEREST RATE. This is a rate of return on invested capital. The term is synonymous with yield rate and discount rate. It does not include any provision for the recapture of investment capital.

(ii) OVERALL CAPITALIZATION RATE. Theoretically, this allows for both return on investment and recaputre of investment capital, but the proportions are usually unknown.

(iii) RECAPTURE RATE. The rate at which invested funds are being returned to this investor is called the recapture rate.

(iv) COMPOSITE CAPITALIZATION RATE. It is a rate composed of interest and recapture with determined proportions and separately fixed amounts.

Security and appreciation of capital

Of all the various considerations that guide the investors, the foremost is the security of the capital. The next is income appreciation. It is possible that he will purchase any property, even when it has some disadvantages as compared with the alternatives, if he is compensated by a higher yield. But if he considers that the income from an investment in real property is absolutely secure, he will look only at the other investments where the income is similarly secured with a view to making comparison of yields. The other consideration may be the prospect of capital appreciation from the investment. Whether it is an investment in the real property market or in other spheres of investment, the prospect of growth will tend to lower the acceptable yield whilst increasing uncertainty or risk attaching to investment will tend to raise the expectation of yield in both the markets. The real estate is often preferred for its prospect of capital appreciation despite low return in rent as compared to other avenues of investment. But bleak prospect of income growth owing to rent restriction laws and hazards of management operate in the opposite direction. A balance-sheet arising out of positive and negative factors ultimately constitute the focal point for decision.

The differences in income appreciation reflected in the yield may also admit of fluctuations over time. There is a difference between variable income investments in the real property market and the general investment market. The exact effect of such difference on the yield will also depend on the date of income change and its expected size. The general rule is that, the nearer in time is the income variation, and the larger and the more certain is its content relative to the present income, the more will be its positive influence on the investor's choice. A contingency, distant in future, may not have appreciable effect.

Rate of interest

The investment market necessarily concerns itself with the rate of interest prevalent under the Government policy. An interest rate is a rate of return on capital. It is usually expressed as an annual percentage of the amount loaned or invested. The term 'interest rate' usually refers to debt capital and not equity capital. If the long-term rate of interest is rising as a matter of Government policy and at the same time yields in real property market remain the same then the investors in the real property market will be tempted to switch over to alternative investments. The wider the gap between rising interest rate in general and stagnating yields in the real property market, the greater may be the number of investors who would rush towards the alternatives for investment. The increase in financial resources in the alternative capital market will again act as a limiting factor in the earning of return by way of interest. Thus, it will be ultimately found that the limits will act as a market force in diverting financial resources from one market to the other till an equilibrium is reached between the two markets in a stable economy.

Valuer's role

The role of a Valuer has to be clearly defined in such circumstances. The Valuer does not attempt to speculate what will be the income to be derived over an existing interest in the future, but rather what the buyers and sellers believe the income to be and hence the value will be. It is the valuation in the estimation of the potential buyers and sellers which determine value and the function of the Valuer is to know how the various characteristics of real property can affect this value and how changes in social, economic and political conditions are likely to influence value.

Profit aspect

It is also necessary to focus on another aspect in the realm of income approach to real property valuation. When a property is leased out on rent, there are two parties—the owner who has to satisfy himself with the stipulated rent, and the occupier who utilises the property for profit or gain. Thus, the value of the property to the owner is quite different from the value of the property to the occupier. The owner can hardly look beyond the stipulated rent with variations permissible under the law or agreement. To him, the reasonable expectation of rent puts a limit to the value of the property in is hand. On the contrary, the value to the occupier encompasses the potentiality of yield the property is capable of.

It is possible that the property may be used for commercial purposes of diverse nature like shop, office, restaurant, cinema-hall, hotel, amusement centre etc. The value should be estimated on the profit approach. It has been appropriately quoted in *Corporation of Calcutta* v *Smt. Padma Devi,*[1] "the distinction between the occupier and the owner, in this connection, is of paramount importance. The occupation value of a property may be, and often is, distinct from the value to the owner. The distinction may probably be emphasised where an artificial statutory maximum is fixed and statutory restrictions prevent an owner from receiving from any tenant a greater amount of rent than the statutory maximum".

The profit approach to valuation is relevant also when the owner himself is the occupier and utilises the property for gain in non-residential uses like hotel, cinema hall, nursing home and the like.

Capitalisation rate

Capitalisation means the method used to convert future benefits to present value by discounting such future benefit at an appropriate rate of return. Capitalisation in perpetuity means capitalising the net future benefits assumed to last permanently or indefinitely. Capitalisation rate means a designated rate of return which converts net future benefits to capital value. Thus the capitalisation rate is a ratio of earning against price of a property.

We can estimate the value of income property by studying the economic relationship between income and value. Income capitalisation is the broad term used to describe this process.

1 AIR 1962 SC 151.

Capitalisation is the process of converting the net income of a property into its equivalent capital value. This recognises a principle known as the "time value of money". The capitalisation process reflects the time value of money by reducing or discounting future income to its present worth. The basis is this proverb—'a bird in hand is worth two in the bush'. The actual mathematics of discounting can be a direct or indirect calculation, depending on the capitalisation technique used.

Income capitalisation techniques are designed to consider three aspects of the future income, namely, its amount (quantity), its quality and its duration. For example, a large income from a risky investment can be less valuable than a smaller income from a very safe investment. Thus, certainty of income and the length of time it will last are as important as the amount of income the property produces.

Value results from the relationship between income and the rate of return. Thus the capitalisation rate generally is defined as a rate of return, or percentage used to convert income into its value equivalent. Such a rate directly or indirectly provides for a return on the investment which we call interest, as well as a return of the investment which we term as capital recovery. The most commonly used capitalisation rate is the overall rate which is calculated by dividing a property's net income by its sale price.

Capitalisation rates are key factors of evaluating the status of real estate markets for they determine the attractiveness of investing in property compared to other assets like bonds, shares, gilts etc. Capitalisation rates defined as the total initial operating income expressed as a proportion of the total market price, are seen to be an important indicator of market valuation yields. A capitalisation rate on a property, when compared with that of another property, should indicate such things as level of risk potential, appreciation in value and general market rates of returns. Thus capitalisation rate can be seen of as a risk-adjusted discount rate. The advantage of capitalisation rate compared with the internal rate of return is that it measures actual (*ex ante*) expectations while the internal rate of return measures the (*ex post*) result. Risk-adjusted discount rate depends on the potential annual variability of the initial yield compared with the investment's expected internal rate of return.

Determinants of capitalisation rate

Capitalisation rates are the results of the following inter-linked determinants:

(*a*) yields on gilts/risk-free assets;

(*b*) inflation rate/expected growth;

(*c*) risk premium;

(*d*) operating expenses.

Like any other assets that people buy and sell, real estate is valued on the basis of the present value of cash flows it is expected to bring to its owner over time.

By 'risk', we mean the uncertainty regarding the expected rate of return from investment. Risk premium can be seen as that part of the expected growth of the property which is not explained by the inflation rate. Thus, growth expectations are generally based on both inflation rates and built-in risk premiums. The measurement of the risk premium is determined by the difference between the actual return and the calculated risk-free capitalisation rate.

Multiplier factor for capitalisation

Regarding multiplier factor for capitalisation of net income from a property, we may refer to the observations of the Supreme Court in *Union of India* v *Shanta Devi*.[2]

The Supreme Court made the following remarks:

> "A perusal of the decisions referred to above and some others which have not been cited here shows that in India the multiplier which is adopted in determining the compensation by the capitalisation method has been 33$^1/_3$, 25, 20, 16$^2/_3$, 11 and 8. The number of years' purchase has gradually decreased as the prevailing rate of interest realisable from safe investments has gradually increased. The higher the rate of interest, the lower the number of years' purchase. This method of valuation involves capitalising the net income that the property can fairly be

2 AIR 1983 SC 1190.

expected to produce and the rate of capitalisation is the percentage of return on his investment that a willing buyer would expect from the property during the relevant period. It was once felt that the relevant rate of interest that should be taken into consideration was the interest which gilt-edged securities or Government bonds would normally fetch. The safety and liquidity of the investment in bonds were relied on as the twin factors to take the view that the interest on gilt-edged securities should alone be taken into consideration. This was at a time when there were not many avenues of safe investments and investment in private commercial concerns was not quite reliable. But from the year 1959-60 circumstances have gradually changed. There are many State Banks and nationalised banks in which deposits made are quite safe. Even in the share market we have many 'blue chips' which command stability and other attendant benefits, such as, the possibility of issue of bonus shares and rights shares and appreciation of the value of the shares themselves. They are attracting a lot of capital investment. A return of 10 per cent per annum on such safe investments is almost assured. Today nobody thinks of investing on land which would yield a net income of just 5 per cent to 6 per cent per annum. A higher return of the order of 10 per cent is usually anticipated. Even in the years 1962 and 1963 an investor in agricultural land expected annual net return of at least 8 per cent. It means that if the land yielded a net annual income of Rs. 8 a willing buyer of land would have paid for it Rs. 100; i.e. a little more than 12 times the annual net income. The multiplier for purposes of capitalisation would be about thirteen."

The Supreme Court in *Veerabhadrappa's* case analyses how gilt-edged securities bear upon the expected return from other investment opportunities like agricultural land etc.

The following observations of the Supreme Court in *Spl. Land Acquisition Officer* v *Veerabhadrappa*[3] regarding certain general considerations which investors of all types

3 (1985)154 ITR 190 (SC); AIR 1984 SC 774; (1984)2 SCC 120.

take into account, do reflect on motivations in the investment market:

> "There are certain general considerations which investors of all types take more or less into account: yield and appreciation possibilities, the ability readily to dispose of the investment, marketability and safety. Investments differ with respect to assurance of income and safety of principal. In the investment market, the quality of investment is evidenced by the yield or return that is produced in relation to market price; higher the quality, the lower the yield. Investors must take into account various types of risks associated with different investment mediums and, therefore, adopt a type of investment that is appropriate to their resources and particular investment objectives.
>
> "As already stated, some 20 to 30 years back; i.e. till the early 50s, it was taken as a settled rule of practice, that the capitalised value of agricultural lands should be arrived at 20 years' purchase having regard to the rate of interest on gilt-edged securities at five per cent. That rule no longer can be adhered to in view of the changed economic situation. In the early '70s, people believed that investment in housing was more secure than other forms of Government securities in respect of safety of investment. Investment in housing involves certainty of labour and effort such as maintenance, collection of rent, payment of taxes, etc. The rate of return expected, therefore, was 1.5% to 2.25% more than what was expected from gilt-edged securities. A person investing his capital in agricultural lands would ordinarily expect a return of 2% to 3% more than what he could obtain from gilt-edged securities or other forms of safe investment such as fixed deposits in scheduled banks, National Savings Certificates, Unit Trusts, etc. or on blue chips; i.e. on stocks and shares in the public or private sector which yield a much greater return".

In this context, we may also refer to the following cases—

(i) *CIT* v *Ashrafi Lal Gupta* (1983)142 ITR 766 (All).

(ii) *CIT* v *New Indian Construction Co.* (1908)123 ITR 68 (Del).

(iii) *CIT* v *Panchanan Das* (1976)116 ITR 272 (Cal).

(iv) *CIT* v *Radhey Mohan* (1985)153 ITR 399 (P&H).
(v) *CIT* v *Inderjit Singh* (1985)153 ITR 372 (P&H).
(vi) *Malabar Hill Co.-op Hsg. Society Ltd.* v *Union of India* (1990)184 ITR 216 (Bom).

It was generally held that tenanted property are to be valued by applying a multiplier to annual yield.

It is relevant here to point out that the rate of capitalisation as provided in Rule 3 of Schedule III of the Wealth Tax Act provides for a multiplier of 12.50 for freehold property and 10.00 for leasehold property. These two multipliers appear to be reasonable having regard to the present day conditions.

Equity yield rate

An *equity yield rate* is a rate of return on equity capital as distinguished from interest as a rate of return on debt capital. Accordingly, yield capitalisation is a method used to convert a series of future benefits to present value by discounting each such benefit at an appropriate yield rate. The equity yield rate incorporates both annual income and capital appreciation. Both interest rates and equity yield rates do reflect correct market conditions and investor's expectations. The source of information on investors' expectation are the investors themselves. Besides, real estate brokers, lending institutions and other market participants are also valuable sources.

Discounted cash flow and annuity

'Cash flow' technically means a measurement that equals cash receipt from an asset minus cash payment on its account over a given period of time. Discounted Cash Flow analysis is a method of evaluating an investment by estimating the present worth of future cash flows after taking into consideration the time value of money.

A discount rate is often derived on an internal rate of return. An internal rate of return is an annualised rate of return on capital that is generated or capable of being generated within an investment or portfolio over the period of ownership. One can also find the present value of each expectant payment of an annuity when there is a series of payments receivable out of the investment at regular intervals.

This approach is generally termed as *discounted cash flow* analysis and applicable to any projected income stream. It can also easily accommodate a projected resale or reversion at the end of the holding period of the investment or termination of an economic life, as the case may be. Discounted cash flow analysis is a programme in which the quantity, variability, timing and duration of a periodic incomes as well as ingredients of reversion are specified and discounted to a present value at a specified rate. *Annuity capitalisation* implicity provides return on investment as well as recovery of investment capital. In this respect, this is different from sinking fund which provides only for the return of the investment capital without reference to the income. As regards land, the annuity is in perpetuity as it extends into the future without termination. Returns to land are often conveniently treated as level perpetuity. But in reality, it may not always be so. Land values and returns thereon undergo historical appreciation. The converse is also true when the returns to land represent a declining income stream. Capitalisation rate can, however, be worked out on the basis of formula for converting an increasing or decreasing perpetuity to an equivalent level perpetuity. Alternatively, returns to land can be treated as an annuity, level or otherwise, with a reversion at the end of the holding period.

Residual capitalisation technique

The *residual capitalisation technique* divides a property into two physical components. It proceeds on the assumption that the value of one of the components is known by previous estimation, while the value of the residual component remains to be investigated into and estimated. There are three residual capitalisation techniques in practice so far as real estate is concerned,—the building residual technique, the land residual technique and the property residual technique.

The *building residual technique* assumes that the value of the land has been determined independently by capitalising the return thereon as level perpetuity or otherwise. Then the income attributed to the building can be converted to an equivalent level annuity or discounted cash flow. In *land residual technique*, on the other hand, the value of the building is known independently and the income to the land treated as residual. The income path of the land is projected into a series of return and this income capitalized into an estimate of land value. The building value is ultimately added back to obtain an estimate of total value. The *property residual technique* separates the income stream into typical net income from operations and a reversion. The reversion is assumed to be realised at the end of the property's economic life or at the end of the specified holding period. The technique consists in the estimation of typical net income, the discount rate, the income path of the property and the reversion. The value of the entire income stream plus reversion is worked out by the method of annuity capitalisation. A few examples of practical valuation are given elsewhere in this book in the chapter on Leasehold Interests.

Thus on an analysis of income approach, the techniques of valuation include the method of income capitalisation on the basis of discounted income rate, discounted yield rate, or discounted cash flow. The techniques may also involve loan-equity analysis and considerations of the building residual, land residual or property residual.

Valuation is an integrated process of all approaches

The discussions above would reveal that income approach is not an easy technique. It is a preferred valuation approach only when reliable income and expense data are available, along with well-supported income multipliers, overall rates and required rates of return on investment. In case of direct income capitalisation, it is necessary to adjudge at the beginning the gross income multipliers which express the ratio of market value to gross income. The process can be further refined by finding out the net income multiplier or the overall capitalisation rates. These multipliers and rates should always be extracted from actual income and sale-price data obtained from properties that have been recently transacted in the market. If such reliable data can be collected in a scientific manner, income multipliers and overall rates tend to provide reliable, consistent and well supported valuation. Thus, income approach is also not an independent system of valuation unrelated to other approaches. The analysis of cost and sales data is often an integral part of income capitalization approach and valuation process as a whole is composed of integrated, interrelated and inseparable techniques to produce a convincing market value of assets. It is interesting to refer to the observations in this context made by the Supreme Court in the case of *Special L.A.O., Devangere* v *P Veerabhadarappa.*[4]

"Market value" is the price which the property may fetch in the open market if sold by a willing seller unaffected by the special needs of a particular purchase. Where definite material is not forthcoming either in the shape of sales of similar lands in the neighbourhood at or about the date of notification under s. 4(1) or otherwise, the court has no other alternative but to fall back on the method of valuation by capitalisation. Normally, the method of capitalising the actual or immediately prospective profits or the rent of a number of years' purchase should not be resorted if there is evidence of comparable sales or other evidence for computation of the market value. The rule as to the number of years' purchase is not a theoretical or legal rule but depends upon economic factors such as the prevailing rate of interest in money investments. The return which an investor will expect from an investment will depend upon the characteristic of income as compared to that of idle security. The main features are—(*i*) security of the income, (*ii*) fluctuations, (*iii*) chances of increase, (*iv*) cost of collection.[5]

4 AIR 1984 SC 774; (1984)2 SCC 120.
5 *Special L.A.O., Devangere* v *P. Veerabhadarappa* AIR 1984 SC 774; (1984)2 SCC 120.

CHAPTER

11

Security—Year's Purchase—Interest

When a person buys a property he does it for two purposes:

(1) To obtain an annual income, *and*

(2) To obtain security for his capital.

If a property produces a net return of ₹ 1,000 per annum and a purchaser desires 6% return on his capital he will pay ₹ 1,000 × $\frac{100}{6}$ = ₹ 1,000 × 16.6 = ₹ 16,666 maximum for the property. If he pays more, he will not have a 6% return on his capital. If he pays less, he will obtain a greater return than 6%. The multiplier of the net rent to obtain capital value is known as the year's purchase. The security of the rent which a property produces is reflected in the year's purchase. For valuation purposes, therefore, security and year's purchase are the same. Security in the form of percentage yield of capital is found by $\frac{\text{Rent}}{\text{Capital}} \times 100$ and year's purchase is found by dividing capital by rent.

Year's purchase or security is a very arbitrary figure. One person may be satisfied with a 4% return on his capital whilst another person may want 7% return. For the purposes of valuation the valuer is mainly concerned with market value and the percentage he applies must be the equivalent to what a reasonable and prudent business man would expect.

Interest may be termed, the payment made for the use in production of capital. A valuer is mainly concerned with land and buildings, therefore, interest is the payment made for the use of land and buildings, and it takes the form of rent. People will pay rent for building because they receive something in return. It may be a place from where he will transact his business, or it may be for a place to live in with his family. He knows that if he did not give the owner some reward for his capital, these facilities would not be available to him. Interest or rent is not merely a payment for the use of capital, but it is a payment for the temporary control of capital in general. If a person invests in a highly speculative concern such as new old mining shares, he will expect a high rate of interest on the capital invested, because he knows that there is no safeguard that the capital will not depreciate, or that the interest paid will be maintained. Whereas, if he invested his money in Government Securities, he knows that his money is as safe as it possible can be, and that the interest will be maintained. His money having all the safe guards that can be expected, he will be satisfied with a moderate return on his capital. It is, therefore, that Government Securities form a datum line from which all other forms of investment are compared.

Interest can vary with supply and demand. In the money market interest will vary according to the amount of money available. At the present time (1997) Government Securities are yielding between 10.5% and 12.5%. There is a plentiful supply of money in the market at present, and if government had floated a loan at 8%, there would have still been buyers. It does not follow, however, that if Government Securities are the datum line that very low or very high rates of interest due to abnormal circumstances will act as the correct datum line for estimating property returns.

In order that the correct relationship between one security and another may be firmly established, it is well to study the essential characteristics of the ideal investment which are:

(1) An absolute safe security.

(2) Stability. Not liable to fluctuation and with every prospect of the income being maintained.

(3) The certainty of realisation.

(4) A fair return by way of interest on the capital invested.

(5) The income must be easy to collect.

(6) The capital must be easily realisable at any time.

Government securities possess most of the qualifications of the ideal security and it is for this reason that comparison is made with Government securities, when a value estimates the security applicable to a certain property, or to a certain income.

The return which an investor will expect from a property will depend on the characteristics of the income, as compared to that of the ideal security. He will consider if the income is secure; if there is the possibility of it being maintained for a considerable period; if the income is liable to fluctuate owing to the vagaries of trade; if the income is liable to increase or be augmented by any means; if the costs of collection are in a reasonable proportion to the amount collected; if the income can be collected easily and this will depend on the class of tenants likely to occupy the premises; if he wishes to realise his capital at any time, is there a reasonable chance of selling the property without making a loss. Having considered all these factors he will then consider what return would be reasonable and that figure will represent the security of the income from which the year's purchase can be easily calculated.

Every case will have to be considered on its merits, all the advantages and disadvantages must be carefully considered, and no person can lay down hard and fast rules which will govern every type of property. All that can be given are figures which will guide and help a valuer to arrive at a correct result, but much depends on the diligence and integrity of the valuer when doing his work. In *Heysham* v *Bholanath Mullick*,[1] the Chief Justice said:

> "We think on the evidence that 16 years' purchase would be a fair allowance. But in saying that 16 years' purchase is a fair allowance in this case, we must not be understood as laying that down as a rule in cases of this kind. Every case must depend on its own circumstances, on the evidence given and the nature of the property. The number of years' purchase which it would be right to allow with regard to one sort of property, might not be a fair allowance for other kinds of property, and we wish to guard ourselves against being understood as laying down any rule as to the number of years' purchase which ought to be allowed. On the

1 11 BLR 1873.

evidence, we think that 16 years' purchase is sufficient to allow in the present case".

This is a very sound judgment, and assessors and values would do well to remember that:

"Every case must be considered on its own circumstances on the evidence given and the nature of the property" and not to rely too much on what has been done in a previous case. There are many previous High Court cases which could be quoted, but each and every case has been considered on its merits and what is fair in one case would obviously be unfair in another and it would be an absurdity to apply a fixed percentage to a particular case because Judge had found that the same percentage was applicable in another case. High Court cases are excellent guides to principle, but must be rigidly avoided on questions of facts unless it can be proved beyond all reasonable doubt that the fact are identical in both cases.

Computation of capital value on the basis of year's purchase or security—examples

After the net rent has been ascertained, this will be multiplied by a sum which represents the security of the rent. The result will be the market value of the premises. The final step to be taken is set out in the judgment of *Raghunathdas* v *Secretary of State*.[2]

"It is common ground that in this case rental should be the basis of calculation, so that after arriving at the net rental what has to be ascertained is the rate of return investors in this class of property expect; for that will determine the number of year's purchase it is proper to allow, after giving due weight to any special conditions that may affect the property, advantageously or otherwise".

The following are a few typical examples of valuations by the rental method. The figures given are only to illustrate the answers and are not to be taken as representing each and every case. They are only a guide and a valuer must exercise his own judgment and discretion when submitting figures.

2 ILR (1905)29 Bom 506.

EXAMPLE 3. A plot of land measuring 3,600 sq. ft. or 5 kottah is let out for ₹ 9,750 per kottah (720 sq. ft.) per month on a 99 years' lease as ground rent. The lessee has erected a substantial building on the site. What is the value of the lessor's interest?

SOLUTION

Rent of land for 5 kottah @ ₹ 9,750 per kottah (720 sq. ft.) p.m. = ₹ 48,750 p.m.

Annual rent = ₹ 48,750 × 12 = ₹ 5,85,000

Years' purchase (Y.P) @ 5.5% p.a. on invested capital for perpetuity $= \frac{1}{i} = \frac{1}{0.055}$ =(×) 18.181818

[i = rate of interest]

Capitalised value of the lessor's interest on the material date of valuation (multiplying annual rent by Y.P.)

= ₹ 5,85,000 × 18.181818 = ₹ 1,06,36,364

say, ... ₹ 1,06,36,000

Assumptions:

(*i*) The leased ground rent is secured.

(*ii*) There is no rent revision clause.

(*iii*) The lease period is for 99 years only.

(*iv*) There is no stipulation for renewal of the lease.

EXAMPLE 4. What is the value of a plot of land 7 kottahs (5040 sq. ft.) in area in a poor locality let out for @ ₹ 4,300 per kottah (720 sq. ft.) per month?

The lessee has erected bustee dwelling on the land. The lessee is liable for property tax on the land and for the whole of the taxes on the structure thereon.

SOLUTION

Rent of land 7 kottah (5040 sq. ft.) @ ₹ 4,300 per kottah (720 sq. ft.)

(@ ₹ 4,300 x 7 kottah) = ₹ 30,100 p.m.

Gross Annual Rent = ₹ 30,100 × 12 = ₹ 3,61,200

Deduction @ 10% for servicing, maintenance etc. on G.A.R. = ₹ 36,120

Further deduction @ 10% on G.A.R. towards property tax	= ₹ 36,120	
Net annual rent (N.A.R.)	= ₹ 3,61,200 – 72,240	
		= ₹ 2,88,960
Years' Purchase (Y.P.) @ 6.5% for perpetuity	$= \frac{1}{i} = \frac{1}{0.065}$	= 15.384615

[i = rate of return on invested capital]

Value to the lessor	= N.A.R. x Y.P.	
	= ₹ 2,88,960 x 15.384615	=₹ 44,45,538
	say	₹ 44,46,000

Assumptions:

(*i*) This is an unsecured ground rent but the lessee's interest is secured by law.

(*ii*) The rent is secured only by the structures.

(*iii*) The Years Purchase of 15.38 is sufficient as security.

(*iv*) Property tax is 10% on vacant land.

EXAMPLE 5. **What is the value of premises consisting of building and land let out for ₹ 5,000 per month inclusive of municipal taxes? The house is about 15 years' old and the rent is fair and maintainable under the relevant rent laws.**

SOLUTION

Gross Annual Rent (G.A.R.)	= ₹ 5,000 × 12 =	₹ 60,000
Less: Outgoings (per annum)		
(*i*) Municipal taxes @ 10% on annual value (Assuming A.V. = ₹ 54,000)	= ₹ 5,400	
(*ii*) Repairs & maintenance @ 10% on G.A.R.	= ₹ 6,000	
(*iii*) Collections/vacancies/bad debts/insurance & contingencies/ service charges etc. @ 10% on G.A.R.	= ₹ 6,000	(–) ₹ 17,400
Net Annual Rent		= ₹ 42,600

Years' Purchase (Y.P.) @ 7.5%

for perpetuity $= \frac{1}{i} = \frac{1}{0.075} = 13.34$

Value = ₹ 42,600 x 13.34 = ₹ 5,68, 284

Say, ... ₹ 5,68,000

Assumptions:

(*i*) Outgoings as per relevant municipal law/rent law.

(*ii*) Value to the owners and not to the occupier.

EXAMPLE 6. What is the value of premises consisting of building and land let out for ₹ 5,000 per month inclusive of taxes? The building is in a poor condition and the balance economic life cannot be more than 30 years. The rent may be maintained provided the repairs are constantly executed.

SOLUTION

Rent per month = ₹ 5,000

Gross Annual Rent (G.A.R.) = ₹ 5,000 × 12 = ₹ 60,000

Less: Outgoings (per annum)

(*i*) Rates ... @ 10% on Annual Value [where A.V.= G.A.R. less statutory deduction @ 10% for repairs, maintenance etc.
= ₹ 60,000 – ₹ 6,000
= ₹ 54,000]
= 0.10 x ₹ 54,000 = ₹ 5,400

(*ii*) Special repairs & maintenance @ 15% on G.A.R. the building being in poor condition = ₹ 9,000

(*iii*) Collections charges/Bad Debts/Vacancies & insurance service charges etc. @10% on G.A.R. = ₹ 6,000 (–) ₹ 20,400

Estimate cost of rebuilding as on the date of valuation = ₹ 2,30,000

1 year's rent to be reserved for dislocation during rebuilding (+) ₹ 60,000

= ₹ 2,90,000

Annual Sinking Fund (A.S.F.) to produce Re. 1 in 30 years @ 3% $= \frac{r}{(1+r)^n - 1}$

$= \frac{0.03}{(1+0.03)^{30} - 1}$

$= 0.021 \times 2{,}90{,}000$

= ₹ 6,090 p.a.

Total deduction (₹ 20,400 + 6,090) =(-) ₹ 26,490

Net Annual Rent (N.A.R.) = ₹ 60,000 – ₹ 26,490 = ₹ 33,510

Year's purchase (Y.P.) say @ 8.5% security for perpetuity $= \frac{1}{i} = \frac{1}{0.085}$ =(x) 11.764706

Value ∴ = ₹ 3,94,235

Say ...... ₹ 3,94,000

Assumptions:

(*i*) Value to the owner on income capitalisation.

(*ii*) Balance economic life for 30 years can be supported only by incurring maintenance expenditure @ 25% of G.A.R.

When you compare this valuation with Example 5, you may say that the value for Example 6 must be confusing. This requires clarification. Assume both the sites have an area of 7,200 sq. ft. of land, value of which is ₹35,000 per 720 sq. ft. and both buildings can be estimated at ₹2,30,000 as prime cost (historical cost).

Then, in *Example 5* —

Land 7,200 sq. ft. @ ₹ 35,000 per 720 sq. ft. = ₹ 3,50,000

Building Prime cost ₹ 2,30,000

Depreciation @ 10% ₹ 23,000

Depreciated value = ₹ 2,07,000

Land and Building (Capital value) Method
= ₹ 3,50,000 + ₹ 2,07,000 = ₹ 5,57,000

According to Rental Method in *Example 5* the value has been estimated at = ₹ 5,68,000

Thus the valuation by the Rental Method practically coincides with that of the Land and Building Method and therefore, the security and deductions taken in *Example 5* are justified.

It is obvious in *Example 6* that the building cannot be treated as a normal standing structure. Old buildings depreciate very rapidly and although it states that the balance economic life cannot be more than 30 years, it may be much less. If the building was estimated for salvage value, it would be—

Land 7,200 sq. ft @ 35,000 per 720 sq. ft.		= ₹ 3,50,000
Old materials valued for salvage purposes @ 15% on Prime Cost of the building	= 0.15 × 2,30,000	
Salvage value		= ₹ 34,500
Therefore, Land + Salvage value		= ₹ 3,84,500

On the rental method estimation the value is ₹ 3,94,000 taking security at 8.5% (*vide Example* 6). This security is on the low side. The rent of ₹ 5,000 cannot be maintained throughout the whole life of the building, especially for such an old building. In order to command the same rent throughout, 8¾% would probably be nearer the correct figure as security.

Because, at 8¾% the value would be ₹ 3,82,971 against the above estimated value of ₹ 3,84,500 for land and salvage value of the building, which is a nearer approximation.

To re-state how the figures at ₹ 3,82,971 has been arrived at, it may be shown as follows:

$$\text{Y.P.} = \frac{1}{i} = \frac{1}{0.875} = 11.428571$$

$$\text{Net annual rent} = \frac{\text{Capitalvalue}}{\text{Y.P.}} = \frac{₹\,3,82,971}{11.428571} = ₹\ 33,510$$

Therefore, capitalised value = 11.428571 × 33,510 = ₹ 3,82,971

This reveals that cross-checking by the capital value method has brought the estimate nearest to the existing situation.

It is interesting to note that in *Example 5* the rental method gives the nearest approximation while in *Example 6*, the capital value method gives the better approximation. Thus cross-checking is a very desirable exercise in valuation.

EXAMPLE 7. What is the value of a 5-storey block of shops, offices and godowns let out for ₹ 3,70,000 per month inclusive of

municipal taxes in a busy shopping centre? There are 48 tenants. The building is in a good state of repair and is 22 years old.

SOLUTION

Gross Annual Rent (G.A.R.) = @ ₹ 3,70,000 p.m. × 12= ₹		44,40,000
Annual value (A.V.)	= ₹ 44,40,000	
Less: (*deductions* for maintenance/ repairs reckoned as 10% of G.A.R.)	₹ 4,44,000	
	= ₹ 39,96,000	
Less: *Outgoings*		
(*i*) Rates assuming @ 30% on A.V. = ₹ 39,96,000 x 0.30	= ₹11,98,800	
(*ii*) Repairs & maintenance @ 10% on G.A.R. = ₹ 44,40,000 x 0.10	= ₹ 4,44,000	
(*iii*) Vacancies and bad debts @ 2%on G.A.R.	= ₹ 88,800	
(*iv*) Collection charges @ 2% on G.A.R.	= ₹ 88,800	
(*v*) Building Insurances @ 1% on G.A.R.	= ₹ 44,400	
(*vi*) Lift, Contingencies & other services @ 3.5% on G.A.R.	= ₹ 1,55,400	
Total outgoings come to		= (–)₹ 20,20,200
Net Annual Rent (N.A.R.)		= ₹ 24,19,800
Multiplying by Year's purchase (Y.P.) @ 8.5% yield on invested capital for perpetuity	$= \frac{1}{i} = \frac{1}{0.085}$	(×) 11.764706
Capitalised value to the owner (freeholder)		= ₹2,84,68,235

Assumptions in calculation

1. The multi-tenanted building has been let out in parcels to statutory tenants governed by Rent Control Act.
2. Repairs and maintenance calculated at not less than @ 15% owing to large number of tenants occupying for commercial use.
3. This being a multi-tenanted premises, charges for collection, insurance, lift etc. reckoned on a reasonable basis.

4. The premises is situated in a good location.
5. There is justification for Y.P. @ 8.5% after considering alternative investment opportunities as follows:
   (*a*) Yield of gilt-edged security varies between 10.5% and 11.5%
   (*b*) Yield of securities for 'blue chips' companies varies between 12.5% and 14.5%.
   (*c*) Potential of the property exists for capital appreciation and income appreciation at a low but steady rate on a continued basis being a multi-tenanted premises.
6. There may be surcharge on property tax levied by municipal authorities for non-residential user of premises but the same has not been taken into account separately; instead, a consolidated rate of 30% on annual value has been assumed.

EXAMPLE 8. What is the value of a 4-storey block of shops and flat in a good locality? Gross Rent, when fully occupied ₹ 1,85,000 per month inclusive of taxes. The building is in excellent repair. Rents are likely to be maintained.

SOLUTION

Gross Rent per month = ₹ 1,85,000

Gross Annual Rent (G.A.R.) = ₹ 1,85,000 x 12 = ₹ 22,20,000

Outgoings—

Lift man, Pump Man, Sweeper } @ 4.5% on G.A.R. = ₹ 99,900

Maintenance of Lift @ 1% on G.A.R. = ₹ 22,200

Electricity (To be borne by the occupiers @ 1% on G.A.R.) for co. .... areas = ₹ 22,200

Municipal Property Taxes (p.a.): Assuming 30% on A.V. or ₹ 19,98,000 x 0.30 = ₹ 5,99,400

Cost of collection @½% of G.A.R. = ₹ 11,100

Insurance @ 1% on G.A.R.	= ₹ 22,200	
Repairs @ 5% on G.A.R. (External repairs to be borne by the owner and internal repairs to be borne by the tenant occupier).	= ₹ 1,11,000	
Vacancies, bad debts & Contingencies	= Nil	
		(–) ₹ 8,88,000
Net Annual Rent (N.A.R.)		= ₹ 13,32,000
Multiplying by Year's Purchase (Y.P.) @ 7.5% security for perpetuity	$= \frac{1}{i} = \frac{1}{0.075}$	= (×) 13.34
Capitalised Value of the Lessor's (freeholders) interest as on date of valuation		= ₹ 1,77,68,880

These are figures taken from an actual valuation as a typical example. The figures for servants, lift, electricity, collection and insurance are actual expenses as prevailed at that time. The actual taxes paid represent an annual value at the time of inspection. Repairs are based on an average of the past 5 years and represent 5%. The cost of collection was 0.5% and vacancies and bad debts were nil. The total outgoings were just 46 per cent. The property was sold 3 months after this valuation was made for ₹ 1,77,68,880 which represents a security of 7.5%.

In making many valuations it is customary to check one method by another method. The Rental Method of valuation should be checked by the Land and Building Method of valuation whenever possible. If you try to analyse a sale of land and buildings, it is rare for the valuer to obtain figures of rent but he can measure and value the building and can check the sale price by the Land and Building Method.

THE CONSTRUCTION, APPLICATION AND USE OF VALUATION TABLES

The valuation of leasehold interests by computing rental value on the basis of year's purchase involves many mathematical calculations dealing with compound interest and to assist valuers to arrive at a speedy and accurate conclusion, valuation tables have been compiled at the end of the book. These tables are in the form of ready reckoners and are very easy to use, but so that a valuer will know which table to use and why, it is necessary for him to have a thorough knowledge of the construction of these tables.

The various tables in use are:

(1) Present value of Re. 1 per annum.

(2) Present value of Re. 1 per annum after a given number of years.

(3) Present value of Re. 1.

(4) Amount of Re. 1 per annum.

(5) Amount of Re. 1 and

(6) Annual Sinking Fund.

Parry's Tables

It should be emphasised that all the tables which the valuer uses are based on the principle of compound interest. All references to Parry's Tables hereafter should be construed as references to Parry's Valuation Tables, revised and enlarged by Philip H. White (1958), London, The Estates Gazette Ltd., 47, Museum Street, W.C. 1, London, U.K. (Eighth Edition).

Amount of one Rupee in a given number of years n, at rate of interest of i, per annum on one Rupee

The object is to find the amount to which Re. 1 will accumulate at compound interest in a given time. The amount at the end of one year will be (1+i). The amount at the end of 2 years will be $i(1+i) + (1+i) = (1+i)^2$, and so on. By the same reasoning the amount at the end of n years will be $(1+i)^n$ ...... **(1)**. Hence the total interest paid on Re. 1 in n years will be $(1+i)^n - 1$. For various i and n, the computed 'amount of one rupee' are available in Parry's Valuation Tables, p. 83-100.

EXAMPLE 9. What is the amount of Re. 1 at 5% in 20 years?

SOLUTION

By Equation 1, Amount $= (1 + 0.05)^{20}$

or, Log Amount $= 20 \times 0.02119 = 0.4238$

or, Amount $= 2.6534$ (Page 90 of Parry's).

PART I

Construction of Valuation Tables

Year's Purchase in Perpetuity.

$$\text{Y.P. in Perpetuity} = \frac{100}{\text{Rate per cent}}$$

EXAMPLE 10. What is the year's purchase in perpetuity of 5%?

$$\text{Y.P.} = \frac{100}{5}$$

$$\text{Y.P.} = 20$$

EXAMPLE 11.

P = Principal.

i = Interest on ₹ 1 for one year.

n = Number of years.

At the end of the first year the amount will have increased by the amount of interest. By the end of the second year the amount will have increased by the interest on the capital and the interest for the first year. This may be set out as follows:

End of 1st year $1 = 1+i$

End of 2nd year $1 = (1+i)(1+i) = (1+i)^2$

Amount of Re. 1 in n years $= (1+i)^n$

EXAMPLE 12. What is the amount of Re. 1 at 3 per cent in 30 years?

SOLUTION

Amount $= (1+.03)^{30}$

log 1.03 $= .0128372$

$\times\ 30$

$= .3851160$

$= 2.427258$ (Parry's Valuation Tables)

The present value of Re. 1

To find the amount which must be invested now in order to accumulate to Re. 1 at the end of n years at the rate of interest, i, (compound interest). If the amount is $(1+i)^n$ at the end of n years the present value is Re. 1. Hence, if the amount is Re. 1 at the end of n years the present value is .... (2).

For present value of Re. 1 table refer pp. 51-66 of Parry's valuation tables.

In other words, the present value of Re. 1 is the present value of the amount of Re. 1 at the end of n years.

The amount of Re. 1 is $(1+i)^n$

Re. 1 is the P.V. of $(1+i)^n$ at the end of n years.

That means an amount of x if invested now will become Re. 1 after n years

Rupees x will become at the end of 1st year $= x + xi = x(1 + i)$

[i = interest of Re. 1 for one year]

Rupees x will become at the end of 2nd year $= x(1+i)(1+i) = x(1+i)^2$

Similarly,

Rupees x will become at the end of nth year $= x(1+i)^n$

As per assumption, $x(1+i)^n$ = Re. 1 or $x = \dfrac{1}{(1+i)^n}$

The following illustrations may explain the equation

What is the present value of Re. 1 in 25 years at 3 per cent?

$$\text{P.V.} = \frac{1}{(1+.03)^{25}} = \frac{1}{2.093774} = 0.477606$$ (*See* Parry's Valuation Tables)

What sum invested now will at 5 per cent compound interest accumulate to Re. 1 in six years time?

Answer. From Equation (2),

$$\text{P.V.} = \frac{1}{(1+i)^n}$$

or, P.V. × Amount of Re. 1 in 6 years @ 5% = Re. 1

$$\text{or, P.V.} = \frac{1}{(1+0.05)^6}$$

or, P.V. = 0.7462154

EXAMPLE 13. What is the present value (P.V.) of a building site which should be ripe for development in 4 years' time, when its value is expected to be ₹ 20,000? Interest to be taken at 5 per cent.

SOLUTION

Value in 4 years @ 5% = ₹ 20,000

P.V. of Re. 1 in 4 years @ 5% is $\frac{1}{(1+.05)^4}$ = 0.8227

P.V. = ₹ 20,000 × 0.8227 = ₹ 16,454

The amount of Re. 1 per annum

These tables are calculated on the basis that Re. 1 will be invested at the end of each year. The figure can be obtained by adding to Re. 1 all the figures given in the table "Amount of Re. 1" up and including one year less than the given term.

Amount of Re. 1 per annum in 1 year at 5% = 1

" " 1 " " 2 years at 5% = 1.05+1

" " 1 " " 3 years at 5% = $(1.05)^2$+1.05+1

and so on

Or

Amount of Re. 1 p.a. $= 1 + (1+i) + (1+i)^2 + ... + (1+i)^{n-1}$ .... (1)

(Amount of Re. 1 p.a.) × $(1+i) = (1+i) + (1+i)^2 + ... + (1+i)^n$ .... (2)

Number (2) – (1)

Or, Amount of Re. 1 p.a. x $(1+i)$ – (Amount of Re. 1 p.a.)

$= \{(1+i) + (1+i)^2 + ... + (1+i)^n\} - \{1 + (1+i) + (1+i)^2 + ... + (1+i)^{n-1}\}$

$= (1+i)^n - 1$

or, Amount of Re. 1 p.a. $\{(1+i) - 1\} = (1+i)^n - 1$

or, Amount of Re. 1 p.a. $(1 + i - 1) = (1+i)^n - 1$

or, Amount of Re. 1 p.a. $= \frac{(1+i)^n - 1}{i}$

To put it in a different way, the amount to which Re. 1 p.a. invested at the end of each year will accumulate in a given time, n years, at the rate of interest i, per annum on each rupee (compound interest) is $\frac{(1+i)^n - 1}{i}$.

This table is calculated on the basis that Re. 1 will be invested at the end of each year. Hence the first payment of Re. 1 made at the end of the first year will accumulate for (n–1) years if the period of accumulation is n years.

Accordingly, the second payment will accumulate for (n–2) years and so on year by year. It is also readily seen that the payment made at the end of (n–1) years will accumulate for one year and obviously the payment made at the end of n years will not accumulate any interest since it will be withdrawn as soon as it is deposited.

From Equation (1), we may write that the amount to which the first payment of Re. 1 will accumulate $(1+i)^{n-1}$, the second $(1+i)^{n-2}$ and so on.

Let the amount of Re. 1 per annum in n years be A

then $A = (1+i)^{n-1} + (1+i)^{n-2} + \ldots\ldots\ldots\ldots + (1+i)^2 + (1+i) + 1$

or, more conveniently $A = 1 + (1+i) + (1+i)^2 + \ldots + (1+i)^{n-2} + (1+i)^{n-1}$

The above terms form a geometrical progression for which the summation is

$$A = \frac{(1+i)^n - 1}{(1+i) - 1} = \frac{(1+i)^n - 1}{i} \ldots\ldots\ldots\ldots\ldots\ldots\ldots (3)$$

For "Amount of Re. 1 per annum Table", refer Parry's Valuation Tables, pp. 103 to 117.

If we have to find out the amount of Re. 1 p.a. for 20 years @ 5 per cent

from Equation (3), $A = \frac{(1+0.05)^{20} - 1}{0.05} = 33.06594$

EXAMPLE 14. What is the amount of Re. 1 per annum for 20 years @ 5 per cent?

SOLUTION

$$\text{Amount} = \frac{(1+0.05)^{20} - 1}{0.05} = \frac{(1.05)^{20} - 1}{0.05}$$

$$= \frac{2.653297 - 1}{.05} = \frac{1.653297}{.05}$$

$$= 33.06594 \quad \ldots\ldots\ldots\ldots\ldots\ldots \textit{(See Parry's Tables)}$$

Annual Sinking Fund

This is the amount of Re. 1 per annum again, the figure at the end of n years is 1 and the annual amount to be invested is required.

If the amount of Re. 1 per annum in n years is $\frac{(1+i)^n - 1}{i}$

The Annual Sinking Fund to provide

$$\text{Re. 1 in n years} = \frac{1}{\text{Amount of Re. 1 per annum in n years}}$$

$$= \frac{1}{\frac{(1+i)^n - 1}{i}} = \frac{i}{(1+i)^n - 1}$$

Annual Sinking Fund Table

To find the sum which, if invested at the end of each year will accumulate at compound interest to Re. 1 in a given number of years, let, the annual sinking fund be S, the period n years and the rate of compound interest i, per annum per rupee.

From the reasoning presented earlier in **Equation (3)** we may write that the first annual instalment will accumulate to $S(1+i)^{n-1}$; the second to $S(1+i)^{n-2}$ and so on year by year.

$$\text{Hence, } 1 = S(1+i)^{n-1} + S(1+i)^{n-2} + \ldots\ldots\ldots\ldots + S(1+i) + S$$

$$\text{or, } 1 = S\,[1 + (1+i) + (1+i)^2 + \ldots\ldots\ldots\ldots + (1+i)^{n-2} + (1+i)^{n-1}]$$

$$\text{Hence, } S = \frac{i}{(1+i)^n - 1} \quad \ldots\ldots\ldots\ldots\ldots\ldots\ldots\ldots\ldots\ldots\ldots\ldots \text{(4)}$$

It may be observed that S in Equation (4) is exactly the reciprocal of A in Equation (3). It should be noted that investment for sinking fund also takes place at the end of each year. This is convenient in dealing with income from real property, which is commonly assumed to be receivable yearly at the end of each year. The sinking fund table is of direct use to the valuer when it is required to know what sum ought to be set aside annually out of income in order to meet some capital expenses accruing liabilities, and thereby avoid the embarrassment of having to meet the whole of a considerable expenses out of a single year's income. Although often neglected in practice, it enables the owner to see precisely how much of the annual return from the property he can afford to treat as a spendable income. The rate of interest return on annual deposits on sinking fund usually varies from 2 to 3.5 per cent. However, if the sum to be set aside annually is considerable, it is possible that an owner may find opportunity for the accumulation of it in his business, or in some other investment at a higher rate of interest.

EXAMPLE 15. What annual sinking fund at 3.5 per cent must be invested to produce Re. 1 at the end of 30 years?

SOLUTION

$$\text{A.S.F.} = \frac{i}{(1+i)^n - 1} = \frac{.035}{(1+.035)^{30} - 1}$$

$$= \frac{.035}{(1.035)^{30} - 1} = \frac{.035}{2.806793 - 1}$$

$$= \frac{.035}{1.806793}$$

$$= .0193714 \quad \textit{(See Parry's Valuation Tables)}$$

The annual sinking fund is also found by dividing 1 by the amount of Re. 1 per annum in n years.

$$= \frac{1}{\text{Amount of Re. 1 per annum in n years}}$$

Present Value of Re. 1 per annum

These tables are divided into 2 classes:

(*a*) Single Rate per cent tables.

(*b*) Dual Rate per cent tables.

The single rate per cent tables give at a glance the present value of Re. 1 per annum at a given rate per cent interest. It is assumed that the invested capital can be redeemed by paying into sinking fund an annual amount which will accumulate at compound interest at the same rate per cent as that at which interest is required on Capital.

The formula to find the year's purchase of Re. 1 per annum for a given number of years is as follows:

$$\text{Y.P. for n years} = \frac{1}{(1+i)} + \frac{1}{(1+i)^2} + \ldots\ldots + \frac{1}{(1+i)^n}$$

Present Value of Re. 1 per annum or Year's Purchase Table (Single Rate) where income is receivable for limited period

It represents the present value of a series of future payments of Re. 1 per annum receivable at the end of each year for a given term of years allowing compound interest.

As already shown in Equation (2) the present value of the first instalment of the income receivable at the end of the 1st year is $\frac{1}{(1+i)}$. That of the second instalment receivable at the end of 2nd year is $\frac{1}{(1+i)^2}$, the present value of the third instalment receivable at the end of the 3rd year is , and so on. Let the present value be V and the term of years n, then

$$V = \frac{1}{(1+i)} + \frac{1}{(1+i)^2} + \frac{1}{(1+i)^3} + \ldots\ldots + \frac{1}{(1+i)^{n-1}} = \frac{1}{(1+i)^n}$$

This is a geometrical progression and the summation is

$$V = \frac{1}{(1+i)}\left[\frac{1-\frac{1}{(1+i)^n}}{i-\frac{1}{(1+i)}}\right] \text{ or } V = \frac{1-\frac{1}{(1+i)^n}}{i} \quad \ldots\ldots\ldots\ldots\ldots\ldots\ldots (5)$$

In the above expression (5), V is nothing but the years' purchase (y.p.) single rate, where the income is receivable for a limited period of years in future.

It must be recognised that the **Equation (5)** has two-fold aspects:

(1) As shown above V represents the present value of a series of future payments of Re. 1 per annum receivable at the end of each year for a period of n years allowing compound interest.

(2) V also represents the sum upon which an income of Re. 1 per annum will yield simple interest at i per annum on the capital V and will provide a sinking fund at i allowing compound interest to accumulate to V at the end of n years as shown below.

Proof

The amount of simple interest per annum on V is V.i., and the sinking fund per annum to replace, i.e. to accumulate V in n years is $\frac{V.i}{(1+i)^n - 1}$ on the basis of the Equation (4) presented earlier. As per (2) above, these together should be equal to the income of Re. 1 p.a.

Hence, we may write: $$1 = V.i + \frac{V.i}{(1+i)^n - 1}$$

$$\text{or, } 1 = V.i\left[1 + \frac{1}{(1+i)^n - 1}\right] = V.i\left[\frac{(1+i)^n}{(1+i)^n - 1}\right]$$

$$\text{or, } V = \frac{(1+i)^n - 1}{i(1+i)^n} \text{ or } V = \frac{1-\frac{1}{(1+i)^n}}{i} \quad \ldots\ldots\ldots\ldots\ldots\ldots\ldots\ldots (5a)$$

It is readily seen that the Equations (5) and (5a) are same, hence the statement at (2) made earlier is also true. So long, while deriving the expression for years' purchase when the income is receivable for certain period of years in future we have made allowance for accumulation of Sinking Fund at the same rate as that at which interest on capital is required and therefore the figure of years' purchase is said to be on a 'single rate' basis when computed by Equation (5). In Parry's Table 'single rate' figures of years' purchase are given in pp. 27 to 35.

It has already been pointed out that the rate of interest on sinking fund policy is usually very low. Hence where interest on capital is expected at comparatively high rates, for instance, @ 5% or even more, it is desirable to adjust the figures of years' purchase so as to allow for the accumulation of sinking fund at a different and lower rate to that at which interest on capital is assumed; figures of years' purchase calculated by allowing different interest rates on sinking fund and capital are said to be 'dual rate' figures as discussed later on.

In the context of the previous discussions it is clear that when the income from some capital invested is receivable for a limited number of years only (such a situation may frequently occur in practice the common example being the interest of the lessee on a leasehold property) the calculation of years' purchase has become slightly complicated by the fact that not only will the investor expect interest on his money throughout the term at the given rate per cent, but he ought also to be setting aside annually out of income the annual sinking fund (set aside at the end of each year during the term) which at compound interest will be sufficient by the end of the term to replace the capital invested. The mathematical aspects of above have already been discussed earlier and presented in Equation (5).

It is, however, interesting to point out that, V as in Equation (5) may be expressed in another form. We have already written that—

$$1 = V.i + \frac{V.i}{(1+i)^n - 1}$$

Again from Equation (4),

$$S = \frac{1}{(1+i)^n - 1}$$

where S is the annual sinking fund to replace Re. 1 at the end of the given term of n years allowing compound interest @ i per rupee per annum.

Hence, we may write $1 = V(i + S)$ or, $V = \frac{1}{(i+S)}$ .... (5b)

EXAMPLE 16. What is the year's purchase at 5 per cent (single rate) for 3 years?

SOLUTION

$$Y.P. = \frac{1}{(1+.05)} + \frac{1}{(1+.05)^2} = \frac{1}{(1+.05)^3}$$

$$= \frac{1}{(1.05)} + \frac{1}{1.05\times1.05} = \frac{1}{1.05\times1.05\times1.05}$$

$$= 0.952381 + 0.907029 + 0.863837$$

$$= 2.723247$$

In accordance with Parry's Tables page 14 the year's purchase is given as 2.723.

If a large number of years were given, this method would be very laborious and the following method will give the same result.

To find the year's purchase (single rate) deduct the present value of Re. 1 for n years from 1 and divide by the rate per cent.

$$\text{Or, } Y.P. = \frac{1-\frac{1}{(1+i)^n}}{i}$$

EXAMPLE 17. What is the year's purchase at 3 per cent (single rate) for 20 years?

SOLUTION

$$Y.P. = \frac{1-\frac{1}{(1.03)^{20}}}{0.03} = \frac{1-0.553676}{0.03}$$

$$= \frac{0.446324}{0.03} = 14.87746$$

Parry's Valuation Table gives 14.877.

EXAMPLE 18. What is the value of a leasehold property producing a net income of ₹ 1,80,000 per annum for the next 33 years assuming that a purchaser requires a return of 5 per cent on his money, and that a sinking fund to replace capital can be accumulated at 5 per cent also.

SOLUTION

From Equation (5), the years' purchase (Y.P.) single rate for 33 years @ 5% is

$$= \frac{1-\frac{1}{(1+i)^n}}{i} = \frac{1-\frac{1}{(1+0.05)^{33}}}{0.05} = \frac{1-0.199872}{0.05}$$

$$= \frac{0.800128}{0.05} = 16.00255$$

or otherwise from Equation (5b), Y.P., single rate for 70 years @ 5% is

$$\left(\frac{1}{i+S}\right) = \frac{1}{i+\frac{i}{(1+i)^n-1}} = \frac{1}{0.05+\frac{0.05}{(1+0.05)^{33}-1}}$$

$$= \frac{1}{(0.05+0.01249)} = 16.00255$$

[S = A.S.F.]

Hence, value of the leasehold property = (net income p.a.) × (P.V. of Re. 1 p.a. or Y.P. for 33 yrs. @ 5%)

Hence, value of the leasehold property

$$= ₹\ (1,80,000 \times 16.00255) = ₹\ 28,80,459$$

Proof:

The fact that the estimated purchase price does allow both for simple interest @ 5% on capital and also an annual sinking fund allowing compound interest @ 5% may be shown as follows.

Interest on ₹ 28,80,459 @5% = ₹ 28,80,459 × .05 = ₹ 1,44,023 p.a.

Annual sinking fund (A.S.F.) to produce ₹ 28,80,459 in 33 yrs.

at 5% (Compound interest) $= ₹\ 28,80,459 \times \frac{r}{(1+r)^n-1}$

$$= ₹\ 28,80,459 \times \frac{0.05}{(1+0.05)^{33}-1}$$

$$= ₹\ 28,80,459 \times \frac{0.05}{(1.05)^{33}-1}$$

$= ₹\ 28{,}80{,}459 \times 0.0124900$

$= ₹\ 35{,}977$ p.a.

Therefore, the sum of the two [*i.e.*, interest on capital and A.S.F. = ₹ 1,44,023 p.a. + ₹ 35,977 p.a.] equals to ₹ 1,80,000 p.a., which is the net income of the property.

Again, from Equation (3), amount of Re. 1 per annum

@ 5% for 33 years is $\dfrac{(1+0.05)^{33}-1}{0.05} = 80.06377$

Hence, amount of 35,977 p.a.
@5% for 33 years = $80.06377 \times 35{,}977$ = ₹ 28,80,455 (approx)

Thus it is also proved that an annual sinking fund of ₹ 35,977 set aside at the end of each year for a term of 33 years will accumulate at the compound interest of 5 per cent, the sum invested which is ₹ 28,80,459 in this case.

Present value of Re. 1 per annum of years' purchase (dual rate) when the income is receivable for a limited period, i.e. terminable on expiry of term

The dual rate tables give at a glance the present value of Re. 1 per annum at a given rate per cent at which interest is required on Capital and allowance is made for the invested Capital to be redeemed by paying into an Annual Sinking Fund at a different rate per cent. In the Dual Rate Tables the values are given for possible investments of Sinking Funds at 2.5, 3, 3.5 and 4 per cent.

The following formula will give the year's purchase according to the dual rate principle:

V = The present value of Re. 1 receivable at the end of n years at the rate per cent at which an Annual Sinking Fund can be invested.

d = the difference between the interest on Re. 1 for one year at the two given rates per cent.

i = the interest on ₹ 1 for one year at the rate per cent at which interest is required on Capital.

$$\text{Y.P.} = \frac{1-V}{i-(V\times d)}$$

The dual rate table gives at a glance the present value of Re. 1 per annum or years' purchase, when the income is for limited period, n years, and when the rate of simple interest on the capital is different from the rate of compound interest on the annual sinking fund deposited at the end of each year for n years to recdem at the end of n years the capital invested. If the rate of simple interest on capital is i per rupee per annum and the rate of compound interest on sinking fund is r per rupee per annum, then by Equation (4), we may write $S = \frac{r}{(1+r)^n - 1}$ ...... (4a) where S is the annual sinking fund deposited at the end of each year for a term of n years to redeem after n years the amount of Re. 1 allowing compound interest of r per rupee per annum.

Also we may write $1 = V.i + \frac{V.r}{(1+r)^n - 1}$

Hence, V or years' purchase (Y.P.) dual rate = $\frac{1}{(i+S)}$, where S is as per Equation (4a).

Figure for years' purchase dual rate basis are available in Parry's Valuation Tables pages 1 to 25. Selecting the rate of compound interest (r) for the sinking fund is also important. The rate of compound interest (r) on the sinking fund should be in the neighbourhood of 3 per cent.

EXAMPLE 19. What is the year's purchase for 6 years at 7 per cent assuming that an Annual Sinking Fund can be invested at 3 per cent?

SOLUTION

$$V = \frac{1}{(1+i)^n} = \frac{1}{(1.03)^6} = .837484$$

$$d = .07 - .03 = .04$$

$$i = .07$$

$$\text{Y.P.} = \frac{1 - 0.837484}{0.07 - (0.837484 \times 0.04)}$$

$$= \frac{0.162516}{0.07 - (0.03349936)}$$

$$= \frac{0.162516}{0.03650064} = 4.45241$$

Parry's Table = 4.452

Another method of calculation of the year's purchase (dual rate) is to divide 1 by the interest required on Re. 1 for one year plus an Annual Sinking Fund necessary to redeem Re. 1 at the end of the term.

The equation is: $\text{Y.P.} = \frac{1}{i + \text{A.S.F.}}$

EXAMPLE 20. What is the year's purchase for 6 years at 7% and 3%? The calculation to be by the second method.

SOLUTION

Y.P. dual rate @7% &

3% A.S.F. for 6 yrs: $= \dfrac{1}{(i+S)}$ [S = A.S.F.]

$$= \frac{1}{i+\dfrac{r}{(1+r)^n-1}}$$

$$= \frac{1}{0.07+\dfrac{0.03}{(1+0.03)^6-1}}$$

$$= \frac{1}{0.07+\dfrac{0.03}{(1+0.03)^6-1}}$$

$$= \frac{1}{0.07+0.01545975} = 4.452$$

Compare the answer to Example No. 16. In this later case S is found from Parry's Tables.

EXAMPLE 21. What difference will it make to the property valuation described in Example 18 if it is assumed that the rate of interest allowed on sinking funds will be 3 per cent only.

SOLUTION

Net income p.a. (Example 18) = ₹ 1,80,000

From the question, $S = \dfrac{0.03}{(1.03)^{33}-1}$ = .018156121

Hence, P.V. of Re. 1 per annum or

Y.P. dual rate for 33 yrs. @ 5%

and 3% $= \dfrac{1}{i+S}$ When, $S = \dfrac{r}{(1+r)^n-1}$

$$= \frac{1}{0.05+0.018156121} = 14.6721965$$

Hence, the estimated value

of the property = ₹ 1,80,000 × 14.6721965 = ₹ 26,40,995

Thus, the valuation on dual rate basis is ₹ 2,39,464 less than the value estimated on single rate basis as in Example 18.

Proof:

Simple interest on ₹ 26,40,995 @ 5% = ₹ 1,32,050 p.a.

Annual sinking fund to produce
₹ 26,40,995 in 33 years @3%
= (26,40,995 × .018156121) = ₹ 47,950 p.a.

Although, in the Examples 18 and 21, the use of single rate and dual rate figures respectively has resulted in a considerable difference in the estimated value, it is quite possible in practice for a valuer consistently using single rate figures to arrive at approximately the same estimate of the market value of a property producing a terminable income as another valuer who consistently uses dual rate tables in valuing such interests. This is possible by analysing the recent sale of similar and comparable properties in the neighbourhood. From the analysis of sale, the years purchase for property sold is found out.

At this stage the valuer will also work out the rates of interest return on capital for single rate and dual rate basis corresponding to the years' purchase figure obtained by analysing the sale as stated. By this approach, the two valuers, one using single rate and one using dual rate tables may have little difficulty in agreeing on the capital value of a property, although their valuations may differ as regards the rate at which the purchaser is presumed to receive interest on his capital.

EXAMPLE 22. A building estate was purchased for ₹ 2.50 crore. A sum of ₹ 50 lakhs was spent at once on roads and other costs of development. During a period of 5 years no return was received from the property. What was the total cost of the property to the purchaser at the end of the 5 years assuming interest at 6.5 per cent.

SOLUTION

If the owner had not tied up ₹ 3.0 crore in the purchase and development of this land, he could presumably have invested the sum in some other investment producing interest at 6.5 per cent and have allowed capital and income to accumulate at compound interest. The cost of the property to him is, therefore, the sum to which ₹ 3.0 crore might have accumulated in 5 years at 6.5 per cent compound interest. Hence,

Capital sum invested ... ... ₹ 3.0 crore

Amount of Re. 1 in 5 yrs. @ 6.5% = $(1+.065)^5$ = 1.370086

Cost to purchaser = ₹ 3.0 crore × 1.370086 = ₹ 4,11,02,580

EXAMPLE 23. A new plantation of timber trees will reach maturity in 40 years time. The original cost of planting was ₹ 200 per acre. The annual expenses average ₹ 20 per acre. What will be the total cost per acre by the time the timber matures, if the cost of land only is ₹ 3,000 per acre, and assuming that interest @ 5% is required on the capital invested?

SOLUTION

The amount of (₹ 3,000 + ₹ 200) = ₹ 3,200 per acre spent towards cost of land and planting is in the nature of a lump sum which has remained unproductive over a period of 40 years. Its cost to the owner is represented by the sum to which it might have accumulated if it had been invested during that period at compound interest. Hence, this part of the calculation requires the use of the Amount of Re. 1 per Table. The expenditure of ₹ 20 per acre on upkeep is an annual payment which has also brought no return during a period of 40 years. Its cost to the owner is represented by the sum to which a series of such annual payments might have accumulated, if placed in some form of investment bearing compound interest. Here, it will be necessary to use the expression for "Amount of Re. 1 per annum" as derived in **Equation (3).**

Hence,

Amount of ₹ 3200 in 40 yrs @5%

= 3,200 × amount of Re. 1 in 40 yrs @5% = ₹ 3200 $(1 + .05)^{40}$

= ₹ 3,200 × 7.04 = ₹ 22,528

Again,

Amount of ₹ 20 p.a. in 40 yrs @ 5%

= 20 × amount of Re. 1 p.a. in 40 yrs @ 5%

$$= ₹\ 20 \times \frac{(1+0.05)^{40} - 1}{0.05}$$

= ₹ 20 × 120.80 = ₹ 2,416

Total cost per acre for period of maturity = ₹ 22,528 + ₹ 2,416 = ₹ 24,944

EXAMPLE 24. An investor recently purchased for ₹ 2,00,000 a freehold property which it is estimated will yield a net income of ₹ 10,000 per annum for the next 30 years. At the end of that time it will be necessary to rebuild at a cost of ₹ 50,000 in order to maintain the income. How should the owner provide for this and what will be the result on the percentage yield of his investment?

Solution

The owner may provide for the cost of rebuilding by means of an annual sinking fund accumulating at say, 3 per cent over the next 30 years as follows:

Annual sinking fund to produce Re. 1 in 30 years @ 3% is given by Equation (4):

$$S = \frac{r}{(1+r)^n - 1}$$

$$= \frac{0.03}{(1+0.03)^{30} - 1}$$

$$= \frac{0.03}{1.427262471} = 0.0210192$$

Cost of rebuilding is given as ₹ 50,000

Hence, amount of sinking fund required per annum = ₹ 50,000 × 0.0210192 = ₹ 1,050.96

say, ... ₹ 1,051

The owner's true income for 30 years will be = ₹ (10,000 – 1051) = ₹ 8,949

₹ 8,949 represents a return of 4.47 per cent on the purchase price.

Example 25. A property is producing a net income of ₹ 500 per month which is likely to be maintained. The building is in a bad state of repair and cannot be expected to last more than 15 years and therefore, requires thorough repairs at the end of 15 years. The estimated cost of rebuilding the existing structure is ₹ 72,000 and the repair works may take about 12 months for completion. What allowance should be made for sinking fund to cover the estimated repair cost and the loss of one year's rent during reconstruction.

Solution

The owner may provide the cost by means of an annual sinking fund @ 3.5% for 15 years.

From Equation (4) annual sinking fund to redeem Re. 1 in 15 years @ 3.5% = .0518251

Amount required in 15 years' time is = 72000 + (500 × 12) = ₹ 78,000

Hence, amount of sinking fund per year = (.0518251 × 78,000) = ₹ 4,042.35

The Tables for 'Annual Sinking Fund' are available in Parry's Valuation Tables pp. 69-81. In the context of the previous discussions, sinking fund may be defined as "the fund set aside annually (at the end of each year) out of the annual income from a capital invested, which at compound interest, will be sufficient by the end of the term of n years to replace the capital invested". It is emphasized that the sinking fund set aside annually is assumed to accumulate at compound interest.

EXAMPLE 26. A leasehold shop in a good market position held for a term having 50 years unexpired at a ground rent of ₹ 1,000 per annum was recently sold for ₹ 50,800. The rental value (free of all outgoings other than ground rent) is ₹ 5,000 per annum.

(a) analyse this sale for the purpose of future reference;

(b) apply the result of your analysis to the valuation of a similar property of leasehold type for a term of 65 years unexpired at a ground rent of ₹ 1,200 per annum and worth a rent of ₹ 6,000 p.a. (free of all outgoings other than ground rent).

SOLUTION

(a) *Analysis of sale*

Estimated net income = ₹ (5,000 – 1,000) = ₹ 4,000 p.a.

$$\text{Years' purchase} = \frac{₹\,50{,}800}{₹\,4{,}000} = 12.7$$

Reference may now be made to the tables of years' purchase for 50 years having value nearest to 12.7 and the rate per cent is found out.

In dual rate tables with sinking fund @ $2^1/_2$% the nearest Y.P. figure is 12.46, which is found at 7 per cent table (p. 8 of Parry's valuation tables). Again, in single rate tables, the nearest figure for Y.P. is 12.97 found $7^1/_2$% tables (p. 30 of Parry's valuation tables).

(b) *Valuation of comparable property*

The dual rate valuation @ 7% capital with sinking fund of $2^1/_2$% and the single rate value on a $7^1/_2$% return.

Dual rate valuation:

Rental value (free of all outgoings other than ground rent)	= ₹ 6,000 p.a.		
Deduct ground rent	= ₹ 1,200 p.a.		
Net income per annum		= ₹	4,800

Multiplied by Y.P. for 65 yrs @ 7% and $2^1/_2$%
(p. 9 of Parry's Valuation Tables)

$$= \frac{1}{(i+S)}$$

$$= \frac{1}{i+\dfrac{r}{(1+r)^n-1}}$$

$$= \frac{1}{0.07+\dfrac{0.025}{(1.025)^{65}-1}} = 13.1$$

Value = ₹ 4,800 × 13.1 = ₹ 62,880

Single rate valuation:

Net income per annum (as above) = ₹ 4,800

Multiplied by Y.P. for 65 yrs @ $7^1/_2$%
(p. 31 Parry's Valuation Tables)

$$= \frac{1}{(i+S)}$$

$$= \frac{1}{i+\dfrac{r}{(1+r)^n-1}}$$

$$= \frac{1}{0.075+\dfrac{0.075}{(1.075)^{65}-1}} = 13.2$$

Value = ₹ 4,800 × 13.2 = ₹ 63,360

EXAMPLE 27. Present value of Re. 1 per annum or years' purchase when the income is for perpetuity or years' purchase for perpetuity.

SOLUTION

The following general expression has already been derived earlier (Equation 5)

$$V = \frac{1 - \frac{1}{(1+i)^n}}{i} \quad \ldots\ldots\ldots\ldots\ldots\ldots\ldots (5)$$

If the income is a perpetual one, obviously, n is infinity and therefore,

$$\frac{1}{(1+i)^n} = \frac{1}{i}$$

Hence, Equation (5) readily reverts to:

$$V = \frac{1}{i} = \frac{100}{\text{Rate per cent}} \quad \ldots\ldots\ldots\ldots\ldots\ldots (6)$$

In Equation (6), V is the years' purchase for perpetuity.

Part II

Deferred incomes

The valuer frequently has to deal in practice with cases where the whole or part of the income from a property will not commence until after the lapse of a certain number of years. In other words, he has to find the present value of a deferred income. In practice, deferred incomes may be:

(*a*) receivable in perpetuity after the expiration of a given number or years;

(*b*) receivable for a limited number of years only after the expiration of a given number years.

(A) DEFERRED INCOME RECEIVABLE FOR PERPETUITY AFTER THE INCOME COMMENCES

RULE 1: Estimate the capital value as though it was commencing at once and then find the present value of that capital sum by multiplying it by the present value of Re. 1 receivable at the end of the term for which the income is deferred.

EXAMPLE 28. To give an illustration, a freehold shop property with a net income of ₹ 1,44,000 p.a. has been leased for a term having 21 years unexpired at a peppercorn. What is the value of the freeholder's interest? Assume the rate of interest return as 6.5%.

SOLUTION

Future net income per annum = ₹ 1,44,000

Multiply by Y.P. for perpetuity @ 6.5% = $\frac{1}{i} = \frac{1}{0.065}$ = 15.38461538

Value if the income was receivable at once

= 1,44,000 x 15.38461538 = ₹ 22,15,385

Multiply by P.V. of Re. 1 in 21 years

@ 6.5% (p. 56 of Parry's) = $\frac{1}{(1+i)^n} = \frac{1}{(1+.065)^{21}}$ = 0.266476083

Present value of free holder's deferred income

= 22,15,385 x 0.266476083 = ₹ 5,90,347

.... (*Method I*)

The above calculation may be expressed in a slightly different way by first deferring the figure of Y.P. and then applying to the income thus:

Future net income per annum = ₹ 1,44,000

Y.P. for perpetuity @ 6.5% = 15.38461538

Multiply by P.V of Re. 1 in 21 yrs @ 6.5% =0.266476083

i.e., $\frac{1}{i} \times \frac{1}{(1+i)^n} = \frac{1}{0.065} \times \frac{1}{(1.065)^{21}}$

= 15.38461538 x 0.266476083 = 4.0996320

Thus, Years Purchase (Y.P.) for perpetuity deferred 21 yrs @ 6.5% = 4.0996320

Value of free holder's deferred income = ₹1,44,000 × 4.0996320 = ₹ 5,90,347

.... (*Method II*)

Rule II: Year's Purchase of a reversion to a perpetuity (after a given number of years) = (Years' purchase for perpetuity)

minus (Years' purchase, single rate, for the no. of years which must elapse before the perpetual income commences)

The illustration above may be solved as follows:

Future net income per annum = ₹ 1,44,000

Y.P. for perpetuity @ 6.5% = 15.38461538

Deduct Y.P. 21 years @ 6.5% = $\dfrac{1}{i + \dfrac{i}{(1+i)^n - 1}}$

$$= \frac{1}{0.065 + \frac{0.065}{(1.065)^{21} - 1}} = 11.28498333$$

(p. 28 of Parry's Valuation Table)

Y.P. for perpetuity deferred 21 yrs @ 6.5%

= 15.38461538 − 11.28498333 = 4.09963205

Value = ₹ 1,44,000 p.a. × 4.09963205 = ₹ 5,90,347

Note. Values of Y.P. of a reversion to a perpetuity (without allowance for Income Tax) are available in Parry's Valuation Table, pp. 37-50.

(B) Deferred Income Receivable for a Limited Period after the Income Commences

Where the deferred income will be receivable for a limited number of years only, the value of the deferred income may be computed by multiplying the future net income with the appropriate figure of years' purchase. At this stage the valuer should decide whether he should use single rate, years' purchase figures or dual rate years' purchase by the rules as explained below.

Years' purchase single rate basis

Rule I: Multiply the years' purchase, single rate, for the period for which the income will be received by the present value of Re. 1 receivable at the end of the period which must elapse before the income starts.

Rule II: Subtract the years' purchase, single rate, for the period which must elapse before the income starts from the years' purchase single rate, for a period extending from the present day upto the time when the income ceases.

Example 29. To give an illustration, what is the present value of a net income of ₹ 10,000 p.a. receivable for a period of 20 years commencing in 10 years time? Assume 5% to be the rate of interest on capital and also the rate at which a sinking fund can be accumulated.

Solution *Applying Rule I:*

Future net income per annum = ₹ 10,000

$$\text{Y.P. 20 yrs @ 5\%} = \frac{1}{i + \frac{i}{(1+i)^n - 1}}$$

$$= \frac{1}{0.05+\frac{0.05}{(1.05)^{20}-1}} = 12.462$$

Multiply by P.V. of Re. 1 in 10 yrs @ 5% $= \frac{1}{(1.05)^{10}} = 0.614$

Y.P. 20 yrs deferred 10 yrs @ 5% = 7.6516

Present value of deferred income = ₹ 76,516

Or, *applying Rule II*:

Future net income		₹ 10,000
Y.P. 30 yrs @ 5%	= 15.372	
Subtract Y.P. 10 yrs @ 5%	= 7.722	
Y.P. 20 yrs deferred 10 yrs @ 5%		= 7.65
Present value of deferred income = ₹ 10,000 × 7.65		= ₹ 76,500

Years' Purchase Dual Rate Basis

Rule: Multiply the years' purchase, dual rate, for the period for which the income will be received by the present value of Re. 1 receivable at the end of the period which must elapse before the income starts.

EXAMPLE 30. To give an illustration, what is the present value of a net income of ₹ 1,000 per annum receivable for a period of 10 yrs, but will not commence until 10 years have expired? Interest on capital is 4% p.a. and that on sinking fund is 2.5% per annum.

SOLUTION

Future net income per annum = ₹ 1,000

Y.P. 10 yrs @ 4% and 2.5%

$$\frac{1}{i+\frac{r}{(1+r)^n-1}} = \frac{1}{0.04+\frac{0.025}{(1.025)^{10}-1}} = 7.736$$

$$= (x)\frac{1}{(1+i)^n} = \frac{1}{(1+0.04)^{10}} = \frac{1}{(1.04)^{10}} = 0.6755642$$

Y.P. 10 yrs @ 4% and $2^1/_2$% deferred 10 yrs = 5.226

Present value of deferred income = ₹ 5,226

Varying incomes

Very often the valuation of deferred income forms part of the calculation involved in finding the capital value of some property, the income from which may be expected to increase or decrease in future. The following are typical examples of such cases:

1. Freehold land let on lease for some term of years at a found rent with the condition of creation of a substantial building by the lessee. When the ground lease expires the free holder will be in possession of the full rack rental value of the land and buildings.
2. Land and buildings at present let on lease at a low rent. When the present lease expires, the owner will be able to relate at the full rental value of the premises. Reverse of the above case may also occur.
3. Property let on lease at a rising rent, *e.g.* for a term of 21 years at a rent of ₹ 2,000 per annum for the first 7 years, ₹ 2,500 p.a. for the next seven years and ₹ 3,000 p.a. for the balance of the term.

In all such cases the mathematical problem involved is that of valuing the present income for the period for which it is likely to endure and then estimating the present capital value of the reversion to a greater or less income in the future.

The second part of the calculation will involve the use of those rules referred to in Deferred Income of this Chapter. Besides the mere mathematics of the question, however, the valuer must exercise his judgment and experience as to the security of the income at the different stages of his calculation.

EXAMPLE 31. What is the present value of a net income of ₹ 1,800 per month receivable for 25 years? 9.5% interest per annum is required on capital.

SOLUTION

Net Annual income = ₹ 1,800 p.m. × 12 = ₹ 21,600

Year's purchase (Y.P.) @ $9^1/_2$% for 25 years single rate

$$= \frac{1}{(i+S)} = \frac{1}{i + \dfrac{i}{(1+i)^n - 1}}$$

$$= \frac{1}{0.095 + \dfrac{0.095}{(1+0.095)^{25} - 1}} = 9.4375777$$

Present value = ₹ 21,600 x 9.4375777 = ₹ 2,03,852

EXAMPLE 32. What is the present value of a net income of ₹ 2,000 per month for 32 years, assuming that the rate of interest required on capital is 8.5% per annum and that the Annual Sinking Fund can be invested at the same rate?

SOLUTION

Annual Net Income = ₹ 2,000 p.m. × 12 = ₹ 24,000

Y.P. at 8.5% for 32 years $= \dfrac{1}{i+\dfrac{i}{(1+i)^n-1}}$ [Here r = i]

$$= \frac{1}{0.085+\dfrac{0.085}{(1+0.085)^{32}-1}} = 10.90$$

Present Value = ₹ 24,000 × 10.90 = ₹ 2,61,600

EXAMPLE 33. What is the present value of a net income of ₹ 2,200 per annum receivable for 21 years? Assume that the rate of interest required on capital is $9^1/_4$% per annum and that a Sinking Fund can be invested at $3^1/_2$% per annum.

SOLUTION

Annual Net Income = ₹ 2,200 p.m. × 12 = ₹ 26,400

Y.P. @ $9^1/_4$% and $3^1/_2$% for 21 years (dual rate)

$$= \frac{1}{(i+S)} = \frac{1}{i+\dfrac{i}{(1+i)^n-1}}$$

$$= \frac{1}{0.0925+\dfrac{0.035}{(1+0.035)^{21}-1}} = 7.9658$$

Present Value = ₹ 26,400 x 7.9658 = ₹ 2,10,298

Proof

Interest at $9^1/_4$% per annum on ₹ 2,10,298 = ₹ 19,453

Amount required in 21 years = ₹ 2,10,298

Annual Sinking Fund (A.S.F.) to produce

Re. 1 in 21 years @ $3^1/_2$% $= \dfrac{r}{(1+r)^n-1}$

$$= \frac{0.035}{(1+0.035)^{21}-1} = 0.0330365$$

Annual Sinking Fund (A.S.F.)
to produce ₹ 2,10,298 in
21 years @ $3^1/_2$% = ₹ 2,10,298 × 0.0330365 = ₹ 6,947
Net Income p.a. = ₹ 19,453 + ₹ 6,947 = ₹ 26,400

If the valuer had failed to take into account the Sinking Fund his value would have been

Net Income per annum = ₹ 26,400
Y.P. @ $9^1/_4$% for 21 years (single rate)

$$= \frac{1}{i + \frac{i}{(1+i)^n - 1}}$$

$$= \frac{1}{0.0925 + \frac{0.0925}{(1+0.0925)^{21} - 1}} = 9.1242271$$

Present Value = ₹ 26,400 × 9.1242271 = ₹ 2,40,880

The difference between ₹ 2,40,880 and ₹ 2,10,298 is ₹ 30,582 which is too high and hence, ₹ 2,40,880 is more than the correct value.

EXAMPLE 34. A net income of ₹ 2,600 per month for 26 years has been purchased for ₹ 2,45,783. Assuming that 4% was taken for the Sinking Fund, at what rate per cent was the purchase made?

SOLUTION

Year's purchase $= \frac{\text{Capital Value}}{\text{Annual Net Income}}$

$$= \frac{₹\ 2,45,783}{₹\ 31,200} = 7.8776603$$

Here, Y.P. has dual rate @ i and
4% on A.S.F. for 26 years $= \frac{1}{(i+S)} = \frac{1}{i + \frac{r}{(1+r)^n - 1}}$

$$= \frac{1}{i + \frac{0.04}{(1+0.04)^{26} - 1}}$$

$$= \frac{1}{i + \frac{0.04}{(1.04)^{26} - 1}}$$

$$= \frac{1}{i+0.0225673} = 7.8776603$$

or, 7.8776603 i + 0.1777775 = 1

or, 7.8776603 i = 1 – 0.1777775 = 0 .8222224

or, i = = 0.1043739

Thus the interest on capital is 10.44%.

EXAMPLE 35. What is the present value of a reversion to a net income of ₹ 3,200 per month receivable in perpetuity after the expiration of 15 years, the rate of interest being 8¾%?

SOLUTION

The lessor's interest is being valued; therefore, single rate table is all that is required.

This can be calculated by two methods—

(*a*) Multiply the year's purchase in perpetuity by the present value of Re. 1 receivable at the time when the income will commence.

(*b*) Subtract the year's purchase for the period before the income commences from the year's purchase in perpetuity.

(a)

Annual Net Income = ₹ 3,200 p.m. × 12 = ₹ 38,400

Y.P. @ 8¾% in perpetuity $= \frac{1}{i} = \frac{1}{0.0875}$

= 11.428571

P.V. of Re. 1 receivable in

15 years' time at 8¾% $= \frac{1}{(1+i)^n} = \frac{1}{(1+0.0875)^{15}}$

= 0.2841587

Y.P. for perpetuity @ 8¾%
deferred 15 years = 11.428571 × 0.2841587 = 3.2475279

Present value = ₹ 1,24,705

Y.P. for perpetuity @ 8¾%

deferred 15 years $= \frac{1}{i} \times \frac{1}{(1+i)^n}$

$$= \frac{1}{0.0875} \times \frac{1}{(1+0.0875)^{15}} = 3.2475279$$

(b)

Annual Net Income = ₹ 38,400

Y.P. @ 8¾% in perpetuity $= \frac{1}{i} = \frac{1}{0.0875}$

$= 11.428571$

Y.P. @ 8¾% for 15 years $= \frac{1}{i + \frac{i}{(1+i)^n - 1}}$

$$= \frac{1}{0.0875 + \frac{0.0875}{(1+0.0875)^{15} - 1}}$$

$= 8.181043$

Y.P. for perpetuity @ 8¾% deferred 15 years $= 11.428571 - 8.181043 = 3.247528$

Present Value ... ... = ₹ 1,24,705

EXAMPLE 36. What is the present value of the reversion to a perpetual net income of ₹ 2,850 per month commencing after the expiration of 17 years @ 11.5%?

SOLUTION

Annual Net Income = ₹ 2,850 p.m. × 12 = ₹ 34,200

Y.P. 11½% for perpetuity deferred 17 years $= \frac{1}{i} \times \frac{1}{(1+i)^n}$

$$= \frac{1}{0.115} \times \frac{1}{(1+0.115)^{17}} = 1.3665622$$

Present Value = ₹ 34,200 x 1.3665622 = ₹ 46,736

EXAMPLE 37. What is the present value of a net income of ₹ 2,800 per month receivable for a period of 10 years, but will not commence until 12 years have expired? A return of 9.5% is required on capital and a Sinking Fund can be invested at the same rate.

SOLUTION

Annual Net Income = ₹ 2,800 p.m. × 12 = ₹ 33,600

Y.P. @ 9.5% for 22 years $= \dfrac{1}{0.095+\dfrac{0.095}{(1+0.095)^{22}-1}}$

= 9.0968763

Y.P. @ 9.5% for 12 years $= \dfrac{1}{0.095+\dfrac{0.095}{(1+0.095)^{12}-1}}$

= 6.9838394

Y.P. @ 9.5% for 10 years deferred 12 years = 2.1130369

Present Value ... ... = ₹ 70,998

Y.P. @ 9.5% for 10 years deferred 12 years

$$= \frac{1}{i+\dfrac{i}{(1+i)^n-1}} \times \frac{1}{(1+i)^n}$$

$$= \frac{1}{0.095+\dfrac{0.095}{(1+0.095)^{10}-1}} \times \frac{1}{(1+0.095)^{12}} = 2.1130369$$

EXAMPLE 38. What is the present value of a net income of ₹ 4,500 per month receivable for a period of 10 years, but will not commence until 10 years have expired? Interest on capital required is 11.5% per annum; a Sinking Fund can be invested at 3.5% per annum.

SOLUTION

Net Annual Income = ₹ 4,500 p.m. × 12 = ₹ 54,000

Year's purchase (Y.P.) shall have dual rate @ 11.5% and 3.5% for 10 years: $= \dfrac{1}{i+\dfrac{r}{(1+r)^n-1}}$

$$= \frac{1}{0.115+\dfrac{0.035}{(1+0.035)^{10}-1}}$$

$$= \frac{1}{0.115 + \frac{0.035}{(1.035)^{10} - 1}}$$

$$= 4.9939731$$

P.V. of Re. 1 @11.5% receivable

for 10 years $= \frac{1}{(1+i)^n} = \frac{1}{(1+0.115)^{10}}$

$$= 0.3367063$$

Y.P. @ 11.5% and 3.5% for

deferred 10 years = 4.9939731 × 0.3367063 = 1.6815022

Present Value = ₹ 54,000 × 1.6815022 = ₹ 90,801

EXAMPLE 39. What is the present value of a sum of ₹ 4,00,000 receivable at the end of 8 years? The rate of interest required on capital invested is 11¾% per annum.

SOLUTION

Amount to be received after 8 years = ₹ 4,00,000

P.V. of Re. 1 receivable in

8 years @11¾% $= \frac{1}{(1+i)^n}$

$= \frac{1}{(1+0.01175)^8}$ = 0.4111684

Present value = ₹ 4,00,000 x 0.4111684 = ₹ 1,64,467

EXAMPLE 40. In 10 year's time an owner will have to find ₹1,50,000 for repairs to his premises. What sum will the owner have to invest now in order to have the ₹1,50,000 in 10 years' time, assuming that the amount will accumulate 12 per cent compound interest?

SOLUTION

Amount to be received after 10 years = ₹ 1,50,000

P.V. of Re. 1 receivable in

10 years @ 12% $= \frac{1}{(1+i)^n}$

$= \frac{1}{(1+0.12)^{10}} = \frac{1}{(1.12)^{10}} =$ 0.3219732

Therefore, sum required of the owner = ₹ 1,50,000 x 0.3219732 = ₹ 48,296

EXAMPLE 41. What is the present value of a man's right to receive ₹ 5,00,000 every 10 years for the next 40 years, the first amount being due in 10 year's time? Assume interest on capital at 11.5% per cent per annum.

SOLUTION

Amount to receive every 10 years = ₹ 5,00,000

P.V. of Re. 1 @ 11.5% in 10 years $= \frac{1}{(1+i)^n}$

$= \frac{1}{(1+0.115)^{10}}$

$= \frac{1}{(1.115)^{10}}$ = 0.3367063

P.V. of Re. 1 @ 11.5% in 20 years $= \frac{1}{(1.115)^{20}}$ = 0.1133711

—do— —do— 30 years $= \frac{1}{(1.115)^{30}}$ = 0.0381727

—do— —do— 40 years $= \frac{1}{(1.115)^{40}}$ = 0.0128530

= 0.5011031

Present value = ₹ 5,00,000 × 0.5011031 = ₹ 2,50,552

We can work out the same in the following way:

$$\text{Present Value} = \frac{A_1}{(1+r)^{n_1}} = \frac{A_2}{(1+r)^{n_2}} + \frac{A_3}{(1+r)^{n_3}} + \text{.........}$$

[Here $A_1 = A_2$ .... = ₹ 5,00,000]

Present Value

$$= \frac{5,00,000}{(1+0.115)^{10}} + \frac{5,00,000}{(1+0.115)^{20}} + \frac{5,00,000}{(1+0.115)^{30}} + \frac{5,00,000}{(1+0.115)^{40}}$$

$$= \frac{5,00,000}{2.9699} + \frac{5,00,000}{8.82058} + \frac{5,00,000}{26.1966} + \frac{5,00,000}{77.8027}$$

= 1,68,356 + 56,686 + 19,086 + 6,427 = ₹ 2,50,555

EXAMPLE 42. What is the present value of a man's right to receive ₹ 60,000 in 2 years' time, ₹ 1,00,000 in 5 years' time and ₹ 1,75,000 in 8 years time? Interest on capital may be taken at 11%.

SOLUTION

Amount to receive after 2 years = ₹ 60,000

P.V. of Re. 1 @ 11% receivable

in 2 years $= \frac{1}{(1+i)^n}$

$= \frac{1}{(1+0.11)^2} = \frac{1}{(1.11)^2} = 0.8116224$

= ₹ 48,697

Amount to receive after 5 years = ₹ 1,00,000

P.V. of Re. 1 @ 11% receivable

in 5 years $= \frac{1}{(1.11)^5} = 0.5934513$

Or, ₹ 1,00,000 × 0.5934513 = ₹ 59,345

Amount to receive after 8 years = ₹ 1,75,000

P.V. of Re. 1 @ 11% receivable

in 8 years $= \frac{1}{(1.11)^8} = 0.4339265$

= ₹ 75,937

Present Value = ₹ 48,697 + ₹ 59,345 + ₹ 75,937 = ₹ 1,83,979

EXAMPLE 43. What will be the total cost (including interest at 11.5%) due to an annual expenditure of ₹ 1,60,000 upon a building for a period of 8 years?

SOLUTION

Annual expenditure = ₹ 1,60,000

Amount of Re. 1 per annum

in 8 years. @ 11.5% $= \frac{(1+i)^n - 1}{i}$

$= \frac{(1+0.115)^8 - 1}{0.115}$

$= \frac{(1.115)^8 - 1}{0.115} = 12.077438$

Total Cost = ₹ 1,60,000 × 12.077436 = ₹ 19,32,390

EXAMPLE 44. A man purchased a plot of land 7 years ago. He was offered a ground rent of ₹ 1,200 per month. He refused the offer as

he considered ₹ 1,600 per month was the value. The land has remained vacant for the whole period. What total loss has been made, assuming that the expected interest on capital is 9.75%?

SOLUTION

Loss of annual income = ₹ 1,200 p.m. × 12 = ₹ 14,400

Amount of Re. 1 per annum in 7 years @ 9.75% $= \dfrac{(1+i)^n - 1}{i}$

$= \dfrac{(1+0.0975)^7 - 1}{0.0975} = 9.4146191$

Total Loss = ₹ 14,400 × 9.4146191 = ₹ 1,35,571

EXAMPLE 45. What will be the amount of ₹ 3,75,000 at the end of 10 years at:

(*a*) 9.5% simple interest.

(*b*) 9.5% compound interest?

SOLUTION

(*a*) Capital at beginning of period = ₹ 3,75,000

Simple Interest (S.I.) on Re. 1 for 1 year = 0.095

" " on ₹ 3,75,000 for 1 year

= ₹ 3,75,000 × 0.095 = ₹ 35,625

Simple Interest for 10 years = ₹ 3,56,250

Amount = ₹ 7,31,250

Alternative Method

Simple interest (SI) $= \dfrac{P \times T \times R}{100}$

$= \dfrac{₹\,3{,}75{,}000 \times 10\text{ yrs.} \times 9.5}{100}$ = ₹ 3,56,250

Amount = P + SI

= ₹ (3,75,000 + 3,56,250) = ₹ 7,31,250

(*b*) Capital at beginning of period = ₹ 3,75,000

Amount of Re. 1 in 10 years @ 9.75% $= (1+i)^n = (1+0.0975)^{10}$ = 2.535393

Amount $= P(1+i)^n$ = ₹ 9,50,772

EXAMPLE 46. A man purchased 5 years ago a plot of land for ₹ 2,00,000. He became involved in litigation and the land could not be sold. He is now free to dispose of it. What amount should he accept so that he does not make a loss? Interest required on capital in 9.5%.

SOLUTION

Capital		= ₹	2,00,000
Amount of Re. 1 in 5 years @ 9.5%	$= (1+i)^n = (1+0.095)^5 =$		1.5742387
Amount = 2,00,000 x 1.5742387		= ₹	3,14,848

EXAMPLE 47. A man has purchased for ₹ 3,47,000 a leasehold property which produces a net income of ₹ 30,000. The lease has 30 years to run. What sum should be placed annually in a Sinking Fund which will accumulate at 3.5% compound interest so that he can redeem his purchase money at the termination of his lease?

SOLUTION

Amount to be redeemed = ₹ 3,47,000

Annual S.F. to produce Re. 1 in 30 years @ 3.5%

$$= \frac{r}{(1+r)^n - 1}$$

$$= \frac{0.035}{(1+0.035)^{30} - 1} = 0.0193713$$

Annual Sinking Fund = ₹ 3,47,000 x 0.0193713 = ₹ 6,722

EXAMPLE 48. What rate of interest did the purchaser of the property described in Example No. 47 obtain on his capital?

SOLUTION

Income	₹	30,000
Annual Sinking Fund	(–) ₹	6,722
Interest on capital:	₹	23,278

Rate per cent $= \frac{23{,}278 \times 100}{3{,}47{,}000} = 6.70$

Rate: 6.7%

EXAMPLE 49. Free hold ground rent of ₹ 1,200 p.m. are secured on a shop property of an estimated rental value of ₹ 10,000 p.m. (free of all outgoings) on full repairing lease. The ground leases are for 80 years, having 19 years unexpired and the building has been kept in a good condition by the lessee. Value the free holder's interest.

SOLUTION

Income for next 19 yrs = ₹ 1,200 p.m. x 12 = ₹ 14,400 p.a.

Multiply by Y.P. for 19 yrs

@ 4.5% single rate $= \dfrac{1}{0.045 + \dfrac{0.045}{(1.045)^{19} - 1}} =$ 12.59

(well secured freehold ground rent)

Capitalised value = 12.59 × ₹ 14,400 = ₹ 1,81,296

Reversion to net rack rent of ₹ 10,000 p.m. = @ ₹ 1,20,000 p.a.

Y.P. for perpetuity @7% $= \dfrac{1}{0.07} = 14.29$

Subtract Y.P. for 19 yrs @7% $= \dfrac{1}{0.07 + \dfrac{0.07}{(1.07)^{19} - 1}} = 10.34$

Y.P. for perpetuity @7%
deferred 19 yrs =3.95

Value on reversion =1,20,000 × 3.95 = ₹ 4,74,000

Present value of the free holder's interest

= ₹ 1,81,296 + ₹ 4,74,000 = ₹ 6,55,296

The figure of 3.95 could also have been obtained direct from the table P.V. of a reversion to a perpetuity (p. 44 of Parry's Valuation Tables) or by multiplying 14.29 by P.V. of Re. 1 in 19 yrs @ 7%.

EXAMPLE 50. Free hold shop property in a newly developing suburb has just been let on a 21 years' full repairing lease to a substantial firm at a rent of ₹ 4,000 p.m. for the first 7 years, ₹ 5,000 p.m. for the next 7 years and ₹ 6,000 p.m. for the balance of the term. The rents mentioned above are free of all outgoings. Value the free holder's interest.

SOLUTION

A. Terms value

(i) First 7 yrs, (rent reserved) = ₹ 4,000 p.m. x 12 = ₹ 48,000 p.a.

Multiply by Y.P. single rate

for 7 years @ 7% $= \dfrac{1}{0.07+\dfrac{0.07}{(1+0.07)^7-1}} =$ 5.39

= ₹ 48,000 × 5.39 = ₹ 2,58,720

(ii) Next 7 years, (rent reserved) ₹ 5,000 p.m. x 12 = ₹ 60,000 p.a.

Y.P. for 7 years @ 7% = 5.39

Multiply by P.V. of Re. 1 = 0.6227497 = 3.35

= ₹ 60,000 × 3.35 = ₹ 2,01,000

(iii) Last 7 yrs, (rent reserved) = ₹ 6,000 p.m. x 12 = ₹ 72,000 p.a.

Y.P. for 7 yrs, @ 7% = 5.39

Multiply by P.V. of Re. 1
in 14 years @ 7% = 0.3878172

Alternately,

Y.P. for 7 yrs @ 7% deferred 14 years

$$= \frac{1}{i+\dfrac{i}{(1+i)^n-1}} \times \frac{1}{(1+i)^{n_1}}$$

$$= \frac{1}{0.07+\dfrac{0.07}{(1.07)^7-1}} \times \frac{1}{(1.07)^{14}} = 2.10$$

= ₹ 72,000 p.a. × 2.10 = ₹ 1,51,200

term's value = (i) + (ii) + (iii)

= ₹ 2,58,720 + ₹ 2,01,000 + ₹ 1,51,200

= ₹ 6,10,920 ..... (A)

B Reversion to estimated rental value

Revision to estimated rental value= ₹ 6,000 p.m. x 12 = ₹ 72,000 p.a.

Y.P. for perpetuity deferred 21 years

@ 7.5% (Parry's Valuation Tables) $\left(\frac{1}{i}\times\frac{1}{(1+i)^n}\right)$

$$= \frac{1}{0.075}\times\frac{1}{(1+0.075)^{21}}$$

$= 13.34 \times 0.2189 \qquad = \qquad 2.92$

$=$ ₹ 72,000 p.a. × 2.92

= ₹ 2,10,240 ..... (B)

Present value of Free holder's interest (A) + (B)

= ₹ 6,10,920 + ₹ 2,10,240 = ₹ 8,21,160

Note. The rents reserved under the lease are valued at a slightly lower rate per cent than the estimated rental value on reversion as they are secured by the lessee's personal covenant to pay the rent.

EXAMPLE 51. What is the value on a 6 per cent basis of the head lessee's interest in a house hold for a term having 14 years as unexpired period in respect of a peppercorn sublet for the remainder of the term of the head lease at a net rent of ₹ 3,000 p.a. for 7 years rising to ₹ 4,000 p.a. for the balance of the term?

SOLUTION

First 7 years, (rent reserved) = ₹ 3,000 p.a.

Multiply by Y.P. @ 6% and
2.5% for 7 yrs (dual rate) = ₹ 3,000 × 5.20 = ₹ 15,600

Reversion to rent ... ... ₹ 4,000 p.a.

Y.P. @ 6% and 2.5% for 7 years ... 5.20

Multiply by P.V. of Re. 1 @ 6%
for 7 years .066 = 3.43

Y.P. dual rate @ 6% and 2.5%

for 7 yrs. deferred 7 years $= \frac{1}{i+\frac{r}{(1+r)^n-1}}\times\frac{1}{(1+i)^{n_1}}$

$$= \frac{1}{0.06+\frac{0.025}{(1.025)^7-1}} \times \frac{1}{(1.06)^7}$$

Value on reversion = ₹ 13,720

Value of head lessee's interest

= ₹ 15,600 + ₹ 13,720 = ₹ 29,320

Note. While valuing the lease-holder's (lessee's) interest provision for some annual sinking fund is invariably made to redeem the capital invested. If the rate per cent of interest return on capital is comparatively high then the rate of compound interest on annual sinking fund is provided at some lower rate and thus the dual rate years' purchase table is used.

CHAPTER

12

Land and Building Method of Valuation

In cost approach to valuation, the Land and Building Method which is known also as the Contractor's method is widely in practice. When land is not developed by buildings erected thereon or where the buildings that are erected do not fully develop the land, it becomes difficult to value a property on the Rental Method of Valuation, and the method that is usually adopted in these cases is to value by the Land and Building Method.

The method may be briefly stated to be:

"To the market value of the land at the material time add the value of the buildings at the material time."

The building value may be the prime cost less accrued depreciation: it may be the old material value of the structure, or something more than old material value, and less than the depreciated value. Many factors have to be taken into account and these will now be discussed in detail.

The value of land depends upon many things:

- Situation,
- Size,
- Shape,
- Frontage and depth,
- Return frontages,
- Width of roadway,

- Vistas *and*
- Nature of the soil and tanks.

Situation

The capacity of a building erected on land to earn a reasonable return on capital expended, is the main feature which will determine the market value of land. There is much more likelihood of a building in the centre of a town producing a higher rent than a similar sized building on the outskirts of a town. A shopping or business and commercial locality will produce higher rents than lands which can only be used for residential purposes, because greater profits can be obtained from premises used for business purposes situated in the locality where the merchants congregate to do their work, than a building situated away from the usual meeting place of merchants. For instance, offices situated near a stock exchange will command higher rents than offices situated in a residential area. In normal times the demand for offices and rooms in the business locality will be appreciable and steady; therefore, high rents will be paid to secure the most advantageous positions. It does not follow that lands situated half a mile away from the Stock Exchange will be less valuable than lands adjoining the Exchange. For 'Brokers' offices the demand will be in the vicinity of the Stock Exchange, but there may be a greater demand half a mile away if the locality is a good and fashionable shopping area. It is this earning capacity of the buildings which determine the value of the land. To give an example, a four-storey building in Chittaranjan Avenue, Kolkata, would probably be used for shops on the ground floor, and residential quarters on the upper floors. A similar sized building in Netaji Subhas Road would probably be used by a Bank on the ground floor, and offices in the upper floors, or offices on all the floors. The demand would be greater in Netaji Subhas Road than in Chittaranjan Avenue, owing to the fact that more profit could be made in Netaji Subhas Road. The buildings may be of the same value, but the land would absorb the difference in the capitalised value of the rents; therefore land value would be higher in Netaji Subhas Road than in Chittaranjan Avenue.

A building costing, say, ₹ 25,00,000 to erect in a residential locality, may bring in a rent of ₹ 12,500 per month. An exact replica of the building situated in the centre of the town and only useful for residential purposes may command the same rent, in fact the rent may even be less. This would not mean that the land value was the same or less. The land value would in all probability be much higher. The building in the centre of the city would undoubtedly not fully develop the land, whilst the value of the two may be the same, the one in the centre of the city would probably be valued as land plus old materials for the building, but the one in the residential locality may be land plus depreciated value of the building. The difference in value of the structures would be made up in the increased land value in the centre of the city.

It will generally be found that land value will be the greatest in the centre of the business and commercial locality, or in the centre of the fashionable shopping district, and the values will fall towards the outskirts of the town. There will of course be rises and falls within each area. In Canning Street, Kolkata, in 1936, land value near the Jewish Synagogue was ₹ 25,000 per kottah for a depth of 40 ft. approximately, whilst only 20 yards away in Sukeas Lane and David Joseph Lane the land value fell to ₹ 6,000 per kottah and less in some cases. At the other end of these two lanes was Radhabazar, where the land value was ₹ 12,500 per kottah for a depth of 60 ft. Canning Street and Radhabazar were both shopping streets, but the rents in Canning Street were considerably higher in proportion than the rents in Radhabazar. Hence the difference in land value. The buildings in the two lanes were mainly godowns and the rents were very low compared to the shop rents on the two streets mentioned. This again accounts for the difference in land value. The value has since increased hundred-fold but the logic of variation remains the same.

When a comparison is made with land of a known value, then the relative merits of the two plots must be very carefully compared. The rental equivalents in rupees per 100 square feet of the shops immediately adjoining each site should be compared. You cannot make a complete valuation on the Rental Method without knowing the value of the land and buildings; in the same way you cannot value by the land and building method without knowing the rents prevailing in the locality, and the higher the land value, the greater care and more details are required especially regarding rents.

In India where temperatures rise to high levels during the summer season there is a great demand for houses facing the prevailing breezes. This is especially so in the residential districts. In Kolkata the prevailing winds during the hot season are from the south, south-east, and there is a very keen demand for south facing plots. The sea-facing plots of Mumbai or Chennai similarly commands great demand.

In Residential Districts values vary according to the direction to which the plot faces and the following is a summary of the order in which they are preferred.

Assume all plots to have similar shape and area, and if the west facing plot on a 40 ft. roadway was priced at ₹ 1,00,000 per kottah (1 kottah = 720 sq. ft. = 66.89 sq. m.) and the same is taken as the base, the value for the other plots would be approximately as under:

South-facing	₹ 1,12,500.00	per kottah	@	12.5 % increase
South-east facing	₹ 1,10,000.00	– do –	@	10 % increase
East-facing	₹ 1,06,250.00	– do –	@	6.25 % increase
North-east facing	₹ 1,03,750.00	– do –	@	3.75 % increase
South-west facing	₹ 1,03,750.00	– do –	@	3.75 % increase
North-facing	₹ 1,02,500.00	– do –	@	2.5 % increase
North-west facing	₹ 1,01,250.00	– do –	@	1.25 % increase

If the south facing plot on a 40 ft. roadway was priced at ₹ 1,00,000.00 per kottah and the same is taken as the base, the value for the other plots would decrease by a percentage approximately as under assuming all plots to have similar shape and area. The diminished value of each type of plot consequent on such decline in percentage of value is also shown below:

South-east facing	₹ 97,770.00	per kottah	@	2.23 %
East-facing	₹ 94,440.00	– do –	@	5.56 %
North-east facing	₹ 92,220.00	– do –	@	7.78 %
South-west facing	₹ 92,220.00	– do –	@	7.78 %
North-facing	₹ 91,110.00	– do –	@	8.89 %
North-west facing	₹ 90,000.00	– do –	@	10 %
West-facing	₹ 88,880.00	– do –	@	11.12 %

This will not apply in all cases. In business localities there is very little difference between north and south facing plots unless the south is completely open, such as facing a park or public open space, and in areas where land values are low directional facing will not affect the value to any appreciable extent. In the case quoted, however, if on the opposite side of the roadway there was in existence a park or large public open space the lands would have a much higher value. For example, the west-facing plot would probably have a value of ₹ 1,05,000 per kottah, whilst the south-facing plot would have a value of at least ₹ 1,25,000 per kottah or even more.

Size

The size of a plot of land will have a very important bearing on the value. You cannot value a large area of land on the same basis as a small plot. There is no definite relationship between plots of 2 and 3 kottahs and plots of 2 and 3 bighas. The Judges in the case of *Rathnamasari* v *Secretary of State,*[1] made the following observations:

> "We do not think that this acquisition of such a small plot of land for which only a small sum of money was paid can be made the basis of valuation for a large plot like the one now in question before us. It is impossible to say that such an acquisition stands on the same footing as the present acquisition, nor can we properly deduce the market value of the land from such an acquisition as that for when very small plots are acquired the actual rates at which they are acquired are not often properly scrutinised, the whole cost of the acquisition being small."

There is a definite relationship between plots of 2 and 3 kottahs, 4 and 6 kottahs, 8 and 12 kottahs, 2 and 5 bighas; you can also ascertain the value of a plot 1 bigha in area from a sale of a plot only 6 to 8 kottahs in area, but it would be impossible to deduce the value of a plot 2 bighas in area from a sale of a 2 kottah plot. (1 bigha = 20 kottahs = 14,400 sq. ft.)

But, how is a large plot to be valued if the only transactions that are available near about the material time are of all small plots? Deductions in that case will have to be made from the

1 AIR 1923 Mad 332.

sale prices of small plots on account of difference in size. No definite rule can, however, be laid down regarding the quantum of such deduction. If the larger plot has a long frontage and is easily divisible into small plots, then necessarily the deduction for difference in size would be less. Here are a few cases where the Calcutta High Court valued large plots on the basis of sales of small plots.

In the case of *State of West Bengal* v *Bibhuti Bhusan Chatterjee,*[2] P.N. Mukherji, J valued 41 acres of land within the municipality of Dhakuria in the South Suburban area of Kolkata on the basis of sales of small plots which were sold as part of a Land Development Scheme. His Lordship made a deduction of 10% on account of the largeness of the size of the land in question. The relevant passage in the judgment of the learned Judge is given below. It does not appear that any Expert was examined in the lower court. After arriving at the rate per kottah from an examination of the sales, His Lordship said:

> "They (the sales) are in respect of lands which with some adjustments may afford a comparable basis for valuing the claimants' C.S. plots. By way of adjustments, deduction will have to be made on account of the largeness of size of the said C.S. plot and its distance from the Dhakuria Railway Station and from the other amenities of bazar, school, etc., which are very much nearer the two Kobala plots. These plots again were in Tanupur locality which appears to have been fairly developed at the time or the two Kobalas and the said plots were sold as part of a Land Development Scheme."

A deduction of 10% was made for the largeness of size and a further deduction of 20% was made for the other factors stated above. It should be noted that the land in question had a long frontage.

In the case of *Province of Bengal* v *Umacharam Law,*[3] His Lordship Mr. Justice Roopendra Kumar Mitter valued 15 Kottahs 7 Chittaks 8 sq. ft. of land on the basis of the sale price of a

2 AIR 1959 Cal 572.
3 48 CWN 609.

plot of land which had an area of 2 Kottahs 9 Chittaks 15 sq. ft. The difference in size of the two plots was taken into account, but percentage of deduction was not separately assessed for that disadvantage. After consideration of the respective advantages and disadvantages of the two plots, His Lordship made a net deduction of 10%.

In the case of *Mohini Mohan Saha* v *Province of Bengal,*[4] 8 bighas 12 kottahs 14 Chittaks of land in South Beliaghata were valued on the basis of transactions relating to plots measuring 1 Kottah 8 Chittaks to 3 Kottahs 8 Chittaks The rate per kottah, namely, ₹ 600 derived from those transactions was assessed for the front belt land of the land in question upto a depth of 60', and then a deduction for size was made on the basis of the evidence of the expert witness examined in the lower court.

In *U.P. Government* v *H.S. Gupta*[5] an estate known as 'Dilkhusa Estate' situated outside the city of Lucknow was acquired in 1947. The learned District Judge found that the net saleable area came to 409952 sq ft. Valuing the same at the rate of ₹ 0.5 per sq ft., the compensation due to the claimant on that footing was ₹ 4,61,196. On an appeal by the Government, the High Court of Allahabad, Lucknow Bench, reduced the value of land to ₹ 14 per sq. ft. and thereby made a deduction in the value of the land from the award of the District Judge by ₹ 53,366. The learned Judges of the High Court while accepting the rate of ₹ 0.5 per sq. ft. as found by the District Judge reduced that rate to ₹ 14 per sq. ft. on the basis of an admission made by the claimant himself in cross-examination that small plots are sold at a higher rate than bigger plots and that price paid for bigger plots cannot be compared with the price for smaller plots and if the Dilkhusa Estate is sold, it would fetch one or two annas per sq. ft. less than if it were sold in plots. The observations of the Supreme Court on this point are set forth below:

> "Having perused the deposition of P.W. 8, we do not think that the construction put upon a stray statement like the one in question should have weighed with the Judges in reducing the price per square foot. That the Scheme

4 85 CLJ 379.
5 AIR 1957 SC 202.

adumbrated in Ext. 52 is a feasible and workable one, designed and set forth some years anterior to the time when the compulsory acquisition was decided upon, cannot be disputed and as the learned Judges of the High Court in concurrence with the District Judge have held that there can be no difficulty in finding purchasers for all the plots in accordance with the lay out of Ext. 52, we do not find any justification for any reduction in the value per sq. ft. * * * Having rightly agreed with the District Judge that Rs. 0.5 per sq. ft. should be taken as the average rate for valuing the land, if the criterion to be adopted is plotwise, we do not find any justification in the learned Judges of the High Court falling back upon the method of blockwise sale specially when we see from the evidence that there is no doubt whatever that there are willing, if not anxious, purchasers for all the plots delineated in Ext. 52. The application of the principle that if the land is to be sold in one block consisting of a large area, the rate per sq. ft. likely to be fetched would be smaller than if an equal extent of land is parcelled out into smaller bits and sold to different purchasers, cannot be reasonably applied to the circumstances in the present case. The High Court should have, in our view, concentrated its attention on the price fetched for the smaller extent of land similarly situated with the same kind of advantages and drawbacks and then applied that test to the facts in the present case. Viewed in that light, it would be proper to consider the Mahanagar Scheme as a nearest approach. In our view, the learned District Judge was right in thinking that Rs. 0.5 per sq. ft. should be the price of the various plots as delineated in Ext. 52. We do not, therefore, think that the reduction of a sum of Rs. 53,356 from the amount awarded by the District Judge is justified."

It may be noted that in the above case it was urged on behalf of the Government before the Supreme Court that the claimant had purchased the property as late as September 1941 for a sum of ₹ 72,000. But that sale was not considered at all by the Supreme Court apparently because of the rise in value of land during the intervening period of six years. Two important principles were laid down by the Supreme Court in the above case—

(*i*) Where a large block of land was divided into plots for sale in pursuance of a development Scheme before the publication of Notification for acquisition and the Scheme is found to be feasible and workable, the valuation should be plotwise and not blockwise, and

(*ii*) if there is reliable evidence that there were willing, if not anxious, purchasers for the plots, no deduction should be made for size.

In every district there is usually a demand for all sizes of plots of land, but there is also a keen demand for one size. In a poor residential locality the demand will probably be for small plots, whilst in a better area the demand will be for bigger ones. In suburbs of towns the demand will be for much larger areas mainly for garden houses. It is the keen demand which fixes values.

An analysis of rents of shops will usually indicate the reduction for size theory. If you have, say, 10 shops adjoining each other, all the same size and all capable of being let for ₹ 2,000 per month each, and if there is a very keen demand for shops, the owner will most probably not grant a reduction in rent if more than one shop room is taken by the same person. If, however, the tenant is a substantial one, some reduction will be made, because the collection of rent will be easier and the risks of vacancies are lessened.

There may not be a very keen demand for shops and some may be vacant and to let. In this case the reduction for size will be evident. If a person takes two shops he will probably pay ₹ 2,000 for the first shop and ₹ 1,750 for the second. If a third is taken, he will probably pay an additional ₹ 1,500 and ₹ 1,500 for a fourth. This reduction of size is reflected in land values. If the size of a normal plot is 6 kottahs, then a plot of 12 kottahs having the same depth would be about 5 to 7.5 per cent less. If the area was 3 times that of the normal plot prevailing in the locality but having the same depth, the value would be 12.5 to 15 per cent less. All this is on the understanding that the depth in all cases is the same.

The value of land has an important bearing on the deduction for size. Land having a high value will need a greater deduction for size than similar sized plots in other areas where land values are very low.

In areas on the outskirts of a town, distinction between areas of, say, 1, 2 to 5 bighas and upwards must be made, and values of any lands between, say, 1 and 10 bighas can be valued by comparison with sales of lands of a similar nature. If a person has taken up an area and developed the land into small plots, he will have incurred expenses in laying out roads, etc., and he will naturally expect a much higher price for his land. Small plots, therefore, in an area where large plots predominate, must be valued by comparison with plots of a similar size. There cannot be any definite relationship between the small 2 kottah plot and land having an area of an acre.

The aspect of comparability of small plots with bigger ones for the purpose of valuation according to sales comparison method has been more elaborately dealt with in Chapter 7 of this book.

Shape

The shape of a plot has a direct bearing on its value. In residential areas people like regular shaped plots, that is, if lands are only about 4 to 6 kottahs; otherwise there may be difficulty in preparing building plans. This is definitely the case with small plots in a shopping area where every inch of space is valuable. Irregular shaped plots in this instance would considerably lessen the value. In districts on the outskirts of a town shape does not play such an important part. Lands slightly irregular in shape will not seriously detract from the value. In fact slightly irregular shaped plots would have an attraction for a garden house. It is impossible to lay down any hard and fast rules regarding reductions for irregular shaped plots. Each case must be carefully considered, when making a valuation, and dealt with in accordance with the information available.

Frontage and depth

The relationship between the frontage of a plot of land and the depth, is an important factor to be taken into consideration when making valuations of land.

In shopping areas the land nearest to the roadside will be the most valuable. This land will be used for shopping space and usually shopping space areas will command the highest rents in a building, with the result that shallow depth plots suitable for shops are the most valuable lands. The ideal plot for shops requiring a 30 ft. depth of shopping space is a plot with a total depth of 40 ft. Certain back space must be left open in accordance with the Building by-laws; therefore, a plot having a depth of only the area required for shops and back space in accordance with the Municipal regulations, will be the ideal plot for small lockup shops in a business locality. Many plots in shopping areas have depths greater than the area required for shopping space only. The front land may have the same value as the shallow depth plot, but the back land value will vary in accordance with the rent that can be realised for the back land. The relationship between front land value and back land value will be described in greater detail later on under the heading of "Comparison of values by belting".

In other areas, generally speaking, the best plots are those have a depth of one and half times the frontage. If the frontage was 60 ft. the best depth plot would be 90 ft. This, however, is not a hard and fast rule. If this land with a 60 ft. frontage was 80 to 100 feet in depth, it would be difficult to prove that the 80 ft. depth plot was more valuable per square yard than the 90 ft. depth plot and similarly it would be difficult to prove that the 100 ft. depth plot was less valuable per square yard than the 90 ft depth plot. Back land does have a lesser value than front land, but this must be dealt with by the Valuer, taking each case separately, and estimating correctly the relationship on the merits of each individual case.

In residential areas more land in depth is required than in shopping areas, and the highest demand is for lands having a depth of twice the frontage of the plot. Here again it would be difficult to prove that plots with a depth of 90 ft. and 110 ft. respectively with a frontage of 50 ft. each are more or less valuable than a plot having a depth of 100 ft. There are limits to everything and any Valuer who tries to prove that 100 ft. depth plot is less valuable than 90 ft. depth plot by a mathematical calculation is simply dealing in absurdities. However, you cannot adopt this rigidly, because you cannot say that a 100 ft. depth plot has the same value as a 90 ft. depth plot and that a 110 ft. depth plot has the same value as a 100 ft. depth plot, and a 120 ft. depth plot is the same as a 110 ft. depth plot and so on *ad infinitum*; otherwise, you would have another absurdity that a 250 ft. depth plot has the same value per square yard as a 100 ft. depth plot. It is as well to put a limit on what may be regarded as the best depth for a plot of land and this may be within 10 per cent of what is regarded as the ideal depth. For instance, if the average plot has a frontage of 50 ft. and the depth 100 ft. then any depth between 90 and 110 feet may be regarded as being of equal value. There is no doubt that a plot having a depth of 150 ft. would be of lesser value than the 100 ft. depth plot, and so if you only have values of 100 ft. depth as a guide, you would estimate the reduction in value of the rear portion before estimating the average value of the whole.

The relationship between frontage and depth will not be the same in all cases. In shopping areas, the narrower the depths (within limits) the more valuable will be the land; but in any residential area, shallow plots will not be of much use, because it not only requires side and back space in accordance with the Municipal regulations, but open space as well to develop a residential plot to its best advantage. Again, in residential areas, frontage is not of such vital importance as for shopping areas. There are many people who would prefer houses situated away from the main road in a more quiet and secluded spot than at the side of a busy thoroughfare, but this does not mean that back lands are of the same value as front lands. There are many disadvantages living on back lands and many advantages living on lands adjoining main roadways, and because a person prefers to live in a quiet spot, that will not enhance the value of his land.

In garden lands situated on the outskirts of a town, frontage on a main road is relatively unimportant from the occupier's point of view; all he requires is an access to his premises. Lands adjoining main roads may be used for other purposes and values are bound to be higher. The relationship between frontage and depth, however, does not matter to any great extent. Provided the land is fairly regular in shape, it may be ideal for development as a garden house.

The question of frontage in relation to depth plays a very important part when dealing with valuations of property in a business and commercial area, and a method of determining the relative values between one position and another will be explained later when "Belting" is discussed.

Return frontages

In shopping areas the amount of frontage in relation to depth is an important factor to be considered. Suppose the normal shop frontage was 40 ft. with a depth of 60 ft. on an important street; let the area be $3^1/_3$ kottahs, therefore there is 12 ft frontage per kottah. If another road joined this road at right angles and both roads were of equal importance the corner plot would have a frontage of 100 ft., that is, 40 ft. on the first road and 60 ft. return frontage on the second road. The corner plot would still have the same area but it would possess 30 ft. frontage per kottah. This would allow a larger amount of goods to be displayed. It would attract customers from both the streets. There would be a likelihood of more trade owing to more people using the two roads. Better facilities would be available for loading and unloading goods. A person would pay more rent to possess a corner shop having all these additional facilities over the single frontage plot and, therefore, values of corner plots are generally higher than single frontage plots.

In residential areas corner plots are an added attraction; better planning of the house is possible with easier access to the roadways, and the rooms will possess more windows thus making the rooms lighted and cooler. In the same way as corner sites in shopping areas, more rent will be paid for corner houses, and the value of the site will be higher than single frontage lands.

It follows that when valuing corner sites the method adopted is to take the single frontage value, and add something for the advantage of the return frontage; what this amount is will depend upon the importance of the return frontage. The single frontage value will be the value of the more important of the two streets, and the amount to be added will depend on the relative value of the street where the return frontage is situated compared to the value of the more important street, where the single frontage value is known.

A good and experienced valuer will never add a percentage on to the single frontage value to represent the increased value of the corner plot but he will add a lump sum per kottah or per unit according to the system of measurement applicable in that particular place.

To give an example, sites in a residential district 5 kottahs in area, south-facing, *B* plot say, on 90 ft. road are selling for ₹ 1,00,000 per kottah.

The value is required for a south and east open corner plot say, *P*. Both roads are 90 ft. wide and of the same importance. The valuer would probably add on ₹ 20,000 per kottah @ 20% for the corner plot.

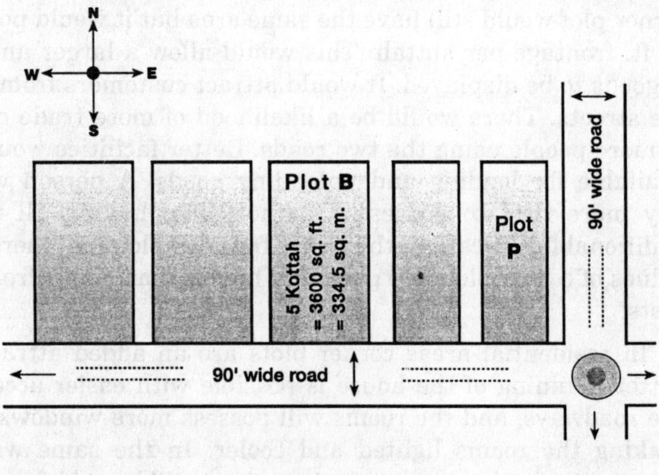

NOT TO SCALE DIAGRAM

This short illustration shows the fallacy of blindly adding a fixed percentage of the single frontage value to represent the corner site value, and because the courts have held in one case that a value should be increased by 20 per cent, this is no guide whatsoever unless you can find a plot absolutely similar in size, shape, situation and value.

In residential areas, the amount to be added will depend upon the relative value of the second street. Assume, you have cross-roads running north and south, east and west; one plot will be south and east open, another south and west open, the third north and east open and the last north and west open. Both the roads are 90 ft. in width, and south-facing single frontage plots are selling for ₹ 2,50,000 per kottah. The south and east open plot will be increased the most since this type of situated plot is likely to get more cool breezes than the others. This will probably be fair if the value is put at ₹ 3,00,000 per kottah. South and west open is not so valuable as south and east open, so this plot will be about ₹ 2,90,000 per kottah. North-facing plots would probably be ₹ 2,30,000 per kottah, and north and east open would be much better than north and west open. East-facing plots would be ₹ 2,40,000 per kottah, so for the advantage of the northern return frontage you would add ₹ 40,000 per kottah this being ₹ 2,80,000 for the north and east open plot; and the north and west open plot would not be more than ₹ 2,70,000 per kottah. To put this into percentages. For south-facing plots with east return frontage add 20 per cent. For south-facing plots with west return frontage add 16 per cent. For east-facing plots with north return frontage add $16^2/_3$ per cent. For north-facing plots with west return frontage add 17.4%. It is obvious that for the advantage of west open, you should not have a greater increase than east or north open; therefore it is ridiculous to add a certain percentage. The minds of intending purchasers work in mysterious ways, they have a passion for corner plots and fantastic prices are paid for corner plots. The average increase found for lands between ₹ 2,00,000 and ₹ 2,50,000 per kottah of single frontage is from ₹ 30,000 to ₹ 50,000 extra per kottah for the return frontage.

If the main road is 90 ft. in width the value of a return frontage on a 60 ft. wide roadway will be much less and again if the land is south-facing overlooking a park or open space the single frontage plot will have a relatively high value and the amount to be added for the advantage of a return frontage will be comparatively small, probably 10 per cent or less.

To continue with lands in residential areas, the increased value for a return frontage on a 30 ft. roadway will be very small. If the value of the single frontage plot had been ₹ 80,000 per kottah, he might still have added ₹ 20,000 per kottah. This represents 25% increase and in the same way he may have added ₹ 20,000 per kottah if the single frontage value had been ₹ 1,20,000 per kottah. This would have represented an increase of $16^2/_3$%.

Some plots have the advantage of a return frontage on a common passage. The increased value due to this will depend entirely on the usefulness of this common passage. Assume, you have crossroads running north and south, east and west; one plot will be open on south and east, say *A*, another open on south and west, say *B*, the third open on north and east, say *C* and the last open on north and west, say *D*.

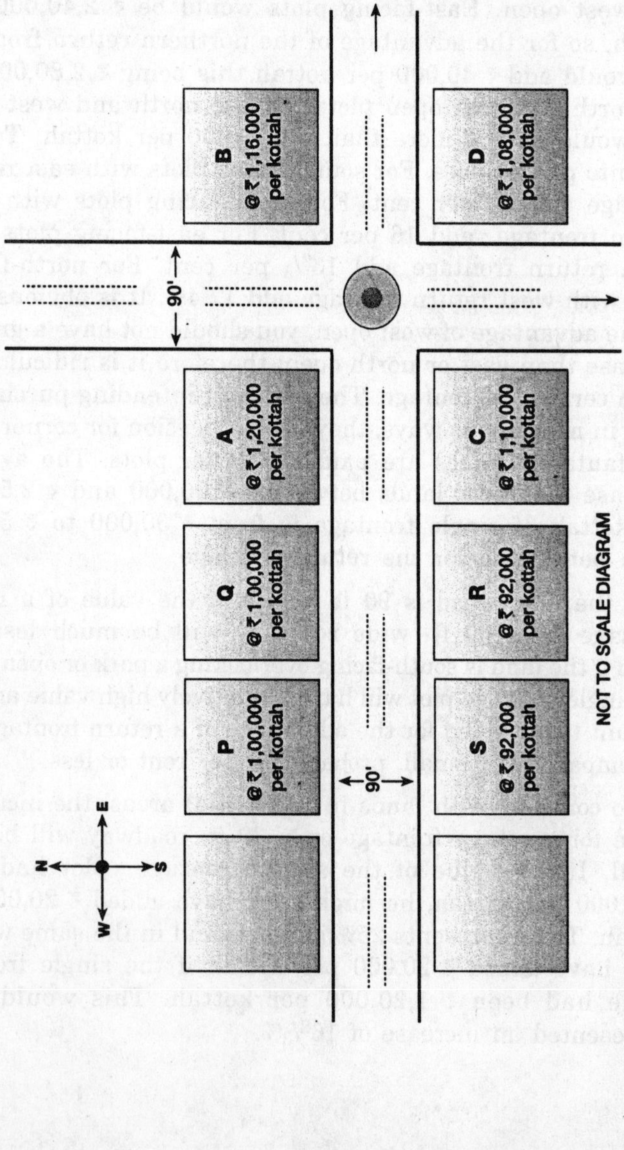

Both the roads are 90 ft. in width and south-facing single frontage plots such as *P, Q* etc. are selling for ₹ 1,00,000 per kottah. The plot open on south and east will increase in value the most since such situation is likely to get more cool breeze than the others. This will probably be fair if the value of plot *A* is put at ₹ 1,20,000 per kottah (i.e. increased @ 20%). Openness on south and west is not so valuable as that on south and east; so the plot *B* will value perhaps @ ₹ 1,16,000 (i.e. increased @ 16%) per kottah. North-facing plots, such as *R, S* etc. would probably fetch @ ₹ 92,000 per kottah (i.e. decreased @ 8%) and plots open on north and east would be much better than those open on north and west. Thus, east-facing plots would be around @ ₹ 96,000 per kottah; and for the advantage of the northern return frontage, you may add @ $16^2/_3$% (i.e. ₹ 16,000 per kottah) thus being ₹ 1,12,000 for the plot *C* open on north and east and the plot *D* which is open on north and west would not fetch more than ₹ 1,08,000 per kottah (i.e. @ 8% increase on south-facing single frontage or @ 12.5% on east-facing plots).

Occasionally in residential areas lands fronting on to a main road have the advantage of a roadway running parallel along the rear of the site. The measure of its usefulness will determine the amount to be added to the single frontage value. The main advantage is that full use can be made of the frontage on the main road. Access for a garage and to the servants' quarters can be had from the secondary road in the rear and this allows for economical planning of the house and the grounds. For plots south facing on a 90 ft. wide roadway having single frontage value of ₹ 2,00,000 per kottah, ₹ 30,000 to ₹ 40,000 per kottah would be the additional value of a 60 ft. wide roadway in the rear. Some people will pay a ridiculously high price for plots of this nature for the purpose of building on the front half, and when they submit plants to the Municipal Authorities the rear half is shown as open land. After the erection of the house they erect a boundary wall across the plot and then sell off the rear portion. If land can in this way be increased in value by the deliberate violation of the Building Rules then nothing must be added for this doubtful advantage.

The value of a return frontage in a business or commercial locality depends entirely on the importance of the secondary road frontage. If the streets are of equal importance and are both of the same width the amount to be added will depend on the locality and value of single frontage plots. Whilst ₹ 50,000 per kottah may be fair to add for the value of a return frontage in a residential area, it would probably be absurd in a locality where values are ₹ 2,00,000 per kottah. If the locality was a shopping area and the values of single frontage lands were ₹ 2,00,000 per kottah the return frontage would be worth about ₹ 20,000 per kottah or in this case 10 per cent. This would apply to lands worth, say, ₹ 1,75,000 to ₹ 2,50,000 per kottah, so the additional value for return frontage would vary from 8 to 11½ per cent. There may be isolated instances where the value may be more or less but that is for the valuer to decide after he has ascertained all the facts of the case. In business localities purchasers will usually pay an additional ₹ 10,000 per kottah for the advantage of a return frontage at the rear of the premises, the reason being that no space need be wasted on the main street, and goods can be handled and despatched by the secondary road. This ₹ 10,000 per kottah would apply to lands varying between ₹ 1,00,000 and ₹ 2,00,000 per kottah single frontage value, but this figure is of course liable to variation in accordance with the importance and usefulness of the secondary road. In the shopping area, the existence of common passages and sewered ditches at the side of a premises do not always tend to increase the value and under no circumstances should a valuer say "I will add on so much per cent for the advantage of the common passage". He should say "the property is increased in value due to the existence of this common passage or sewered ditch by so much per kottah". The usefulness of these second frontages can be measured very accurately if a valuer will take trouble to thoroughly inspect the whole of the neighbourhood, and carefully consider all the advantages (if any) that a property can derive from, and due to the existence of a return passage.

Lands on the outskirts of a town are a different proposition altogether. In areas where garden land predominates, a return frontage is of very little value especially when plots have average areas of 4 or 5 bighas (one acre of land admeasures 3 bighas). In these areas values are low compared to values in the centre of town and nothing should be added for the return frontage unless the valuer is absolutely satisfied that the property is capable of deriving extra benefit over and above that enjoyed by the single frontage plot.

Width of roadway

The width of the roadway in front of a plot of land must be taken into account when estimating the value of the site. As a general rule, there is a better prospect for fuller development of land abutting on wider roads as Floor Space Index (FSI) or Floor Area Ratio (FAR) generally favours the wider roads. It does not follow that the wider a roadway the greater the value. This would be an absurd proposition. In many business and shopping localities, such as Cotton Street and Cross Street in Kolkata, values are very high. These streets are all very narrow and it is extremely doubtful, if these streets were made 100 ft. in width, values would rise or even be as high. It is interesting to note that the highest land values in Kolkata are in narrow streets where the roads are hardly of sufficient width for two cars to pass, and where the traffic must all proceed in one direction only. It does not follow that when the police schedule a street as one-way only, values will fall in that street. In many cases, two-way traffic would only cause endless confusion and traffic blocks, with the result that people would avoid those streets, business would suffer, rents would fall, and there would be a consequent drop in land value. This is not typical of Kolkata; it applies to all large towns and cities in India and other countries. The role and character of the road is important to consider in valuing its abutting plots of land. In wide streets you have a fashionable or popular side where the majority of the people walk, and where most of the business is done, with the result that values on one side will be higher than values on the opposite side. This does not apply to narrow streets where the majority of the customers wander down the centre of the road noting prices of articles exhibited for sale on either side. It is well to note at different times of the day which side of the roadway the majority of the people walk. This will then considerably assist a valuer who knows according to a recent sale the value of one site, and he wishes, by comparison, to value another site, say, 100 to 200 yards away. It, of course, does not follow that in all cases where roads are widened values will fall. In the Ahiritola Area of Kolkata which consisted of a network of narrow streets, the majority of the sites were small and values ranged between ₹ 2,000 and ₹ 4,000 per kottah during 1940's. The Calcutta Improvement Trust made an 84 ft. wide roadway right through the centre of this area and values on this new roadway did vary generally between ₹ 5,000 and ₹ 7,000 per kottah during those days. There are many other instances of this. In the Radhabazar area values varied from ₹ 7,000 to ₹ 12,000 per kottah during 1940's and when a 100 ft. wide roadway was made running through this area, sites on the new road were sold for ₹ 20,000 per kottah in those days. Of course, the prices have soared manifold high since then. It follows, therefore, that no rules can be laid down in business and shopping localities concerning the variation of value according to the width of the street. Each case must be carefully considered in accordance with the evidence found in each locality.

In some cases in residential areas a different state of affairs exists. The more open space that is available the more valuable will be the building sites. For instance, in an area where small plots are in great demand, there cannot be much open space around the buildings; therefore, the wider the roadways, the more air space will be available, and the buildings will have the advantage of the cool breeze especially during the hot summer season. If sites facing south on a 30 ft. wide roadway were of ₹ 2,00,000 per kottah, south facing on a 60 ft. roadway would fetch ₹ 2,20,000 per kottah, whilst on a 90 ft. wide roadway the values would be ₹ 2,50,000 per kottah, and it would be quite reasonable to expect that the same-sized plots facing south on a 200 ft. wide roadway would command a value of over ₹ 3,00,000 per kottah. Usually what happens is that the wider the roadway the larger the plot, and the larger the plot, the value decreases, with the result that in a building estate you have various sized plots according to the width of the roadway, there being very little difference between the values. Although it would be possible to obtain the highest prices for small plots, it is not economical to lay out a building estate in small plots abutting on very wide roads. Because, FSI or FAR is an important consideration. In metropolitan and major cities, high-rise buildings in residential and commercial zones have pushed land prices sky-high in recent times. Individual houses on small plots are gradually receding as distant dreams.

In garden house lands the width of the roadway does not matter to any appreciable extent. Plots are usually measured in bighas and not kottahs, with the result that each individual plot makes its own provision for south open to get the advantage of any cool breeze. The whole area will be practically open, therefore an extra 20 ft. wide roadway will not affect the value of the lands. As a general rule, however, a plot accessible from a roadway will naturally be more valuable than a plot accessible from a narrow lane or common passage, owing to the access being better and the upkeep of the roadway being borne by the Corporation and also because higher FSI or FAR is available on the frontage of wider roads.

Vistas

In certain circumstances a property may be increased in value if it has an uninterrupted view. For instance, a property may be situated on a roadway running east and west. Immediately in front of the property there is a road running north and south. This property may, therefore, have a clear and uninterrupted view down the whole length of the north to south roadway. This vista may give the property a higher value than the adjoining properties. In residential areas a site having a vista on the south may be increased in value by a considerable amount. A plot on a 60 ft. wide roadway having a south open vista down a 90 ft. or 120 ft. wide roadway would probably have a value equal to a south-facing plot on a 90 ft. roadway. If the value of a single frontage plot on the 60 ft. wide roadway was ₹ 2,00,000 per kottah, the south open vista down the 90 ft. roadway may increase the value of the land by ₹ 40,000 per kottah. On the other hand, a south open plot of land on a 90 ft. wide roadway having a south open vista down a 60 ft. wide roadway would probably only have a value of ₹ 10,000 per kottah more than the single frontage plot on the 90 ft. wide roadway.

Plots that are north facing and which possess a vista down a roadway running north and south will only be increased in value by a relatively small amount. The single frontage plot on a 60 ft. roadway if north facing may be worth ₹ 1,80,000 per kottah; if it had a vista down 90 ft. wide roadway, the value may be increased by ₹ 10,000 per kottah, whilst a single frontage plot north facing on a 90 ft. wide roadway may only be increased by ₹ 2,500 per kottah, if the vista is along a 60 ft. wide roadway. Partial vistas in a residential area are of very little value unless they are on the south side, that is, in districts where the prevailing cool breezes are from the south. The same principle regarding estimation of the value applies to vistas as it does to corner plots. You cannot add on a percentage to represent the increased value of the land, but a lump sum per kottah can be added to the single frontage value plot which will be equivalent to the value which the land will be increased in price, due to the existence of this vista.

In garden house lands in the suburbs of a town, vistas are of very little importance; there is usually such an abundance of open land in the vicinity that a vista down another roadway will not increase the value.

The estimate of the value of a vista in a business and commercial locality is a much more difficult proposition. If a shop can be seen from a long distance away that shop will certainly have a good advertisement value, especially if the nature of the goods that are sold in the shop require an elaborate display. The fact of a plot being south open and having the advantage of the cool breeze does not play a very important part in business localities unless the upper floors are let for residential purposes.

The site occupied by St. Andrew's Church, Dalhousie Square, Kolkata, possesses one of the finest vistas in the city. This Church can be plainly seen from the Southern end of the Red Road about one mile away. If this site had been used for commercial purposes instead of religious purposes, the increased value due to the existence of this vista over the single frontage value would have been an appreciable amount.

If a plot possesses a vista in a business and commercial locality, and the value of a similar sized single frontage plot is known, then the valuer must estimate what will be the increase in rent that will be paid because of this vista, and the capitalised value of that increased rent will be the amount to be added on to the value of the single frontage plot.

EXAMPLE 52. What is the value of vista in a business locality of a plot having an area of 8 kottah (i.e. 5,760 sq. ft.). The value of single frontage land in the locality is ₹ 1,00,000 per kottah (i.e. 720

sq. ft.). Increased rent that can be expected due to the existence of this vista is ₹ 500 per month.

SOLUTION

Gross Rent ₹ 500 per month x 12 = ₹ 6,000 p.a.

Outgoings:

Say, 30% of Gross Rent = ₹ 6,000 p.a. x 0.30

= (–) ₹ 1,800 p.a.

Net Rent = ₹ 4,200 p.a.

Multiplying by the Years' Purchase

(Y.P.) @ 8% on perpetuity $\frac{1}{i} = \frac{1}{0.08}$ = (x) 12.5

Capitalised value of the amenities of vista = ₹ 52,500

Vista valuation reckoned per kottah (720 sq. ft.)

$= \frac{₹ 52{,}500}{8 \text{ kottah}}$ = ₹ 6,562.50

Value of land as increased by vista

= ₹ 1,00,000.00 + ₹ 6,562.50

= ₹ 1,06,562.50 per kottah

Nature of the soil and tanks

Generally, the nature of the soil in Kolkata is unsuitable for building large structures without making some special provision for support of the foundations. It is usual, when erecting multi-storey buildings, to support the foundations on concrete piles driven into the ground. This not only gives a substantial foundation for the building, but is an added protection against small earth tremors that are experienced occasionally in the locality. In the centre of the city in shopping and business localities the soil is fairly constant throughout, and owing to the provision of modern services in the way of an ample supply of filtered and unfiltered water, tanks have now become unnecessary for the provision of a supply of water, with the result that very few tanks exist in the city today. In residential areas and in localities in the suburbs of the city many tanks are found varying in depths, and the valuation of tanks presents a very difficult problem.

The courts have adopted during the past few years a Rule of Thumb Method of valuing tanks at one-half the value of solid land. This is really an absurdity. The value of a tank plus the cost of filling that tank with good earth and after being left out for a sufficient number of years for it to consolidate, the value should equal to solid land value. Therefore, it follows that a tank 6 ft. deep should not be valued at the same rate as a tank 7 or 8 ft. deep, nor at the same rate as one 4 or 5 ft. deep.

The earth for filling tanks is usually excavated from lands in rural areas which are cheap in value but which are accessible by fairly good roads.

The usual method of filling a tank is simply to dump the soil into the water from the sides of the tank. At the bottom of a deep tank there is usually about 3 to 4 feet of silt. When the tank has been filled with earth, this silt acts as a cushion and for some years there is bound to be movement of the soil laterally as well as vertically whilst the silt is drying up. By this method at least 10 years must elapse before the land can be said to be sufficiently consolidated for erecting, say, a one or two storied building without having to drive piles.

A freshly filled tank with good earth can be said to have a value equal to solid land value deferred 10 years at 5 per cent or deferred 10 years less than the number of years the tank has been filled. The following figures will illustrate the multiplier to give effect to the previous statement:

Tank just filled		Multiply by	... .6139133	say	.61
" filled	1 year	" "	... .6446089	"	.64
" "	2 years	" "	... .6768394	"	.68
" "	3 "	" "	... .7106813	"	.71
" "	4 "	" "	... .7462154	"	.75
" "	5 "	" "	... .7835262	"	.78
" "	6 "	" "	... .8227025	"	.82
" "	7 "	" "	... .8638376	"	.86
" "	8 "	" "	... .9070295	"	.91
" "	9 "	" "	... .9523810	"	.95
" "	10 "	" "	... 1.0000000	"	1.00

These figures will, of course, not apply if the tank has been filled with rubbish, then the land will never become the same value as land composed of good earth only, especially if in a residential district.

The best way of filling a tank is to dewater the tank, that is, to pump all the water out. The silt at the bottom will dry and shrink to about I foot in depth, that must also be dug out. The earth must then be filled in layers. This will enable the lorries to consolidate the newly filled soil to an appreciable extent, and if this is done in the dry season, after three monsoons the land will have consolidated and will probably be fit for building thereon. The extra cost of filling will be about 25% more than the normal method and this will just about offset the saving on the period required for consolidation, the initial value being .86 against .61 in the case of a tank-filled in the ordinary way.

From these figures it will be seen that, to take 50 per cent of the solid land value as the value of tank land, is just an approximation and a very approximate approximation at that. Every case of the tank values should be carefully considered including the sales of tank filled lands.

The value of tanks depends upon:

(*a*) the situation of the tank,

(*b*) the depth of the tank,

(*c*) the commercial value of the tank,

(*d*) the amenity value of the tank,

(*e*) the value of the surrounding solid lands,

(*f*) the cost of available earth for tank filling *and*

(*g*) the cost of transport of the earth to the tank.

The value of tank filled lands depends upon:

(*a*) the depth of the tank,

(*b*) the type of material used for filling the tank,

(*c*) the time when the tank was filled,

(*d*) the method employed for filling the tank, *and*

(*e*) the value of the surrounding solid lands.

EXAMPLE 53

A case-study on valuation

Let us consider a hypothetical case of property having the following particulars as depicted in the diagram below:

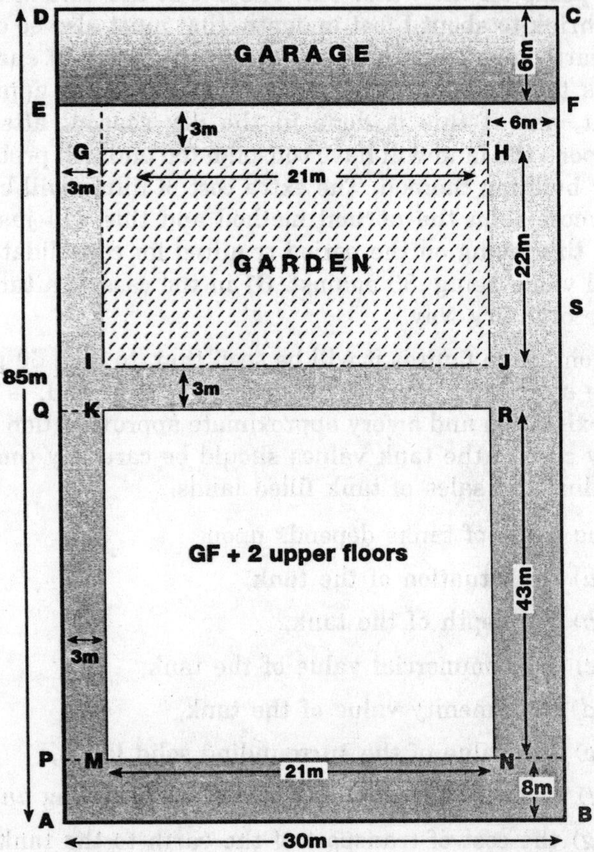

(*i*) Area of land ABCD = 2550 sq. m.

(*ii*) Built-up area of garage DEFC = 180 sq. m.

(*iii*) Built-up area of the building KMNR

Ground floor	=	903 sq. m.
First floor	=	903 sq. m.
Second floor	=	462 sq. m.

Total = 2268 sq. m.

(*iv*) Permissible Floor Space Index (FSI) at present 1.33

(*v*) Balance of FSI potential

Construction allowed	= 2550 sq. m. × 1.33	=	3392 sq. m.
Construction carried out		=	2268 sq. m.
Balance potential	= 3392 – 2268	=	1124 sq. m.

Assume

1. Tenure of land—freehold

2. Built-up area of garage—free of FSI

3. The entire property is let out at a gross monthly rent of ₹ 50,000 and the net monthly rent works out at ₹ 30,000 and the entire building was let out immediately after construction in 1965.

4. The tenants are protected under the Rent Control Act and it is difficult for the owner to recover possession of the premises due to protection to tenants against eviction under the said law.

5. The building is 50 years old, being built in 1965 but the construction is very good and as per the opinion of the structural engineer, it is capable of taking the load of two additional floors after carrying out modification costing ₹ 10,00,000.

Problem

Find out the value of the property on behalf of the owner for the purpose of sale.

Solution exercise

As the property falls under the category of rented property having balance FSI, a prudent purchaser will take into consideration the following factors before buying the property:

(*i*) The property can be expected to yield only the rental income from the building let out.

(*ii*) As the tenants are protected under the rent control law, they can file an application for fixation of standard rent. If the rent charged is in excess of such standard rent, there is possibility of the contractual rent being reduced to the level of standard rent through the intervention of the appropriate authority under the said law.

(*iii*) As the building was constructed in 1948 in accordance with the building rules and regulations prevailing at that time, the question of consuming the balance FSI shall have to abide by the rules and regulations laid down by the municipal authorities at the present moment.

Enquiries reveal

(*a*) that the tenants have the right to file application for fixation of standard rent under the existing rent control law even after 50 years of occupancy;

(*b*) that under the existing rules and regulations for development of property, any lay-out on sub-division of vacant land in a residential zone shall provide open space as given below:

For plots within 1001 sq.m. to 2600 sq.m. in area 15%

(*c*) that recreational space has to be provided in respect of plots falling within the category of above size which shall not be less than 450 sq.m. The minimum dimension of such reserved recreational space shall in no case be less than 7.5 metre in length and if the average width thereof is less than 24 metre, the length shall not exceed $2^1/_2$ times of the average width;

(*d*) that as regards Floor Space Index/Built-up area calçulations, the following rule prevails at the moment for any new development:

Plot size	*Maximum coverage permissible for FSI*
1001 to 2600 sq.m.	2210 sq.m.

(*e*) that under the existing rules, building line shall be at least 3 metres away from the boundary of recreational open space;

(*f*) that under the existing rules, the minimum side open space to be kept for any building is 4 metres but if there is already a deficiency in this regard, the municipal authorities' may charge premium at the prescribed rate for allowing the deficiency to remain for future construction;

(*g*) that the property falls under Residential Zone as per Development Plan in force in 1998;

(*h*) that the property is not covered under any acquisition proceedings or street alignment;

(*i*) that the title of the owner to the property is clear and free from any encumbrance whatsoever.

APPROACH TO VALUATION

The valuation shall consist of two parts:

(*a*) Capitalised value of land with building.

(*b*) Value of balance FSI.

Capitalised value

The net standard rent according to the rules for fixation thereof works out at ₹ 20,000 p.m. which is less than the net contractual rent @ ₹ 30,000 p.m. Therefore, the net standard rent requires to be capitalised at the appropriate rate in perpetuity. As tenants are protected under the rent control law, the possibility of the premises reverting back to the owner is remote. One can only expect rent in perpetuity.

While deciding the rate of capitalisation, the following factors need be considered—

- risk
- alternative investment
- market trend.

Having regard to the above, the rate of capitalisation adopted in this case is 15% in perpetuity.

Thus, capitalised value $= ₹\ 20{,}000 \times 12 \times \frac{100}{15} = ₹16{,}00{,}000$

Value of balance FSI

As the plot in question has an area of 2550 sq.m. the open space to be kept under the new rules is 15%.

Permissible built-up area = 2550 × 0.85 = 2167.5 sq.m.

Since this is less than 2210 sq.m. the entire area could be covered. But permissible construction has to be confined to 2167.5 sq.m.

Therefore, total floor area now available under FSI = 2167.5 × 1.33 = 2883 sq.m.

Construction already carried out = 2268 sq.m.

Balance FSI = 2883 – 2268 = 615 sq.m. instead of 1124 sq.m.

Again out of the garden area GHJI (21 × 22) sq.m. or 462 sq.m. an area of 450 sq.m. needs to be statutorily reserved as recreational area under the new development rules. So, there is no scope for any horizontal expansion for the building.

But in order to develop vertically, there is a snag. The existing open space PMKQ is only 3 m. instead of 4 m. as required under the rules now in vogue. This can be obviated only on payment of a premium for deficiency to the municipal authorities which work out at ₹ 15,00,000 in this case.

Thus, Balance FSI = 615 sq.m.

Value of balance FSI @ say, ₹ 10,000 per sq.m. = 615 × ₹ 10,000 = ₹ 61,50,000

Value of the property

(*a*) Capitalised value		=	₹ 16,00,000
(*b*) Value of balance FSI		=	₹ 61,50,000
Less (liabilities) :	Total	=	₹ 77,50,000
(*i*) Cost of modification estimated by Structural Engineer	= ₹ 10,00,000		
(*ii*) Premium for deficiency in open space	= ₹ 15,00,000		
	₹ 25,00,000	(–)	₹ 25,00,000
			₹ 52,50,000

Explanation

The formula for fixation of standard rent differs from State to State. The amount fixed in this case is in accordance with the rent control law in force in Bombay which is discussed elsewhere in this book.

CHAPTER

13

Land Characteristics

Land in the context of valuation may be described as a site or parcel on the surface of the earth which is separate and distinct as a piece of land having defined physical boundaries and capable of being separately conveyed. We have already said that 'property' as a broad term includes movables, immovables and intangibles which are held under the right of ownership as well as rights falling short of ownership. Immovable property again includes 'land, benefits to arise out of land, and things attached to the earth, or permanently fastened to anything attached to the earth', as defined in the General Clauses Act. In our present treatise, we concern ourselves primarily with urban land as a species of property and enquiry into its characteristics from the point of view of valuation.

To look at from another angle, land is actually real property or real estate divorced from any building or improvements upon it. It may be recalled that real property is the sum of the rights in land, or rights arising out of building/improvements to the land and its appurtenants. Real estate on the other hand refers to the physical land and its improvements. When we look at land as such, we have to exclude from it such features as site improvements, structures, fences, concrete, special landscapes and the like. Such land is a free gift of nature, inelastic in characteristic and rights thereto evolved through a historical process of transformation of human society.

The quantum of usable land in an urban area may for all practical purposes be regarded as fixed. However, a land which has been previously unusable may be brought to use due to technological advances or improved devices. But, more or less, there is limit to its elasticity in response to demand. While the extent of land is fixed, diversion from one use to another is quite possible. Such diversion would again depend on the market forces of supply and demand in each segment of use like residential, commercial, industrial, institutional, storage and the like.

Macro-economic forces, such as, population, density, transportation and competitive use are important factors that determine land value. Legal factors are no less important. Restrictions imposed by rent control laws, fiscal levy on transfer of property, ceiling on possession of urban land, zoning regulations imposed by planning authorities—all go a long way in determining the potential value of the land. The above forces operating on land value may not be confined to the local or the regional boundaries. In fact, these forces may be operative at national or even international level. The movement of population and economic activities consequent on globalisation or political factors like influx from neighbouring countries, authorised or unauthorised, do affect land value in a particular region or neighbourhood. So does remittances from outside or gains speculated by exchange rate fluctuations. There is also perceived pressure from the parallel economy that operate outside the authorised flow of money within the country or clandestine investments thriving on artificial differences in purchasing power parity between one country and another. Monetary phenomena like deficit financing, inflation or deflation do also cast their shadow on land values.

In this backdrop, the major factor that determines urban land value is location or *situs*. The factor of location is a comprehensive concept that includes proximity to schools, shopping centres, public transport, hospitals, amusement centres and the like; frontage to arterial road, communication nodes, seashores, river banks and the like; current as well as potential use; zoning, easement or similar restrictions; availability of amenities and public services; soil characteristics and topography; neighbourhood and environment. The last of these factors, viz., neighbourhood and environment is gradually gaining more and more content with considerations as regards vista, view, air rights, escape from pollutions surrounding land uses, open spaces, parks and gardens. Size, shape and dimension of land are other factors that determine value.

We discuss below a number of features relating to land that have attracted judicial decisions on pertinent issues.

(A) VACANT LAND

How to value a strip of land, say, 6 feet wide by the side of a public road which has a fairly long frontage on that roadway and which forms the front-part of an owner's land? The strip taken as an independent plot is unbuildable, as no building can be constructed on such a narrow width; but the entire plot of which the strip forms a part is a good building site. This question arose in the case of *State of West Bengal* v *Bibhuti Bhusan Chatterjee.*[1] The acquired land in that case was 6 feet wide by the side of a public lane in Dhakuria and it was acquired by the Municipality for widening that lane. The acquired land formed part of a plot which had an area of .41 acre (24.8 kottahs). It was held by Their Lordships that "the acquired strip should be valued as part of the claimant's plot, whose part it formed, taking into account its (*i.e.* the plot's) value to the owner with all its existing advantages and all its possibilities and potentialities. The court has, therefore, to find the average rate per kottah of the main plot and value the acquired strip at that rate. If the acquired strip were the only land belonging to the claimants at the site and not a part of a bigger plot belonging to them, the strip would then be valued on the basis of valuations of similar strips and as the strip 6 feet wide cannot constitute a building site, in valuing it, the standard of valuation of building plots would not be of any assistance". Their Lordships proceeded to determine the average rate per kottah of the main plot taken as a whole and fixed that rate for the acquired strip. It would be seen that the learned Judges' decision was as stated by them based on the principle that value of the land to the owner must be the basis for determination of the market value of the land acquired under the Land Acquisition Act. It was stated by Their Lordships in the case that it was a case of first impression.

1 AIR 1959 Cal 572.

It is submitted that there is one Privy Council case from Ceylon (Sri Lanka as was then known), *The Municipal Council of Colombo* v *Kuna Manavanna Sunapana Chettiar*,[2] to which reference may be made. The facts were more or less similar to the facts of the Calcutta case. There was, however, one distinguishing feature in the Ceylon case and that was that no building could be built on the acquired strip by reason of the restriction imposed by the Colombo Municipality. It does not appear that the Privy Council case was cited at the bar before Their Lordships who decided the case in *State of West Bengal* v *Bibhuti Bhusan Chatterjee*.[3]

The facts of the Ceylon case were as follows: The Municipal Council of Colombo defined street lines for widening of a road and later on compulsorily acquired the land within such street lines. The effect of the inclusion of the strip of land between street lines was to prevent it from being dealt with as a building land. It had an area of about 3 quarters of an acre and formed a part of the respondent's estate having an area of over 11 acres, bounded on the west by a road called 'Bambalapitia Road' and on the south by 'Vijira Road'. The acquired strip was 1140 ft. long with a width between 28 feet to 32 feet and abutted on Vijira Road, for the widening of which, it was acquired. It was held by all the courts that the acquired strip as a separate entity was obviously unsuitable for development as building-site on account of its size and shape. The Collector awarded ₹ 5 on account of the value of the land (token value). The Supreme Court of Ceylon by a majority judgment applied the principle which had been laid down by that court in a previous case that in a case in which a small strip of land of little intrinsic value forming part of a larger estate of the owner was acquired, the proper method of valuing it was to ascertain the market value of the entire estate and to assign to the land acquired a proportion of that value. Following that principle the whole estate of the respondents was valued at ₹ 50,000 per acre. The value of the acquired strip was assessed on that basis at ₹ 28,412. As for the building restrictions on the acquired land, the learned Judges thought that it would be unjust to take them into account in the facts of the case.

2 51 CWN 504.
3 AIR 1959 Cal 572.

Mr. Justice Kenneman took a different view. He thought that the inclusion of the acquired strip within building lines had the effect of preventing it from being built upon and that it could not, therefore, be valued as a building land. He, however, expressly stated that it would not be correct to value the strip as a separate entity since on account of its shape and size it might be of no use to a prospective purchaser. On a consideration of the evidence adduced by the respondent of a possible development of Respondents' Estate by building houses upon it and using the acquired strip as gardens or yards appurtenant thereto he valued it at ₹ 19,360.

It will be seen that the Supreme Court of Ceylon valued the acquired strip on the same principle as was adopted by Mr. Justice P.N. Mukherjee in the Calcutta case referred to above.

On appeal to the Privy Council the Judicial Committee held that the Supreme Court had valued the acquired strip on a wrong principle.

> "The owner of the acquired land who is notionally the vendor cannot also be the purchaser and the fact that he owns other land in the neighbourhood is irrelevant for the purpose of ascertaining the market value of the land acquired, though such fact is the foundation of a claim for severance and injurious affection of other properties.
>
> "In valuing the acquired strip as part of the rest of the land of the owner, which is not either notionally or actually in the market the Supreme Court has not ascertained the market value of the acquired strip, but has attempted to ascertain the loss sustained by the owner by reason of the acquisition of the strip."

The Privy Council held "that a fresh offer made by the Appellants founded on a correct basis would not differ materially from the previous offer and Their Lordships could not see anything in the evidence to suggest that, that offer was inadequate". In Their Lordships' opinion, as no damage to the remaining land had been proved, the claimants were not entitled to get anything on account of injurious affection thereto by reason of acquisition.

It will be seen from the above that the principles enunciated by the Privy Council are not based on any consideration of the building restrictions that were imposed on the land by the Municipal Council of Colombo. Shortly stated, the principle is that what is acquired must be valued as an independent plot with all its existing advantages and disadvantages. If it is unsuitable as a building site it must be valued as such even though the entire plot of which it forms a part may be a good building site. In the result though the value of the strip as a part of the entire plot to the owner was about ₹ 20,000, its value on acquisition was determined at ₹ 5.

It is submitted with the greatest respect that in determining the market value of the acquired strip the well-recognised principle of determining compensation on the basis of value to owner does not appear to have been taken into consideration by the Privy Council. The method adopted by the Supreme Court of Ceylon and by the Calcutta High Court in *State of West Bengal* v *Bibhuti Bhusan Chatterjee*[4] is based on that principle. It is unfortunate that the Privy Council case was not cited before their Lordships in the Calcutta case.

Strips of land are often acquired in execution of street alignments. It is, therefore, desirable that the conflict in the two decisions should be resolved by our courts in near future.

In discussing vacant land, it is important to understand what land actually means and includes as a legal term. A number of judicial decisions has reflected on this issue on the basis of Land Acquisition Act of 1894.

The definition of the word "land" in s. 3(*a*) of the L.A. Act (now s. 3(*p*) of the Right to Fair Compensation and Transparency in Land Acquisition, Rehabilitation and Resettlement Act 2013) is not exhaustive for the use of the "inconclusive verb" included in it. It shows the legislature intended to lump together in one single expression "land" several things or particulars such as soil, building on it, and other interests in it, which all have separate existence and are capable of being dealt with either in a mass or separately as the exigencies of each case arising under the Act may require.

4 AIR 1959 Cal 572.

This was observed in the case of *Government of Bombay* v *Esufali Salebhoy.*[5]

Trees are "things attached to the earth" and are included in the definition of land under s. 3(*a*) [now s. 3(*p*)] and which must be applied in the construction of s. 23 of the Act[6] (now s. 28).

The same view was reiterated in a much later case. It was held, trees standing on the land acquired are "things attached to the earth" and hence they are included in the definition of land in s. 3(*a*) of the L.A. Act and that definition must apply in construing s. 23 of the Act. The value of the trees as are on the land must be included in the market value of the land on which the allowance of 15% should be given under s. 23(2) of the L.A. Act.[7]

Trees are things attached to the earth and are thus included in the definition of land in s. 3(*a*) [now s. 3(*p*)] of the Act and this definition must be applied in the construction of s. 23 [now s. 26] of the Act. The value of such trees as are on the land when the notification under s. 4(1) [now s. 11] is made is included in the market value of the land on which statutory allowance of 15% is to be calculated under s. 23 of the L.A. Act.[8] In assessing the market value of the trees the relevant date is the date of publication of the notification under s. 4.[9]

Various types of trees and valuation thereof

Where a person whose lands are acquired asks the same to be valued as vacant land to be used for the purpose of erecting buildings, he could not at the same time claim the value of the trees on it. An issue on this point was raised in *Secretary of State* v *Duma Lall Show*[10] wherein it was decided that the trees would be valued separately as timber after they are cut down. The aspect of valuation of such trees came in for decision in *State of Haryana* v *Gurcharan Singh.*[11] It was

5 12 Bom LR 34; 5 IC 621.

6 *Krishna Bai* v *Secretary of State for India-in-Council* 42 All 555; AIR 1920 All 101; 18 ALJ 695; 57 IC 520.

7 *Chaturbhuj Pande* v *Collector, Raigarh* AIR 1969 SC 255.

8 *Socklofing Tea Co.* v *Collector of Sibsagar* AIR 1977 Gau 61.

9 *State of Himachal Pradesh* v *Liaq Ram* AIR 1987 HP 14.

10 13 CWN 487; ILR (1917)40 Mad 233.

11 AIR 1996 SC 196.

observed that market value of the land is determined twice over and one on the basis of the value of the land and again on the basis of the yield got from the fruit-bearing trees. The definition of land includes the benefits to arise from the land as defined in s. 3(*a*) of the L.A. Act [now s. 3(*p*) of the new Act of 2013]. After compensation is determined on the basis of the value of the land from income applying suitable multiplier, then the trees would be valued only as fire-wood and necessary compensation would be given. It is settled law in catena of decisions that when the market value is determined on the basis of the yield from the trees or plantations, 8 years multiplier shall be appropriate multiplier at the maximum. For agricultural land 12 years multiplier shall be suitable multiplier at the maximum.

Trees cannot be valued once again for arriving at total compensation payable to owners of forest land when the value of the trees is taken into consideration while valuing the forest in case of acquisition of land as forest.[12]

Lands have been valued as homestead lands and the entire land under acquisition including the lands over which trees stand have been valued as homestead lands on the basis of their market value. Under the circumstances, if compensation on the capitalised value of the income from the trees were awarded, it will result in the portion of the land over which the trees stand being valued twice.[13]

If a land is almost wholly covered with trees, the market value should be determined for the land including the trees as a whole and not by valuing the trees separately from the land, because the land wholly covered with trees cannot yield any usufruct independent of the usufruct of the trees, and, without the trees such a land would have very little value.[14]

Land situated on outskirts of growing town

Where the land to be acquired was admittedly situated on the outskirts of a town which was growing and the area in which the land was situated was also developing as an industrial site, and the land was purchased by the owner not for

12 *Niranjan Singh* v *State of U.P.* AIR 1979 SC 1547; (1979)3 SCC 758.

13 *Manzarul Haque* v *State of Bihar* AIR 1985 Pat 84.

14 *Surendra Nath Biswas* v *State of Bihar* AIR 1962 Pat 406.

agricultural purposes but for the establishment of a workshop or industry, the land should be valued not merely as a vegetable garden but also with reference to other uses to which it can be put in future.[15]

Whether development cost is to be reckoned in making the valuation

It is settled law that a deduction has to be made for development of land. In *Special Tehsildar, Land Acquisition, Vishakapatnam* v *Amangala Gowri*[16] the Supreme Court has reviewed earlier case laws and stated:

> "In *Tribeni Devi* v *Collector of Ranchi*[17] this court held that 'in order to develop that area at least the value of 1/3 of the land will have to be deducted for roads, drainage and other amenities'.
>
> "In *Kaushalya Devi* v *Acquisition Officer, Aurangabad*[18] this court held that deduction of 1/3 was reasonable. In *Vijay Kumar Moti Lal* v *State of Maharashtra*[19] one-third was deducted towards developmental charges in undeveloped area. In *Vijaysingh Liladhar* v *Special Land Acquisition Officer*[20] the deduction of one-fourth by the High Court was not challenged in this court and was upheld. In *Special Land Acquisition Officer, Bangalore* v *T. Adinarayan Setty*[21] deduction of 25 per cent was held to be reasonable. It is to be noted that in building regulations, setting apart the lands for development of roads, drainage and other amenities like electricity etc. are conditions precedent to approve layout for building colonies. Therefore, based upon the situation of the land and the need for development the deduction shall be made. Where acquired land is in the midst of already developed land with amenties of roads, drainage, electricity etc. then deduction of 1/3 would not be justified. In the rural housing schemes relating to weaker sections

15 *Rajeshwari Poddar* v *Sub-Collector of Berhampur* AIR 1964 Ori 12.
16 (1991)1 SCC 218.
17 (1972) SCC 480.
18 (1984)2 SCR 900.
19 (1981)2 SCC 719.
20 (1988)3 SCC 760.
21 AIR 1959 SC 429.

deduction of 1/4 may be justified. On that basis, this court in *R. Dharma Rao* case upheld deduction of 1/5 because the owner while obtaining the layout had already set apart lands for road and drainage. Therefore, deduction of 1/3 would be reasonable. In fact in *Tehsildar, Land Acquisition, Vishakapatnam* v *P. Narasing Rao*[1] a Division Bench of the High Court surveyed judgments of the High Court relating to housing schemes of Vishakapatnam upholding deduction of 1/3 to be reasonable. Accordingly we hold that 1/3 of the market value should be deducted for development of the lands."

(B) LAND-LOCKED LAND

One of the most difficult problems that confront a valuer is to make a valuation of land-locked land, that is, land not having an access to any roadway, common passage or sewered ditch. If a plot of land has an access on to a sewered ditch, then it must be valued as land on a sewered ditch and not land-locked land. To understand how land without an access can be valued, it is interesting to see how land can be land-locked.

A large plot of land having road frontages on the North and South may be partitioned. The portion fronting on the North Road may be allotted to *A*, the portion fronting on the South Road may be allotted to *B*, and the centre portion may be allotted to *C*. The three owners may be brothers and no question is raised by them concerning *C*'s right of way across the land of *A* or *B*. *C* leaves the district and *A* sells his portion without reserving a right of way for *C*. In course of time *B* sells his portion and *C* still being away does nothing to preserve the access to his land. *C* returns and finds that his land is now completely land-locked.

In the same way *C* may have a right of way across the land of *B*, but *C* may be living in another district and the land being of little value, he does not trouble to arrange for any one to safeguard his interest. In course of time *C*'s access is encroached upon by *B* and *C* fails to exercise his right within the prescriptive period, thereby losing his right of access.

1 (1985)1 APHJ 99 (AP).

To quote an actual case: *A* owned a plot of land on Shambunath Pandit Street, Kolkata, the northern half consisted of a self-contained pucca building, the southern half being open land. *A* sold the pucca building without reserving any access to his land. To the south of this piece of open land was a small strip of land owned by the Government which had an access on to Maharatta Ditch Lane. *A* took a lease of this land, thereby giving himself an access on to his own land. The Government is not bound to give *A* a perpetual lease of the strip of land and if at any time they decide to grant a lease to any other person, then *A*'s land becomes land-locked.

The value of land is governed by the economic laws of supply and demand. The supply of land-locked land is constant whilst the demand varies according to the number of the adjacent owners. Land situated on a main road for sale is capable of having an unlimited number of prospective purchasers, whilst land-locked land can only be sold to one of the adjoining owners. It cannot be imagined that any outsider would be purchasing land-locked land unless he knows that he can come to some arrangement with one of the adjoining owners concerning an access to the land. It follows, therefore, that if a plot of land-locked land had, say, 2, 3 or 4 different adjoining owners, these 2, 3 or 4 owners could bid amongst themselves for the purchase of the land. Actually if the land would not improve their properties to any appreciable extent, very little would be paid for it. On the other hand if the land-locked land was surrounded by land in one ownership that person could pay what he wished for the land, and the owner of the land without the access would be compelled to accept. If he did not, then he would only be robbing himself, as the land must be valueless to him. It follows in the case of land-locked land surrounded by a built up area that the value to the owner is *nil,* and the value to the adjoining owners is the price they are willing to pay. Land-owners are not philanthropists and they are not likely to pay more than they need for land, and the value cannot be more than one quarter the belt value of the land, assuming it had an access on to the roadway. That is, the land must be belted back from the main road as though it formed part of the roadside land and one quarter the value is all that should be paid.

Land-locked land in an agricultural district will not vary to a great extent from the value of the surrounding lands. These lands which are virtually land-locked, have an access along the *als* of the adjoining lands. As soon as these lands become ripe for building development, a different state of affairs exists and they then become fully land-locked and only worth approximately one quarter the value of the surrounding lands.

Several cases of land-locked land have been decided in the Calcutta Improvement Tribunal and the following are extracts from two judgments of Dr. S.C. Banerjee, the President:

1. *Case No. 95 of 1922*—"In valuing a property of this kind the market value of land on the roadside is of no assistance and I think the Collector was right in valuing the land in question on the basis of sales and awards in respect of other land-locked properties."

2. *Case No. 156 of 1922*—"Evidence regarding the valuation of lands abutting on the road or having access from that road by a well-defined passage would be of little or no use in valuing a land-locked property like the land in question."

This latter case was in respect of No. 117, Dhakuria Road, Calcutta. The Land Acquisition Collector awarded ₹ 220 per kottah and the Tribunal after comparing the sale of another plot of land-locked land increased the award to ₹ 250 per kottah.

Immediately adjoining and to the North of this plot of land-locked land was land with a frontage on Dhakuria Road and this was valued at ₹ 1,225 per kottah.

Needless to say, the prices quoted above are very old and have no relevance in the present day. But the cases are quoted only to show how land-locked lands are devalued.

The land-locked land came in as an issue in *Mumtaz Alikhan (dead) by LR* v *Collector, Rampur, U.P.*[2] The court observed that in modern days, land which is not accessible and locked from all sides, is practically worthless. Pedestrians may go but people having vehicles will refuse to go. So, for a modern civilised man, this land is practically worthless or useless. This fact of the situation of land in dispute has been

2 AIR 1996 All 71.

correctly taken note of by the District Judge. So, the land is very peculiar and that a lot has to be done in the assessment of compensation which should be assessed at a diminished rate which has been done by the District Judge as well as by the Special L.A.O.

(c) Common Passage

Land used as common passage and the plots abutting on the common passage have frequently been acquired in execution of the Calcutta Improvement Schemes. On such acquisitions, the plots abutting on the common passage would be valued by taking into account easement rights enjoyed by them on it. But, what about the value of the common passage?

This question arose in a case before the Calcutta Improvement Tribunal. It was contended by the Government that no separate compensation was payable as the existence of the passage was considered at the time of valuing the plots served by it which were acquired with all interests in it. The Tribunal negatived that contention and on the basis of expert evidence adduced by the claimant valued the common passage land at $^1/_4$th the value of the surrounding lands.

On appeal, *Secretary of State* v *Dulali Bala Debi,*[3] the High Court held that the decision of the Tribunal was correct and in conformity with the method followed in awarding the compensation for the land covered by the common passage, or passage land. In the course of their judgment, Their Lordships referred to the case of the *Chairman, Howrah Municipality* v *Khetra Krishna Mitter.*[4] Though Their Lordships in this case declined to lay down any rule of general application for guidance of acquiring authorities, awards are now generally made in the case of acquisition of common passage land at $^1/_4$th the value of surrounding lands.

(d) Bustee Land

Bustee land is a species of encumbered land. *Bustee* land is land let to tenants at will who pay rent to the owner of the land and utilise the land generally by erecting huts, in a portion

3 AIR 1938 Cal 75.
4 ILR 33 Cal 1290.

of which they live and the remaining portion is let out to their sub-tenants.

Rents paid by the tenants to the owners are often found to be low, that is to say, rents have no relation to fair rents which the land should yield having regard to its market value. The tenants in their turn are found to realise a good rental from their sub-tenants which is out of all proportion to the capital invested in the construction of the huts.

Private transactions of *bustee* lands are not at all common because the owner if he wanted to sell his *bustee* land generally always cleared the site by evicting the tenants before the sale. If, however, an owner wanted to sell his *bustee* land without taking the trouble of clearing the site he may not get the same price of his *bustee* land as for other lands.

It cannot be said that because owners of *bustee* lands charge and get low rents, therefore *bustee* lands are not capable of yielding a fair rent. There are instances where *bustee* lands were yielding fair rent in Kolkata. There can be no doubt that if the owners of *bustee* lands cared or wanted to charge fair rent they would get it. It has to be remembered that the hut-owners, as a rule, make large profits by letting a portion of their huts and would gladly meet the demand of the owners, rather than lose all their capital and profits by leaving the land.

It may be noted that hitherto no difference in the assessment of market value was sought to be made in cases of compulsory acquisition of extensive areas of *bustee* land in Kolkata. At the present time, however, it appears that the Judges are inclined to uphold the contention that the market value of *bustee* lands should be assessed at a figure which is less than the market value of other lands on the ground of restriction on the rights of owners regarding eviction and increase of rents by the operation of the Thika Tenancy Act. It remains to be settled by authoritative decisions how far the rights of owners to get full market value have been affected by the operation of the Thika Tenancy Act or otherwise in cases of compulsory acquisition of their *bustee* lands.

The question to be decided is whether by the Thika Tenancy Act tenancies in a *bustee* have become in any way encumbrances on the *bustee* land which may reduce its market value to the owner when it is acquired free from all encumbrances.

The Thika Tenancy Act has undergone a major change in the meantime. The Calcutta Thika Tenancy (Acquisition and Regulation) Act 1981 has been passed in replacement of the earlier enactment with a view to acquisition by the State Government of the interest held by the erstwhile owners in the land comprised in the *thika* tenancies. Thus, the *thika* tenants owning the huts or structures have come to occupy the some directly under the Government and substituted as landlords. On the other hand, the sub-tenants now occupy the rooms or spaces within the *thika* tenancy as a direct tenant under him duly protected by the rent control law in force. But the diminution of the value of *bustee* land as an encumbered species still remains on account of the restriction on the rights of owners regarding eviction or increase of rent under the laws in force.

(E) BELTING METHOD/RECESS LANDS

You cannot value a property by what is sometimes called "The Belting Method of Valuation", but by the Belting Method it is possible to estimate the value of one plot of land fairly accurately in comparison with another plot of known value. It is very rare that in a district, plots of land are all of the same size and shape, and possessing similar amenities; and a valuer may have to value an irregular shaped plot and the only known values are for regular shaped plots; in the same way he may have to value a regular shaped plot in relation to an irregular shaped plot of known value. Again, the normal depth of plots in a street may be 60 ft.; the valuer may have to value an isolated plot having a depth of 160 feet. If sufficient data are available, the area of plots in a locality can be reduced to units; then by taking into account frontage, depth, shape and size it is possible to compare one plot with another fairly accurately.

Belting method of valuation—meaning

It is necessary to turn to judicial decisions for an appreciation of the topic.

For evaluating land, a method often adopted is the "belting method" described in *CIT* v *Madho Properties Ltd.*[5] as: "nothing more than a method of calculation in which the value of the portion of the land nearest to the main thoroughfare i.e. the front belt is first ascertained in usual manner on objective data. Thereafter the value of the other portions are determined taking into account the progressive decrease in value according to the distance from the front".

It has already been explained that frontage land has a greater value than back land; so when making comparisons by Belting, the very first step is to ascertain to what depth of the land does the maximum value extend. Having decided this point, the standard of measurement applicable in that district will become units. In Kolkata the measurement is by kottahs; therefore, having found that the area of the land to which the maximum value extends is 4 kottahs, this would become 4 units. The next step is to ascertain the relationship regarding the value of the back land to the front land. If it is found that the back land value is one half of the front land value, then the back land area would be divided by 2 to convert the kottahs into front belt units.

This method has become recognised by the courts and before explaining its application in detail, the following are a few extracts from judgments of the High Courts commenting on this system and which should be carefully studied.

Mr. Justice MacLeod in his judgment in the case of *Government of Bombay* v *Karim Tar Mahomed,*[6] said:

> "When determining the value of frontage land the depth is a question of supreme importance. What is a suitable depth must primarily depend on the character of the buildings in the locality but in an ordinary shop and *chawl* locality like the one I have to deal with it has been the custom for surveyors to calculate the depth at 100 feet. In the next place the value of a building frontage must depend on the higher rents that can be obtained for the shops or rooms facing the street, and as the proportion of these rents to

5 (1981)131 ITR 380 (Cal).
6 ILR (1909)33 Bom 325.

the lower rents of the back rooms decreases, so does the value of the whole frontage land decrease.

* * * *

"There are two alternatives in this case, either to take a deep frontage which must have a piece of back land of very little value, or to take a lesser frontage, which, while increasing the value of the back land, would at the same time increase the proportion of back land to the front land. But I must decline to accept as a hard and fast rule that back land must be worth half the frontage land. That would only lead to absurdities."

This case points out that depth of a plot must be carefully considered as well as the rents obtained for the front and rear portion and that no hard and fast rule can be laid down regarding the respective values of front and back land. This latter proposition was expounded in the case of *Guru Das Kundu Chowdhury* v *The Secretary of State for India in Council*,[7] by the Chief Justice Sir Francis Maclean:

"It is difficult to lay down in these cases any hard and fast rule as to what is the relative proportion of value as between the back land and the frontage land, but it is at least reasonable in seeking to fix that proportion to bear in mind how far land stands back from the road."

Belting method—a gradually recognised process

The belting system has obtained gradual recognition, although its indiscriminate use has found disfavour from courts in view of arbitrariness it may often involve. But the fact remains that just and fair valuation can hardly ignore the resort to belting method in urban scenarios and in a developing economy. The following judicial decisions will bear out the fact that there is a growing tendency to recognise the method rather than discard it.

In the case of *K.K. Pillai* v *State*[8] it was observed that valuation by belting system, by artificially dividing the property into belts or plots, is generally discouraged for the obvious

7 18 CLJ 244.
8 AIR 1953 Trav-Co 177.

reason that it involves a considerable extent of arbitrariness. It was again held, "Belting method can be resorted to only in cases where extensive lands having road only on one side is to be valued. It will not be suitable in cases where the plot acquired has roads and lanes on its three sides."[9] But a more reasoned view has been expressed in *Balbir Singh* v *State of Haryana*.[10]

> "The system of carving out land by acquisition authorities into different belts or blocks for awarding compensation on that basis higher and lower, though have some element of arbitrariness, is now judicially recognised by courts. But this belting system is not so universally applied in each and every case. It is applied where the application of the system is justified and each case is decided on its own merits."

A discordant note is again heard in the case of *Kehar Singh* v *State of Punjab*.[11] It was observed in the instant case that the courts of law would generally be disinclined to categorise the land and would be inclined to evaluate the entire land at a flat rate whenever it has got the potentialities for being used for residential, commercial and industrial purposes. The fact that the land being situated in a compact block is another consideration which must weigh with the court to do away with the belting system. The location of the land in the urban area is another factor leaning towards the grant of flat rate when the entire land is acquired by one notification. Even suburban properties near or around the Municipality town can have the same potentialities until and unless evidence to the contrary is produced.

The same view is echoed in *P.R. Modi* v *Collector, Durg*.[12] It was held, the method of valuation by belts i.e. by artificially dividing the land into plots, is generally discouraged for the obvious reasons that it involves a considerable extent of arbitrariness. Court will not be able to appreciate how best

9 *Ananthan Pillai* v *State of Kerala* 1961 Ker LJ 352; *Chander Prakash* v *State of Haryana* (1994)2 PLR 353.

10 (1983)85 Punj LR 148.

11 (1992-1)101 Punj LR 148.

12 AIR 1975 MP 75.

the land can be used without the advice of the opinion of experts in town planning, layout and designing and assessing valuation.

But the belting principle was applied for the acquisition of a large area of undeveloped land in *Sahib Singh Kalha* v *Amritsar Improvement Trust.*[13] The tribunal classified the lands into two belts for purposes of town development making provisions for amenities for town life, road, drainage, electricity connection, water connections etc. as such involved deduction of the cost of the factors required to bring the undeveloped lands at par with the developed lands.

In a case for acquisition of land *Ludhiana Improvement Trust* v *Brijeshwar Singh Chhal,*[14] it was held that levelled-up land and low lying land cannot command the same market rate. Therefore, fixation of market value at uniform rate would be improper. The L.A.O. classified the lands as levelled up land and low lying land and awarded compensation at different rates. So, the High Court was clearly in error in holding that the belting system cannot be adopted and compensation has to be paid at uniform rate.

Adoption of belting method for the purpose of valuation of land is not illegal and held appropriate in *Mathura Prasad Raigharia* v *State of West Bengal.*[15]

Where a large area of land in an urban area or locality is sought to be acquired, then in determining the market value the method of belting is appropriate as lands having frontage on the main roads in urban areas are always more attractive than the lands which have no frontage. This was the view in *State of West Bengal* v *Musst. Nurjahan Sakil.*[16]

Thus the principles of valuation by dividing the land acquired into front land and back land, though not always viewed with favour, has long been followed. Even in an earlier judicial decision *Prem Chand Boral* v *The Collector, Calcutta,*[17] it was held, "the frontage is no doubt valuable—if instead of

13 AIR 1982 SC 940; (1982)1 SCC 419.
14 (1996)7 SCC 188.
15 AIR 1971 SC 465.
16 AIR 1985 Cal 39.
17 ILR 2 Cal 103.

calculating the whole area together we were to estimate the front land at ₹ 100 and the back land at ₹ 60 the result will be the same".

The value of the land abutting on the road or main road is very much higher in a business locality than the value of the land in the rear side of the road. But in case of a residential area, the value of the two types of plots, on the road and a bit off from the road, should be taken as the same. Hence reduction in market value should be based on reasonable calculations and considerations.[18]

Where a large extent of the land is required for being laid out in smaller plots as house sites, allowance has to be made for the space which will be taken up for roads and the cost of the rest of the amenities including the cost of laying roads as without such roads, the land cannot be valued as house sites. Though the price paid for the small plot of land cannot normally be the sole basis for determining the market value to a large extent, still the court can take into consideration that price. The market value of a plot abutting the main road will necessarily have to be higher than the value of plots in the interior.[19]

A very long stress of agricultural land alongside G.T. Road 3 kms. in length was acquired and the L.A.O. awarded compensation by belting the land in three categories and fixing separate rates therefor. The High Court ultimately reduced it into two categories enhancing rate per sq. yd. The appellant not satisfied with the order of the High Court made appeals praying for uniform rate @ ₹ 42 per sq. yd. on the basis of a previous sale instance of a land which was part of the acquired land. The appellant also urged that since the land was acquired for building purposes, its quality as agricultural land should not have weighed with the courts. The Supreme Court held that the tiller's effect to keep his land more productive could not be lost sight of in awarding compensation and belting had kept regard to the quality of the land. No supportive material on record could be pressed in support of uniform rate of compensation. The only sale instance produced was a small

18 *Jiwan Lall* v *Collector, Ranchi* 1968 Pat LJR 140; 1968 BLJR 496.
19 *V. Kannia Lal* v *Collector of Madras* AIR 1966 Mad 82.

one with fully constructed house on it and a godown facing the road. Though normally belting is not resorted to as pointed out by the appellant, the Supreme Court did not discard the belting system adopted by court and lean towards uniformity in the instant case.[20]

In *G. Ramesan* v *State of Kerala*,[21] two categories of land were acquired; one abutting road and the other in low lying area. In the case, belting procedure could be adopted on the principle that no willing buyer in the open market would be prepared to purchase these two categories of land at the same rate. So, the order of the High Court applying belting system was upheld.

When a large area has been acquired, the claimant ought to have adduced evidence about the length and breadth of the area to show that land adjacent to National Highway is such that breadth will not make any difference in nature of use. As no such evidence is available, the principle of belting can be applied to ascertain market value of the acquired land. When there is no material to come to the conclusion that principle of belting would not be applicable, classification by the L.A.O. has rightly been accepted by trial court.[22]

Similarly, it was held in *Mirza Nausherwan Khan* v *Collector, L.A., Hyderabad*:[23] "There is no doubt that when the court has to deal with valuation of an extensive plot of land in a city, the strip that adjoins an important road will have a higher value than what is in the rear for obvious reasons of potential user or commercial exploitation. While no general principle can be laid down in these matters, local circumstances guide the courts."

Criteria for valuation in belting method

A broad approach regarding criteria to be adopted for the belting method are contained in the observations of the Supreme Court in *Mathura Prasad Rajgharia* v *State of West Bengal*[1] where it was laid down as follows:

20 *Sher Singh* v *State of Haryana* AIR 1991 SC 2048 (DB).
21 AIR 1997 SC 2159.
22 *Diptilata Panigrahi* v *L.A. Collector, Balasore* AIR 1995 Ori 294.
23 (1975)1 SCC 238.
1 AIR 1971 SC 465.

"Where a large area of land in an urban locality is sought to be acquired in determining the market value, 'the method of belting' is appropriate. It is common knowledge that lands having frontage on the main roads in urban areas are always more attractive than the lands which have no such frontage. No objection was raised before us against the adoption of the method of belting. It was also accepted that of the land under acquisition the front belt would be 100 feet deep: the second belt of 150 ft. deep and the rest may be included in the third belt. No objection was again raised to the opinion of the Tribunal that the price of the second belt should be taken at 75% per kottah of the value of the land per kottah in first belt; and the price per kottah of the third belt should be taken at 50% of the value of the land per kottah in the first belt."

Alaul Huq v *Secretary of State for India in Council*,[2] is a case where the front land had a very high value and back land had a relatively low value. An extract from the judgment of Mr. Justice Mookerjee follows:

"We, therefore, accept the contention of the claimant that the front portion of the land acquired should be valued at ₹ 2,000 per kottah. But this necessarily leads to the two important questions, as to the extent of the front land, and the mode of valuation of the back land. It is not disputed on behalf of the appellant that this basis of calculation is applicable only to the front portion to a depth of 16½ feet as in the case of godowns situated on the opposite side of the road. Now as the frontage of the land is stated to be 75 feet, the portion upon which the hypothetical godowns could be built would cover an area of 1¾ kottah. There would thus still remain in the back an area of 4 kottahs and 14 chittacks. How is this portion to be valued? It was suggested on behalf of the appellant that this portion ought to be valued at half the rate allowed for the front portion. In our opinion this is an unfair estimate. As observed in the case of *Government of Bombay* v *Karim Tar Mahomed*[3] it cannot be taken as a hard and fast rule that back land must be

2 (1910)11 CLJ 393.
3 ILR (1909)33 Bom 325.

worth half the frontage land. The specially high value of the front portion in the present case is due to the possibility of the erection of godowns which might be let out at a very profitable rate of rent. The back portion evidently cannot be used for any such exceptionally advantageous purpose. But, although there are no materials on the record on which we can say with absolute precision what ought to be taken as a fair value for the back land, it is manifest that if the front portion is valued at ₹ 2,000 a kottah, the award which has been made by the District Judge for the whole is insufficient; because if ₹ 2,000 is allowed for the front portion of $1^3/_4$ kottah, the remainder according to the award works out at about ₹ 65 per kottah, and there can be no possible doubt that ₹ 65 for the back land is too low a rate. Upon the materials before us, we are of opinion that if the front portion is valued at ₹ 2,000 a kottah, the back portion should be valued at not lower than one-fifth of that rate, namely, ₹ 400 a kottah. If this is done, the total value works out to ₹ 5,450 which gives approximately a rate of ₹ 820 per kottah. In our opinion the claimant is entitled to an award at this rate."

Situations that call for application of belting method

In the case of *CIT* v *Madho Properties Ltd.*[4] the issue whether the belting method had become obsolete was considered. The Calcutta High Court stated:

"We are unable to accept the contentions of the Revenue that in valuing the land in the instant case the "belting method" was not appropriate or that such method has become obsolete. In none of the decisions cited at the Bar the belting method has been held to be obsolete or entirely rejected.....

...... in our opinion, the controversy has been set at rest by the Supreme Court in *Mathura Prasad Rajgharia.*[5] Though there was no dispute before the Supreme Court whether the belting method should be adopted or not the Supreme Court clearly laid down that where a large area of land was being acquired in an urban locality, the method of belting for determining the value thereof was

4 (1981)131 ITR 380 (Cal).

5 *Mathura Prasad Rajgharia* v *State of West Bengal* AIR 1971 SC 465.

appropriate and that it was common knowledge that land in urban areas having a frontage on the main road was more attractive than the land which has no such frontage. The said observations appear to have been made *de hors* any concessions and is intended to lay down the law. Observations of the Supreme Court even if *obiter* would be binding."

In determining compensation the value fetched for a small plot of land cannot be applied to lands covering a very large area. The large area of land cannot possibly fetch a price at the same rate as the sale of small plots. The valuation of lands by belts ought to be done in a scientific and logical manner. There is no question of applying belting if the acquired land is small since uniform value cannot be obtained for the entire land. This was the view of the Supreme Court in *Collector of Lakshimpur* v *Bhuban Dutta.*[6]

The case of *Nityagopal Sen Poddar* v *The Secretary of State*[7] is also very important. This case states that the belting system can be perfectly scientific if sufficient data are available showing relative values according to the distance from the main road. The system is practically useless when dealing with garden lands which are usually sold by the bigha or acre. The system is an artificial system and cannot be resorted to as a hard and fast rule. The following is an extract from the judgment:

> "Now so far as the system of belting is concerned it is a system which is widely used, but its value as a system depends much upon a variety of facts. If data are available showing the proportion at which the value of land diminished accordingly as it is situated at a particular distance from a main road or thoroughfare, the system would be perfectly scientific. In the absence of any such data also, it may be assumed that in big cities where land sells by kottahs or yards or feet there is such a proportion as common experience shows. For instance, in land acquisition or improvement schemes in and near about Calcutta, land is generally divided into blocks facing some

6 AIR 1971 SC 2015; (1972)4 SCC 236.
7 AIR 1933 Cal 25.

particular street or road or lane and each block is divided into three belts, the first to a depth of 60 feet or so on the road frontage, the second to a depth of about 150 feet thereafter and the third consisting of all land behind, and the relative values of the three belts are fixed in the proportion of 100, 66.6 and 50. But in place and localities where lands are sold by bighas or acres, and there is no real evidence of such proportionate diminution in value, the system is based on no sound principle and must be regarded as a method not quite satisfactory. Of course, there is almost always a distinction in value between front lands and back lands everywhere, but that distinction would not obviously justify a recourse to the belting system in each and every case. It is a highly artificial system and cannot be resorted to as a hard and fast rule.[8] Nor again can there be any hard and fast rule that back land must be always of less value than front land or that the proportion should be one to a half or that there must be a certain proportion at a certain distance from the road."[9]

The following observations made by Mr. Justice R.P. Mukherjee in the case of *Mohini Mohan Saha* v *State of West Bengal*,[10] should also be noted in this context:

"The unit value of the first belt of the land in question should, therefore, be made dependant on the first belt being of depth similar to those contiguous plots on the valuation of which market value is to be ascertained. When determining the value of a portion of the land having road frontage, the depth must primarily depend on the nature of the plots, the locality where they are situate as also the character of the use the land is put to ....

8 See *Secretary of State* v *India General Steam Navigation and Railway Co. Ltd.* (1909)36 Cal 967; 36 IA 200 (PC); *Raghunath Das* v *Collector of Dacca* (1910)11 CLJ 612; *The Collector* v *Ramchandra Harishchandra* AIR 1926 Bom 44.

9 See *Collector of Poona* v *Kashinath Khasgiwala* (1886)10 Bom 585; In the matter of *Government of Bombay* (1908)33 Bom 325; 10 Bom LR 660; *Alaul Huq* v *Secretary of State* (1909)11 CLJ 393; *Guru Das Kundu Chowdhury* v *Secretary of State* (1913)18 CLJ 244.

10 85 CLJ 379.

"If the area be a commercial one where buildings erected on the roadside fetch a higher rent from shops let out on the road, such depths as can be utilised for the erection of an utilisation as shops will be regarded as reasonable depth of the first belt. The character of the business and the nature of shops in a particular area may differ from those of another area. In the Burrabazar area in Kolkata, the depth of the first belt may differ from the first belt in the Bentinck Street area. For residential areas also, the depth of the first belt allowed in Calcutta varies from place to place. It is well known that the building sites in the purely residential areas in North Kolkata differ from those in the more developed area in Ballygunj in the South and both differ from the Chowringhee area. In places which may be deemed to be a factory area, the question of the application of the belting method or of the depth of the first belt may sometimes become either unimportant or even immaterial.

"No general or uniform rule can be laid down for all cases where belting method is applied as to what the depth of the first belt should be. The question has to be decided with reference to the particular area and the nature of evidence, as may be available in a particular case."

In this case, the Calcutta Improvement Tribunal fixed on a consideration of the evidence, 60' as the depth of the first belt. The High Court held that there was no error of law on this question which can justify interference by the High Court.

In the case of *Sushil Chandra Ghose* v *Satish Chandra Ghose*,[11] a question arose as to the depth of the first belt of premises No. 6, Charakdanga Road, in Narkeldanga. The premises had a depth of 90'. The first belt was taken by the lower court upto a depth of 60'. It was contended *inter alia* that the entire premises which has a depth of 90' should be taken as the first belt land. Their Lordships (Mukherjee & Guha, JJ.) accepted the contention and made the following observations:

11 A.O.D. No. 459 of 1928 (unreported).

"Belting, it is admitted on all hands, depends on the development of the locality and on the average type of houses and it may also depend, as Mr. C.K. Sarkar, the Expert examined on behalf of the Plaintiff says, 'on the width of the road'. Judged by the admitted test, the house standing on the lands to be valued, itself affords the most satisfactory data on which a Valuer should proceed unless, of course, there are indications that there is anything extraordinary about it. Mr. Johnstone, the Expert, examined on behalf of the Defendants has proceeded upon an average taken from two premises on Charakdanga Road. It is doubtful if, in taking the depths of those premises he took into account the back lands which were vacant or the privies etc. But, apart from that, there were several instances put to him of buildings in and about the locality which had depths of 90', if not more. There is very little reason why those instances should be ignored."

In *Province of Bengal* v *Uma Charan Law*,[12] the acquired land, 70, Nimtolla Ghat Street had a frontage on that street which was to its south and another frontage on Kundu Chowdhury Lane to its north. The land had a north-south depth of about 200'. After determining the rate of ₹ 5,150 per kottah for the front belt land on Nimtolla Ghat Street of that premises, Their Lordships belted the land into two belts and fixed the value of the second belt land which had frontage on Kundu Chowdhury Lane at ₹ 4,250 per kottah. The relevant passage from the said judgment is quoted below:

"We think that for the purposes of valuation, the acquired land, plot No. 70, ought to be divided into two belts. As the frontage is about 53 feet, the first belt ought to be taken to be of a depth of 106 feet. But, instead of proceeding on nice calculation, we think that plot No. 70 is to be divided into two equal belts, each belt being half of the total area. The belt on Nimtolla Ghat Street is to be valued at Rs. 5,150 a kottah.

"Then there remains the valuation of the other belt. If premises No. 70 had no recess frontage on Kundu

12 48 CWN 609.

Chowdhury Lane, we would have valued the second belt at two-thirds of the rate of the front belt. But the fact that the second belt has a recess frontage must be taken into consideration. We think that the second belt ought to be valued at the rate of Rs. 4,250 per kottah."

An analysis of the above figures would show that Their Lordships in valuing the second belt land which had frontage on Kundu Chowdhury Lane made a deduction of 17.48% from the value of front belt land on Nimtolla Ghat Street in place of the usual 33⅓rd per cent on account of the additional frontage. If the usual ⅔rd value is given to that belt, then an allowance has to be given to the entire premises for the advantage of the second frontage on Kundu Chowdhury Lane. According to Their Lordships' valuation of the premises, that allowance would work at 10.8% for the entire area. It does not appear from the report that any transaction of land on Kundu Chowdhury Lane was produced in that case.

A plot of land accessible by and abutting on a passage from a public street cannot be valued by adopting the belting method from that public street. If it has no frontage on that public street, but only on a passage therefrom, it cannot be said it is in a certain belt on that street. In the case of the *Secretary of State for India in Council* v *Bhupati Nath Deb*,[13] the acquired land was approached by a common passage from Beadon Street. The claimant's expert Mr. Shorsbree was of opinion that the land should be valued on the basis of its being on the third belt of a property with a frontage on Beadon Street. The Calcutta Improvement Tribunal did not quite accept that opinion but gave the land 75% of the 'belting value' instead of the full value of a third belt plot on Beadon Street. On appeal by the Government, it was held by the High Court that:

> "As the land was actually cut off from the Beadon Street frontage by a large piece of land in different ownership, the Tribunal should have discarded all notions of the plot being a third plot on Beadon Street and valued it according to its actual disposition at the material date. Propinquity and easy access rather than frontage on Beadon Street were elements to be taken into account in valuing this land."

13 68 CLJ 90.

Information prerequisites to belting method

In a Kerala case, *Mariam* v *State of Kerala*,[14] held that where it is a case of large urban lands, part of such land will be of more value than the rest. In such a case, the valuation depends upon the advantageous situation of that part in comparison to the rest. A rational basis for determining the depth of each belt should be the scientific approach as below:

(*i*) the immediate contiguity to the main road;

(*ii*) easy access to the road where there is no frontage on the main road.

If different values are adopted without any intelligible data, the valuation cannot be accepted.

If this belting system is to be applied with any degree of accuracy, then it is necessary to have certain information from which to work. For instance, you may have two plots of land both having a frontage of 50 feet, both equally well situated, one has a depth of 60 feet and the land value is known to be ₹ 2,00,000 per kottah (720 sq. ft) and the other one has a depth of 160 feet and its value is required to be ascertained or estimated. Before this can be done with any degree of accuracy, it is necessary to know what are the rents of the shops within the first 60 feet depth and what are the rents of the rooms in the rear of the premises. A problem of this sort does not require any elaborate calculations. The area of the smaller plot is 4 kottahs, 2 chittacks and 30 square feet. The area of the larger plot is 11 kottahs, 1 chittack and 35 square feet. The larger is $2^2/_3$ times more in area than the smaller; therefore, it would be necessary to deduct between 20 to 25 per cent, say, $22^1/_2$ per cent, for size and the depth from the value. The calculation would be—

11 K. 1 Ch. 35 sq. ft. or 11.12 kottah (8000 sq ft.)* @ ₹ 2,00,000 per kottah	=	₹ 22,24,000
Deduct 22.5% for size and depth	= (–)	₹ 5,00,400
Value	=	₹ 17,23,600

* [1 Kottah = 720 sq. ft. and 1 Ch. = 45 sq. ft.]

14 AIR 1980 Ker 176.

Before one could arrive at a decision regarding the percentage deduction to allow one must inspect and ascertain the rents of the properties in the locality. It may be that the ground floor for a depth of 60 feet would let for ₹ 25 per sq. ft., first floor ₹ 12 per sq. ft.; second floor ₹ 10 per sq. ft.; and third floor ₹ 9 per sq ft. For lands at the rear of the 1st 60 feet depth ground floor would let for ₹ 13 per sq. ft.; first floor ₹ 9 per sq. ft.; second floor ₹ 8 per sq. ft.; and third floor ₹ 7 per sq. ft. The respective rental values of the front and rear portions would, therefore, be:

	Front	*Rear*
Ground Floor	₹ 25 per sq. ft.	₹ 13 per 100 sq. ft.
First Floor	₹ 12 per sq. ft.	₹ 9 per 100 sq. ft.
Second Floor	₹ 10 per sq. ft.	₹ 8 per 100 sq. ft.
Third Floor	₹ 9 per sq. ft.	₹ 7 per 100 sq. ft.
	₹ 56	₹ 37

The rental value of the rear portion is therefore 37/56 of the front portion or 0.661 or say, $^2/_3$rds that of the front portion. The rental factor can only be taken as a guide and if the rent actually works out at $^2/_3$rds for the rear portion compared to the front portion, something less should be taken to give the correct relationship between the land values, because the rent is a product of the land and building and in the example given the buildings on the front and back portion have the same value; therefore, there must be a greater difference in the land value than by taking a proportion of the rent. But for the purposes of this calculation it is assumed that the land in the 2nd belt is $^2/_3$rds that of the land in the first belt. If you wish to reduce this down to units of front belt you have—

1st belt 60 ft. deep 4.1667 kottahs	=	4.1667 units
Remainder 100 ft. deep 9.1666 kottahs @ $^2/_3$rds of 1st belt	=	6.1111 units
	=	10.2778 units

The land value is now ₹ 2,00,000 per unit and not ₹ 2,00,000 per kottah; therefore, the value is:

10.2778 units × ₹ 2,00,000 per unit = ₹ 20,55,560

Adjustment of large size when compared with sale of small plot

The Supreme Court in *Bhagwathula Sumanna* v *Special Tahsildar Land Acquisition Officer, Vishakapatnam Municipality*[15] stated:

> "In awarding compensation in acquisition proceedings, the court has necessarily to determine the market value of the land as on the date of the relevant notification. It is useful to consider the value paid for similar land at the material time under genuine transactions. The market value envisages the price which a willing purchaser may pay under *bona fide* transfer to a willing seller. The land value can differ depending upon the extent and nature of the land sold. A fully developed small plot in an important locality may fetch a higher value than a larger area in an undeveloped condition and situated in a remote locality. By comparing the price shown in the transactions all variables have to be taken into consideration. The transaction in regard to smaller property cannot, therefore, be taken as a real basis for fixing the compensation for larger tracts of property. In fixing the market value of a large property on the basis of a sale transaction for smaller property generally a deduction is given taking into consideration the expenses required for development of the larger tract to make smaller plots within that area in order to compare with the small plots dealt with other sale transactions."

In *Kaushalya Devi Bogra* v *Land Acquisition Officer,*[16] the Supreme Court stated as under:

> "When large tracts are acquired, the transaction in respect of small properties do not offer a proper guideline......In certain other cases this court indicated that for determining the market value of large property on the basis of a sale transaction for smaller property a deduction should be given."

15 (1991)4 SCC 506.
16 (1984)2 SCC 324 (335-36).

We shall also refer to the observations of the Supreme Court in *Administrator General of W.B.* v *Collector, Varanasi*:[17]

"The principle that evidence of market value of sales of small, developed plots is not a safe guide in valuing large extents of land has to be understood in its proper perspective. The principle requires that prices fetched for small developed plots cannot directly be adopted in valuing large extents. However, if it is shown that the large extent to be valued does admit of and is ripe for use for building purposes; that building lots that could be laid out on the land would be good selling propositions and that valuation on the basis of the method of a hypothetical layout could with justification be adopted, then in valuing such small sites in the area at or about the time of the notification would be relevant. In such a case, necessary deductions for the extent of land required for the formation of roads and other civic amenities; expenses of development of the sites by laying out roads, drains, sewers, water and electricity lines, and the interest on the outlays for the period of deferment of the realisation of the price; the profits on the venture etc. are to be made.

"The proposition that large area of land cannot possibly fetch a price at the same rate at which small plots are sold is not absolute proposition and in given circumstances it would be permissible to take into account the price fetched by the small plots of land. If the larger tract of land because of advantageous position is capable of being used for the purpose for which the smaller plots are used and is also situated in a developed area with little or no requirement of further development, the principle of deduction of the value for purpose of comparison is not warranted."

It was held in *Collector of Lakhimpur* v *Bhuban Chandra Dutta*,[18] that when a large area of land under acquisition is the subject-matter, it cannot fetch the price of the rate at which smaller plot or plots are sold. One aspect which, however, should weigh is that determination of the value of large extents

17 (1988)2 SCC 150 (157).

18 AIR 1971 SC 2015; (1972)4 SCC 236.

of acquired lands on the basis of the prices fetched by smaller plots must be a matter of last resort and should be adopted when there is no possibility of determining the market value of acquired lands on the basis of comparable transactions of large extents. Therefore, where a sale deed or an agreement to sell relating to a small extent of land is produced by the claimant, in the enquiry held for determination of compensation payable for his large extent of land, the court is not always bound to determine the market price of such large extent of acquired land on the basis of the price fetched or to that fetched by small extent of land covered by such sale deed or agreement to sell.

Computation of valuation of lands under belting system

An experienced valuer will have a very good idea how much one plot of land is worth compared to another without making a valuation a problem in mathematics, but Courts and Judges are not valuation experts and it is perhaps as well to produce a valuation based on the belting method of comparison, as this will be more easily understood by the layman and more likely to be accepted than an opinion based on a wealth of experience, although experience will certainly give the best and most accurate valuation.

This first item in "Belting" is to decide what shall be the depth of the first belt. A local inspection usually solves this quite easily. In shopping areas it varies from 50 to 80 feet in depth, but the boundary line between the first and second belt is usually clearly defined, there being a sharp fall in the rents of the rear portions. It may be, if the plot is very deep, that you will find still lower rents farther away from the main road: this will indicate a 3rd belt. The difficulty in belting is to estimate the correct value of the belt in relation to another and in shopping areas you will very rarely find the rents of the 2nd belt more than 50 per cent of the first belt, there being only a slight difference between the 3rd belt and the 2nd belt. In shopping areas you also get another belt known as the shopping belt, falling within the first belt. This shopping belt invariably commands a high rental and the relationship between the shopping belt (which has now become the first belt) and the second belt is very marked and the second belt will generally be found to be only 40 per cent or less in value than the shopping belt value. The greater the depth of the first belt, the less will be the difference between the 1st and 2nd belt. The smaller the depth of the 1st belt the greater will be the difference in value between the 1st and 2nd belt. In the case of *Alaul Huq* v *Secretary of State for India*[19] the front belt was found to be ₹ 2,000 per kottah, but this was only for a depth of 16½ feet and for the back land the value was placed at ₹ 400, being only one-fifth of the value of the front land.

There is no hard and fast rule that the second belt is one and half times the depth of the first belt, although the courts invariably follow this rule of thumb method. There must be a reason for everything. If back land irrespective of depth was capable of commanding a certain rent, then there would be no question as to the depth of the 2nd belt; the whole would be 2nd belt. If, however, it was found that the rent fell steadily in accordance with the distance from the main road, then there would be some justification for adopting the 2nd belt one and half times the depth of the first belt. If the land was of great depth, it may extend to a 4th belt and in dealing with land in shopping areas having a high value, you would continue belting until you arrived at a value for the lowest value land which represented its rental value compared to the rents and the value fixed for the 1st belt. The depths that are generally adopted are 2nd belt one and half times the depth of 1st belt; 3rd belt, one and half times the depth of the 2nd belt.

In residential areas the depths of each belt will be greater than in shopping and commercial localities and the differences in value between each belt will usually be less. The normal house requires a greater depth than what is required for a shop or business premises and the depth of the first belt is generally 100 feet. In areas where plots are fairly extensive, the first belt may be 150 feet and the 2nd belt one and half times the depth of the 1st belt, the remainder being 3rd belt. This applies where lands in the 1st belt are of a low value, because the back land cannot be of a lesser value than the

19 11 CLJ 393.

lowest value of lands in the locality. In residential areas there is not the larger difference in value between the 1st belt and the 2nd belt and usually there is very little information available which will be a guide to the 2nd belt value except the sale of tandem plots, and these are usually sold at approximately two-thirds the value of the front plots. The 2nd belt value is therefore taken at two-thirds the value of the 1st belt and the 3rd belt is taken at one-half the value of the first belt or three quarters the value of the 2nd belt.

Sales of land are the best guide to belt values. If you have two sales of different depths from which to form your basic values, it is comparatively easy to find the value of a third plot. To give an example:

EXAMPLE 54. Plot No. 1 having a frontage of 50 feet and a depth of 100 feet sold for ₹ 4,85,000. Plot No. 2 having a frontage of 80 feet and a depth of 200 feet sold for ₹ 11,25,000. What are the respective values of the 1st and 2nd belt?

(Calculations made in terms of local measurement of kottah: 1 Kottah = 720 sq. ft. or 66.89 sq. mtr.).

SOLUTION

Plot No. 1

Area— 50' × 100' = 5000 sq. ft. (6 K. 15 Ch. 5 sq. ft)

= 6.9444 kottahs

= 6.95 kottahs say (464.51 sq. mtr.)

Value $= \dfrac{₹\ 4,85,000}{6.95} =$ ₹ 69,784 per kottah

Plot No. 2

Area 80' × 200' = 16000 sq. ft. = (22 K. 3 Ch. 25 sq. ft.) = 22.23 kottahs. The area being roughly 3 times that of the normal plot the value will be $12\frac{1}{2}$ per cent less than normal value on account of size. Therefore, to arrive at normal value, if one-eighth has been deducted for size, add one-seventh:

Sale Price = ₹ 11,25,000

Add $\dfrac{1}{7}$ = ₹ 1,60,714

Normal Value = ₹ 12,85,714

Sketch 1

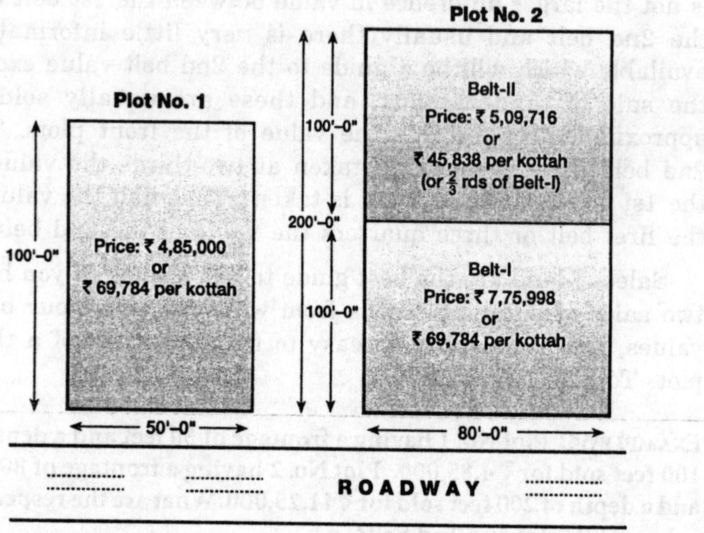

1st belt value—

80' × 100' = 8000 sq. ft. = 11.12 kottahs

@ ₹ 69,784 per kottah = ₹ 7,75,998

2nd belt value—

80' × 100' = 8000 sq. ft. = 11.12 kottahs

@ ₹ 45,838 per kottah = ₹ 5,09,719

Normal value – 1st belt value

= ₹ 12,85,714 – ₹ 7,75,998 = ₹ 5,09,716

1st belt value ₹ 69,784 per kottah = 1 unit

2nd belt value ₹ 45,838 per kottah = $\frac{45{,}838}{69{,}784}$ unit

or $\frac{2}{3}$ rds of 1st belt value.

If you now wish to find the value of a third plot the process will be easy. The first belt of 100 feet will be valued at ₹ 69,784 per kottah and the 2nd belt up to 150 feet will be valued at two-thirds the value of the first belt and so on, due allowance must be made for size.

Irregularities in shape of plots of land are covered by the Belting Method. This only means that difference in depths of plots can be adjusted by the belting method. A plot of land irregular in shape cannot have the same value as another plot of land regular in shape, even though both may have the same depth, as was observed by Mr. Justice R.P. Mukherjee in the case of *Mohini Mohan Saha* v *Province of Bengal*:[20]

> "Division into belts does not provide for other peculiarities of the land in question. It was urged that where a land is valued by dividing the property into belts, no deduction is allowable under the law for largeness, shape and other special features of the plot. This proposition cannot be supported."

Recess land—what it means and how valued

If the side of the plot forms with the frontage an angle greater than a right angle, then the land included in that area, which does not fall between two perpendicular lines extended at right angles from the extremities of the frontage, is known as *recess land*. This recess land is valued at three-quarters the value of the belt value. This deduction for recess land is derived from many actual transactions. For example, if the first belt value was 1, and the second belt value was $^2/_3$, the first belt value, then the recess first belt would be $^3/_4$ of $1 = {}^3/_4$, and recess second belt would be $^3/_4$ of $^2/_3 = {}^1/_2$. In the same way if the second belt was $^1/_2$, recess second belt would be $^3/_4$ of $^1/_2 = {}^3/_8$th. The following example will illustrate these points.

EXAMPLE 55. Land to a depth of 60 feet in the area is valued at ₹ 70,000 per kottah (*i.e.* per 720 sq. ft.) and 2nd belt value is $^1/_2$ of 1st belt value.

The area marked *A* will be 1st belt land. *B* will be recess first belt. *D* will be second belt and *C* will be recess second belt.

20 85 CLJ 379.

Sketch 2

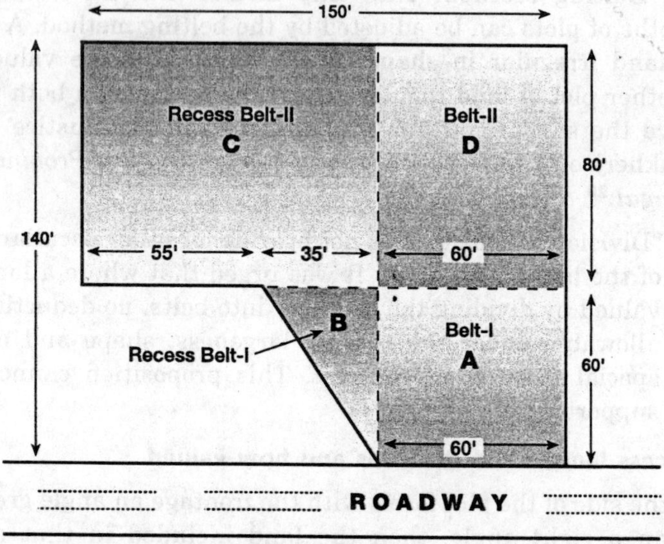

The calculation for units is as follows:

1st belt— 60' × 60' = 3600 sq. ft = 5 kottahs @ 1 = 5.00 units
(each kottah of 1st belt taken as 1 unit in term of value)

1st belt recess— 60' × $\frac{35}{2}$ = 1050 sq. ft
= 1.4583 kottah @ $\frac{3}{4}$ of 1 = 1.0937 units

2nd belt—80' × 60' = 4800 sq. ft
= 6.67 kottah @ $\frac{1}{2}$ of 1 = 3.34 units

2nd belt recess—80' × 90' = 7200 sq. ft
= 10 kottah @ $\frac{3}{4}$ of $\frac{1}{2}$ = 3.75 units

= 23.1283 kottah = 13.1837 units

A total of 23.1283 kottahs is thus converted into 13.1837 units of equal value.

Value = 13.1837 units × @ ₹ 70,000 per unit = ₹ 9,22,859

Average value per kottah = $\frac{₹\ 9,22,859}{23.1283}$ = ₹ 39,902

If the land shown as *C* in the above example had extended much beyond its western boundary, the value of *C* would have lessened in value. The first belt was 60 feet in depth. The second belt would have extended up to one and half times this depth, 90 feet. Recess 2nd belt land would extend sideways one and half times the depth of the belt and in this case that would be one and half times 90 feet = 135 feet. Any land extending eastwards or westwards in the second belt up to a distance of 135 feet would be valued as recess second belt, that is at three-quarters the value of the second belt. If the land had extended beyond 135 feet, then the excess amount would be known as recess—recess second belt and the value would be three-quarters of recess value, that is $^3/_4$ of $^3/_4$ or $^9/_{16}$th of second belt value.

The following sketch will help to make this clear:

Sketch 3

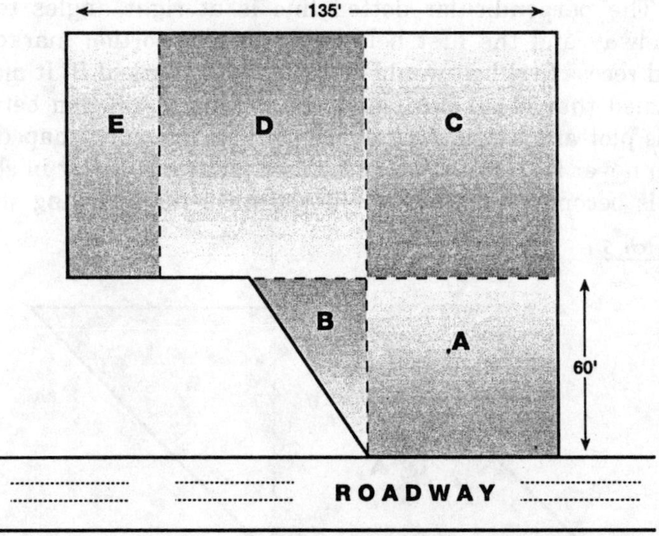

As in the previous example—*A* is first belt 60' deep. *B* is recess first belt. *C* is second belt and *D* extends up to one and half times the second belt, that is 1.5 (60 × 1.5) = 135 feet. The remainder of the land shown marked E is recess—recess second belt.

Sometimes lands have to be valued which are not rectangular in shape, although the sides may be parallel. The belting method takes these irregularities into account. The following area of land has to be valued, all falling within the first belt.

Sketch 4

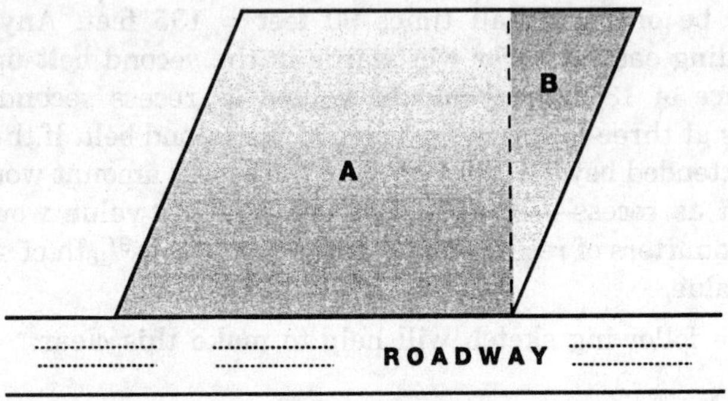

The perpendicular dotted line is at right angles to the roadway and the first belt would be the portion marked *A*, and recess first belt would be the portion marked *B*. It may be argued that it is ridiculous to make any distinction between this plot and a rectangular plot, but an irregular shaped plot can never be of the same value as a plot rectangular in shape. This becomes more obvious if you have the following shape.

Sketch 5

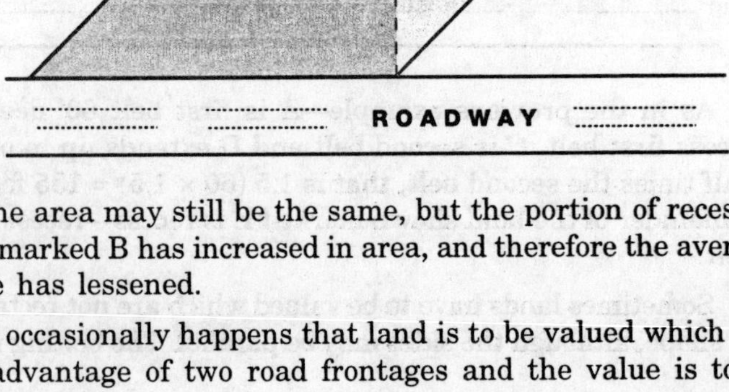

The area may still be the same, but the portion of recessed land marked B has increased in area, and therefore the average value has lessened.

It occasionally happens that land is to be valued which has the advantage of two road frontages and the value is to be determined by comparison of value by belting. In this case belting is done from both road frontages and if the values of the two frontages are not the same, then the whole of the land is belted from each road frontage on the same plan and the highest value of each portion is taken. For instance, a portion of the land belted from road *A* having a value of ₹ 1,20,000 per kottah for the 1st belt may fall within the 2nd belt. This piece of land may be the same as recess 1st belt when belted from Road *B* which has a 1st belt value of ₹ 1,00,000 per kottah. Belted from road *A* the value would be $^{2}/_{3}$rds of ₹ 1,20,000 or ₹ 80,000 (if the 2nd belt value is $^{2}/_{3}$rds that of the 1st belt). Belted from Road *B* the value would be $^{3}/_{4}$ of ₹ 1,00,000 or ₹ 70,500 per kottah. The value taken would be ₹ 80,000 per kottah, because this is the higher value. When belting is adopted for land which has the advantage of 2 frontages, nothing more need be added for the advantage of 2 frontages, if the land is belted from both frontages, but this does not apply to small corner sites which must be treated as explained previously.

Sketch 6

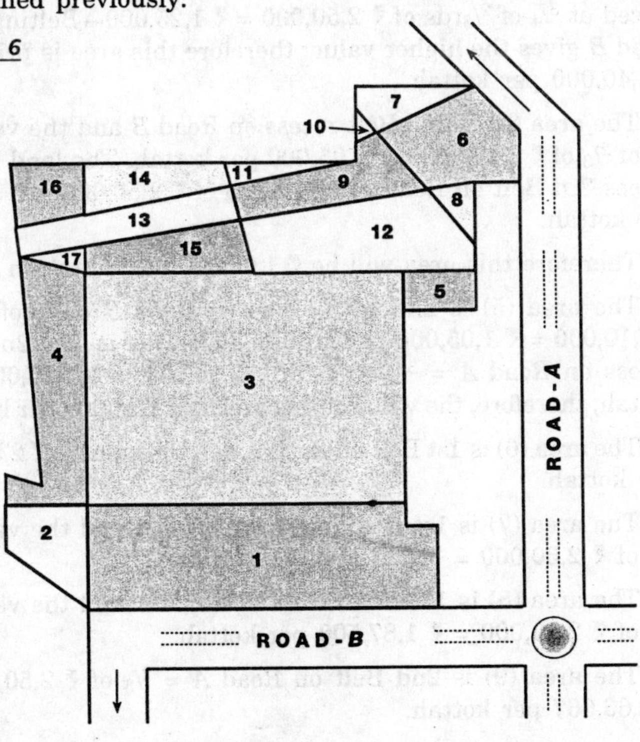

EXAMPLE 56 (Sketch 6)

This is a typical example of a plot of land having two road frontages in a city. Land on Road *A* is worth ₹ 2,50,000 per kottah for the first 60 feet and for the purpose of this example the second belt is assumed to be $^2/_3$rds the value of the first belt. The land value on road *B* is ₹ 2,10,000 per kottah for 60 feet deep and second belt is also assumed to have a value of two-thirds that of the first belt.

To value this land by comparison with the belting method you must belt the land from both frontages.

The area (1) is first belt of Road *B*. The value is ₹ 2,10,000 per kottah.

The area (2) is recess 1st Belt on Road *B* and the value is therefore $^3/_4$ of ₹ 2,10,000 = ₹ 1,57,500 per kottah.

The area (3) is 2nd on Belt Road *B* and the value is $^2/_3$rds of ₹ 2,10,000 = ₹ 1,40,000 per kottah. If this area had been valued from Road *A*, a part would have been 2nd Belt Recess priced at $^3/_4$ of $^2/_3$rds of ₹ 2,50,000 = ₹ 1,25,000—Belting from Road *B* gives the higher value: therefore this area is priced at ₹ 1,40,000 per kottah.

The area (4) is 2nd Belt recess on Road *B* and the value is $^3/_4$ of $^2/_3$ of ₹ 2,10,000 = ₹ 1,05,000 per kottah. The land is also recess 3rd Belt on Road *A* = $^3/_4$ of $^1/_2$ of ₹ 2,50,000 = ₹ 93,750 per kottah.

Therefore this area will be ₹ 1,05,000 per kottah in value.

The area (5) is 2nd belt recess on Road *B* = $^3/_4$ of $^2/_3$ of ₹ 2,10,000 = ₹ 1,05,000 per kottah. This area is also 2nd Belt recess on Road *A* = $^3/_4$ of $^2/_3$ of ₹ 2,50,000 = ₹ 1,25,000 per kottah; therefore, the value of this area is ₹ 1,25,000 per kottah.

The area (6) is 1st Belt on Road *A* and the value is ₹ 2,50,000 per kottah.

The area (7) is 1st Belt recess on Road *A* and the value is $^3/_4$ of ₹ 2,50,000 = ₹ 1,87,500 per kottah.

The area (8) is 1st Belt recess on Road *A* and the value is $^3/_4$ of ₹ 2,50,000 = ₹ 1,87,500 per kottah.

The area (9) is 2nd Belt on Road *A* = $^2/_3$ of ₹ 2,50,000 = ₹ 1,66,667 per kottah.

If belted from Road *B* the land would be 3rd Belt on Road *B* = 1/2 of ₹ 2,10,000 = ₹ 1,05,000 per kottah.

The value is therefore ₹ 1,66,667 per kottah being the higher one.

The computation of value of each plot can be done in this manner for areas market 10 to 19%. The pricing is shown in terms of kottahs as per land measurement system locally in vogue in West Bengal. One kottah is equivalent of 720 sq. ft. or 66.89 sq. meters. Thus, the pricing can be converted to any other standard system without injury to the logic of computation.

No hard and fast rule in Belting Method of Valuation

Belting method as has been held is a highly artificial method and as such no hard and fast rule can be laid down regarding the method to be adopted for assessing compensation. An irregular piece of land measuring 4 bighas 8 kottahs abutting to the west on Banamali Vidyasagar Lane (24, Cockler Lane and 45, Lake Road) in south Calcutta was valued by the Calcutta Improvement Tribunal by giving an average rate per kottah for the entire land treated as a single block. The Government appealed to the High Court and the principal contention of the appellant was that the Tribunal committed an error of law by giving an average rate per kottah for the entire land and not by dividing the land into successive belts and giving diminishing rate according to several belts into which the lands fell. Their Lordships Mr. Justice Rupendra Kumar Mitra and Mr. Justice Akram held in *Province of Bengal* v *Jaynarayan Fetepuria*,[21] as follows:

> "It appears that the learned Judge has considered this matter and on a consideration of the situation, size, shape and frontage of the land came to the conclusion that the belting method is not a suitable one in the present case for the purpose of valuation. I do not think that he has committed any error of law regarding this matter or applied any wrong principle in fixing an average rate per kottah on the basis of accepted awards; no hard and fast rule can be

21 82 CLJ 18.

laid down and each case must be considered in view of its own special features."[22]

There may be cases where in valuing a property on a certain roadway transactions are not available of the lands on the same roadway but on less important or more important roadways in the neighbourhood. In such cases both the experts and courts have to make guess work having regard to the relative importance of the two roads. In the case reported in *Government of Bombay* v *Century Spinning Manufacturing Co. Ltd.*;[23] the land to be valued abutted on a 40' road and 60' road, in the suburbs of Bombay. There was evidence of a transaction of land abutting on Worli Road, a 100 ft. wide road in the neighbourhood. On the basis of that transaction Chief Justice Beaumont inferred the value of the land in suit and observed as follows:

"Now the Worli Road is not only the main road but it is common knowledge that it is the main artery by which all motor traffic or at any rate fast motor traffic leaves Bombay because the road connects upto the road to Thana which divides into the road which goes to Poona and South India and the road which goes to Nasik and North India. A factory erected on that road is bound to possess considerable value from the advertisement point of view because motorists passing by that road will see the name of the factory and may carry the name in their memories. If I had to make a guess without assistance of any evidence I should say that a site to be used for commercial purposes on a main road of that character would be worth something like twice as much as site not on the main road."

The case of *Narsingdas* v *Secretary of State*,[24] may be usefully studied as an example showing how a court of law (Chief Justice Sadilal and Harrison, J) of the Lahore High Court valued a piece of land in the absence of sales of comparable lands by making assumptions and adjustments on the basis of an accepted award of back land without any frontage. It appears that in 1908 the appellant had purchased

22 *Nityagopal Sen* v *Secretary of State* ILR 59 Cal 921 at 925.
23 ILR (1942) Bom 403.
24 AIR 1922 Lah 327.

the plot in suit and the adjoining area, the plot in suit doubtless forming the most valuable portion of his purchase at the rate of ₹ 690 per kanal. In 1914 Government acquired from the appellant 10 kanals 8 marlas of land out of the area purchased in 1908 and immediately behind the present plot at the rate claimed by him viz. ₹ 2,000 per kanal.

In 1917 the present plot measuring 4 kanals 15 marlas 120 sq. ft. was notified for acquisition. The Collector awarded a sum of ₹ 9,553 and 5 annas/4 pies as market value at the rate of ₹ 2,000 per kanal. On reference to the District Judge the award was confirmed. On appeal the High Court found that the evidence produced by the parties was extremely meagre and afforded extraordinarily little help, and observed as follows:

> "Land values vary in Lahore with the most astounding rapidity and, once the recognised business highway of the Mall is excluded, the value of land on the adjoining feeder roads must be largely a matter of guess-work, and while it is obviously true that propinquity is an important element, it is impossible to say at what rate the values of frontage sites vary inversely with their distance from the Mall. At present there is only one important shop on a feeder road namely, that of M/s. Maxe Minck on the Ferozepore Road adjoining the Central Circus. The day will doubtless come unless the development of Lahore be retarded in some way, when shops will be built on other feeder roads, but there is no immediate prospect of this happening and the site in question not being on the business highway the prices paid for land on the Mall afford no help whatever."

The High Court also found on evidence that although before the war, prices were rising rapidly, during the war the prices were at a standstill and land could be obtained in 1917 at the same price as in 1914. The High Court then proceeded to value the land in suit in the following manner:

> "We find ourselves therefore reduced to one piece of evidence only, which is the fact that in April 1914 just before the war Government acquired from Rai Sahib Narsingh Das, the objector, 10 kanals and 8 marlas of land out of the area purchased in 1908 and immediately behind the present plot at Rs. 2,000 a kanal. It is a truism that in calculating the

value of a plot of land the price previously paid for a portion of the same area affords infinitely the best material which can possible exist. We have explained that prices were stationary during the war and, if this area of 10 kanals had been of precisely the same quality as that now in dispute, the matter would be settled by the price then paid and accepted without objection, for the order of the Collector shows that this was the valuation claimed by the owner himself. The land, however, though otherwise as desirable and as well situated had no frontage on any road and the difficult point to be decided is how far the existence of frontage and of a disproportionate area of frontage as compared with the whole affects the market price. Here again we must repeat that it is not a question of valuing the site of a possible shop but of the site of a building, which in the nature of things required an entrance from the road but did not depend for its prosperity on the amount of shop window, which could be constructed. Looking at the property acquired by Rai Sahib Narsingh Das as a whole and as comprising in Ewberys building sites adjoining the main business thoroughfare of Lahore, we may assume that every purchaser of a plot would demand some frontage, and the whole area would be cut up into portions of a convenient size combining such frontage with a reasonable area at the back, the measurements being presumably not less than those of a square. We also assume that the price would vary inversely with the depth as measured from the road and that the available sites would also decline in value as the distance from the Mall increases. Here the area behind had already been acquired by Government in 1914 and the price paid was Rs. 2,000 a kanal. Had the present plot been added to provide a frontage and the whole sold as one compound, we think it fair to assume that the value of the whole would have been Rs. 2,400 as against the Rs. 2,000 actually fixed for land without any frontage. The area now in suit is 4 kanals, 15 marlas, 120 square feet, the adjacent area previously acquired measure 10 kanals, 8 marlas. The total area of the two is therefore 15 kanals, 3 marlas and 120 square feet. At Rs. 2,400 a kanal the price of the combined plot is Rs. 36,424. The price paid excluding the 15 per cent for compulsory acquisition is

Rs. 30,353-5-4. The difference therefore is Rs. 6,070-10-8 and this was to be added to Rs. 9,553-5-4 the price already paid giving a total of Rs. 15,624 to which has to be added a further sum of Rs. 2,343-9-0 on account of compulsory acquisition.

"While it is quite true that within reasonable limits the narrower the plot sold on a thoroughfare the higher the price this only applied to shop sites and for other purposes such as the building of officers or residential houses a certain depth is essential. It is obvious that a site without a frontage had not the same value as one with a frontage but, at the same time, it must not be forgotten that the settler of a narrow strip of frontage deprecates the value of the land behind, which should have been added to it and the converse proposition is equally true.

"To look at it in another way if the value of a normal site on the Montgomery Road be X, a kanal, and the value of the back hall be X-2 it does not necessarily follow that the remaining portion of frontage is worth 3X-2 but rather that, if the pieces be sold separately, the total price will be less than that of the economic plot sold as a whole. We have, however, allowed that full 3X-2 as the figure we have assumed for a normal site with a frontage has been so assumed without any certain guide and as we do not know how far the figure would fall below 3X-2 we make no further assumptions but allow the whole of the difference .... All, therefore, that can be said is that the value of the various portions of the area purchased by Rai Sahib Narsingh Das must vary enormously infinitely, the most valuable portion being that nearest the Queen Statue and as we know the value of a plot at this end without a frontage, we can only reach the value of the frontage, which would naturally go with it by assessing the whole and increasing the price of this portion by the amount of the deficiency.

"We, therefore, accept the appeal in so far as to raise the price for the land in suit to Rs. 17,967-9-0 and for this sum we give the appellant a decree."

It should be noticed that what was acquired in 1914 at the rate of ₹ 2,000 per kanal was back land and part of the owner's land which had frontage on Montgomery Road though the acquired portion did not have any frontage. The learned Judges of the Lahore High Court valued the front land acquired in 1917 at a rate of about ₹ 3,288 per kanal. The increase over the rate of back land works out at about 64%.

The judgment of the Lahore High Court was affirmed by the Privy Council in *Lala Narsingdas* v *Secretary of State.*[25] Their Lordships observed as follows:

> "Now the principle upon which valuation of properties compulsorily acquired should be measured has been repeatedly laid down by this Board and by the House of Lords to use the word to be found in *Fraser* v *City of Fraserville.*[26] "It is the value to the seller of the property in its actual condition at the time of expropriation with all its existing advantages and with all its possibilities executing any advantage due to the carrying out of the scheme for the purpose for which the property is compulsorily acquired". Their Lordships are unable to find that this principle has been departed from by the High Court in the judgment that they have formed. The learned Judges appeared to examine the cases of sales of property in the District and rejected those which from their different locality and the different possibilities of value due to their position were in their judgment inapplicable and to have dealt with this case by considering the value of the land immediately adjacent at the rear and excluded from the road as determined by actual sale then to have assumed that the land in dispute was added with the advantages of the frontage and thus to have fixed a value for the whole and then taken the fractional value of this same road by the ratio of the area of the land in question to the entire block and given to it the whole added value due to the frontage. Their Lordships see nothing wrong in the court being thus guided to their conclusion and the question as to the amount which they thought right to add for the advantageous position that the present property acquired their Lordships are not prepared to examine."

25 29 CWN 822.
26 1917 AC 194.

Belting approach in high-rise buildings

The fact that the land was being purchased for construction of multi-storeyed buildings cannot rule out the application of the belting method. In the methods of valuation of land adopted in advanced countries like U.S.A. where 'high rise' buildings are common, the distance of different parts thereof from the main thoroughfare is taken into account and the 'depth factor' is introduced in the calculation of such value. Similarly, in a shopping complex, facility of accessibility is important. Easy accessibility makes for saving of time in shopping and is an attraction to clientele in a hurry. Thus shops on the ground floor will command a greater premium than those at higher levels. Availability of lift service or escalators are other factors which have a bearing on valuation. Ground floor shops facing the road also have an advantage in the matter of window display. The aforesaid are some of the factors which are taken into consideration in foreign countries in evaluating vertical shopping complexes.

This principle is applicable to high-rise buildings as was observed in *Madho Properties'* case (supra) and can be taken to be an extension of belting principle to vertical dimensions as well.

CHAPTER

14

Building and Estates

(A) Depreciation and Obsolescence of Building

The apportionment of value between depreciable amount and residual amount of 'land and building' is a significant topic to be discussed in the context of valuation. While the land component of a premises does not generally depreciate in value and may often appreciate due to development in surrounding areas, buildings have always a limited life. There are, however, exceptions in case of land too. For example, the land may have limited life due to depletion on account of extraction of minerals; or restrictions in use in future imposed through planning regulations or municipal building code; or any legislative intervention declaring the land as surplus to be vested in the State. But in normal circumstances land remains to be a residual amount in the valuation of real estate, leaving the building to be valued as a depreciable asset. That is why depreciation is an important aspect to be focussed upon in the valuation of building in particular.

Depreciation as a concept

The word 'depreciation' has been variously interpreted. The *Webster's Dictionary* (1951 edition) defines depreciation as 'an act of lessening or crying down price or value'; or in other words, "the falling of value; reduction of worth". As for building, depreciation is the measurement of wearing out through consumption, or use, or effluxion of time. A building also undergoes diminution in value due to obsolescence which is a factor different from depreciation to be discussed later on.

The concept of depreciation has been crystallized through a process of precision over the time. Earlier it was confused with repair and maintenance or replacement to keep the property in a state to command its existing value, but now it is conceived as a state of physical condition measured by wear and tear. It was earlier believed that a property maintained in a state of good physical condition could not have suffered much depreciation inasmuch as the property remains good as new. But such outward appearance is not a reliable index of the intrinsic worth of the property. Depreciation is a fact and it is the loss not restored by current maintenance. Depreciation results in a cost of service and it is an allowance for consumption of capital.

Depreciation accounting

Thus, depreciation accounting is an estimate which aims to distribute the cost or other basic value of tangible real property, less salvage, if any, throughout the estimated useful life of the asset. It is a process of allocation in a systematic and rational manner the element of decay inherent in all real estates. Depreciation for the year is the reckoned portion of the total charge under such system allocated to the year.

There are several methods of computing depreciation. In the Straight Line method, the cost of an asset less its salvage value is distributed or written off at a uniform rate for its complete service life. In this method, the crux of computation lies in realistic evaluation of salvage value and correct estimation of service life of the asset.

In the Sinking Fund Method, an amount is set aside every year and invested at compound interest so that after a specified period, one gets predetermined value of the asset less deduction for salvage. The sinking fund is a reserve built up by accumulating periodic allocations expanded with compound interest and is meant to meet the future liability of replacement. Thus there are two components in a sinking fund, one representing annual deposits of reckoned depreciation and the other is the interest on the depreciation reserve. The method calls for determining the present worth of the asset beforehand.

There is another method known as Written Down Value method in which the percentage rate for depreciation remains constant throughout whereas the capital base goes on reducing every year by an amount equal to the depreciation for that year. The result is that the quantum of the amount reckoned as depreciation dwindles with the reduction of the capital base in each successive year. It thus differs from the straight line method wherein the quantum of depreciation amount is constant being distributed throughout the service life of the asset at a uniform rate.

Repair, maintenance and depreciation

REPAIRS and replacements are intended to restore a run down building to good physical condition. It is a process of mending or replacing broken or worn out parts or overhauling so that the building retains its essential useful value and continues to render the services originally intended for.

MAINTENANCE, on the other hand, is a cost in valuation directly charged as operating expense while depreciation is an allocation out of prior expenditure. Maintenance costs are paid from current income as they are incurred, while depreciation is allotted as a cost equal to the inevitable write-off starting from the property new till the end of its useful life. Of course, efficient maintenance can prolong the useful life of a real estate and control depreciation cost to a certain extent, but no property can be rendered good as new by any standard of maintenance. Deferred maintenance can add to the misery of a building resulting in an accumulation or aggravation of maintenance work reflected in larger operating charges payable from current income. Good maintenance behaves in the opposite direction. But depreciation costs are inescapable and a sound accounting procedure would try to achieve an equitable distribution of depreciation cost over the years.

It is only the realisable site value which is exempt from the charge to depreciation. So also the other salvageable materials from which there should be an appropriate deduction towards the cost of demolition. Thus, depending upon the situation, an apportionment for depreciation as between land and building of a real estate may be arrived at either after deducting from the cost or valuation of the property the value of the land for its existing use; or, by making an assessment of the net replacement cost of the building.

Obsolescence

Like depreciation, obsolescence is also a factor that erodes the value of an asset. But there is a difference: obsolescence arises out of extraordinary situation in cases of wear and tear while depreciation is inherent in the asset as a process of physical decay over the time that is inevitable. The valuation process should in appropriate cases reflect on the aspect of obsolescence as on depreciation, to arrive at the sound value.

Obsolescence has been defined in *Webster's Third New International Dictionary* (Unabridged 1961 Edition) as under:

> "A factor included in depreciation to cover decline in value of assets due to invention of new and better processes or machines, changes in demand, in design or in the art, and other technical or legal changes but not to cover physical depreciation."

Obsolescence may be of three kinds: economic, functional or technological. Another type of obsolescence termed as statutory obsolescence has also been in vogue.

Economic obsolescence takes place when it is found that the expenditure for repair, replacement and maintenance of the building is much higher than what would be found in a modern facility capable of achieving the same level of services by replacement of the existing building. In other words, age and condition of the existing building demanding probable cost of its future maintenance as well as services may often prove too high as compared with that of a modern building. Thus, economic obsolescence is perceived.

Functional obsolescence takes place when the suitability of a building in the present use cannot be adapted to a changed demand. For example: a building for residential purpose in a growing commercial area may be more profitably exploited if it could have been opened up on the road front for accommodating a commercial activity like departmental store, retail business, computer services, etc. But if the construction of the building absolutely prohibits such conversion of use, the property suffers from incurable internal obsolescence. The obsolescence becomes curable if some additions and alterations can pave the way for adaptation to a proposed use. Likewise, a property which has a potential for industrial use becomes functionally obsolete if the planning regulations for zoning prohibits its user for industrial purposes. But again, if the zoning regulations remain for a limited period, the obsolescence becomes curable after elapse of such period.

TECHNOLOGICAL OBSOLESCENCE appears in an era of fast changing building technology. Buildings supported by walls are no more valid for construction beyond a height where framed structure has appeared to be the appropriate technology. Likewise, structural designs for high-rise buildings are also different. So, with the change of time, the design and construction of buildings can profit by the latest innovations. The purpose of a building is to provide shelter and protect belongings against sun, shower and wind. Again, the construction of a building has to conform to certain basic safeties, viz., structural safety, health safety, fire safety, constructional safety etc. Both these can be served by alternative building technologies at work. Quite a number of options are available on the structural designs as regards load, foundation, wood, masonry, concrete, steel, prefabrication or systems buildings as well as building services. Besides, horizontal sprawl of buildings may be conveniently replaced by vertical rise so as to leave more area for better uses including means of access, parking space, landscape etc.—a field where the architects have a major role to play. The prescribed Floor Area Ratio (FAR) or Floor Space Index (FSI) under the Municipal Building Code offers a variety of options as regards coverage and height of a building. On all these considerations, a building of the present day may often be obsolete for continuance in future due to sheer technological reasons. While functional obsolescence arises out of constraints in building uses, technological obsolescence arises mainly due to fast changes in technologies and innovations.

Composite property consists of land and buildings. Obsolescence can affect either or both. Land becomes obsolete when there is an instance of building encumbering the site, or where the bare land would have been more valuable than the combined entity of land and building. There are other cases where the buildings do not adequately develop the site, and to that extent it may be said the land is suffering from obsolescence.

STATUTORY OBSOLESCENCE occurs when enforcement of statutory restrictions affect the value of land and building. Laws are enacted on environmental considerations imposing zoning restrictions or controlling height or coverage of buildings. These restrictions or controls have bearing on the value of land or building. As for example, when zoning restriction is promulgated under planning law that prohibits building uses other than residential or commercial, in any particular area, the availability of land for multiple purposes in that area becomes banned under the statute. Likewise, hazardous use of buildings on land may be completely prohibited in areas other than that earmarked for that purpose. Such planning law restricts the supply of land for such hazardous use. The result is rise or fall of the price of land in the affected areas coupled with a corresponding change in the value of buildings for different uses in the planning area. This is a typical case of statutory obsolescence. Similar obsolescence can be brought about by coastal regulations or restrictions on riverside lands imposed under relevant law. As and when new aerodromes are built or microwave towers raised, the neighbouring buildings may come to experience restrictions in heights resulting in statutory obsolescence. Similarly, the fiscal laws may often affect constructions for particular purposes. High rate of property tax may render building of new premises less rewarding in some cities. Capital gains tax may take away the fruit of improvements if it amounts to an appropriation beyond what is reasonable. All these may be termed as statutory obsolescence.

Prime cost and depreciated value

The aspects of depreciation and obsolescence came up for judicial decision in a number of cases. To the value of the land must be added the depreciated value of the building, that is, the present day market value of the building. This does not mean that the value is the actual cost of erecting a similar structure, less an amount equal to the depreciation of the building. A person may spend a considerable amount on a structure for his own personal whims and fancies. This additional expenditure may not have a market value and accordingly it cannot be included. An extract from the judgment of Mr. Justice Broomfield in the case *Ismailji Mohomedalli Bohori* v *District Deputy Collector, Nasik*[1] is to the point:

"No accounts of the expenditure on these wells have been produced, and I think it is quite clear that there is no reliable evidence before the court to show even what the cost of construction was. Moreover, the cost of construction would not necessarily be the amount to be awarded by way of compensation. There is no evidence to show that the outlay on these wells or pits whatever it amounted to was successful or profitable. We do not even know that any water was found and there is no evidence to show that any of the wells was ever used. That being so, it is clear that the claimant has not made out any case for further compensation in respect of these wells. I agree with the order proposed by my learned brother."

The usual method is to ascertain the prime cost of a building and to deduct therefrom depreciation to give the present day market value.

As was laid down by the Privy Council in *Harichand* v *Secretary of State*,[2] this method is, what is commonly known as 'Contractor's Method'. "The subject to be valued being a building apart from the site, the principle of fixing value by ascertaining the cost of reproducing the building at the present time and then allowing for depreciation in consideration of the age of the building and for the costs of such repairs as might be required, apart from depreciation, is quite a well-known and recognised method of valuing buildings for the purpose of compensation".

The prime cost is the value a similar structure will cost to erect taking into account all the ornamental features which have a market value. The following are a few of the methods which can be adopted for estimation of the prime cost:

The building must be measured up very carefully and a schedule prepared of all the quantities of the various materials used in the construction. These will have to be priced and a sum added for the labour involved in construction. To this must be added a sum for builder's profit and risks. This is a

1 AIR 1933 Bom 37.
2 44 CWN 5.

very laborious task and is usually undertaken by a quantity surveyor. An intimate knowledge of the prices of every article from a nail to a bath that is used in the building is required and they must be the prevailing rates at the material time. Prices before the war were fairly constant but since the war began prices have varied very widely, and there has not been uniform increase. As a commodity becomes scarce prices rise. The issue of permits for buying steel, put up the prices of second-hand girders an appreciable amount, then the fixing of prices caused a boom in the black market. Therefore, any abnormal increases in prices of materials caused by temporary legislation and scarcity of commodities, due to the war, should be disregarded.

This list is only very brief and does not include the many hundreds of small items necessary to make up the building and is only intended to give a general idea of prices at a given time.

Prime cost of landed property in bustees

In ascertaining the prime cost of *bustee* huts, a valuer should carefully examine the materials used. In the case of *Mathura Prasad Rajgarhia* v *Province of Bengal*,[3] the Expert for the claimant had estimated the prime cost of a *bustee* hut taking the rates of first-class materials. On appeal, the High Court did not accept that estimate on the ground that "In a *bustee*, the materials used are not first-class".

Buildings can be valued by taking the external measurements and obtaining the cubical contents and then applying a rate per cubic foot to represent the prime cost. This is probably the best way providing the valuer has a thorough knowledge of building values. Buildings vary considerably in price.

Another method which is on the same principle, is to measure the area of the building and to take a value at so much a square foot. This will then depend on the height. A valuer must be careful in his evidence in law courts regarding values of buildings. Many valuers give a value for the building which really represents the value of the whole of the completed

3 AOD No. 214 of 1948 (unreported).

structure, they then proceed to add on many extra items which have already been included in the value. Others attempt to value the prime cost of a building assuming the building to be modern in every respect whereas the building may be constructed of small bricks denoting a great age, and mainly wooden beams. If there are a number of steel beams in the building they will be of recent origin and will have been placed there probably to prevent the building from falling down.

Entropy is the arrow of time. The universe is exposed to sure decay. But it is possible to cause delay in the process of decay through measures for preservation in a confined to a sector at the cost of the others. After ascertainment of the prime cost of a building the present day value is required. This is found generally by making a deduction to represent the depreciation of the building. No fixed percentage can be given for this item because it must vary with every case. One method is to take nothing for the first 5 years and then to take 5 per cent for every six years. This is an absurdity. Many newly erected buildings after 5 years will show numerous defects usually caused by using unseasoned timber and lack of supervision during erection. Every case must be treated on its merits after a thorough inspection has been made. The minimum depreciation will be half per cent per annum but in most cases much more. There are, of course, exceptions to every rule. A building of the type similar to Government House will not have a depreciation as high as half per cent per annum, the reason being that much more than the normal amount will be spent each year in repairs and renovations. Huts and *bustee* dwellings depreciate very rapidly. A hut 5 years old may have depreciated between 25 and 50 per cent and a valuer must exercise great care when making a valuation of a *bustee* for compulsory acquisition. He should not be deceived by a plentiful display of colour-wash on the walls which has been put on to hide serious defects in the structure.

The Contractor's method of valuing a building as laid down by the Privy Council in *Harichand's* case,[4] is not strictly followed by valuers. They usually deduct from the estimated prime cost a certain percentage on account of what they say

4 44 CWN 5.

'age and condition'. They do not separately assess the two factors. Be that as it may, age of a building should be carefully ascertained by valuers. In doing so, the valuer should not depend on his eye-estimate. Proper enquiries should be made by him. He should search the municipal assessment records, examine sanctioned plan and other relevant authentic papers which are likely to give the correct age of the building. In *Ganesh Properties Ltd.* v *State of West Bengal,*[5] His Lordship Mr. Justice S.R. Das Gupta accepted the contention put forward by the advocate, "that an ordinary Engineer and Surveyor cannot be said to be an Expert specially skilled in the art of finding out the age of the building".

The depreciated value of a building is not always the correct figure to add to the value of the land to arrive at the value of a property. The building may have to be valued as old materials. A good guide is to value the premises first by the rental method. If the value of the land *plus* the depreciated value of the structures closely approximate to the rental method of valuation, then the full value of the structures should be taken. If the value by the rental method of valuation is less than the value of the land, then there can be no justification whatsoever to take more than old material value of the structures. If the value by the rental method comes midway between the value of the land and the value of the land *plus* the depreciated value of the buildings, then the buildings can be said to be worth something between old material value and standing structural value and it is advisable to take the mean of the two values.

(B) Building, Retirement and Remaining Life

Buildings must by their nature have a limited life. While lands have a residual value, the physical property in the form of building decreases in value with age and use, as there is always a decline in the amount and character of the future services it can render before it will be retired. It has also been observed that good maintenance can prolong useful life but does not overcome internal forces that ultimately cause the retirement of the physical property. Physical condition alone is not the

5 AOD 59 of 1954 (unreported).

sole measure of the diminution in value in service capacity. While depreciation in terms of physical condition is often apparent and bear a direct index of the depreciated value of a property, the value depreciation owing to diminishing capability for delivery of services cannot be observed and takes place silently. Viewed in this light, the forces operating to bring about the ultimate retirement of a property from services may include wear and tear, decay, action of the elements, inadequacy, obsolescence or restrictions imposed for public purposes and the like. In retirement accounting, therefore, the amount charged to production expenses each year is the cost, less salvage value of the property, retired that year. As the diminution in value is the loss not restored by current maintenance and is due to all the factors causing the ultimate retirement of the property, such expenses charged each year is termed as retirement expenses.

Remaining life

It is always difficult, if not impossible, to put a precise life to a building or a group of buildings but it is necessary to undergo an exercise to estimate the remaining life. The allocation of a single life to all types of buildings would not be appropriate; user of building differs from case to case; besides, the level of maintenance and repairs is a major factor to be taken into consideration. The life of a new building can usually be extended within a reasonable limit by a higher standard of maintenance or minor improvements as and when occasion demands. So each building should be considered individually. At the end of the useful life of a building, the full potential of the site for redevelopment within existing planning framework would be realisable. A reasonable allowance towards cost of demolition of the worn out buildings may often be required to be made from the price likely to be fetched in the open market in respect of the site with potential for redevelopment. Since the physical property in a building decreases in value before it will be retired, the basic measure of the amount of this decrease in value is the decrease in the present worth of the service remaining with the building. In other words, the amount which is the difference between the value new and the present worth of the future services remaining with the building after allowing for salvage value, if any, should be the appropriate measure of the decay looked at from the angle of retirement of a property. It is in this way that the depreciated value of buildings may be estimated on the basis of their remaining useful life.

Depreciation as in the law for compulsory acquisition

The principles evolved by courts for incidental heads of compensation, such as "depreciation" have not fully charted the area. In fact, there is no clear statutory provision for "depreciation" in s. 23(1) of the Land Acquisition Act 1894 (now s. 28 of the Right to Fair Compensation and Transparency in Land Acquisition, Rehabilitation and Resettlement Act 2013) except such incidental heads of compensation as (*i*) *Secondly,* for standing crops or tress (*ii*) *Thirdly,* damage for severance (*iii*) *Fourthly,* damage for injurious affection to other property or the claimant's earnings (*iv*) *Fifthly,* reasonable expenses incurred for change of residence or place of business (may be classified as disturbances) (*v*) *Sixthly,* diminution of profits of land between declaration under s. 6 (now s. 19) and taking of possession.

In England, however, provisions for compensation for 'depreciation' of land are provided in the Compulsory Purchase Act 1965 as under:

(A) Depreciation and actionable nuisance.

(B) Depreciation resulting from taking claimant's land on account of plugging of price, severance, injurious affection, nuisance from severed land.

(C) Depreciation not resulting from taking claimant's land, but caused on account of use by public works.

(D) Actual loss suffered by depreciation.

A good number of English case decisions have illustrated the point. But the Indian law for compulsory acquisition being not specific on the point of depreciation, has remained in a somewhat nascent stage.

(c) Land with Buildings

Land with buildings is viewed in a different perspective than bare land as such. Land and buildings once merged in each other as if married to each other to become one unit, and neither land nor building can thereafter be valued separately. A building once erected on or married to the site, as it is technically often termed, takes unto itself a value which may be either greater or less than the cost of erection depending upon the market situation. If the building properly and economically develops the land, the total value of the complete entity may be worth more than the sum of the individual valuer. In such cases, the excess of the composite value over the sum cf the individual values is ascribable as the builder's profit. But there may also be instances to the contrary. It is generally impossible to arrive at the true value of the whole by addition of the parts.

The cost of a building is not necessarily its value, either when new or still more so when it is old. In the case of a completely new building, if it is suitable to the site and adequately develops the land, it is likely that its cost would approach its value. If otherwise, value would clearly be less than its cost. To take an extreme example, an excellent building on the middle of a desert with the anticipation that habitation may soon grow there, may turn out to be a futile investment. On the other hand, there may be instances where a tiny cottage in the heart of a city assumes immense value due to spurt of commercial growth all around. This acts as a warning against taking cost of construction as a criterion of value and highlights the overall feature that land and building lend their characteristics to each other to make up the total value. The locational advantages of the land may give a unique worth to the building erected on it and on the other hand, the building may develop the land so as to bring out its potential worth to the fullest extent.

Land as three-dimensional entity

The potential of land for building purposes is again a technological question. Though land is a two-dimensional entity having only length and breadth, building provides the third dimension to it in the form of vertical rise. This is based on the legal concept of land as a potential volume of cubical space with boundless height and depth. This is significant because technological development continue to expand our ability to utilize the earth's sub-surface as well as air space. In urban areas in particular, engineering advances have dramatically affected land use and, therefore, highest and best use considerations. The development of steel-framed building construction, the passenger-elevator, deep tunnel excavation techniques and communication technology are some examples of technological changes that have helped shape our urban sky-line as well as underground uses. A sub-surface right to use profitably the underground portion of a designated property is becoming entrenched day by day in metropolitan cities. Air rights are emerging as incorporeal rights associated with the use, control and regulation of air space over a parcel of real estate. Thus land is gradually presenting an idea of a three-dimensional entity. As density of building in urban area increases, fewer sites are available for new construction and land value escalates. As early as in 1902, air rights in New York city were beginning to be developed. Air rights can be transferred there in various ways. Often, the air rights to one property are shifted to another within the same building zone under legal planning regulation. The transfer of air rights allows developers to adjust the density of land use by dispersal of the thrust of new constructions. Air rights can be sold and may also be sub-divided. In this way, Transferable Development Rights (TDR) emerged in the real estate industry in USA since the 1970's. A transferable development right is a right of construction that cannot be used by the landowner on a particular land due to restrictions—legal, planning or otherwise—but can be sold to landowners in another location within the same jurisdiction. Thus, landowners in the preservation district are assigned development rights which they cannot use to develop their own land through additional construction but can sell to landowners in the development district where such further constructions are permissible under zoning regulations of planning laws. The concept has lashed the shore of our country too. In the city of Mumbai, Transferable Development Rights can be negotiated as an incorporeal property right on the strength of certificate issued under the Development Control Regulations for Greater Bombay, 1991.

Monopoly rights

The discussion is not complete unless we refer to the rights as conferred on the holders of intellectual property in matters of patent, copyright, design and trade mark ensured in the relevant fields of law. The Patent Act of India had protected the monopoly rights of patent holders in 'products' and 'processes' for sixteen years. The World Trade Organisation mainly dominated by the western powers as if in exercise of activities in the quaternary sector of ecomomy, recommended such monopoly rights extended to twenty years as because they are sure to explore better methods of performance of such products and processes through Research and Development (R&D) involving huge investments which creates an 'Entry Barrier' for other countries however, much they are required to amend such duration of protection extended to twenty years in obedience to enmembership of WTO. The result is perpetuation of monopoly rights in favour of western countries in the relevant field of production. The obsolescence caused to the intermediate products is another burden in the economy of the developing countries.

Valuing land with buildings

Quite a number of judicial decisions have reflected on various aspects of valuation of land with building particularly in the context of compulsory acquisition. The catena of such decisions do not strike a uniform note but present a fairly reasonable approach to be adopted as a tool for valuation purposes.

Land and building constitute one unit and the value of the entire unit must be determined with all its advantages and its potentialities. The purpose of acquisition is to acquire all interests which clog the right of the Government to full ownership of the land. The court has to value the unit and then apportion the compensation among the persons entitled thereto. This rule cannot be departed from merely because the receiver in whom the *benami* rights in the land with buildings were vested failed to raise an objection to the quantum of compensation awarded to him. Where the value of the building is to be determined, regard must be had to what may be called the life expectancy of the building. In the case as no evidence was adduced to show the condition of the building acquired the market value was determined on the basis of the actual rental value.[6]

6 *Collector of Kistna Masulipatam* v *S.R.Y. Sivarama Prasad* AIR 1938 Mad 33; (1937)2 MLJ 744; ILR (1938) Mad 431.

When the property sold is land with building, it is often difficult to secure reliable evidence of sale instances of similar land with buildings proximate in time to the date of notification under s. 4 of the Land Acquisition Act 1894 (now s. 11 of the Right to Fair Compensation and Transparency in Land Acquisition, Rehabilitation and Resettlement Act 2013). Therefore, the method generally resorted to in determining the value of the land with building is the method of capitalisation of return actually received etc. Compensation cannot be determined by ascertaining the value of the land and the "break-up-value" of the building separately. The land and the building constitute one unit, and the value of the entire unit must be determined with all its advantages and potentialities. Under s. 23 of the Land Acquisition Act 1894 (now s. 28 of the Right to Fair Compensation and Transparency in Land Acquisition, Rehabilitation and Resettlement Act 2013). Compensation has to be determined by taking into account the market value of the land at the date of notification and the damages, if any, under any head *secondly to sixthly* in s. 23(1).[7]

The land, buildings standing thereon and standing crops and trees on the land constitute one unit, and the value of the entire unit has to be determined with all its advantages and potentialities. Necessary consequences will be that only one award has to be rendered for the unit.[8]

It has been held by the Supreme Court in the case of *Administrator General of West Bengal* v *Collector, Varanasi*[9] that it is permissible to value property estimating separately market value of land with reference to the date of preliminary notification and add to it value of structures as at that time. So, the District Judge was justified in assessing the value of the structures separately or that the valuation on this score was not excessive.[10]

7 *State of Kerala* v *P.P. Hassan Koya* AIR 1968 SC 1201.

8 *Sharan Pal Singh* v *State of Punjab* AIR 1991 P&H 98 relied on *State of Kerala* v *P.P. Hassan Koya* AIR 1968 SC 1201 and distinguished *Ranjit Singh* v *Union Territory Chandigarh* AIR 1983 P&H 308; 1983 PLJ 290.

9 AIR 1988 SC 943.

10 *Collector L.A., Darjeeling* v *Sudhangsu Sil* AIR 1992 Cal 246 (DB); *Sharan Pal Singh* v *State of Punjab* AIR 1991 P&H 98.

In the determination of market value of property comprising building and extensive land, building is not on the entire piece of land under acquisition and the existing structures not indicating realisation of full developmental potential of the land, it was held, property cannot be treated as one unit with building. So market value of building and land underneath can be evaluated separately.[11]

Land with building could be valued in either of the two methods:

(1) If valuation is to be made on rental basis it should be on the basis of the net rent. Twenty years' purchase is regarded as an approximately correct estimate of the value of a substantial building which is likely to stand for a reasonably long period.

(2) If the land and the building are to be separately valued the proper method is to find out the value of the building on the basis of the value of the materials by appointing a building commission for the purpose and the value of the land on the basis of the value of land in the locality similarly situated.[12]

An important decision was given by the Supreme Court regarding the valuation of land with buildings in *State of Kerala* v *P.P. Hassan Koya.*[13] A piece of land with a building standing thereon which was used for business purposes and fetched as monthly aggregate rent of ₹ 332.50P was acquired by the Government under the L.A. Act 1894. The L.A. Officer determined the compensation payable @ ₹ 10,000 per acre for the land and for the houses standing thereon at their break-up value. In a reference it was held that the method adopted by the L.A. Officer to be wrong and proceeded to determine the market value of the land and the building by capitalizing the net rent received from the same and taking into consideration the return from gilt-edged securities at $3^1/_2$%, awarded the compensation at 35 times the net annual rent. On appeal the High Court determined the compensation by multiplying the net rent $33^1/_2$ times, that being in their view

11 *Hiralal* v *State of U.P.* AIR 1994 NOC 147 (All).

12 *State of Trav-Cochin* v *Rama Krishna Iyer Narayana Iyer* AIR 1955 Trav-Co 132.

13 1968 SCA 362.

the true multiple derived from the return based on the current return from gilt-edged securities. In dismissing the appeal preferred by the Government the Supreme Court observed as follows: "Agree with the Trial Court and the High Court that the method adopted by the L.A. Officer for determining compensation payable for extinction of the interest of the holder of the land and of the building separately was unwarranted. In determining the compensation payable in respect of land with buildings compensation cannot be determined by ascertaining the value of the land and the *'break-up'* value of the building separately. The land and building constitute one unit and the value of the entire unit must be determined with all its advantages and its potentialities. Under s. 23 of the L.A Act compensation has to be determined by taking into consideration the market value of the land at the date of the publication of the notification under s. 4(1) and the damage, if any, sustained by the person interested under any of the heads mentioned in *Secondly* to *Sixthly* in s. 23(1) of the L.A. Act.

"As observed by the Judicial Committee in *Vyricherla Narayana* v *Revenue Divisional Officer, Vizagapatnam.*[14]

"There is not in general any market for land in the sense in which one speaks of a market for shares or a market for sugar or any light commodity. The value of any such article at any particular time can readily be ascertained by the price being obtained for similar articles in the market. In the case of land, its value in general can also be measured by a consideration of the prices that have been obtained in the past for land of similar quality and in similar positions and this is what must be meant in general by 'the market value' in s. 23. An instance of sale which is proximate in time to the date of notification under s. 4(1) of the L.A. Act in respect of land similarly situated and with similar advantages and which is proved to be a transaction between a willing vendor and a willing purchaser would from a reliable guide for determining the market value. The value which a willing vendor might reasonably expect to receive from a willing purchaser in respect of a house, generally depends upon a variety of circumstances including the

14 66 IA 104.

nature of the construction, its age, situation, the amenities available, its special advantages and a host of other circumstances. When the property sold is land with building it is often difficult to secure reliable evidence of instances of sale of similar lands with buildings proximate in time to the date of notification under s. 4. Therefore, the method which is generally resorted to in determining the value of the land with buildings specially those used for business purposes is the method of capitalization of return actually received or which might reasonably be received from the land and the buildings.

"That method was rightly adopted by the Trial Court and High Court. The unit under acquisition is used for business purposes and has a prominent situation in the town of Calicut. There was a clear evidence about the rental of the building and the Trial Court proceeded to capitalise the net annual rental having regard to the rate of return of $3^1/_2$% from gilt-edged securities by multiplying it by 35 items. The High Court has slightly reduced the multiple.

"It cannot be laid down as a general rule applicable to all situations and circumstances that a multiple approximately equal to the return from gilt-edged securities prevailing at the relevant time forms an adequate basis for finding out the market value of the land. But in this case the Trial Court and the High Court were of the view that a multiple based on the return from gilt-edged securities was the approximate multiple for determining the value of the property under acquisition, and no ground has been suggested for not accepting the basis and the rate of capitalization adopted by them. It is relevant to note that the same multiple which has been adopted in other cases relating to land and the buildings acquired under the same notification under which the land of the respondent was acquired has not been challenged by the State."

The principles laid down in the above case are very important and must be borne in mind in valuing lands with buildings particularly business. It is, however, submitted that the Supreme Court in the above decision has not laid down any hard and fast principle that all lands with buildings must be valued as one unit by capitalizing the rent actually received or which might be reasonably received from the lands and the buildings. The other method of valuation of lands with buildings is to find out the value of the land and then add to it the value of the building which is commonly known as the Land and Building Method, has not been completely ruled out and can be adopted in a proper case. In *T. Adinaryan Setty* v *Special L.A. Officer*[15] on one of the plots in suit there was a newly constructed building which was tenanted at the material time. The Mysore High Court found the value of the land and added to it the value of the building. In the appeal against that judgment as reported in AIR 1959 SC 429, the Supreme Court while modifying the judgment of the High Court as regards the value of the land did not interfere with its valuation of the building.

It may be relevant in this context to refer to two decisions of the Calcutta High Court in *Madan Mohan Burman* v *Secretary of State,*[16] and *Province of Bengal* v *Uma Charan Law.*[17] In the first case the High Court held that it is permissible to deduce the value of land from the sale price of a land with building by deducting the value of the building from the sale price. In the second case before the High Court valued the land in suit on the basis of the sale price of land with buildings as its integral part by simply deducting the value of the building.

The other question raised in the case has also great importance. After finding out the net rental of the property (presumably by deducting the outgoings from the actual rentals) the High Court determined the compensation by multiplying the net rent 33$^1/_3$ times, that being in its view the true multiple derived from gilt-edged securities and that was approved by the Supreme Court. In other words, a multiple approximately equal to the return from gilt-edged securities prevailing at the relevant time was taken and the net annual rent was multiplied by that multiple. It is submitted that the case *Province of Bengal* v *Board of Trustees for the Improvement of Calcutta,*[18] was not cited before the Supreme Court for the consideration

15 AIR 1954 Mys 71.
16 AIR 1925 Cal 481.
17 48 CWN 609.
18 50 CWN 825.

of Their Lordships. In that case, Calcutta High Court discussed the question of return from land and gilt-edged securities and held that the return from land should be 1% higher than that from gilt-edged securities and consequently the multiplier for capitalization of the annual rental would be at a lesser figure than that for gilt-edged securities.

(D) Hypothetical Building Scheme

The hypothetical building scheme consists in an attempt to value a parcel of land by means of figures based on a calculated financial result of a notional erection of buildings on the land, and its notional development in the most profitable manner. The land to be valued is thus imagined as covered with as many houses or shops of profitable character as can be reconciled with possible development in response to future demand. The courts of law have admitted evidence on such hypothetical building schemes in the matter of assessment of compensation for land compulsorily acquired. Thus this method has attained the stature of a recognized method of valuation although this technique of valuation has not found favour for various reasons. This technique known also as land residual method revolves around determination of land potentiality, on the basis of the following assumptions:

(*a*) That the subject land will be married to hypothetical buildings to generate the best possible market rent;

(*b*) That the outgoings assumed on the subject land developed with buildings would not undergo any change during the period from the date of valuation till the last unit of occupancy under the scheme is sold out;

(*c*) That the cost of construction will remain constant throughout the above period, i.e. from the date of valuation till the last unit of occupancy is constructed;

(*d*) That the rent realizable on occupancy of the hypothetical scheme will remain undisturbed from any intervention by way of rent restriction;

(*e*) That the subject land is capable of being put to the highest and best use in accordance with the notional development as conceived in the hypothetical building scheme.

Thus it is a method full of hypotheses and assumptions, and its validity depends on the sustainability of each of them. If any one of them fails, the method will be of no use. The most important proposition that one can ascertain the value of land by deducting the cost of construction from the capitalized rental income is not correct as land once married to the building cannot be separated out by any known process and it is not possible to ascertain in what proportion the intangible value generated by the marriage can be allocated separately to land and building. In the next place, the promulgation of rent control laws completely upsets the assessment of rental income which lies at the basis of the scheme model. The other assumptions also call for adjustments on which there may not be any unanimity amongst valuers. The method pushes enquiry back into causes which create a notional demand in a reasonable market whereas the other methods of valuation ascertain demand direct from the market.

In spite of all these infirmities this technique was put to test in a number of judicial findings, of course, with due care and considerations as evident from the discussions therein.

Although the law is very definite upon this point, there is still a tendency for valuers to estimate the value of a vacant plot of land by capitalising the assumed rent that can be obtained from a building, if erected on the land, then to deduct the cost of the building to ascertain the value of the land. Some courts still allow evidence of this nature to be put in, and upon which no reliance whatsoever can be placed. It has already been explained that from a rental valuation of land and buildings you cannot deduct the value of the buildings to arrive at the value of the land. Now in this case you are expected not only to deduct the value of the building from the land, but you must assume the cost of the building, the rent that can be expected, the numerous outgoings and the security. It would be a simple matter for a valuer to make a calculation on this basis and to arrive at any value that was required for the land, but under no circumstances can it be called a sound valuation or any reliance placed upon it exclusively.

In the same way when valuing land and structures consisting of a one-storey building which does not develop the site, no reliance whatsoever can be placed on evidence which is based on the assumption that extra floors can be erected on the building, the capitalisation of an assumed rent, then deduction of the cost of the extra floors that are assumed to be erected.

The case of *Government of Bombay* v *Merwanji Muncharji Cama,*[19] is very definite on this point and an extract from the judgment is therefore quoted below:

> "This brings us to the question whether the hypothetical building scheme should in any case have been accepted by the court as a guide to its decision. This question was argued as a preliminary point, and we intimated to counsel that our decision was against the admissibility of the scheme. Our opinion is grounded mainly on the following reasons: In the first place the scheme depends entirely on the validity of three propositions, of which the first is that the present market value of land on which buildings have been erected can be ascertained by deducting the cost of construction from the capitalised nett annual rental. Then it is asserted that the prospective market value of land which is now vacant can be ascertained by deducting the estimated cost of the buildings which, it is supposed, can be erected on the land from the capitalised nett annual rent which it is estimated such buildings will produce. Lastly, it is asserted that the present market value of the land can be ascertained by making certain deductions from the prospective market value. It is clear that, unless the first proposition is true, the other two propositions cannot be true and the hypothetical building scheme is out of court. In our opinion the first proposition is not true. The balance remaining after deducting cost of construction of buildings *in esse* from the capitalised value of actual rents received must, we think, be regarded as including builder's profits, which will depend on the capital, skill and experience at his disposal; it is therefore an unknown quantity and has no necessary connection with the "market value of the land", which is the figure to be ascertained under s. 23 of the Land Acquisition Act. In our opinion the market value of land means simply the price which, at the given time and

19 (1908)10 Bom LR 907.

place, land would fetch on sale according to the then rates of the market; and this value depends on general pre-existing considerations apart from the individual projects of a particular purchaser. To express the same thing in other words: land is a marketable commodity of one description, and land with buildings on it is a marketable commodity of another and a different description; and there is no known process by which from the ascertained value of land *plus* buildings as an investment it is possible to deduce the value of the land alone.

*** *** ***

In the matter of the Land Acquisition Act X of 1870; *Munji Khetsey*,[20] a case decided in 1890 by Farran, J, sitting with assessors. There the claimant's experts sought to derive the present value of neighbouring land on which a chawl had been built from the joint value of the land and chawl, and suggested that the value so derived should be applied to the land then under reference. This method was rejected with little ceremony by the learned Judge in these words: "When we have before the court evidence of actual purchases and sales of land in the vicinity, in none of which does the actual price given even remotely approximate to that figure (*i.e.*, the figure arrived at by this method), it is plain that there must be something intrinsically unsound in the calculation or its basis. It would be easy to point out wherein this unsoundness consists. It is, however, unnecessary to do so, for this method of arriving at the value of land has not been adopted by the court". Three years later this same method, as applied to imaginary buildings and not to neighbouring buildings, was tendered on behalf of the claimant in *Municipal Commissioner for the City of Bombay* v *Syed Abdul Huk Kurmolker*[21] and the Court observed: "We do not think that such a basis of valuation should be accepted in any case, certainly not where there is any more practical basis to work on". That decision has the high authority of Sir Charles Sargent, CJ, and we may note in passing that in the case now before us there is sufficient

20 ILR 15 Bom 279.
21 ILR 18 Bom 184.

evidence of sales of land in the vicinity, and the prices so indicated do not in general approach the figure deduced from the hypothetical scheme.

"Then we think that a scheme of this sort, considered as evidence, is bad as being too remote, speculative and conjectural. We do not lose sight of the decision of the Privy Council in *Secretary of State for Foreign Affairs* v *Charlesworth, Pilling & Co.*,[22] where Their Lordships point out: "It is quite true that in all valuations, judicial or other, there must be room for inferences and inclinations of opinion which, being more or less conjectural, are difficult to reduce to exact reasoning or to explain to others. Everyone who has gone through the process is aware of this lack of demonstrative proof in his own mind, and knows that every expert witness called before him has had his own set of conjectures of more or less weight according to his experience and personal sagacity. In such an inquiry as the present relating to subjects abounding with uncertainties and on which there is little experience, there is more than ordinary room for such guess-work, and it would be very unfair to require an exact exposition of reasons for the conclusions arrived at."

* * * * * * * * *

It is true that the opinion of an expert witness is admissible in evidence not only when it rests on the personal observation and inquiry of the witness himself or on facts within his own knowledge, but also when it is founded on the case as proved by other witnesses at the trial; and, under s. 51 of the Evidence Act, when the opinion is admissible, the grounds upon which it is based are also admissible. But we understand it to be settled law that an expert may not be asked purely speculative hypothetical questions having no foundation in the evidence, in other words, before the expert witness is entitled to give evidence on the hypothesis, a sufficient foundation for it must be laid by due evidence *aliunde* of the facts assumed.

This is the view taken on the subject in the recognised text books on the law of evidence (*e.g.* Wharton s. 452., Phipson

22 28 IA 121 at p. 139.

2nd Ed., p. 364, Amir Ali and Woodroffe under s. 46) and followed in the American Courts: see *Storey* v *Union of Bank*[23] and other cases cited in Volume XII of the *American and English Encyclopaedia of Law*.

* * * * * * * * *

And in this case, as we have noticed, these conjectural calculations are the less admissible inasmuch as the record contains sufficient evidence of a simple and direct character to guide the court to its determination. Indeed we cannot resist the conclusion that these hypothetical schemes are not really intended to assist an inquirer to ascertain an unknown figure, but are designed as arguments to afford some support for a figure already otherwise fixed upon and settled. It is apparent that nothing is easier for the calculator than to shape and adjust his figures so as to bring about the result desired without introducing any one variation large enough to be pronounced wholly improbable. But in our opinion no intending purchaser would allow his purchase to be decided by complex calculations of this kind involving so much risk of error as to be practically worthless.

* * * * * * * * *

But apart from that, we consider there is a clear decision on the question in *The Collector of Poona* v *Kashinath,*[1] where Sir Charles Sargent, CJ, says: "The value of the property should be determined not necessarily according to its present disposition but laid out in the most lucrative and advantageous way *in which the owner could dispose of it,* which in the present case it was urged by the respondent No. 1 and not disputed by the appellant, would be by laying it out for building purposes. The question then is what would be its market value if so laid out, and the most reliable evidence on that question must be the rates per square foot at which similar building land sites in the neighbourhood have recently been sold".

* * * * * * * * *

We agree with the principle laid down in *Fink* v *Secretary of State for India*[2]: "If it is shown that a person has paid a

23 34 Ala 687; *Bush* v *Long Island R. Co.* 10 NY App Div 535.

1 ILR 10 Bom 588.

2 ILR 34 Cal 604.

certain price for a block of neighbouring land similarly situated and possessing similar advantages with a view to some profitable disposal thereof, there is no reason why another block of land the subject of acquisition should not be similarly valued. The probability of a person purchasing the land for a similar purpose is an element for consideration if the probability is not so remote that it ought to be held purely speculative, so that other things being equal, of two blocks of land, the block under acquisition should be taken to be of equal market value with the other block. The general principle cannot be denied".

An extract from the case of *Government of Bombay* v *Karim Tar Mohamed,*[3] regarding this same point is given below. Here counsel tried to argue that the *Merwanji Cama* case was in his favour, but the judgment is again very definite on the point:

> "I have already decided in an interlocutory judgment in this reference (which can be incorporated herewith) that evidence of hypothetical building schemes is irrelevant to the question of finding the market value of land. It is difficult to suppress the belief that seems to exist almost universally amongst surveyors in Bombay that market values can be ascertained in this way. Otherwise it should not be necessary to keep on giving reasons to the contrary. The belief that a hypothetical scheme can be a guide to market values ascertained by other means is equally fallacious. However much conclusions may differ, the road which leads to the determination of land values is short and straight. By the ingenuity of Counsel and surveyors, attempts, often successful, are made to divert the road on the grounds that the diversions will lead to an infallible result. They only lead to waste of time."
>
> * * * * * * * * *
>
> The interlocutory judgment was as follows:
>
> MACLEOD, J.— I have already decided this question in what I thought sufficiently plain language in the reference of In re: *Dhanjibhoy Bomanji* and everything I said in that judgment on this question may be taken as incorporated in this. Mr. Robertson argues that though that decision might

3 ILR 33 Bom 325.

be right in the case of a piece of land of 21,000 square yards, it would not follow that it would apply to the case of a piece of land measuring 3,500 square yards. I can see no distinction. In the first place there can be no relation between the capitalised rent of land and actual buildings and the market value of the land. It follows that there can be no relation between the capitalised imaginary rents of imaginary buildings and the market value of the land. Mr. Robertson has cited In re: *Merwanji Cama.* That case is not binding on me, though I would follow it if I could possibly agree with the decision. If it does decide that hypothetical building schemes are relevant, I have already expressed my view on that question in *Dhanjibhoy's* case. These hypothetical calculations are not founded on fact. There are a number of factors each of which can be varied to an indefinite extent and therefore the permutations and combinations of these factors are practically infinite. I happen to know exactly how those calculations are made and I am perfectly aware that if Mr. Chambers thought the land was worth ₹ 15 a square yard, he could turn out an equally plausible scheme to support that figure. Mr. Robertson argues that if I disallow this scheme as irrelevant, it follows I must hold any hypothetical building scheme is irrelevant. In my opinion it is. As long as opinions may differ as to the building to be put on a piece of ground there can be no certain fa^tor on which the valuation can be founded. That is the root of the matter. If the building is certain, *i.e.* one of which there cannot be two opinions, and there may possibly be cases in which it can be, then there is no longer an hypothetical building scheme. The failure to recognise this guiding principle can only result in enormous waste of time and money.

On the impact of hypothetical building schemes on valuation, the onus lies on the claimant. Thus, it was held in the case of *Narsingdas* v *Secretary of State*[4] hypothetical building schemes are the usual basis of valuation in case of building lands, but the course there contemplated is that a surveyor should be called who would unfold a scheme giving

4 AIR 1928 Lah 263; 112 IC 797.

details of the amount to be spent and estimating probable returns which could be tested in cross-examination. A claimant cannot ask the court to value his land on that basis where he has not adopted this course.

In the valuation of land on the basis of a hypothetical building scheme the valuer has to ascertain the maximum value of each plot laid out in the most lucrative manner in the light of the potentialities and in doing so, expenses which may have to be incurred for developing the land in the most profitable manner have evidently to be taken into account. A land cannot be parcelled into building plots for residential purposes unless proper and adequate roads are demarcated and prepared and it is only by the reservation of land for roads that the building plots acquire a substantially higher rate than the overall rate of land regarded as a single unit. This principle was evolved in the case of *Addl. Special L.A.O.* v *Shantaram Sharmrao Ghole.*[5]

So, a hypothetical layout of building plots in the acquired land similar to that of the layout of building plots actually made in the similar other land has to be prepared. The price fetched by the sale of building plots in the layout actually made should form the basis for fixing the total price of the acquired land with building potentiality. In ascertaining such potentiality it has to be enquired if plots similar to other plots had been made in the actual layout of land and sold by taking into account plus factors and minus factors involved in the process. The market value of the acquired land with building potentiality can then be regarded as the total amount of prices of sales of all the building plots envisaged in the hypothetical layout of building plots minus the losses which could have been suffered or expenses incurred in making the hypothetical layout of building plots projected on the acquired land at a par with the developed layout of building plots.

As decided in *P. Ram Reddy* v *L.A.O.*[6] prices fetched by sales of building plots which may become available could be of building plots in either a fully developed layout of building plots or in an undeveloped layout of building plots situated in

5 AIR 1960 Bom 448.
6 (1995)2 SCC 305.

the vicinity of the acquired land with building potentiality. Then how much of land out of the acquired land becomes available to be made into plots similar to those in the developed layout of building plots or in the undeveloped layout of building plots has to be found out. So, whether the acquired land has building potentiality or not and the market value of the acquired land with building potentiality are to be determined with reference to the material to be placed on record or made available in that regard by the parties concerned and not on surmise, conjectures or guess-work.

(E) BUILDING ESTATE

The valuation of building estates is an entirely different proposition from the hypothetical building schemes. Known also as the developer's method of valuation, the technique consists in ascertaining value of land if sold in lots rather than sold in one block. Land must be valued having regard to all its potential possibilities when laid out in its most advantageous manner, and if an estate would be worth more, if sold out in small plots, then a scheme should be framed showing the most "advantageous manner" it can be laid out. To quote again the case of the *Government of Bombay* v *Karim Tar Mohamed*:[7]

> "The owner in claiming compensation can seek to prove either what the property would fetch, if sold in one block, or what is the present value if he plotted out the property and sold it in lots."

On the outskirts of large towns and cities there are many vacant lands which would be capable of being developed as a building estate. Before any attempt can be made to value an estate, the essential features and characteristics of a good building estate must be thoroughly understood.

Land near a city passes through three phases:

(1) Agricultural land.

(2) Accommodation land.

(3) Building land.

7 ILR 33 Bom 325.

At one time the land will only be worth the capitalised rent receivable for agricultural land and the rent will only be a rent for that purpose. Gradually the city will expand and a demand will be set up for accommodation land for use as market gardens, school playing fields and recreation grounds. The rent will be higher than for agricultural land and the land will have increased in value. The city will continue to expand and the land will become known as 'ripe for building development'.

The demand for any land in a locality is caused by the wants of the inhabitants. As and when the population of any district increases, the demand for land becomes greater and prices are bound to rise. A slow increase in the rise of population in a district means a slow increase in the value of lands. A large influx of people to a locality will cause an immediate rise in land value to an appreciable extent. This packing of large masses of people into a confined space has led to high prices being paid for land. At the present time transport facilities have improved considerably and this has been the means of people being able to live some distance away from their work, and town-dwellers nowadays measure distance by time and not by miles. A long period of peace, prosperity, stable Government, low taxation and general enlightenment has led to a demand for more and more houses, and the discovery of more rapid means of transport has caused a shifting of the population to other areas.

When land becomes ripe for building development it must be accessible to the city. Transport facilities must be good and fares low and there must be a good bus service; a tram service or a rapid transit system like underground railway would be an additional attraction. The site should also be easily accessible to a Railway Station. The estate should have access on to a main roadway and better still if a main roadway passes through the centre of the site. It is the main roadway which will give the site publicity value. The cost of the land must be low, otherwise the speculator will have no margin for profit and enterprise. The estate must be capable of an economical development and an expert must be consulted to advise on the best and most economical method of layout. The lie of the land must be suitable for natural drainage and sewerage disposal facilities must be available. The area of the land should be large enough for economical development, but not too large, otherwise the initial cost may be prohibitive and the supply may greatly exceed the demand which might easily cause a loss to be made. The land must be suitable for all classes and types of development; small plots for the poorer people, larger plots for the richer and space available for markets, open spaces and places of amusement. There must be a demand for land in the locality, otherwise the scheme will be doomed to failure before it is half completed. There must not be any restrictive statutes or municipal regulations which will hamper the sales of land or the erection of buildings on the site. The title of the land must be absolutely sound without any clogs or defects, otherwise the land will not sell at a price anywhere near the proper and correct value. There must not be any easements over the land such as rights of way which cannot be extinguished or alternative routes offered through the estate roadways. The boundaries of the estate should be fairly regular in alignment, otherwise around the boundary of the estate will be numerous plots of irregular shape and these will have a lesser value than regular shaped plots.

The development of an estate is done in the following manner:

(1) Purchase of the whole of the land free of all easements and encumbrances.

(2) Filling in all the tanks and raising low lands.

(3) Preparing plans of new roads which will develop the estate to the best advantage.

(4) Executing the engineering works, such as road making and the installation of modern services such as sewerage, drainage, water and lighting; and

(5) Selling the land available for sale in the most advantageous manner.

There is no finality whatsoever in building estate schemes. Different surveyors will devise different schemes, all of equal merit. It may be even possible to make a profit out of a bad scheme, but good and well thought-out schemes will certainly make more profit.

The best method of testing various schemes as well as comparing the merits and demerits of various layouts is to calculate the cost per foot frontage. The formula is—

$$\frac{\text{Cost of Estate + Cost of roads \& incidental expenses}}{\text{Total building frontage in feet}} = \text{Cost per foot frontage}$$

The development of roadways in a scheme should be as far as possible level, roads are generally laid along contour lines to avoid gradients. Gradients should not be more than 1 to 40 unless absolutely necessary.

Losses on a building estate may be caused by:

(1) Paying too high price for the land.
(2) Buying too large area.
(3) Under-estimating the cost of development.
(4) Becoming involved in litigation.
(5) Unattractive scheme of development.
(6) Depreciation owing to the use made of adjoining lands.
(7) Competition.
(8) Financial difficulties.
(9) Lack of well-directed energy.
(10) Slumps.
(11) Restrictive provisions of planning law.

These different issues are mainly self-explanatory. Care should be taken to see that the estate is not bordering on land used for a tannery or other offensive trade. Competition is absolutely fair, but if there are many other estates in the neighbourhood, the supply of plots of land may exceed the demand and you may have a slump in land values. A financier should not embark on speculation in a building estate unless he is in a position to acquire the whole of the estate and make all the development roads and can wait a little while for a return on his capital.

The following table shows how the economic "Law of Diminishing Returns" applies to building estates and how a slump occurs:

Stage	No. of plots	Demand for same	Market value per kottah	Remarks
A	1000	1,50,000	1,50,000	Excessive profits.
B	1000	1,25,000	1,40,000	Profits reduced but still large.
C	1000	1,00,000	1,20,000	Normal profits.
D	1000	99,900	1,15,000	Poor market, small profits.
E	1000	95,000	1,00,000 or less	Slump.

The time taken in passing from one stage to another may be very rapid and care should be taken to see that the demand always exceeds the supply. This can easily be done by only putting on the market a limited number of plots at one time and although it will take slightly longer to dispose of the whole of the land in the estate, much better prices will be realised.

In making a valuation of a building estate the first item is to ascertain the Gross Income. The Gross Income is found by adding together the whole of the values expected to be realised for each plot of land. The land will be plotted out into suitable sized plots and prices placed upon each plot. The prices should be the normal expectation if sold in the best possible manner. There may be too many plots to put the whole on the market at one time; therefore provision must be made for putting them on the market in stages so that the best prices may be obtained.

The next step is to ascertain the present value of the estimated realisation. Some of these plots, especially those situated at the side of existing roadways, will be capable of being sold immediately. As the engineering works progress, more land will become available for sale and an estimation must be made of the period of time which is likely to elapse before all the lands are sold. A well laid-out scheme which is estimated to be all sold within 5 years, may be disposed of as follows:

1st year	... ...	30 per cent
2nd "	... ...	22.5 " "
3rd "	... ...	17.5 " "
4th "	... ...	15 " "
5th "	... ...	15 " "
		100 per cent

The present value of the estimated realisation is therefore found by deferring the Gross Income half the period, that is likely to elapse before all the plots are sold. If the period is 4 years, then the Gross Income will be multiplied by the Present Value of Re. 1 in 2 years' time at 6 per cent; if the period is 6 years, the Gross Income will be multiplied by the Present Value of Re. 1 in 3 years' time and so on. The result is the present value of the estimated realisation.

For the present value of the estimated realisation must be deducted the various outgoings which may consist of the following items:

1. Any capital sum which may have to be paid to any of the adjoining owners to provide an access across his land, or any sum which may have to be paid to extinguish any easement right. This will be deducted in full because the amount will have to be paid immediately.

2. *Engineering costs.* This item will consist of all charges for road making, laying of footpaths and kerb stones, laying of sewerage mains, filtered and unfiltered water mains and lighting of the streets. To this must be added the fees for preparation of the plans and supervision charges, as the work must be done in a competent manner so that the roads will be taken over by the Municipal authorities after they are completed, otherwise their maintenance will become a perpetual burden on the estate. The whole of this amount will not be payable immediately, amounts will have to be paid to the contractors as and when the works proceed; therefore the total engineering costs should be deferred half the period they are likely to take to be completed. For instance, if it is estimated that the whole of the engineering works will be completed within 3 years, then the total engineering costs should be deferred $1^1/_2$ years at 6 per cent, that is, the total cost should be multiplied by the Present Value of Re. 1 in $1^1/_2$ years at 6 per cent.

3. *Other costs incidental to purchase.* This item will include solicitors' and any legal costs. The purchaser usually pays the cost of the conveyance, so this item will not be large. Land Agents' commission will also come under this heading. These costs will be spread over the period during which the whole of the plots are being sold: therefore the total cost must be

deferred half the period. If it is estimated that the last plot will be sold in 6 years' time, the total cost under this item will be deferred 3 years at 6 per cent, that is, the total cost will be multiplied by the Present Value of Re. 1 in 3 years' time at 6 per cent.

4. *Advertisement costs.* This item will have to be spent immediately to start the scheme off. Boards will have to be erected on the site and numerous leaflets printed for distribution. The total cost will be the deduction to make.

5. *Developer's Risks and Profits.* This is sometimes known as Adventurer's Risks and Profits. The Speculator who is providing the capital for the purchase of the land and the cost of the development not only deserves to derive interest on his money, but there must be a good margin for profit owing to the risks that he is taking. For instance, if a slump occurs, he will undoubtedly not only suffer a loss in capital, but he will not make or receive any interest on his capital that he has invested. In a highly speculative concern at least 20 per cent of the ultimate realisations must be allowed, that is, 20 per cent of the present value of the estimated realisation. If there is a great demand in the locality for plots of land and there is only this one estate capable of being developed, an allowance of 15 per cent may be made. This item should never be less than 15 per cent and this can be taken as the absolute minimum.

The final stage in the valuation is to deduct the total of the outgoings from the present value of the estimated realisation, the result will be the valuation of the estate.

If a speculator wishes to know how much he can afford to pay for an estate, the same calculation must be made taking 20 per cent for developer's risks and profits, the balance being the purchase price of the estate. Care must, of course, be exercised in estimating the present value of the estimated realisation and the outgoings and too optimistic a view should not be taken since so many things nowadays can upset a calculation.

EXAMPLE 57. What is the present value of the following estate which is now ripe for building development. The estimated cost of engineering works completed is ₹ 42,78,500. The estimated Gross

Return from lands available at immediate rate is ₹ 1,11,31,750. Let us assume, 3 acres of land worth ₹ 16,20,000 will not be sold immediately but reserved for cinemas and markets.

[1 kottah = 720 sq. ft.; 20 kottahs = 1 bigha; 3 bighas = 1 acre]

SOLUTION

Gross return expected from land for sale = ₹ 1,11,31,750

This sum will not be realisable at once. Part of it will be received immediately and the last sale is expected in 3 years' time, so defer the gross return by 1½ years @ 10% calculated as

$$\frac{1}{(1+i)^n} = \frac{1}{(1+0.10)^{1.5}}$$

$$= \frac{1}{(1.1)^{1.5}} \qquad = \qquad 0.87$$

Present value (P.V.) = ₹ 1,11,31,750 x 0.87 = ₹ 96,84,623

Add:

Value of lands not at present for sale = ₹ 16,20,000

It is proposed not to sell it at once, but reserve for cinema, markets, etc. for 3 years Defer 3 years @ 10% calculated as

$\frac{1}{(1.1)^{1.5}}$ or 0.75 estimated for ₹ 12,15,000

Present value of estimated realisation = ₹ 1,08,99,623

Deduct:

(*i*) Cost of road-making, sewers, water mains, lighting and all engineering works ₹ 42,78,500

This work will take 3 years to complete

Defer 1.5 years @ 10% calculated as

$\frac{1}{(1.1)^{1.5}}$ estimated at 0.87

= ₹ 37,22,295

(*ii*) Engineering and supervision charges, say, @ 12½% on ₹ 37,22,295 = ₹ 4,65,287

(*iii*) Finance charges @ 15% on (*i*) + (*ii*) for 1 year = ₹ 6,28,137 (*iv*) Legal charges, commission on sales and other costs incidental to purchase, say, @ 5% on ₹ 1,08,99,623 = ₹ 5,44,981

(*v*) Advertisement cost @ 1½% of ₹ 1,08,99,623 = ₹ 1,63,494

(*vi*) Developer's risks and profits @ 20% of ₹ 1,08,99,623 = ₹ 21,79,925

= ₹ 77,04,119

Surplus for the site (land)

= ₹ 1,08,99,623 – ₹ 77,04,119

= ₹ 31,95,504 or estate

Let X be the value of the estate.

Stamps duty, legal charges etc. @ 10% (say) = 0.10X

Therefore, site value + stamp duty, legal charges etc. + finance charges for 1.5 years @ 15% on land value and stamp duty etc.

$$= (1.10X) \times (1.10)^{1.5}$$

Add: Developer's profit @ 15% in land value and stamp duty $= (1.10X) \times (1.10)^{1.5}$

Surplus for the site or estate

$$= [(1.10X) \times (1.10)^{1.5}] + [(1.10X) \times (0.15)]$$

$$= [(1.10X) \times (1.1536897)] + [(1.10X) \times (0.15)]$$

$$= 1.269X + 0.165X$$

$$= 1.434X$$

₹ 31,95,504 = 1.434X

$$X = \text{Value of the estate} = \frac{₹\ 31{,}95{,}504}{1.434} = ₹\ 22{,}28{,}385$$

Assumptions:

(*i*) Project period is 3 years

(*ii*) Booking starts after 1 year.

(*iii*) Sale starts after $1^1/_2$ years.

EXAMPLE 58. An interesting case was reported in the Estates Gazette of 18th April 1942, and extracts are given below:

A claim for compensation was made against the Minister of Supply arising out of the compulsory acquisition of land in the Northolt and Yeading (Middlesex) districts. The claim was heard by the Official Arbitrator, Mr. A. Lloyd Thomas at the Chartered

Surveyors Institution on January 6th, 7th and 8th 1942. The compensation was to be assessed in accordance with the Acquisition of Land (Assessment of Compensation) Act 1919. The effect of the war on values was clearly indicated in the valuations submitted by both parties.

SOLUTION

The expert for the claimant submitted the following valuation:

			£
Frontage—			
Residential 17,650 ft. at £ 6 per ft. frontage			1,05,900
Add: Shop 500 ft. at £ 20 per ft. frontage			(+) 10,000
			1,15,900
Roads and Sewers—		£	
Contract Price		44,900	
Deduct:			
(*i*) Paid to Contractors	8,450		
(*ii*) Retention Money	947		
(*iii*) Work done yet to be paid for	75		
(*iv*) Estimated value of work to be completed on that part of the estate not being purchased by the Ministry of Supply	1,117	(–) 10,589	
		34,311	
Add: Contribution to be paid to the Hayes and Harlington U.D.C. towards the cost of a surface water sewer in Brook-side Road		(+) 3,000	
		37,311	
Deduct: Contribution by White Hart Estates Ltd. to Broadlands (London), Ltd. towards the cost of surface water sewers		(–) 4,195	(–) 33,116
			82,784

	C/f.	£ 82,784
Deferrer—		
800 plots available. Normal period development 4 years. But defer for further 3 years for period of war conditions. Deferrer 3 + $\frac{4}{2}$ year = 5 years. Present Value of £ 1 in 5 years on the 5½% (per cent) Tables		.7651
		63,339
Value of 3½ acres reserved in the development as an open space for playing fields, etc., 3½ acres at £ 350 per acre	1,225	
Defer for the period of war conditions—three years: P.V. £ 1 in three years on 5½% (per cent) Tables	(x) 0.8516	1,043
		64,382
Adventure's profit and risk 15 per cent		9,657
		54,725
Add:		
Value of work on foundations oversites and brickworks on plots Nos. 50 and 52, Douglas Crescent and cost of surface water and soil drains north of No. 1, Douglas Crescent		110
Value of land taken		54,835

(NOTE: £ 54,725 ÷ 66$\frac{3}{4}$ acres = £820 per acre).

Consequential Damage

Approximately one acre of land outside and adjacent to the south-west corner of the land taken would normally drain on to the land taken. This cannot now be effected.	
Estimated depreciation	400

It was obvious that the arbitrator would reduce this valuation. In the first place the whole of the cost of road making has been deducted instead of spreading these costs over a number of years and secondly the adventurer's risks and profits have been deducted from the net amount and not from the present value of the estimated realisation. Further 15% is on the low side considering the speculative nature of this valuation.

The District Valuer of the Acquiring Authority submitted the following valuation:

Market Value—5th June 1940

			£
1. *Frontages*—			
(*a*) Residential—17,650 feet at £5 15s		=	101,488
(*b*) Shop—500 feet at £15		=	7,500
			1,08,988
It is considered that the estate would require at least six years for development under normal conditions, therefore, take three years the average of six years and add six years for the duration of the war and the re-establishment of normal conditions, i.e. P.V. of £1 for nine years at 6%			.5919
			64,509
Less Adventurer's share 20%			12,902
			51,607
2. *Roads and Sewers*—			
Deduct the balance of the cost of roads and sewers as per pre-war contracts	£34,310		
This will probably be expended in the first four years, therefore, take two years as the average of four years and add six years for the duration of the war and the re-establishment of the Normal conditions, i.e., P.V. of £1 for 8 years at 5%	.6768		
3. *Surface Water Drainage*—	£23,221		
Deduct from (2) the difference between monies to be received from the White Hart Estates for surface water facilities, *viz.* £4,195 and the liability of Broad-lands (London) Ltd. to the Local Council, viz. £3,000 *i.e.* £4,195 – £3,000 = £1,195			
Not receivable for six years until development can proceed—therefore take P.V. £1 for five years at 5% = .746	£891		(–) 22,330
			29,277

	c/f.	£ 29,277
4. *Back Land*—		
$3\frac{1}{2}$ acres at £200 per acre, *add*		700
5. Money throw away on foundation, etc., estimated original value £110 take 50%, *add*		55
6. Injurious affection by severance to one acre, *add*		200
Total as at 5th June, 1940	=	30,232

After hearing the evidence on both sides the arbitrator made the following award on 27th February 1942—

(1) I assess the compensation payable to the claimants at £40, 136 in respect of their freehold interest in the land, including consequential damages to one acre or thereabouts of land adjacent to the south-west corner of the site.

(2) The Acquiring Authority to pay £674 towards the costs of the claimants.

(3) The Acquiring Authority to refund to the claimants the sum of £3, the prescribed fee paid on this application herein to the Reference Committee for the selection of an Official Arbitrator.

(4) The Acquiring Authority to pay the fees on this award.

From a careful perusal of the reported evidence, I consider that the figures of the District Valuer would be taken as correct but not his pessimistic outlook concerning the duration of the war. If the claimants' figures were taken for this item then a valuation would be as follows:

		£
Estimated Gross Return	=	1,08,988
It is assumed that the land will take 4 years to develop after the war which may last 3 years.		
P.V. of £1 in $(\frac{4}{2} + 3) = 5$ years @ 6%	=	.74726
Present Value of Estimated Realisation	=	81,442
Less Adventurer's Share 20%	=	16,288
		65,154

		C/f.	65,154
Less Roads and Sewers	34,310		
It is assumed that it will take years to construct after the war.			
P.V. of £1 in 5 years @ 5%	.7835		
	26,881		
Surface Water Drainage. Money to be received	1,195		
Not receivable until after the war 3 years. So P.V. of £1 in 2 years @ 5%	.907		
	1,084		25,797
			39,357
Back Land			700
Money wasted on foundations			55
Injurious affected			200
			40,312
Arbitrator's Award		=	40,312

It is, of course, wrong to take different percentage when calculating the present value. The whole of the undertaking is of a speculative nature and six per cent should have been taken throughout. This would have given a slightly higher figure than the amount awarded by the Arbitrator. No allowance was made for legal expenses, commission or other incidental charges.

(F) HIGH-RISE BUILDINGS

The skyline of major cities have witnessed a remarkable change in recent decades with high-rise buildings dominating the city centres, commercial hubs, as well as densely populated residential areas. New legislations regulating the enterprise of promoters of such high-rise buildings have been a recent phenomenon since a promoter is a person who builds not for his own use but for transfer to others. It stems primarily from the apartment ownership law that features since the early seventies in our country conferring transferable and heritable right to the occupant of each individual flat comprised in the multi-storeyed building. The era prior to that had seen either individual ownership or joint ownership over land and buildings and not concurrent ownership that lie at the core of the Apartment Ownership Acts passed by almost all the states of India one after another. Of course, co-operative housing law had been in vogue initially in the State of Maharashtra and gradually adopted by the other states providing a legal framework for co-operative ownership of multi-storeyed buildings with individual flats allotted to each member offering him a perpetual occupancy right therein together with proportionate share in the areas of common uses and facilities which is heritable but transferable only under limitations. The apartment ownership laws have relaxed the limitations as respects transferability creating a vast market for promoters' enterprise in the realm of real estate all over urban India. A regulatory legislation to control, guide, and provide norms for the enterprise of promotership became inevitable after various abuses in promotership surfaced. But only six states in India have responded to this urgency and enacted laws for regulation of the promoters in the matter of construction of multi-occupancy buildings and transfer of flats therein. These are Maharashtra, Gujarat, West Bengal, Andhra Pradesh, Karnataka and Punjab. The national Capital of Delhi manages the situation by pressing into application a few relevant provisions of Apartment Ownership Law of the State of Delhi.

The aspect of valuation of immovable property is quite pronounced in the enterprise of developers and promoters. The expectation of profit, which is the driving force behind the enterprise necessarily entails an exercise to determine the value of the land and/or building before promotion of construction and compare it with the estimated value the property might obtain after completion of construction. The expected value of the property in its diverse uses again weighs with the intending purchasers of flats/units. The extent of right conferred on the intending purchaser is again a preponderant consideration. Under the relevant law, the promoted property, which is a high-rise mutli-storeyed building, has to be administered after transfer of all flats to intending purchasers by the promoter, by an Association of Apartment Owners, which generally cannot impose any embargo on transfer. In other words, the members of the Apartment Owners' Association, which means the individual flat-owners have a free hand in effecting subsequent transfer of flats if need be. But, the situation is different when a high-rise multi-storeyed building comes into existence with the promotership of a Co-operative Society. In this case, the Co-operative Society is technically the owner of the entire building and members are the allottees of individual flats. They have absolute right as respects heritability but so far as transferability is concerned, the members' option to do so comes within the ambit of the consent of the Co-operative Society thereto. This is a clog, which generally attaches to Co-operatives buildings and has a meaningful reference to valuation. The extent to which the market value of the flat corrodes depends upon the extent of authority exercisable by the Co-operative Society under the relevant bye-laws.

(G) ENVIRONMENTAL FACTORS

Environmental factors are becoming increasingly important in recent times in all sorts of property valuation. The property market has now become sensitive to the detrimental effects of contamination caused to property due to pollution of air, water, soil etc. Environmental hazards caused by noise, vibration, fume, dust or radiation are also equally responsible for decay of property. Visual pollution is being recognized as a factor that calls for clean-up. The subject of contamination is an ever-widening matter for research and dissemination of information. The laws of the land are increasingly taking note of adverse effect of contamination and providing for regulatory measures to prevent as well as cure the environmental hazards caused by various kinds of pollution. Contamination may be both physical as well as non-physical. Physical contaminants are substances present in or around the subject property in such measurable quantities as to have a harmful environmental impact, viz., substances that are ignitable, corrosive, toxic or impairer. Non-physical substances, such as intrusive light or noise or electro-magnetic radiation, are also considered contaminants although they cannot be identified as physical substances inherent in the subject property.

As we scan a building in the light of environmental factors, several issues do arise. A building is intended to provide for certain safeties, viz., structural safety, health safety, fire safety and constructional safety. The structural design of the property and the materials provided must be such that do not make use of corrosive or toxic substances. Apart from all engineering requirements as regards foundation or load, internal gadgets including electrical installations, and wood-work should not expose the property to potential of fire. The protection against fire must also provide for sufficient means of exit. The means of access to the building ought to conform to the minimum requirement. The lighting and ventilation ought to be in conformity with the habitable standards as regards supply of fresh air for respiration of occupants and dilution of inside air to prevent vitiation. Again, when the building is constructed, proper rules should be observed as regards stacking of building materials and scaffolding so that the passers-by are not inconvenienced. As regards building services, the most important item from environmental point of view is the disposal system for wastes and effluents. The disregard of any of the above items beyond a reasonable proportion may expose the building to environmental questions that call for a remedy.

The environmental question obtains dimension and importance according as the use to which the building is put. If the building is meant for industrial use, environmental requirements demand additional ventilation, temperature control in work-room, lighting, water supply system, sanitation, safety from operating machines, means of access, canteen, first aid, rest room and the like. Besides, discharge of effluents both in air and water as well as exhaustion or emission of all other wastes ought to be reduced to a limit of ecological tolerance. If again, the building is meant for congregation or assembly of any character, the precincts must provide for sufficient parking space and lobby floor. If the building is meant for use as transport terminal, the appurtenant land should be enough for loading and unloading activities. Thus, every building use has its own requirements which, if not observed adequately, environmental degradation may be caused.

The concept of neighbourhood has introduced further requirements as regards aesthetic designs, landscape and greeneries to go along with the building activities. The advertising signs and outdoor visual structure in buildings are also required to bc regulated to ensure a desirable standard of neighbourhood.

Stigma and cost of cure

From the point of view of valuation, it is necessary to note that the market is beginning to recognize that contaminated properties or, so to say, buildings handicapped by environmental factors, suffer from a condition of obsolescence. Such properties are even stamped with a stigma which makes the property less desirable in the market. A stigma acts in the opposite way to 'goodwill'. It is an identifiable factor which affects market value as determined through the sales comparison method. But contaminated or environmentally hazardous property may be redeemed and redeveloped into valued assets after incurring a cost of cure. The cost to cure an environmental handicap necessarily lessens the value of the property as the utility of the property can be restored only by incurring such cost. This would then be added to the accrued depreciation, because current replacement cost of a new building would be based on the assumption of a presumably clean and environmental-friendly one. The cost to cure includes all expenses associated with the clean-up. But it must be understood that the stigma often prevails even after the clean-up and declines only over time and disappears perhaps after additional restorative efforts are demonstrated. Viewed in this light, the effect of stigma on value may often be out of proportion to cost of cure. The valuation process should be suitably adjusted to take due consideration of all such relevant aspects. It is, therefore, absolutely necessary that a valuer must have some background knowledge about the contaminants and their effects on property value in general as well as environmental factors that lessen the value of a building in its marketability in particular. The requirements for regulation should be clearly understood by a valuer to assess the nature and gravity of obsolescence that a stigmatised building suffers from. The cost to cure gives an idea to the valuer as to the discount to be allowed in assessing the depreciated cost of a stigmatised building or a building-estate. Thus, making valuation is complex in such cases as because circumstances are different for each affected property and adequate comparable sales are difficult to obtain and are often unavailable. Nevertheless, as in all other types of property valuation, the three approaches to value are recognized and may be used. The highest and the best use after appropriate adjustments arising out of environmental issues may be a good guide to valuation.

CHAPTER

15

Cost Approach to Valuation

Cost and value are sometimes confused because cost and value are often equal when the property is new or proposed. Cost relates to the supply side of the property. In order to supply goods and services in demand, it is necessary to work out the monetary sacrifice in terms of materials and labour and estimate if in the long range such sacrifice or costs prove economically rewarding in terms of value or return. Since creation of value without incurring expenditure on costs of production is unthinkable, there is justification of reliance on costs as a measure of value but it is not correct to say that cost is equal to value. A building may be constructed at a huge cost but there is no certainty that it would fetch the same amount if sold in the market since price is determined by the forces of demand and supply which again depend on many factors other than cost of production. The proverbial "hotel building in a desert" is a typical illustration on this point. But it is possible that the supplier may withhold the property from the market if its cost of production is not covered. For valuation or estimating price such individual choice of a particular supplier to withdraw is of course irrelevant if his decision exerts no influence on the market.

But there are properties which are not marketable in nature, nor yield any income the capitalisation rate of which may indicate the value. It is this category of properties that abide by cost approach to valuation, e.g. school, hospital, temple, city hall, Government and semi-Government office buildings which are neither investment property nor marketable ones.

These are basically non-investment properties acquired, held or produced in the expectation that they will yield benefits to their owners in the form of use and/or provide service to the society without any stipulation for direct monetary return. These institutional buildings may conveniently be valued through estimating current construction cost and subtracting accrued depreciation and adding estimated land value,—an exercise which in substance is the cost approach to valuation. In this approach, the replacement cost is first ascertained and therefrom total depreciation during the age of the asset is deducted by giving due weightage to functional, technological and economical obsolescence. The difference between the replacement cost and the cumulative depreciation gives the NET CURRENT REPLACEMENT COST.

At this point, it must be clarified that it is the replacement cost and not reproduction cost that must be considered in a determination of value. REPRODUCTION COST measures the extent of sacrifice necessary to reproduce a replica or an identical structure using the original designs, material and building specifications. REPLACEMENT COST, on the other hand, are those required to construct a substitute structure at current prices having similar utilities, using current designs, materials and building standards, according to prevalent market. Modern methods of construction and designs may offer savings in both labour and material costs as compared to methods in vogue many years ago. It therefore stands to reason that reproduction costs cannot truly measure value as because reproduction of a structure may involve wasteful practices. The replacement cost is more relevant as because all properties, no matter how diverse their physical attributes may be, are substitutable economically in terms of service utility or income productivity. The economic concept of substitution thus sets a limit on value as set by an acquisition of an equally desirable substitute property.

The replacement cost should also be distinct from historical cost. The HISTORICAL COST of a property is the purchase price paid at the initial time of acquiring the asset plus additions made subsequent to purchase. Historical cost is computed without considering depreciation. But as we have seen, there are three steps in the application of cost approach:

(a) Estimate current construction cost of the improvements;

(*b*) Subtract accrued depreciation; and

(*c*) Add the value of the land.

The estimate of current construction costs should include both direct and indirect costs that would be incurred in building and marketing the property, including normal profit.

Cost can be estimated in four ways—

(*i*) Comparative unit method;

(*ii*) Cost summation method;

(*iii*) Quantity survey method;

(*iv*) Trended original cost method.

Comparative unit method

In comparative unit method, the DIRECT AND INDIRECT COSTS are expressed on a per sq. foot, per cubic foot or in other unit basis. While the UNIT COST can be obtained or developed from local cost data, adjustment can be made to account for building features that differ from those included in the basic data. The comparative unit schedule could be applied to any building of any dimension to arrive at the replacement cost.

The method of estimating building cost by cubic metre volume is more accurate in general than the method of estimating cost by sq. foot. as because cost of buildings depends not only on their plinth area but also on volume of the building. By this method the volume or cubic content of the proposed building is worked out and multiplied by the rate per cubic volume of similar building at that locality constructed recently. So preparation of such an estimate depends on (*i*) determination of total volume in cubic metre of the proposed building and (*ii*) determination of present rate per cubic metre of similar building constructed recently at that locality. The formula for determination of total volume in cubic metre is 'Length × Breadth × Height': length and breadth are taken from the external dimensions of the building above plinth level and this is the plinth area of a building.

There are different rules of measuring the height of a building. To measure the height of a building the bottom level may be considered from ground level or from top of foundation-concrete or from half the depth of foundation up to plinth level or up to 15 cm below the finished surface of lowest floor (according to the American Institute of Architects). But there is no fixed rule. Choice of any one of the above rules may be made and applied for both the proposed and existing buildings. The cost of a building depends also on the depth of foundation. But the cost of construction per metre depth from ground level and per metre height from above the ground level is not the same. So the rule to determine the height of a building from half the depth of foundation should be more appropriate and this is normally followed in India.

Cost summation method

In the cost summation method the cost of individual construction components (e.g. foundation, walls, concrete, wood etc.) are computed on a per "unit-in-place" basis. The total cost of each component is found by multiplying these varied per unit costs by the number of units (sq. foot, length etc.). The component costs are then summed up and combined with applicable indirect cost to obtain a total replacement cost estimate. The unusual or special purpose properties may conveniently be valued on such basis of costing.

By this method approximate estimates are prepared for type-designed structures or units consisting several works after comparing with the past records of expenses for such works. The estimate of a building is prepared considering the cost of building structure, cost of internal water supply, sanitation and electrification works. But allocation of cost for external services, if any, should be provided in the total estimate. The external services include—(1) clearing site, including the demolishing of any old building, damage of existing roads or adjacent property that may occur due to construction of the building, or (2) forming site approach roads or paths, (3) fences, gates, boundary wall, shades etc., (4) laying of water supply, drainage, electric cables, gas mains, fire mains lines from the property line to service main, (5) turfing or planting trees etc.

The costs to be computed may be either actual cost, or capital cost or prime cost. The ACTUAL COST is the actual expenditure involved in order to complete a work excluding profit but including all other incidental, establishment and travelling charges. All such expenditure in connection with the work are accounted regularly in a register book and are summed up after completion to know the *actual cost*. This is not the estimated cost and generally maintained for the builder's own satisfaction.

The term CAPITAL COST is used to indicate the actual amount incurred in connection to complete a work. The expenditure required for surveying, designing, planning, drawing, supervision, legal expenses, travelling, taxes, charges for electricity and water supply fees, establishment, contingencies and all other miscellaneous charges required in connection with the work are included in the capital cost. But the capital cost does not include profit and interest due to investment of money. Cost of land where required are also included in the capital cost.

PRIME COST is the net cost or purchase cost of articles at shop, and refers to the supply of the articles only and not to the carrying out of work. No profit for such supply of materials is reckoned. During preparation of an estimate it is not always possible to specify the exact type or brands of materials required as in the case of door and window or water supply and sanitary fittings according to the choice of the owner. The owner may supply such articles or may instruct a contractor to purchase such articles for the work. The fitting and fixing charges are paid separately. In order to execute such items of work a reasonable amount is provided in the estimate as PRIME COST.

Quantity survey method

In quantity survey method, all the various labour and material costs are separately itemised, as INDIRECT COST. This method tends to produce the reproduction cost estimate rather than a replacement cost estimate and may be useful to contractors while bidding on construction projects.

The process involves finding out the quantities of works from the detailed measurements of various items of works in a scheme. The estimator takes off the various dimensions from the plan, sections and drawings and tabulates them in a measurement sheet also called dimension paper.

BILL OF QUANTITIES or schedule of quantities is a complete list of all items of work involved in connection with the estimate for a project together with the description, quantity and unit of rate against each item of work. When the bill of quantities are multiplied by their corresponding rates of the items and totalled it gives the estimated cost of the project. Bill of quantities is also required to calculate the quantities of different materials required for the project.

During execution of a project there may be certain type of works which are not included in the schedule and cannot be paid by measurements viz., special type of architectural works, dismantling partition wall under water, taking out root of trees during earthwork in excavation for foundation, trenches etc. Costing on the basis of actual quantity of materials and labour hours required to complete the job is denoted as *'Day Work'*. The prices are to include cost of materials, labour, overhead, supervision charges and profit. The total cost may take into account all these items.

Trended original cost method

The trended original cost method involves the trending over time of historical cost of factors obtained from a construction cost index. It can be useful in the valuation of complex-structures for which the comparative unit or unit-in-place methods would be either inapplicable or difficult to apply. It is particularly necessary to have an uptodate construction cost index for the purpose and the original cost figures should be accurate.

INDEX OF BUILDING COST indicates the comparison of cost for any specified item in percentage basis over a certain year with respect to the price of a particular year known as "base year". By this method the approximate cost of construction of a building may be worked out.

Consider the year 1987 is based with datum = 1 for the construction cost for a specified type of building at a place and the construction cost index at that place for same type of building in the year 2014 is 2.50. So the index indicates the cost of construction in the year 2014 is 150% more than that in the year 1987. There are various methods for preparing the cost index number but any of the methods to estimate building cost does not give realistic results because rise in cost for all the building materials and labour are not uniform and vitiated by heterogeneity.

The above four methods are not to be taken as exhaustive. Other techniques of estimating are also in vogue. One such is the BAY-METHOD. *The approximate estimated cost by Bay-method = Number of bays in the proposed structure × cost of one such bay.* Bays are compartments or similar portions of a structure. When the area of a structure consists of similar cabins or parts such as a godown, a railway platform, factory shades etc., these are built up with intermediate columns or with roof trusses on walls placed at equal distances with same roofing on top of those supporting members. The area may then be divided from centre to centre of the supports and each division treated as a Bay. The cost of construction of one bay may give a reasonable estimate of all others.

This is a reliable estimating process but the following points should be considered:

(*i*) End bay should be considered separately due to its end wall (Gable Wall).

(*ii*) Current rate per bay should be worked out from the previous recorded rate.

(*iii*) The location, specifications and drawings should be the same.

The cost data may be available from the sources of Government publications and ought to be supplemented or modified with locally gathered cost data. The cost data should also be updated or revised periodically. Regardless of source, cost data should be valid against cost of bench-mark properties. Local modification is necessary to fine tune them for the purpose of application in a particular case.

Accrued depreciation

The concept of depreciation as well as the different methods of computing depreciation have been discussed earlier in this book.

Accrued depreciation is the difference between the current replacement or REPRODUCTION COSTS NEW, and the current market value of an improvement or building. As we have already seen, depreciation represents the physical wear and tear coupled with obsolescence of any kind. It is generally the practice to estimate depreciation on a percentage basis. Property with unusual circumstances can be treated on an exception basis. As discussed earlier, the physical wear and tear accounting for depreciation gets offset to a varying extent by the standard of maintenance and repair. Again, curable obsolescence can also be attended to by appropriate measures of restoration or remodelling. Hence, accrued depreciation represents the effective age rather than actual age. Ordinarily, it is reasonable to assume that the actual age and effective age are the same but when there are reasons to hold a contrary view, the effective age must be separately estimated as a variation from the average. Having regard to the physical condition of the building, an upward or downward percentage adjustment to effective age may have to be made according as the physical condition of a subject building is found above average or below average relative to the condition of similar structure of approximately the same age. In any case, the actual age ought to be a guide to the effective age.

Once effective age has been estimated, accrued depreciation can also be estimated. This can be done by a number of ways. An estimate can be made on account of physical deterioration through elapse of time in accordance with predetermined formula and doing necessary adjustment for particular obsolescence. Again, properties may be classified with reference to type of construction or any other relevant features obtained from the sales data, if available. An estimate of total depreciation may be made from market-derived schedules in respect of each category and applied. A module of depreciation deduction for application in individual cases may also be prepared. Another method is to express building restoration on a per unit basis and the relate such building restorations to property characteristics available in terms of effective age. The application of multiple regression analysis can also be tried if sufficient and accurate sales data are available.

Value of land

In estimating land value for the purposes of cost approach, the sales data constitute the primary source. When data for sale of vacant land are acquired, the land residual method can be resorted to. It means that the estimated construction values are subtracted from sale price. The resulting land residual can then serve as substitute for vacant plot sale in determining average unit value of land. Thereafter, adjustment on account of size, depth, shape, utilities, ingress and egress and similar factors can be made. Another method of land valuation may be the capitalisation of land rent from the cost of development method. In the latter, it is necessary to estimate the present value of projected net revenues from development and sale of land. Then, there may be the subtraction method in which land values are simply calculated as a percentage of the total value estimate for the entire property arrived at by the sales comparison approach or income approach. Once estimated, the land values should be reviewed and updated.

In view of the known fact that the documents of transfer, very often than not contain a gross undervaluation of the transacted property, whether in a sales transaction, or in a gift or mortgage. This often poses a stumbling block in the way of relying on the document of transaction for the purpose of valuation of land or property comprising both land and building. In such cases, the best way to assess the correct market value of property is to look at the transactions in land acquisition or value of registered transactions of collateral security in mortgages to the Banks. Because, in such cases, people have a tendency to over-value the land/property for obtaining higher rates of compensation or of advances, as this cause may be. Whether the uppervalue of land or property recorded in the document of conveyance and the lower value given in the transactions registered, an approximation to the market value can be reached by resorting to prudent 'plus' and 'minus' factors.

Depreciated replacement cost as basis of valuation

We have so far discussed valuation by ascertaining the replacement cost of a property and deducting accrued depreciation therefrom. The property means land and building. The land value is ascertained and added to the estimated current cost of the building as reduced by accrued depreciation as on the date of valuation. The properties valued by such cost approach are generally institutional in character and non-marketable in nature. There are, however, properties which are also non-marketable, although not institutional in character but having all features of an investment. Oil refineries, giant chemical works, power stations, dock installations etc. fall under this category.

In these cases, the buildings are no more than structures or cladding for highly specialised plant; or the buildings and site engineering works are operational in nature and directly related to the business of the owner. Being so, it is unlikely that these properties would attract open market transactions and they may not obtain value to anyone other than the owner of the company or someone acquiring the entire undertaking. The cost approach to valuation is mended as depreciated replacement cost in such cases in order to measure the present worth of the property to the company after taking into account all factors of depreciation and obsolescence as well as the balance economic life of the property.

A DEPRECIATED REPLACEMENT COST basis of valuation thus requires an estimate of the open market value of the land in its existing use and an estimate of the new replacements cost of the buildings and other site works, from which deductions are then made to make appropriate allowances for the age, balance life, condition, obsolescences and other factors which lessen the worth of the asset in comparison with a new replacement. It does not necessarily approximate the realisable market value of the asset in question and only indicates the value to the organisation in occupation of the assets as existing on the date of valuation. Being considered as value to the business, the estimate is subject to the adequate potential profitability or service potential of the asset. While valuing the land, regard has to be given to the manner in which it is developed by the existing buildings and site works and the extent to which the full potential value thereof has thus been realised. The gross replacement cost of the building shall take into account a modern substitute building with the latest technology available for providing the similar advantages, facilities and uses under existing conditions of geographical location and legal permissibility.

CHAPTER

16

Benefit Approach to Valuation—Infrastructure Investments

Approaches to valuation

Development of infrastructure is a major component of economic growth as measured in terms of Gross Domestic Product. Infrastructure supports the superstructure of production of goods and services and also conditions the potential for the future. The role of infrastructure generally goes unnoticed by common man who thinks that his individual resources and earnings are enough for his well-being. It has also as a result failed to attract private investment. While consumer goods have a direct demand in the market and also capital goods to the producers, the infrastructure has throughout been a matter of public enterprise at the behest of Government, local authorities and statutory bodies. But, as a matter of fact, each taxpayer contributes to the huge public expenditure on infrastructure through his tax-payment which is only mobilised through the agency of the Government for providing the bulk delivery services in the form of such infrastructure. The common man is also the recipient of the services of infrastructure which in no small measure supports the living system in any country. Thus, enjoyment of a piece of land and building, however spacious or full of amenities it might be, loses all value unless the abutting road gives it infrastructural support, pursuit of avocation, however remunerative it might be, falls far short of expectations, unless the supportive infrastructure of road or railway communication makes the journey to and fro a reasonably tolerable experience; trade and commerce however flourishing on its own wings are arrested in growth if the infrastructure of ports and airstrips does not provide the pace of movement of merchandise; industry comes to a halt if failure of energy supply takes away its breath. In fact, the acquisition of property and its beneficial enjoyment take two different routes,—one is direct acquisition through marketing mechanism with exclusive possession as the mode of enjoyment and the other is acquisition via payment of tax through the agency of public authority and common use along with other members of the community. Each mode is complementary to the other towards exploiting the maximum benefit from expenditure.

Infrastructure in developing countries

The bulk communitarian services in the form of infrastructure pose a more difficult problems with the developing countries than those of the capital-rich nations. First of all, infrastructural development whether in roads or bridges, ports or airstrips, railways or navigation, electricity or telecommunications, sanitation or water-supply, power house or dams, need huge deployment of funds in fixed assets compelling the nation to part with liquidity of resources so sunk. The return is not immediate. In so far as marginal value of money to a capital-starved country is much greater than that to a rich nation, the situation calls for greater sacrifice for a developing nation. Marginal value of money means the value added by the last unit of money expended. Law of diminishing return prevail as we go on spending money more and more in the same direction of consumption since the capacity to spend in the developed country is much more than what a developing country, do have the developed economy exhausts the value of the marginal expenditure in a quicker pace than what prevails in the developing one. In the second place, the sheer inequalities of income status pronouncedly in-built in the population profile of an under-developed economy do not permit the burden of expenditure to be distributed evenly throughout the citizenry. Thirdly, the capacity to exploit the infrastructural opportunities is also not uniform which makes for inequalities to aggravate. Fourthly, the infrastructures are not safe as public properties. Last but not the least, sustainability becomes the first casualty from the viewpoint of both maintenance and continuity.

Too many claims for too scarce resources

The deployment of fund for infrastructural projects come from public finance since the assets are not generally marketable and the income stream there from stretches to an uncertain futurity and private enterprises do not find any profitability in them. Being capital investments, it entails curtailment of present consumption for the country as a whole. The exploitation of benefits out of infrastructure is very often a long-drawn process. In the course of planning, the countries like India generally adopts the principle of starting too many projects over which the available resources are thinly distributed. The result is that all of them are dragged on beyond economic viability. This becomes the inevitable fate of a developing economy perplexed with too many claims on too scarce resources. A rational basis of priority is the only answer to it and firm adherence to the accepted principles of priority *sine qua non.*

Income inequality and regional imbalance

Inequality of income and opportunities coupled with regional imbalances have proved to be a hydra-headed monster on the way to sustainable development. Inequality cuts with both edges of the blade. The fiscal devise of funding demands the broader shoulders to bear the heavier burden. A large section of the community below the level of fiscal liability have no share in the burden but infrastructural services are usually meant to serve all and sundry. This is one paradox. Again, inequality of opportunities arising out of disparity in income as well as regional imbalances results in differential scale of exploitation of infrastructural facilities though financed by the same public exchequer. Thus, an international standard attained of an airport terminal has no meaning to a vast rural population who may never have an opportunity to enter the arena of an airstrip, nor an investment to further enrich the posh localities of the National Capital Territory. To the elites, these are, however, extremely conducive to economic pursuits. A develcped country that can squeeze its population within the same bracket of comparable income and opportunities stands in distinctive advantage both in distribution of burden as well as exploitation of facilities. Thus development of infrastructure in a developing economy is inextricably linked with a sweeping economic reform and revision of entitlements.

The capital-intensive methods of production are gradually pushing the countries of the world towards an era of jobless growth. The rich are getting richer and the poor poorer. While the market forces at work are inevitably leading to such inequalities, the challenges is combat it through interventions is becoming more and more difficult for only Government.

Pricing infrastructure services to users

An argument is often made to price the services of infrastructure directly to users. This is equally difficult to enforce nor often morally justifiable in an economy vitiated by wide disparity of income. If water-supply is priced equally for all, it may result in its complete denial to the poorest income bracket. If, for the same reason, sanitation does not reach all sections of the community on account of slum-dwellers being unable to pay for the facility, the ultimate epidemic of diseases may not spare any one. There is perhaps no escape from bulk communitarian services being meant for the community as a whole irrespective of distinctions. This socio-economic aspect needs a serious consideration in any serious endeavour to resolve the *impasse*. One of the ways to solution may be found in cross-subsidy amongst the consuming classes. To take the example of water-supply, individual house connections may be made available only on adequate payment while conceding public standposts to the poorer section; private individual toilet for each tenement or house but public toilet duly maintained for squatter colonies; individual telephones to households on usual rentals matched with provision for public booth as recently developed in the nook and corner of the country. But this approach is again service-specific and may not be a ready answer in all areas. However, the experiences in each field is a pathfinder to the other.

Joint ventures in infrastructural projects

The participation of private capital in infrastructural projects is one of the big issues to be faced. Public enterprise has reached its limiting point. While budgetary allocations have become difficult, recourse to borrowing from agencies abroad has landed the country into an ever-widening debt-trap. Internal borrowings may be mopped up but that too depends on attractive terms of yield. In this situation, a devise to tap resources from the private sector in joint ventures may be step in the right direction. The message of joint venture is still full of substance. The economic resources at private hands may be looked upon as complementory by the Governments resources. In the changed contest, the private enterprise ought to discover the similar elements of common benefit derivable from various infrastructural projects and partner with the Government for implementation which assures them a cushion against uncertainties of trade depression and also a reasonable but steady return.

Valuation of infrastructure is a necessity

A scientific basis for valuation of infrastructural project is a dire necessary. Evaluation will ease out the option for the most viable one in preference to the other competing claims. Valuation of infrastructure is an emerging field. Infrastructural assets being non-marketable and also not being meant for immediate return, have to be valued in terms of long-range benefits expected to emanate from the project in various phases and in multiple directions. The assessment of present worth of all future benefits is the major purpose of valuation. If this is scientifically worked out, the private enterprise may find a secure ground to partner with the Government in this field. This seems to be an approach appropriate in the present context which may come to the aid of developing countries like India in the realm of development of infrastructure.

We have seen in our earlier chapters that there are three usual approaches to valuation of real estate comprising lands and buildings as well as rights appurtenant thereto. The market approach is the most appropriate method where there is scope for sales comparison. The investment properties are usually valued with income approach while the cost approach provides the key to valuation of lands and buildings which are neither marketable nor meant for investment.

Again, the three approaches are often interrelated, integrated and supplementary in application. There is element of sales comparison in the income approach to valuation as capitalisation rate has to be fixed upon a market study of different alternatives of investment. In the cost estimation of cost approach, reference to market is indispensable. Costing again is an essential exercise in determining profit for the purpose of application of income approach. But can we assume that these three approaches amongst themselves exhaust all eventualities of the exercise of valuation in respect of all categories of assets? What about public works of the Government like roads, bridges, transport terminals, railways, communication lines etc.? No doubt, they involve the investment of huge sum of money though not meant primarily for profit or income, but go by the name of development. The advancement of public utilities is the primary objective of such public expenditure which creates infrastructure for further investment, both public and private. In other words, the laying of infrastructure acts as a catalytic agent for further growth which is not limited to the mere cost incurred in land and building. Since this species of properties is never marketable, the question of sales comparison does not arise. But, nevertheless, valuation is an important exercise which can throw light on the desirability of deploying funds for one project of infrastructure rather than on another. In each deployment of fund, the maximum return is expected and the expectation of return is sought to be maximised in the distribution of resources amongst various infrastructural projects. The internal rate of return takes us to some level of assessment in the field of valuation. But that is also not always adequate. Just as valuation is not an accounting exercise of price but a reasonable estimate as to what the price ought to be after taking into account all relevant considerations, valuation of infrastructure does not rest only with working out the internal rate of return but entails an estimate of the total benefit arising out of it which includes its multiplier effect on the economic front and its spread-effect on the social front measurable in value. There is a conventional method of working out the cost-benefit ratio of a project. But such ratios have relevance primarily in accounting for the economic viability and not beyond it. The process of charting out the contours of the area of total benefit achievable stage by stage caused by multi-facet thrusts of an infrastructural project and finding out the present worth of all such future benefits in a dynamic scenario is a different exercise altogether. This ushers in the relevance of a fourth approach in the field of valuation which is the 'benefit approach'.

Uniqueness of infrastructure as an asset

For example, when a vital road link is established, it may open up brisk economic activity in diverse directions which would have remained dormant for decades or centuries had the linkage not been established. This spurt in economy may invite investments paving the way for multiplier effect to turn the wheel of prosperity and development. On the other hand, similar investment on another road may not obtain the same value in terms of linkage when sufficient economic activities are not propelled. The value of investment thus differs in terms of benefit accrued. Let us assume the Salt Lake City in Kolkata with as well as without the Eastern Metropolitan Bye-pass that provides an express corridor to connect areas of the Salt Lake City with successive intersections for entering into different regions of the city. The Salt Lake City is primarily a satellite 'bed-room town' the dwellers of which are under occupational compulsion to commute to different parts of the main city of Kolkata. The absence of an express corridor like Eastern Metropolitan Bye-pass would have crippled their economic life for all time to come. So this has brought a tangible economic benefit to millions of people and that too for all time to come. Compared with it, even an extension of State Highway along a not-too-potential region with similar investment may be relegated to a lesser preference. The estimate of benefits provides the clue to the choice and the cost factor becomes irrelevant.

Think of India's railway system which has transformed the way of life of the Indian people. Might be, the rulers of the by-gone century might have calculated the cost of its construction, laying and convergence against the economic return on quick transfers of indigenous raw materials for exportation and movement of army personnel to quell the rebellions, the ultimate benefit has been the transformation of the way of life throughout the length and breadth of the country. Can the cost provide a real estimate of its value? Surely, the value worth its connotation must take note of all the benefits that directly or indirectly have come out of it and are convertible in monetary terms of valuation given the sophisticated methods available in the computer age.

What is the value of the Statue of Liberty in New York or the Eiffel Tower in Paris? Can cost provide any clue to valuation? Being wonders of the world, they have attracted billions of people from all over the world and shall continue to do so throughout the foreseeable future. So is India's Taj Mahal where perhaps more money will be necessary for its preservation than was required for its original construction as because the cost of construction is only a poor estimate of its value. Here too, a different approach to valuation is called for which justifies all expenditure for maintenance and preservation. The income approach do not provide answer to the requirements. The income from millions of visitors to the coffers of the statutory authorities is only a fragment of the total economic impact of these wonders of the world. The very fact of convergence of a large number of people from all around the globe on a perennial and steady scale for a foreseeable span of centuries has provided a fertile ground for the growth of numerous ancillary avocations, economic pursuits, professions and the like which have an indelible impact on development as triggered by a multiplier effect. The growth takes place along a wide spectrum encompassing urbanisation, souvenir trade, tourism industry, transport, hotels, cafeteria, literature, general business and so on. If valuation is an art of estimating the present worth of future benefits, it is the benefit approach to valuation which claims to be the best method to be deployed for an assessment of the worth of such objects.

Growth of private enterprise in infrastructure

As a matter of fact, private enterprises have already started gathering around infrastructural projects all over the globe amongst countries, which are on the path of privatisation. Once privatisation is introduced it becomes necessary to estimate the value of the infrastructural project from the viewpoint of return on investment to the private investor. Alongside, the Government estimates its recurring gain from the terms of agreement with the private investor and the residual gain after the period of agreement expires. Thus, the value to the private entrepreneur is different from that to the Government or public body. A brief look may now be taken at the types of private participation or joint venture, as it may be called, that have emerged so far.

(1) *Build-Own-Operate (BOO)*

It is a contractual agreement whereby a project developer is authorised to finance, construct, own, operate, and maintain an infrastructural development facility that enables the developer to recover the total investment costs plus a reasonable return thereon through collection of tolls, fees, rentals or other charges from the users of the facility. Under such agreement the developer is also empowered to assign the operation and maintenance of the facilities to an external operator for gains.

(2) *Build-Operate-Transfer (BOT)*

It is a contractual agreement whereby the project developer finances and undertakes the construction of a given infrastructural facility including operation and maintenance over a fixed term. The project developer recovers his return on investment as well as the investment itself through collection of tolls, fees, rentals, charges, and etc. not exceeding a prescribed limit. At the end of a fixed term the infrastructural facility in its entirety vests in the Government or the public body with all its potential for yield.

There are many other variations to these broad outlines according as the situation demands. For example, the persons ousted from the area in consequence of the infrastructural development may have to be compensated or rehabilitated. This may require sharing of expenses between the Government and the investor. The agreement may require a premium to be paid to the Government or local body either in lump or periodically in which case the infrastructural property takes the character of a leasehold during the tenure of the agreement.

Constraints of usual methods of valuation

If a project is that of a dam or a thermal power installation with a limited horizon of durability and purpose, the cost approach or, more precisely, the depreciated replacement cost, may provide a sound estimation of value as discussed in the preceding chapter. But that is not the case with the infrastructural projects that are open-ended like laying of cable communication lines, satellite network, telecommunication etc. Even a public enterprise which provides the key industries like steel or petroleum or chemicals falls under this category since they provide the potential for multiple end-use and are a catalyst of a plethora of subsidiary investments, income and employment. Investments for development of human resources are now subjected to economic analysis for estimating benefits arising out of monetary inputs. In doing so, such investments are treated as that for development of social infrastructure. The economics of education work out the value of investment in human capital in the field of education with reference to the ultimate return it provides to the community. We come across exercise to work out the value of inputs in health programme by measuring the series of expected return to the community by a healthier manpower. These are similar open-ended projects in the sense they provide only the infrastructure upon which the edifice of a better performance can be built for the entire population. The total benefit lies in an estimate of the value of improved performance projected to be rendered by the built-up human capital in quantified monetary terms. On the same analogy, the benefits arising out of physical infrastructure comprising lands, buildings and other capital assets can be subjected to estimate as a series of expected monetary return in successive stages reduced to present worth which do not abide by the conventional income approach, nor attract the cost approach or market approach.

'System' valuation

We may take this analysis to other areas of expenditure by the public exchequer designed to achieve designated social goals. We may think in terms of "system valuation" which brings public expenditure on specific projects like universal literacy program, empowerment of weaker sections, entrepreneurship development program, thrift and credit program through self help groups, women's development programs, safeguards for Scheduled Castes and Scheduled Tribes, and a host of similar activities for development of human resources, the achievement of which can be placed under the scan of analysis from the valuation point of view. The preamble to the Constitution of India outlines the ultimate objectives to be realized in a broad manner by each of these projects directly or remotely aimed towards those ends. Now, along with development of natural resources or processing of commodities or services through industrialization, augmentation of agricultural output, etc. the development of human resources contribute in no small measure to the process of value-addition in all the above fields. So, legitimately the techniques of valuation need to be extended to such fields particularly in the less developed countries where a vast area of human resources remain to be tapped for utilization to their rated capacity, just as the rated capacity or installed capacity of plants and machineries enter into the field of valuation for accounting in income method or market approach to valuation. We may cite the example of Japan or Korea or Taiwan or Singapore—the tiger economies of the East, where employment of human resources to the rated capacity is the key to the understanding of their productivity leading to relative prosperity which is a significant issue in business valuation.

Non-monetised area—valuation

A further reflection would take us to the non-monetised area of the economy which booms in the traditional countries where a host of economic activities are still confined within the family or community and not yet exposed to the market. On the contrary, the so called advanced countries of the world are exploring newer and newer pastures for consumer goods by exploiting the process of division of labour to the utmost. The marketing strategies create utilities for the new species of products in the consumers' enclave. The capital formation acts as booster to the production while the capacity for investment is monopolized by the advanced countries. In this way a new era of economic colonialism divides the countries who invests after elaborate research and development and the countries where the vast population provides the potential for marketing. Because investment arises out of saving which again is dependent on the excess of income over expenditure on consumption, with marginal propensity to consumer as the determinate factor.

In this way, mother's care in the form of cooking has been replaced by fast food or home delivery services; grandmothers' baby-sitting by creches; fathers' tutoring by tutorial homes; and the like. Many activities of processing within the household, which are still a distinguishing feature of traditional communities, are gradually moving out of the non-monetised arena and swelling the market for finished items for immediate consumption. Even, child-bearing is going to create a market for surrogate mothers. On the infrastructural side, spots of scenic beauty are now being brought within the nexus of commercial tourism. The above analysis leads us to the necessity of estimating the monetary value of goods and services that are yet in the non-monetised area but have opportunity cost for availability in the monetised sector. Now the question is what should be the appropriate methodology of valuation in each of such cases?

Inquest for a new approach to value infrastructure

The methodology of valuation under the benefit approach ought to take account of a multi-stage and multi-pronged situations of development consequent on investments in infrastructure. It should trace the 'accelerator' effect as well as the 'multiplier' effect induced by the investment. For example, the construction of a vital bridge to connect a pair of cities lying across a major river may have the immediate effect of traffic flow initially served by animal power but gradually improved by diesel or petroleum or electricity reflecting on the carrying capacity of vehicles, and pedestrian movement between the two cities. The improvement in circulation of goods and services quantified in monetary terms as also the monetary value of time saving may provide the immediate basis of valuation at the first stage. But the stimulus of development do not end here. Since the bridge is projected to last for centuries and serve the purpose of linkage throughout this period and even beyond it as because, at the termination of its economic life the question would inevitably arise for its replacement rather than discontinuation of the established linkage, the process of valuation ought to take into consideration the subsequent stages of economic development which the conventional cost-benefit analysis may not perhaps capture. The hinterland of both the twin cities would now have a growth pattern conditioned by the linkage of the bridge. The land value at both ends encompassing a spread all around depending on the impact would undergo an upward trend together with a gradual change in the land use pattern. More warehouses and storage facilities would perhaps replace the residential blocks; the network of commerce and trade would now be woven on a changed perception of prospects; inmigration to both the cities will find a new impetus leading to wider jurisdiction; location of strategic operations within the domain of the public authorities will undergo a gradual review. In short, the complexion of growth after a century may perhaps be altogether different from what was before and the metamorphosis may come about in different stages by silent steps.

Since valuation is an exercise that offers the challenge of assessing the present worth of all future benefits, the mode of valuation in case of major infrastructural investments like satellites, railway terminals, air strips, ports, national highways, bridges etc. ought to be different from the usual income approach, sales comparison or cost approach. When the development is assessed on a single direction like impact on traffic movement consequent on investment on highways, the rate and quantum of growth at different stages may be computed by taking into account the 'accelerator' effect on the single track of value-addition. But as multiple avenues of growth are identified and that in different stages, the 'multiplier effect' comes into consideration.

While estimating the value to the private entrepreneur the income approach provides the appropriate method for valuation. As a regular market for privatisation develops amongst bidders, domestic or international, the market approach may provide a suitable methodology for valuation. But, for a Government or a public body which embarks on such infrastructural project whether out of its own fund, or joint venture with a private investor, has to fix its priority for such project investment with due regard to the total benefit, whether on account of the "accelerator effect" or a "multiplier effect". We take the meaning of the two expressions in a somewhat technical sense. The "accelerator effect" as we have said is a development on the same track or pursuit. For example, if the development is considered in the transport sector it may mean a stage of development from non-motorised to motorised, from lightweight vehicle to heavyweight vehicle, from two-wheelers to fourteen-wheelers. If the infrastructure is in the building sector, it may mean an impulse for development from a single-storied cottage to multi-storeyed high-rise buildings. From mere residential building uses to multiple uses. If the infrastructure in the communication sector is taken into account, it may take the shape of a movement from cable connection to wireless communication. On the other hand "multiplier effect" takes into consideration the growth pattern of diverse streams and shades. An infrastructural growth in highway communication may trigger growth of industries, townships, and avocations along with providing faster movement. A port may cater to the need of a hinterland in diverse direction—inland dry port, container industry, communication links, warehouses, subservient occupations, habitat, industrial and commercial growth and what not. An industrial township by its multiplier effect can command the entire gamut of a counter-magnet to a metropolitan city. The question is how to estimate the total benefit on a multiplier basis, while a private tenderer calculates only immediate return on investment. A planning authority of our country always has to answer it. A valuation strategy can attempt simulating the project on the computer to find out the second order differential equation, i.e. the rate at which the rates change over time, and, if possible, the third order rates being the rate at which the rates that are changing, are changing in a scenario of development triggered by multiplier effect or accelerator effect, as the case may be such simulation is not unknown in the scientific world today. This would lead to an approximation nearer to reality. It has to be remembered that an infrastructural project lays an indelible mark on the socioeconomic life for duration beyond centuries as because improvement of techniques always takes us beyond the immediately perceptible horizon.

CHAPTER

17

Valuation of Leasehold Interests

A lease is the outcome of the rightful separation of ownership and possession. The owner retains to himself the incidence of ownership by realising rent or accepting premium and makes over to the lessee the right to enjoy possession of the property during the period of lease. The lessor is also entitled to reversion of the property unto himself on termination of the period of lease. A lease, therefore, is the transfer of a right to enjoy property. It creates an interest in the property by virtue of the contract of lease which may be either oral or written.[1] A lease is not a mere contract, but a transfer of interest in land.[2] It creates a right *in rem*.[3] The person acquiring a leasehold right, in the ordinary course, has a right to transfer the property further.[4]

Lease defined

A lease has been defined in s. 105 of the Transfer of Property Act in the following manner:

> "A lease of immovable property is a transfer of a right to enjoy such property, made for a certain time, express or implied, or in perpetuity, in consideration of a price paid or promised, or of money, a share of crops, service or any other thing of value, to be rendered periodically or on

1 *Tirtha Ram Gupta* v *Gurubachan Singh* (1987)10 Reports (SC) 84.
2 *Juthika Mullick* v *Mahendra Y. Bal* (1995)1 SCC 560.
3 *Anwar Ali* v *Jamini Lal* 43 CWN 797; ILR (1939)2 Cal 254; AIR 1940 Cal 89.
4 *Latika Rani* v *State* Cal LT (1989)2 (HC) 333.

specified occasions to the transferor by the transferee, who accepts the transfer on such terms.

"The transferor is called the lessor, the transferee is called the lessee, the price is called the premium, and the money, share, service or other thing to be so rendered is called the rent."

Lease distinguished from licence

A lease has to be distinguished from licence. A licence is defined in s. 52 of the Indian Easements Act as "a right to do or continue to do, in or upon the immovable property of the grantor something which would, in the absence of such right be unlawful, and such right does not amount to an easement or an interest in the property". Thus a licence does not create any estate or interest in the property to which it relates.[5] It is the creation of an interest in immovable property which distinguishes a lease from a licence, the latter being limited to a right to possess on permission or authorisation. For the purpose of deciding whether a particular transaction is a lease or a licence, the question of intention of the parties is to be determined, and such intention has to be inferred from the facts and circumstances of each case. It is essential to look to the substance of the agreement, and not merely to the form.[6] In *Associated Hotels of India* v *R.N. Kapoor*,[7] the following principles were aptly laid down for ascertaining whether a transaction is lease or licence:

"(*i*) to ascertain whether a document creates a lease or licence the substance of the document must be preferred to form;

(*ii*) the real test in the intention of the parties—whether they intended to create lease or licence;

(*iii*) if the document creates an interest in the property, it is a lease, but, if it only permits another to make use of the property, of which legal possession continues with the owner, it is a licence; and

5 *Lall* v *Dunlop Rubber Co.* (1968)1 SCR 23; (1968)1 SCJ 644.

6 *Board of Revenue* v *A.M. Ansari* (1976)3 SCC 550; (1976)3 SCR 1032; *Rajbir Kaur* v *S. Chokosiri & Co.* (1989)1 SCC 19; *K.A. Bashir Ahmed* v *T.S. Sarangpurwalla* AIR 1988 SC 184; (1988)1 SCC 155.

7 AIR 1959 SC 1262; (1960)1 SCR 368; 1960 SCJ 453.

(*iv*) if under the document a party gets absolute possession of the property, *prima facie* he is considered to be a tenant; but circumstances may be established which negative the intention to create a lease."

A licensee is not entitled to notice to quit before eviction.[8] It is recoverable by the grantor and is automatically determined when the grantor makes an assignment in favour of another. So, the licence is not assignable by the licensee, nor does it entitle him to sue strangers in his own name.

Lease distinguished from easement

The grant of an easement is not a transfer of property. It is a right which a person enjoys in another man's property whether as a right of way, or right to light or support. An easement is defined in s. 4 of the Easements Act of 1882 as "a right which the owner or occupier of certain land possesses, as such, for the beneficial enjoyment of that land, to do and continue to do something or to prevent and continue to prevent something being done, in or upon, or in respect of certain other land not his own." The land which enjoys the right is called the dominant heritage and the land on which the liability is imposed is called the servient heritage. Enjoyment of an easement peaceably without interruption and for 20 years results in its acquisition by prescription under s. 15 of the Easements Act. Otherwise, an easement may be created by a grant, express or implied; or may arise as an easement of necessity under s. 13; or may be acquired by virtue of a local custom under s. 18 of the said Act.

An easement must be distinguished from an interest in property like lease. An interest in land entitles the holder thereof to a certain user of the land and correspondingly it withholds that particular user from the owner thereof. The person in whom the right vests by way of lease becomes all in all entitled to its enjoyment to the exclusion of any other person, even the owner himself. The right to an interest in property is exclusive while that to an easement is only restrictive of the user of the property.[9] A right of easement does not create an

8 *Lall* v *Dunlop Rubber Co.* (1968)1 SCR 23; (1968)1 SCJ 644; *Sri Upendra Mondal* v *Bhajahari Mondal* AIR 1991 NOC 107 (Gau).

9 *Clifford* v *Hoare* 43 LJC 225.

interest in land. Claim to the ownership of land and also to a simultaneous right of easement on it is inconsistent.[10] An easement cannot be created unless there are two distinct heritages but it is not so in a lease or interest created in land. No plaintiff would be allowed to take the impossible position of being owner of the land and of having a simultaneous right of easement over the land.[11]

An easement should also be distinguished from a restrictive covenant in an agreement for lease. A restrictive covenant is a limitation of the manner in which one may use the demised land, and may or may not involve a grant. While easements are creatures of statute, the covenants are based on agreement. In other words, easements arise by an act of law while restrictive covenants arise by act of parties. On the same ground, an easement cannot be dislodged unless extinguished by authority of statute law. But a restrictive covenant becomes purposeless when the servient tenement is acquired for a legal estate by a *bona fide* purchaser for value without notice of the existence of the covenant, as provided in s. 40 of the Transfer of Property Act.

From the grantor's point of view, a lease is distinctly different from an easement created by grant. By a lease the owner of the land retains his ownership but parts with possession. But by the granting of an easement, the owner retains both ownership as well as possession. The grantee gets merely a right to the limited use of the owner's land but not possession thereof. Thus, where by a *kabuliyat* a person has been given merely a passage over the land, the *kabuliyat* is not a lease deed but creates only an easement in favour of the grantee.[12]

Lease how created

A lease of immovable property for a term not exceeding one year and not reserving a yearly rent can be made by an oral agreement accompanied by delivery of possession. A lease from year to year, or for any term exceeding one year, or reserving

10 *Narendranath* v *Abhoycharan* ILR (1907)34 Cal 51.

11 *Laxman Patnaik* v *Cuttack Municipal Council* AIR 1985 Ori 90; (1984)58 Cut LT 195; (1984)1 Ori LR 1062.

12 *Haran Chandra* v *Shyama Charan* AIR 1940 Cal 447; *Ram Prasad Mondal* v *Snehalata Ghosh* 71 CWN 17; AIR 1967 Cal 369.

a yearly rent can be created only by a written document which must be executed by both parties and duly registered as required under s. 107 of the Transfer of Property Act.

Lease how terminated

As provided in s. 111 of the Transfer of Property Act, a lease of immovable property may terminate in any of the following manner:

(*a*) by efflux of the definite period of time for which the lease was made, i.e. by reversion;

(*b*) where such time is limited conditionally on the happening of any event,—by the happening of such event;

(*c*) if the lessor's interest is a limited one, the lease comes to an end as soon as such interest of the lessor is determined; thus a lease given by a tenant for life is void at his death;

(*d*) by merger, i.e. when the lessor acquires the lessee's interest;

(*e*) by express surrender of the lease by the lessee;

(*f*) by implied surrender;

(*g*) by forfeiture on ground of breach of condition, or the lessee repudiating the lessor's title or lessee declared an insolvent in which case the lessor may exercise his right of re-entry over the land;

(*h*) by notice in writing; periodic tenancies are terminated by notice to quit; as breach of condition only makes the lease voidable, the forfeiture is not complete unless and until the lessor gives notice that he has exercised his option to determine the lease.[13]

Rent control legislation

The provisions of the Transfer of Property Act have been largely modified in their application to the urban areas where rent control laws have been promulgated with a view to protection of the rights of tenants against the arbitrariness of landlords. The arbitrariness of landlords became pronounced in the

13 *Asghar* v *U.P. Government* (1954) ALJ 346; *Tatya Saolya* v *Yeshwanta Kondiba* 52 Bom LR 909.

aftermath of the great wars which visited incessant migration of population from rural to urban areas and resultant housing shortages. Thus during or after the First World War (1914-1918), the Bombay Rent (War Restrictions) Act 1918, the Calcutta Rent Act 1920 and the Madras City Tenants Protection Act 1922 came into force. The spate of legislation on this line got a further fillip during and after the Second World War (1939-1946). All the States in India enacted rent control law, the primary purpose of which was the fixation of criteria for determining fair rent or standard rent to be legally realisable by the landlords from the tenants. The legislations also prescribe the grounds on which alone a tenant could be evicted by the landlord. The net effect of the provisions of such legislations is to override a number of important rights otherwise available to the lessor or landlord under the Transfer of Property Act. In matters not covered by the rent control legislations, the provisions of the Transfer of Property Act, however, still continue to govern the relationship between a landlord and a tenant.

The following is a list of rent control legislations which are in force in the municipal urban areas of different States:

(1) Andhra Pradesh Buildings (Lease, Rent and Eviction) Control Act 1960.

(2) Assam Urban Areas Rent Control Act 1972.

(3) Bihar Buildings (Lease, Rent and Eviction) Control Act 1982.

(4) Bombay Rents, Hotels and Lodgings House Rates Control Act 1947.

(5) Chhattisgarh Rent Control Act 2011.

(6) Delhi Rent Control Act 1958.

(7) East Punjab Urban Rent Restriction Act 1949.

(8) Gangtok Rent Control and Eviction Act 1956.

(9) Goa, Daman and Diu Buildings (Lease, Rent and Eviction) Control Act 1968.

(10) Haryana Urban (Control of Rent and Eviction) Act 1973.

(11) Himachal Pradesh Urban Rent Control Act 1987.

(12) Jammu and Kashmir Houses & Shops Rent Control Act 1966.

(13) Jharkhand Building (Lease, Rent & Eviction) Control Act 2012.

(14) Kerala Buildings (Lease and Rent Control) Act 1965.

(15) Madhya Pradesh Accommodation Control Act 1961.

(16) Meghalaya Urban Areas Rent Control Act 1972.

(17) Mizoram Urban Areas Rent Control Act 1974.

(18) Mysore (Karnataka) House Rent Control Act 1967.

(19) Orissa House Rent Control Act 1967.

(20) Pondicherry Buildings (Lease and Rent Control) Act 1969.

(21) Rajasthan Premises (Control of Rent and Eviction) Act 1950.

(22) Tamil Nadu Buildings (Lease and Rent Control) Act 1960.

(23) Tripura Buildings (Lease and Rent Control) Act 1975.

(24) U.P. Urban Buildings (Regulation of Letting, Rent and Eviction) Act 1972.

(25) West Bengal Premises Tenancy Act 1997.

It is not only in the urban municipal areas that the contractual matters arising out of lease have been statutorily modified in departure from the provisions of the Transfer of Property Act. In the rural areas, the agricultural tenancies and particularly share-cropping have been brought under the purview of land reforms legislations. Thus, the land reform laws of different States do also override the provisions relating to lease under the Transfer of Property Act, to the extent there are specific safeguards for tenants and other regulatory measures provided in the land reform legislations. Besides, there are other State laws inforce that affect agricultural land-holdings in the rural sector.

For the valuation of leasehold interests of the lessor and the lessee in respect of a property subject to a lease the following facts will have to be carefully ascertained:

(1) Nature of the property.

(2) Fair rent which the property may be estimated to yield as on the date of valuation.

(3) Leasehold rent and the unexpired period of the lease.

(4) Special terms and conditions, if any, in the deed of lease affecting the interests of the lessor and lessee.

Having ascertained the nature of the property and made an estimate of the fair rent which such a property may be expected to yield, the net income of the lessee from the leasehold property will be the surplus, if any, of the fair rent over the leasehold rent for the unexpired period of the lease. The value of the lessee's interest will therefore be the present value of the said income for the unexpired period of the lease on the basis of the security of the fair rent having regard to the nature of the property.

On acquisition of a leasehold property, the compensation payable on account of market value may be determined on many hypothetical considerations. The leasehold rent may be taken into consideration if it is a fair rent. Generally speaking, Collectors do not separately assess the value of the lessor's interest and the value of the lessee's interest in the property, but determine the market value of the property on the basis of comparable transactions.

After the market value is determined of a leasehold property, question of appointment of the total compensation money as between the lessor and the lessee would arise. The lease may contain a special covenant as to apportionment of the compensation money in the event of acquisition of a leasehold property. In such a case, compensation money will be apportioned between the parties in accordance with that special contract. In the cases of those leases where there are no such special covenants or where it is stated that compensation money in case of acquisition will be divided between the lessor and the lessee according to law, the ordinary law would prevail and the question is not free from difficulty. In answering the question, the following observations of Biswas, J. in *Surendra Nath* v *Peary Charan,*[14] should be kept in view:

"It seems to be only common sense that as between lessor and lessee, the acquisition should not place either party in a better or worse position than he was before the acquisition. The acquisition transforms the property into a certain sum

14 42 CWN 1191.

of money, but the rights of parties relatively to this sum ought to be the same as they were with reference to the property. Where a property is subject to a lease, theoretically speaking, the total compensation for the property should be the sum total of the compensation payable in respect of the interests of the lessor and the lessee. If the total compensation is not, however, arrived at by separately calculating the interests of the lessor and lessee, it seems to us that the amount should be divided between them in such proportion as would represent the value of their respective interests."

In that case, the High Court remanded the case to the lower forum (Calcutta Improvement Tribunal) to be dealt with *de novo* in the light of the principles indicated in that judgment.

Two cases of apportionment of the compensation money awarded for leasehold properties decided by the Calcutta High Court on an appeal from the Calcutta Improvement Tribunal are given below which may be profitably studied by valuers.

In the case of *Sitanath Pal* v *K.C. Basu,*[15] the facts were as follows:

The acquired premises collectively known as Lalbagan Bustee in Chitpur Area of Kolkata along with other properties were the subject-matter of a lease dated 13th September 1918 for a period of 90 years starting from a rent of ₹ 5,401 per month for the first 10 years and thereafter increasing by 12½% for every subsequent period of 10 years over what was payable for the preceding period. The lessee was given the right to remove or alter the existing buildings or structure and to erect and build new buildings. The tenants in the demised premises were monthly tenants and tenants-at-will with only a precarious interest in the land. The property was acquired in pursuance of a declaration published on 23.12.1943. Possession was taken by the Collector in February-March 1945. The lease had 63 years to run from the date of possession which was taken to be the material date for valuation of the respective interest of the parties.

The rent payable for the acquired properties which formed only a part of the several leasehold properties was determined

15 A.O.D. No. 80 of 1948 (Cal) (unreported).

at ₹ 1,240 per month at the material time. A sum of ₹ 10,28,785 plus S.A. thereon was awarded by the Collector on account of market value of the acquired properties.

The learned President of the Calcutta Improvement Tribunal assessed the fair rent at 4 per cent of the value and capitalised the profit rental of the lessee at 5½% security. On that basis a sum of $\frac{₹ 4,55,201}{14}$ inclusive of S.A., was awarded to the lessees and the balance to the lessors. The lessees appealed to the High Court and a cross-objection was filed by the lessor. The Appeal was heard by G.N. Das and K.C. Das Gupta, JJ. Their Lordships allowed the appeal and dismissed the cross-objection. Extracts from the judgment of Mr. Justice K.C. Das Gupta, who delivered the judgment of the Court are given below which will throw a good deal of light in the matter:

> "Three different principles were considered by the learned President for application to this case. The first was that the lessee's interest should be valued by calculating the present value of what he would have received during the unexpired portion of the lease, if the land had not been acquired and that this (with the S.A.) should be awarded to him and the balance of the compensation money should be awarded to the lessor. The second principle considered is that the lessor's interest should be valued by calculating the present value of what he would have received during the unexpired portion of the lease and adding to it the present value of the reversion that would have fallen in on the expiry of the lease, if the land had not been acquired and that this total sum (with S.A.) should be awarded to the lessor and the balance of the compensation money should be awarded to the lessee. The third principle that was considered by the learned President was that the lessee's interest and the lessor's interest should be valued separately and the compensation money should be apportioned between the lessor and the lessee in the same proportion as the value of the lessor's interest, thus calculated, bears to the lessee's interest, as calculated. The learned President accepted the first of the above principles for application to the facts of these references.

"The second question is as regards the actual calculation of the value of the lessee's interest or the lessor's interest that becomes necessary for the application of the correct principle ....It is necessary to decide first which of the three principles should be chosen for application to the facts of the present case for apportioning the compensation awarded. The last of the three principles mentioned above was applied in the case of *Surendra Nath* v *Peary Charan.*[16]

"I have no doubt in my mind that this is the correct principle to apply whenever it is possible to value the lessee's interest and lessor's interest with approximately an equal degree of certainty. Just as in assessing the compensation to be paid to the lessee and the lessor together, the intention is to put the owner of the land as nearly as possible in the same position economically as if the land had not been acquired, the intention in apportioning the total compensation between the two interests is to ensure that *vis-a-vis* each other the lessor and lessee are left as far as possible in the same position as if the land had not been acquired. Obviously, the best way of ensuring this is to value the lessee's interest and the lessor's interest separately and then to divide the compensation money in the same proportion. Suppose, for example, the total compensation awarded for the owner's interest—comprising the lessor's interest and the lessee's interest—is Rs. 1,000 and that calculating separately the lessor's interest is found by the Court to be Rs. 800 and the lessee's interest to be Rs. 400. If the first of the above 3 principles is applied, the lessee will get Rs. 400 and the lessor Rs. 600. That would mean that while the lessee would be as nearly as possible in the same economic position as he was before, the lessor would be worse off by getting Rs. 600 while his loss is Rs. 800. If the second of the above 3 principles is applied, the lessor would get Rs. 800 and the lessee Rs. 200. That will mean that while the lessor is as well off as he was before, the lessee is worse off because he gets Rs. 200: while his loss is equivalent to Rs. 400. It is only by applying the third principle that we can attain the desired result of a fair

16 42 CWN 1191.

distribution of the loss or gain as the case may be between the lessor and the lessee.

"In a large number of cases, however, while the lessee's interest may be capable of valuation with a fair degree of certainty, the calculation of the lessor's interest is a much more uncertain process. In this class of cases the Court will necessarily have to adopt the first of the principles mentioned. There are other cases where the lessor's interest is capable of valuation with a fair degree of certainty, but not so the lessee's interest. In such cases, the Court will necessarily have to adopt the second of the principles mentioned above.

* * * * * * * * *

"My conclusion is that at least when valuing the lessee's interest for the purpose of apportionment, the chances of most advantageous disposition of the land have to be taken into account. It must be admitted, therefore, that there is some amount of uncertainty in calculating what the lessee would have obtained. It is well to remember, however, that the uncertainties which Mr. Gupta (Advocate for the lessee) has mentioned and similar other concertainties are day after day being taken into consideration by persons who are purchasing land. In investing money on land, these people decide after taking into account all the uncertain factors, what rate of interest can be fairly expected from investment of this nature, what the actual rent is likely to be, taking an average over the future years. The margin of errors in these calculations is not likely, in my opinion, to be very great. Thus, if Rs. 10,00,000 is the market value of some property now, it may be reasonably assumed that prudent men expect that over a number of years the property will fetch a net income which prudent men consider now to be a reasonable return on this amount. These expectations may well be belied. Natural calamities, like flood, or earthquake may do considerable damage, the Corporation rates may be increased so much as to leave very little to the owner, the city of Calcutta may cease to be a great centre of commerce and industry. Or the reverse may take place. The Corporation may decrease its rate to a nominal figure; there may be favourable climatic changes tending to make Calcutta a health resort; Commence and Industry may prosper enormously.

"But, on the whole the expectations of prudent men may be taken as the safe guide by the courts in matters like this, where absolute certainty is impossible of attainment. I am of opinion, that the degree of certainty with which the lessee's interest can be valued in the present case cannot be considered to be negligible.

"In any case, it seems to me that the degree of certainty which we can hope to attain in calculating the lessee's interest is decidedly greater than what can possible be hoped for in valuing the lessor's interest. The calculation of what the lessor would have got from the land in the 63 years that still remained of the lease should not be difficult. But, the valuation of the reversion that would have fallen in at the end of 63 years is almost impossible to calculate in view of the term in the lease that all buildings that the lessee may erect will pass to the lessor. If the reversion was offered for sale in the market, a willing purchaser will take into consideration the chances of any such building coming to him. But these chances are very difficult to assess.

"On all these considerations, I have come to the conclusion that in the facts of this case, lessee's interest can be valued with considerably greater certainty than the lessor's interest and so the court below was right in applying to this case the first of the three principles mentioned earlier.

"In assessing the value of the lessee's interest, the court below, as has been stated earlier, calculated the average fair return from the property to a 'full owner' at 4 per cent of the amount assessed as the market value. It has been contended on behalf of the respondents that land is considered to be such a good security that a willing purchaser would have at the date of the declaration for the acquisition expected no more than $2^1/_4$% or $2^3/_4$% return on the amount invested. Mr. Mullick who followed the Advocate-General for the respondents vehemently argued that land is even better security than gilt-edged security and taking into consideration the yield on gilt-edged security at the relevant date, the investors would gladly invest in land, even if it was expected to yield $2^1/_4$% or $2^1/_2$%. The two Expert witnesses have disagreed as regards the comparative security of land and gilt-edged security and, in my judgment, their opinions are of little assistance. There can be little doubt that the investment in land has a peculiar fascination for many Investors in this country and other things remaining the same, they would be prepared to accept a lesser interest on investment in land. But other things are not the same. While the return of the gilt-edged securities and other securities would be liable to income-tax only, the income from landed properties in Calcutta would be liable to Corporation rates in addition to income-tax. Past experience shows that these rates keep on mounting. The risks of having to resort to litigations for realising income from land are much greater than for realising the income from securities.

"A further consideration which is bound to weigh with the prospective purchasers of bustee land is the probability of the State imposing special burdens on the owners of such land for the welfare of bustee tenants. Taking everything into consideration, prudent purchasers of bustee land such as was acquired in this case would not, in my judgment, offer a price on which the expected return would work out at less than 4 per cent. The court below, therefore, rightly calculated the return to the 'full owner' of such properties at 4 per cent of the market value .... The more difficult question to my mind is what security table is to be applied in calculating the present value of the amounts that the lessee would have expected to receive year by year. The court below accepted $5^1/_2$% table...........The judgment does not show that the court below considered the different factors that determined the Security Table to be applied. The 'Security' in each table—whether it be 2 per cent, $2^1/_2$ per cent, 4 per cent, 5 per cent or $5^1/_2$ per cent or more or less—is really the rate of interest which a prudent investor would demand on the principal he would invest in payment of the present price of the future expectations so that the principal and interest would together be equivalent to the amount of the future receipt. When a Bank advances money on a Bill of Exchange, which would mature 3 months hence, the Bank would take into consideration the risk of the Bill not being honoured in deciding the rate of discount. Similarly, the present purchaser of the right to get what the lessee would receive, say, 1 or 2 or more years hence, would take into consideration the risk of his not getting it at all or getting less against the advantage of having his capital invested for a period. In my judgment, the risk of the expected receipts not being realised in part or in full is approximately of the same nature and degree as those which the purchasers of the full owner's interest in land have to take into account in deciding what rate of return should be insisted upon. This rate has been calculated by the court below at 4 per cent and for the reasons given above. I have accepted this as correct. In my judgment, the same rate, namely, 4 per cent should be taken as the rate which the investors would ask for on the amount invested in payment of the present price of the future expectation of receipts so that the principal and interest would together equal the amount expected in future. The present value of each year's receipt for the next 63 years that remained of the lease has, therefore, to be calculated according to the 4 per cent security table. The sum total of the values thus calculated of the expected return for each of the 63 years being 4 per cent on the market value of the 'full owner's' interest less the rent payable for that particular year is admittedly Rs. 4,89,636. My conclusion is that the lessee should be given this sum plus 15 per cent S.A. out of the total sum of Rs. 10,28,758 plus 15 per cent S.A. that has been awarded by the Collector for the 'full owner's' interest and the balance should be given to the lessor".

The lessee preferred an appeal to the Supreme Court where the parties came to a settlement.

The other case is *Santosh Kumar Dhur* v *Nanda Kishore Mullick.*[17]

Bare land out of premises No. 35 and 35/1, Lower Circular Road popularly known as 'Mullick Bazar' was acquired by the Calcutta Improvement Trust in connection with their Alignment Scheme. Two-thirds share of the entire property was leased to the Appellants for 25 years in the first instance with an option of renewal for another 25 years on the expiry

17 AIR 1958 Cal 56.

of the said fixed first term of the same period. The renewal was to be on the same terms as the original letting.

At the date of the Collector's taking possession, the lease had 21 years to run and then of course there was the option for another 25 years. A sum of ₹ 1,93,535/6/8 ps. inclusive of S.A. was awarded as the market value of the owner's interest (lessor's plus lessee's interest) for $^{2}/_{3}$rd share in the property.

There was no question of abatement of rent in this case as the lessee had agreed that he would go on paying the full rent in spite of the acquisition and the lessors had accepted the position. The lessor, therefore, in this case was only entitled to value of his reversion.

The learned President found that the net income of the lessee from the acquired property was ₹ 106 per month. As regards right of renewal for a further period, the Tribunal did not take that into account in assessing the lessee's interest. He capitalised this net income at 10 per cent security for 21 years and arrived at the valuation of ₹ 11,000 on account of the lessee's interest. He calculated the lessor's interest, namely, the reversion at 5 per cent interest for 21 years and obtained the figure of ₹ 59,450 as the value of his reversion.

The learned President then struck the proportion between the two values, the lessee's and lessor's, namely, ₹ 11,000 and ₹ 59,450 and apportioned the compensation money in that proportion between the two parties, the lessee getting ₹ 30,191/12/6 and the lessor ₹ 1,63,343/10/2. In making the apportionment as above, he relied upon and applied the principle enunciated by the High Court in the case of *Surendranath* v *Peary Charan.*[18]

The lessee appealed to the High Court.

On the question of the lessee's right of renewal for a further period, which was not taken into account by the Tribunal, the High Court held that "the lessee is to be compensated for the loss of his rights and advantages under the lease by reason of the acquisition. The option of renewal is undoubtedly one of

18 42 CWN 1191.

such rights and its loss has to be taken into account in assessing the lessee's portion of the compensation money"

Taking all facts into consideration including the fact of the existence of the Alignment over the acquired land Their Lordships fixed the effective unexpired period of the lease at (21 plus 15) 36 years giving the lessee the benefit of $^{3}/_{5}$th of his optional renewal period.

On the question of the actual income from the acquired land, the High Court after an examination of the evidence came to a finding that the net income of the disputed share in the acquired land would be ₹ 165 per month or roughly ₹ 2,000 per annum. Then Their Lordships proceeded to state as follows:

> "Reasonable security so far as the Appellant is concerned would be in view of the above assessment of income 8 per cent and the effective unexpired period of his lease would be, as already stated, 36 years. The lessor's rate of interest should be taken at 5 per cent in valuing his reversion at the end of 36 years. Admittedly also the lessor would not be losing any rent during the lease period as the acquisition notwithstanding, the lessee would continue to pay the whole rent of Rs. 1,501 per month reserved under the lease for his occupation of the remaining part of the unacquired portion of the demised property."

To value two interests, therefore, we have the following data:

(1) *for the lessee*—The net income of ₹ 2,000 to be capitalised at 8 per cent security for 36 years' purchase, and

(2) *for the lessee*—The reversion at the end of 36 years to be valued at 5 per cent interest rate".

On the vexed question of apportionment, Their Lordships after a review of the authorities including the above unreported case of *Sitanath Pal* laid down the following principles:

> "The suggested methods may be broadly put under two heads:
>
> (1) *Value one of the interest*. The lessor's or the lessee's—deduct it from the total valuation and award the remainder for the other interest; and

(2) *Value both interests.* If the total award does not reasonably correspond to the sum total of the two valuations, apply the rule of proportion, or in other words, divide the total compensation money between the two interests in proportion to their respective values.

"Which method is to be applied in a particular case will, of course, depend upon its circumstances and considerations of justice may sometimes usefully aid this determination. ...... In apportioning the compensation money between the landlord and the tenant, the court will have to bear in mind the two modes of apportionment enumerated in (1) and (2) above and will apply that which suits a particular case or the facts before it. In doing so, it will, of course, consider the possibility of valuing both the interests and failing there, it will pay due attention to the comparative degree of certainty of the one or the other of the two valuations and then apply the suitable method of apportionment according to its finding on that question.

* * * * * * * * *

"It is also the duty of the court to prevent obvious or gross injustice and as already stated that may sometimes assist in the determination of the correct method of apportionment and in checking up whether the correct method is being applied.

* * * * * * * * *

"In general, however, the first method may fairly be applied where one only of the two interests can be conveniently and reasonably valued, while the other cannot and where both interests can be conveniently and reasonably valued with fair or fairly equal amount of certainty, the second method based on the rule of proportion ought to be employed. To such a case, the first method should not be applied as its application would be attended with obvious injustice except where the sum total of the two valuations would coincide or practically coincide with the award-money or at least reasonably approximate the same. This is almost self-evident as in all other cases, the residue part would be either more or less than the value of the corresponding interest and the difference would not be negligible. It is eminently fair in such cases to apply the rule of proportion to distribute the difference between the total award money and the sum total of the two valuations whether the excess or the deficiency be in the one or in the other as between the two parties.

"In calculating the values, however, for applying the rule of proportion, it would be useful to remember that the potential values of the two interests (by which, of course, we mean the present values of their potentialities) should not be altogether disregarded."

Valuation of the two interests was made by the High Court in the manner following:

Bearing in mind what we have said above, the relevant calculation in the present case would be as follows:

(1) *Value of the lessee's interest*: Net rental of ₹ 2,000 p.a. to be capitalised at 8% security at 36 years' purchase. That gives us ₹ 2,000 × 11.717193 *i.e.* ₹ 23,434.

(2) *Value of the lessor's reversion.* Award for land and building: ₹ 1,65,625. Present value of ₹ 1 in 36 years at 5% is 0.1726574. Therefore, the value of the lessor's reversion is ₹ 1,65,625 × 0.1726574 *i.e.* ₹ 28,596.

The proportion then would roughly be 23434/28597 which means that the lessee's share would be 23434/52031 and the lessor's 28597/52031.

The total award money including S.A. is ₹ 1,93,535. The distribution in the above proportion would give us the figure of ₹ 87,165 in the lessee's 23434/52031 share and the remainder, namely, ₹ 1,06,370, which corresponds roughly to the other proportion 28597/52031 in the lessor's share.

It will thus be seen that the apportionment of the compensation money awarded for a leasehold property between the lessor and the lessee is a very difficult and complicated matter which can only be determined by a court of law on materials placed before it by the parties. It is clearly beyond the capacity of Land Acquisition Collectors who should themselves refer it to court under s. 30 of the Land Acquisition Act[19] (now s. 76 of the new Act of 2013).

Lease premium and deposit

The Supreme Court in *A.R. Krishnamurthy* v *CIT,*[1] held that ownership is a "bundle of rights". There can be transfer of one such right out of the bundle of rights and lease of immovable property is a transfer of one such right. The price paid for the modicum of ownership which the landlord transfers to the tenant is often described as *salami* or premium. Valuation of particular rights out of the total bundle of rights transferred in terms of money, may be difficult, but nevertheless an evaluation is possible and can be made.

There is a difference between a deposit, and a premium. A premium in terms of s. 105 of the Transfer of Property Act, is price paid, i.e. once for all outgoing of money in return of transfer of certain rights in the land. A deposit on the other hand is an amount which is returnable on fulfilment of certain conditions.[2]

Licence, given to make a structure on roof—how to value such right?

When a right to construct alone (terrace right) is transferred there is no transfer of any undivided share/interest in the land on which the superstructure exists. Nevertheless the transferee though ownership does not vest in him has acquired a valuable property right in the nature of access to value-in-use. The right in the superstructure which he constructs will be co-terminus with the life of the existing building on which it has been constructed. The value of the right to construct could be equated to a percentage of the savings effected in not having to purchase an undivided share in the land for making the construction. There is a correlation as well between the reduced value to the erstwhile absolute owner after such construction and the value of construction right. In view of the practice of this kind of licence coming into greater use because of housing shortages in cities, the question of valuation is bound

19 *Rabindra Kumar Bose* v *S.K. Banerjee* 63 CWN 851.

1 (1989)176 ITR 417.

2 *CIT* v *Bazpur Co-op. Sugar Factory Ltd.* (1988)172 ITR 321 (SC).

to arise and an appropriate valuation has to be worked out with practical approach in each particular case.

Valuation of right in remainder on actuarial basis

Right in remainder is a right in property subject to life interest. The remainderman's right is not that of a mere *spes successionis* and is a right *in praesenti* partaking of the same nature as the property itself in which the right of remainder vests.[3] It is not just the difference in value of property as reduced by life interest in view of uncertainty of duration of life interest.

Where assessee had a property by way of bequest but subject to life interest in favour of assessee's mother, the value to be adopted should be discounted adequately for the encumbrance as pointed out in *CWT* v *V. Pugalagiri*[4] in following words:

> "While the assessing authority did not accept this, the Appellate Authority, applying the observations of the Supreme Court in *CWT* v *Trustees of H.E.H. Nizam's Family (Remainder Wealth) Trust,*[5] upheld the method of the interest of the remainderman as put forward by the assessee. The Tribunal also accepted the valuation so made. We have carefully considered the order of the Tribunal and we find that the course adopted by the Appellate Authority as well as by the Tribunal, in the absence of specific rules in regard to the valuation of the interest of the remainderman, is quite correct and is also fully supported by the observation of the Supreme Court in the decision referred to earlier. It has been pointed out by the Supreme Court that the value of the remainderman would be the present value of his right to receive the corpus of the property at an uncertain future date and such valuation should be done on an actuarial basis and that taking the future value of the asset to be received at a later date, its present value had to be discounted. That precisely had been done by the Appellate Authority and was also upheld by the Tribunal. Ultimately, the whole question revolves round the method of the valuation to be adopted, in the absence

3 *WTO* v *Miss Meher Toos Vakily* (1989)31 ITD 293 (Andh).
4 (1995)212 ITR 156 (Mad).
5 (1977)108 ITR 555.

of any specific rule in that regard. We are, therefore, of the view that no referable question of law as such can be said to arise out of the order of the Tribunal."

Relative valuation as between lessor and lessee

The valuation of the lessor's interest is different from that of a lessee. While the mathematical illustrations hereafter would give an idea as to relative values thereof, the judicial decisions in a few cases reflect on the aspect of apportionment of compensation as between a lessor and a lessee.

In apportioning the compensation money awarded under the L.A. Act between the landlord and the tenureholder, the court ought to proceed on the principle of ascertaining what the value of the interest of the landlord is on the one hand, and that of the tenant on the other, and to divide the sum awarded between them in accordance with these values. Where the rent is fixed in perpetuity the landlord is not entitled to more than the capitalised value of his rent.[6]

Where the land leased in perpetuity on a fixed rent is required under the L.A. Act and the question is as to the proportion in which compensation should be divided between the lessor and the lessee, the court ought to proceed on the principle of ascertaining what is the value of the interest of the *zamindar* on the one hand with which he has parted and that of the tenant on the other, and to apportion the compensation money between them in accordance with those values.[7]

In apportioning compensation paid for land acquired by the Government between the occupancy tenants and the landlords, the proportion of interests of the landlord and the occupancy tenant in the land acquired may be fairly taken to be the same as that between the *malikana* paid by the tenant to the landlord and the land revenue.[8]

In arriving at the value of the property the lease-rent derived by the landlord should be taken into consideration,

6 *Batan Singh* v *Nathu Birju* AIR 1961 P&H 503; *Dinendra Narain Roy* v *Titu Ram* ILR 30 Cal 801.

7 *Hakim Singh* v *Collector, Gurdaspur* AIR 1932 Lah 123(2).

8 *Ram Kishen* v *Jati Ram* AIR 1931 Lah 649.

besides other matters in the particular case and also what the owner was actually receiving from the property and what would be the amount of loss to him by the acquisition. The value to the seller of the property in its actual condition at the time of the sale should be taken into consideration.[9]

Where compensation is assessed on the basis of *lease-rent* actually received, regard must be had whether the lease was one for a considerable period and the rent was likely to be received for a long time.[10]

The valuation of ordinary leasehold was on 20 years' purchase taking into consideration the terms of the lease, the amount and the age of the lease.[11]

Where land is given in permanent lease at fixed rent and the same is acquired, compensation to the landlord and tenant should be given in the ratio of 25:75.[12] In another case compensation to landlord and tenant was apportioned in the ratio 7:7.[13] Where land given in lease for 99 years was acquired the lessor was entitled to compensation of 25% only.[14] Merely on the basis of mutation entries showing the claimant as qualifying tenant, he cannot be treated as a tenant to claim share in compensation as tenant under s. 23 of the L.A. Act.[15]

In case of *Nazul* land on perpetual lease by Government with right of re-entry on breach of covenants, the lessee was not held to be entitled to the whole compensation amount determined by the Collector. Compensation apportioned between lessee and lessor was 75:25.[16]

9 *Government of Bombay* v *Merwanji Muncherji Cama* 10 Bom LR 907; *Sreemutty Swarnamanjuri Dasi* v *Secretary of State* AIR 1928 Cal 522; 32 CWN 421; 49 CLJ 54; 55 Cal 994; 112 IC 706.

10 *Ismailji Mohamedalli Bohori* v *District Collector, Nasik* AIR 1933 Bom 37; 34 Bom LR 1457.

11 *Radha Charan* v *Secretary of State* AIR 1943 All 238.

12 *Sharad Chandra* v *State* AIR 1987 Guj 55; *Bai Saraswati* v *Bharat Khand Textile Co.* AIR 1967 Guj 36 (DB).

13 *Indraprastha Ice and Cold Storage Ltd.* v *Union of India* AIR 1987 Del 171.

14 *Union of India* v *Ajit Singh* AIR 1987 Del 151.

15 *Durga Das* v *Collector H.P.* (1996)5 SCC 618; AIR 1996 SC 2786.

16 *Inder Parshad* v *Union of India* (1994)5 SCC 239.

A freehold land normally commands higher compensation while the land burdened with encumbrances secures lesser price. The fact of a tenant in occupation would be an encumbrance and no willing purchaser would willingly offer the same price as would be offered for a freehold land.[17]

A leasehold from the Govt. was acquired. The lessee had only seven years' lease-hold rights in the land and thereafter the land would stand revested to Govt. High Court directed compensation for land within ceiling limit to be apportioned between lessee and Govt. on 50:50 basis. As the State did not question the apportionment, Supreme Court declined to interfere.[18]

The valuation of a premises held in use and occupation has often to be made for assessment of damages. The question arises if the damages are to be assessed in accordance with the rent method or by applying the income or profit method or the cost method. The Supreme Court held that the award of the arbitrator was improper as the Arbitrator did not consider at all the rent method for assessing damages and instead applied the income or profit method and even in doing so, erred in not taking into account the expenses, the cost of investment etc. The award thus stood vitiated.[19]

Let us now turn to a few practical examples which are relevant in valuation of leasehold properties from differents angles and under varying situations.

Salami or Premium

EXAMPLE 59. **A person is negotiating for a 21 years lease of a premises worth a net rent of ₹ 3,500 per months. He is willing to pay a *salami* and a rent ₹ 2,000 per month. He requires 9.5% interest on his capital. What *salami* should he pay?**

SOLUTION

The Lessee will save ₹ 1,500 per month in the way of rent. He will have to pay a *salami* equivalent to the present value of the profit rental. He will also

17 *M.B. Gopala Krishna* v *Special Deputy Collector, L.A.* (1996)3 SCC 594.

18 *Ratan Kumar Tandon* v *State of U.P.* AIR 1996 SC 2710.

19 *Union of India* v *Banwari Lal and Sons Private Limited* (2004)5 SCC 304.

pay into a sinking fund to recover of the end of the lease the amount he will have to pay as *salami*.

Rack Rental Value	=	₹	3,500 p.m.
Less: Rent reserved under lease	=	₹	2,000 p.m.
		₹	1,500 p.m.

Profit Rental = ₹1,500 p.m. × 12 = ₹ 18,000 p.a.

Multiplying by years' purchase (Y.P.) @ 9.5% and 3.5% for an Annual Sinking Fund Deposit (A.S.F.D.) for 21 years

$$= \frac{1}{(i+S)} = \frac{1}{i+\dfrac{r}{(1+r)^n - 1}}$$

$$= \frac{1}{0.095+\dfrac{0.035}{(1+0.035)^{21}-1}}$$

$$= \frac{1}{0.095+\dfrac{0.035}{(1.035)^{21}-1}} = (\times)\ 7.8102675$$

Salami = ₹ 1,40,584.82

Say ... ₹ 1,40,585

In the above Example, the problem has been approached from the lessee's point of view. However in such cases, the amount appropriately determinable by the lessor may also be estimated. The lessor knowing that the property would ultimately revert to him, will probably be satisfied with a security slightly lesser than that of the lessee, say, at 5½ percent interest on his capital. Also the possibility is that the lessor will not start a Sinking Fund. Let us calculate the *salami* from the lessor's point of view. Assume that the lease is for a term of 21 years, the Rack Rental value is ₹ 300 per month and rent reserved in lease deed is ₹ 200 p.m. If no *salami* is to be received by him, then present value of the premises would be:

Net rent of the property per annum = ₹ 3,600

Y.P. @ 5½% for perpetuity $= \frac{1}{i} = \frac{1}{0.055}$ = (×) 18.1818

Present value = ₹ 65,455

However, if *salami* is received the rent would be = ₹ 2,400.00 per annum for 21 years and then will be ₹ 3,600.00 per annum after the term of lease.

(*a*) Net rent for first 21 years = ₹ 2,400 p.a.

Multiplying by Y.P. single rate @ 5½% for 21 years

$$= \frac{1}{i + \frac{i}{(1+i)^n - 1}} = \frac{1}{0.055 + \frac{0.055}{(1+0.055)^{21} - 1}} = (\times)\ 12.275$$

= ₹ 29,460

(*b*) Net rent after 21 years = ₹ 3,600 p.a.

Multiplying by Y.P. @ 5½ for perpetuity deferred 21 years

$$= \frac{1}{i} \times \frac{1}{(1+i)^n}$$

$$= \frac{1}{0.055} \times \frac{1}{(1+0.055)^{21}} = (\times)\ 5.9065$$

= ₹ 21,264

Present value = ₹ 29,460 + ₹ 21,264 = ₹ 50,724

Salami = ₹ 65,455 – ₹ 50,724 = ₹ 14,731

Therefore, in the above example we see that from the lessee's point of view a *salami* of ₹ 12,649 is to be paid but from the lessor's point of view a *salami* of ₹ 14,731 is more appropriate. A figure somewhere between these two may perhaps be negotiated.

EXAMPLE 60. Take the same property as quoted in the preceding example. If the lessor had stated that he required a premium or *salami* of ₹ 1,40,585, what rent should be reserved in the lease?

SOLUTION

Net Rent of the property = ₹ 3,500 p.m. × 12 = ₹ 42,000 p.a.

Salami = ₹ 1,40,585

Interest on ₹ 1 for 1 year @ 9.5% = 0.095

A.S.F. to produce ₹ 1 in 21 years @ 3.5%

$$= \frac{r}{(1+r)^n - 1} = \frac{0.035}{(1+0.035)^{21}-1}$$

$$= \frac{0.035}{(1.035)^{21}-1} = 0.0330365$$

Annuity which ₹ 1 will purchase @ 9.5% and 3.5%

$$= 0.095 + 0.0330365$$

$$= 0.1280365$$

Reduction in Rent = ₹ 1,40,585 × 0.1280365 = ₹ 18,000 p.a.

Rent to be required in lease = ₹ 24,000 p.a

= ₹ 2,000 p.m.

EXAMPLE 61. 14 years ago a man took a 21 years lease of a premises on payment of *salami*, and rent which was equivalent to a net rent of ₹ 3,000 per month. The net Rack Rent of the property is ₹ 5,000 per month. He now wishes to cancel his existing lease and to take a new lease for 21 years at the existing rental. What would be a fair premium or *salami* for him to pay? Assume interest on capital is required at 9% and sinking fund of 3%.

SOLUTION

Net Rack Rent	=	₹ 5,000 p.m.
Less: Rent reserved in lease	=	₹ 3,000 p.m.
		₹ 2,000 p.m.
Profit rental	=	₹ 2,000 p.m. × 12 = ₹ 24,000 p.a.

Multiplying by years' purchase (Y.P) at 9% and 3% for 14 years

$$= \frac{1}{(i+S)} = \frac{1}{i + \frac{r}{(1+r)^n - 1}}$$

$$= \frac{1}{0.09 + \frac{0.03}{(1+0.03)^{14} - 1}}$$

$$= \frac{1}{0.09 + \frac{0.03}{(1.03)^{14} - 1}} = 6.7328126$$

and present value of ₹ 1 @ 9% for 7 years

$$= \frac{1}{(1+i)^n} = \frac{1}{(1+0.09)^7}$$

$$= \frac{1}{(1.09)^7} = 0.5470342$$

Y.P. dual rate 9% and 3% for 14 years deferred 7 years

= 6.7328126 × 0.5470342 = (×) 3.6830791

Salami to be paid = ₹ 88,393.81

Say ... = ₹ 88,394

EXAMPLE 62. Assume that is the case quoted in example No. 61 the lessee was not in a position to pay the *salami*, but he wished to cancel his existing lease and take a new lease for 21 years. What rent should be reserved in the lease?

SOLUTION

Rent reserved in old lease = ₹ 3,000 p.m. × 12 = ₹ 36,000 p.a.

Salami for extension = ₹ 88,394

Therefore, Annual Equivalent of that sum for 21 years new lease period, @ 9% and 3%

either, A.E. = V(i + S)

$$\text{or, A.E.} = \frac{\text{Capital value or sum paid}}{\text{Years' purchase}}$$

$$\text{A.E.} = 88{,}394\left(i + \frac{r}{(1+r)^n - 1}\right)$$

$$= 88{,}394\left(0.09 + \frac{0.03}{(1+0.03)^{21} - 1}\right)$$

$$= 88{,}394\left(0.09 + \frac{0.03}{(1.03)^{21} - 1}\right)$$

= 88,394 (0.1248717)

= ₹ 11,038 p.a.

New rent = ₹ 36,000 p.a. + ₹ 11,038 p.a. = ₹ 47,038 p.a.

or virtual rent

Alternative Method:

Rent Receive in old lease = ₹ 36,000 p.a.

Salami for extension = ₹ 88,394

Interest on Re 1 for 1 year @ 9% = 0.09

A.S.F. to produce Re 1 in 21 years @ 3%

$$= \frac{r}{(1+r)^n - 1}$$

$$= \frac{0.03}{(1+0.03)^{21} - 1}$$

$$= \frac{0.03}{(1.03)^{21} - 1} = (+)\ 0.0348717$$

= 0.1248717

Annual equivalent = ₹ 88,394 × 0.1248717 = ₹ 11,038

New rent or virtual rent = ₹ 47,038 p.a.

EXAMPLE 63. Shop premises were let 15 years ago for ₹ 4,500 per month inclusive of taxes. The lease was for 21 years and a *salami* of ₹ 5,00,000 was paid. The Rack Rental value at present is ₹ 12,000 per month. What is the lessee's interest in the property?

SOLUTION

Lessee's Interest of the leasehold property as on date

Annual Gross Rack Rental

= ₹ 12,000 p.m. × 12 = ₹ 1,44,000 p.a.

Less:

(i) Assuming 15% on it as outgoings = ₹ 50,000 p.a.

(ii) Rent Reserved per annum in lease = ₹ 4,500 p.a. × 12

= ₹ 54,000 p.a. = ₹ 1,04,400 p.a.

Profit rental per annum = ₹ 39,600 p.a.

Multiplying by Year's Purchase (Y.P.) dual rate at 12% and 3.5% for 6 years on expired of lease

$$= \frac{1}{i+S} = \frac{1}{i + \dfrac{r}{(1+r)^n - 1}}$$

where S = A.S.F.D.
$i = 0.12$
$r = 0.035$
$n = 6$

$$= \frac{1}{0.12 + \frac{0.035}{(1+0.035)^6 - 1}} = 3.667460922$$

$= 3.667460922 \times$ ₹ 39,600 = ₹ 1,45,231

Lessee's interest = ₹ 1,45,000

EXAMPLE 64. In the case quoted in Example No. 63, what is the lessor's interest in the property?

SOLUTION

Lessor's interest of the leasehold property as the date

(A) Term:

Unexpired period of lease for 6 years

Annual Rent received in lease @ ₹ 4500 p.m. × 12 = ₹ 54,000 p.a.

Less: Assuming 35% as outgoing on it (–) = ₹ 18,900 p.a.

Net Annual Rental = ₹ 35,100 p.a.

Multiplying by Y.P. single rate @ 7.5% for
6 years unexpired period of lease (well secured)

$$= \frac{1}{i + \frac{i}{(1+i)^n - 1}}$$

$$= \frac{1}{0.075 + \frac{0.075}{(1+0.075)^6 - 1}}$$

$$= \frac{1}{0.075 + \frac{0.075}{(1.075)^6 - 1}} = 4.6938464$$

Term's Value = ₹ 1,64,754 (A)

(B) *On Reversion*

Reversion to Rack Rent = ₹ 1,44,000 p.a.

Less: *Outgoings*
say, 35% on ₹ 1,44,000 p.a. = (–) ₹ 50,400 p.a.

Net Rent = ₹ 93,600 p.a.

Multiplying by Y.P. single rate @ 8% for perpetuity deferred 6 years

$$= \frac{1}{i} \times \frac{1}{(1+i)^n} \quad \text{[assuming 8\% as normal security]}$$

$$= \frac{1}{0.08} \times \frac{1}{(1+0.08)^6}$$

= 12.5 × 0.6301696 = (×) 7.8771203

= ₹ 7,37,298 (B)

Therefore, Lessor's Interest = (A) + (B)

= ₹ 1,64,754 + 7,37,298

= 9,02,052 = ₹ 9,02,000

NOTE: This has to be matched with an estimate of future rack rent to arrive at its present worth on discounted method of calculation.

EXAMPLE 65. A man takes a 99 years' lease of a plot of land and pays a ground rent of ₹ 10,000 per month. He erects a building on the site at a cost of ₹ 65,95,000. What is the Virtual Rent?

SOLUTION

Land = Ground Rent = ₹ 10,000 p.m. × 12 = ₹ 1,20,000 p.a.

Building = ₹ 65,95,000 @ 10%
(assuming 10% as prevalent gilt-edged security) = ₹ 6,59,500 p.a.

Virtual Rent = ₹ 1,20,000 p.a.+ 6,59,500 p.a. = ₹ 7,79,500 p.a.

EXAMPLE 66. What is the virtual rent of a tenant who purchased 7 years ago a lease for ₹ 10,00,000. The lease had 50 years to run and the reserved rent was ₹ 15,000 per month. The house was in a dilapidated condition and be immediately spent ₹ 4,00,000 on repairs. Two years later he erected a garage costing ₹ 2,50,000 and last year he added another floor on the portion of the house costing ₹ 5,00,000.

SOLUTION

Rent reserved in lease = ₹ 15,000 × 12 = ₹ 1,80,000 p.a.

Cost of lease ... ₹ 10,00,000

Repairs ... ₹ 4,00,000

₹ 14,00,000

Annual equivalent (A.E.) of ₹ 14,00,000 @ 9.5% on invested capital and @ 3% for A.S.F.D. for 50 years is:

$$A.E. = V (i + S)$$

V = Capital sum
i = rate of return on invested capital
S = A.S.F.D.
r = rate of return on A.S.F.D.

$$= V\left(i+\frac{r}{(1+r)^n-1}\right)$$

$$= 14,00,000\left(0.095+\frac{0.03}{(1+0.03)^{50}-1}\right)$$

$$= 14,00,000 \times 0.1038654 \qquad = ₹\ 1,45,412 \text{ p.a. (i)}$$

Cost of Garage ... ₹ 2,50,000

A.E. @ 9.5% and 3% for 48 years

$$= 2,50,000\left(0.095+\frac{0.03}{(1.03)^{48}-1}\right)$$

$$= ₹\ 2,50,000 \times 0.1045777 \qquad = ₹\ 26,144 \text{ p.a. (ii)}$$

Cost of Extra floor ... ₹ 5,00,000

A.E. @ 9.5% and 3% for 44 years

$$= 5,00,000\left(0.095+\frac{0.03}{(1.03)^{44}-1}\right)$$

$$= ₹\ 5,00,000 \times 0.1062298 \qquad = ₹\ 53,115 \text{ p.a. (iii)}$$

Virtual or Sitting Rent = Rent Reserved + (i) + (ii) + (iii)
= ₹ 1,80,000 + ₹ 1,45,412 + ₹ 26,144 + ₹ 53,115= ₹ 4,04,671 p.a.

= ₹ 33,723 p.m.

EXAMPLE 67. What is the virtual rent of a house to a tenant who paid a premium of ₹ 2,00,000 for a lease of 21 years at an annual monthly rent of ₹ 2,500 per month, the lessee doing all repairs?

SOLUTION

Rent reserved in lease = ₹ 2,500 p.m. × 12 = ₹ 30,000 p.a.

Salami or Premium (V) = ₹ 2,00,000

I. Annual Equivalent (A.E.) of the premium

$$= \frac{\text{Capital Value (V)}}{\text{Years' Purchase (YP)}}$$

$$= \frac{V}{\text{Y.P. Dual rate @ 10\% \& 3\% on invested capital i.e. premium and Annual sinking fund (ASF) for 21 years}}$$

$$= \frac{V}{\frac{1}{i+S}} = \frac{V}{\frac{1}{i+\frac{r}{(1+r)^n-1}}}$$

$$= \frac{2,00,000}{\frac{1}{0.10+\frac{0.03}{(1+0.03)^{21}-1}}}$$

$$= \frac{2,00,000}{7.4144497} \qquad = ₹ \quad 26,974 \text{ p.a.}$$

II. A.E. $= V(i + S)$

$$= V\left(i+\frac{r}{(1+r)^n-1}\right)$$

$$= 2,00,000\left(0.10+\frac{0.03}{(1.03)^{21}-1}\right)$$

$$= 2,00,000 \times 0.1348717 \qquad = ₹ \quad 26,974 \text{ p.a.}$$

Rent Reserved in lease	=	₹ 30,000 p.a.
Add: Annual equivalent for the premium paid ₹ 2,00,000 at the time of entrance of the lease for the lease period 21 years.	=	(+) ₹ 26,974 p.a.
	=	₹ 56,974 p.a.
Add: @ 10% of ₹ 56,974 for repairs and maintenance	=	(+) ₹ 5,700 p.a.
Virtual Rent	=	₹ 62,674 p.a.

EXAMPLE 68. A person has purchased a plot of land for ₹ 2,50,000. He has built a house on the said land costing ₹ 6,00,000. It is estimated that the building will have a probable life of 80 years, @10% (Ten percent) interest in the whole cost is expected. What is the virtual rent?

SOLUTION

Cost of the land = ₹ 2,50,000

Annual equivalent (A.E.) $= \dfrac{\text{Cost of the land}}{\text{Y.P. for Petetuity}}$

$$= \frac{₹\ 2{,}50{,}000}{\frac{1}{i}} = \frac{₹\ 2{,}50{,}000}{\frac{1}{0.10}}$$

$$= \frac{₹\ 2{,}50{,}000}{10} = ₹\ 25{,}000 \text{ p.a.} \ldots (1)$$

Cost of the building = ₹ 6,00,000

It's Annual equivalent (A.E.)= $\dfrac{\text{Cost of the building}}{\text{Y.P. duel rate at 'i' on invested capital and 'r' on ASFD for 'n' period (years)}}$

$$= \frac{₹\ 6{,}00{,}000}{\text{Y.P. @10\% \& 3\% for 80 years}}$$

$$= \frac{₹\ 6{,}00{,}000}{\dfrac{1}{i + \dfrac{r}{(1+r)^n - 1}}}$$

$$= \frac{₹\ 6{,}00{,}000}{\dfrac{1}{0.10 + \dfrac{0.03}{(1+0.03)^{80} - 1}}}$$

$$= ₹\ 61{,}867 \text{ p.a.} \ldots (2)$$

Virtual Rent p.a. = (1) + (2)

= ₹ 25,000 + ₹ 61,867 = ₹ 86,867

EXAMPLE 69. What is the value of a property let on lease having 9 years to run at a net rental of ₹ 3,000 per month. The Full Gross Rental of the premises is ₹ 8,000 per month.

SOLUTION

Value of the Freehold Interest of the leasehold property.

A. Term:

Net Rental = ₹ 3,000 p.m. × 12 = ₹ 36,000 p.a.

Multiplying by Y.P. single rate @ 8% for the unexpired period of lease 9 years

$$= \frac{1}{i + \frac{i}{(1+i)^n - 1}}$$

$$= \frac{1}{0.08 + \frac{0.08}{(1+0.08)^9 - 1}} = (\times)\ 6.2468879$$

Term's Value = ₹ 2,24,888 (A)

B. Reversion to Full Gross Rent: ₹ 8,000 p.m. × 12 = ₹ 96,000 p.a.

Less: Outgoings (including repairs maintenance, property taxes, insurance etc.) @ 45% on it = 0.45 × ₹ 96,000 = (–) ₹ 43,200 p.a.

Net annual rent = ₹ 52,800 p.a.

Multiplying by Y.P. for perpetuity @ 7% deferred 9 years

$$= \frac{1}{i} \times \frac{1}{(1+i)^n}$$

$$= \frac{1}{0.07} \times \frac{1}{(1+0.07)^9} = (\times)\ 7.77$$

Reversionary Value = ₹ 52,800 × 7.77 = ₹ 4,10,256 (B)

Lessor's interest

= Term's Value (A) + Reversionary value (B)

= ₹ 2,24,888 + ₹ 4,10,256 = ₹ 6,35,144

EXAMPLE 70. 'A' leased to 'B' a plot of land in 1988 on the following terms (accounting year: April to March):

April 1988 to March 1998 ₹ 2,000 per month, Lessee to pay all taxes.

April 1998 to March 2008 ₹ 2,500 per month, " " " " "

April 2008 to March 2018 ₹ 3,000 per month, " " " " "

April 2018 to March 2028 ₹ 3,500 per month, " " " " "

The lessee is to erect structures worth at least ₹ 10,00,000 and to fill up the tank. After the expiration of the lease, the structures revert to the Lessor. The area of land is 15 kottah. Land on the same road for a depth of 40'–0" is selling for ₹ 3,40,000 per kottah. Buildings have already been constructed costing ₹ 5,00,000. It can be assumed that the value of the land will not fall below the present value.

What is the value of the Lessor's interest in 2013?

SOLUTION

The highest ground rent is very well secured and the security for capitalisation of these Ground Rents may be taken at 6.5%.

(A) Term:

(1) 2013 – 2018

Ground Rent = ₹ 3,000 p.m. × 12 = ₹ 36,000 p.a.

Multiplying by Y.P. Single rate for 5 years @ 6.5%

$$= \frac{1}{i + \frac{i}{(1+i)^n - 1}}$$

$$= \frac{1}{0.065 + \frac{0.065}{(1+0.065)^5 - 1}} = (\times)\ 4.155679438$$

= ₹ 1,49,604 ... (1)

(2) 2018–2028

Ground Rent = 3,500 p.m. × 12 = ₹ 42,000 p.a.

Multiplying by Y.P. single rate for 10 years @ 6.5% deferred 5 years

$$= \frac{1}{i + \frac{i}{(1+i)^n - 1}} \times \frac{1}{(1+i)^n}$$

$$= \frac{1}{0.065+\dfrac{0.065}{(1+0.065)^{10}-1}} \times \frac{1}{(1.065)^5}$$

= 7.188830223 × 0.729880836 = (×) 5.246989413

= ₹ 42,000 × 5.246989413 = ₹ 2,20,374 ... (2)

Therefore,

Term's Value	= (1) + (2)	
	= ₹ 1,49,604 + 2,20,374	= ₹ 3,69,978 ... (A)

(B) Reversion after (2028 – 2013) = 15 years to the lessor

Land:

1st Belt ...	7 kottah	=	7.000 Units
2nd Belt ...	8 kottah	=	5.340 Units (2/3rd of the 2nd belt)
	15 kottah	=	12.340 Units

12.34 Units @ ₹ 3,40,000	= ₹	41,95,600
Deduct: @ 15% on it for size	(–) ₹	6,29,340
	= ₹	35,66,260 ... (3)

Buildings:

Prime Cost	= ₹	5,00,000
Allow 20% Depreciation	(–) ₹	1,00,000
Depreciated Value	= ₹	4,00,000 ... (4)
On reversion, total value : (3) + (4)	= ₹	39,66,260
Multiplying by deferred factor @ 6½% i.e. $\frac{1}{(1.065)^5}$ for 15 years	(×)	0.388826524
Reversionary value after 15 years	= ₹	15,42,187 ... (B)

Value of the Lessor's Interest in 2013 = (A) + (B)

₹ 3,69,978 + ₹ 15,42,187 = ₹ 19,12,165

EXAMPLE 71. What is the lessee's interest in the premises as described in Example 70.

SOLUTION

Rental value of the premises

Value of land = ₹ 35,66,260

Buildings

Prime Cost	= ₹	5,00,000
Less: Depreciation	(–) ₹	25,000
Depreciated value (total life being 40 years which comes down to the lessee to 16 yrs. as the balance of life).	= ₹	4,75,000

Value of land and Buildings

= ₹ 35,66,260 + ₹ 4,75,000 = ₹ 40,41,260

Security @ 8½% ...... (×) 0.085

Net Rack Net = ₹ 3,43,507 p.a.

Say .... ₹ 3,44,000 p.a.

2013-2018 .... (1)

Net Rack Rent	=	₹ 3,44,000 p.a.
Rent paid	= (–)	₹ 36,000 p.a.
Profit rent:		= ₹ 3,08,000 p.a.

Multiplying by Y.P. dual rate @ 8.5% and 3.5% for 5 years

$$= \frac{1}{(i+S)} = \frac{1}{i + \frac{r}{(1+r)^n - 1}}$$

$$= \frac{1}{0.085} = \frac{1}{i + \frac{0.035}{(1+0.035)^6 - 1}} = (\times)\ 3.683493966$$

= ₹ 11,34,516 ... (1)

2018-2028 ... (2)

Net Rack Rent	=	₹ 3,44,000 p.a.
Rent paid	=	(–) ₹ 42,000 p.a.
Profit rent:		= ₹ 3,02,000 p.a.

Multiplying by the Y.P. dual rate @ $8^1/_2$% and $3^1/_2$% for 10 years deferred 5 years

$$= \frac{1}{i + \frac{r}{(1+r)^n - 1}} \times \frac{1}{(1+i)^n}$$

$$= \frac{1}{0.085+\frac{0.035}{(1.035)^{10}-1}} \times \frac{1}{(1.085)^6}$$

$= 5.874 \times 0.6650$

$= 3.90$

$\therefore$ 3.90 × ₹ 3,02,000 = ₹11,77,800 ... (2)

Lessee's present value

= ₹ 11,34,516 + ₹ 11,77,800 = ₹ 23,123,16

Here, Lessee's interest > Lessor's Interest.

EXAMPLE 72. What is the value of the following property which is being acquired under the Land Acquisition Act? The date is 2013. The property was leased by A to B on a 30 years, lease from 1995 on the following rentals:

1st year of the lease (1 yr.)	**₹ 8,500 p.m. (1995-1996)**
2nd year to 6th year lease (5 yrs.)	**₹ 9,000 p.m. (1996-2000)**
7th to 12th year lease (6 yrs.)	**₹ 10,000 p.m. (2001-2006)**
13th to 18th year lease (6 yrs.)	**₹ 11,500 p.m. (2007-2012)**
19th to 24th year lease (6 yrs.)	**₹ 13,500 p.m. (2013-2018)**
25th to 30th year lease (6 yrs.)	**₹ 16,500 p.m. (2019-2024)**

After 2 years B erected a building on the land costing ₹ 20,00,000. In 2007, 'B' sub-leased the property to 'C' for the unexpired term of the lease, less 7 days, at a monthly rent of ₹ 30,750 inclusive of all taxes and repairs. In 2010, 'B' agreed to reduce the rental to ₹ 25,500 per months owing to trade depression (with 50% outgoings liability). 'C' sub-let the premises room by room, the gross rental when fully let was ₹ 35,500 per month.

SOLUTION

To ascertain the Market Value (M.V.) for the purpose of compensation under Land Acquisition Act.

(A) Gross Annual Rent (single letting) = ₹ 25,500 p.m. × 12

Gross Annual Rent (G.A.R.) = ₹ 3,06,000 p.a.

Less:

Outgoings:

i) Property Taxes (P.T.) ... 36% on G.A.R. = ₹1,10,160
[G.A.R. = 10% on G.A.R.
A.V. = ₹ 2,75,400 assuming
P.T. @ 40% on A.V.]

ii) Repairs and maintenance (External 5% & Internal 5%) ... 10% on G.A.R. = ₹ 30,600

iii) Vacancies ... Nil

iv) Collection charges ... $2^1/_2$% on G.A.R. = ₹ 7,650

v) Bad Debts ... Nil

vi) Insurance ... 1% on G.A.R. = ₹ 3,060

vii) Sundries ... 2% on G.A.R. = ₹ 6,120
(Services, maintenance etc.)

... 51½% on G.A.R.= ₹ 1,57,590

(–) ₹ 1,57,590

Net Annual Rent (N.A.R.) = ₹ 1,48,410

Multiplying by the Years' Purchase (Y.P.)

as Security @ $9^1/_2$% for perpetuity = $\frac{1}{i} = \frac{1}{0.095}$ = (×) 10.52631579

Capitalised Value of the leasehold property as on date of valuation = ₹ 15,62,211 .. (A)

(B) Again,

Gross Rack Rental per annum = ₹ 35,500 p.m. × 12 = ₹ 4,26,000

Less:

Outgoings:

i) Municipal Property Taxes ... 36% on it

ii) Repairs and Maintenance ... 10%

iii) Vacancies ... Nil

iv) Bed debt ... Nil

v) Collection charges ... 2½%

vi) Insurance ... 1%

vii) Sundries ... 2%
(Services, maintenance etc.)

... 51½% (–) ₹ 2,19,390

Net Annual Rack Rental = ₹ 2,06,610

Multiplying by the Year's Purchase (Y.P.) single rate @ $9^1/_2$% p.a. yield as prospective return on invested capital for perpetuity

$= \frac{1}{i} = \frac{1}{0.095}$ (×) = 10.52631579

Capitalised Value (×)= ₹ 21,74,842

NOTE: The district is one which has declined slightly in recent years. There is not much prospect of the original rent of ₹ 30,750 per month being restored. The deductions allowed for the single letting are fully justified and if anything are on the low side, very little repairs have been done to the building and more than $7^1/_2$ per cent will have to be spent to maintain the rent. The deductions allowed in the second method are fair. Parts of the premises were vacant and there are bound to be many bad debts. The value being between one and two lakhs and the fact that the district is one which has declined in value, the $6^1/_2$ per cent security is on the high side and probably a fairer security would have been $6^3/_4$ per cent. Having regard to the two valuations made, a fair value for the premises would be (average of the two) ₹ 18,00,000.

EXAMPLE 73. What is the value of the Lessor's, Lessee's and Sub-Lessee's interest in the property described in Example 72?

SOLUTION

(A) Lessor's Interest ('A)

(1) Term (2013-2018)

1st 6 years Ground Rent (i) = ₹ 13,500 p.m. × 12 = ₹ 1,62,000 p.a.

Multiplying by Y.P. single rate @ $7^1/_2$% for 6 years

$$= \frac{1}{i + \frac{i}{(1+i)^n - 1}}$$

$$= \frac{1}{0.075 + \frac{0.075}{(1+0.075)^6 - 1}} = (\times)\ 4.6938464$$

= ₹ 7,60,403 ... (i)

Next 6 years Ground Rent (2019 - 2024)

= ₹ 16,500 p.m. × 12 = ₹ 1,98,000 p.a.

× by Y.P. single rate @ 7½% for 6 years deferred 6 yrs.

$$= \frac{1}{i + \frac{i}{(1+i)^n - 1}} \times \frac{1}{(1+i)^n}$$

$$= \frac{1}{0.075 + \frac{0.075}{(1+0.075)^6 - 1}} \times \frac{1}{(1.075)^6}$$

= 4.69384642 × 0.647961518 (x) 3.041431851

= ₹ 6,02,204 ... (ii)

Thus, Term's Value = (i) + (ii) = ₹ 6,02,204 + ₹ 7,60,403

= ₹ 13,62,607 **(1)**

(2) On Reversion

Reversion after 12 years to Rack Rent = ₹ 35,500 p.m. × 12

= ₹ 4,26,000 p.a.

Less:

Outgoings: 56% on it (–) ₹ 2,38,560 p.a.

Net Annual Rent = ₹ 1,87,440 p.a.

Net Annual Rent = ₹ 1,87,440 p.a.

× Y.P. @ 9½% for perpetuity deferred 12 years

$$= \frac{1}{i} \times \frac{1}{(1+i)^n}$$

$$= \frac{1}{0.095} \times \frac{1}{(1.095)^{12}}$$

= 10.526316 × 0.3365352 = 3.5424758

= ₹ 6,64,002 ... (2)

Lessor's Interest = Terms' Value (1) + Reversionary Value (2)

= ₹ 13,62,607 + ₹ 6,64,002 = ₹ 20,26,609 (A)

(B) Lessee's Interest ('B')

Term's Valuation

1st 6 years Rent Received (2013-2018)

= ₹ 25,500 p.m. × 12 = ₹ 3,06,000 p.a.

Deduct: (*i*) For Ground Rent: ₹ 1,62,000 p.a.

(*ii*) For outgoings @ 56% on ₹ 3,06,000 ₹ 1,71,360 p.a.

The burden is 50% to the lessee and 50% to the sub-lessee @ ₹ 85,680 each = (–) ₹ 2,47,680 p.a.

Net Annual Income ₹ 58,320 p.a.

Multiplying by Years' Purchase (Y.P.) for 6 yrs, dual rate @ 9½% and 3½% on A.S.F.D.

$$= \frac{1}{(i+S)}$$

$$= \frac{1}{0.095 + \frac{0.035}{(1+0.035)^6 - 1}} = (\times)\ 4.0376599$$

= ₹ 2,35,476 .. (i)

(ii) For next 6 yrs. (2019 - 2024)

For next 6 yrs. Rent Received = ₹ 3,06,000 p.a.

Deduct

(*i*) Ground Rent
₹ 16,500 p.m. × 12 ... ₹ 1,98,000 p.a.

(*ii*) Outgoings ... ₹ 85,680 p.a. = (–) ₹ 2,83,680 p.a.

= ₹ 22,320 p.a.

Multiplying by Y.P. dual rate for 6 yrs.
@ $10^1/_2$% and $3^1/_2$% deferred 6 years

$$= \frac{1}{i+S} \times \frac{1}{(1+i)^{n_1}}$$

$$= \frac{1}{i + \frac{r}{(1+r)^n - 1}} \times \frac{1}{(1+i)^{n_1}}$$

[Here, $n = n_1 = 6$ yrs]

$$= \frac{1}{0.105 + \frac{0.035}{(1.035)^6 - 1}} \times \frac{1}{(1.105)^6}$$

= 3.88096 × 0.5493211 = (×) 2.1318932

= ₹ 47,584 (ii)

Lessee's Interest = ₹ 2,35,476 + ₹ 47,584 = ₹ 2,83,060 (B)

(c) Sub-Lessee's Interest

The Sub-Lessee has a lease of the premises from the Lessee on payment of ₹ 25,500 per month. The Lessee pays 50% outgoings. The Sub-Lessee receives ₹ 35,500 per month when fully let. Therefore he has a profit of ₹ 10,000 per month. He has to bear the remaining 50% of all outgoings (since first 50% bears the lessee). Therefore, he is not receiving any gain at present. If he (Sub-Lessee) can reduce the vacancies or bad debts, he will make a slight profit. A fair award for compensation to the Sub-Lessee would be the balance of the award:

Award		= ₹25,00,000 (say)
Lessor's Interest	= ₹ 20,26,609	
Lessee's Interest	= ₹ 2,83,060	
	= ₹ 23,09,669	(–) = ₹ 23,09,669
Balance		= ₹ 1,90,331

The Sub-Lessee would therefore get ₹ 1,90,000 (say).

(C) Sub-lessee's Interest ('c')

Gross Annual Reck Rental: @ ₹ 35,500 p.m. × 12
= @ ₹ 4,26,000 p.a.

Less

(i) For ground rent paid to the lessee = @ ₹ 3,06,000 p.a.

(ii) 50% outgoings p.a. = @ ₹ 85,680 p.a. = @ ₹ 3,91,680 p.a.

Annual profit rental of the sub-lessee = @ ₹ 34,320 p.a.

Multiplying by the Y.P. dual rate for 12 years (2013-2024) @ 11½% and 3½% on invested capital ASFD) considering all risks factors, hazards etc.

$$\frac{1}{0.115+\dfrac{0.035}{(1.035)^{12}-1}} = (\times) \quad 5.4500998$$

= ₹ 1,87,047

Capitalized value of the sub-lessee's interest as on date = ₹1,87,047 (say)

A CASE STUDY

EXAMPLE 74. This Case Study relates to office apartments on ownership basis located in Dalamal Chambers on New Marine Lines Road near Bombay Hospital at Mumbai and Tulsiani Chambers in Nariman Point at Mumbai.

FACTS

A. OFFICE APARTMENT IN DALAMAL CHAMBERS

Land: Lease hold. *Lessor*: Bombay Municipal Corporation

Lease is expiring around the year 2000 A.D. There is no renewal clause. There is a covenant to surrender the entire building with fixtures to lessor without claiming any compensation. The Supreme Court in case of K.R. Dhairaman reported in AIR 1958 SC 789 has held that such a covenant is a valid covenant.

Ground Rent: ₹ 1 p.a. which is almost free

Type of Construction: RCC frame structure 30 years old with estimated economic balance life of 30 years.

Rate prevailing: Exact data not available as on date of valuation: ₹ 15,000 to ₹ 17,500 per sq. ft.

Date as on which valuation is made 31.3.1997.

B. OFFICE APARTMENT IN TULSIANI CHAMBERS

Land: Lease hold. Unexpired period of lease is more than 60 years. Provision in the lease for further renewal for a period of about 90 years.

Ground Rent: ₹ 1 per sq. ft. per month of built-up area of the apartment (approximate).

Type of Construction: Similar to Dalamal Chambers mentioned above.

Rate prevailing per sq. ft. on valuation date: ₹ 14,000 to ₹ 16,000 per sq.ft.

If comparison of the above two property is made with regard to physical, social economic and legal factors, then rate per sq.ft in Dalamal Chambers ought to be much less than the rate prevailing in Tulsiani Chambers as legal factors has very adverse effect on marketability, though social, economic and physical factors are the same.

Query:

— Can the buyers of property in 'Tulsiani Chambers' be considered imprudent in the transaction?

or

Have the buyers taken a risk?

Opinion:

Under the circumstances, the best thing is to enquire with the lessor about the policy. If the policy of the lessor is to renew the lease, then the buyers of apartments in Dalamal Chambers are not imprudent. If policy is to acquire, then the buyers are imprudent.

CHAPTER

18

Valuation of Easements

An easement is a right which the owner or occupier of certain land possesses, as such, for the beneficial enjoyment of that land, to do and continue to do something, or to prevent and continue to prevent something being done, in or upon, or in respect of, certain other land not his own.[1] An easement is in essence a restriction on the natural rights of an owner which he is otherwise entitled to enjoy as incidents of his ownership.[2] It is a right which is carved out in favour of a dominant heritage and is imposed on a servient heritage. A person cannot acquire an easement over his own land because all acts done by him over his own land are acts done in exercise of his rights as owner of the land and the prime requisite of *animus* for acquisition is thereby absent. Similarly, no co-owner can claim an easement against the other co-owners.[3]

The essential features of an easement are the following:

(*i*) It is a right enjoyed by any person or occupier over the land of another person.

(*ii*) It is incorporeal in nature but imposed on a corporeal property.

(*iii*) It generally confers no right to the dominant heritage to share in the profits from the servient heritage which distinguishes an easement from *profit a prendre*.

1 Section 4 of the Indian Easements Act 1882.

2 *Guman Singh* v *Umrao Singh* AIR 1924 Nag 69.

3 *Margabhai* v *Motibhai* AIR 1932 Bom 513.

(iv) The ownership of the easement is separate and distinct from the land to which it is attached and it cannot be transferred except along with the dominant heritage.

Positive and negative easement

A positive easement is a right vested in dominant owner to make use of the servient tenement which otherwise would amount to trespass or nuisance. The following are some of the examples of positive or assertive easements obtained by grant or acquisition:

(*a*) right of way;

(*b*) right to discharge rain water through the land of another;

(*c*) right to take water across a neighbour's land;

(*d*) right to tunnel under another's land;

(*e*) right to graze cattle over the land of another;[4]

(*f*) right to advertise on land belonging to another.[5]

Under the English law, easement is distinguished from *profit a prendre*. But, it would appear from the above list of positive easements that Indian law of easement includes *profit a prendre*.

A negative easement is a right which a dominant owner enjoys by enforcing a restrictive enjoyment of the servient tenement some of the examples of which are as follows:

(*a*) right to receive air through a defined channel,

(*b*) right to receive light for a building,

(*c*) right to receive support for a building from adjoining land or building,

(*d*) right to receive a flow of water from an artificial stream.

But the lists above are only illustrative and not exhaustive. Environmental factors have amplified the jurisdiction of easement in recent times. Pollution caused by noise, vibration, effluents, emission and the like have necessitated safeguards by way of rights in the nature of easement over others property.

4 *Meraji* v *Kanaji* AIR 1953 Sau 39.

5 *Sri Sri Iswar Gopal Jew* v *Globe Theatres* AIR 1947 Cal 200.

Easement and restrictive covenant

But an easement should not be confused with a restrictive covenant. A restrictive covenant is always negative and is an equitable doctrine and applies where there is no privity of contract or estate. It is negative in the sense that it merely binds the covenantor to refrain from doing a thing without requiring him to do any positive act.

Easement and public right/customary easement

An easement is distinct from a public right which is a right not restricted to the person owning the land but is exercisable by any one whether he owns land or not, merely by virtue of the general law. It is also different from a customary right in that a customary right is exercisable by all who are included within the custom independently of the ownership of a dominant heritage and independently of any grant. But as a right of privacy, an easement may arise out of local custom as discussed in the preceding chapter in which case it is known as customary easement. In case of customary easement a phenomenon is said to be happening from time immemorial when the date of its commencement is not within the memory of man or the date of its commencment is shrouded in the mists of antiquity.[6]

Easement and licence

An easement should also be distinguished from a licence. The chief distinction between an easement and a licence to use land in a particular manner is that whereas an easement cannot be extinguished merely at the will of the grantor except in certain specified modes, a licence is generally revocable at the will of the grantor. Moreover, an easement is a right *in rem* which runs along with the land whereas a right in licence is a right *in personam* which is merely personal and cannot generally be assigned.

The basis of a right of easement is generally a grant from the servient owner. It may be expressed or implied or presumed from continued user for a certain period or it may be inferred from a long and continued practice of user that gives rise to an equitable right. On the other hand, legal easement is an

6 *Rudrayya* v *Vekayya* AIR 1961 SC 1821.

easement capable of subsisting in law which has been validly created, namely by statute, deed or prescription or arises out of necessity as recognised by law. The law relating to easements and licences was codified in India under the title of the Easements Act 1882. This has been discussed in details in the preceding chapter.

Easement as discussed in case laws

Easement as a right different from lease has also been discussed in the preceding chapter. Every property has a natural right to receive light perpendicularly but a property has not the right to receive an unlimited amount of light horizontally across another owner's property.

The right to receive a reasonable amount of light across another owner's property is known as an Easement and an Easement as already stated may be defined as:

> "A privilege without profit which the owner of one property has a right to enjoy in respect of that property in or over the property of another person."

When a property has enjoyed a privilege from time immemorial it is said to have acquired a prescriptive right, and for the purpose of ascertaining whether or not an easement has been created the property must have had uninterrupted enjoyment of the privilege for a period of not less than 20 years.

The property which enjoys the right is known as the "Dominant Tenement" and the property over which the right is enjoyed is known as the "Servient Tenement".

To give an illustration, the gable end of a house may extend up to the boundary of another person's property which consists of vacant land. There may be numerous windows in this gable end and these windows may have enjoyed light and air for a period over 20 years. This property will have acquired an easement right over the adjoining land and the owner of this adjoining land will be restricted to a certain extent regarding the buildings he erects on the land. He cannot build right up to the boundary of his land thereby completely blocking out the light of his neighbour nor will he have to build a long distance away so that the light entering all the windows of the dominant tenement is not at all affected. The owner of the dominant tenement cannot claim the full benefit of existing amenities of light and air but only to such portions of them as is essential for the enjoyment of the premises.

In the course of his duties a valuer may have to value this "Right to Light" and he must therefore thoroughly understand how much light a person is entitled to, and a study of some of the classic High Court cases makes this point quite clear. The Indian courts have constantly referred to two cases of the English Court and therefore these two cases which are important are quoted somewhat at length.

An action was brought by the Home and Colonial Stores to restrain Mr. Colls a builder from erecting a building 42' high over an old building 19' high. The owners of the dominant tenement complained that their ancient lights would be affected. The Courts held that although their lights had been affected there was sufficient for ordinary user. The case went to the Court of Appeal who reversed the judgment and ordered the building to be pulled down. The case now known as *Colls* v *Home and Colonial Stores Ltd.,*[7] went to the House of Lords and the appeal was allowed, the judgment of the Lord Chancellor was as follows:

> "My Lords,—In this case, which was tried before Mr. Justice Joyce, the learned Judge gave judgment for the defendants upon the ground that the plaintiff had failed to prove any actionable wrong, although he found that the erection of the buildings of which the plaintiff complained had appreciably diminished the light which the plaintiff had previously enjoyed. The Court of Appeal, as I understood their judgment, though this was wrong, had ordered a mandatory injunction to pull down the premises so as to restore all the light that had been previously enjoyed. If this principle should be sanctioned by Your Lordships, it would be for the first time that, in this House at all events, such a principle had been determined. My Lords, I do not deny that authorities may be found for it, some of which have been cited at the bar; but I do not think that the exact question which is now in debate had ever been brought

7 [1904] AC 179; [1904-07] All ER (Rep) 5 (HL).

before this House until now. The question may be very simply stated thus. After an enjoyment of light for twenty years, or if the question arose before the Act for such a period as would justify the presumption of a lost grant, would the owner of the tenement in respect of which such enjoyment has been possessed be entitled to all the light without any diminution whatsoever at the end of such period? My Lords, if that were the law it would be very far-reaching in its consequences, and the application of it to its strict logical conclusion would render it almost impossible for towns to grow, and would formidably restrict the rights of people to utilise their own land. Strictly applied, it would undoubtedly prevent many buildings which have hitherto been admitted to be too far removed from others to be actionable: but if the broad proposition which underlies the judgment of the Court of Appeal be true, it is not a question of forty-five degrees, but any appreciable diminution of light which has been enjoyed (that is to say, has existed uninterruptedly for twenty years) constitutes a right of action, and gives a right to the proprietor of a tenement that has had this enjoyment to prevent his neighbour building on his own land. My Lords, I do not think that this is the law. The argument seems to me to rest upon a false analogy, as though the access to, and enjoyment of light constituted a sort of priority right in the light itself. Light, like air, is the common property of all or, to speak more accurately, it is the common right of all to enjoy it, but it is the exclusive property of none. If the same proposition against which I am protesting could be maintained in respect of air, the progressive building of any town would be impossible. The access of air is undoubtedly interfered with by buildings which are being built everyday round London. The difference between the town and country is very appreciable to the dweller in cities when he goes to the open country or to the top of a mountain or even a small hill in the country, but would the possessor for twenty years of a house on the edge of a town be at liberty to restrain his neighbour from building near him because he had enjoyed the free access of air without buildings near him for twenty years? No doubt this is an extreme case, but it is one of extreme cases which tries the principle. The truth is that though there were objections to ask a jury whether the enjoyment *talis qualis* was such that they might presume a lost grant when nobody supposed that such grant was ever really made, yet it gave the opportunity of considering what was the extent of the supposed grant, and if anything so extreme as I have just supposed were claimed, no jurymen in their senses would have affirmed such a grant. The statute upon which reliance is placed in this case illustrates the danger of attempting to put a principle of law into the iron framework of a statute. The statute literally construed by the use of the words "the light" would mean all the light which for twenty years has existed in the surroundings of the tenement which has enjoyed it; yet, singularly enough, there has been a complete uniformity of decision upon the construction of the statute that it has made no difference in the light conferred, but is only concerned with the mode of proof; but though I quite concur with this construction, which is supported by an overwhelming body of authority, yet I cannot think the language of the statute has led to some of the decisions which your Lordships are now called upon to review. Certainly, in the older decisions which have been brought to your Lordships' notice in Mr. Bray's very able argument, the proposition which, as I have said, underlies the judgment, now under appeal, finds no place. Lord Hardwicke, long ago in 1752 (*Fishmonger's Company* v *East India Co.* [1752]1 Dickens 163), dealing with this very question, the alleged obstruction to light, laid down what I believed to be law today. "It is not sufficient", he said, "to say that it will alter the plaintiffs' light, for then no vacant pieces of ground could be built on in the city, and here there will be 17 ft. distance and the law says that it must be so near as to be a nuisance". Lord Cranworth, in *Clark* v *Clark,*[8] adopted the same test, and his observation, though a subsequent decision of his seemed to throw doubt upon it, has received the assent of some of the most learned Judges who ever sat upon the English Bench. I think that the whole subject has been confused by certain decisions which were dependent upon the facts proved, and were

8 [1865]1 Ch App 16.

incautiously reported as laying down principles of law, when they were, in my view, only intended to be findings of fact in that particular case. At all events, I am prepared to hold that the test given by Lord Hardwicke is the true one, and I do not think better example could be found than the present case to show to what extravagant results the other theory leads. The owner of a tenement on one side of a street 40 ft. wide seeks to restrain his opposite neighbour from erecting a room which, when erected, will not then be of the same height as the house belonging to the complaining neighbour, and the only plausible ground on which the complaint rests is that on the ground floor he has a room not built in the ordinary way of rooms in an ordinary dwelling house, but built so that one long room goes through the whole width of the house to a back wall which has, however, no window at the back or sides, and which was, therefore, at the back of it, too dark for some purposes without the use of artificial light even before the building on the other side of the street was erected. I think that no tribunal ought to find as a fact that the building is a nuisance; and altogether apart from the inappropriateness of the remedy by injunction, I am of opinion that the plaintiff has no cause for action against the defendant. The test of the right is, I think, whether the obstruction complained of is a nuisance, and, as it appears to me, the value of the test makes the amount of right acquired depend upon the surroundings and circumstances of light coming from other sources, as well as the question of the proximity of the premises complained of. What may be called the uncertainty of the test may also be described as its elasticity. A dweller in towns cannot expect to have as pure air, as free from smoke, smell and noise as if he lived in the country and distant from other dwellings, and yet an access of smoke, smell and noise may give a cause of action, but in each of such cases, it becomes a question of degree and whether in each case it amounts to a nuisance which will give a right of action. My Lords, I have not thought it necessary to enter into a discussion of the authorities, because I think it has been most carefully and accurately done by Mr. Justice Wright in *Warren* v *Brown,* reported in 1900. Of course, my Lords, it must be taken that the foundation of this judgment rests upon the finding of fact by Mr. Justice Joyce, that the buildings of the defendant had not so materially interfered with the light previously enjoyed by the plaintiff as to amount to a nuisance. It follows that, in my judgment the case of *Warren* v *Brown* was rightfully decided by Mr. Justice Wright, and ought to have been affirmed by the Court of Appeal. It was, however, reversed in accordance with the same views which guided that Court in the case now under review. For the reasons I have given I have to move your Lordships that the judgment of the Court of Appeal be reversed, and the judgment of Mr. Justice Joyce restored, and that the respondents do pay to the appellant the costs both here and below". The other noble Law Lords read judgments to the same effect.

The effect of the judgment in *Colls'* case was slightly qualified by the case of *Jolly* v *Kine.*[9] It was narrated—

"The first question was whether the plaintiff had a cause of action. This had to be considered in the light of the recent decision in the House of Lords, where the learned Law Lords said the 'question is whether the obstruction amounts to a nuisance which causes a right of action', and 'not how much light is left, but whether the plaintiff had been deprived of such light as to constitute a current nuisance'. That in this case there has been an obstruction of light sufficient to be left was clear and beyond dispute and was not contested. But the question was whether there was left light for all practical purposes, for business or occupation. Upon this depended plaintiff's right to maintain the action. He saw no reason to alter his opinion as to the drawing room, and testing it by what Lord Lindley said in the House of Lords' decision, he could not admit the obstruction to be an actionable one. It was an obstruction as having regard to surrounding circumstances the plaintiff might have anticipated. As far as he could judge, the drawing room was a well-lighted room for its appointed purpose as a drawing room. Taking this room alone, plaintiff has no cause of action. At the second trial a new cause of action arose,

9 [1907] AC 1.

and that was whether there was an actionable right in regard to the light in the hall. The evidence was clear that this part of the house enjoyed a large proportion of light, a considerable proportion of which was obstructed. Taken alone, his Lordship could not regard it as a nuisance in the words of the House of Lords' judgment. The great cause of complaint had been the obstruction of light to the morning room. It was an exceptionally well-lighted room and was now such. For the complete enjoyment of such a room cheerfulness was essential. That there had been a large obstruction of light by the erection of defendant's house was abundantly clear and that it interfered with the cheerfulness of the room. His Lordship was convinced that the character of the room had been altered, and although it was a well-lighted room it had lost one of its chief charms and advantages. In determining whether this was a nuisance he must take into consideration all the surrounding circumstances, and he had come to the conclusion that the obstruction of light to the morning room was a nuisance within the meaning of the authorities on that subject. Plaintiff having a cause of action was entitled to relief, and the next question was what form the relief was to take. Defendant knew there were ancient lights to be respected.

"It appeared to him to be a case where damage would not be commensurate with the damage done, and it was his duty to grant a mandatory injunction. Taking the hall alone, he could not see a case for injunction, but for damages. But he should make the injunction extend to both, and should order the defendant to pull down so much of his house as caused a nuisance to plaintiff by obstructing the light to the morning room and the hall as the same existed previous to the erection of defendant's house. Defendant is to pay the cost of the trial. Plaintiff would be well advised to accept a substantial sum to put an end to the litigation."

The compromise having failed the defendant appealed to the Court of Appeal (15th December 1904, before Lord Justices Vaughan Williams, Romer and Cozens-Hardy). Vaughan Williams, LJ stated:

"That the law would not interfere in these cases unless there was an interference with the comfortable and profitable occupation of the property. The rule laid down by the House of Lords in *Colls* v *The Home and Colonial Stores* was logically justifiable. It was convenient that people should not be allowed to enforce a right to such an extent that the enforcement of their rights would interfere with the good and progress of the community. That was what he understood to be the meaning of the judgment of the House of Lords. The principle laid down by the various Law Lords as to the main method, that was to say, what was generally essential to constitute a cause of action, was a nuisance. The loss must be substantial, according to the character for which the premises were used, and unless it amounted to that there was no cause of action. A given percentage of loss of light was not sufficient. But it must be an interference with the comfortable and convenient occupation of the premises within the notions of citizens in this country. Now he had to apply that test to this case. He thought, whether one treated this matter as one of prescription or lost grant, that the defendant's house could have been carried out without obstructing the plaintiff's windows in the way it did. On these facts, had there been an obstruction which had rendered the house substantially less comfortable than heretofore? He thought there was evidence upon which to come to that conclusion. He did think that there would be an interference with the light coming to the plaintiff's rooms, according to the notions of mankind in this country. He did not think that under all the circumstances he could differ from the finding of fact of the learned Judge in the Court below. The conclusion he came to was that according to the ordinary notions of mankind the house had been substantially made less comfortable and less enjoyable to the plaintiff. This being the evidence of facts, he came to the evidence of the experts, and he agreed with that evidence that the house had been damaged in its value. He believed that both parties had acted according to what they believed to be their honest legal rights. He thought that the case was one for damages and not for a mandatory injunction, and to that extent only they differed from the judgment of Mr. Justice Kekewich. He thought there should be an inquiry in chambers as to the damages. His opinion was that it was damaged to the extent of about £25 a year."

The other Lords Justices concurred.

In India these two English cases have been closely followed and the Privy Council case of *Paul* v *Robson*[10] establishes the same points.

In this case which was an appeal in an action for damages for the infringement of the appellants' alleged rights to light and air, the Judicial Committee held that though there were concurrent findings of fact in the Courts below, yet the grounds of appeal did not relate to those findings but to the question whether the Courts below had taken the proper view of the legal rights of the appellants, and whether accordingly, the test which they had applied on the question of the infringement of the appellants' rights was the correct one. That was a pure question of law which admittedly turned upon the interpretation to be given to the decision of the House of Lords in *Colls* v *The Home and Colonial Stores,*[11] when considered in connection with the later decision of the House of Lords in *Jolly* v *Kine.*[12]

In the judgment of the House of Lords in *Jolly* v *Kine,*[13] there was an authoritative exposition of the decision in *Colls*' case,[14] and it was established that the law as stated by Lord Davey is the law as laid down by that decision, and that it accurately formulated the law on the subject. Court of first instance adopted Lord Davey's opinion, and applied it consistently to the findings of fact to which he came; and the Appellate Court had substantially taken the same test. Their Lordships, therefore, affirmed the judgments of the courts below, and dismissed the appeal.

The judgment of Their Lordships was delivered by Lord Moulton: "The action in which the present appeal is brought is an action in which the appellants sued the respondents for infringement of certain rights of light possessed by them in connection with premises known as 7, Esplanade East, Calcutta, of which they owned the freehold. The respondents had erected a building known as 8, Esplanade East,

10 AIR 1914 PC 45.
11 [1904] AC 179.
12 [1907] AC 1.
13 [1907] AC 1.
14 [1904] AC 179.

Calcutta, lying to the east of the appellants' premises and so situated that the western walls of the respondents' buildings were parallel to and at a distance of 17 feet from the eastern wall of the appellants' building. The ground on which the respondents' building was erected had for more than 20 years previously been occupied by much lower buildings, and it is conceded that the appellants had acquired rights of light thereby for the windows on the east side of the premises. The new buildings of the respondents greatly exceed in height the former buildings upon the site and decreased the amount of light coming to the eastern windows of the appellants, and it is in respect of this interference with the access of light to their windows that the appellants brought the action.

"In truth the grounds of appeal do not relate to these findings of fact, but to the question whether the Courts below have taken the proper view of the legal rights of the appellants, and whether accordingly the test which they applied as to whether those rights had been infringed was the correct one. This is a pure question of law, and it was admitted by counsel for the appellants that it practically turns upon the interpretation to be given to the well-known decision of the House of Lords in the case of *Colls* v *The Home and Colonial Stores,*[15] when considered in connection with the later decision of the House of Lords in *Jolly* v *Kine.*"[16]

Their Lordships do not consider that it is either necessary or profitable to go into the history of the divergent views in respect of the nature and extent of rights of light acquired by prescription that prevailed in the courts prior to the decision in *Colls*' case.[17] It suffices to say that one stream of authorities gave countenance to the view that by the enjoyment of light of a period of 20 years, there could be acquired an indefeasible right to the enjoyment of a like amount of light in the future. The conflicting stream of authorities countenanced the view that nothing constituted an infringement of rights of light

15 [1904] AC 179.
16 [1907] AC 1.
17 [1904] AC 179.

which did not amount to an actionable nuisance, so that the amplitude of previous enjoyment was no measure of the rights acquired thereby. This conflict of views was fully recognised by the noble Lords who took part in the decision of *Colls'* case[18] and there can be no doubt that it was their intention to decide between them and to lay down the law in such a manner as to prevent uncertainty in the future.

Mr. Justice Stephen takes, as expressing the law laid down by this decision, the following quotation from the opinion of Lord Davey in that case:

> "The owner .... of the dominant tenement is entitled to the uninterrupted access through his ancient windows of a quantity of light, the measure of which is what is required for the ordinary purposes of inhabitancy or business of the tenement according to the ordinary notions of mankind."

The single question in these cases is still what it was in the days of Lord Hardwicke and Lord Eldon whether the obstruction complained of is a nuisance? And the Court of Appeal, although they do not so directly base their judgment on the above passage in Lord Davey's opinion, appear to Their Lordships to have substantially taken the same test. But in Their Lordships' opinion it is not necessary to examine minutely the verbal differences between the expressions used in the Court of Appeal and by the Judge of first instance. They accept in full the findings on fact of the Judge of first instance, and they are of opinion that he has consistently applied to them the legal test above formulated. The only question therefore is whether it accurately formulates the law on the subject.

It is evident on reading the opinion of Lord Davey that he intended the passage to be a precise formulation of the rights of a dominant tenement in respect of ancient lights, and his opinion was formerly accepted by Lord Robertson who also took part in the decision. The opinion of the Lord Chancellor in that case is equally clear on the essential points that the easement acquired by ancient lights is not measured by the amount of light enjoyed during the period of prescription, and that there is no infringement unless that which is done amounts to a nuisance. It has been suggested that a different

18 [1904] AC 179.

view is to be found in the opinions of Lord Macnaghten and Lord Lindley, but although there are passages in these opinions which might if they stood alone indicate that those noble Lords considered that to some extent the amount of light enjoyed in the past might influence the rights acquired for the future, there is no reason to think there was any intention on the part of those noble Lords to differ from the conclusion of their colleagues. It must be taken therefore that the House of Lords adopted the formulation of the law given by Lord Davey as above-mentioned.

But if any doubt remained on the point it is in Their Lordships' opinion set at rest by a consideration of the subsequent decision of the House of Lords in the case of *Jolly* v *Kine.*[19] In that case Mr. Justice Kekewich had found as a fact that the obstruction amounted to a nuisance, but in the course of his judgment said that the room affected was 'still a well-lighted room'. He gave judgment for the plaintiff. On appeal to the Court of Appeal there was a division of opinion among the Judges. Romer, LJ., held that under the decision on *Colls'* case[20] the finding that it was still a well-lighted room was fatal to the plaintiff's claim. Vaughan Williams and Cozens Hardy, L.JJ., held to the contrary. On appeal to the House of Lords their Lordships were equally divided and accordingly the appeal was dismissed. But this division of opinion was not due to any doubt as to the law to be applied. The Lord Chancellor gives his opinion on the law as laid down in *Colls'* case[21] in the following words:

> "The right of owner or occupier of a dominant tenement to light is based upon the principle stated by Lord Hardwicke in 1752, in *Fishmongers' Company* v *East India Company,*[1] that he is not to be molested by what would be equivalent to a nuisance. He does not obtain by his easement a right to all the light he has enjoyed. He obtains a right to so much of it as will suffice for the ordinary purposes of inhabitancy or business according to the ordinary notions of mankind having regard to the locality and surroundings. That is the basis on which the decision of this House proceeded."

19 [1907] AC 1.
20 [1904] AC 179.
21 Ibid.
1 [1752]1 Dick 163.

Lord James of Hereford concurred in the judgment delivered by the Lord Chancellor.

These cases definitely establish the principle that no property can have a monopoly of light. The test is whether or not the obstruction is a nuisance and sufficient to warrant an action. After the obstruction is made, is the amount of light sufficient for the ordinary user for ordinary purposes of inhabitancy or business? There is no such thing as a right, either to an unlimited amount of light or to an uninterrupted flow of breeze. In the case of *Bagram* v *Khettranath Karformah*[2] Mr. Justice Norman said:

> "To give a right of action (in the case where there is no express contract on the subject) for the interference with the access of air to dwelling houses by building on adjoining land, the obstruction must be such as to cause what is technically called a nuisance to the house; in other words, to render the house unfit for the ordinary purposes of habitation or business."

The law on the subject is very clear. If an easement is interfered with the plaintiff can either go to the courts and obtain an injunction to restrain the defendants from doing any act which will be a nuisance or they can claim damages. The question of damages in these cases will be a question of fact and should present very little difficulty, but other cases may arise which are much more difficult to estimate and that is when an easement is totally extinguished.

When a property as acquired under the Land Acquisition Act or the Right to Fair Compensation and Transparency in Land Acquisition, Rehabilitation and Resettlement Act 2013, it is acquired free of all easements and encumbrances and the owner of the dominant tenement is entitled to receive out of the award for the servient tenement a sum as compensation for the loss he will sustain by the complete extinguishment of his easements. Existing textbooks do not assist the valuer to any appreciable extent regarding the method of apportionment of the amount awarded to the servient tenement. The Calcutta Improvement Tribunal have decided cases in the past and

2 3 BLR OC 45.

which have been followed rather blindly. If a case lays down a certain proposition regarding one property it can only be followed if the property in dispute is absolutely identical and again the proposition put forward was the opinion of a valuer to suit an individual case. Before actually giving a formula which will be more applicable to adopt generally a perusal of the case referred to will be of interest.

The case was No. 139 of 1918 and the award was made by Dr. S.C. Banerjee, President of the Calcutta Improvement Tribunal. The Land Acquisition Collector had awarded ₹ 80,939-3-9 for a piece of bare land at 248, Bowbazar Street, Calcutta. The dispute which was the subject of the award was the apportionment of this sum. The President in his award *inter alia* said:

"The basis of the claims of the claimants is this. They allege that the premises in Giri Babu Lane and Gangadhar Babu Lane which I have mentioned above and of which they are respectively the owners have some windows and other openings in respect of which they had easements of light and air over premises No. 248, Bowbazar Street the effect of the acquisition of which has been the extinction of those easements. They contend that the compensation which has been awarded for the premises No. 248 represents the market value of that property released from their rights of easements and they claim to be entitled to some share of the compensation.

It has been established by the evidence that each of the premises Nos. 17 and 18, Giri Babu Lane and Nos. 21 and 22, Gangadhar Babu Lane had some ancient windows through which it has enjoyed the access and use of light and air over premises No. 248 peacefully as an easement without interruption for a period of more than twenty years previous to the date of the declaration under which premises No. 248 has been acquired in this case and that consequently each of the said premises had, previous to that date, acquired an easement of light and air in respect of those windows over the premises No. 248, Bowbazar Street.

By virtue of the proceedings taken under the Land Acquisition Act premises No. 248 has vested in the Crown free from all encumbrances; the effect of the acquisition therefore has been to extinguish the easements which the premises Nos. 17, 18, Giri Babu Lane and 21, 22, Gangadhar Babu Lane had over No. 248 and the compensation which has been awarded in respect of the market value of No. 248 represents the market value of the land released from the burden of those easements. Claimants Nos. 3, 4 and 5 have adduced some evidence to show the extent to which the value of their respective premises have been injuriously affected by the extinction of the easements. In my opinion that evidence is wholly irrelevant to the question which requires adjudication in this case. Under the definitions contained in the Land Acquisition Act the easements which affected premises No. 248 were part of the "land" acquired and the claimants who were interested in that land; as such, they may be entitled to a share in the compensation awarded in respect of the market value of the "land" and also to compensation, under s. 23(1), (4) of the Act, for damages sustained by them by reason of the acquisition injuriously affecting their other property, namely, the premises to which these easements were appurtenant. In the present case the Collector has awarded no compensation in respect of the injurious affection of those premises. The only compensation which the Collector has awarded in this case is in respect of the market value of the land acquired, that is to say, the premises No. 248 released from the easements and the sole question for determination on this reference is the apportionment of that compensation between the several parties interested; the owners of the other premises cannot successfully contend that their claim in respect of the injurious affection of their own premises should be satisfied out of the market value paid for the land in No. 248 and it follows that no such claim can be entertained on this reference. The question to be determined on this reference is this, namely, how much of the compensation awarded in respect of the market value of the land in this case represents the value of each of the several easements as affecting that land, or, in other words, what is the difference between that market value and the value which No. 248 would have fetched if it had been sold subject to the easement appurtenant to each one of the dominant tenements; the difference in each case would represent the value of the easement which was enjoyed by the tenement concerned in so far as such easement affected the premises No. 248.

It was contended on behalf of the Bank that the value which would have been paid by any private purchaser for No. 248 if it had been sold subject to the easements would, for all practical purposes, have been the same as what has been awarded by the Collector as its market value, for the restrictions which would have been imposed on such a purchaser by reason of his purchase being subject to the easements of light and air would not have been more burdensome than the restrictions which are imposed on the owner of any land in Calcutta by the provisions of the municipal building regulations relating to the proportion of the total area permitted to be built upon and the leaving of spaces at the rear and sides when buildings on his land whether such land is subject to any easements of light and air or not. Premises Nos. 17 and 18, Giri Babu Lane are on the north and Nos. 21 and 22, Gangadhar Babu Lane are on the east of No. 248; it was argued that for a building to be erected on No. 248 the north would be the rear and the east would be one of the sides and that under the building regulations the owner of No. 248 notwithstanding that he may not be bound by the easements would not be able to build thereon without leaving on his north and east open spaces which would be sufficient to leave to the owners of the other premises the access and use of so much light and air as they were entitled to have by virtue of their easements. I am not satisfied that that would be so. The premises No. 248 is a large area and it is not likely to be used for the erection of only one house; if it is used for the building of more houses than one then the question as to which would be the rear and which would be the sides would depend on the layout and it is only at the rear that the building regulations are positive in requiring the leaving of the open space, and further more it is always permissible under those regulations to erect boundary walls to a height which would be sufficient to close some of the windows unless their owners can claim easements in respect of them. Learned vakil for the Bank argued in the next place that no owner of land possessing ordinary prudence would build a house without leaving open spaces at his rear and sides so as to make the house comfortable and fit to command an adequate rent so that, in fixing the prices which he would be prepared to pay for the land, it would make no difference, to him that the leaving of such open space would also be necessary owing to the existence of easements in the neighbouring premises which he has got to respect. But I think it would always make a difference to the purchaser of the land if in the matter of the leaving of open spaces he were left at the liberty to follow his own wishes and convenience instead of being subject to any compulsion one to the existence of paramount rights in others. In my opinion it would be reasonable to presume that there would be a difference between the value of a piece of land sold free from the easements and its value if it is sold subject to those easements; that in the opinion of the expert witness, Mr. A.L. Chandra, and I accept it to that extent, the question of the amount of the difference does not, however, admit of being dealt with any exact method and can be answered only approximately.

Two methods were suggested by Mr. A.L. Chandra for estimating the difference. Asked with reference to premises No. 18, Giri Babu Lane he said that on the one method he would estimate the difference at ₹ 50 per kottah. I do not think that this can be a sound method. No. 248 was a comparatively large area, the easements appurtenant to any one of the surrounding premises could not have affected the whole of No. 248 and I do not see how the diminution in the value of No. 248 due to the easements in respect of any one of the surrounding premises can be estimated at a rate distributed over the entire area of No. 248. The other method suggested by Mr. Chandra is this: He would ascertain what area of land should be left open in No. 248 so as to leave the easements in respect of any particular premises unfringed and he would estimate the diminution in the value of No. 248 due to the existence of those easements at one-fourth of the full market value of that land. This seems to me to be a sound method of dealing with the question and I accept it.

To ascertain the quantity of land which should be left open in premises No. 248 so as to leave uninfringed the easements of light and aid in respect of each of the four neighbouring premises it is necessary to bear in mind the extent of the legal right conferred by those easements. The law on the point is well settled; I need only quote the following passage from the judgment of the Lord Chancellor in *Jolly* v *Kine* where, referring to *Colls'* case he observed as follows:

"The right of the owner or occupier of a dominant tenement to light is based upon the principle stated by Lord Hardwicke in 1752 in *Fishmongers Company* v *East Indian Company*, that he is not to be molested by what would be equivalent to a nuisance. He does not obtain by his easement a right to all the light he has enjoyed. He obtains a right to so much of it as will suffice for the ordinary purposes of inhabitancy or business according to the ordinary notions of mankind having regard to the locality and surroundings. That is the basis on which the decision of this house proceeded"—[1907] AC 1.

That passage was quoted as applicable to the law of British India in *Paul* v *Robson*[3] by Lord Moulton delivering the judgment of the Judicial Committee. The law on the subject as laid down in *Colls'* case,[4] which was accepted as the law for British India in *Paul* v *Robson* is that the test of right acquired under an easement of light is whether the obstruction complained of is a nuisance (per Halsbury LC at p. 185, per Lord Davey at p. 204, per Lord Lindley at p. 212); and in ascertaining whether the property of the plaintiff is in fact injured or his comforts or convenience in fact materially interfered with, by an alleged nuisance, regard is had to the character of the neighbourhood and the pre-existing circumstances *H. Helm's Smelting Co.* v *Tipping*.[5] The right to air stands on the same footing as the right to light; where the claim is based on easement, to give a right of action for interference with the access of air the obstruction must be such as to amount to a nuisance and in the absence of express grant, mere uninterrupted enjoyment for upwards of twenty years cannot confer a right to enjoy without obstruction the south breeze, or the breeze coming from any other particular direction; the right to air is co-extensive with the right to light and where there is sufficient adit for light, it will be presumed that there is sufficient adit for air.[6]

Applying the principles to which I have just referred to the case before me I find that the locality in question is a crowded

3 ILR 42 Cal 53.
4 [1904] AC 179.
5 11 HLC 642.
6 *The Delhi and London Bank* v *Hem Lal Dutt* ILR 14 Cal 839.

locality with two-storeyed buildings separated by narrow lanes the average width of which may be taken as about 10 or 12 feet. Having regard to the nature of the locality I am of opinion that the owner of no house with ancient windows in this locality can successfully complain of nuisance if his neighbour builds at a distance of 12 feet from his ancient windows and I would take 12 feet as the width of land which the owner of No. 248 would have to leave open in front of the ancient windows if he had to abstain from infringing the easements enjoyed by those windows.

The south face of the building in No. 17 is shown on the plan, *Ex. A,* and the acquired premises No. 248 is shown on *Ex. 3* and the south face of No. 18 is shown on the plan *Ex. 1.* To protect from infringement the ancient windows in No. 17 the owner of No. 248 will have to leave open strip of land measuring, roughly speaking, 50' × 12'. The value of the easement enjoyed by No. 17 so far as they affect the market value of No. 248 is therefore equivalent to one-fourth of the value of that strip of land valued at the rate of ₹ 2,000 per kottah which is the average rate at which the whole of No. 248 has been valued in the award; the amount comes to ₹ 416.

As regards No. 18, the ancient windows, leaving out of consideration two small openings in the two rooms marked "poultry" and "kitchen" on *Ex. 1,* covered a frontage of 48'10" on No. 248. The value of the easements enjoyed by those windows so far as they affected the market value of No. 248 is therefore equivalent to one-fourth of the value of a strip of land in No. 248 measuring 48'10" by 12' at the rate of ₹ 2,000 per kottah, or roughly, ₹ 400.

Premises No. 248 was to the west of the premises Nos. 21 and 22 both of which are single-storeyed buildings. Premises No. 21 has a frontage of about 22 feet with two windows in that length of frontage on No. 248; No. 22 has a frontage of about 30 feet on No. 248 and there are four windows in that frontage. The amounts by which the value of No. 248 was depreciated by the easements which Nos. 21 and 22 had over it are respectively ₹ 183 and ₹ 428.

The claimant No. 6 did not appear at the hearing in support of his claim which must, therefore, stand dismissed.

The result is that out of the compensation money awarded in respect of the market value of premises No. 248.

₹ 416 is awarded to the claimant No. 3.

₹ 400 is awarded to the claimant No. 4.

₹ 183 and ₹ 428 are awarded to the claimant No. 5, and the balance left after payment of ₹ 199-9-9 to the Chairman of the Calcutta Corporation, is awarded to the claimant No. 2.

I direct that the parties do bear their own costs on this reference.

I assess the hearing fee at ₹ 50".

The first question a valuer must answer is what is the value of the servient tenement encumbered with the easements of the dominant tenement and what is the value of the servient tenement unencumbered with any easements of adjoining properties; the difference is the amount that can be claimed by the dominant tenement out of the award for the servient tenement.

It may happen in a particular case that the acquisition of easements of light and air causes such serious damage to the dominant tenement that the amount recoverable from the servient tenement in the manner indicated above is not adequate to compensate the damage caused. In such a case an additional amount will have to be paid as damages to the owner of the dominant tenement by the acquiring authority.

The principles of assessing compensation payable on acquisition of servient tenement were laid down by His Lordship Mr. Justice Roopendra Kumar Mitter in the case of *Bishnuprosad* v *Benoy Krishna*:[7]

> "If the servient tenement is acquired under the Land Acquisition Act, on acquisition it would vest in the Government freed from the easement of the owner of the dominant tenement (section 16). The owner of the dominant tenement would accordingly be entitled to compensation for the loss of his right ...... The owner of the acquired premises would not be entitled to the full market value of

7 AIR 1945 Cal 142; 49 CWN 203.

> his property. The easement depreciated its value to him. He can only have the value of beneficial enjoyment thus restricted by the easement affecting it. This accords with principle .... A sum of money should, therefore, be deducted from its 'full market value' and the balance should be awarded to its owner. But the sum, so deducted, would not necessarily be the value of the easement, the right of the owner of the dominant tenement, which had not been acquired, but which easement would be destroyed on the acquisition of the servient tenement. The amount representing the value of the right may be more or may be less than the sum that is to be deducted from the 'full market value' of the acquired premises in making payment to the owner thereof."

If, therefore, the value of the easement right is more than the sum so deducted, the excess must be paid by the Government to the owner of the dominant tenement. If the value is less, the gainer will be the acquiring authority.

The next question is what is the reasonable amount of light that a property can expect. This is answered very simply by the Municipal Building Code applicable for the purpose. If it states that the minimum amount of space which must be left between buildings is six feet, then for a single-storey building having easement rights their apportioned value out of the servient tenement may be estimated at one-quarter the value of a six feet strip of land running horizontally and having a length which covers the whole of the windows on the ground floor.

For a building two storey in height a slightly wider strip of land would be required to allow the ground floor windows a reasonable amount of light and for all general purposes it can be assumed that the rental value of the ground floor is twice that of the first floor, therefore, the strip of land now required to compensate for the easement rights is 9 feet. If the dominant tenement had window openings both on the ground floor and the first floor the apportioned value of these easements out of the award for the servient tenement would be one-quarter the value of a 9 feet strip of land which covered the window openings.

There must be a limit to the width of this land which must be left between buildings and that can reasonably be put at 12 feet; therefore for buildings having window openings on three or more floors the apportioned value of the easements out of the award for the servient tenement would be one quarter the value of a 12 feet strip of land covering in length the window openings.

To summarise generally the apportioned value of easements out of a hypothetical award for the servient tenement as narrated above may be as follows:

Single-storey building

Ground floor	:	$^1/_4$ value of 6 feet strip

Two-storey building

Ground floor	:	$^1/_4$ of $^2/_3$ value of 9 feet strip
First floor	:	$^1/_4$ of $^1/_3$ value of 9 feet strip

Three-storey building

Ground floor	:	$^1/_4$ of $^1/_2$ value of 12 feet strip
First floor	:	$^1/_4$ of $^1/_4$ value of 12 feet strip
Second floor	:	$^1/_4$ of $^1/_4$ value of 12 feet strip

Four-storey building

Ground floor	:	$^1/_4$ of $^2/_5$ value of 12 feet strip
First floor	:	$^1/_4$ of $^1/_5$ value of 12 feet strip
Second floor	:	$^1/_4$ of $^1/_5$ value of 12 feet strip
Third floor	:	$^1/_4$ of $^1/_5$ value of 12 feet strip

EXAMPLE 75. **The servient tenement which consists of open land has been acquired by the Land Acquisition Collector for ₹ 400 per sq. ft. The dominant tenement has easement rights consisting of window openings on the ground floor extending 40 ft. in length. To what apportioned amount out of the award for the servient tenement is the dominant tenement entitled? Assume that the minimum space which must be left open between buildings is 6 ft.**

SOLUTION

Area of strip of land to cover
the window openings = 6' ft. × 40' ft. = 240 sq. ft.

Apportioned value

240 sq. ft. @ 1/4th of (₹ 400 per sq. ft. × 240)

= 1/4 of ₹ 96,000 = ₹ 24,000

EXAMPLE 76. The servient tenement which consists of open land has been compulsorily acquired for ₹ 400 per sq. ft. The dominant tenement has easement rights consisting of window openings on the ground and three upper floors extending 60 ft. in length. What is the apportioned value of these easements out of the award for the servient tenement?

Assume that the width of the land must be left open between buildings is 12 ft.

SOLUTION

Area of strip of land to cover

the window openings = 12 ft. × 60 ft. = 720 sq. ft.

Apportioned value

720 sq. ft. @ 1/4th of (₹ 400 × 720)

= 1/4 of ₹ 2,88,000 = ₹ 72,000

EXAMPLE 77. Taking the property quoted in the above example, assume that there had not been any window openings on the ground floor. What would have been the apportioned value for the window openings on the upper floors?

SOLUTION

Area of strip of land to cover

the window openings = 12 ft. × 60 ft. = 720 sq. ft.

Apportioned value

720 sq. ft. @ 1/4th of (3/5th of ₹ 2,88,000)

= 1/4th of ₹ 1,72,800 = ₹ 43,200

EXAMPLE 78. The servient tenement has been compulsorily acquired. The premises consisted of a single-storey building extending to the dominant tenement. The land value was ₹ 400 per sq. ft. the dominant tenement has window openings on the 1st, 2nd and 3rd floors extending 60 ft. in length. The window openings on the 3rd floor had only been in existence for 18 years but the 1st and 2nd floor openings had been in existence over 50 years. What

apportioned amount out of the award should be allotted to the dominant tenement?

SOLUTION

Area of strip of land to cover
the window openings = 12 ft. × 60 ft. =720 sq. ft.

Apportioned value

720 sq. ft. @ $^1/_4$th of ($^1/_2$ of ₹ 2,88,000)

= $^1/_4$th of ₹ 1,44,000 = ₹ 36,000

Explanation. The servient tenement being a single-storey building, the effective value of easement for the dominant tenement would consist only in respect of three storeys and the ground floor is left out of consideration. Out of the three-storeys of the dominant tenement, there is no prescriptive right for the third floor opening of the window. Thus the easement right of the first and second floor of a presumed three storeyed buildings has only to be valued which comes to ($^1/_4$th + $^1/_4$th) i.e., $^1/_2$ of the strip of land.

EXAMPLE 79. The servient tenement has been compulsorily acquired. The premises consisted of a three-storeyed building situated 8 ft. away from the dominant tenement. The dominant tenement had window openings extending 30 ft. on the ground and three upper floors. The closing of these window openings will reduce the letting value of the premises by ₹ 500 per month.

What amount should be awarded to the dominant tenement out of the award for the servient tenement and what amount should be claimed for damages?

The land value is taken at ₹ 400 per sq. ft.

SOLUTION

Area of strip of land to cover the window openings
on the ground, 1st and 2nd floors = 8 ft. × 30 ft. = 240 sq. ft.

Apportioned value

240 sq. ft. @ $^1/_4$th of ($^4/_5$th of ₹ 400 × 240)

= $^1/_4$ of $^4/_5$ of ₹ 96,000

= $^1/_4$ of ₹ 76,800 = ₹ 19,200

Explanation. Since this is valuation in respect of easement rights for the ground, 1st and 2nd floor out of a four-storeyed building comprised in the dominant tenement, the apportioned value of easement will work out to $^1/_4$th of $(^2/_5+^1/_5+^1/_5)$ i.e., $^1/_4$ of $^4/_5$.

Apportioned value for the 3rd floor window opening

Area of strip of land to cover the window openings on 3rd floor	= 12 ft. × 30 ft.	= 360 sq. ft.
360 sq. ft. @ $^1/_4$ of $^1/_5$ of ₹ 96,000		= ₹ 4,800

Explanation. The width in case of the 3rd floor is taken as 12 ft. instead of 8 ft. as the dominant tenement stands above the servient tenement in respect of the 3rd floor.

Apportioned value out of the award for servient tenement	= ₹ 19,200	
	(+) ₹ 4,800	
		= ₹ 24,000
Loss in rent @ ₹ 500 p.m.	= ₹ 6,000	
Allow 30% outgoings	(–) ₹ 1,800	
Net rent	= ₹ 4,200	
Security 6.5%	= 15.385	
		= ₹ 64,617
Deduct amount awarded		= (–) ₹ 24,000
Damages		= ₹ 40,617

CHAPTER 19

Valuation of Land and Building Subject to Restrictions

The value of an encumbered property will certainly have a lesser value than unencumbered property. As decided in the case of *Commissioner of Wealth Tax* v *P.N. Sikand*,[1] and *Commissioner of Wealth Tax* v *Raghabar Narain Singh*,[2] the market value of encumbered property would be depressed to the extent of the burden cast by the restrictions on the property. But even if there is a permanent restriction on transfer, still the property can be valued as held in *Ahmed G.H. Ariff* v *Commissioner of Wealth Tax*.[3] The restriction would only generally depress the value of the property as pointed out in *Commissioner of Wealth Tax* v *Rajkumari Bhubaneswari*.[4]

Restrictions on the user of land may obtain various forms. For example, some of the plots which are near the airport are subject to restrictions with regard to the height of the buildings to be constructed. Such restrictions adversely affect the market value. Restrictions may also be imposed by covenants of lease. In *Shafkat Hussain* v *Collector, Amaraoti*,[5] it was, however, held that inalienability is not a factor that emaciates

1 (1977)107 ITR 922 (SC).
2 (1984)146 ITR 228 (SC).
3 (1970)76 ITR 471 (SC).
4 (1995)215 ITR 198 (Raj).
5 AIR 1933 Nag 208; *Province of Bengal* v *Board of Trustees* AIR 1946 Cal 416.

compensation payable on acquisition of land. The acquired land in these cases were granted on inalienable tenure. On the question whether the inalienability in the grant would have any relevance at the time of fixing compensation, the High Court opined that in determining the compensation payable, the element of non-transferability of land cannot enter into consideration. But it must be understood that payment of compensation is a limited question that arises only in the context of compulsory acquisition of land. As a general proposition, it stands to reason to say that the value of the property with a statutory restriction would be less than the value of the property without any such restriction. In later cases of compulsory acquisition the views were accordingly relaxed and held that a restriction against alienability and partibility would be relevant while determining compensation.[6] The Supreme Court held in *Special L.A. & Rehabilitation Officer, Sagar* v *M.S. Seshagiri Rao*[7] that the compensation payable to the owner is only the market value of the interest acquired as clogged by the right of the State. This is discussed below in details.

The following is the summary of the principles derived from English cases of valuation of land subject to restrictions as to user, as given by Cripps in his *Compulsory Acquisition of Land* (11th Edition): "All restrictions attached to the land in the hands of the owner (including the likelihood of its continuance) must be taken into consideration. This proposition is an example of the rule that it is the value to the owners and not the value as taken to the promoters which must be considered. A restrictive covenant limiting the use of the land or a statutory restriction on development of the land falls within the above principles. The possibility of the removal of the restrictions must, however, be taken into account."

Lands subject to resumptions by Government without compensation

In the case of the *Special L.A. & Rehabilitation Officer, Sagar* v *M.S. Seshagiri Rao,*[8] 11 acres and 38 gunthas of land was

6 *State of Maharashtra* v *G.N. Ghorpade* 1985 Mah LR 500; 1985 Mah LJ 170.
7 AIR 1968 SC 1045.
8 AIR 1968 SC 1045.

granted by the Government of Mysore to the respondents in form Appendix-E to the Mysore Land Revenue Rules with the condition that in the event the Government requiring the land for any reason whatsoever, the grantee shall surrender the land to the Government without claiming any compensation. This land was notified under s. 4 of the L.A. Act (now s. 11 of the Fair Compensation and Transparency in Land Acquisition, Rehabilitation and Resettlement Act 2013) and subsequently by notification under s. 17(4) of the L.A. Act, Government dispensed with the inquiry under s. 5A of the Act and obtained possession of the land. The L.A. Officer did not award any compensation for the land and awarded ₹ 1,495 for improvement claimed to have been made to the land by the grantees. In a reference under s. 18 of the Act, the District Judge agreed with the L.A. Officer. In appeal, the High Court of Mysore set aside the award and remanded the case to the District Court with a direction to determine the compensation payable to the grantees according to law. The High Court observed that since the Government had failed to exercise their right which it had under the terms of the grant and had adopted the procedure prescribed by the L.A. Act, compensation for acquisition under the L.A. Act and the process by which the grantees were to be deprived of the land must be followed. Against that order of the High Court, the Government appealed. The Supreme Court maintained the order passed by the High Court subject to the modification that the market value of the interest of the grantees in the land at the date of the notification under section 4, shall be determined and paid to the grantees in addition to the compensation paid for the improvement in the land. In the course of their judgment Their Lordships observed as follows: "It is true that after obtaining possession of the land in pursuance of statutory authority under section 17, the Government of Mysore could not seek to exercise the option conferred by the terms of the grant. But on that account in assessing compensation payable to the grantees existence of the condition which severely restricted their right could not be ignored. The grantees were entitled to compensation for the land of which the ownership was vested in them. The measure of that compensation is the market value of the land at the date of the notification and the measure of that market value is what a willing purchaser may at the date of the notification under section 4 pay for the right to the land subject to the option vested in the Government."

* * * * * * * * *

"The High Court had observed that the Government availing itself of the machinery under the L.A. Act for compulsory acquisition and treating the subject-matter of the acquisition as not belonging to itself but to others is under an obligation to pay compensation as provided in the Act, and that the Government was incompetent in the proceeding under the L.A. Act, to put forward its own title to the property sought to be acquired so as to defeat the rights of the persons entitled to the compensation." The Supreme Court observed that the above propositions, so broadly stated, are not accurate. The Act contemplates acquisition of land for a public purpose. By acquisition of land is intended the purchase of such interest outstanding in others as clog the right of the Government to use the land for the public purpose. When the land is owned by a single person the entire market value payable for the deprivation of the ownership is payable to the person; if the interest is divided, for instance, where it belongs to several persons or where there is a mortgage or lease outstanding on the land or the land belongs to one and house thereon to another or limited interests in the land are vested in different persons, apportionment of the compensation is contemplated. The Act is, it is true, silent as to the acquisition of the partial interest in the land. But it cannot be inferred therefrom that interest in land restricted because of the existence of the rights of the State in the land cannot be acquired. When land is notified for acquisition for a public purpose and the State has no interest therein the market value of the land must be determined and apportioned amongst the persons entitled to the land. Where the interest of the owner is clogged by the right of the State the compensation payable is only the market value of that interest subject to the clog.

The Supreme Court disagreed with the High Court of Madras that when land is notified for acquisition and in the land the State has an interest that makes the land subject to restrictive covenant in favour of the State, the State is estopped from setting up its interest or right in the proceedings for acquisition. The State in a proceeding for acquisition does not acquire its own interest in the land, and the Collector offers and the Civil Court assessed compensation for acquisition of the interest of the private persons which gets extinguished by compulsory acquisition and pays compensation equivalent to the market value of that interest. There is nothing in the Act which prevents the State from claiming in the proceeding for acquisition of land notified for acquisition that the interest proposed to be acquired is a restricted interest.

Their Lordships quoted in this connexion, with approval the observations made by Batchelor, J. in *Government of Bombay* v *Usufali Salebhai.*[9]

Land in cantonment area

In this connexion three Privy Council cases may be referred to:

(1) In the case of the *Secretary, Cantonment Committee, Barrackpur* v *Satish Chandra Sen,*[10] the Government notified for acquisition a plot comprising $5^1/_4$ bighas of land with a house upon it situated in Barrackpur Cantonment. The Collector valued the building at ₹ 11,467 and the land at ₹ 9,510/10 annas. But refused to award the value of land to the respondent on the ground that the land being Cantonment land was the property of the Government. The Special L.A. Judge held that the respondent was entitled to the value of the land also. The Secretary of State appealed to the High Court, but the appeal was dismissed. The matter was taken before the Privy Council by the Government. The Privy Council held that in the cantonments a peculiar tenure known as military or cantonment tenure has grown up, the characteristics of which are that private persons settling on land within Cantonment have ownership in the buildings they erect but property in the soil remains as in the Government.

9 ILR 34 Bom 618 at p. 636.
10 35 CWN 173.

Their Lordships elaborated the proposition that when Government acquired immovable property under the L.A. Act, it is for the person claiming compensation to establish his title to it affirmatively. On a review of the evidence laid in the case Their Lordships held that long possession of the land with houses standing upon it was not in the circumstances any proof of title but was more consistent with a cantonment tenure. In the result the Privy Council allowed the appeal of the Secretary of State holding that the respondent had not established his title to the land as apart from the buildings.

(2) The case of *Harichand* v *Secretary of State,*[11] was the case of acquisition of land together with building in the Cantonment of Peshwar. In that case the Government prior to the proceedings for acquisition, had given notice that the land has been resumed by them and they were desirous of acquiring the buildings thereon under the provisions of the L.A. Act. Thereafter proceeding for acquisition were initiated with respect to the buildings and not in respect of the land underneath. The Privy Council held that the Government being the owner of the land, there can be under the L.A. Act proceedings for the acquisition of only buildings standing thereon and accordingly notification of an intention to acquire only the buildings of the land is valid and constitutes a proper foundation of the proceedings.

(3) The case of *Secretary of State* v *Sri Narayan Khanna,*[12] was also a case of acquisition of Cantonment land. In this case also the Government gave notice of resumption to the owner, resumed the land and instructed the Government of the U.P. to acquire the buildings under the L.A. Act. The District Judge estimated that the value of the buildings if newly constructed would be ₹ 30,858 and after deducting the amount of depreciation the District Judge held that the respondent was entitled to ₹ 22,816 together with usual 15% allowance. It may be noted that land with the building had been leased out by the owner to the Government for 10 years at a rent of ₹ 325 per month. On appeal by the respondent the Allahabad High

11 44 CWN 5.
12 46 CWN 921.

Court increased the value of the building to ₹ 31,426. The High Court arrived at the figure by capitalizing the annual rental of the building at $8^1/_2$ years' purchase, the court deciding that 12% per annum simple interest may be taken to be a reasonable interest to accept from house property. The contention of the Secretary of State that the basis of valuation adopted by the High Court was incorrect, was upheld by the Privy Council. It was held that the two principles of assessing compensation for the buildings apart from the site, is to ascertain the cost of reproducing the building at the time of the compulsory acquisition, allowing for depreciation in consideration of age and condition of the buildings and for the cost of necessary repairs. Their Lordships held that District Judge applied the correct principle in valuing the buildings and restored the decree of the District Judge.

Land dedicated for user as public road

In the case of *Manmotho Nath Mitter* v *Secretary of State,*[13] certain public roadways within the zamindary of the appellant were acquired for the construction of the Kidderpore Docks. It was found that the sub-soil remained the property of the appellant, but the land was dedicated for the user as a public road by the ancestors of the appellant. The High Court held that the owner was entitled to no compensation because the land as road-land had no separate market value or at any rate it had not been proved to have any separate market value. On appeal, the Privy Council affirmed the decision of the High Court. Lord Hobhouse, in delivering the judgment of the Board observed that the land as a roadway had no market value which was in a way conceded by the counsel of the Appellant. His contention was that when compensation was actually awarded the road had been broken up and the land freed from the burden of the road and was capable of being used for any purpose. This argument was repelled by Lord Hobhouse on the ground that the increase in value of the acquired land which accrued from the use to which it would be put after acquisition must be disregarded.

13 ILR 25 Cal 194; AIR 1924 Cal 574.

Reference may here be made to the case of *Gajanan* v *Asstt. Collector of Salsette.*[14] In this case, over a part of the acquiring land there was a public right of way. The Bombay High Court expressed the opinion "although there may have been a public right of way over the 226 yards it does not follow that the claimant was entitled to no compensation".

Land used for public benefit

In *Chairman of Howrah Municipality* v *Khetra Krishna Mitra,*[15] a burning ghat with certain structures thereon was acquired. The Collector awarded ₹ 1,013/14 on account of the market value of the site of the burning ghat and also awarded certain other sums for the structures and damages. Dispute arose in that case between the parties as to the apportionment of the compensation money. Mukherjee, J, in course of the judgment, discussed all the important English cases on the point of valuation of land subject to restricted user, including the Privy Council case of *Manmatho Nath Mitter*. It was not suggested in that case that the valuation of burning ghat as made by the Collector was erroneous or that the property had no market value.

In valuing land the restrictions of the uses to which it could be put must be kept in as also the chances of those restrictions being discharged. Where a portion of a churchyard was acquired for forming a new street, the plaintiff rector was not entitled to any compensation as the lands were to him without any value. The basis on which compensation for lands are taken to be assessed is the value of the lands to the owner as it existed at the date of the notice to treat and not their value when taken to the promoters.[16]

The English authorities on this point including the case of *Manmatho Nath Mitter* were considered by the Calcutta High Court in the case of *Province of Bengal* v *Board of Trustees for the Improvement of Calcutta.*[17] That was a case for determination of the compensation for requisition of land

14 AIR 1924 Bom 54.
15 ILR 33 Cal 1290.
16 *Corrie* v *McDermott* [1914] AC 1056.
17 50 CWN 825.

belonging to the Calcutta Improvement Trust in Lake Area under the Defence of India Act 1939. The compensation was to be assessed on the principles laid down in s. 23(1) of the Land Acquisition Act. A question arose in that case regarding assessment of the compensation payable for the requisition of the Lake Park which the Calcutta Improvement Trust owned and held for the benefit of the public and which in law cannot put to any other use. Mitter, J. who delivered the judgment in the High Court laid down that compensation must be tested no doubt by the loss to the owner, but, in estimating his loss, it is legitimate to disregard the restrictions to ownership which was existing at the time of acquisition either by voluntary sacrifice of pecuniary benefit by the owner or by competent authority or by rules of law. The case of the Park was found to be very similar to the case of Lord Shand's award in the *Princess Garden* case (Edinburgh). In that case, a strip of land in West Princess Garden in Edinburgh was acquired by a Railway Company. By an Act of Parliament, the Edinburgh Corporation were prohibited from ever building on the land or alienating it; but were bound to keep it for all times as a public garden. Lord Shand who delivered the award, however, accepted the contention of the Corporation that as the Corporation had used the grounds for a purpose more valuable to them and to the community they represent than building purposes, at least its fair and full value or the highest value of the land as building ground should be allowed. Following that case, Mitter, J., held that the Calcutta Improvement Trust is entitled to compensation for the Park on the same basis as building sites.

Land subject to covenant not being an easement

In *Government of Bombay* v *Century Spinning Manufacturing Co. Ltd.*,[18] the acquired land was conveyed to the claimant by two conveyances by the Bombay Improvement Trust. The land was conveyed as freehold, but subject under both the conveyances to certain restricted covenants. In the first conveyance, the user was confined to residential purpose, office and such classes of shops as were not prohibited by the grantor

18 ILR (1942) Bom 403; AIR 1942 Bom 105.

and under the second conveyance, the user was restricted to shops, chawals, offices, residences, godowns, and a wireless broadcasting station. Under neither conveyance, grant was there and any power to use as factory. The building was restricted to ground floor and three upper floors and certain spaces were to be left unbuilt upon. The Collector awarded certain compensation as the market price of the land and a sum of ₹ 100 was awarded to the Bombay Municipality who succeeded the Bombay Improvement Trust. The owner made a reference under s. 18. Wadia, J. valued the acquired land on the footing that the claimants possessed an unrestricted freehold and deducted from that value a sum of ₹ 100 awarded to the Municipality who had made no reference. His valuation was at the rate of ₹ 14/8 per sq. yard. On appeal Their Lordships, Beaumont, CJ. and Sen, J. held that the learned Judge had misconceived the true position. In the course of his judgment, Beaumont, CJ. observed: "Now in this particular case we are dealing with restrictive covenants which are not an easement but have many features analogous to an easement. The Land Acquisition Officer assumed for the purpose of this case that the Municipality as the person entitled to the benefit of the covenants was a party interested within the meaning of the Act. But, he considered that their interest was not seriously affected and as I have stated, he awarded them only a nominal sum of ₹ 100. From that part of the award, there is no appeal and we are not, therefore, concerned, to consider whether the Municipality were entitled to make any claim or if they were, whether the amount awarded to them is inadequate. But, it is perfectly plain to my mind that the restrictions of the nature imposed upon the land to be acquired by the conveyances of 1924 and 1928 must prejudicially affect the value of the land. It is quite impossible to say that the existence of those covenants, although they may be of no benefit to the Municipality, depreciates the land by only a nominal sum. The argument of the claimant would really produce this amazing result that if a man had acquired a land at a low price because it was subject to a covenant not to build upon it, nevertheless, if the land was acquired under the Land Acquisition Act, he would be entitled to claim the market value although that market value be based on its value as a building site. Such a proposition is preposterous. There is nothing in the Land Acquisition Act to suggest that any person interested is to be paid for anything excepting the interest which he possesses and as the claimants in this case only possessed an interest in the land subject to restrictive covenants, they can only be paid compensation for such land. The learned Judge deducted from the sum awarded to the claimants a sum of ₹ 100 paid to the Municipality and that seems to me to show a misconception of the true position". The acquired land was then valued by Their Lordships on the basis of transactions of lands subject to restrictions more or less onerous. Market value was finally assessed at the rate of ₹ 10/8 per sq. yard. Thus restrictive covenants are quite relevant considerations in determining compensation and shall accordingly be borne in mind in assessing the market value of land.

A similar issue came up for consideration before the Supreme Court in *P.N. Sikand* v *CWT*.[19] In this case, the assessee had acquired a plot of land in Delhi from a person, who under the original agreement of lease, was prohibited from parting with her interest in the land except with the sanction of the Chief Commissioner and even if transfer of her interest was effected with such sanction, the lessor (the President of India) was entitled to recover, at the time of the transfer, 50 per cent of the unearned increase in the value of the land being the difference between the consideration already paid and the current market value. The agreement also conferred on the lessor a pre-emptive right to purchase the property after deducting 50 per cent of the unearned increase, and further provided for forfeiture and re-entry in the case of breach of any of these conditions. On the question whether 50 per cent of the unearned increase in the value of the land which was payable to the lessor, was deductible in ascertaining the value of the property for the purpose of wealth-tax, the Supreme Court held that it had to be deducted in ascertaining the value of the property, whether it is taken as a limitation or restriction attached to the property in question, affecting its value to that extent or as a debt owed by the assessee on the valuation date.

19 (1974)96 ITR 424.

If the restriction on transfer is to operate in respect of property which is to be acquired then the compensation payable could be taken as the market value.[20]

Charge on property as encumbrance

It was held in *Commissioner* v *Smt. Sarala Devi*,[1] that the outstanding dues of the deceased, to the extent they have the effect of being a charge on the property in the hands of the heir would depress the fair market value of the property in the hands of the heir. Appropriate deduction has to be given for such liabilities in determining the value in the hands of the heir, because the heir is being considered as the hypothetical seller *vis-a-vis* the property of which value is to be determined.

Mortgage as an encumbrance

This issue came up for consideration in *Commissioner of Income Tax* v *Daksha Ramanlal.*[2] In that case a property subject to mortgage was received under a gift. Subsequently the mortgage was redeemed by the donee paying ₹ 25,000. The property was then sold. The court after referring to the cases of *Ambat Echukutty Memon* v *Commissioner of Income Tax*,[3] and *Smt. S. Valliammai* v *Commissioner of Income Tax*[4] held that though the Kerala and Madras High Court have taken the view that when a capital asset is received by an assessee in one of the modes specified in s. 49 of the Income Tax Act what has to be taken into consideration is the cost of acquisition to the previous owner and any sum paid by the assessee for removing any encumbrance thereon cannot be deducted while computing the capital gains on sale of such property, such a view cannot really prevail. In the opinion of the Gujarat High Court, when a person who has mortgaged the property transfers it to another person, what he transfers is only those rights which he possesses. The transferee would get the property subject to

20 *Gouri Prasad Goenka and Family* v *CWT* (1993)203 ITR 700 (Cal); *CWT* v *K.S.R. Mudaliar* (1984)150 ITR 619 (Mad).

1 (1995)214 ITR 695 (Ker).

2 (1992)197 ITR 123 (Guj).

3 (1978)111 ITR 880 (Ker).

4 (1981)127 ITR 713 (Mad).

the rights created by the previous owner in favour of others. When the assessee discharged the mortgage by paying ₹ 25,000 to the mortgagee, what he did was to purchase that right or interest which the mortgagor did not then possess and which the mortgagee had in the property. When the assessee sold the property, he did not merely sell the right, title or interest which he had received from the donor but also the right, title or interest which he had purchased from the mortgagee. Accordingly, the Gujarat High Court held, payment of ₹ 25,000 to the mortgagee for removing that encumbrance was certainly the cost of acquisition of the interest of the mortgagee and, therefore, that was required to be taken into account for the purpose of computing the total cost of acquisition of the property which the assessee sold and thereby made capital gains.

Onerous gift as encumbrance

In *Smt. P. Subbammal* v *Commissioner of Gift Tax*[5] it was held that in so far as movable property is concerned that an agreement that the donee will pay the gift tax do not create any charge on the gifted property. Since this is only an arrangement whereby the donee discharges the legal liability of the donor, the gift tax payable by the donee will not depress the value of the gifted property. The liability of the gift tax is a post-gift liability and arises only subsequent to the gift and not earlier.

Where the liability is such as to make the gift an 'onerous gift' the market value of the gifted property would, however, get depressed. This was the view upheld in *Commissioner of Gift Tax* v *Biswanath Pal,*[6] and *CGT* v *K.A. Shaik Dawood.*[7] An onerous gift is one where the gift would be defeated if the liability of the donor is not discharged by the donee. The market price of the property for gift tax purposes would stand depressed as a willing buyer would have to discharge the liabilities to obtain possession of the property from the seller in a hypothetical market.

5 (1995)214 ITR 331 (Ker).
6 (1970)76 ITR 39 (Cal).
7 (1983)139 ITR 261 (Mad).

Property encumbered by the urban land ceiling law

Surplus land of the landowner was acquired under the Urban Land (Ceiling and Regulation) Act 1976 and the retainable land was acquired under the Land Acquisition Act. It was held that compensation for the land so acquired could not be assessed on the basis of the market value payable under the U.L.C. Act, but on the basis of the L.A. Act.[8]

In *Gordhandas Purshottamdas Patel* v *Appropriate Authority*[9] it was found that the purchase of property under Chapter XXC of the Income Tax Act without considering the effect of Urban Land Ceiling Act vitiated the exercise of power for pre-emptive purchase under the said provision. In *Commissioner of Wealth Tax* v *Ranganatha Mudaliar*[10] it was observed that the land in such cases has to be evaluated in two parts. Excess land, whether notified for takeover or not, has to take into consideration, restrictions and prohibitions on transfer and hence the value of that part of the land can only be the compensation receivable for excess land under the relevant land ceiling law.

Property subject to restrictions under rent control law

Apart from restrictions imposed by covenants of lease, urban lands and buildings within municipal areas of the country are subjected to statutory restrictions under the relevant rent control laws of the respective State as soon as a tenancy is created. Premises let out by the landlord to the tenant attract the provisions of such rent control laws which are intended to protect the interests of the tenants by way of fixation of standard rent or fair rent as well as safeguards against eviction. Such provisions operate in addition to or supplemental to the terms of lease and general provisions under the Transfer of Property Act; and accordingly, valuation of rented property in municipal areas is substantially conditioned by the restrictive laws of rent control specific to the respective State. The topic has been elaborately covered in other chapters as it constitutes

8 *Sadasiv Durgaji Ambhore* v *State of Maharashtra* 1992 Mah LJ 1300.
9 (1996)217 ITR 62 (Guj).
10 (1984)150 ITR 619 (Mad).

a special field of study and references may be made to those chapters for details as regards impact on the market value of properties so encumbered with tenancies.

Valuation constraints due to rent restriction

The provisions of the rent control laws devising fixation of fair rent differ from State to State. A list of the statutes operating in different States in the realm of rent restriction has been given in an earlier chapter. It would appear from the provisions for fixation of fair rent therein that the value of the leasehold property has been estimated primarily on a cost approach. Thus the West Bengal Premises Tenancy Act 1997 in its s. 17 lays down that the fare rent for a year in respect of any premises constructed and let out after the year 1984, shall be fixed on the basis of annual payment of an amount equal to six and three-fourth per cent per annum of the aggregate amount of actual cost of construction and the market price of the land on the date of commencement of construction. Cost of construction shall includes the cost of water supply and sanitary and electric installation. Delhi Rent Control Act 1958 similarly does not define what standard rent is but s. 6 of that Act merely lays down the procedure for fixation of standard rent. The major principle for determination of standard rent is the computation on the basis of 10% per annum of the aggregate amount of the actual cost of construction and the market price of the land comprised in the premises on the date of commencement of construction. The percentage of 10% is applicable only where the rent so calculated exceeds twelve hundred rupees per annum. In this case too, rent can be revised or increased only on certain specified contingencies. The Rent Control Act prevalent in Mumbai does not specify in terms of actual figures the rate of return allowable to a landlord for his investment in land and construction work. There is a famous case decided in the court of law known as the *Talati's* case which has laid down the principle for determination of reasonable rent of any premises with reference to the existing return on gilt-edged securities. According to successive judicial decisions, the reasonable return which was assessed at $4^1/_2$ per cent on the value of land and $5^1/_2$ per cent on the cost of building in 1940's was gradually raised to 7 per cent on the value of land and 8 per cent on the cost of construction during 1960's, the flexibility being dependent on the upward movement of the return on gilt-edged securities. The position is therefore quite anomalous.

It may be mentioned in this context that there was a terrible pressure for revision of the rent control laws in order that a reasonable return may be assured to the investors in real estate. At the present moment, the income as well as the capital invested in urban real estate are eroded due to inflationary spiral. The right of the tenants being safeguarded by rigid conditions for their eviction, premises once let out virtually becomes the property of the tenants in perpetuity, subject only to routine payment of standard rent or such rent as is reasonable with reference to principles for determination of standard rent. The valuation of the leasehold property to the owner thus gets constrained by the limit of rent that the owner can legally expect by letting out the premises, vide *Padma Devi's* case.[11] The value to the occupier however is different. It includes all the advantages he enjoys by occupation. The occupancy may fetch him a return in terms of profit on business or amenities for pursuit of avocation or a sheer enjoyable stay. But in terms of value, the tenant also suffers from the constraint of inalienability as he has no right to dispose of his interest in the property at market value or sublet it without the consent of the owner. The situation is therefore a very complex one from the point of view of valuation. Quite a number of categories of properties and leasehold interests at present lie outside the scope of the rent control laws in their existing statutory structure. The present pressure of the property-holders is to add to this area of exemption and circumscribe the scope and applicability of the rent control laws. There was accordingly a move all over India to amend the Rent Control Laws to respond to the realities of the situation and relax the privilege of protection that the urban tenants have so far enjoyed. One of the thrust area of the proposed changes is to restore the property to the owner after the expiry of a specified period. In that case, the reversionary

11 AIR 1962 SC 151.

right of the owner would add to the value of the property to him. If the grounds for eviction or ejectment of the tenant are liberalised in favour of the owner, then the value of the property to him would enhance correspondingly. Again, if the fixation of fair rent or standard rent is subjected to liberal increase or revision and initially determined on more liberal terms on market approach rather than on cost approach, the value of the property in the hands of the owner will go up after extricating itself from the constraints of legal restriction.

"Fair Rent" as per West Bengal Premises Tenancy Act 1997

(1) ***When house was constructed and let out after 1984***

Fair rent per annum of the demised property comprising land component and the building $= 6\frac{3}{4}\%$ [(Aggreegate amount of actual cost of construction) + (Current price of the land on the date of commencement of construction)] per annum

(2) ***Tenancy subsists for 20 years or more and the house was constructed in or before 1984***

(A) FOR RESIDENTIAL PURPOSE:

Fair rent per annum = [(Existing rent per annum as on 1.7.1976) + (3 times (not more than 3 times) of the existing rent per annum)] – Increase in respect of rent (if any)

(B) FOR COMMERCIAL PURPOSE:

Fair rent per annum = [(Existing rent per annum as on 1.7.1976) + (5 times (not more than 5 times) of the existing rent per annum)]

(3) ***Tenancy subsists for 10 - 20 years and the house was constructed in or before 1984***

(A) FOR RESIDENTIAL PURPOSE:

Fair rent per annum = [(Existing rent per annum as on 1.7.1986) + (2 times (not more than 2 times) of the existing rent per annum)] – Increase in respect of rent (if any)

(B) FOR COMMERCIAL PURPOSE:

Fair rent per annum = [(Existing rent per annum as on 1.7.1986) + (3 times (not more than 3 times) of the existing rent per annum)]

Limitations/Exceptions

(1) *Residential purpose*

(A) FAIR RENT AS APPLICABLE IN THE AREA OF THE KOLKATA MUNICIPAL CORPORATION AND HOWRAH MUNICIPAL CORPORATION

When rent is upto @ ₹ 6,500 per month @ ₹ 78,000 per annum

(B) FAIR RENT AS APPLICABLE IN OTHER MUNICIPAL AREAS OTHER THAN THE KOLKATA MUNICIPAL CORPORATION AND HOWRAH MUNICIPAL CORPORATION

When rent is upto @ ₹ 3,000 per month *i.e.* @ ₹ 36,000 per annum

(2) *Non-Residential purpose*

(A) FAIR RENT AS APPLICABLE IN THE AREA OF THE KOLKATA MUNICIPAL CORPORATION AND HOWRAH MUNICIPAL CORPORATION

When rent is upto @ ₹ 10,000 per month @ ₹ 1,20,000 per annum

(B) FAIR RENT AS APPLICABLE IN OTHER MUNICIPAL AREAS OTHER THAN THE KOLKATA MUNICIPAL CORPORATION AND HOWRAH MUNICIPAL CORPORATION

When rent is upto @ ₹ 5,000 per month i.e. @ ₹ 60,000 per annum

CASE STUDY:

Considering a land component measuring 3 cottahs located & situated within the jurisdiction of the Kolkata Municipal Corporation. upon the land there is a 2 storied RCC roofed brick built residential building & structures, where the ground floor having approximate built-up area 1250 sq.ft. which is under the occupation of a single monthly tenant occupier paying @ ₹1050 per month. The 1st floor measuring about 850 sq. ft. as built-up area under the occupation of the owner of the property. We are going to ascertain the fair rent per annum & per month of the tenant occupied ground floor portion of the above referred property.

Pictorial view of the above reference

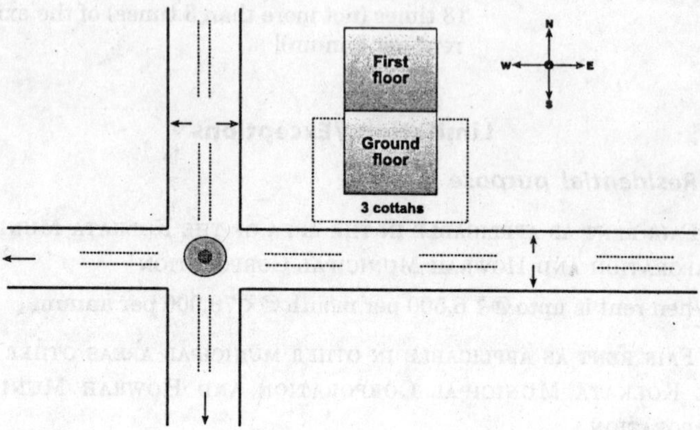

Case I: When house was constructed and let out after 1984

Data: (i) House was constructed in the year 1992

(ii) Actual cost of construction of the ground floor including proportionate cost of foundaton & building services = ₹ 3,80,000

(iii) As on 1992 land price ₹ 5,00,000 per cottah

(iv) For 1.97 cottahs as undivided proportionate land component, land value = ₹ 9,85,000

Fair rent of the ground floor of the property comprising: (i) undivided proportionate share of the land and (ii) the building & structures of the tenant occupied ground floor = $6\frac{3}{4}$% [(Aggreegate amount of actual cost of construction) + (Market price of the land component on the date of commencement of construction)]

per annum = $6\frac{3}{4}$% [₹ 3,80,000 + ₹ 9,85,000]

= $6\frac{3}{4}$% [₹ 13,65,000] per annum

= @ ₹ 92,138 per annum

= @ ₹ 7,678 per month

NOTE:

Total constructed area: GF + FF = 1250 + 850 =2100 sq.ft.

Total land area: 3 cottah = 3 x 720 sq.ft =2160 sq.ft.

For 2100 sq.ft. constructed area, land area = 2160 sq.ft.

For 1 sq. ft. constructed area, land area is = $\frac{2160}{2100}$ sq.ft.

= 1.02857 sq.ft.

For 1250 sq.ft. GF (T/o) Constructed covered area, proportionate land area = $\frac{2160}{2100}$ x 1250

= 1285 sq.ft.

= 1.78 cottah

Clog on alienation affecting value

Besides all that are discussed above, restrictions are often imposed on alienation of property held under common ownership such restrictions adversely affect market value. For example, there are housing societies owning vast land and building which imposes restriction on membership; one society of co-operative housing in Bandra, Mumbai allows membership only to Catholics, some societies restrict their membership only to vegetarians; membership of housing co-operatives confined to occupational groups is quite common. Such societies often exercise a right of pre-emption to transfers taking place within. These are instances of clog on alienation having considerable impact on value of property, the extent of diminution in value, depending on the nature of clog in each case.

It may be pointed out in this context that a restraint on alienation in absolute terms is void under s. 10 of the Transfer of Property Act, which lays down as follows:

> "Where property is transferred subject to a condition or limitation absolutely restraining the transferee or any person claiming under him from parting with or disposing of his interest in the property, the condition or limitation is void, except in the case of a lease where the condition is for the benefit of the lessor or those claiming under him:

Provided that property may be transferred to or for the benefit of a woman (not being a Hindu, Muhammadan or Buddhist), so that she shall not have power during her marriage to transfer or charge the same or her beneficial interest therein."

A condition partially restraining alienation is valid. In the case of partial restraint s. 10 is not attracted.[12] If the restraint is on the mode of alienation it is not a restraint within the meaning of s. 10.[13]

What is important here to note is that a lease is an exception to the rule against an absolute restraint on alienation. This exception arises from the very nature of a lease which is a transfer of property for a time, or in perpetuity, but in which the lessor necessarily retains an interest. Thus, a condition in a lease that a lessee shall not sublet or assign is valid. It is immaterial in this context that the lease is a permanent lease and the restraint is also permanent.[14] An assignment by operation of law, such as a sale in execution, or a sale of the property of a company by an official liquidator does not also constitute a breach of the condition restraining alienation. In *Golak Nath* v *Mathura Nath*,[15] the Calcutta High Court held— "we take it to be clear law in India, as in England that a general restriction on assignment does not apply to an assignment by operation of law taking effect *in invitum* as a sale under an execution".

Restriction repugnant to interest created

Section 11 of the Transfer of Property Act states "where, on a transfer of property, an interest therein is created absolutely in favour of any person, but the terms of the transfer direct that such interest shall be applied or enjoyed by him in a particular manner, he shall be entitled to receive and dispose of such interest as if there were no such direction." This section refers to a restriction on the enjoyment of property, while

12 *Jagan Naik* v *Cheddi Dholr* AIR 1973 All 307; 1973 All LJ 202.
13 *Mata Prasad* v *Nageshar Sahai* (1925)47 All 883; 91 IC 370.
14 *Abhiram* v *Shyama* (1909)36 Cal 1003; 36 IA 148; *Raja Jagat Ranvir* v *Bagriden* AIR 1973 All 11.
15 (1893)20 Cal 273 (278).

s. 10 refers to a restriction on the transfer of property. But both the sections rest on the same principle that a condition repugnant to the interest created is void. In other words, where a property is transferred absolutely, it must be transferred with all its legal incidents. But it must be remembered that s. 11 does not apply unless the transfer creates an absolute interest in the transferee. For example, it does not apply to a lease which is a transfer of a limited interest, and the lessee is bound by the conditions and covenants expressed or implied, restricting the mode of enjoyment of the property by the lessee. When a gift is made only in respect of usufruct and not the absolute interest, covenant restrictive of alienation was held not to be void on ground of repugnancy.[16] In *Tulk* v *Moxhay*,[17] it was held that the transferor may impose conditions restraining the enjoyment of land if such restrictions are for the benefit of its adjoining land. This principle has however, been recognised in the exception added to s. 11 by way of a second paragraph provided thereto.

16 *Jagdeo Baksh* v *Jwala Prasad* (1913)15 OC 345; 15 IC 244 (246).
17 (1848)2 Phill 774.

CHAPTER

20

Valuation of Assets—Property other than Real Estate

(A) AGRICULTURAL LAND

Agricultural land, orchard, plantation and forest are property different in nature from land and building. The characteristics of agricultural land is that it yields crops and does not offer potential for use as building sites. Crops are of seasonal nature and the yield varies from land to land, so also the quality of the yield. Needless to say that crops have immense diversity, so the valuation technique for agricultural land is based on its own method in the assessment of income and it constitutes a different stream of valuation. But agricultural lands in proximity to cities and towns and also those situated in the fringe area assume a transitory character. These are lands agricultural in present use but have potential for non-residential use in future. It is a common feature to witness agricultural land abutting on national highways and other important communicational routes being gradually converted into factory premises since facilities for transport and proximity to agricultural raw materials are conducive to location of industries on a particular spot. In the fringe areas of cities and towns, the expansion of urbanisation engulfs the agricultural land for residential use. Such trends have qualified a number of judicial decisions on compensation payable for compulsory acquisition of agricultural land. It was held in *Collector, Raigarh* v *Dr. Hari Singh Thakur*[1] that agricultural

1 AIR 1979 SC 472.

lands, merely by their proximity to city or town become endowed with their special adaptability, as a building site. While it is not suggested that unfairly low value should be offered; on the other hand, the temptation to over-generosity must be equally resisted. Such generosity at the public expense reacts against the development and against the prosperity of the country and imposes an unnecessary burden on the taxpayers. In another case *K. Padmaraju* v *Senior Regional Manager, FCI, Hyderabad,*[2] it was held that lands which are fertile and capable of double crops and have access to railway station and cinema hall were to be given due weightage for such consideration in the matter of assessment of compensation. In *Delhi Shimla Catholic Archdiocese* v *Union of India,*[3] the High Court held that the fact that the acquired land abuts the railway line and road and is contiguous to an expanded industrial estate gives real potential value to the land which should be considered in assessing compensation. In *Collector of Dacca* v *Hari Das Bysack,*[4] it was held long back that the proper method for ascertaining the market value of agricultural land situated within a municipal area is to ascertain what will be their market value if they were put to most lucrative use having regard to their condition, local position and advantage. Again, in the *State of U.P.* v *Janki Das (through LR),*[5] it was held that where an agricultural land is acquired in a municipal area, its potential value as a building site can be taken into account.

As per the report of the L.A.O. in his award, there was no development of the land though it was situated within the master plan of the Municipal limits and remained as agricultural land. Though sanction was obtained for converting it into non-agricultural land, but the same was done with the knowledge of proposed acquisition and to inflate the market value. Further, all the sale deeds produced related to small agricultural lands purchased on square foot basis and offered no reasonable basis for enhancement of compensation. This

2 (1996)10 SCC 613.
3 AIR 1980 Del 240.
4 14 IC 163.
5 AIR 1966 All 273.

was the decision in the case of *Kamalabai Jageshwar Joshi (Smt.)* v *State of Maharashtra.*[6]

The acquired land had no potential value of any kind and was pure and simple agricultural land. *Held,* High Court was not justified in taking into account future developments and the rates fixed by the District Judge based on factual matrix was confirmed.[7]

Income capitalisation and years' purchase

The above decisions are in the context of land acquisitions. As a matter of principle, when land yields an income and is put to valuation, the proper method of ascertaining market value will be the income capitalisation method.[8]

This was reiterated by the Supreme Court in the case of *Additional Special LAO* v *Y.B. Chalwadi.*[9]

The land under acquisition were *madikattu* in which two dry crops of groundnuts in the first season, jowar or cotton in the Rabi season were being raised. It was held, ten years' multiplier would be the proper method in determining the total market value by following the method of capitalisation which is just and reasonable in the absence of any other acceptable evidence. The number of years' purchase may, however, vary with individual cases. In *Collector* v *Shiva Devi,*[10] 15 years' purchase rule was applied for the purpose of capitalisation of profit in respect of agricultural land.

Where evidence as to value of land *per se* is not available and an evidence of income of such land is available, the capitalised value of such income may be taken as market value. Where sales transacted are available, comparable sales data offer a satisfactory guidance for valuation. Thus, in *Collector, Bilaspur* v *Daulat Ram,*[11] it was held that in assessing the market value of *abadi land* the average price

6 AIR 1996 SC 981; (1996)1 SCC 669.
7 *State of Haryana* v *Joginder Singh* (1997)3 SCC 628.
8 *Special Tehsildar, Land Acquisition* v *R. Sundersekhar* (1992)1 MLJ 378.
9 AIR 1994 SC 1836.
10 1987 (Supp) SCC 526.
11 AIR 1965 HP 7.

of the land on the basis of sales transactions produced and entered in the mutation records should be the guiding factor and in doing so the whole land should be assessed at the same time.

There have been a number of judicial decisions in which the compensation for acquiring agricultural land was assessed on the basis of years' purchase the number of which varied from case to case depending on circumstances in each case. It is interesting to have an overview of some of these cases that would reflect the approach and trend in this behalf.

In the case of *Union of India* v *Shanti Devi,*[12] it was observed as follows:

"The number of years' purchase has gradually decreased as the prevailing rate of interest realisable from safe investment has gradually increased—the higher the rate of interest, the lower the number of years' purchase. This method of valuation involves capitalising the net income that the property can fairly be expected to produce and the rate of capitalisation is the percentage of return on his investment that a willing buyer would expect from the property during the relevant period". In this case 15 years' purchase rule was applied. The net annual income from a land is arrived at by deducting from the gross annual income all outgoings such as expenditure on cultivation, land revenue etc.

In the absence of definite data, computation of market value by capitalisation method by adopting 16 years' net yield is permissible.[13]

Evaluation of the market value on the basis of annual yield applying multiplier of ten was held appropriate. In such a case determination on the basis of sale instances of lands sold in developed area was held illegal as the land was situated in undeveloped area.[14]

What is the proper multiplier to be applied for arriving at the market value of any land if the income method is adopted

12 AIR 1983 SC 1190.

13 *Land Acquisition Zone Officer* v *Dumbeeru Pradhan* AIR 1991 Ori 271.

14 *Vithalbhai Bakorbhai* v *Executive Engineer, Capital Project* (1996)3 SCC 592.

depends upon the nature of the agricultural land and the kind of crop raised on it. There is no invariable rule that in the absence of evidence of sales of similar lands and the only evidence the net income, the net income should be multiplied by 20 (twenty) in order to arrive at the market value. The multiple of 20 is applied where the rate of return expected is 5% of the capital invested.[15]

In the case, in assessing the market value of agricultural land by the capitalisation method a multiplier of 10 (ten) was considered adequate. It was also held that the extent of land has also a bearing in fixing the multiplier. But in case of fruit-bearing agricultural land 15 years' multiplier was held proper and fair.[16]

In case of valuation on the basis of yield of agricultural land, it was held that multiplier of 10 would be proper and not multiple of 16 as applied by the lower court.[17]

For the purpose of determination of market value of land ten years' multiplier was held proper.[18]

In the determination of compensation on the basis of yield, statistics from Agriculture Department as to the nature of crops and price prevailing at that time were not produced either by the claimants or by the Government. Therefore, oral evidence including that of the *sarpanch* was relied upon to determine the compensation on the basis of the yield by the reference court whose award was confirmed by the High Court. *Held,* multiplier of 10 years should be applied and deduction of 50% towards cultivation expenses should also be made.[19]

In case of agricultural lands if there are no sales of comparable lands the value must be found in some other way. One method is to take the annual net income of the land and to capitalise it by a number of years' purchase. The number of years varies with the nature of crops and its duration. When there are transactions of sales of similar lands, the value on the basis of capitalisation of net income method may be

15 *Channaveerappa Gouda* v *L.A.O.* AIR 1974 Mys 42.
16 *State of Kerala* v *Paily Mani* (1994)2 Ker LJ 362; (1994)2 Ker LT 444.
17 *Collector, L.A.* v *Ganaram Dhoba* (1996)1 SCC 631.
18 *Special L.A.O.* v *Virupax Shankar Nadagouda* (1996)6 SCC 124.
19 *State of Gujarat* v *Rama Rana* (1997)2 SCC 693; AIR 1997 SC 1846.

ascertained in order to countercheck whether the value as reflected in the sale transactions actually represents the true market value. The ascertainment of the net income for the purpose of capitalisation and the selection of multiple for capitalisation involve an interplay of diverse factors which require a careful analysis and assessment. The court as a rough and ready measure treated 50% of the gross yield as net income from the principal crops ignoring the yield from subsidiary crop.[20]

For the valuation of agricultural land, statistics for the year 1957 showing the yield in that area was about 10 bags per acre, but statistics for the year 1983 when the notification under s. 4(1) was issued not produced. *Held*, in view of the considerable improvement since 1957, compensation at 22 bags per acre fixed by the High Court not improper.[21]

The process of ascertaining the number of years' purchase is often made to depend on the return available from alternative investment. Thus in the case of *Special L.A.O., Hassan* v *M.S. Mallesha*[22] it was observed that the investment in agricultural land is guided also by expectancy of income from other safer sources.

One of the well-known methods of valuation is the method of capitalising the net income by employing a proper multiple, which is called the number of years' purchase value, which depends upon the rate of return which a prudent man/investor in the class of property would expect in the relevant year. A person investing his capital in agricultural land ordinarily expects a return of 2% to 3% more than what he could obtain from gilt-edged Government security. When the rate of return has to be determined the valuer has to start with the rate of return from gilt-edged security in the year 1971. When the Government securities earn 5% return, an investor in agricultural lands would automatically and naturally expect a higher rate of at least 7% return. If an investor in agricultural lands like dry and wet lands in the State would expect a minimum of 7% return in the year 1971 the proper multiple

20 *Special L.A.O., Devangere* v *Kotraiah* AIR 1977 Kant 33.
21 *Collector, L.A.* v *Ganaram Dhoba* (1996)1 SCC 631.
22 AIR 1975 Kant 165.

to be employed for the purpose of capitalisation cannot exceed 15% which is the multiple adopted by the L.A.O.[1]

Valuation on square yard basis

Determination of market value of agricultural land on the basis of square yard has not been preferred by judicial decisions. This is a method which generally finds application in valuation of urban land. But where the agricultural land is developed so as to command potential value, valuation on the basis of square yard was held as not improper. The following are some of the decisions in this behalf.

Determination of market value of 33 bighas of acquired agricultural land on square foot basis is illegal. It is only when the land is found to possess potential value then only the market value could be determined on square yard basis.[2]

Agricultural lands converted for non-agricultural purpose situated within the municipal limits, but had no potential value as there was no development in the area. In such case determination of compensation on acreage basis is proper and not on comparable sales of small pieces of land. Claimants are entitled to payment of interest and *solatium* on enhanced compensation.[3]

Where agricultural land is not developed and not fit for construction of houses and as such possessed of no potential value, then the determination of market value on bigha basis instead of yard basis is proper.[4]

Valuation of agricultural land serviced by facilities

In some of the judicial decisions, the value of the agricultural land was adjudged with due consideration to facilities available to the land whether by the bounties of nature or by contrivances involving investment like irrigation.

While determining compensation in respect of acquisition of land on the basis of agricultural income, the lower court took into consideration several factors like rainfall, vagaries of climate,

1 *Special L.A.O., Hassan* v *M.S. Mallesha* AIR 1975 Kant 165.

2 *State of Madhya Pradesh* v *Hari Shankar Goel* (1997)2 SCC 487.

3 *State of Maharashtra* v *Digambar Bhimshankar Tandale* (1996)2 SCC 583.

4 *Basant Kumar* v *Union of India* (1996)11 SCC 542.

invasion by insects and calamities like untimely rain, shortage of rain, cyclone, famine, severe heat etc. and irregularity in supply of canal water if there be any, and other factors which may have varying effect on the agricultural production from year to year; the method was not erroneous. There is no exact yardstick for measuring the net income and there is also no exact yardstick for arriving at the fair market value of the land on the basis of the agricultural produce. Valuation of land itself is a matter of guesswork, and after arriving at such a figure of net income per year, it will have to be capitalised by applying a proper multiplier. In the instant case of acquisition of land in the year 1969, the High Court adopted the multiplier of 12.5 in computing capitalised value of land.[5]

Market value of agricultural land has to be determined under the L.A. Act with reference to the date on which preliminary notification was published in the State Gazette proposing its acquisition and according to the price which a buyer interested in agriculture would have paid for it to the owner having regard to its soil, the irrigation and other facilities, it commanded for its maximum utilisation for agricultural purposes. The highest factor is the irrigation facility that is the water supply which it can command for crops to be grown in it. Where river water or tank water is unavailable or is insufficient for cultivation of agricultural land open irrigation wells are sunk raising stone or brick or cement walls or by use of cement rings. The advantage which an agricultural land may have because of the irrigation facility it had from the irrigation well, could only enhance the value of agricultural land depending upon the water yield from the well. When such lands are acquired, the value of the land will have to be determined taking into consideration the irrigation facility it had from the well. In this situation the irrigation well in an acquired agricultural land, cannot have a value apart from the value of the agricultural land itself. In the instant case, the L.A.O., the Civil Court and the High Court determined market value of the irrigation wells and nature of crops grown in them and awarded compensation to the owners. Thus, they have proceeded on a misconception that the market

5 *State of Gujarat* v *Kathi Malsiya Vaghe* AIR 1992 Guj 79 relied on *Special L.A.O., Davangere* v *P. Veerabhadrappa* AIR 1984 SC 774.

value of the irrigation wells had to be determined according to their construction costs and paid compensation independently of the compensation payable for the agricultural lands which was wholly unwarranted. So, the question of granting further enhanced compensation by the Supreme Court for irrigation wells situated in their acquired agricultural lands would not arise.[6]

There is no exact yardstick for measuring the net income and there is also no exact yardstick for arriving at the fair market value of the land on the basis of the agricultural produce. Valuation of land itself is a matter of guesswork, and after arriving at such a figure of net income per year, it will have to be capitalised by applying a proper multiplier. The lower court took into consideration various factors like rainfall, vagaries of climate, invasion by insects and calamities like untimely rains, shortage of rain, cyclone, famine, severe heat, and other factors which may have effect on the agricultural production from year to year. The method was held not erroneous in view of the above stated considerations. The High Court applied the multiplier 12.5 in the case in 1969 in computing capitalised value of land.[7]

In the case, the Special L.A.O. treated part of the land as irrigated one and part as non-irrigated, though there is a pucca well present in the land on the date of notification, with engine fixed on well and water is being supplied to the whole land from it. The District Judge held the whole land is irrigated and classified the entire land as under irrigation. In view of the above evidence on record High Court disagreed to hold that part of the land is non-irrigated.[8]

Where the land acquired is agricultural land and compensation is claimed on the basis of agricultural land including its potentialities, the hypothetical purchaser would consider the entire area in dispute to be subject to irrigation and would pay for the entire area as irrigated and agricultural land less area market as *ghair mumkin.*[9]

6 *Janardhan Reddy* v *Special Deputy Collector, L.A., Karimnagar* AIR 1995 SC 186.

7 *State of Gujarat* v *Kathi Malsiya Vaghe* AIR 1992 Guj 79.

8 *Raval Maneklal Motiram* v *State of Gujarat* AIR 1991 Guj 137.

9 *Surjan Singh* v *East Punjab* AIR 1957 Punj 265.

Agricultural land with trees or grass

There are particular methods of valuation when an agricultural land comprises standing trees or commercial grassland. The issue came up for judicial decision in a few cases and there have been divergent views depending on peculiar circumstances of each case. Thus it was held that in evaluating market value of acquired property namely, land and building or the lands with fruit-bearing trees standing thereon, the value of both would not constitute one unit but separate units. In the former case the trees are to be separately valued as timber and deduct therefrom the salvage expenses to cut and remove the trees from the land. Otherwise, on the basis of annual income of fruit-bearing trees, appropriate capitalisation would be proper.[10]

Where agricultural lands are valued as building sites, the claimants are not entitled to ask that trees standing on the lands should be separately assessed and valued as fruit-bearing trees since what is awarded is an inclusion price.[11]

Where land is valued as agricultural land it is reasonable to ascertain the capitalised income of fruit-bearing trees in which case the period of computation of value should be taken as only ten years. But if the site is valued as a house site, the trees thereon cannot be valued on that basis (i.e. as fruit-yielding trees). At best, the value of the trees as timber or fuel alone can be taken into account. For otherwise the valuation will really result in duplication of values.[12]

In assessing compensation in respect of *danga* lands growing *sabai* grass the Supreme Court observed that since after one crop was taken for 7 to 10 years, another crop could be raised after an interval of one to two years. So, the compensation to be awarded to the landowners should be 20 times the annual income from the land. Compensation fixed as ₹ 800 per acre for *danga* land growing *sabai* grass and ₹ 50 per acre for other

10 *Koyappathodi M. Ayisha Umma* v *State of Kerala* AIR 1991 SC 2027.
11 *Tharosaruma* v *Deputy Collector, Cochin* 77 IC 347; 1923 MWN 682; 18 LW 356; 45 MLJ 339; 33 MLT 48.
12 *State of Madras* v *Alameluthayammal* AIR 1970 Mad 184 dissenting from *Rabindradhar Barua* v *Collector, Kamrup* AIR 1982 Gau 17.

danga land held correct. Price of *sabai* grass at ₹ 4 per maund was also approved.[13]

(B) ORCHARD

'Orchard' generally means land covered with fruit-bearing trees within a notional or actual enclosure. It is distinct from agricultural land in the sense that agricultural land is filled up with seasonal crops harvested in such manner that the land is laid bare after harvesting operation. But orchards remain perennially covered with fruit-bearing trees. The fruits are harvested as season's yield while the trees remain standing during the entire period of their fruit-bearing life. After such economic life is over, the trees are felled for use as timber or fuel and if the owner intends to keep the orchard intact, new plantations are made. Thus, land together with the trees constitute the capital which yield an income by way of fruits. But, in case of agricultural land, the bare land qualified by soil fertility is the capital and the grains reaped are the income.

Forest

Another species of land use with growing trees is 'forest'. Still another is 'plantation' to which we shall turn as our next topic. In forest, large tracts are covered with trees and undergrowth meant generally for supply of timber for furniture, log for constructional purposes, raw material for industries, fuel for domestic use and fodder for animals. Besides, ecological reasons need woodland to be maintained. Forests are different from orchards in that the usufruct of the forest generally consists of the tree itself or its branches or leaves while in the orchard, it is mainly the fruit. Looked at from this angle, the capital asset of a forest, akin to agricultural land, comprises the land and its soil fertility since the tree itself is regarded as crop. When the trees are already full grown as standing timber, the role of the land is that of a mere warehouse for storage of timber in natural state. In a case for compulsory acquisition of forest, the evidence disclosed that tree had been planted by the Government in its scheme of afforestation of lands and that the income from them was always appropriated by the Government under the agreement entered into with the landlord

13 *State of W.B.* v *Shyamapada* (1976)3 SCC 66.

paying him as advance a fixed sum therefore. The acquisition being made after the expiry of the agreement period, the Court held, it was fallacious for the landlord to ask for the value of the trees towards compensation for the acquired land.[14] This judgment thus reflects how the trees in the forest are treated as yield of the land and not as part and parcel of land as the capital for production.

Whether trees can be valued separately from land

In *Jute and Gunny Brokers (P) Ltd.* v *State of Bihar,*[15] the orchard sought to be acquired was wholly covered with trees it was held that its market value should be determined for the land including the trees as a whole and not by valuing the trees separately from the land for the simple reason that the land being wholly covered with trees cannot yield any usufruct independent of the usufruct of the trees, and without the trees such a land may have very little value.

When an orchard or a plantation is acquired the land and the plants cannot be separately valued independently of the value of the land. If the land is to be used for building sites the plant growth has to be removed and only timber value of the plant growth can be taken into account. The existence of the plants has a bearing upon the enhancement in the market value of the land.[16]

The question has been elaborately discussed in the case of *State of Kerala* v *Mariamma Abraham,*[17] where land together with trees has been considered as a single income-yielding unit. When the land has been fully planted to the best advantage from the point of view of income, capitalisation of the net annual income derived from the trees might be a safe mode of arriving at the market value. But this method must fail where the plantations are scattered here and there and the bulk of the land is bare land. In such cases, where the improvements yield an income, a fair way of assessing the value of the improved land would be to deduct from the total

14 *Raja Niranjan Singh* v *State of U.P.* (1979)3 SCC 758; AIR 1979 SC 1547.
15 AIR 1980 Pat 225.
16 *A.K. Ahmed* v *Special L.A.O. C.I.T.B.* (1974)2 Kant LJ 1.
17 AIR 1969 Ker 265.

area, the area necessary for or occupied by the improvements since the area would not be available for any other purpose, value the balance as bare land, and add to the capitalised value of the income derived from improvements. However, even non-yielding improvements (unless they are worthless and cannot really be regarded as improvements) would add to the market value of bare land, and, in case of such improvements, their present cost less depreciation might be a proper addition. And, where the improvements consist of non-yielding trees, their fuel or timber value must be added to the value of the land as bare land without any deduction made for standing space. For, if the trees are felled and sold, the entire area without any deduction in area would be available for sale as bare land *plus* the fuel or timber value of the trees whether yielding or non-yielding standing on it, and the deductions made on account of standing space for yielding trees should not have the result of reducing. The capitalised value of the income of the trees is not the value of the trees alone but as including also the value of the land necessarily occupied by them in order to produce the income, the tree with necessary land being the income producing unit, not the tree itself.[18]

Separate compensation cannot be awarded for fruit growing trees standing on the land. When a garden is acquired the proper method of valuation is not to value the land and the trees separately. Thus when cocoanut garden or mango garden is acquired, the market value of the garden should be considered.[19]

Under the definition of land under s. 3(*a*) of the L.A. Act (now s. 3(*p*) of the Right to Fair Compensation and Transparency in Land Acquisition, Rehabilitation and Resettlement Act 2013), the land would include trees standing thereon. Therefore, the value of the trees should not be excluded in calculating the 15% allowed by the statute.[20]

The value of the trees is to be added to the value of the land to find the market value and to calculate *solatium* at the rate of 15% to be paid on the same.[1]

18 *State of Kerala* v *Mariamma Abraham* AIR 1969 Ker 265.

19 *L.A.O., Tumkur* v *T.S. Aswathanarayana Rao* AIR 1974 Kant 112; (1974)1 Kant LJ 129.

20 *Krishna Bai* v *Secretary of State* ILR (1920)42 All 555; 57 IC 520.

1 *Mugneeram Bangur & Co.* v *State of W.B.* AIR 1974 Cal 369.

Where land is valued with reference to its potentiality for building purposes and on the basis of prices fetched by small sites in a hypothetical layout, the tree grown of the land cannot be valued independently on the basis of its horticultural value or with reference to the value of the yield. But this principle does not come in the way of awarding the timber value or the salvage value of the tree grown after providing for the cost of cutting and removing.[2]

Income capitalisation or market value—only one method to be adopted

In the case of *Joginder Singh Saini* v *State of Haryana,*[3] the issue arose whether in the valuation of an orchard both income capitalisation as well as computation of market value could be applied. The court held that there can be two ways of assessing the market value of an orchard, namely—

"(*i*) to find out the value of the annual produce from the orchard and capitalise the same by 20 times. This would give the total market price of the land under the fruit-bearing trees as also the wood in the trees. However, it is made clear that over and above this capitalised value the claimants would not be entitled to market price of the land under the orchard, nor for the wood in the trees, as the capitalised value would include the price of all these,

or

(*ii*) the market value of the land underneath the orchard *plus* the market value for the wood in the trees."

Claimants are permitted to choose the higher of the two values. In case of purchase, the purchaser would also judge the value of the same on the basis of its annual produce and that is why it would be on the basis of the capitalised value. If that does not suit the claimant, then the other reasonable method would be to allow him the price of the land underneath the orchard *plus* the wood in the tree. Naturally, he would like to have the higher value. While the claimant who has

2 *Administrator General of W.B.* v *Collector, Varanasi* AIR 1988 SC 943.

3 AIR 1981 P&H 170.

only Eucalyptus trees will have one method of evaluating the market value, the owner of the orchard would be entitled to claim market value on either of the two methods.

In case where the land is occupied entirely by the trees, the market value has to be determined either, on the basis of the value of land or on the basis of the income of the yielding by trees, and in no case double value can be adopted. But in case where a large extent of land only, some trees are situated scattered here and there, then the value of the trees cannot reflect the correct market value and, therefore, some margin has to be given if the trees are merely income yielding trees, then the income has to be calculated on the basis of actual yielding, plus 20 times capitalisation. If the trees do not bear any fruits then they have to be valued as firewoods and accordingly market value has to be determined.[4]

Where a large number of trees are planted on a small bit of land, such a land cannot be used as house sites unless the trees are removed. In that case it may be reasonable to say that the valuation of the site as a house site includes the valuation of the trees also. The trees can be valued as firewood. But where there are only a few trees, it is not necessary to remove the trees. Their continued standing would only enhance the value of the house site. In course of discussion and argument in the instant case, the learned judge referred to the case of *State* v *Alameluthayammal*,[5] and observed that if the site is valued as house site then to value the trees separately and then add their value to the house site value will be duplication and so only one of the two has to be valued.[6]

Factors enhancing or affecting value of orchard

In the case of *Nageswar Rao* v *Special Deputy Collector*,[7] the Andhra Pradesh High Court identified a number of considerations that affect the value of an orchard. According to the observations therein:

(*a*) the valuation of an orchard should take into consideration the condition of the soil, noting its

4 *Gopu Manikyam* v *L.A.O. and District Social Welfare Officer, Eluru* (1988)1 Andh LT 699.

5 AIR 1970 Mad 184 (DB).

6 *L.A.O., Khammam* v *Katia Venkaiah* AIR 1981 AP 310.

7 AIR 1959 AP 52.

fertility. The valuer should see whether the soil has hard pan or plousole and whether the method of cultivation in the past has been proper or improper. The depth of the soil, salinity, alkalinity, subsoil condition, drainage facility, irrigational facilities, e.g. wells, pumpsets etc.

(*b*) the actual condition of the trees, if affected with pests or suffering from improper fertilisation, whether pruned properly, the number of replacements, the variety of trees, their richness in yield, etc. should be considered. Whether there is any bad stock or scaly bark, or gummosis, and the age of the trees are also relevant factors. In India the approved method of fixing the valuation of orchards is to capitalise their net income at the number of trees and other circumstances.

Thick plantation beyond a certain limit would render such an orchard a total failure from the commercial point of view. In such an eventuality, proper growth, production and productivity would become a casualty and, in no case, the owner thereof would reap any benefit from this type of orchard. Actually, it may then be a losing proposition. No profit is likely to accrue from such an orchard and it is highly doubtful if such apple trees would fetch any market value whatsoever within the ambit of s. 23(1) of the L.A. Act.[8]

Orchard price as basis of valuation

In the valuation of orchard it will be the orchard price which should be made the basis of assessing the profits and not the wholesale price or retail price. As per the Report in the case the market price of orange is considered in three aspects, viz. (1) orchard price, being the price in the garden; (2) wholesale price, being the price in a recognised wholesale market, and (3) retail price. When an income is derived annually for several years to come, it is necessary to find the present worth of the income to be derived in future years at a reasonable rate of interest; generally 5% per annum (*sic*). In the case of properties yielding income permanently, capitalised value is measured by twenty times the annual profit.[9] The owner whose orchard was acquired

8 *State of Himachal Pradesh* v *Amba Dutta Dhanta* 1987 Sim LC 48.
9 *Collector of Raigarh* v *Chaturbhuj Pande* AIR 1964 MP 196.

went up in appeal before the Supreme Court.[10] The Collector awarded a sum of ₹ 59,494/6 annas as compensation. On a reference the District Judge valued the trees at ₹ 2,19,220 and in all awarded a sum of ₹ 3,29,480 for the land and the trees. The orchard comprised orange, musambi and guava trees. On appeal against that judgment the High Court reduced the value for the land and the trees. The trees were valued at ₹ 58,566. In giving to this valuation of the trees the High Court relied on official reports and pamphlets published by certain individuals as to the yield from orange, musambi and guava trees, the average span of life of those trees and the market value thereof and reassessed the compensation for the trees. On appeal, the Supreme Court observed that those documents were looked into by the learned Judges of the High Court after conclusion of the arguments. This was irregular from the point of view of procedure. Their Lordships held that the claim of the appellant was highly exaggerated one and the evidence of the witness supporting that claim was unaccountable. In those circumstances the claimants could not have any complaint and since the Government had not appealed, their Lordships did not interfere with the judgment of the High Court.

Orchard having potential value

In *Ranjit Singh* v *Union Territory of Chandigarh*[11] blind application of income capitalisation in the matter of valuation of an orchard with total disregard to its potential value has been disfavoured. It has been observed that to work out the market value of the orchard lands on the basis of the annual value or according to the formula known as capitalisation, is most likely to work to the prejudice of the claimant whose land under the fruit trees has enormous potentiality to be utilised as residential or commercial area. In such a case the value of the fruit trees or the orchard has to be assessed independently of the value of the land or in other words the potentiality of the land to be utilised for residential or commercial purposes. So, the case was remanded back to redetermine the market price of the trees of the claimants in accordance with law.

10 *Chaturbhooj Pande* v *Collector of Raigarh* AIR 1969 SC 255.
11 AIR 1983 P&H 308.

In determining the market value, when the court puts a fictitious value of certain property on account of its potentiality for building purposes, then the rate allowed by the court should be taken as an inclusive rate nothing can be allowed in addition for the trees standing upon the land.[12]

Capitalisation rate

When the method of income capitalisation has been adopted, orchards have been valued in accordance with different capitalisation rates varying with circumstances of each case.

Where there are different types of trees on the land under acquisition separate valuation for each type of tree has been held proper. Fruit-bearing trees likely to bear fruits for a number of years, for example, mango trees, were valued at 20 years' annual rental.[13]

For cocoanut trees ₹ 3 was taken as the annual income and 10 years' purchase was allowed as the value for the cocoanut trees.[14]

In another case, it was observed that the approved method of valuation of orchard is to capitalise the net income at a number of years' purchase with reference to the nature of the trees and other circumstances. In the case, the court capitalised the net income at 15 years' purchase to determine the market value of the cocoanut grove and the orange orchard.[15]

In another case, the net income from an orchard was capitalised at 15 years' purchase to determine the market value of the orchard.[16]

(c) Plantations

Plantation is different from agricultural land, orchard or forest. It is an estate on which the land is used for commercial yields

12 *Collector of Thane* v *Chaturbhuj Radha Krishan* AIR 1926 Bom 356; 95 IC 513; 28 Bom LR 548.

13 *Rajammal* v *Headquarters, Deputy Collector, Vellore* 25 IC 393; AIR 1915 Mad 356.

14 *Shanmuga Velyudu Mudaliar* v *Collector of Tanjore* AIR 1926 Mad 945; 23 MLW 336.

15 *Kompalli Nageswara Rao* v *Special Deputy Collector* AIR 1959 AP 52.

16 *Elias M. Cohen* v *Secretary of State* AIR 1918 Pat 625(2); 2 Pat LJ 615.

like tea, coffee, cotton, rubber etc. It is different from the forests in that the trees are not generally felled nor vegetations uprooted. The yield is plucked or tapped. The typical yield of a tea estate is 'two leaves and a bud'. In rubber plantation, the juice is tapped and not any fruit. Thus the capital asset in plantations consists of the land together with the trees or vegetations thereon which are perennially maintained akin to an orchard. But it is distinguished from an orchard in that the yield is not fruit but a substance which requires to be further industrially processed in order to qualify for consumption. Plantation of tea, coffee or rubber being an estate in itself, comprises township with a number of structures, houses, factories and of course, captive hinterland for plantations. It is a common practice in valuing such property to itemise each piece of machinery and equipment and determine the cost new, from contemporaneous price list. To this cost is added the transportation and installation cost. As regards deduction therefrom, allowance is given for physical depreciation and obsolescence. The various buildings and structures on the asset side are valued by estimating their individual replacement cost new and deducting therefrom the reasonable depreciation. The land is appraised by the sales comparison method as if vacant. Plantations have a definite life and therefore are a kind of decaying asset. The losses are compensated by new plantations to keep the stock in perpetuity. Thus, the valuation of the plantations as such has to take into consideration the factors like health of the bushes or trees, expected life of the saplings, crop return, maintenance, agro-climatic conditions etc. The value of the whole property is taken to be as the sum of the value calculated for the portions. However, it does not follow that the value of the enterprise as a whole is equal to the sum of the values of those fractions in spite of the fact that each of these fractions were correctly valued. In valuing the whole property as a going concern the aspect of goodwill is to be taken into account as a major intangible asset. If the plantation is a profitable one as a going concern, its value in entirety will be larger than the value obtained by adding the value of its fractions. The difference between the two can be attributed to the intangible item called 'goodwill'. Normally, such an enterprise would never be sold in parts or fractions, but as a whole on a going concern basis; and hence, this method of valuation is much appropriate.

It is often necessary to ascertain the investment value of the property for purposes other than sale. In such a case, an alternative method of valuation often followed in practice involves the forecasting of the earning capacity of the subject assets and calculating the present worth of the series of monetary returns therefrom. The capitalisation of the potential profit in this manner constitutes the basis for investment value. Since this process envisages the determination of the value contributed to the business by all the individual assets, it may suffer from the infirmities of valuation by fractions and not as a whole. When the element of goodwill is found absent and valuation as a going concern do not indicate any excess of investment value as a whole over that obtained by adding the value of the fractions, the method based on earning capacity of component assets may prove useful.

There are a few judicial decisions relating to valuation of different kinds of plantations like tea, coffee, rubber, sugarcane, etc. The decisions are mainly in the context of compulsory acquisition but it has been held in *Murlidhar Barua* v *State of Assam*,[17] that there can be no scope for determination of the compensation for the acquired land as a tea estate. If a tea estate is to be acquired as an estate, resort must be had to some other legislation. It cannot be acquired under the Land Acquisition Act 1894. Similarly, it was held in *V. Narayana Gajapatiraju* v *R.D.O.*[18] that if any estate is acquired as a unit there can be no scope for determining the compensation in accordance with the provisions of s. 23 of the Land Acquisition Act (now s. 28 of the Right to Fair Compensation and Transparency in Land Acquisition Rehabilitation and Resettlement Act 2013). In the matter of *Hemendra Prasad Baruah* v *Collector Sibsagar, Assam*,[19] a different issue however arose. In this case s. 7(1A) of the Assam Land (Requisition and Acquisition) Act 24 of 1948 [at present Assam Land (Requisition and Acquisition) Act 15 of 1964] or the larger one stipulated under s. 7(1) was attracted. The simple statutory test that settles the issue is to find out whether the land acquired is lying fallow or uncultivated. It was held, if a small

17 AIR 1977 Gau 44.
18 AIR 1939 PC 98.
19 AIR 1976 SC 908.

amount of compensation is awardable, s. 7(1A) of the Act really would be applicable. On the other hand, if it is a tea garden, the quantum is under s. 23 of the L.A. Act.

In *State of Madras* v *Matha Gowder*[20] a different question arose as regards quantum of compensation payable on acquisition. But a minor issue on valuation was also decided. In this particular case, notification under s. 4(1) of the Land Acquisition Act 1894 [now s. 11(1) of the new Act of 2013] was made on different dates from June 1956 to December 1957 for acquisition of tea or coffee estates. But the Superintending Engineer, Electrical got into the possession of the lands before those notifications to expedite the Kundah project and the tea or coffee estates thereby destroyed. The owners had been paid compensation partly or fully for the coffee and tea plants at certain rates per plants. Government objected to such payments and fresh proceedings started. The High Court held that the court below was right in holding that lands should be valued as vacant lands because on the dates of notification there were no tea or coffee plants. It was also observed that the part payment of compensation for plants is not to be treated as payment under the L.A. Act and cannot be allowed to be set off against the compensation payable under L.A. proceedings. The owners would be entitled to compensation for the vacant lands at rates determined by court below without any deductions for part payments. It is to be noted that where there are still tea or coffee plants as on dates of notifications, the court may value them as such and allow part deductions of compensation if and where it had already been paid for the plants.

Coffee trees—valuation thereof

In the area of the coffee estate abutting the railway line, half an acre of coffee plantations should be injuriously affected as there would be no shade trees to protect them. The claimant can get damage at 50% of the value of the land in respect of that half an acre coffee plantation. By the acquisition, the coffee estate was cut into two pieces one smaller on one side of railway and the other larger one on the other side of the line. The claimant has to take a circuitous route of about 2 to

20 AIR 1966 Mad 393.

3 furlongs on account of the bifurcation by railway line. If the blocks were large enough for economic management, there would be no depreciation. But in the case, the smaller portion was depreciated in value by about ₹ 1,000 an acre. The report of the commissioner stated that out of the smaller portion of the bifurcated coffee estate 1½ acres was fallow and hence the compensation was reduced from ₹ 4,000 to ₹ 3,000 taking into account 1½ acres as fallow, out of 4 acres 20 gunthas, being the smaller one.

Again, the market value of half an acre of coffee land injuriously affected was fixed as ₹ 3,000, but as the claimant is entitled to get only damages for injurious affection, hence, 50% of ₹ 3,000, i.e. ₹ 1,500 was awarded by the L.A.O.[1]

The acquired coffee plantation was planted with *Robusta* coffee in 50% of the land and in the remaining land with *Arabic* coffee. It was held that there was no justification for enhancement of compensation in respect of lands planted with *Robusta* coffee since it was not as valuable as *Arabic* coffee.[2]

Rubber trees—valuation thereof

The basis for determining the annual income in case of rubber trees is the usual method of conducting test tapping of rubber trees. Trees tapped once in two days yield more than those tapped everyday. The yield depends on the number of trees, their age, attention given to them, the season etc. So, all such factors are taken into consideration to determine the yield by test tapping. The court will take considerable care in making use of the data obtained by such test tapping for determining the annual income. In the instant case, the basis for determining the land value adopted for the purpose of capitalising the income was by the use of data obtained by such test tapping. The court decided that the multiple to be adopted for the purpose of capitalising the income for the particular season in 1965 would be 16. When once capitalised value of the income is adopted as the basis for determining

1 *Special Land Acquisition Officer* v *M.S. Siddalingiah* (1974)1 Kant LJ 463.

2 *Special Tahsildar (L.A.) Modernisation of Vaigai Channel Scheme* v *Managing Director, Alavai Industries (P) Ltd., Madurai* (1982)2 MLJ 390.

the land value there is no scope for awarding any additional value for the land separately.[3]

In the case compensation for rubber trees was assessed by the capitalisation method by multiplying the gross annual income by 12.[4]

Sugar-cane growing land—valuation

Sugar-cane, strictly speaking, cannot be taken as an yield from plantation as the entire plant is uprooted after maturity of crop. But it resembles plantation in the aspect that the yield is quite often industrially processed for production of sugar. It was held in the case of *Special Land Acquisition Officer* v *Kalist Monterio,*[5] that the proper method of determination of market value of land is to adduce evidence of contemporaneous sale of similar lands and to produce or lead evidence as to the net yield after meeting cultivation expenses and adopt a proper multiple for capitalising the value. The appropriate multiple depends on the nature of the crop raised in the land. The adoption of the multiple of 20 may not always be justified in the case of agricultural lands. It depends upon the return of the investments of the investor and his expectation in this regard. In case of sugar-cane crop, the same cannot be grown in the same land each year and the duration of the crop is more than one year in the same land.

(D) TANK, FISHERY AND WELL

Land is used not always for construction but often also for excavation. When used as a tank, the land obtains value as a water reservoir for multiple purposes—irrigation, bathing, washing, drinking, sporting and the like. Similarly, wells are in common use for supplying water for the purposes of drinking and irrigation. Tanks assume commercial importance with exploitation as 'tank fishery'. There has been a few cases that relate to valuation of tank, fishery and well in the context of acquisition under the Land Acquisition Act.

In *Special L.A.O.* v *Virupax Shankar Nadgouda,*[6] the claimant for compensation based his claim on the basis of yield

3 *State of Kerala* v *Geevarghese Kathanar* 1980 Ker LT 880.

4 *State of Kerala* v *Varghese Joseph* (1989)2 Ker LT 51 (SW).

5 (1973)2 Mys LJ 333.

6 (1996)6 SCC 124.

of crops. He draws water from a well for the land. It was held that he cannot get separate compensation for the well and the reference code was found wrong in granting compensation for the well and applying 15 years' multiplier. Where the entire agricultural land is supplied with water from a pucca well on the land fitted with an engine, it was held that the entire land had to be treated as irrigated land and no part could be treated as non-irrigated.[7] It was again held in *State of Bihar* v *Madheshwar Prasad*[8] that when a well is used for irrigation of land, it cannot be separately valued. In the same vein, the Supreme Court decides in *State of Bihar* v *Ratanlal Sahu*[9] that where water is being used from the tank and well for cultivating land, no separate value can be granted for the same.

Tank fishery

In the case of acquisition of 'tank fishery', 16 years' purchase or 16 times of annual profit was fixed as compensation having regard to expected return from the property, security or stability of such return and its duration, costs of collection prevailing rate of interest, etc.[10] In the case of *Ananda Behara* v *State of Orissa,*[11] it was held that s. 5(*a*)(*iii*) of Estate Acquisition Act 1954 (West Bengal) or s. 4(*a*) of Bihar Abolition of Zamindaries Act 1949 or under Madhya Pradesh Abolition of Proprietary Rights Act 1959 and Orissa Estates Abolition Act 1951 etc. make "fishery" in the 'estate' a part of the land and so immovable property. The right to catch and carry away fishes in a tank or lake is a licence with a grant, i.e. is a *profit a prendre* and is regarded as a benefit to arise out of the land.

In *State of West Bengal* v *Ganesh Chandra Mitra*[12] the court adopted the method of valuing tanks at one and half of the value of solid land. In *Salil Kumar Ghosh* v *State of Orissa,*[13] it was held that in respect of tank, the actual cost of excavation of the tank should be taken into account.

7 *R.M. Motiram* v *State of Gujarat* AIR 1991 Guj 137.
8 (1996)6 SCC 197.
9 (1996)10 SCC 635 relying on *O. Janardhan Reddy* v *Special Deputy Collector, L.A.* (1994)6 SCC 456.
10 *State of West Bengal* v *Belarani Devi* (1984)1 CLJ 10.
11 AIR 1956 SC 17.
12 AIR 1972 Cal 333.
13 AIR 1957 Ori 76 (DB).

(E) MINERAL PROPERTY

Mineral properties are fixed assets in limited supply which, if consumed, cannot be replaced on the same location. They are, therefore, known as wasting assets. They are also non-mineral wasting assets which exhaust their resources in proportion to the consumption. Waste disposal sites and burial grounds are examples of non-mineral waste assets. Minerals form part of the corpus of the land and may be owned along with surface. It is also possible to have varying rights with regard to such mineral-bearing land, such as, the right to extract minerals in varying terms and conditions or leasing of the surface under a separate title. As a general rule, all mineral property belong to the State in conformity to its power of eminent domain. Lease of surface land or the right of extraction is the title that a private person or an organisation may obtain.

Minerals are found at varying depths below the surface, from surface itself down to thousands of metres. It is possible to dispose of minerals separately from the surface, either by selling or leasing strata of minerals, and retaining the surface, or by disposing of the surface and retaining the strata of minerals. This disposal of minerals can be selective, that is selecting certain types or strata of minerals. Where the deed of severance is clear and unambiguous there is generally no difficulty in deciding whether or not a particular mineral is included in the reservation. But it often happens that lack of clarity leads to confusion. For example the surface may be *china clay* and the properties of *keolin* therein may have a dominant use for the manufacturing of high quality paper, which might not have been contemplated at the time of grant. This subsequent discovery of more value may give rise to competing claims unless the documentation is clear. As a matter of fact, "mines and minerals" in a grant generally means what passes for in the mining parlour or commercial world. Hence, the necessity for precision with future change in technology in vision.

Another controversy arises with regard to establishing ownership of minerals when there is the question of the removal of the right of support of the adjacent or superjacent land. Where the surface and minerals are in the same ownership there is no problem; but if it is otherwise, problems may arise when minerals are severed from the surface, which is dependant on the minerals for support. There is a presumption of a right of support for the surface unless by necessary implication or express words it is made clear that there is a contrary intention. The problems of support equally apply as between adjacent owners of land and a right to remove support from superjacent surface may or may not extend to a right to remove support from the adjacent land, depending upon the construction of the deed of severance and the law of the land applicable.

Considerations for valuation

It is not easy to lay down a distinct valuation process for this species of land that bear the minerals since such land may be on the surface or also beneath the sea. The mineral valuer is principally interested in the dimensions of mineral deposits and therefore in the quantity of minerals present, together with the proportion of the constituent upon which the economic value of the deposit depends. It is important that a deposit should not only be sufficiently large, but that it should also have a value of sale, sufficiently high, to provide an adequate return on capital invested after costs of working have been deducted. A knowledge of mining geology can enable him to draw the correct inferences. But it is relevant to outline certain distinct characteristics of such property which have definite bearing on the process of valuation. First of all, it is an essential characteristic of an wasting asset that when consumed, it cannot be replaced on the same location which means that a land bearing minerals will have no value when that mineral-bearing portion comes to an end of its useful life. In other words, mineral extraction consumes the land over a period of time. Thus, the concept of existing use can include both the interior surface use of the reserved land and its eventual consumption for mineral working. But that should not lead to an admission that the land becomes absolutely devoid of value on the expiry of its existing use. The question of after-use of the property persistently arises in the realm of valuation. Thus the normal concept of existing use may be modified to include the after-use value even though this may involve a change of use. The value of the after-use may often be a significant proportion of the valuation. In any assessment of after-use value, proper consideration must be given to restoration liabilities which may be imposed under the law for the time being in force. Much would depend on the planning regulations that lay down the relevant conditions.

The valuation of the mineral deposit in production will usually encompass not merely the cost of extraction of deposits but also the cost of exploration carried out to identify reserves and the cost of opening up and developing the deposits.

The mineral valuer has generally to consider the mineral deposits in four classes—superficial, beds, veins, and masses. Superficial deposits originated when material were deposited on the eroded surface of the earth. The deposition may be caused by the erosion and re-deposition of older rock fragments by the action of rivers or by glacial action. For example, sand and gravels found in the river valleys which are of significant economic value. Beds are an integral part of the formation in which they occur. Thus coal seams are composed of the metamorphosed remains of plant material. In another class of bedded deposit, the value as mineral deposits may depend upon chemical changes which have occurred in the materials originally forming the bed. The mineral valuer has to consider not only the extent to which alteration has taken place which will depend on the nature of the overlying stratum and the movement of water through it. Mineral veins are the result of infilling of fissures and faults in the earth's crust. They are largely vertical or near vertical, but may also be horizontal amongst the adjoining beds. Evaluation of veins is far more difficult as keen observation is necessary to reveal a pattern which will enable predictions to be made in order to arrive at an equally reliable opinion of value. Masses are irregular bodies having no definite geometrical shape. Most masses owe their origin to the filling of cavities or to changes in soluble rocks. Some of the masses are connected with igneous rocks and show a greater tendency to regularity in shape, which account for economic value. Igneous masses are very often of value for use as road-stones and sometimes as building stones and constructional aggregates.

Royalties and rents

A lease of property in the usual sense is the grant by one to another of the use of the property for a fixed term. At the end of the term the property is handed back to the lessor for his further use. The terms of the grant provide for the payment of a rent or royalty as well as the way in which it can be used. The difference between mines and minerals is that the terms for return of the property is at the end of the lease in a state fit for further use which is relevant in the case of mines but cannot be so in the case of minerals. In the case of extraction of minerals, they can be leased for extraction either in whole or in part. Often the term is for such duration as to enable all the minerals to be worked. A mining lease has two important features which distinguish it from other leases. First is the method of payment of rent and second is the general aim of the agreement applicable to a wasting asset.

Mining leases usually contain provision for surface rent or royalty or both. Surface rents are payable periodically at a fixed sum. Often, a minimum rent is fixed regardless of the amount of minerals extracted while in other cases rent takes into account the occupancy of the land and quantum of minerals consistently extracted.

Royalties payable on the leasehold is another consideration that enter into valuation. This is to be compared in the light of the volume and quality of the recoverable and saleable reserves. The likely rates of future output is also a pertinent consideration. Then comes the question of costs of operation with regard to current and potential profitability. Generally speaking, the cost of operation escalates with extraction in remote zones. But potential profitability depends on prices of the output at the current and future market rate. The location of the mineral property is another factor. If it is situated in proximity to the area of demand with good transport facilities, the potential profitability is enhanced, but existence of mines and minerals do not always abide by such laws of economics and may require infrastructure to be subsequently built up as new sites are discovered.

After-use and interim use of land

Conditions of tenure is yet another major factor. Unless the minerals to be valued are severed from the surface, the valuation will include elements of value of the surface as well as of the minerals. It may quite happen that the extraction is deferred in the future and the question of use of the land during the interim period consistent with its ultimate use for extraction may arise as an issue for valuation. The surface land scheduled for extraction ought to have a potential for another use at the date of valuation if the extraction is deferred. It is a consideration reverse of after-use. While in after-use the valuation has to take account of the potential of the user after the expiry of the useful life of mineral deposit, in the issue under consideration, the process of valuation has to take account of the interim use of the land prior to extraction. Thus the concept of open market value for existing use may have to be suitably modified in case of mineral property.

Fixed plant and machinery in mineral assets

Last but not the least, mineral assets normally include the ancillary buildings and site improvement and very often the fixed plant and machinery. The buildings will normally fall into the category of specialised buildings and have to be valued on the basis of depreciated replacement cost. It may be necessary to place a value on the site of the buildings and that on the plant which is additional to the value of mineral reserve. The plant and machinery might have a life co-extensive to the wasting assets which they serve. After which they may have only salvage value. All these considerations may enter into valuation of the plant and machinery which of course are to be valued in accordance with the other normal guiding principles.

Whether sub-soil right is included in lease

Interesting questions arise in the realm of land acquisition as to whether the land-owner is entitled to compensation for quarries and mines that pass on to the Government along with the land acquired or should such mines or quarries by taken as property of the State by virtue of its power of eminent domain for which no compensation is payable under the Land Acquisition Act. In the case of *State of Mysore* v *Swamy Satyanand Saraswati, Rajchur,*[14] the question arose whether the land-owner was entitled to sub-soil rights by virtue of the *pattas* granted in favour of his predecessor in-interest by Nawab Salar Jang III. The property was acquired for the Tungabhadra Project under the Hyderabad Land Acquisition Act 1946. The

14 AIR 1971 SC 1569.

pattas only indicated that the grant was for the purpose of cultivation or grazing of cattle with express reservation of the trees on the land to the grantor. But the land which is a large block contained hillock of granite. The issue was raised as to whether the land-owner was entitled to compensation on the basis of the sub-soil rights to the hillock. The Supreme Court answered it in the negative holding that the grant was to allow the user of the surface only and it would be wrong to presume, in the absence of any express mention in the lease, that the sub-soil rights were also conferred thereby. A different approach was, however, taken in the case of *Special Tehsildar, Land Acquisition, Yerraguntla* v *Kamalagangi Reddy,*[15] wherein it was held that the owner of a surface of the land is entitled *ex jure* to everything beneath the land and in the absence of any reservation in the grant, mineral necessarily pass with the rights to the surface. So a transfer of the right to the surface conveys right to minerals underneath unless there is an express or implied reservation in the grant.

Whether possession of mine includes possession of land

The issue was approached from another angle in the case of *P.P. Chakraborty* v *Coal India Ltd.*[16] Here the question arose as to whether the possession of the mines includes possession of the land as well. The court answered in the affirmative. The land in dispute was covered by coal mines of which the mine and not the land vested in the Central Government under the Coal Mines (Nationalisation) Act 1973. It was held that the possession of the mines includes possession of the land and hence a direction as to delivery of possession of land to the landowner was improper. Instead, the authority were directed to determine compensation payable to the landowner under s. 23 of the Land Acquisition Act 1894 (now s. 47 of the Right to Fair Compensation and Transparency in Land Acquisition, Rehabilitation and Resettlement Act 2013).

Valuation method as decided by courts

In *State of Kerala* v *Malayalam Plantations Ltd.*,[17] the question of the ascertaining the value of quarry came up for decision.

15 AIR 1990 AP 124.
16 AIR 1991 NOC 97 (AP).
17 AIR 1981 Ker 1; ILR (1981) Ker 1.

It was held that the quarry acquired can be valued on a capitalisation basis or on a quantitative basis. The special adaptability of the land for quarrying purposes is important for fixing the amount of compensation. In *Additional Special L.A.O., Mangalore* v *A. Anantha Bhatt,*[18] it was decided that if the value of ten quarry were to be assessed independently, such assessment becomes a part of the compensation payable to land. It will not be correct to compute the value of the land and the quarry separately awarding compensation in regard to both. An area covered by granite rock has to be valued as one unit and not separately as land and granite.[19] In another case *Additional Special L.A.O. Ports, Mangalore* v *K.T. Alva*[20] the authority for whom the acquisition was made, had inspected the site and were satisfied that granite was available in abundant quantity for the purpose of construction of Mangalore Port. The L.A. Judge took the rate of yield as notified by the Government as the basis and adopted the multiple of 20 to arrive at the market value. The same was held as the valid method.

Factors affecting valuation

The royalty rate charged for a mineral generally reflects all the circumstances that effect the value of the mineral. The factors which influence royalty rates may be as follows:

(*a*) *Quality of the mineral.* The royalty rates are levied generally on the basis of physical and chemical characteristics of the mining property. Metally ferrous minerals can be refined in processing to meet a specification and in this case ratio of rock-to-ore might influence the royalty level. The other features like quality of deposits or beds and the extent of veins and masses are also important.

(*b*) *Contamination of the mineral.* External contamination arises when a volume of lower grade material has to be extracted with more valuable ones. The contamination may be removed by washing or

18 AIR 1972 Mys 313.
19 *A.K. Ahmed* v *Special L.A.O., CITB* (1974)2 Kant LJ 1.
20 AIR 1976 Kant 99.

screening, which involve processing cost that affect valuation. As for example, coal with high ash content is considered impurities. A limestone chemically changed to dolomite is an example of intrinsic contamination, which cannot be readily removed.

(c) *Water table.* Almost all mines work minerals from beneath the natural water table and thus require more or less constant pumping. In extreme cases pumping costs may render the mining uneconomic for use while provision for surface run off, cut off drains etc. may ease the problem.

(d) *Ease of working.* Geological factors may cause the deposit to be inclined at a high angle, folded or faulted, where the stratum has to be torn apart and the mineral displaced laterally or vertically. Igneous rocks sometimes display columnar jointing which can make working conditions hazardous. Some rocks are more easily worked than others in the way that they fragment well on blasting or require a minimum of crushing whereas the others may need more expensive processes. Where a mineral deposit is highly disturbed the costs of working may go up. All these factors enter into valuation.

(e) *Access to the market.* The importance of markets within easy reach is needless to emphasise. The distance which a mineral can economically be transported clearly depends in the location of the mine and the vicinity of disposing of the finished good.

(f) *Supporting surfaces.* Availability of water and electricity are quite important. Transport from the operation to the main node of communication is another big factor. Where a large number of staff are employed, housing facilities and other infrastructure for community living poses a big consideration. Railway linkage is very worthy criterion and so also the proximity of the highways. Last but not the least, the applicability of the town and country planning parameters and the environmental factors cannot be ignored.

(F) PLANT AND MACHINERY

Plant, machinery and equipment collectively constitute an exclusive class of property other than real estate and are accordingly classified as tangible assets for accounting purposes. As tangible asset, such property may admit of the following situations of market transactions:

(*i*) plant and machinery may be purchased and sold as isolated asset;

(*ii*) plant and machinery may be purchased and sold in conjunction with a variety of other tangible and intangible assets that constitute a business or industrial undertaking as a whole;

(*iii*) plant and machinery in the nature of building or structure which are usually considered to form part of building service installations or as claddings for industrial installations.

Plant, machinery or equipment—what it means

In common parlance, 'plant and machinery' usually refers to 'installations and support facilities for manufacturing in an industry designed to perform a specific predetermined function to enhance the productivity or operating facility in manufacturing or processing of products, from the stage of raw materials to finished goods'. But as we have seen plant and machinery can be conceived as tangible asset other than in industrial use; for example, for rendering specific building services or as an isolated marketable asset, particularly machinery or equipment which are often marketed as independent apparatus whether for industrial use or other purposes. But the fact remains that capital assets like plant and machinery worth the nomenclature are mostly the result of the industrial revolution and accordingly appear in our mind in the context of industries where they are treated as fixed assets. All said and done, 'plant' includes assemblage of assets that may comprise specialized structures, machinery or equipment, the purpose of the structure being to offer support facility to the installations. 'Machinery' is a produced means of production using power, electrical, mechanical or manual and employed as apparatus for definite function in a process of production. 'Equipment' on the other hand includes ancillary assets that are used to assist the productive function in an enterprise, viz. trailors, lorries, tractors, computer installations, photo-copier, telephone system, fire-engine and the like.

Distinctive considerations in valuation

In the context of valuation, plant, machinery and equipments involve considerations, somewhat different from real estates. We have seen that each real estate has some unique feature and that being so, one is not an exact substitute for the other. In the method of market comparison, we look for a comparable asset and not an identical asset and adjust the value of the subject asset with due consideration to the plus and minus factors of the comparable assets. This uniqueness arises out of the fact that land and building are immovable property imbedded in a particular location which cannot be mechanically reproduced except *in situ*. But plant, machinery and equipments though often imbedded on earth are regarded as fully replaceable assets. In view of this, the market value of plant, machinery and equipment rests on the assumption that a prudent purchaser would pay no more for an asset than the cost of acquiring an equally functional substitute in the market.

Again, the cost of the substitute, often includes such costs as would be necessary to make the asset productive, viz. transportation, installation, attachment to utilities and start-up. These costs are sometimes called "make-ready" costs or costs on "turn-key" basis. This is more pronounced when plant and machinery are considered as a fixed asset working in conjunction with other tangible and intangible assets in an operating concern or act as an installation and support facility for processes or manufacturing.

Machinery and equipment valued in isolation

Being assets substitutable in nature, the value of any individualised machinery or equipment depends on the following major factors:

(*a*) physical—type, model, capacity, make etc.

(*b*) social—taste and preferences of consumers using products manufactured by the machinery.

(*c*) economic—demand and supply, availability of money and credit, interest rate.

(*d*) legal—taxation policy, regulation of industry, environmental protection.

Thus the process of valuation requires the preparation of an inventory in the form of a Schedule which is very important from valuation point of view as substitutability would abide only by such specifications. The extent of details to be included in such a Schedule is a matter of judgment of the valuer but information on the following points are relevant in the preparation of inventory:

(*i*) description;

(*ii*) model, serial number and maker's name;

(*iii*) client's own plant reference number;

(*iv*) size or capacity;

(*v*) age;

(*vi*) reference to any special foundations, service connections, accessories as the case may be;

(*vii*) modifications, renovations carried out after installation;

(*viii*) energy consumption;

(*ix*) environmental and other legal restrictions if any;

(*x*) usage;

(*xi*) record of production and maintenance.

Valuation of such individualised item of machinery or equipment is best done with market approach. When there is an established product market for such items, the sale price between a willing buyer and willing seller at arm's length transaction offers the most reliable data for valuation.

Valuation of plant and machinery as building

Plant and machinery which are in the nature of building and structure have obtained distinctive consideration in the realm of rating. The Common Law of England recognized that any plant and machinery sufficiently affixed to land or buildings become rateable as part of that property. The judicial decisions also reiterated the view. In the case of *Smith* v *Willesden Union* (1919), it was held that in valuing the hereditament, the assessment must be based on the rent that would be paid for the land, buildings and plant and machinery on the assumption that the hypothetical landlord has provided it, whether or not, he in fact has done so.

Building services that are within plant, machinery and equipment may include electricity, gas, water, space heating, hot water, air-conditioning and ventillation, fire security, drainage, and lifts and gantries, among others. Accordingly, the Rating and Valuation Act 1925, identified in U.K. four classes of rateable plant and machinery in its Third Schedule. The Valuation for Rating (Plant and Machinery) Regulations 1994 which is now in vogue in U.K. has embellished the Schedule with additions in all the four classes of rateable plant and machinery. This long list identifying plant and machinery as part of building and structure is also reflected in the municipal legislations in the different States all over India in order to bring them within the ambit of rateability. In this way, plant and machinery forming a part of building service installations and enumerated as such in the relevant Schedule of the municipal laws of our country constitute a distinctive category. They *inter alia* comprise the following items—

— air-conditioning plant with ducting;
— electrical installations for Plant and Machinery;
— water and sewerage installations;
— chimneys and boilers;
— brick or concrete structures, foundation, and tanks associated with plant;
— effluent treatment plant;
— overhead cranes and steelwork for crane;
— alarm installations;
— underground as well as overhead tanks.

Needless to say, the above list is not exhaustive but only illustrative. The lists in the relevant Schedule are amended from time to time.

It may be necessary to provide an apportionment of value as between:

(*a*) land and buildings; and

(*b*) plant and machinery which forms part of a building.

In such circumstances, the valuation is of the whole and an apportionment is made of the overall value on treating the plant and machinery as a part of the hereditament and it is the rental value of the entire hereditament that is required to be worked out for the purpose of apportionment. The method of valuation is usually on cost basis considering the plant and machinery either as separate items within a rental valuation or as items within a property valued on the contractor's method. In other words, computation of value for apportionment is made by reference to—

(*a*) the value of the land plus the net current replacement cost of the buildings; and

(*b*) the net current replacement cost of the plant and machinery.

In any case, plant and machinery should not be regarded as an "add on" at the end of the valuation. The rateable value of the property is a usually a prescribed percentage of the capital value worked out on cash basis as above. The rateable value provides the taxable base for levy of municipal rate as fixed by law.

Valuation of plant and machinery operating in conjunction

The valuation of plant and machinery in such case is a complex process as it pertains to a wide spectrum of items with inherent characteristics and functions working in conjunction with the subject plant and machinery. Amongst the issues to be considered in the valuation of plant and machinery are the specific utility or usefulness of the asset, its contribution to the production of goods and services and its potential to contribute to the profitability of the business. It is ultimately a matter of techno-commercial evaluation and requires a thorough understanding about the role of the machine, its useful economic life, aspects of depreciation and obsolescence. Finally, the contribution of each item to productivity would depend upon the value of the business as a going concern. The value acquired by the whole brings allocation of higher value to the parts of fractions.

Useful Economic Life

A plant and machinery extensively used or not properly maintained may become useless much before its normal life as against a plant or machinery of the same type which is well looked after with maintenance and servicing done as per established norms. When plant and machinery has been sparingly used, it may have a considerably longer residual life, notwithstanding the years of use. Thus it is necessary to make a physical evaluation of each plant and machinery to arrive at the remaining age or estimate the balance economic life after proper judgment.

The following aspects pertinently arise in determining the balance economic life:

(*a*) existing physical condition and rate of use;

(*b*) year of acquisition;

(*c*) routine and special maintenance, including; reconditioning, rebuilding or retrofitting, *vis-a-vis* depreciation;

(*d*) operational efficiency, and contribution to productivity *vis-a-vis* obsolescence.

Depreciation

Depreciation is loss in value that may be caused by deterioration, decay, wear and tear or damage of any kind which changes the physical condition so as to reduce usefulness. In case of plant and machinery, depreciation adversely affects its value to a potential buyer. The method of reckoning depreciation in case of plant and machinery has to take the following considerations in view:

(*a*) Age and estimated economic balance life;

(*b*) Present capital value to be recouped in instalments during the remaining life of the asset and not lump sum amount at the end of life;

(*c*) Rate of recovery at an increasing rate for a period in the beginning and decreasing rate subsequently;

(*d*) Value of plant and machinery to decline slowly in the beginning and faster during mid-life and maximum at the end;

(*e*) History of repairs and maintenance;

(*f*) Rate of yield declining during the remaining life;

(*g*) Factors for consideration of a willing buyer and a willing seller;

(*h*) Number of working hours per shift per day, applicable during a defined period;

(*i*) Wear and tear *vis-a-vis* maintenance;

(*j*) Effect of surrounding weather conditions, and environment;

(*k*) Anticipated scrap value.

Obsolescence

Obsolescence may be identified in four aspects,—technological, functional, economic or statutory. Technological obsolescence arises due to change in design and materials of construction of the plant and machinery under consideration. It is usual to find the emergence of sophisticated items in the market with improved efficiency, reduced occupancy of space and optimum energy consumption. It is often found economic to replace the existing plant and machinery with the latest technology in the field for increasing the rate of production or reducing the operating cost and the old plant and machinery rendered technologically obsolete.

Functional obsolescence arises when a machine already in function loses its optimum capacity owing to a decline in cooperation from its operating counterparts. It may arise due to a variety of internal reasons. The company might have been compelled to commission a machine of high rated capacity simply because a low-rated one is not available. In such situation the operating counterparts may not be geared to give the machine an opportunity for optimum output resulting in functional obsolescence. Non-availability of spares and accessories, faulty design and wrong location of installations are the other usual factors that give rise to functional obsolescence.

Economic obsolescence arise due to factors external to the plant and machinery itself. This could be due to changes in the fashion or design or otherwise change in demand of the product manufactured; or shrinkage in supply of raw materials and labour; or new legislations affecting taxes or duties on the product.

Obsolescence caused by new legislative measures imposing environmental control or zoning restrictions; or construction or building restrictions in sea-coasts or in the vicinity of airports or for enforcing any town and country planning law may be characterised as statutory obsolescence.

Approaches to value

It has already been stated that valuation of plant and machinery operating in conjunction with other items of productive functions present a complex situation which is entirely different from others. Such plant and machinery are only part or fraction of a 'whole'. The value of the whole depends upon the income stream derivable as business; or its marketability for an adequate monetary return; or utility measuring both monetary and non-monetary return. The portion comprised in a particular plant and machinery can be evalued either as fraction or part depending on the purpose for which valuation is made. It is a common practice to value such itemised piece of plant and machinery by determining the cost new of each item from which depreciation is deducted. The value of the whole property is then reported as the sum of the values of the parts or fractions. By considering each portion separately and independently of the whole, each portion has been treated as a fraction but it does not follow that the value of the enterprise as a whole is equal to the sum of the values of these fractions in spite of the fact that each of the fractions was correctly valued.

In determining the value of the whole property, the following considerations necessarily arise. If the industry is a successful going concern with an earning expectancy more than sufficient to pay fair annual rate of return on the sum of the values of the fractions, then apart from the tangible assets, we can discover another part in the form of intangible assets like "goodwill of the business" that account for the total earning expectancy exceeding the annual return allocated to tangibles. The intangibles like goodwill, patents, know-how etc. often account for the value of business in much larger proportion than the contribution of the tangibles. Hence this constitute a separate field of study which is dealt with in the next section of this book.

As for the present, it may be said that if the earning expectancy of the whole is less than sufficient to pay a fair annual rate of return on the sum of the values of the fraction, then the value of the whole property may be either the amount obtained by capitalizing this earning expectancy, or the sum of the liquidating values of the physical fractions, whichever is higher. It is presumed that there is no intangible element in such situation which can lend a higher value to the whole property. An income approach to valuation perhaps gives the best tool of measurement in such situation as it bears reflection of the total depreciation of all assets and a full account of the obsolescences that depreciate the value of all assets in aggregate. The income approach cannot segregate specific assets in the process of valuation as it becomes very difficult to identify the value of specific assets without same sort of arbitrary allocation. The value of the whole property, can thus be determined by income approach with much better approximation than through the market or cost approach. If, the liquidation value of each fraction has to be ascertained instead of the earning expectancy of the whole property, resort can be had only to the market approach. Since there may often be a difficulty of availability of comparable sales, adequate care has to be taken to identify the marketable features of the individual fraction like age of the machine, its condition, features including accessories, location, manufacturer, price, quality, quantity etc. for the purpose of comparison.

A few court cases reflect on valuation of plant and machinery in our country. In dealing with the question of the vires of Metal Corporation of India, Acquisition of Undertaking Act XLIV of 1965, the Supreme Court made some important observations in *Union of India* v *Metal Corporation of India Ltd.*[1]

> "It is common knowledge that there has been an upward spiral in prices of machinery in recent years. The cost price of machinery purchased about 10 years ago is a consideration not relevant for fixing compensation for its acquisition in 1965. The principles must be such as to enable the ascertainment of its price at or about the time of acquisition. Nor the doctrine of written down value accepted in the income tax law can afford any guide for ascertaining the compensation for the used machinery acquired under that Act. Under the general scheme...........the artificial

1 AIR 1967 SC 637; (1967)1 SCR 255.

rule of depreciation evolved in income tax purposes has no relation to the value of the assets viz. machinery, buildings, plant etc. The doctrine of inherent work of a machinery has no relevance in the matter of giving compensation for its acquisition at a particular point of time, for the simple reason that the worth of an article depends upon the market condition obtaining at the time of its acquisition. It is impossible to predicate, irrespective of such conditions that a particular machinery has a fixed value for all times."

The said Act was held void being violative of Article 31(2) of the Constitution of India.

The Supreme Court after reviewing the evolution of the law pertaining to compensation for compulsory acquisition upheld the validity of the principle of capitalising the net profits as the sole factor for determining the compensation payable for acquisition of a public limited company. It was further held that tangible and intangible property of a public utility undertaking may not be valued separately. So, the principle for a valuation of the undertaking including the machinery is not open to challenge as the legislation held valid.[2]

Appropriate approach in valuation of plant and machinery

In valuation of plant and machinery, cost approach rests mainly on principles of substitution. Valuer compares an existing facility to its modern counterpart. But it fails to assess a full measure of economic obsolescence in its objectivity as it blindly computes the costs.

The market approach is reliable if only appropriate market data are available. But comparable sales offer an unsurmountable problem. Even when there are sufficient sales, we may not have sufficient knowledge as to whether the sale is induced by compulsion, liquidation, or speculation. Transaction of identical asset is another big question. A valuer shall have to take care to identify the age of the machine, its condition, features including accessories, location, manufacturer, price, quality, quantity, and etc. for the purpose of comparison of sales.

2 *Oriental Gas Ltd.* v *State of West Bengal* (1979)1 SCC 171.

The income approach is perhaps the best measurement of the total depreciation of all assets and bears reflection of the rationale behind all business decisions. The relative strength of income approach is its ability to project the full amount of economic obsolescence and at the same time measure the value of all assets in aggregate, not achievable through the use of market or cost approach to that extent. Of course, the income approach cannot segregate specific assets in the process of valuation as it becomes very difficult to identify the value of specific assets without some sort of arbitrary allocation. In spite of such infirmity, it is the only approach for valuation of a going concern business where an appropriate overview of contribution of each asset working capital, fixed or intangible, is called for as a whole.

(G) BUSINESS VALUATION

Business valuation is a complicated process as business has a large area as its hinterland comprising innumerable influences that account for its success or failure. The range of the hinterland is contoured by factors—economic, social and no less political or even diplomatic. The productivity of the assets is no doubt a fundamental factor. The assets as we have seen may be tangible or intangible or financial assets. The tangible assets include land and building, plant and machinery, equipment, etc. The intangibles include intellectual property like copyright, patent, trademark, design, trade secrets, managerial efficiency as well as intellectual capital like human resources employed. The other intangibles are good will, effective contacts, sales promotion, advertisement, etc. No less important in such valuation is the prospect of business triggered by prevailing technological changes, fashion, environmental norms, political patronage etc. In the present global context, availability of foreign funds in capital inflow and outflow and even political stability, nature of governance, diplomatic relations amongst nations, create conditions for thriving of business prospects or its decline. As regards social factors,—taboos or prejudices, or religious perceptions—do often bear upon business. Unseen factors are also at play. A tsunami may devastate all business hopes, or may open up economic avenues for re-construction; the outbreak or sudden bird flu or a mad cow disease may prove disastrous to business.

It is quite imaginable how difficult it is to assess a correct valuation of business for any purpose whatsoever. But the foreseeable factors provide a reliable data for appraisal. In general terms the value of a business consists of the contributions made by (*a*) net fixed assets, together with, (*b*) net current assets, along with (*c*) goodwill, as well as (*d*) other intangibles if any.

Issues for valuation consideration

The following practical issues pertinently arise for consideration in business valuation.

1. How the market is growing?
2. How the Company's efforts are directed towards increasing share in the market domain. For example, (*a*) formation of subsidiaries, (*b*) contracts at hand, (*c*) distribution channels (*d*) whether sales strategy is distributed over a large number of customers so that one single customer cannot decide the fate of the Company.
3. Company's position *vis-a-vis* competitors.
4. Mode of payment for contracts like advances, period for payment, credit facilities etc.
5. Advertising and sales promotion strategy.
6. Barriers to new entrants of competitors.
7. Capacity of trained personnel and scope for out-sourcing or sub-contracting.
8. Whether the buildings, offices, plant or machinery are owned or leased and the terms thereof.
9. Whether the process is capital-intensive; if not, the availability of skilled personnel at reasonable rate.
10. Foreign tie-up possibilities foreign market potentials, impact of legal framework *vis-a-vis* globalisation.
11. Flexibility in personnel management and the legal impediments to rationalisation involving discharge of hands.
12. Financial analysis of the project including analysis of past performance and projection for future.
13. Non-operating assets and their potential.

14. Research and Development in technology holding threat for obsolescence.

(H) RELEVANT DATA FOR BUSINESS VALUATION

Financial statements and other financial data

1. Annual financial statements for the last five years.
2. Interim financial statements for the recent 12 months and the preceding 12 month period.
3. Union Government's prescribed income tax returns for the last five years.
4. Copies of any forecasts or projections.
5. List of subsidiaries or other businesses in which the subject company has an ownership interest, together with their financial statements.
6. List of cash accounts and any significant cash investments.
7. Aged accounts receivable listing.
8. List of items comprising inventory (quantity, description, and cost) and information on inventory accounting policies.
9. Fixed asset register or depreciation schedule.
10. List of items comprising significant other asset balances.
11. Accounts payable listing, preferably aged.
12. Analyses of significant accrued liabilities.
13. List of payables and other interest-bearing debt.
14. List of items comprising significant other liability balances.
15. Schedule of sales by product for each period from which an income statement is obtained.
16. List of accounts comprising significant major expense captions on the income statement, unless that data is presented on the income statement.
17. Copies of sales, capital, or operating budgets.
18. Copies of any business plans.
19. Schedule of officers' and directors' compensation.
20. Schedule of key person life insurance.

21. Reports of other professionals or consultants for appraisal, if any.

Other operating data

22. Brochures, price lists, catalogues, or other product information.
23. List of stockholders or partners, showing the amount of stock or percentage owned by each person.
24. Organization chart.
25. List of five largest customers and suppliers and the total amount of sales and purchases respectively, for each during the last year.
26. Details of transaction with related parties.

Legal documents

27. Copies of significant leases and loans, including receivables and payables.
28. Copies of stockholder or partnership agreements, including any stock option agreements.
29. Minutes of board of directors meetings.
30. Copies of any buy-sell agreements and/or written offers to purchase or sell company stock.
31. Copies of key managers' employment contracts.
32. Copies of any major sale or purchase contracts.
33. Details of any litigation, including pending or threatened law suits.
34. Detail of any employee benefit plans, including pension plans, profit-sharing plans, and employee stock option plans.
35. Collective bargaining agreement.
36. Reports of examination issued by Government agencies.
37. Attorney's invoices/billing statements.

Other company data

38. Detail of transactions in the company's stock during the last 5 years.
39. List of any of the following:
    (*a*) Patents
    (*b*) Copyrights.

(c) Trademarks.

(d) Similar intangibles.

40. Details of any contingent liabilities (such as guarantees or warranties) or off balance sheet financing (such as letters of credit).

41. Resumes or a summary of the background and experience of all key personnel.

42. Copies of any other value indicators, such as property tax appraisals.

(I) ECONOMIC DATA

National economic data

43. Data on economic trend (GNP, inflation, employment levels, etc.).

Regional and local Economic and Demographic Data.

44. Data on regional and local demographics and economic conditions. Possible sources of such data include.

Market data

45. Appraisals of specific assets, if appropriate.

46. Data on market rates of return.

Valuation techniques for business enterprise by income approach

RATE OF RETURN. There are various techniques for appraisal of investment in business. One of them is assessment by accounting the rate of return on capital employed which is simply the profit produced by an investment expressed as a percentage of capital outlay.

PAY BACK COMPUTATION. Under this technique, the time taken for the income flowing into an investment to recoup the capital outlay is determined. To take an example, let us consider the following chart.

Year	Out flow	Inflow
0	₹ 50,00,000	
1		₹ 10,00,000
2		₹ 10,00,000
3		₹ 15,00,000
4		₹ 15,00,000
5 onwards		₹ 15,00,000

By the end of the 4th year, total income of ₹ 50,00,000 will have been received; therefore the investment will pay back the outlay within 4 years.

Ratios in business valuation

The value of a business is the synergic effect as reflected in the financial statement or seen through any other alternative analysis, as a result of the combined productivity of net Current Assets (CA) and net Fixed Assets (FA) together with intangibles including goodwill, if any. The productive efficiency of capital employed, both CA and FA, would depend upon factors including security as well as liquidity of capital, regularity and security of yield or income, capital appreciation prospects, ease of purchase or sale etc. The financial assets ought to admit of divisibility of holdings and guard against inflation by security in real income.

A ratio is nothing but a mathematical relationship of two quantities that provides a qualitative assessment and meaning to one key financial statement item relative to the other. The most important financial statements which are commonly used for the purpose are the statement of profit and loss and balance sheet for a particular period. These statements are usually analysed for a period of several years and the same are compared with similar data of other companies in the same industry and often with that of the entire industry averaged as such. In comparing ratios, it is important to ensure that the ratios are compiled on the same basis as those with which they are being compared. For example, all ratios should be computed using ending balances in the balance sheet if they are being compared to industry data or ratios of companies which also use balance sheet accounts. If, however, the average of the beginning and ending of the balance, or the beginning balance of the balance sheet is used, the same criterion should be followed. When a ratio is compiled using both an income statement variable and a balance sheet variable, the balance sheet variable would ideally represent the average amount for the period for which the income statement variable was calculated.

The ratio analysis help locating areas of comparative strengths and weaknesses of different companies. The ratios may be, classified under the following major heads:

(*i*) Liquidity ratio;

(*ii*) Profitability ratio;

(*iii*) Activity ratio;

(*iv*) Leverage ratio.

In liquidity ratio the purpose is to assess the short term solvency of the business so that the revenue earning cycle may go unhampered. It is intended to reflect the self-liquidating nature of the Current Assets (CA) so as to cover the Current Liabilities (CL). The financial institutions and banks are known to assign much importance to it in lending funds. A deteriorating ratio of CA against CL, i.e. $\frac{CA}{CL}$ is taken as an evidence of corporate failure, the quantum of current assets available being unable to meet the short-term financial obligations. The standard ratio, whether 1:1 or 1:5 or 2:1, depends upon various factors like type of industry, business policy, future expectations, cost of credit etc. No definite standard can be prescribed as a general rule.

Sometimes 'quick assets' meaning current assets less inventory and pre-paids are considered against current liabilities to arrive at an acid-test.

The factors that affect the profitability or earnings of any business are reflected in profitability ratio being expressed as percentage of return on capital employed during a given period. The return can be influenced by increasing the turn-over of capital by sales promotion and/or by reducing the capital employed for achieving a target figure of sales. The earnings in such case represent only earnings out of operations and generally speaking, non-operating capital such as investments, loans for non-business purposes, sale of fixed assets etc. are left out of account. Consequently, interest do not enter into such accounting which is confined to earnings before interest. Since the objective is to ascertain what is the ultimate earnings of the company out of share holders' funds, it is customary to ascertain the ratio of pre-tax earnings against total assets or as against net sales or as against stock holders' equity. Because, the rate of taxation payable by the company is not within its managerial competence. The utmost the company can do is window dressing of income and asset towards minimum tax liability. The ratio of gross profit meaning net sales minus cost of sales as against net sale, is also a mode of ascertaining profitability.

To summarize, the profitability ratio consists in—

(*a*) $\dfrac{\text{Pre-tax earnings}}{\text{Total Assets}}$

(*b*) $\dfrac{\text{Pre-tax earnings}}{\text{Net sales}}$

(*c*) $\dfrac{\text{Pre-tax earnings}}{\text{Stock holders' equity}}$

(*d*) $\dfrac{\text{Net sales minus costs of sales}}{\text{Net sales}}$

The activity ratio is the most important item for consideration in business valuation. It reveals the level of performance achieved by corporate efforts. It mainly reflects the optimisation of the use of working capital through effective inventory control and also financial handling that achieves quick realisation of the receivables and a regular or smooth cash flow on turn-over of sales. The fixed assets like land, building, plant, machinery and equipment must be put to efficient use towards productivity and ultimate sales. Hence, the ratio of net sales to fixed assets comes in. The average age of inventory is an important consideration. Hence, a ratio is struck between it and cost of sales. Of course, the age of inventory is very much industry-specific and no fixed standard can be prescribed. But the trend of use may reflect efficiency in control. The following ratios pertinently arise in assessing the level of performance:

(*a*) Age of receivables

$$\frac{\text{Average accounts receivables} \times 365 \text{ days}}{\text{Net credit sales}}$$

(*b*) Total asset turnovers

$$\frac{\text{Net sales}}{\text{Total Assets}}$$

(*c*) Sales to working capital

$$\frac{\text{Net sales}}{\text{Working capital}}$$

(d) Age of inventory

$$\frac{\text{Inventory} \times 365 \text{ days}}{\text{Cost of sales}}$$

(*e*) Sales to Net Fixed Assets

$$\frac{\text{Net sales}}{\text{Property, Plant \& Equipment}}$$

(*f*) Sales to Gross Fixed Assets

$$\frac{\text{Net sales}}{\text{Property, Plant \& Equipment plus Accumulated Depreciation}}$$

The Leverage ratio seeks to study the composition of funds deployed by a business unit. The options available can be broadly classified under two heads, viz., (*a*) funds borrowed by issue of debentures bearing fixed interest to be paid together with obligation for repayment as 'Debt'; and (*b*) 'Equity' being fragmental ownership by issue of shares of the company with obligation to service the capital in the form of dividends. The development of the capital market has brought into use various hybrid combinations of the two. A higher proportion of borrowed funds increase the return to the company by what is commonly known as 'trading on thin equity'. But this also exposes the business to the risk of inability to meet the repayment obligation in the event of business failure. There was a time when the lending financial institutions used to insist on 'Debt: Equity ratio' around 2:1. This was taken as reflecting net worth and accepted as bench mark ratio. But with the increase of market nexus and prospects of business in an era of globalisation, a level of 1:1 or even lower is considered acceptable. The leverage arises out of the cumulative advantage derived from the capital structure of the business unit as chosen. The leverage ratio focuses on the long-term component of the total debt and indexes the prospect of the company's business. The business projects with long gestation period have a substantial component of long-term debts which is material for determining such ratio. Thus, the following ratios are generally considered in this context:

(*a*) $$\frac{\text{Long-term debt}}{\text{Stockholders' equity}}$$

(*b*) $$\frac{\text{Fixed Assets}}{\text{Long-term debt}}$$

(*c*) $$\frac{\text{Earnings before Interests \& Taxes}}{\text{Interest Expenses}}$$

Valuation methods

The followings valuation methods are generally adopted for business valuation. The method that is considered most appropriate for any company or ownership interest, has to be carefully selected out of them. Normally, two or more valuation methods are chosen for application with a view to cross-checking the results. The methods not adopted should also be reasoned for.

A. Discounted future return methods:

(*i*) Discounted net cash flow;

(*ii*) Discounted future earnings.

B. Capitalised returns methods:

(*i*) Capitalisation of earnings;

(*ii*) Capitalisation of gross cash flow;

(*iii*) Capitalisation of net cash flow.

C. Value multiples against comparative companies on the basis of:

(*i*) Price: earning ratio;

(*ii*) Price: gross cash flow ratio;

(*iii*) Price: dividends ratio;

(*iv*) Price: book value ratio;

(*v*) Price: revenues ratio;

(*vi*) Price: net asset value ratio.

D. Underlying asset methods:

(*i*) Net asset value or adjusted book value;

(*ii*) Liquidation value.

For an understanding of the ratios, the discussions hereinbefore or elsewhere in the relevant chapters of this book may be helpful. If the above methods of valuation are found not sufficient to reflect the market health of the company. On analysis of the excess earnings or data from actual transactions or any documented offers in respect of the relevant companies stock or any relevant evidence from enforceable contracts may help formulation by rules of thumb.

Appropriate approach in valuation of plant and machinery

In valuation of plant and machinery, cost approach rests mainly on principles of substitution. Valuer compares an existing facility to its modern counterpart. But it fails to assess a full measure of economic obsolescence in its objectivity as it blindly computes the costs.

The market approach is reliable if only appropriate market data are available. But comparable sales offer an unsurmountable problem. Even when there are sufficient sales, we may not have sufficient knowledge as to whether the sale is induced by compulsion, liquidation, or speculation. Transaction of identical asset is another big question. A valuer shall have to take care to identify the age of the machine, its condition, features including accessories, location, manufacturer, price, quality, quantity, and etc. for the purpose of comparison of sales.

The income approach is perhaps the best measurement of the total depreciation of all assets and bears reflection of the rationale behind all business decisions. The relative strength of income approach is its ability to project the full amount of economic obsolescence and at the same time measure the value of all assets in aggregate, not achievable through the use of market or cost approach to that extent. Of course, the income approach cannot segregate specific assets in the process of valuation as it becomes very difficult to identify the value of specific assets without some sort of arbitrary allocation. In spite of such infirmity, it is the only approach for valuation of a going concern business where an appropriate overview of contribution of each asset working capital, fixed or intangible, is called for as a whole.

Business valuation is a growing subject. It encompasses tangible assets, intangible assets and financial assets too. Since business stands on multiple factors each of which merit consideration in the valuation process, a detailed treatment of all complexities and varieties is out of reach in a short treatise. However, a perspective to understanding the basic issues is provided hereafter.

Plant and machinery as we have seen are valued as fixed asset contributing to a business. Since all business investments are aimed at profit, it is usual to assess the rate of return on investment on each item of plant and machinery employed. This does not depend entirely on the inherent productive capability of plant and machinery. As matter of fact, plant and machinery are inanimate asset and their productivity depend not only on their intrinsic efficiency but also in the manner in which those are employed and productivity realised. This leads us to the bigger issues of business including the level of management and goodwill earned. When the entire business assumes greater values owing to efficient management creating goodwill and bringing in other intangibles like patent copyright, technical knowhow etc., the operating plant and machinery obtain better earning capacity as integral part of the whole business. Again, as the business assumes prospects, it has its reflection on the equity which means the stocks and shares not bearing fixed interest. Thus business valuation involves an enquiry into the relationship as amongst earnings, equity and assets of an organisation.

We have discussed in the preceding section how plant and machinery are valued as fixed assets under different situations. In our present discussion, we shall focus attention on business as a whole or, in other words, the relationship between earnings and assets. In the next section, we shall switch over to the aspect of equity, i.e. stocks and shares.

The important aspect in determination of value based on projected earnings is the evaluation of projected earnings and the assumptions that may have been made in establishing such projections. Considerations must be given to the future business plan and strategy to be adopted by the company as regards future expansion and capital expenditure, projections on sales and revenues, need for further capital expenditure and increased working capital requirements, prospects for the industry and for the company among other relevant factors. The reasonableness and realisibility of the projections have to be examined closely in reference to the past performance of the company. Sometimes such projections are highly speculative and based on estimates and guesses as regards managerial efficiency and future prospect of business, the validity of which cannot always be assured. It is for this reason that it may be appropriate to discount these projections and assess the projected earnings on a scientific basis.

Discounted cash flow technique

The discounted cash flow technique is one of the most rigorous approaches to valuation of business. It uses the future expected cash-flows from the business for determining the value of the business. It recognises that money has a time value by discounting the future cash flows at an appropriate discount rate that reflects the risk in those cash flows. The valuation exercise which is basically an income approach projects sales, expenses and profits of the enterprise and then makes adjustments for non-cash expenditures like depreciation and for any infusion of equity capital required to achieve the forecasted profits and then discount the resultant net cash flow back to its present day value. While some experts consider capitalisation of income and discounted cash flow as separate valuation tools in fact both require an earnings analysis of the enterprise and both are therefore variant forms of income approach. Earnings may denote past earnings, projected earnings, realised earnings and cash flow. Under the method of capitalisation of past earnings, past earnings over a period of a business cycle are averaged and then capitalised by an appropriate capitalisation rate to arrive at the value of the business entity. The past earnings may, however, exclude unusual items of repairs, lump sum retirement compensation, abnormal bad debts, remuneration to proprietors, capital expenditure etc. One business cycle would normally be a period of at least 3 to 5 years. But it must be understood that a record of past earnings is a very unreliable measure of future earnings. As buyers of a business are generally forward looking and would be more interested in future earnings, valuation on the basis of future earnings has gained more importance as an income approach to business. Past earnings provide only a possible index of future earnings.

The Discounted Cash Flow (DCF) analysis involves the determination of the following:

(1) the nature of the future cash flow;

(2) the timing of the cash flow, i.e. explicit forecast period;

(3) appropriate discount rate to be applied to cash flows;

(4) the continuing value, i.e. the cumulative value of the cash flows beyond the explicit forecast period.

The major hurdle in applying the DCF technique is the practical difficulty involved in forecasting reliable cash flows. It is most commonly used where future cash flow can be estimated with a fair degree of certainty. Besides, the DCF technique to be effective needs explicit forecast of free cash flows for at least one trade cycle which would normally be a period of at least 3 to 5 years with data on expected capital investments and increased working capital requirements for such period. That is why it is commonly relied upon in the case of valuation of manufacturing concerns.

Another problem is posed by the indefinite life of the business to be valued. This could be tackled by separating the value of the business into two time periods,—during and after an explicit forecast period. The value of the business would then be the present value of cash flows during the explicit forecast period plus the present value of cash flows after the explicit forecast period.

Under the DCF method the time value of money is recognised by applying a discount rate to the future free cash flows to arrive at their present value. This discount rate should reflect the opportunity cost to all the capital providers, shareholders and creditors, weighted by their relative contribution to the total capital of the company. This is commonly referred to as the weighted average cost of capital. The opportunity cost to the capital provider equals the rate of return the capital provider expects tc earn on other investments of equivalent risk. Free cash flows are the correct operating cash flows generated by the company that are available to all providers of the company's capital both debt and equity. They are equal to the sum of the cash flows paid to or received from all the capital providers by way of interest; new borrowings, and debt repayment in case of debt-holders; dividends, share issues and share repurchases in case of equity-holders.

It is computed as operating profits of the company after tax and also after adding back depreciation and interest expenses and making adjustment for investments in working capital, capital expenditure and increase in other assets.

The value of the business after the explicit forecast period is known as the continuing value. The calculation of the continuing value may be made by capitalising the cash flow for the final period of the explicit forecast period into perpetuity using appropriate rate of return and factoring for an element of growth in the future years, without the need to forecast the company's case flows in detail for an indefinite period.

Asset valuation method

The asset valuation method focuses more on the balance sheet than on the capitalisation of projected earnings. All assets, tangible and intangible, are adjusted to reflect their market value as opposed to book value shown on the financial statement. In theory, it is equivalent of the aggregate market value of all tangible and intangible assets, less all outstanding liabilities indicating the market value of ownership equity, or net assets. A careful analysis is required in estimating net asset value. The net tangible assets of the enterprise are the main instruments in generating profits earned or to be earned by the enterprise in the future. The existence of an unusually high value of fixed assets in relation to earning capacity would not by itself suggest that the business had any added value. Rather it may indicate efficient use of assets. Similarly, a high earning capacity compared to a low value of fixed assets may not necessarily indicate efficient use of assets. In fact, it is not uncommon to find major investments in machinery and equipment virtually eliminated from the balance sheet yet the assets are still utilised in operation. The fixed assets capitalised at original cost and depreciated over its economic life are often shorter than the asset's productive life resulting in a deemed 'write off' in the accountant's version of the asset. This is because, intangible assets and goodwill do not generally appear on the accountant's balance sheet, unless they have a cost basis. An assets used over its economic life may often appreciate rather than depreciate in value. Thus, it is extremely necessary to find out the exact relationship between the value of assets and the capitalised value of earnings.

Earnings and assets

We may think of three situations as we try to find out the relationship between capitalised value of earnings and value of assets. First, an enterprise may be reaping abnormal profit as it benefits from excess earnings and its asset structure includes significant intangible assets. The excess earning might be due to preponderance of intangibles in the form of an advantageous lease, an established business name, a unique location, a recognized trade mark, and personal contacts. In these circumstances, the intangibles are the first to lose value as earnings decline. Conversely, the tangible assets obtain more intrinsic worth as easily identifiable assets to support the value of the business. Because of their physical existence, they offer greater investment security than intangibles. As for example, bankers would readily accept such tangible assets for loan collateral but seldom accept patent right or trade marks for security. In follows that the business enterprise value increases rapidly with earnings when the enterprise includes intangible assets than when comprised solely of tangible assets.

In the second place, we may come across the opposite situation when the business is worth only net liquidation value. This may be caused by economic depreciation due to an inefficient plant lay out, burdensome labour rates, product obsolescence, inefficient management or general economic depression. Individually, the fixed assets may be in excellent condition but collectively, incapable of generating sufficient projects to justify an investment worth the market value. At this point tangible assets suffer from maximum economic depreciation and earning capacity, in spite of excellent physical condition of the assets, is just adequate to provide a fair return on investment at liquidation value.

Going concern value

Thirdly, we come across a going concern which is a business whose capacity of earnings provides a fair return on investment greater than liquidation value. Investors look at both earnings and assets when buying and selling business. Both deserve consideration when valuing a business. A business which is expected to continue in operation may have a value as a going concern. Mitra's *Legal & Commercial Dictionary*, 6th Ed. defines a 'going concern' as 'a business in actual operation and working order, in which the transfer of ownership would effect no interruption of business. A valuation of a business on the basis of a going concern is higher than on a break-up value'. Going concern means continuation of operation of an entity in foreseeable future. An enterprise is generally viewed as a going concern so long as it has neither the intention nor the necessity of liquidation, nor of curtailing materially the scale of operations. In the valuation context, going concern value is essentially a business valuation concept rather than a concept of individual property valuation. The concept involves valuation of a continuing enterprise from which allocations or apportionments of overall value may be made to constituent parts as they contribute to the whole, but none of the components by themselves constituting market value.

The concept of a going concern is akin to the definition of a 'representative firm' as given by Alfred Marshall. He defines the representative firm as one "which has had a fairly long life, and fair success, which is managed with normal ability and which has normal access to the economies external and internal, which belong to the aggregate volume of production; account being taken of the class of goods produced, the conditions of marketing them and the economic environment generally".[3] The concept is further made transparent by the assumption that the size of the representative firm does not alter for Marshall assumes that although "the firms rise and fall but the representative firm remains always of about the same size as does the representative tree of a virgin forest".

Is it possible to ascertain the value of a going concern?

In *Syndicate Bank Ltd.* v *Addl. CIT*,[4] Karnataka High Court held that as in the case of goodwill which is a self-generated assets where it has not been paid for, it is possible that the cost may not be ascertainable.

If the cost cannot be ascertained, it goes without saying that in cases of valuation of a going concern where it is a running business, the same difficulties would arise. But the mere fact that there is difficulty in valuation can hardly ever avoid the necessity of valuation. Business changes hands. They are being taken over by others from persons who have established them. In case of conversion of individual business into partnership or where there is reconstitution of a business or where a firm's business is taken over by a company, or where a company merges or amalgamates with another, there may arise the necessity of valuation of the business as a going

3 Marshall; *Principles of Economics,* p. 265.

4 (1985)155 ITR 681.

concern. The sellers and purchasers may have different perceptions as to the real value of the business but ultimately it is settled as a bargain after negotiations with or without the help of the valuer. Valuers are often called upon by both parties or in arbitration proceedings to give their own opinion of the value of the business as a going concern.

In *Shri Krishna Gyanodoy Sugar Limited* v *State of Bihar,*[5] the matter was valuation of a sugar undertaking, which was acquired under the Bihar Sugar Undertakings (Acquisition) Act 1985. The undertaking was valued on the basis of book value and the question arose as to whether the method adopted was reasonable or not. It involved interference of the court in technical matters. The Apex Court held that the manner in which the valuation of the property should be undertaken may be either according to book value or any other value that reflects the true valuation. As no material was placed before the court to show as to what method other than that on the basis of book value could have been reasonably adopted and as because book value is one of the approved methods, the court refused to enter into the question and rejected the plea of valuation on a basis other than book value.

Going concern value and itemised sale

Courts have held that there would be no inference of independent sale of any of the assets comprised in the going concern since what is transferred is the concern itself and not any of the assets on a disjunctive basis. It is, however, possible that even a going concern may be sold by way of itemised sale. Tax consequences would be different when a business is sold as a going concern, since in such a case what is sold is the business itself as an asset. In an itemised sale, the tax consequences would be the same as in the case of sale of each of such assets taken over independently.

The question as to the manner in which a going concern could be valued is not capable of a precise answer. The ascertainment of cost in the case of a person selling the business as a going concern can be even more complex. There may even be difficulty in ascertaining whether what is sold is a slump sale of a business as a going concern or it is only an itemised

5 (2003)4 SCC 378.

sale. Where there is an annexure to such a sale agreement giving valuation of each asset, there is sometimes an inference possible that it is an itemised sale. But such individual asset valuation by itself need not go against the inference of sale as a going concern.

To sum up, going concern value of an enterprise is the value created by an established business with promise for continuity. In valuation, an attempt is made to derive the capitalised value of the profits of that business reflecting turnover and contingent liabilities. The enterprise to be valued may be a large concern of complex business comprising substantial intangibles together with tangible assets. It can also relate to a single property like a hotel, departmental store etc. whose value is derived on market approach by referring to sales transactions of similar trading activities. Again, the going concern concept may be further extended to include public sector undertakings with infrastructure assets and also organisations which are meant more for services than for trading viz., sporting complex, community halls etc.

While a going concern as a whole may be valued on the discounted cash flow technique or on the asset-based method, as discussed earlier in the relevant context, the individual assets operating as components of the going concern assume so much of value as they individually contribute to going concern entity. Thus, such individual asset can be said to possess a value-in-use, measured through subjective tests usually applied by owners of the enterprise or by a valuer possessing specific expertise. Such value-in-use is the measure of the value to the business or value to the owner. If an individual asset do not contribute at all, and is considered as surplus, it will attract only salvage value or at best, value in alternative use.

As regards specialised properties which do not sell on the open market but required by public authorities for the provision of services, the going concern value is appropriately derived by the Depreciated Replacement Cost. This entails a market valuation of the land for its existing use and an estimate of the gross current replacement cost of the buildings, plant, machinery and equipment from which deductions are made to allow for age, condition, obsolescence and environmental factors.

Replacement cost in this context ought to be distinguished from Reproduction Cost.

Intangible assets

An intangible is usually defined as a capital asset having no physical existence, its value depends on the rights that possession confers upon the owner. It is an asset that is not corporeal. Trade marks, trade names, organization costs, and goodwill are examples of intangibles which are generally considered to have no limited term of existence and no natural limited life. However, the economic life of each of these is definitely limited unless efforts or expenditure are continually made for maintenance and replacements. There are, however, intangibles which have a maximum legal life. Patents, copyrights, and some franchises will have a limited life because of the very nature of themselves; only rarely will the economic life exceed their legal life. If circumstances permit the value to extend beyond the legal life, the cost or other value should be amortized over this economic life; but without the legal protection, the value beyond the legal life is too uncertain to be included in the amortization schedule. Often the economic life falls short of the legal life due to obsolescence and fall in market demand. Each intangible is usually unique and cannot be compared with other similar items. And because of this uniqueness, meaningful and relevant price indexes cannot be found to compute specific replacement costs. The only practical process of valuation is, therefore, the actual input value—historical cost—or cost adjusted for changes in general purchasing power although neither of these can command exclusive reliance.

The most important single characteristic of intangibles is the high degree of uncertainty regarding the value of the future benefits to be received. In most cases, the possible values may range from zero to very large amounts. Some intangibles relate to the development and manufacture of a product, and others relate to the creation and maintenance of the demand for the product. Patents and copyrights reflect primarily the former; trade marks and trade names reflect primarily the latter. Goodwill may represent either or both. All, however, represent benefits that are highly uncertain and difficult to associate with specific revenues or specific periods.

Both tangible and intangible non-monetary assets derive their economic value from the expectations of future earning power. However, many tangible assets have value in alternative uses, and their value to the firm can, at least in part, be compared with their physical condition, their replacement cost, the market value for used assets, and the market for the product of the enterprise. But, most intangible assets represent the development of exclusive processes or products or the protection of marketing superiority, none of which can be transferred to alternative uses. Although their value is derived from expected future revenues, it is impossible in most cases to determine what part of the revenue results from the intangibles and what part from other assets and services.

An alternative view of intangible assets is that they arise only from conditions of imperfect competition. Patents, copyrights, and franchises grant the firm special partial monopolistic powers or rights to limit direct competition. Therefore, these rights do not add directly to the wealth of the economy and are differentiated from plant and equipment, which are productive assets. However, this distinction is not clear because the rights associated with the owning of productive property may also be at least in part the result of imperfect competition.

Increasing importance of intangible assets

Intangible assets such as know-how, patents, brands, licenses, etc. are increasingly becoming a subject-matter of trade and transfer in the business transactions. Rapid advancement in technology, globalisation of business and keen competition to increase market share in global markets has increased the value of intangible assets. For knowledge and service organisations, profits are generated almost entirely through the successful management of their intellectual capital. This contrasts with the manufacturing organizations whose profits rely substantially on the intangible assets such as brands, technical knowledge, distribution-networks etc. that are increasingly becoming value drivers. Intangible assets are becoming key differentiators in the operating performances and results between companies operating in similar industries or economies. In companies having valuable brands such as

Coca-cola, Pepsi, IBM, Microsoft, McDonalds etc. the intangible assets may have much higher values than their tangible assets.

The purposes that compel increasing applicability importance of intangible assets are not far to seek. The following are a few examples of such purposes.

(*a*) *Transaction support sale*: At the time of exchanging the intellectual property, the price must be determined and so valuation option must be conducted.

(*b*) *Bankruptcy*: Intellectual property values play an important role in bankruptcies. Value opinions are needed for presentation in court as debtors salvable for assets that can satisfy their losses.

(*c*) *Licensing*: When the owner of intellectual property is considering licensing a property, the outright value is also a valuable consideration.

(*d*) *Strategic alliances*: Often two independent entities come together to form a third party for the purposes of exploiting new technology with their individual contribution and identification of intangibles is needed.

(*e*) *Infringement damages*: A growing trend in litigation involves patent and trademark infringement. The damage analysis is directed at determining the damages caused by the infringer in terms of amount.

(*f*) *Inter-company transaction*: The transfer of intellectual property between related parties comes under the security of various taxation authorities. As a result, the valuation of patents and trade marks is needed.

(*g*) *Collateral bases of financing*: As intellectual property becomes the dominant asset of companies, it also becomes the primary collateral on which banks are willing to make loans. Banks are asking for valuation options for patent, trademark and copyright as security for their loans.

(*h*) *Accounting requirements*: In some instances the value of intellectual property and intangible assets must be valued so that appropriate property and estate tax bases can be determined, as patents, trade marks or copyrights are the part of estate.

Valuation of intangible assets

Valuation of intangible assets is a complex exercise, as the non-physical form of intangible assets poses the difficulty of identifying the future economic benefits that the enterprise can expect to derive from them. Physical assets such as plant and equipment acquired for use in developing or providing goods or services to consumers often have alternative uses. For example, they can often be sold or may be used in the production of different goods or services. In addition, their component parts can have value in use or exchange. Many intangible assets do not have alternative uses and cannot be broken down into component part for resale. This characteristic of intangible assets adds to the difficulty of determining with sufficient certainty the value of such assets. Intangible assets normally do not have an active market. Many times, intangible assets are not separable from the business and hence it is difficult to value them separately from the business.

Valuation of intangible assets is a separate topic by itself. There are three main approaches used in valuing intangible assets:

(*i*) Cost Approach;

(*ii*) Market Value Approach;

(*iii*) Economic Value Approach or Income Approach.

The value must evaluate the methodology options available according to credibility, objectivity, relevance and practicality. These must be considered in context of the individual characteristic of the asset under review and the specific circumstances of the valuation. In many cases, the nature, quality and quantity of information available will guide the selection. Each case is different from others inasmuch as the role played by intangibles differs from firm to firm; so also the degree of protection entitled to and the potential of contribution of each species of intangibles. Hence, valuation norms are mere guidelines.

Cost approach

In cost approach, expenditures incurred in developing the asset is aggregated. Cost as measured by purchase price is a relevant factor where the asset has been acquired recently.

One common characteristic of most of the intangibles is that they cannot be separated from the firm or the physical property of the firm. They exist and have value only in combination with the tangible assets. Because of this, they are frequently considered to represent residual benefits after all tangible assets are specifically identified.

When intangibles are acquired by purchase, individually or as a part of a basket purchase, the determination of cost is similar to the computation of the cost of plant and equipment under like circumstances. When intangibles are acquired by self-development, however, the computation of their cost involves all of the difficulties of self-constructed assets plus some additional problems of its own. Most of the costs of patents, trade marks, and trade names are joint costs. Many patents may emerge from joint research and development expenditures, and several trade marks and trade names may be advertised jointly. These problems can be solved by the use of known costing methods, but the results are likely to be arbitrary if they include allocated joint costs. To the extent that they do, the valuations are likely to be meaningless.

Although cost approach is recommended for tangible assets in certain cases other valuations may be acceptable and are occasionally recommended. But for intangibles, there must be compelling evidence that some other valuation is more appropriate. Even when intangible assets are donated to the firm, there is a general reluctance to record any value in the accounts because of the high degree of uncertainty regarding whatever valuation may be chosen.

When intangibles are acquired through the issuance of capital stock, the determination of cost is a difficult, if not almost impossible, problem. In this case, cost may be considered to be either the fair value of the stock given or the fair value of the rights acquired, whichever is the more evident. If the stock does not have a current market price, the determination of the cost of the intangibles is extremely difficult because the intangibles generally have no market value either. It is inappropriate to assume that cost is equal to the par value or stated value of the shares issued in exchange.

Valuation by amortization

In quite a number of situations, the cost approach to valuation of intangibles proves inadequate. Amortization is the method that often provides the plausible solution.

Most intangibles that are generated gradually by the firm through annual expenditures are charged immediately to expense. However, intangibles that are acquired through a lump sum purchase or that are developed through extraordinary identifiable expenditures are frequently capitalized and amortized similarly to the depreciation allocations of plant and equipment. Once the initial valuation to be amortized is determined, the major factors to be estimated are (1) the useful life of the asset; and (2) the pattern of allocation to the several periods of the life of the asset. The residual or scrap value is generally non-existent or immaterial.

Intangibles can be classified on the basis of how they are acquired, whether they can be specifically identified, or whether their lives are limited and can be estimated or are indeterminate. According to the traditional accounting structure, if resource out lays are incurred in order to benefit future periods, the cost should be capitalized and allocated to the future periods. It does not matter how the intangible asset was acquired. However, from the point of view of semantic interpretation, the intangible asset acquired must be identifiable. An intangible asset is assumed to be identifiable if it is acquired from other enterprises or individuals. For intangible assets that are developed by the firm, the costs should be charged to expense unless the asset is specifically identifiable, has a determinable limited life, and is not inherent in the continuation of the business. Although one of several methods of classification can be used, the classification according to whether the asset has a limited life or an indeterminate life does provide a useful breakdown in studying the alternative allocation procedures and their effects.

Market value approach

In comparable market value approach, intangible assets are valued by reference to transactions involving similar assets that have occurred recently in similar markets. The approach is possible if there is an existence of an active market in which arm's length transactions have occurred recently involving comparable intangible assets and adequate information on the terms of the transactions is available. This method, where practicable, normally satisfies the criteria of credibility, objectivity and relevance.

Economic value approach or income approach

This approach is based on the cash flows or earnings attributable those assets and the capitalization thereof, at an appropriate discount rate or multiple. Some of the key parameters used in this approach are projected revenues, projected earnings, discount rate, rate of return etc. The information required can be derived from either internal sources, external sources or both. In this approach the value has to identify the cash flows-earnings directly associated with the intangible assets like the cash flows arising from the exploitation of a patent or copyright, licensing of an intangible asset etc. This approach can be put to practice only if cash flows arising from the intangible assets are identifiable from the management accounts and budgets, forecasts or plans of the company. In most situations of valuation of intangible assets, the economic value approach is used, because of the uniqueness of intangible assets and the lack of comparable market data for the use of market value approach.

Intangibles other than intellectual property

Confidential information; trade secrets, know how etc. are also intangible assets that contribute to the business though there is no remedy of protection to them under the copyright law. But that does not expose them to indiscriminate traffic. It is well settled that information imparted in confidence, especially information acquired by the employees or agents in course of deployment are not to be freely disclosed. The courts will restrain the use of it if it is in breach of good faith. Such acquire of information must not make use this advantage to the prejudice of him who gave it, unless the letter so consents. This restraint follows from the principle of equity even though there may not have been any contract to the effect, written or implied. The essence of the principle is that a person who has obtained confidential information because of the accessibility given in confidence is not allowed to use it as a springboard for activity detrimental to the interest of the given, even when all the features of such information have published or can be ascertained by actual inspection by members of the public. The acquirer is thus placed under a specific disability in the field of competition in order to ensure that he does not get an unfair start without paying for the confidential information so obtained. Unconscious use of confidential information is also a breach of confidence. There is however, no liability when discloser is in the public interest or when the person divulges only such information which get by actually going to a public source.

Know-how

Know-how consists of all those technical and commercial knowledge as are acquired by a person by dint of his skill and experience. It is essentially different from trade secret or confidential information. All employer as a general rule is not entitled to impose a restriction which will prevent the employee from using his skill, aptitude and efficiency in alternative employment after leaving the job that helped him to develop such skill. Breach of confidence does not hold good in case of know how learned in course of employment.

Goodwill

There are several intangibles that contribute to the business but no separate accounting of which is possible as a distinct item. Nevertheless, they have the effect of promoting goodwill and for reasons of such characteristic features of silent contribution, these intangibles form part of their business and cannot be parted with except as an integral component of, the business itself. Thus managerial skills, particular contracts, customer linkage, motivation of human resources, effective advertising strategy are significant contribution to the growth of business. They together create an impact of synergy on the build up of goodwill.

When a business as a whole is acquired by another firm the excess of the price paid in stock or other assets over the fair value of the separable tangible and intangible assets acquired, less obligations assumed represents the amount paid for goodwill. The favoured definition of goodwill comes from the *Shorter Oxford Dictionary* and reads as follows:

"The privilege granted by the seller of a business to a purchaser of trading as his recognised successor; the possession of a ready-formed connections with customers considered as a separate element in the saleable value of a business".

In *Star Industrial* v *Yap Kwee Kor*,[6] Lord Diplock stated as follows:

"Goodwill as the subject of proprietary right is incapable of subsisting by itself. It has no independent existence apart from the business to which it is attached. It is local in character and divisible; if the business is carried on in several countries a separate goodwill attaches to it in each. So when the business is abandoned in one country in which it has acquired goodwill; the goodwill in that country perishes with it although the business may continue to be carried on in other countries".

The goodwill is territorial in nature. The owner of trade mark or business name may have goodwill in a country without having any place of business there. Goodwill is the whole advantage, whatever it may be, of the reputation and connection of the firm which may have been built up by years of honest work or gained by lavish expenditure of money. Goodwill is inseparable from the business to which it adds value.[7]

Goodwill is frequently thought to arise from advantageous business relationships, good relations with employees, and favourable attitudes of customers. These favourable attitudes may be due to an advantageous location, an excellent reputation and name, monopolistic privilege, good business management, strategic advertisements and other factors.

The importance of goodwill was thus recognised by the Supreme Court in *R.C. Cooper* v *Union of India*[8] in the following words:

"Goodwill of a business is an intangible asset. It is the whole advantage of the reputation and connection formed

6 [1976] FSR 256 (269) (PC).
7 *Commissioner* v *Miller* [1901] AC 217 (223-225).
8 AIR 1970 SC 564.

with the customers together with the circumstances making the connection durable. It is that component of the total value of the undertaking which is attributable to the ability of the concern to earn profits over a course of years or in excess of normal amounts because of its reputation, location and other features. Goodwill of the business is, therefore, the value of the attraction to customers arising from the name, and the reputation for skill, integrity, efficient business management, efficient service."

The decision of the Tribunal in *Desu Venkata Subba Rao v WTO, Hyderabad*[9] sets out the following passage from the *Text Book on Accountancy* by William Pickles, 4th Ed. (brought out by the English Language Book Society and Publisher):

"The goodwill is an intangible, but not necessarily a fictitious, asset representing the value—however difficult its appraisement may be—to its owner of benefits arising from the business in question, such as the sole right to enjoy the profits of the business, and, where goodwill has been acquired, the sole right of succession to the advantages of the business which have been built up in the past. Goodwill arises mainly (*a*) by personal reputation of the owners, (*b*) by reputation of the goods dealt in, (*c*) by site monopoly or advantage, (*d*) by access to sources of supply, e.g., large quotas, (*e*) for patent and trade mark protection, (*f*) effectiveness of publicity, (*g*) reputation of the firm's goods and methods, (*h*) relationship between firm and personnel, and (*i*) growth element.

"The purchaser of goodwill acquires the trade marks, patents, copyrights, etc. of the business as well as the benefits of contracts and all the benefits accruing from the location, reputation, connection organization and other exceptional features of the business. The purchaser will seek to express the sum payable in terms of the compounded or capitalized value of an annuity of future deferential or 'super' profits, that is those profits in excess of the marginal return normally arising."

The name of the firm is thus a very important part of the goodwill of business. So also descriptive words, surnames or

9 (1983)6 ITD 341.

geographical names indicating source of origin or manufacture of the product traded by the firm. Goodwill is capable of being sold or charged or bequeathed by will. Trade mark, trade name and get-up form part of the goodwill of business. The transfer of goodwill of a business confers on the transferee the exclusive right to carry on the business transferred, the exclusive right to represent himself as carrying on such business, and as against the transferor the exclusive right to use the name under which the business has been carried on. The sale of the business and goodwill carriers with it the right to use the old firm's name. The sale of the business is a sale of the goodwill, whether the word 'goodwill' is mentioned or not. Any unregistered trade mark vested in a company would pass with an assignment of its goodwill by the company. In the absence of any express restrictive covenant, the vendor of a business is at liberty to set up a competing business, but he may not solicit the customers of the business of which he has sold the goodwill and so deprive the purchaser of the benefit of that which he has bought.

The unstable character of goodwill was stressed by the Supreme Court in *CIT* v *B.C. Srinivasa Setty*[10] wherein it was pointed out that "because of its intangible nature remains unsubstantial in form and nebulous in character".

Delhi High Court in *CWT* v *K.N. Khanna*[11] recognised goodwill for wealth-tax purposes as a capital asset though it is intangible in form. However, it has, now, no relevance for wealth-tax as at present goodwill is not one of the assets liable for wealth-tax.

Before estate duty was withdrawn, valuation of goodwill was a matter of contention in many cases. In *CED* v *Mrudula Nareshchandra*,[12] the Supreme Court had held that interest of a partner passes on his death even if partnership deed provided otherwise. Goodwill was considered relevant for gift-tax purposes in *CGT* v *V.A.M. Ayya Nadar*[13] and *CGT* v *P. Gheevarghese.*[14]

10 (1981)128 ITR 294.
11 (1971)81 ITR 117.
12 (1986)160 ITR 342.
13 (1969)73 ITR 761 (Mad).
14 (1972)83 ITR 403 (SC).

Passing off

This is an actionable wrong for any person to pass off his goods or business as and for the goods or business of another person by whatever means that result may be achieved. The law of passing off has been extended to professions and non-trading activities as well. Thus passing off is a form of tort. The law of passing off based on common law, has remained substantially the same over more than a century though its formulation has changed over the time. The object of the law is to protect the goodwill of a business, its entitlement to reputation and destructiveness as against infringement by dishonest competitors. The principle is that 'no man is entitled to represent his goods as being the goods of another man, and no man is permitted to use any mark, sign or symbol device or other means whereby, without making a direct' false representation himself to a purchaser who purchases from him, he enables such purchaser to tell a lie or to make a false representation to somebody else who is the ultimate customer.[15]

There has been a plethora of litigation on the allegation of passing off. To quote only a few, injunction was granted against the use of the term 'Spanish Champagne',[16] in *Dent* v *Turpin*,[17] two firms were trading under the name 'Dent' as watch-makers, it was held that either could prevent a third person from carrying on the same business under the same name. Similar cases may be found in *Sherry* case,[18] *Scotch Whisky* case,[19] and *Advocoat* case.[20]

Accounting of the intangibles for valuation

Serious attention has been given in the recent years to discuss the above issues on accounting treatment for intangible assets and International Accounting Standard (IAS 38) has been issued in July 1998 and is to be effective for financial statements covering accounting periods beginning on or after 1st July 1999. Earlier application is encouraged.

15 *Singer* v *Loog* [1881]18 Ch D 395 (412).
16 *Bollinger* v *Costa Brava* [1961] RPC 116.
17 [1861]2 J&H 139.
18 [1969] RPC 1.
19 [1970] RPC 489.
20 [1980] RPC 31 (HL).

The International Accounting Standards Committee (IASC) started a project to develop an International Accounting Standard on Intangible Assets in 1989. However, the project became a priority in 1993 after the IASC completed its project on "Comparability and Improvements of Financing Statements", which resulted in revisions to 10 International Accounting Standards, including IAS 9, Research and Development Costs and IAS 22, Business Combinations.

The recognition of an item as intangible asset for accounting purposes requires an enterprise to demonstrate that the item meets the:

(*a*) definition of intangible assets;

(*b*) recognition criteria set out in the standard.

An intangible asset should be recognised if and only if:

(*a*) it is probable that the future economic benefits that are attributable to the asset will flow to the enterprise; and

(*b*) the cost of the asset can be measured reliably.

It is probable that the future economic benefits especially attributable to an intangible asset will flow to an enterprise if, and only if, the enterprise can demonstrate:

(*a*) how the intangible assets is expected to enhance the net inflow of future economic benefits to the enterprise;

(*b*) the enterprises ability an intention to use the intangible assets; and,

(*c*) the availability of adequate technical, financial and other resources to enable the enterprises to obtain its expected future economic benefits.

From an accountant's point of view, a balance sheet is a simple statement, drawn up on a historical costs basis and gives a summary of all transactions of the business since its inception. It signifies the financial position of a company at any given point of time and is in no way viewed as a statement of value. However, at the other end of the spectrum are those who would like to change the basis of the balance sheet reporting by switching from a historic cost approach to one which values assets an on "existing use" to the business. Thus, the contention is that all the assets as the balance sheet should be reviewed and revalued on a regular basis and the balance sheet should be a proxy for a company's worth or value. This brings to the fore the demand for valuing intangible assets and reflecting them in financial statements.

If an intangible asset is acquired separately, the cost of the intangible asset can usually be measured reliably and such cost of intangible assets can be recognized in the accounts. If an intangible asset is acquired in a business combination, the cost of that intangible asset is based on its fair value at the date of acquisition. The exceptional treatment of allowing fair value on initial recognition is permitted because in such situation main issue is of allocation of total cost of acquisition to various assets acquired according to their respective fair values. If the cost (i.e. fair value) of an intangible asset acquired as part of a business combination in the nature of acquisition cannot be measured reliably, that asset is not recognized as a separate intangible asset but is included in goodwill.

The useful life of an intangible asset may be very long but it is always finite. Uncertainty justifies estimate of the useful life of an intangible asset on prudent basis. If control over the future economic benefits from an intangible asset is achieved through legal rights that have been granted for a finite period, the useful life of the intangible asset should not exceed the period of legal rights unless:

(*a*) the legal rights renewable; and,

(*b*) the renewal is virtually certain.

There may be both economic and legal factors influencing the useful life of an intangible asset; economic factor determine the period over which future economic benefits will be received; legal factors may restrict the period over which the enterprise controls access to these benefits. The useful life is the shorter of the periods determined by these factors.

In addition, Impairment of Assets of an enterprise should estimate the recoverable amount of the following intangible assets as least at each financial year-end, even if there is no indication that the asset is impaired. The recoverable amount should be determined and impairment losses recognized accordingly.

Goodwill, in general, is recorded in the books only when some consideration in money or money's worth has been paid for it. Whenever a business is acquired for a price (payable either in cash or in shares or otherwise) which is in excess of the value of the net assets of the business taken over, the excess is termed as 'goodwill'. Goodwill arises from business connections, trade name or reputation or an enterprise or from other intangible benefits enjoyed by an enterprise.

As a matter of financial prudence, goodwill is written over a period. However, many enterprises do not write off goodwill and retain as an asset. Goodwill arising on amalgamation represents a payment made in anticipation of future income and it is appropriate to treat is as an asset to be amortised to income on a systematic basis over its useful life. Due to the nature of goodwill, it is frequently difficult to estimate is useful life with reasonable certainty. Such estimation is, therefore, made on a prudent basis. Accordingly, it is considered appropriate to amortise goodwill over a period not exceeding five years unless a somewhat longer period can be justified.

Factors which may be considered in estimating the useful life of goodwill arising on amalgamation include:

(*a*) the foreseeable life of the business or industry;

(*b*) the effects of product obsolescence, changes in demand and other economic factors;

(*c*) the service life expectancies of key individuals or groups of employees;

(*d*) expected actions by competitors or potential competitors; and

(*e*) legal, regulatory or contractual provisions affecting the useful life.

Methods of valuation

Valuation of intangible rights poses problems. One, they are not tangible and hence physical verification or even estimation are not possible. Second, all of them source benefits in future. Historical costs incurred in creating them are of lesser use to know its value. Third, to a large extent they are unique and hence there is no adequate market for this rights and comparable transactions are also of relatively limited use for valuing them. Quality of valuation depend to a large extent the quality of data that go into estimating cost and expected benefits from the asset under consideration.

We have earlier referred briefly to the different approaches to valuation—cost approach, market approach and income approach (or economic value approach) together with limitation in application of each. We are now concerned with the methods to carry out the approach is actual practice. With regard to intangibles, cost is only a factor for assessment of income which is the ultimate object of accounting in a business. Market approach is ordinarily relevant when a particular intangible asset is separately acquired in an active market for such transactions which does not always happen. Thus, the various methods of valuation emanating from an income approach can throw bright rays of light in determining the economic value of an intangible asset. The various such methods in practice are briefly narrated below which take into account the estimated life of the intangibles within the parameters of statutory provisions.

Valuation of goodwill

There are four methods usually adopted for valuation of goodwill:

(1) Valuation on the basis of super profits;

(2) Valuation by capitalisation of future maintainable profits;

(3) Valuation on the basis of the mean between the tangible assets value and capitalised value of the yield;

(4) Valuation of a number of years' purchase of past profits.

A rough and ready method usually followed is to take it as being worth 1 to 3 years' purchase of annual average profits of past three or five years. It should be emphasised that goodwill can only have a market value to the extent it is transferable. When the purchase price of a going concern exceeds the sum of the valuations of all individual assets other than goodwill, the excess may be assumed to represent the payment for the specific intangible attributes that build up the goodwill. However, specific values cannot be assigned to each of the characteristic components of goodwill individually.

There is, therefore, a fallacy in recounting the specific attributes of goodwill such as advantageous location, excellent reputation, trade names, brand name etc. Because, a total valuation of goodwill cannot be computed by adding the sum of these components. Goodwill has to be viewed as a whole and as overall impact on the business.

A common approach to measure goodwill often assumes that it represents the present discounted value of expected future earnings (or cash payments to equity-holders) in excess of that which may be considered a normal return. But the assumption that the tangible assets can earn only a normal rate while other factors are responsible for the excess is a fiction. In the ultimate analysis, it is doubtful if goodwill is at all a severable asset. That is why goodwill is hardly reported in the financial statements.

The return on assets (ROA) method

ROA is the ratio of a company's average earnings (average pre-tax earnings of a company over three to five years) divided by average tangible assets over the same period of time.

This ratio is compared with the industry average to calculate the difference. If this difference is zero or negative, then the company does not have excess intellectual capital compared with its industry average and the value of its intellectual capital is assumed to be zero. However, if the difference between the company's ROA and its industry average tangible assets to calculate the average annual excess earnings. Dividing excess earnings by the company's average cost of capital, one can derive an estimate of the value of its intellectual assets.

The main advantages of this are that it is simple to use the formulae and all required information is available in historical financial statements.

Discount cash flow method

This is one of the most accepted methods of valuation of any asset that promises benefits in future as because valuation requires identification, separation and quantifications of earnings available in the cash flow statements. This method essentially requires estimation of expected cash flow from the asset under consideration. For example, buying a copyright of particular computer programme. The buyer needs to estimate the net cash flows he is going to get from the given programme. He needs to appraise his existing infrastructure whether it can sustain and exploit the potential of the programme. Not only that needs to make an appraisal of age such computer programmes when the industry itself is subject high level of technological obsolescence. It is also important to assess appropriateness of discount rate, terminal value tax rate etc. Discounted cash flow analysis is the comprehensive appraisal technique of intellectual property in Income Approach. Investment here takes into consideration the estimated future cash flow on the basis of useful life on legal permissibility as well as appropriate discounting on the basis of time value of money. Cash flow equals cash receipt minus cash payment over a given period of time.

Royalty method

This approach is prevalent in arriving at value for licensing the use of trade mark or brand by third party. This method is based on the economic theory of deprival value, whereby it is assumed that a business does not own the asset and hence it has to pay royalty for its use to the owner of the asset. The value of the asset is the capitalized value of after-tax royalty that company is relieved from paying as a result of ownership of the asset. Alternatively, value is best on what royalty the asset commands in the market, if is transferred or licensed to a third party. An extension to this method is marginal royalty method whereby one evaluates the value of potential incremental royalty if the rights are conferred to third parties over and above used by the owners.

Complexities arise when one incorporates provisions of minimum royalty and excess royalty. This means for certain level of sales or below that level, minimum royalty is paid, and for sales above these minimum levels another incentive structure is created for excess royalty. It can be made more complicated by incorporating additional provision of renewal of licence subject to minimum performance. Estimation of this excess royalty is quite subjective area in practice. Internationally, when the structure of royalty is complex and depends upon more than one certain variable, Monte Carlo simulation model is prepared to evaluate the proposal.

Monte carlo model

It is worth considering a model which has been practised in some quarters in this context. Monte Carlo modelling refers to a technique designed to simulate the expected outcomes of uncertain future events. It works by first describing a set of possible future events using probability distribution—often normal distribution—and then conducting may trial runs to see what outcomes develop. The advantage of this method is many uncertain events can be combined together in complex ways in single trial run. Once model is developed and trials are conducted, one can look at the distribution of outcomes and gain useful insights into the most likely (as well as least likely) results. For example, when all outcomes could be clustered together in a small range, it means that the result is highly probable. Alternatively, there might be several clusters of very different outcomes with each being equally likely. Often there is a range of outcomes with a single peak being the most likely. Value of each outcome is then discounted to present and averaged to get estimated value for licensing the asset. Consider an example of determining value for licensing trade mark with following assumptions in different situations:

- Revenue for the first year be ₹ 1,00,000 and rate of discount 14%

	Year 1		Year 2			Year 3		
Case	*Cost Ratio*	*Royalty*	*Growth*	*Cost Ratio*	*Royalty*	*Growth*	*Cost Ratio*	*Royalty*
Normal	0.5	0.20	1.20	0.5	0.20	1.20	0.5	0.20
Best	0. 4	0.22	1.15	0.4	0.22	1.15	0.4	0.22
Worst	0.6	0.18	1.00	0.6	0.18	1.00	0.6	0.18

NOTE: Cost and growth are calculated with respect to revenues and royalties are calculated on the basis of contribution (revenue less cost).

A sample 500 trial runs through Monte Carlo simulation suggest that most likely (average or present values) value for licensing is in range of ₹ 29,000 – ₹ 30,000. Different assumptions and conditions would reflect different values for the asset under consideration.

Direct intellectual capital method

The direct intellectual capital (DIC) method focuses on measuring the value of intellectual capital by first identifying its various components and then directly evaluating them. Components of market assets (such as customer loyalty), intellectual property (such as patents), technology assets (such as know-how), human assets (such as education and training), and structural assets (such as information systems) are in the focus of the DIC. After these components are all measured, the total value of a company's intellectual capital can be derived. The DIC method is the most complex, but also the most accurate means of measuring intellectual capital.

Option pricing method

Intellectual property like patent has a limited protection for monopoly in marketing as guaranteed under the statutory regulation. Nevertheless, it is quite possible that it may not have enough marketing possibility at this initial stage but with growing popularity it may have tremendous potential which may extend its useful life much beyond the period of legal protection. The existing risk less rate of interest is a factor that enters into the arena in such situation which gives an option to the owner of the business to introduce the patent just now when the investment for it may not earn sufficient margin of project or at a later period when the commercial exploration becomes more profitable from the view point of pricing and margin above risk less return from interest. The important factor for consideration is that if the economic value of the patent is restricted only to its protected life, say for 17 years, then for every year 1/17 part of the projected income is lost. But if the potential for commercial exploitation spills over the protected life, the consideration turns different and an options pricing become relevant.

As every right gives you an option to exercise or not, intellectual property right also gives you an option whether to exploit it yourself, sell it, license it, differ it, or forget it. Discounted cash flow method of valuation assumes passivity of the investment. It ignores to value the asset that may not generate revenues currently but holds potential to reward firm substantially. Hence, valuing by discounted cash flow method, firms with unutilized but unexpired patents will always be under-valued. While option pricing approach to value such intellectual property rights that are yet to be activated provides valuable insight into the value of the firm.

(J) STOCK SHARES AND DEBENTURES

Shares entitle the shareholder to certain rights in respect of the company. Those rights are right to share in profits by way of dividend, right to take part in management of the company and right to share in surplus assets of the company on liquidation. Bonus shares are often issued without varying the original right of the shareholder. In other words, rights of a shareholder after issue of bonus shares neither increase nor decrease but remain the same. Though the number of share certificates held by the shareholder increase with acquisition of bonus share, there is no increase in rights denoted by the same. Coming to the issue of right shares, the cost of acquisition of right shares, could be the amount subscribed towards the right shares as increased by the amount of depression in market value of the original shares due to issue of such right shares. Such amount of depreciation in market value of shares will have to be calculated by comparing market quotation of shares before and after issue of right shares.

The origin of shares can be traced with the growth of joint stock companies in the wake of industrial revolution. Huge capital amount were sunk in illiquid assets—as giant enterprises came into existence employing big plants and machineries for industrial processing and manufacture. At this stage it became necessary to strike a dichotomy between the owner of the fixed assets and the group of persons entrusted with the management. The ownership again could hardly comprise a single provider of capital but instead, came to be shared by a large group of investors each having a unit ownership in the assets of the company. Thus each small unit of ownership was given a share corresponding to the monetary contribution. Then came the question of easy transferability of such shares in order that the capital deployed could obtain perfect liquidity. In such situation the ownership of the company rests on an amorphous collection of shareholders unconnected with one another like hotel guests coming in and coming out. That is how the stock, shares and debentures in the form we find came into existence.

Stock, shares or debentures are negotiable instruments, the assignment of which is effected under the Negotiable Instruments Act by endorsement and delivery. The provisions of the Transfer of Property Act as respects actionable claims are not applicable to stock, shares or debentures, as laid down in s. 137 of the said Act. The assignment of shares may be by way of sale, mortgage or pledge. In case of mortgage, the right to enjoy is given, while in a pledge, no such right accrues.

Need for valuation

The need for valuation of shares arises on account of the following among other reasons:

(*i*) Sale.

(*ii*) Premium determination.

(*iii*) Amalgamation or Merger.

(*iv*) Tax purposes.

In these instances there may not always be statutory provisions which define value or which impose conditions or methods under which the valuation must be made. Having regard to the fact that the valuation of the same shares may be required for a variety of different reasons or purposes, the inescapable conclusion is that though different values may exist for different purposes, it cannot be too strongly emphasised that a valuer can only arrive at one value for one purpose.

Market value established by actual sales does not necessarily represent the value to holder who does not wish to sell, neither is the value, to a holder necessarily coincident with the value to a prospective purchaser. Therefore, different concepts of value may be identified such as intrinsic value, market value, holding value, fair value, tangible assets value, value as a going concern, and realisation value. In any exercise of value determination, the basic principle will be that the fair value should be such as is determined between a willing buyer and a willing seller having regard to the purpose of the valuation.

Methods of valuation

The methods of valuation of shares can be broadly divided into two categories:

(*a*) Balance sheet or asset based valuation.

(*b*) Profit and loss account or income based valuation.

Since the earliest days the balance sheet or asset based valuation techniques have been used to determine value of shares. These methods include values based on original cost, sales value or replacement cost methods of determining value of shares. As the concepts and principles of valuation developed and evolved, there has been a shift to the Profit and Loss based or income based valuation techniques as being more representative and appropriate basis of valuation of shares especially where the company is a going concern. Even in India as elsewhere the concept that valuation of shares of a company as a going concern is primarily to be based upon its earnings has been judicially accepted.

Principles of valuation as determined judicially

The Supreme Court in *C.W.T.* v *Mahadeo Jalan*[21] has emphasised this aspect and laid down the following principles for valuation of shares in a limited company:

(*i*) Where the shares in a public limited company are quoted on the Stock Exchange and there are dealings in them, the price prevailing on the valuation date is the value of the shares.

(*ii*) Where the shares are of a public limited company which are not quoted on the Stock Exchange or of a private limited company, the value is determined by reference to the dividends if any, reflecting the profit-earning capacity on a reasonable commercial basis. But, where they do not, then the amount of yield on that basis will determine the value of the shares. In other words, the profits which the company has been making and should be making will ordinarily determine the value. The dividend earning method or yield method are not mutually exclusive; both should help in ascertaining the profit-earning capacity as indicated above. If the results of the two methods differ an intermediate figure may have to be computed by adjustment of unreasonable proportion of profits.

(*iii*) In the case of a private limited company also where the expenses are incurred out of all proportion to the

21 AIR 1973 SC 1023; (1973)3 SCC 157; (1972)86 ITR 621.

commercial venture, they will be added back to the profits of the company in computing the yield. In such companies, the restriction on Share Transfers will also be taken into consideration as earlier indicated in arriving at a valuation.

(*iv*) Where the dividend yield and earning method break down by reason of the company's inability to earn profits and declare dividends, if the setback is temporary then it is perhaps possible to take the estimate of the value of the shares before setback and discount it by a percentage corresponding to the proportionate fall in the price of quoted shares of companies which have suffered similar reverses.

(*v*) Where the company is ripe for winding up, then the break-up value method determines what would be realised by that process.

(*vi*) As in *Attorney General of Ceylon* v *Mackie*,[1] a valuation by reference to the assets would be justified whereas in that case, the fluctuations of profits and uncertainty of the conditions at the date of the valuation prevented a reasonable estimation of prospective profits and dividends.

Value of shares in a going concern

It may be noted that the aforesaid principles laid down by the Supreme Court lays emphasis on the profit-earning capacity of an undertaking to determine its value where such undertaking is a 'going concern'. It is only where the company is ripe for winding up that the break-up value method or the net asset value basis of valuation is to be adopted. The various methods or combinations thereof used to establish value of shares of a company as a going concern are:

Stock market quotations

This may be the simplest method of determining value of shares of the company, where the shares are listed on one or more recognised stock exchanges. The market price of shares as quoted on a stock exchange is normally considered as the fair value of the shares of that company especially where such

1 [1952]2 All ER 775 (PC).

quotations are arising from shares being regularly and freely traded in subject to the element of speculative support that may be in-built in the value of the shares. The Supreme Court in *CWT* v *Mahadeo Jalan,*[2] has observed:

> "Where shares in a company are bought and sold on the stock exchange and there are no abnormalities affecting the market price, the price at which the shares are changing hands in the ordinary course of business is usually their true value. These quotations generally reflect the value of the asset having regard to the several factors which are taken into consideration by persons who transact business on the stock exchange and by the buyers who want to invest their money in any particular share or shares."

Stock market quotations however may not always be regarded as fair value of shares. There could be situations where the value of the shares as quoted on stock exchanges may not be regarded as a proper index of the fair value of the shares. This could be in situations where the market values are fluctuating in a volatile capital market due to factors totally unconnected with the earnings of the company. There could also be special situations where the market has information of a likely takeover bid, which may have the effect of pushing up the market price of a particular company's share.

There could be situations where a large block of shares were to be released in the market it may have the effect of weakening the market price of the shares. However, there are also situations where a parcel of shares sufficient to carry a special resolution may have a higher value, because such an interest was substantially equivalent to absolute ownership. This principle was propounded by Williams, J. in *Martin's* case. It must be remembered that there is a point beyond which size would increase the unit value rather than reduce it and that is when the holding approaches a controlling interest. Similarly in case of amalgamation of companies, where it is a question of evaluating the shares of one company against those of another, the volume of transactions and number of shares available for trading on the stock exchange over a reasonable period would have to be of a comparable standard for the

2 AIR 1973 SC 1023 at 1026.

evaluation to be meaningful. In view of the above limitations the London Stock Exchange stated that Stock Exchange Quotations are not related directly to the value of the company's assets, or to the amount of its profits, and consequently these quotations, no matter what date may be chosen for reference, cannot form a fair and equitable basis or rational basis for compensation. Lastly, for valuing shares of companies whose shares are not listed this method is not available. However, to the extent that the market values of listed shares of a particular industry reflect a relation between price and earnings, i.e. the Price Earnings Ratio, P/E Ratios as they are popularly known may be a useful tool in determining the price of unlisted shares of a company.

Capitalisation of past earnings/maintainable profits

The past earnings of a company form a very useful basis of determining fair value of the shares of a company. In determining the value on this basis the past earnings need to be adjusted to take account of several factors which may affect value. Apart from the possibility that the earnings statements may be falsified or they may not confirm to 'good accounting practice' adjustments may be necessary for several other reasons such as:

(*i*) Elimination of unusual items;
(*ii*) Remuneration of proprietors/promoters;
(*iii*) Valuation of inventories/stocks;
(*iv*) Depreciation;
(*v*) Income Tax;
(*vi*) Adjustment to expenditure/income;
  — Abnormal repairs;
  — Lump sum retirement compensation;
  — Abnormal bad debts;
  — Capital expenditure.

Another important aspect in determining value based on past results is to select an appropriate period for which past results should be considered. No specific length of time can be laid down. The period should be sufficiently long to cover a business cycle. In selecting the past results that portion of the past profits must be selected that best represents the maintainability of the profits. What is required is not so much the future but the current earning capacity or maintainable profits.

The third aspect that may be required to be taken account of is the changes in capital invested, during the period under examination. The capital may have increased or decreased. The average capital employed during the period which has generated the earnings reflected in the accounts must be taken into account in establishing the value of the shares. Some other factors which need to be taken account of are, income from surplus funds invested in securities, the commencement of a new business, the results of which are not reflected in the past and changes in the business that may have taken place after the balance sheet date which have a material impact on the maintainable profits.

Finally, the fourth aspect is the determination of an appropriate rate of yield to be sought on capital invested in a business.

Unreliable as sometimes stock exchange quotations are, they afford the best available approach to the determination of the yield, both to establish the riskless rate applicable to gilt-edged securities and as a basis of comparison where there are stocks with characteristics sufficiently similar to the shares or business being valued. This yield value may have to be appropriately adjusted for certain factors like, lack of negotiability due to non-listing of shares on stock exchanges, restrictive clauses in articles of association, net tangible asset backing, upward or downward trends in profits, quality of management etc. among others. The adjusted yield reflected in comparable stocks can be used to capitalise the maintainable profits to determine the value of the shares of the company.

The final value of the shares will further depend upon factors such as minority or majority holding, additional capital requirements to maintain yield, shares having differing rights etc.

Value based on future/projected earnings

Current thinking on valuation emphasises the importance to be placed on prospective earnings in determination of value of an enterprise. All competent appraisers recognise that a record of past earnings taken by itself is a very unreliable measure of future earnings. It is argued that when earnings have once been 'realised', they are water under the mill and have no direct bearing on what the property in question is now worth.

Two methods have normally been applied for determining 'value' based on projected profitability:

(*a*) Capitalisation of Projected Earnings.

(*b*) Discounted Cash Flow (DCF) Technique.

Capitalisation of projected earnings

The process of determining the value of the shares based on projected earnings is similar to that adopted for determining value of shares based on capitalisation of past earnings discussed above.

The important aspect in determination for value based on projected earnings is the evaluation of the projected earnings and the assumptions that may have been made in establishing such projections. Consideration must be given to the future business plan and strategy to be adopted by the company as regards future expansion and capital expenditure, projections of sales and revenues, needs of further capital for capital expenditure and increased working capital requirements, prospects for the industry and for the company among several other relevant factors. The reasonableness and realisability of the projections have to be examined closely having regard and keeping in mind the past performance of the company. Often the projected earnings may be the subject of appraisal by lenders. More reliance may be placed on such appraised projections in determining value of the shares.

The projected earnings of a company as a basis of determining value is often subject to the criticism that such projections are highly speculative and are based on estimates or guesses as to future business conditions and managerial efficiency, the validity of which cannot adequately be assured. It is for this reason that apart from a proper evaluation of the projections, since these projections are in the realm of future probabilities and are subject to various contingencies, it may be appropriate to discount these projections appropriately in determining the value of the shares or business based on such projected earnings.

Discounted Cash Flow (DCF) Technique

Under the traditional method, the future maintainable profits are capitalised to arrive at the value of the business. The DCF technique is one of the most rigorous approaches to the valuation of a business. It uses the future expected cash flows from the business for determining the value of the business. It recognises that money has a time value by discounting these future cash flows at an appropriate discount rate that reflects the riskiness of these cash flows. The value of company's equity is equal to the sum of the present value of the various future cash flow streams that ultimately add up to the cash flows to the equity holders in terms of dividend, share repurchases and share issues. Rather than value the equity directly as the present value of the various cash flows to the shareholders, the equity is valued as the present value of the operating free cash flows less the present value of the cash paid to and received from the company's debt-holders.

Net asset value

Although valuation on a going concern basis primarily uses the income yield for determination of value, the value based on assets of an enterprise cannot be wholly ignored. Some attention must be given to the underlying strength indicated by the net tangible assets of the enterprise which are the main instruments in generating the profits earned or to be earned by the enterprise in the future.

In certain special circumstances, even when the valuation is on the basis of the 'going concern' concept, it may be necessary to give added importance to the intrinsic worth of the assets of the enterprise. This is especially true where the transfer of shares results in a transfer of controlling interest in the enterprise. In this situation, the owner of shares, who enjoys controlling interest would expect a fair compensation for his disinvestment which will not only take into account the earning power of the shares but also the real worth of the assets, rights over which he would relinquish on transfer of the shares.

In other words one has to look at the market value of the assets rights to which the owner would be relinquishing on diminution of his interest in the equity of the company. The true value of the property in such a situation to its owner necessarily takes account of all the direct and indirect advantages that the property affords its owner.

Valuation of stock in dissolution

In *Commissioner of Income Tax* v *Popular Automobiles*,[3] the issue was how to value the closing stock of a firm dissolved when the valuation takes place after dissolution followed by the discontinuation of business. The Revenue agreed that there is a distinction between cases where there is a continuation of business after dissolution and cases where there is a discontinuation of business after dissolution. In this case, the assessee pleaded that the dissolution of the firm was followed by discontinuation of business and accordingly it valued the closing stock at cost or market price whichever is less. Held that such closing stock was to be valued at the market rate. The decisions in *A.L.A. Firm* v *Commissioner of Income Tax*[4] and *Shakti Trading Company* v *Commissioner of Income Tax*[5] were followed.

In *Shakti Trading Company* v *Commissioner of Income Tax*[6] the assessee was a registered firm. As a result of death of one out of its six partners on 6th February 1984, the firm was dissolved it was reconstituted with effect from the next day 7th February 1984, with the remaining five partners. The Tribunal held that, as the business of the firm was never discontinued but was taken over on succession by another firm, the closing stock of the assessee firm as on 6th February 1984, had to be valued at cost or market price whichever is lower. On a reference, the High Court held that the closing stock had to be valued at market price. On appeal, the Supreme Court reversing the decision of the Madras High Court, held that since there was no cessation of business, the closing stock had to be valued at cost or market price, whichever is lower. It is an established rule of commercial practice and accountancy that where there is no discontinuance of business the closing stock is to be valued at cost or market price,

3 (2002)255 ITR 499 (Ker).
4 (1991)189 ITR 285 (SC).
5 (2001)250 ITR 871 (SC).
6 (2001)250 ITR 871 (SC).

whichever is lower. The decisions in *G.R. Ramachari & Co.* v *Commissioner of Income Tax*[7] and *A.L.A. Firm* v *Commissioner of Income Tax*[8] were distinguished.

(K) INTELLECTUAL PROPERTY

"Intellectual property" has come to be internationally recognised a major contributor to the 'goodwill' of a going concern comprising the attributes of patents, industrial designs, copyright, trade marks, know-how and confidential information. It is a sub-set of 'intangible assets' that include both 'intellectual capital' as well as 'intellectual property'. All these expressions need to be explained at the outset in order to avoid confusion and clarity of understanding, as because; they often tread the common pasture.

Asset and goodwill

An 'asset' is a resource from which future economic benefits are expected to flow to the enterprise. An 'intangible asset' is an asset without physical substance but capable of yielding economic benefits. Some of the intangible assets are identifiable like patents, copyrights, trade marks, etc. But some are not identifiable such as 'goodwill' except as a resultant phenomenon. In fact, 'goodwill' represents future economic benefits from synergy between identifiable assets and from factors that do not meet the criteria for recognition as an intangible asset, such as, excellent management, outstanding workforce, market penetration, effective advertising etc. Thus 'goodwill' is the resultant of combination of various factors which places an enterprise in a superior position as compared to its competitors and enables each firm to earn super profits.

Intellectual capital and intellectual property

'Property' is an asset which is capable of acquisition, possession and disposal. Viewed in this light, an intellectual property must also be something which can be acquired, possessed and transferred. It must be the product of intellect arising out of human skill, intelligence, ideas, inventions or any other creative faculty. In that sense, the man himself possessing the particular

7 (1961)41 ITR 142 (Mad).
8 (1976)102 ITR 622 (Mad)

gift of skill or intelligence has to be rightly termed as 'intellectual capital' of which 'intellectual property' is the product. Because, skill, intelligence or any other creative faculty cannot be separated from the person who possesses it and hence not transferable as a property. But nevertheless, it is an asset since it gives a yield or is fountain of benefits of value. Thus, an intangible asset does embrace within its definition both intellectual capital and all its products in the form of intellectual property whether as patent or as copyright, or as design or any other innovative step capable of being treated as property. The productive human resources, in fact constitute the intellectual capital which cannot be transferred except by way of 'brain drain' or other forms of lure.

Intangible asset and intellectual property

'Intangible asset or property' is again distinguishable from 'intellectual property' as such. Intellectual property of whatever species is in the nature of intangible asset but all intangibles are not intellectual property. Patents, designs, copyright and industrial know-how have always been recognized as having the attributes of intellectual property. It cannot be doubted that these are the products of intellectual efforts and creative activity in the field of applied arts or technology in manufactures, but the creation of trade mark has very little to do with intellectual creativity, although it certainly merits inclusion as an intangible property of a company or business. So also is goodwill. The scope of intellectual property is expanding very fast and attempts are being made by persons to create new creative ideas to seek protection under the umbrella of intellectual property rights. The proportion of contribution of intangible assets *vis-a-vis* tangible assets in a modern going concern may be estimated as going up between 70%-80% as against 30%-20% from tangible assets. The productivity of tangible assets is again heavily dependent on intangible assets that the manufacturing concern operates. The relationship *inter se* of the intangible assets in their conjoint effect may be expressed as the company's goodwill, being symbolized or identified in trade marks or brand names; protected by patents, copyrights or designs; and enriched by confidential information and industrial know-how.

Laws on intellectual property

There are many similarities in the law relating to the different species of intellectual property in regard to the nature of the property, the mode of its acquisition, the nature of the rights conferred, commercial exploitation of those rights, enforcement of those rights and the remedies available against infringement of those rights. The law again differs from country to country but generally agree to the basic tenets or statutory regulations and the objectives of legal control.

With the growth of intangibles in enterprises, intellectual property has gradually surfaced as a species of assets. But it must be understood, there is always some intellectual contribution also in the product resulting from physical labour and conversely, product driven by intellect do also find expression in some physical form. But certain intangible products like copyright, patent, etc. are regarded as an altogether different kind of asset from consumable goods or physical articles. The distinguishing feature is that in an intellectual property, the tangible element is an insignificant component of the total value. A book may have a negligible component of value in terms of paper, printing and binding but account for enormous value in terms of thought, precepts or information contained therein. Again, any form of intellectual service is not an intellectual property. A violinist may be hired for presenting a concert before an audience. But this musical service is not regarded as a property. But if he brings out a cassette of his own, it becomes an intellectual property. In that sense, an intellectual property must be a product by itself having the elements of utility, scarcity and transferability. It is primarily the outcome of an individual's creative instinct which finds a place of value in the market.

In recent times, there has been a strong pressure from all quarters to afford protection to intellectual property rights in order that the value of the product may not be diluted by reckless reproduction and the producer gets his due. Hence the laws on intellectual property. In earlier times, the diffusion of knowledge was so slow that an invention could be fully exploited by the inventor long before others were about to copy it. But there has been a qualitative change in modern technology in the case of reproduction of books, films, video tapes and so forth opening up a flood-gate of the possibility of pirating once the intellectual property is available in the market. With the proliferation of cassettes and computer software and the rapid rise of cheap reprographic facilities, the matter of protection has taken on a new urgency in the last decade or so. It is because a product of intellectual creativity has come to be seen as a financially valuable asset to be exploited for economic purposes that the society started to take cognizance of it and indeed, created laws for its protection.

Rights with regard to intellectual property are thus very often statutorily reserved for a limited period exclusively in favour of the inventor or creator in the form of patent, copyright etc. The WTO has decided to extend the period of patent rights to twenty years. India as an enlisted country of WTO had to amend the relevant provision of law accordingly. It is not impossible for an advanced country to perpetuated its patent right by a continuous attempt through research and development for a substitute that renders the earlier product or process obsolete. This is a real threat to the developing countries which are unable to afford huge investment in R&D and consequently have to serve the role of consumers in a market economy.

Nature of intellectual property in its different species of patents

Intellectual property of whatever species consists of a bundle of rights created with the owner for use of such rights, grant licenses to others, or to sell that right to a third person. Thus, a patent when granted confers on the patentee the exclusive right to use the invention during the term of the patent, or as long as it is in force on payment on renewal fee. The patentee may assign his rights or grant licenses to use the invention. There is a general obligation cast on the patentee to work the invention on a commercial scale either by himself or through licensee. If the patentee does not do this, any interested person may obtain a compulsory license from the Government authority to work the patent. This is the general philosophy about patent although the laws may differ from country to country about the details like term of patent, renewal provision or the eventuality for compulsory license. In India, in respect of patent related to drug or medicine or substances used as food, the term of patent is five years from the date of sealing the patents or seven years from the date of filing complete specifications. This may not be the same in most other developed countries.

The idea behind patent is to confer a monopoly right to the inventor for a limited period to market a patented product or patented process of manufacture. The object is to encourage and develop a new technology in that industry because, an inventor may disclose the new invention only if he is rewarded; otherwise he may work it secretly and the invention may ultimately be lost to the industry. But the patent laws are also mindful of fact that the inventor should not be allowed to play havoc with its vested right for undue gain. That is why disclosure to the public of the invention is provided for, through licensing on reasonable term and other forms of transfer. If the inventor withholds such disclosure, the law generally provides for compulsory disclosure at the command of the governmental authority so that the commercial exploitation of the invention may not be unreasonably prejudiced.

It may be noted that a patent does not give the patentee an omnibus right to use the invention as such. It gives him only the right to exclusively use or make patented article or use the patented process. The value of patent system is demonstrated by the fact that in almost all advanced countries the number of patents granted has shown a phenomenal increase. A good number of them are foreign patents which is common in pharmaceutical field. Attempts are being made from time to time by international associations for the protection of industrial property by introducing more and more uniformity and harmonisation among national patent systems. The International Convention for the Protection of Industrial Property as well as GATT (now WTO) and TRIPs agreements are examples of attempts at such harmonization.

Designs

The consumers are very often influenced in their choice of purchase of an article, not only by practical utility or quality, but also by its appearance. That is how designs have emerged as a significant species of intellectual property. Many simply choose the article which cateches their eyes. An article with a particular design may sell better than one without it. That is how design acts as a stimulus to sales. The law provides for designs registration in order to ensure that the originator of a profitable design is not deprived of his reward by others copying it without permission. The law everywhere ensures that the designs which are functional are not registrable as design. The drawings or diagrams on the basis of which the articles are made artistic, may come within the definition for protection under the copyright laws but the object of the law of design is to provide that only the features of shape, configuration, pattern, ornaments or composition of lines or colours applied to any article whether in two dimensional or in three-dimensional forms are given protection through registration. To give examples, shape and configuration are three-dimensional in case of a bottle, vase and so on; while patterns or ornamentals are two-dimensional in case of textile, wallpaper etc. A design may be the shape of a washbasin, a motor car, locomotive engine or any material object whatsoever. But the appeal must be to the sense of sight of human beings. Like patents, design also gives a monopoly of marketing to the author but only for a limited period. If the design is not used by other traders even after the expiry of the monopoly period it may mature into a trade mark which is entitled to protection under a different statute. Design can be licensed or assigned like patent.

Trademark

A trademark is not a registerable design though it is a visual symbol. It may take the form of a word, a device, mark, brand, name, label, signature, letter, number, shape of goods, packing or combination of colours which is intended to give an indication to the purchaser to give an identification as to an manufacturer or quality of the goods, or to provide an indication of the trade source or origin from which the goods come. It gives the purchaser a satisfactory assurance of the quality of the article he is buying, the particular quality or the product of a particular market not being apparent to the eye. Under modern business conditions, a trade mark performs four functions—(1) it identifies the product and its origin; (2) it guarantees its unchanged quality; (3) it advertises its product; and (4) it creates an image for the product. Licensing or assignment of trademark is permissible. Registration gives a protection of monopoly use; if not registered, it also gives a right to be defended against unauthorized use by others as a tort. This is usually called the right against passing off on false representation. The idea is to prevent the hi-jacking the good will of another enterprise with a view to undue gain.

Trademark is capable of transmission and assignment. But unlike other species of intangibles, it is not a product of intellectual creativity but of marketing strategy; and it is not limited by any period of tenure during registration or statutory subsistence. It pertains to a product for an indefinite period.

Copyright

The object of copyright law is to protect the author of the copyright work from an unlawful reproduction or exploitation of his work by others. In ancient times creative writers, musicians and artists wrote, composed or made their work mainly for fame and recognition rather than to earn a living or make profits. Copying was also laborious and expensive process. But things have changed with time. Knowledge, skill or creativity is now a marketable article and at the same time, copying or duplication has become so easy, cheap and convenient. Hence the idea of protection of this leading species of intellectual property which every country has adopted. The Indian law on copyright prevalent since 1957 protects the following classes of work:

(*a*) Original literary, dramatic, musical and artistic works,

(*b*) Cinematograph films, and

(*c*) sound recording.

Literary work includes computer programmes, tables and compilations including computer databases. The period of copyright protection extends to the lifetime of the author and sixty years thereafter from the beginning of the calender year next following the year in which the author dies. The author can retain the copyright to himself, or assign it or give license in favour of others. As a property, it can be transferred, inherited or disposed of by testamentary document. In addition to civil remedy, the Copyright Act enables the owner to initiate criminal proceedings against an infringer in appropriate cases. Apart from the Berne Convention and Universal Copyright Convention, works of International Organizations like UNO and its agencies as well as the Organization of American States are granted copyright protection in India. Works of foreign authors first published in India are granted protection on a reciprocal basis. Another distinguishing feature in the matter of copyright is the provision for registered copyright societies exercising administration of licensing on behalf of its members.

In business valuation as discussed earlier, we consider the contribution of intangibles to business for estimating the value thereof, but an intellectual property, since it is a product by itself, has also to be valued either according to the market approach or cost approach or the income approach according as the contingency or purpose warrants as a distinct item, if separately accounted for, in accordance with similar methods or principles.

Impact of intangibles including intellectual property on economy

Valuation consideration's on intangibles including intellectual property lead upwards to certain macro-economic issues that have meaningful implications in a globalised world. Economy is gradually being drawn towards dependence on heavy capital investments with liquidity of assets banished more and more to distant recesses. At the dawn of economic life, the participants to the production of commodities and services were confined in a simple process to labour and natural resources. The subsequent stage of development introduced capital and enterprise. Thus, land, labour, capital and organisation formed the chief factors of economic production with the advent of industrial revaluation. The technological revolution followed by information age of the last few decades has brought us to the doorstep of a new era. Capital has already needed huge investment to be sunk in monetary fund and given rise to joint stock companies for spread of shares and debentures with the result of infusing liquidity to capital assets so sunk in investment. The other alternative has been a system of capital participation by banks and financial institutions as fund mobilisers who step in through mortgage or hypothecation or leasing of high-valued assets. Large investment also means large scale production and a marketing strategy matched to it. Quest for market tracked the path of colonisation at one stage of global history. Now information age has brought in an advanced nexus of global communication introducing newer techniques of management and marketing strategy. Simultaneously, intangible assets including intellectual property have assumed preponderant role in the dominating sector of economic production. The secondary and tertiary sectors have undergone a sea change with more and more investment in Research and Development which revolutionises the primary sector of production as well. Multinational enterprises have occupied the front stage of economy as well as political support that sustains it. This leads to a parallel growth of entry barriers to industries fostering monopoly or oligopoly. In this scenario the world has been divided into capital—rich countries with multi-national enterprises (MNEs) in commanding height and capital-starved countries at the receiving end. The international distribution of research and development (R&D) activities of MNEs is highly uneven, depending along with other factors on the foreign direct investment (FDI) received by the countries, as well as resources and environment prevailing in the subject country for technical upgradation. The treatment of intellectual property among other policy instruments rights can also be an important factor on a country's ability to attract R&D investment from MNEs.

A number of studies have analysed the phenomenon of overseas R&D. As for example, Patel and Pavitt (1991) analysed the importance of overseas R&D in generation of technology for the 686 largest manufacturing corporations by examine the origin of patents obtain by them in USA (Vide Journal of International Business Studies, vol. 22, No. 1, pp. 1-22) Jaffe (1986) finds that the pay off in terms of patents, projects or market value to a firm's own R&D is higher in technological areas, where there is much R&D undertaken by other firms (Vide American Economic Review, vol. 76, No. 5, pp. 984-1001). OECD (1994) studies show that for Japanese firms, the effect of a skilled labour force on the decision to invest abroad is highly important. (Vide The Performance of Foreign Affiliates in OECD Countries, OECD Paris) Mazzoleni and Nelson (1998) made remarkable findings (Vide Research Policies, vol. 27, pp. 273-821) which has been further discussed by Prabuddha Sanyal of American University, Washington DC (Vide Journal of Intellectual Capital, vol. 5, No. 1, 2004, pp. 59-76). It reveals that there are great opportunities in broadening and strengthening patent rights in the areas of production in certain industries like chemical, aircraft, semi-conductor etc. Because, it will entail heavy entry barriers for new firms with adverse implications for firms in developing economies. Rather weaker patent protection is desirable for group of industries like food and chemicals if technology has to flow across boundaries. Incidentally the Indian law on patents is already responsive to this situation, inasmuch as the term of legal protection of patents in general is twenty years from the date of filing of the application for patent. The duration of registration of all semi-conductor layout design under the relevant Act passed in the year 2000 in India, is ten years from the date of application or the date of commercial exploration, whichever is earlier; with no provision for renewal. Entry barrier is a major factor for consideration in the wake of capital-intensity propelled by the growth of the role of intangibles in production. At the further end lies investment in infrastructure which is mostly controlled by the public sector of the governmental administration. The complexion of the Government in power again has much to weigh in this sphere.

Contrary to popular belief, the above studies have revealed that the strength of patent protection in developing economies does not appear to be of any significance for R&D investments. On the other hand, the R&D based in industrialised economies, being more creative and development oriented needs stronger intellectual property regimes. However the above inferences should be treated with caution and is only tentative, given the limitations of measuring the strength of intellectual property rights regimes to a general rule. The major determinants for investment in R&D in another country is the market size of the host country, availability of skilled labour force, benefits derived from localised spill-over providing scope for adaptations of product or process, policy environment, technological infrastructure etc. Much can be achieved with trade and intellectual property agreement at global level, inviting proactive role of organisations like WTO, WIPO or TRIPs Agreements.

(L) GEM AND JEWELLERY

Professional jewellery appraisal as a distinct entity from a jeweller and separate from a gemologist evolved since the 1970s during which gems and jewellery gained widespread popularity as investments. While gemologists could identify and grade and jewellers could come up with a price for gems and jewellery, few of them were qualified to vouch for the value thereof. Valuation involves an estimate and judgment on the price and state logically the reasons thereof. Moreover, no uniform appraisal standards were known. Now professional jewellery appraisers are on the brink of a new vocation. Banks, insurance companies and governmental agencies have been relying more and more on the judgment of professional appraisers. According to the definition as given in Explanation 1 of s. 2(*ea*) of the Wealth-tax Act, "jewellery" includes—

(*i*) ornaments made of gold, silver, platinum or any other precious metal or any alloy containing one or more of such precious metals, whether or not containing any precious or semi-precious stones, and whether or not worked or sewn into any wearing apparel;

(*ii*) precious or semi-precious stones, whether or not set in any furniture, utensils or other article or worked or sewn into any wearing apparel.

The task of valuing jewellery for Wealth-tax purposes is now assigned to registered valuers and a valuer of jewellery, under rule 8A(9) of Wealth-tax Rules, must have been, for a period of not less than five years, a sole proprietor or partner in a partnership firm carrying on jewellery business which has on an average annual turnover of not less than ₹ 15 lakhs or profit (including fees for valuation of not less than rupees fifty thousand) in the last three accounting years immediately preceding the year in which the application for registration as a valuer is made by him.

The sources of information on which a professional appraiser on gem and jewellery has to rely are actual prices compiled from quotations by wholesale and retail dealers, manufacturer's price lists, auction sale reports and different literature on the subject. In an Indian text, the *Arthasashtra* developed between the fourth and the sixth century A.D. a body of rules and standards regulating taxes and other charges were applied to diamonds and precious stones.

For valuation of gems and jewellery, it is essential for an appraiser to he trained in various manufacturing methods, experienced in buying and selling and the various levels of value of stones and metals from source to consumer. It is necessary for him to be equipped with the knowledge of current wholesale and retail prices of gemstones and jewellery with access to verifiable data. It should be borne in mind that appraising is a discipline different from gemology and an appraiser's main field of operation is in the market when transaction's take place rather than a gemological laboratory.

Gems and jewellery as personal property have now a growing investment market with rising potential for investment. Material properties are customarily divided into 'real and personal'. Real property comprising 'real estate' and rights/interests arising out of it assume a dominant role in business matters. Personal property also known as chattels are relegated to secondary treatment in valuation. But there has since been a growth of vast financial investments in personal property and the valuation problems inherent in buying, selling and insuring these goods have surfaced since investment potentials in arts, antiques, stamps, coins, sculpture, gems and jewellery have grown in volume, necessity has arisen to study, rationaliser, define and codify the appraisal standards. The appraisal includes both qualitative opinion on the items and estimation of value in monetary terms.

Value in gems and jewellery depends primarily upon the relationship of the item to the person, to the culture and to the social, regional and geographical background. Historically, the use and demand began with self-beautification. Precious metals had a long user in coins for circulation by the Governmental authorities. The Indian women look upon ornaments and jewellery as security for rainy days and possessory pride. Even if ornaments and jewellery cannot be openly displayed or used for self-beautification due to consideration of law and order, the assets find their safe resting place in bank lockers in perpetuity, sometimes pressed into use on festival occasions and even if that is not possible, preserved as storage of value. The gems, jewellery and precious metals do also represent congealed wealth within a physical dimension as minimum as possible, possessing reasonable liquidity and capable of being hidden outside the gaze of unwarranted persons or authorities. Besides, these are assets with relative stability in value lent by the elements of scarcity, utility, and transferability; and being so, have a good demand for investment. Vintage jewellery transcend into a higher echelon of valuation hued by association of history, antiquity, fame or rarity.

The duties of an appraiser in such circumstances consist of the following functions:

(1) to identify the item for appraisal;
(2) to research and establish its identity, make, age, origin and other relevant particulars;
(3) to specify the appropriate market of buying and selling;
(4) to determine the proper approach to value;
(5) to be ready to offer full narrative description of factors for identical reproduction;
(6) to be able to support his judgment before the clientele.

Valuation market

Production cost of an item of gem or jewellery may not be its intrinsic value; rather it is the estimated amount of cost to produce a piece of jewellery by assembling the separate components, making a complete piece and finishing it. On the other hand a buyer's fascination for an item may not be the true value. While the price actually paid may provide an evidence, the value shall remain to be estimated as an expected amount under specific market conditions.

The market may be an 'estate' which is an omnibus word used to describe numerous markets in the jewellery industry. Again, the market may be an auction market or a bankruptcy proceeding. In another view, the market may be wholesale or retail each having its own characteristic.

Market value

Transactions in an estate generally abide by the fair market value the auction market generates the highest and best value while bankruptcy proceeding bring in the liquidation value.

For wholesale value, the appraiser may have to research for prices at mine sites, cutting centres, dealer-to-dealer in order to arrive at a reasonable estimate. The retail price essentially depends upon replacement cost with a comparable item or an exact replica in quality and utility.

Valuation estimate of an antique jewellery is, however, a difficult one since it cannot be exactly replaced in today's market. However, the valuation estimate thereof must bear a reflection of the sum required to replace the antique specimen with an item of same specification, motif, skill of workmanship, subject to the availability of a like article in the current market-place.

Valuation approaches

It would follow from the above discussion that cost approach has a limited application in the field of appraisal of gems and jewellery. It may be used to determine the wholesale price or wholesale value where reference to the mine site or at the cutting centre is of significance.

The cost approach can never determine the fair market value, nor is it used to estimate the replacement value in antique jewellery. The retail replacement new for insurance purpose may often be determined by the cost approach.

The market data comparison approach is the best method of appraisal. But it requires a thorough research in the market for comparable data and analysing each of the comparable properties and constant updating of information.

The comparable attributes of gems and jewellery may comprise the following:

- distinctive features/design;
- quality of the article;
- condition;
- age;
- origin and manufacture;
- factor of scarcity;
- market for transaction.

But the most important requirement is the collection of data or relevant information. The following are the usual sources:

— jewellery firms and establishments;
— price catalogues in circulation;
— sales representatives and dealers;
— auction houses;
— manufacturers;
— trade shows, exhibitions and fairs;
— jewellery industry magazines and literature;
— sales advertisements;
— computer information services.

Sometimes, the market provides a range of prices in which case the statistical method of working out the mode, median or mean may approximate the correct market value or the fair market value.

Since gems and jewellery have also an investments market where speculative dealings are as well in vogue, the income approach is often called into play. In income approach too the expected income is compared with alternative avenues of investments in a market situation. Thus, market data comparison approach plays the dominant role in the field of valuation.

(M) CURRENCY

How value of money is determined has been a subject of intense debate among the economists. The metre measures distance, but what measures the metre? Well, the distance itself. Similarly, money measures goods and services, but what measures money? "The amount of goods and services" is the reply. Value, as we know, is the ratio of exchange between two goods and money measures that value through the medium of price. What money can buy depends on the level of prices. When price level rises, a unit of money can purchase less goods than before and money is said to have depreciated in value. Conversely, a fall in price signifies that the purchasing power of a unit of money rises and money is then said to appreciate in value. An attempt has been made to explain the determinants of the value of money by the Quantity Theory as developed by Irving Fisher, an American economist. According to it, the total quantity of money in circulation together with instruments of credit like cheque, drafts, bills etc. as multiplied by the velocity of circulation of money determines the total volume of money supply. It gets fully distributed over the total turnover of goods and services as multiplied by price. He puts it in the form of an algebraic equation of exchange as M.V. = P.T., where M represents the total quantity of money and V is the velocity of circulation while P is the price and T stands for the trade or goods exchanged. In spite of criticisms raised against this equation, we may say that although the exact relationship between the supply of money and its value as indicated by the equation may not hold good, yet the theory in a general way explains the phenomenon of changes in price level and consequent inflation or deflation.

Value of currency under gold standard

What we are concerned in our present topic is not exactly the value of money but the value of currency. The value of a particular currency depends upon the forces of demand and supply reflected in the exchange rates in the international arena. As the value of a unit of money or currency means its purchasing power measured in terms of commodities and services, it is urgently necessary for facility of international transactions that the value of a currency remains stable. There was an attempt by the world community to stabilize the value of currencies by tying them up to the gold standard. Under the gold standard, the supply of gold is the primary factor in determining the quantity of money. Discovery of new gold mines, increase of supply from old mines and diversions from non-monetary uses of gold, sooner or later reaches the Central Bank's vaults and increases its reserves. The issue of notes bears a fixed ratio to this reserve. Under a pure gold standard, gold can be converted into coins at the option of the holder of the gold. Increase in the quantity of coins and notes in due course increases the reserves of the banks, and leads to the creation of more bank credit. Thus the quantity of money increases in cautious steps. For about 60 years spanning both sides of the turn of the twentieth century, the international payments systems operated on the gold standard. This did not mean that all international payments were settled in gold, but each country was prepared to pay in gold and by keeping to the rules of the system, ensured that its Balance of Payments was never in heavy deficit. The gold standard was virtually abandoned in 1931 and ended later with the Bretton Woods Conference. For a few years, the international payments system relied upon free or floating exchange rates to adjust deficits and surpluses. But this experiment was also not successful and after the Second World War the system of managed flexibility representing a partial return to gold came into vogue. In this changed pattern, it is in the last resort that creditor countries could insist on being paid in gold.

Sterling balance

So far as India is concerned, the rupee currency was tied up with the Sterling Area comprising the majority of the Commonwealth countries headed by U.K. This gave rise to development of sterling as a reserve currency. Since Britain was the main source of manufactured goods as well as the main customer for raw materials and also the main source for investment funds, many countries of the Commonwealth found it beneficial to keep the reserves in London. Thus sterling balances that accumulated in London were as good as gold to the overseas countries. The gold reserves of the Sterling Area in London virtually provided the standard in relation to which the individual member's currencies were valued.

Dollar supremacy and IMF

From the end of the First World War and more specially after 1945, the American dollar challenged and surpassed sterling as the reserve and trading currency. The ten years after the war saw an unprecedented demand for dollars. The American economy assumed an insuperable position. In this scenario, the International Monetary Fund has assumed the task of regulatory control for maintaining stable exchange rates. As a matter of fact, the IMF has been holding the reins ever since the Bretton Woods Conference of 1944 provided the system of managed flexibility. The objectives of the IMF have been to establish a system of convertible currencies and stability of exchange rates. The system of managed flexibility required a member to declare the par value of its currency in terms of gold or the U.S. dollar, which was itself priced in terms of gold at $35 per ounce. The success of the IMF in maintaining stable exchange rates led to increasing activity in its other role of providing currency to members in temporary balance of ayments difficulties. Gradually, a revolving pool of currency was created in the IMF to enable the members to tide over their difficulties of balance of payments marked by a borrowing right for each member determined by a complex formula. Under the system that ultimately developed, as a member draws foreign currency from the IMF, it must deposit corresponding amounts of its own currency.

Special drawing rights

At the initial stage when the Fund was established, the drawing right of a member was determined by its quota or contribution to the fund. The members were required to contribute 25 per cent of their quota in gold or U.S. dollars and the remainder in their local currency. With the increase of quota in 1978, this ceased to be the case. Members are now entitled in case of future increase in quota to deposit 75 per cent in local currency and 25 per cent in Special Drawing Rights (SDRs). Thus, there has been an important introduction of a new kind of international money in the form of Special Drawing Rights on which the value of currency of a particular country depends. The SDRs are automatically available to members and are regarded by them as part of the reserves. The SDRs exist only on the books of the Fund and can be transferred only between members. They cannot be used in international trade for the purchase of goods and services but may be transferred to the accounts of other members in exchange of foreign currencies. In this way, SDR is virtually a 'paper gold' the efficacy of which depends on the willingness of surplus countries to accept it and provide their currency in exchange. A small rate of interest is payable by debtors to creditors. As yet SDRs form but a small proportion of world reserves and can hardly replace the gold standard but has constituted an important stage in the development of world liquidity linked to the growth of trade. So far as valuation of a currency is concerned, everything would depend upon the strength of the currency as reflected in its purchasing power and consequent demand in the world market. The fact remains, the exact worth of a currency in terms of purchasing power may be artificially enhanced by superior bargaining power in the world trade and even by political domination. During the days of colonisation, the subject nations used to suffer mostly because of political domination. In the era of free world, the domination is imposed by the bigger economic powers exercising compulsions on the world trade market by sheer bargaining strength extraneous to purchasing power parity. This belies the golden theory of market value which means the estimated price as determined between a willing buyer and a willing seller in a market situation uninfluenced by any compulsion or extraneous circumstances.

(N) ANTIQUITIES, ARTS AND ARTEFACTS

Fine art, painting and sculpture often command high value as intellectual property. There has been a growth of the market in the sense of local, national or international. The value is manifold when a piece of art or artefact earns the distinction of uniqueness and, of course, historical association. But rarity or uniqueness does not by itself make a piece valuable. It must have specific comparables to be valuable. The paradox is that the masterpieces of art derive value when they cease to be generally marketable and withdrawn from open market. But even if so withdrawn, they obtain high value with reference to rare comparables in a specialised restricted market in the estimation of connoisseurs. This is the process that brings appraisal award to outstanding work of art or craftsmanship, rare book, manuscript; vintage car or legendary idol.

Historicity is an important factor as well as antiquity. One hundred years has been generally accepted as the qualifying age for antiquity, whether the object is a coin, sculpture, manuscript or inscription. Until recently, an antique was regarded as anything produced prior to 1830. However in 1966 the United States of America passed a new tariff permitting the duty-free importation of 'antiques made prior to one hundred years before their date of entry'. This has now been accepted as the usual criterion of an antique by most countries. One hundred years has been the accepted age in Britain for an antique to be exempt from Value-Added Tax, and also under the Hallmarking Act 1973 in respect of gold and silver.

In India, the Ancient Monuments Preservation Act 1904 (Act 7 of 1904) provides for preservation of ancient monuments and of objects of archaeological, historical or artistic interest. The Ancient Monuments and Archaeological Sites and Remains Act 1958 (Act 24 of 1958) provides the following definitions:

Section 2(*a*). "Ancient monument" means any structure, erection or monument, or any tumulus or place of internment, or any cave, rock sculpture, inscription or monolith, which is of historical, archaeological or artistic interest and which has been in existence for not less than 100 years, and includes—

(*i*) the remains of an ancient monument;

(*ii*) the site of an ancient monument;

(*iii*) such portion of the land adjoining the site of an ancient monument as may be required for fencing or covering in or otherwise preserving such monument, and;

(*iv*) the means of access to, and convenient inspection of, an ancient monument;

Section 2(*b*). "Antiquity" includes—

(*i*) any coin, sculpture, manuscript, epigraph or other work of art or craftsmanship;

(*ii*) any article, object or thing detached from a building or cave;

(*iii*) any article, object or thing illustrative of science, art, crafts, literature, religion, customs, morals or politics in bygone ages;

(*iv*) any article, object or thing of historical importance, and;

(*v*) any article, object or thing declared by the Central Government by notification in the Official Gazette, to be an antiquity for the purposes of this Act, which has been in existence for not less than 100 years.

Section 2(*d*). "Archaeological site and remains" means any area which contains or is reasonably believed to contain ruins or relics of historical or archaeological importance which have been in existence for not less than 100 years and includes (*i*) such portion of land adjoining the area as may be required for fencing or covering in or otherwise preserving it, and (*ii*) the means of access to, and convenient inspection of, the area.

Section 2(*j*). "Protected monument" means an ancient monument which is declared to be of national importance by or under this Act.

Valuation considerations

Valuation of antiquities offer a considerable challenge. Condition is certainly a very significant consideration in value. Authenticity must be unquestionable when a piece of workmanship or craft relates to the aesthetic quality representing a particular period or preserves the style of an era or age. Original cost is not as important as a credible statement of current value based on long experience of the valuer. Any way, a specialised knowledge developed by a fair degree of prior experience reinforced by currently researched comparables would be the best equipment for a valuer. There is no substitute for experience as well as basic knowledge. Collection of hobby materials like stamps, coins etc. often attract high sentimental value. But in that case, market is the better judge where the objects are freely transacted.

A few court cases in India, particularly in the field of compulsory acquisition, touch upon certain aspects of determination of market value. In *Special L.A.O.* v *A.L. Srikantaraj,*[9] it has been held that a temple has no real market value. In awarding compensation its special significance including the sculptural and archaeological value are required to be considered. In *Secretary of State* v *Shanmugaraya Mudaliar,*[10] the Government acquired a granite hill on the sea beach near Chennai where seven pagodas of Mahabalipuram stood as ancient monument and also there were certain temples and carvings on that granite hill.

It was held by the Privy Council that they had no market value, as they never had been and was never likely to be a source of income. So, the right course of proceeding was to estimate the rent at which possibly the whole plot might be leased on the basis of how much rent a portion of the plot when leased for quarries had in fact been obtained for the *zamindar*. The purchase money might be properly calculated at 25 years' purchase of such rent.[11]

Again, in the case of *Vishnu Narayana Vaidya* v *District Deputy Collector, Kolaba,*[12] it was held that "Section 21 of the Ancient Monuments Preservation Act 1904 (Act 7 of 1904) clearly applies to the purchase of movable antiquities or relics and the compensation which may have to be paid for incidental damages caused by the removal or protection of such objects

9 (1992)3 Ker LJ 748.

10 ILR 16 Mad 369 (PC); 20 IA 80.

11 *Secretary of State* v *Shanmugaraya Mudaliar* ILR 16 Mad 369 (PC); 20 IA 80.

12 AIR 1918 Bom 245; 42 Bom 100.

of historical interest or art value. In ascertaining the market value of such movable antiquities and the amount of compensation to be paid to adjacent owners for acts done under the Act, being clearly indicated and by implication defined in s. 20 the provisions of the L.A. Act 1894 (repealed and replaced by the Right to Fair Compensation and Transparency in Land Acquisition, Rehabilitation and Resettlement Act 2013) as enumerated in s. 21 of the Ancient Monuments Preservation Act 1904 only are to guide the court for the determination of market value for the purpose. Since, the enumerated sections do not include ss. 18, 53 and 54 of the L.A. Act, there is no right of appeal from the authorised purchasing officer of the Government to Civil Court. Sections 10 and 21 of the Ancient Monuments Preservation Act 1904 deal with different classes of objects; so, where the Government actually acquires immovable property under s. 10 of the Act *ibid*, it is intended that the owners shall have full rights which they would have under the L.A. Act 1894.

CHAPTER

21

Valuation of Different Fiscal Purposes

(A) RATING

Rating originated in England as far back as the year 1601 and was given legal authority by the Poor Relief Act of that year and thus contemplated payments for the support of persons unable to maintain themselves, and the Act remained in force for over 300 years. It was held as far back as 1633 that assessments ought to be made on the visible estate of a resident in the town in which he dwelt. To look at the origin of this term, to 'rate' is to apportion a fixed amount between the members of a specified community. The amount raised by 'rating' is entirely governed by the municipal expenditure and the system of rating has no connection with it. It seems equitable that as far as possible every responsible resident should bear his or her share of the expenses incidental to the running of the town administration, because everyone derives benefit from the municipal services rendered.

There are different systems of rating in force in different countries, some purport to assess the rate on capital value, and others on annual value, some on the capital value of land only, others on the capital value of land and buildings jointly, or separately, as the case may be. Thus there is a bewildering variety of systems in practice. In India, following the British tradition, the word 'rate' is understood to mean a tax for local purpose imposed by the local authorities the basis of which is the annual value of lands, and buildings arrived at by adopting different recognised modes of making the levy. If the rental value of the lands and buildings can be easily estimated such as residential or commercial property the annual value is the gross annual rent it can reasonably be expected to fetch. If the property is industrial, it becomes difficult to assess the rental value since such property is not meant to be tenanted or let out. Besides, industrial property comprises also plant and machinery under the Indian laws, plant and machinery which are in the nature of building or structure as generally listed in a Schedule annexed to the respective municipal legislation, are also subject to municipal taxation. Such property is valued on a capital basis and then a statutory percentage of the capital value is reckoned as the annual value upon which the prescribed rate of taxation is imposed. The institutional property like community hall, school, hospital, etc. is also not subject-matter for tenancy. So, these properties are valued on the land and building method and the annual value is reckoned as a statutory percentage thereof which is generally lower than that for industrial property. Tax is levied in accordance with the prescribed rate of imposition upon the quantum of annual value so determined. There is application of the income method of valuation as well. The trading or income-generating assets like cinema hall, hotel, restaurant, petrol filling station, cold storage etc. are valued in a different approach the basis of which is income or profit. Then the annual value is usually worked out to provide the tax-base. In any situation the payment of municipal dues entails the exercise of working out the annual value in accordance with the principles as laid down in law and embroidered by judicial decisions.

The properties of the Central Government are exempt from municipal taxes under Article 285 of the Constitution of India, except in respect of such property as was liable to tax before the 1st April 1937. But the Central Government as a matter of policy have undertaken to pay service charges in lieu of taxes to the municipal authorities according to scale fixed from time to time.

Thus the urban property in India may be categorised in the following manner in the context of rating:

(*i*) Domestic or commercial property that are rentable assets.

(*ii*) Industrial property.

(*iii*) Institutional property.

(*iv*) Other income-generating assets.

(*v*) Central Government property.

It is the domestic houses or commercial property which constitute the bulk of assets subjected to municipal taxation and provide the major source of municipal revenue. But the rent thereof cannot be left exclusively to market forces for determination although the value thereof has to be determined only under the rental method. The reason is the rent control laws universally in enforcement in the urban municipal areas of India in all the States. This topic has been discussed in the earlier chapters of this book and the scenario as shaped by different judicial decisions are given hereafter. The property the value of which cannot be easily estimated by the rental method like industrial undertakings, institutional property or other profit-generating assets do not come under the purview of these decision as those are valued under a different approach altogether.

For the purpose of municipal taxation in respect of house property or commercial property the usual practice is to arrive at an annual valuation which forms the base for imposition of rates. The Annual Rateable Value (ARV) is worked out by an artificial method of valuation on the basis of the gross annual rent which the house property may reasonably fetch from year to year including service charges but less an allowance of usual 10 per cent towards cost of repair etc. In this way ARV has almost become a variant of gross annual rent. The idea of including service charges towards computation of the gross annual rent is to exclude the possibility of evasion of a component of rent which go by the name of service charges. An irregular practice had developed in some quarters to show a portion of the rent as payment towards service charge like payments for furniture, lifts, darwans etc. so that the actual rental may find a lower base of annual value for imposition of municipal rate. This loophole is sought to be plugged by including all service charges towards computation of gross annual rent. Again, an amount equal to 10 per cent is usually deducted towards cost of repairs and maintenance so that the house property may remain in a physical state to command the gross annual rent. This percentage is again arbitrary and not realistic but this is permissible statutory deduction. Thus, for determination of annual value, the following are the ingredients to be taken into account:

(*i*) The gross annual rent at which the land or building might at the time of assessment be reasonably expected to let from year to year.

(*ii*) Service charges, if any, to be included in gross annual rent.

(*iii*) An allowance of 10 per cent towards cost of repairs etc. for deduction.

The municipal laws in India have, in a general way, taken the rental value of properties as the basis for imposition of house-property taxation. It is the annual value or the Annual Rateable Value which forms the basis of such taxation. The general method of determination of ARV of house-properties, again, is similar under different municipal laws. It is the "gross annual rent at which the land or building might at the time of assessment be reasonably expected to let from year to year" which forms the general basis for determination of the ARV under most of the municipal laws. The different High Courts and the Supreme Court have interpreted this expression "rent at which the land or building might ... be reasonably expected to let...." in their different decisions from different angles of viewing. These decisions, together with certain earlier decisions of the Privy Council, provide the legal framework within which the principles of valuation of urban properties have developed. We may now discuss some of these decisions of law courts and trace the track of evolution of the principles of valuation through such decisions.

Padma Devi's case

In *Corporation of Calcutta* v *Smt. Padma Devi*,[1] the Supreme Court laid down two principles of valuation under the Calcutta Municipal Act (C.M. Act) 1923. First, that in the matter of assessment of land and building to consolidate rating the criterion is the rent realisable by the landlord and not the value of holding in the hands of the tenant. It is the value of the property to the owner which forms the standard in making

1 (1962)3 SCR 49; AIR 1962 SC 151.

such assessment. Secondly, for the purpose of assessment to rates, the premises is deemed to be vacant and is deemed to be capable of being let. The test of reasonableness of the gross annual rent at which the building may reasonably be expected to let is the rent which the landlord may realise if the house is let under a bargain between a willing lessor and a willing lessee uninfluenced by extraneous consideration, and in determining the reasonableness of expectation of the landlord in the matter of rent, a law which imposes penal consequences cannot be ignored. In this case the standard rent of the premises was fixed by the Rent Controller. Under s. 3 of the West Bengal Premises Rent Control (Temporary Provisions) Act 1950, the landlord is debarred from realising any amount excess of standard rent and s. 33(*a*) of the said Act provides for a penal provision for realisation of such an excess amount. It appeared from this decision that the Supreme Court in interpreting the provisions of s. 127(*a*) of the C.M. Act 1923 had introduced a new principle of valuation of properties by equating reasonability with legality as to the expectation of rent.

L.I.C.I.'s case

In *Corporation of Calcutta* v *Life Insurance Corporation of India*[2] the Supreme Court went a step further and gave another dimension to the theory propounded in *Padma Debi's* case. In this case the standard rent of the premises was not fixed by the Rent Controller, yet the Supreme Court held that the standard rent is the maximum amount which could be taken into account in assessing the building to the consolidated rate. This decision was made on the basis of a notional concept of standard rent based upon the provision of s. 9 read with s. 2(10)(1) of the Rent Act 1950, which runs as follows:

> "Section 9. Standard rent in relation to any premises means:
>
> (*a*) ....
>
> (*b*) .... the rent .... at which it would have been fixed if application were made under the said section."

Guntur Municipal Council's case

In *Guntur Municipal Council* v *Guntur Town Rate Payer's Association,*[3] the Supreme Court further developed the concept

2 AIR 1970 SC 1417.
3 AIR 1971 SC 350.

of notional existence of fair or standard rent. The Hon'ble Court held that there is no distinction between the fair rent which has actually been fixed by the Rent Controller and those in respect of which no such rent has been fixed. It further held that when the Controller has not fixed the fair rent, the municipal authorities will have to arrive at their own figure of fair rent in accordance with the principles laid down in the Rent Control Act. In this decision also reasonable expectation of rent is made co-extensive with lawful expectation of rent by the landlord. The Hon'ble Court held that the landlord cannot lawfully expect to get more than the fair rent payable and under the Rent Control Act, and, therefore, asked the municipal authorities to assess properties on the basis of such lawfully expected fair rent.

Devan Daulat Rai Kapoor's case

In *Devan Daulat Rai Kapoor* v *New Delhi Municipal Committee*,[4] the Supreme Court developed a new concept of notional fair rent and norms of reasonableness as to expectation of rent. The Supreme Court in this case held that even if the tenant has lost his right to make the application for fixation of standard rent and the landlord can lawfully demand the agreed rent, the municipal committee is bound to assess annual value of a building on the basis of standard rent determinable under the Delhi Rent Control Act 1958. This decision is based upon two principles enunciated by the Supreme Court. First, the hypothetical tenant would be entitled to make an application for fixation of the standard rent and the limit of the standard rent determinable under the Rent Act would, therefore, inevitably enter into the bargain and circumscribe the rate of rent at which the building could reasonably be expected to be let. No hypothetical tenant would ordinarily agree to pay more rent than what he could be made liable to pay under the Rent Act. Secondly, the Rent Control Act, lays down the norms of reasonableness in regard to the rent payable by the tenant to the landlord. The Legislature has laid down the standard of reasonableness, and it would not be right for any court of law to say that the landlord may reasonably expect to receive rent exceeding the measure provided by this

4 AIR 1980 SC 541.

standard. It is by applying the principle of hypothetical tenancy in this form that the Supreme Court could give a go-by to the universally accepted principle of present user (*Rebus sec Stantibus*) and adopted the theory of prospective user. In propounding the theory of norms of reasonableness, the Hon'ble Court has introduced ethical consideration in place of extra-legal consideration and has, therefore, made a radical departure from its earlier views as expressed in *Padma Debi's* case and in *LIC's* case.

East India Commercial Company's case

In *Corporation of Calcutta* v *East India Commercial Co. (P) Ltd.*,[5] the High Court at Calcutta made a momentous decision in the matter of valuation of lands and buildings for the purpose of assessment to consolidated rate under the provisions of the C.M. Act 1951, when the West Bengal Premises Tenancy Act 1956 was regulating relations between landlords and tenants in West Bengal. This decision was made after considering all the earlier decisions of importance. Here the Hon'ble Court reaffirmed its earlier views equating reasonable expectation of rent with its lawful expectation. This decision is mainly based upon the provisions of the W.B. Premises Tenancy Act 1956, specially that of s. 4, which has imposed an obligation on the tenant to pay the agreed rent until the fair rent is fixed. The Hon'ble Court held that the West Bengal Premises Tenancy Act 1956, itself having recognised the contractual rent and having made it payable by the tenant, there would be no bar on the assessing authority to assess the annual value with reference to such contractual rent. The High Court at Calcutta, distinguished the points in issue from those arising for decisions of the Supreme Court in *Guntur Municipality's* case and *Devan Daulat Rai Kapoor's* case on the ground that unlike the Delhi Rent Act and Andhra Pradesh Rent Act, the W.B. Premises Tenancy Act recognised the contractual rent and equated the contractual rent with the fair rent determinable under the statute. Moreover, unlike the West Bengal Rent Control Act (Temporary Provisions) 1950, the W.B. Premises Tenancy Act 1956 does not provide for a penal clause in its s. 30 for realisation of rent in excess of standard rent.

5 AIR 1982 Cal 479; 1982(1) CHN 360; 86 CWN 926.

Ratnaprova's case

In *Indore Municipal Corporation* v *Ratnaprova*[6], the building in question was a hotel and as such the premises was not let out on rent. Again there was a *non-obstante* clause in s. 138(*b*) of the M.P. Municipal Corporation Act 1966, which reads as follows:

"The annual value of any building shall, notwithstanding contained in any other law for the time being in force, be deemed to be the gross annual rent at which such building together with its appurtenances and furniture that may be let for use or enjoyment thereof might reasonably at the time assessment be expected to be let from year to year". In coming to a decision in the above case, Their Lordships considered the view taken in *Padma Devi's* case which was subsequently followed in the *L.I.C.'s* case. *Guntur Municipal Council's* case and also in the case of *New Delhi Municipal Committee* v *M.N. Soi,*[7] but distinguished that the common feature in all those above cases were that the premises in question were let on rent and also there was no *non-obstante* clause in the provision for determination of annual value in the respective Municipal Acts. But in *Ratnaprova's* case, the premises was a hotel and admittedly, it was not let on rent. Moreover, there was a *non-obstante* clause in the relevant Municipal Act".

Considering the above distinguishing features, Their Lordships held, "it would not be a proper interpretation of s. 138(*b*) of the Act to ignore the significance of its *non-obstante* clause altogether. That is why we have taken the view that it would be a fair and reasonable interpretation of section 138(*b*) to hold that as no standard rent has been fixed so far in respect of the hotel, the Municipal Commissioner was justified in adopting another suitable criterion for determining the annual value of the building. There is, in fact, nothing in the Act to make it obligatory for the Commissioner to follow the provisions of the M.P. Accommodation Control Act instead of the *non-obstante* clause and to limit the annual value to any standard rent the building might fetch under the Act".

6 AIR 1977 SC 308.
7 AIR 1977 SC 302.

As because in *Ratnaprova's* case the premises was a hotel and the *non-obstante* clause was there in the relevant Municipal Act, the Supreme Court considered it permissible to fix the reasonable rent of the premises without regard to the M.P. Accommodation Control Act 1961. The Court has, nevertheless, by necessary implication evolved the idea that even the *non-obstante* clause in the Municipal Act is of no avail in case where the standard rent of the building is capable of being fixed under the relevant provisions of the Rent Act, in this case being the M.P. Accommodation Control Act.

Balbir Singh's case

In *Balbir Singh* v *Municipal Corporation, Delhi,*[8] the Supreme Court dwelt elaborately on the provisions of the Delhi Rent Act, particularly with reference to the provisions wherein the principles for determination of standard rent in almost all conceivable classes of cases are laid down and finally decided that the rateable value of premises whether residential or non-residential, cannot exceed the standard rent but it may in given cases be less than the standard rent. Within the upper limit of standard rent as formulated by the Rent Act, the assessing authority would have to determine as to what is the rent which the owner may reasonably expect to get if the premises are let out. But for a hypothetical rent, the authorities would necessarily evaluate factors, such as, size, situation, locality and condition of the premises and the amenities provided therein. The assessing authorities would also consider the rent of premises constructed earlier in the locality so that the disparity should not be disproportionately large. This decision gives a new dimension to the determination of annual rateable value vis-a-vis the provisions in the Rent Act. This decision establishes the proposition that the rateable value of a building, whether tenanted or self-occupied is limited by the measure of standard rent arriving at by the assessing authority by applying the principles laid down in the Rent Act and cannot exceed circumstances.

DETERMINATION OF "RATEABLE VALUE" RATIO DECIDENDI IN BALBIR SINGH'S CASE REITERATED. In the case of *Common Cause*

8 AIR 1985 SC 339.

Registered Society v *Union of India*,[9] the Division Bench of the Supreme Court comprising Ranganath Misra, J, and M.M. Dutta, J reiterated the earlier three-Judge Bench decision of the Supreme Court in the case of *Dr. Balbir Singh* v *Municipal Corporation of Delhi*,[10] in which the manner of determination of "Rateable value" was elaborately examined. It was recalled in the later case that the Supreme Court had in the earlier case of *Dr. Balbir Singh* classified the properties into four categories:

(*i*) self-occupied;

(*ii*) partly self-occupied and partly tenanted;

(*iii*) restrictive leasehold on which construction is raised; and

(*iv*) where the property has been constructed in stages.

So far as this fourth category is concerned, the court in *Balbir Singh's* case had answered the question as to how the rateable value is to be determined when the premises at the first stage of construction are to be assessed. In such case, the assessing authorities would first have to determine the standard rent of the premises, keeping in the mind the upper limit fixed by the standard rent and various other factors. But when any addition is made to the premises at a subsequent stage, three different situation may arise. First, the addition may not be of a distinct and separate unit of occupation but may be merely by way of extension of self-occupation. Secondly, the addition may be an extension of an existing tenancy and thirdly, the addition may be of a distinct and separate unit of occupation. In this first case, the original premises together with the additional structure would have to be treated as a single unit and reasonable letting value has to be determined subject to the upper limit of the standard rent. In this second case, standard rent of the tenancy would be liable to increase owing to additions and such increased rent would be the standard rent for rateably purpose, and reasonable letting value shall be subject to this upper limit so fixed by standard rent. In the last case, the rateable value shall have to be determined on the basis of the formula laid down for premises which one

9 AIR 1987 SC 2211.

10 (1985)2 SCR 439; AIR 1985 SC 339.

partly self-occupied and partly tenanted. The basic point to be remembered is that the formula for determination of standard rent cannot be applied for determining the standard rent of addition, as if that addition was the only structure standing on the land. That is to say, the assessing authority cannot work out the standard rent of such additions by applying the statutory principle of $7^1/_2\%$ of the Delhi Rent Act on the aggregate amount representing the cost of construction of this additional structure together with market price of land. In *Balbir Singh's* case, this matter came up for pointed examination and it was held that the market price of land cannot be added twice over, once while determining the standard rent of the original structure and again while determining the standard rent of the additional structure. Once the addition is made, the formula for determination of standard rent can be applied only once and in relation to the premises as a whole and where the additional structure consists of a distinct and separate unit of occupation, the standard rent would have to be apportioned in the manner indicated in the earlier part of the judgment. Thus, the Supreme Court in this later case finds that "this court has categorically decided that the market value of land is not added over again", and on this score, declined to make any further clarificatory order on the issue holding that "there is no ambiguity which requires clarifications".

It was observed by B.N. Kirpal, J, in the case of *Express Newspapers Ltd.* v *Municipal Corporation, Delhi*[11] thereof "In the present case, therefore, the value of the land as in 1958 has to be added to the cost of construction of the old building. Therefore, the market price of a part of the same land as in 1978 when construction of the new building started cannot be added to the cost of construction of the new building while determining the standard rent of the said building."

The above view was reiterated by the Supreme Court in *Common Cause Society* v *Union of India*,[12] while declining relief to the Municipal Corporation of Delhi on the matter in issue. It was *inter alia* observed "this court had, therefore, normally indicated the when at different stage additional construction was raised on the property already valued, the

11 (1987)31 DLT 369 (para 38).
12 (1987)32 DLT 406; AIR 1987 SC 2211.

market value of the land was not taken into account while fixing the valuation of the pre-existing construction".

The same issue arose for determination in the case of *Municipal Corporation of Delhi* v *Pragati Builders and N.R.D.C. of India*,[13] wherein the assessee has raised the impinged construction in two phases, the first phase covering a land area of 3056 sq.ft. and the second phase, an area of 4044 sq.ft. and thus, a total area of 7100 sq.ft. The issue was with regard to the quantum of the cost of the land to be taken into account for determining rateable value. The trial court was of the view that while determining the rateable value of the first phase only, proportionate cost is to be taken into consideration. But, Their Lordships felt that the above view was contrary to law as laid down by the Supreme Court in the case of *Dr. Balbir Singh* v *N.C.D.*,[14] as well as other decisions cited above. Accordingly, Their Lordships held that the market value of the land cannot be added twice over once while determining the standard rent of the original structure and again while determining the standard rent of the additional structure. Once the addition is made the formula set out in the relevant provisions of the municipal law can be applied only in relation to the premises as whole and standard rent may be apportioned accordingly for the additional structure. The cost of the entire land at the commencement of the first phase of construction has to be taken into account for determination of rateable value on the basis of standard rent as per law laid down by the Supreme Court in *Balbir's* case.

Rating of plant and machinery

Plant and machinery is as a general rule outside the purview of municipal taxation in India. Because, in our country industry and commerce by and large remain with the domain of the Central Government and only to a limited extent with the State Government for regulatory and taxing purposes. Though the local Government has no taxing power with regard to plant and machinery, which lie at the core of industry and allied business activities it nevertheless is empowered to levy property tax. With the growing technology of building and building

13 AIR 1991 Del 212.

14 AIR 1985 SC 339 (part 19).

services, land and building nevertheless includes now-a-days a lot of components which are in the nature of plant and machinery, viz., lifts, air-conditions, water installations, fire equipments, transformers, etc. Thus, it becomes meaningless if plant and machinery, which are in the nature of building and structure, are kept outside the purview of the fiscal powers of the local Government. Accordingly, the Indian laws on the municipalities incorporate a schedule carrying a list of plant and machinery, which are considered as components of building and structure to be taken into account in rating as an exception to the general rule that prohibits plant and machinery entering into the domain of municipal fiscal powers.

The above exception is also modelled after the British law on the subject of rating. To trace the history thereof we have to turn the leaves from the pages of the evolution of rating in UK already discussed earlier. It is to be noted that the exemption list as provided in the schedule of British law is updated after review by the expert bodies from time to time. Almost on the same lines, the Indian laws on rating also have undergone changes.

Latest trend

A new trend in the field of municipal taxation in India surfaces with the verdict of the Supreme Court of India in the case of *Griha Yajamanula Samkhya of Andhra Pradesh*[15] which was followed in *Kamala Mills* in Mumbai.[16] The Apex Court came to the relief of Municipal authorities in India in the field of municipal property taxation by laying down that it is possible to give a free hand to the municipal authorities to determine the annual valuation of taxable proportions by ignoring the provisions of fair rent in the real control legislation, if the relevant municipal laws provide for a complete code for determination of annual valuation.

This has unleashed a new trend in rating by a method known as 'Unit area based assessment' which means the laying down of self-assessment system by providing after market analysis a 'unit-area rate of assessment' for a particular locality

15 *Commissioner, Hyderabad Municipal Corporation* v *Griha Yajamanula Samkhya* AIR 2001 SC 2046.

16 AIR 2003 SC 2998.

which has only to be multiplied by the area of his occupancy by the ratepayer. Thus, the objectivity as well as transparency of assessment is assured by eliminating any subjective element on the part of this municipal assessment personnel.

The above system came into practice in Patna and spread out in other major cities like Ahmedabad, Delhi, Bangalore, Hyderabad and also Kolkata.

In Kolkata, a 'Unit Assessment Cell' was formed in awardness with the provisions of the KMC Act 1980 to give shape to the above move. The first step therein is divide the municipal wards into appropriate valuation blocks and thus categories them in hierarchical orders of valuation by an expert body known as the Municipal Valuation Court references to valuation at this stage is the 'market value' of property transactions as new ordered by the appropriate authority like the Inspector General & Registration of this State Government is respect of transfer of property. The next step is to assess the acceptability of the such division and cicatrization by the rate-payers at large through another independent body known as the Anomaly Review Council. The third step has again with the Municipal Valuation Committee to determine the base unit area value of each individual property after applying a multiplication factors arrive at the market value theory varying according to locations, use, age, quality structions, occupancy status etc. It lies with the individual rate payer to assess his dues by a system or self-assessment with the case may be and after taking into account the rate as imposed by the Corporation within range of 6% to 20% as prescribed in the Act. The owner of the property determines the extent of his occupency will the help of qualified experts. The 'annual value' of any property shall comprise the total occupancy of the rate proper and multiplying the same by the finalised base unit area value. The property due will comprise the tax payable on the total occupancy in accordance with the rate promulgated by the corporation.

Rating in UK

As the Indian law on local Government including rating closely follows the develop in UK it is necessary to go into the history of development in UK for a proper appreciation of the perspective of rating system in Indian.

Although rating in various forms had existed in UK for several hundred years before 1601, it is the Poor Relief Act of that year which can fairly be said to be the commencement to the rating system as we know today. The purpose of that Act was the relief to the poor and to this end overseers were appointed who were authorised in order to carry out their duties, to raise money by taxation of every inhabitant, Parson, Vicar and other, and of every occupier of Lands, Houses, Tithes impropriate, Proprial of Tithes, Coal-mines, or saleable underwoods in such competent sum or sums of money as they shall think fit. The important words to extract from their provision are: "by taxation of every inhabitant ...... and every occupier ......". The effect was to levy rates on every inhabitant for personal estate and every occupier for real estate. Thus, personal estate was rateable and remained so until the Poor Rate Exemption Act 1840, which said ... "It shall not be lawful for overseers of any Parish, township or village to tax any inhabitant thereof, as such inhabitant in respect of his ability derived from the projects of stock-in-trade or any other property, for or towards the relief of the poor". Thus, from 1601 to 1840 both real and personal estate were rateable in UK.

The purpose of the Poor Relief Act, sometimes known as the statute of Elizabeth, was to bring relief to the poor, and it was the culmination of a variety of efforts to deal with the problem of caring for the poor and the sick, a problem which arose due to dissolution of the monasteries and convents by Henry VIII in 1535 and 1539. Up to that time, it was the monks and nuns who had cared for the poor and the sick. For the next two or three centuries, it was there principally for the relief of the poor that the Poor Rate continued to be levied. Today, however, the General Rate (the national successor of the Poor Rate) is levied for the whole range of service for which rating authorities are responsible to practice the 1601 Act, was not finally repealed until the General Rate Act 1967, which is a consolidating Act and the Act under which the General Rate came to be levied. However, the Poor Rate Exemption Act 1840, which mitigated the rigours of the taxpayers holding personal property by exempting them. In that the General rate is levied on the value of the occupation on real estate only, together with incorporated rights such as advertising rights and sponsoring rights such as advertising rights and sporting rights. 'General rate' is a tax on value of occupation. It is therefore, necessary to define occupation. As per-requisite to determine occupation, there must be occupation of a 'hereditament'—i.e., the unit of occupation on assessment of which the rates will be levied. 'Hereditament' is defined in the s. 115 of the relevant Act as "property, which is or may become liable to a rate, being a unit of such property, which is, or would fall to be, shown as a separate item in the 'Valuation List'. The term 'occupation' has no statutory definition; in consequence it has been the subject of many legal decisions. Thus, the necessary ingredients to constitute a rateable occupation have been determined by the Courts of England as follows:

(*a*) The occupation must include actual possession, legal or otherwise.

(*b*) There must be an overt act of user—not just on intention to occupy.

(*c*) The occupation must be exclusive.

(*d*) The occupation must be of benefit to the occupier although this does not mean that it must be pecuniary benefit.

(*e*) The occupation must be for not too transient a period.

In the legislature history and practice in England upto 1925, rate for the purpose of local taxation meant a tax on the annual value of lands and buildings liable to such taxation.[17]

Since 1990, there have been fundamental changes in the rating system, mainly affecting domestic property.

From the early 1970's the conservative party were committed to a reform of the system, which had fallen into disrepute, perhaps mainly because a revaluation was badly needed. The Community Charge, or 'poll tax', that replaced the rating of domestic property, fared much the same as its predecessor in 1377, very nearly producing a repeat of the peasant's revolt in 1381. The Community Charge was itself replaced in 1991 by the Council Tax, a system under which tax is charged upon domestic property according to its capital

17 *Godhara Borough Municipality* v *Godhara Electricity Co. Ltd.* AIR 1968 SC 1504.

value. However, this capital value does not have to be determined precisely, there being 8 'bands' of value into which each domestic property has been placed.

These bands are as follows:

Valuation band	Range of values as at 1st April 1991
A	Up to £ 40,000
B	£ 40,001 – £ 52,000
C	£ 52,001 – £ 68,000
D	£ 68,001 – £ 88,000
E	£ 88,001 – £ 120,000
F	£ 120,001 – £ 160,000
G	£ 160,001 – £ 320,000
H	Over £ 320,000

The amount of tax charged on properties in each band is a proportion of the tax charged by a council on band D.

These proportions are as follows:

Valuation band	Proportion of band D
A	6/9
B	7/9
C	8/9
D	One
E	11/9
F	13/9
G	15/9
H	Two

For example, the tax charged in respect of a property in Band A will be 6/9 of that charged in respect of a property in Band D and that charged on a property in Band H will be twice that charged on a property in Band D.

Non-domestic property remains within a rating system very much the same as that which existed prior to the changes in 1990, a system consolidated by the General Rate Act 1967. The relevant legislation now is the Local Government Finance Act 1988 as amended by the Local Government and Housing Act 1989.

Rating in USA

In USA, property tax assessments, levies and rates are administered under a completely different pattern. The system rests on a relationship among appraised value, assessed value, tax levies and tax rates.

The *appraised value* of a property is an appraiser's judgment as to the full market value on a specific appraisal date. It is the responsibility of assessors to determine the appraised value of each parcel of property in their jurisdictions.

The terms *assessment* and *assessed value* are often interchangeable. Assessment may refer to the assessed value of a single parcel of property, the total assessed value of all properties within the boundaries of the tax jurisdiction, or the assessed value of any group of properties.

Assessed values are usually based on the appraised value of property. The term *appraised value* distinguishes full value from assessed value when the assessed value is a proportion of full value. According to various laws, the assessed value of property for tax purposes must represent either the full fair market, or cash, value of the property or a specified percentage of such value. Whether assessments are at full value or a proportion thereof is usually a constitutional or legislative policy decision, not an administrative one.

A *property tax levy* is the total amount of money to be raised from the property tax, as set forth in the budget for the local Government or tax jurisdiction. This levy, whether higher or lower than the preceding year, is determined by the budget-making authority of the local Government. It is usually recommended by an administrator (for example, a mayor or school superintendent) and adopted by the local legislative body (city council, county board, or board of education).

The nominal *tax rate* is simply a mathematical expression of the relationship between the tax levy and the total assessment for the jurisdiction: the levy amount is divided by the assessment amount to give the nominal tax rate.

The tax rate is usually expressed as dollars per \$100, mills per dollar, or dollars per \$1,000 of assessed value. The tax for each parcel is calculated by multiplying the parcel's assessed value by the nominal tax rate for the jurisdiction so that the tax for each parcel is at the same percentage of assessed value; the tax is, therefore, a tax according to value.

The *effective* tax rate, although mathematically related to the nominal tax rate, is not directly used in the calculation of property taxes. It is the proportion of tax dollars to full, or market value and may be calculated for all properties, a single parcel, or any group or stratum of properties (for example, residential property). If variations exist in the levels of assessment for different classes of property, effective tax rates will also vary among the classes. The effective tax rate is the only way to compare the effect of the property tax across jurisdictions. To calculate the effective tax rate, divide the property tax by market value. For example, the effective tax rate of a property with a market value of $1,00,000 and a property tax of $1,200 is

$$\frac{\$1200}{\$100000} = 0.012 = 1.2 \text{ per cent}$$

If properties are appraised at market value, the effective tax rate can also be calculated by multiplying the nominal tax rate by the assessment ratio or assessment level (proportion of assessed to appraised value) for the property in question. For example, if a property is appraised at its full market value and the assessment ratio is 0.05, and the nominal tax rate is 2.6%, then the effective tax rate is 0.05 × 0.026 = 0.13 per cent.

(B) Stamp Duty on Transfer of Property

The system of collecting duties through the requirement of affixing stamps to documents and various transaction instruments has been in existence in India for a long time. Under the Constitution, the power to levy Stamp Duties is divided between the Centre and the States. The Stamp Duties mentioned in the Union List are levied by the Centre but the proceeds are assigned to and collected by the States where they are levied. The Stamp Duties in the State List are levied and collected by the States. The instruments which are of importance to trade and industry in the Union list ensure uniformity of rates imposed throughout the country in regard to those instruments. Also, the Central Government is able to keep the level of the Stamp Duties on important instruments at a fairly low level so that they do not add too much to business costs. In regard to instruments placed in the State List, one often finds widely varying rates among the different States, and in some cases, as for instance in respect of Conveyances, the rates have been fixed at high levels. Both these features create problems.

Even a casual survey of the realm of Stamp Duties indicates that the structure, the relevant definitions, the rates of duty in many cases and the manner of administration leave much to be desired. To mention only the major problems, the differing rates of duty on many instruments lead to diversion of economic activity and also loss of revenue to some States. Secondly, the revenue motive has been dominant in designing the structure and fixing the rates. Even simple fees have been sought to be converted into taxes. The economic consequences and the question whether a particular "Stamp Duty" is a fee or a tax has been ignored or neglected. Thirdly, even the revenue objective is not always fulfilled because high rates in many cases not only retard the growth of the economy by reducing the long-term buoyancy of revenue but also cause avoidance, evasion and distortion. Fourth, the fixing of different *ad valorem* rates of Stamp Duty and the method of collecting duties through the fixing of stamps or the use of stamp paper are causing severe hardship to transactors of business. Stamps of the required denomination or magnitude are often not available and, it often becomes necessary to fix a large number of stamps on documents making the entire package of documents too bulky and cumbersome. Lastly, the system of sale of stamps mainly through vendors is found to suffer from weaknesses during the whole process starting from the printing of stamps in the Security Printing Press to the retail sale by vendors. We need to consider also the question of appropriate burden of Stamp Duty to be imposed on the citizens, keeping in view the level of other property-related duties payable by them. This is the equity aspect of the problem of Stamp Duties.

Stamp duty, whether a fee or tax

When one scans the list of instruments subject to Stamp Duties one finds that most of them are documents used for transactions in commerce and industry while others are related to property transactions. The requirement to affix a stamp on several of these documents is mainly to impart evidentiary value to the documents concerned. This being so, in such cases the Stamp Duty is to be looked upon as a fee charged for according that status. Good examples are stamps to be affixed to receipts, proxies and bills of exchange.

If a given Stamp Duty is really a fee then the fee should be commensurate with the cost of rendering the concerned service. If the cost of rendering a service is very small and hence the Stamp Duty has to be low, then it may not be worthwhile levying and collecting the Duty. If a Stamp Duty is intended to be a tax, then one must examine whether it satisfies the criteria for a good tax, i.e. whether it satisfies the canon of economic efficiency, whether it is related to ability to pay and whether it can be administered easily without too much trouble to the tax collector and to the tax-payer. The case for abolishing a duty which brings little revenue would be greater if it at the same time acts as a hindrance to the smooth flow of business. While, theoretically and legally, all the Stamp Duties enumerated in the Constitution can be used by the Governments as a means of raising revenues, both the nature of the instrument and the possible impact of a given duty on the flow of economic activity and on cost of production will have to be kept in view.

Clearly, the Stamp Duty on property transfers is intended to be a tax since there is a separate registration fee. What is the rationale for this tax? It can be justified as a tax on part of wealth as well as a tax on realised capital gain. However, if there is a recurring tax on property based on current annual or market value and also a global capital gains tax, the case for a high rate Stamp Duty becomes weak. The combined incidence of the property tax, the capital gains tax, the Stamp Duty and the Registration fee should be kept in view.

The Indian scenario

Stamp Duty on Conveyances is one of the largest single sources of revenue to State Government in spite of considerable undervaluation and avoidance through non-registration.

In India, the structure of Stamp Duty on Conveyances varies from State to State. In some States there is a flat *ad valorem* rate expressed as a percentage of market value. This rate is usually high, e.g. 10 per cent in West Bengal, 13 per cent in

Tamil Nadu (including surcharge). In other States a progressive rate schedule is adopted. There is little justification either for a high rate or for a progressive system. Since there exists a property tax in all the State and a capital gains tax is levied by the Central Government, there is hardly any justification for a high rate of Stamp Duty or for any significant progression. Besides, a high rate of duty leads to avoidance through undervaluation of property. The buoyancy of revenue from Stamp Duties could be enhanced through the adoption of moderate rates. The underlying assumption for adopting a progressive system of Stamp Duties on conveyances seems to be that the higher the value of property transferred, the proportionately richer must be the buyer and the seller. This is not necessarily true. A simple moderate rate of tax would be the ideal solution to adopt. Otherwise, a large proportion of property transactions have already found an escape route from fiscal levy through clandestine deals in real estates by non-registration, particularly in the metropolitan cities in India.

A moderate rate combined with proper valuation would yield adequate and buoyant revenues.

Valuation of property

In administering the Stamp Duty on Conveyances, the valuation of property plays a crucial role. As already stated, because of the generally high rates of Stamp Duty on Conveyance prescribed by different States there is a very strong tendency for undervaluation of property. On the other hand the correct determination of market value is beset with many problems. Properties or real estates differ in terms of location, occupational use, age, quality of construction the state of repair and neighbourhood. All these factors are taken into account when the market determines the value of any given property. It is of course difficult independently to assess what would be the market value of any property. The value mentioned in the property transfer deed cannot be accepted as a matter of routine, particularly when relatively high rates are levied, because such acceptance would lead to under-valuation being acted upon. On the other hand, if the discretion to question the value is given to the Registrar or Sub-Registrar, one would be creating avenues for harassment, corruption and collusion. Hence, several States have endeavoured to fix guidance values for properties in various localities. For valuation purposes, the value of a property is to be decomposed into two parts: the value of land and the value of building. The valuation of such land and building should follow the market approach, or cost approach, or income approach, or a combination of approaches as each case may appropriately demand. All the approaches to value and methods, involved have been discussed elaborately in the earlier chapters. It is important to emphasise that the job of valuation should be completely taken away from those who would be involved in collecting the tax.

Five adjoining buildings of the same measurement and quality situate in the same locality may not account for the same value. Because, in valuation what matters is not only the brick and mortar and the other materials of the buildings or the land but other factors like the purpose of valuation or nature of interest of the occupants therein. Though valuation is computed in respect of the land and building, nevertheless it involves some purpose in which the consideration of the occupancy rights or other interests are to be taken into account. In our given case of five similar buildings, one might have been subjected to easements enjoyed by the adjoining owners; in another, the land might have been obtained on a lease for a term of fifteen years while still another for ninety-nine years. One of the premises might have been mortgaged for building loans, while the other given on rent to a tenant governed by the prevalent rent control law. There may be instance of another owner letting out his premises on tenancy at a monthly sum which being above the prescribed ceiling takes it outside the purview of the rent control law. Thus, encumbrances are significant factors in valuation of real estate along with other factors like location, usage of building, neighbourhood, and etc. Much depends on the purpose for which valuation is made and the person for whom the valuation is made. These aspects have been discussed in detail in other chapters of this book.

Problems in the matter of registration

In the case of Conveyances, registration has given rise to several problems causing hardship to people involved in transfer of properties as well as to the Government department dealing with registration. First, there is the requirement that before a property can be registered, the buyer of the property will have to obtain no objection certificates on three matters:

(*i*) For clearance under the Urban Ceiling Act;

(*ii*) An income-tax clearance certificate under section 230(*a*) of the Income-tax Act; and

(*iii*) A no objection certificate from the appropriate authority which could acquire property for the Government which is considered to be undervalued in the transaction deed under Chapter XX-C of the Income-tax Act.

The delay in obtaining these clearances causes trouble both to the people who want to get their deeds registered and also the registration offices. The Registrar's office is thus being used to implement the provisions of other Acts.

What is meant by conveyance or transfer

The word 'conveyance' has been defined in s. 2(10) of the Indian Stamp Act 1899 in the following manner:

"'Conveyance' includes a conveyance on sale and every instrument by which property, whether movable or immovable, is transferred *inter vivos* and which is not otherwise specifically provided for by Schedule I.

Some of the State Governments have modified the above definition by State amendments of the Act.

The definition of 'conveyance' inserted under the Bombay Stamp Act 1958, as amended in 1985, is as follows:

"(*g*) Conveyance includes:—

(*i*) a conveyance on sale;

(*ii*) every instrument;

(*iii*) every decree or final order of any Civil Court;

(*iv*) every order made by the High Court under section 394 of the Companies Act, 1956 (I of 1956) in respect of amalgamation of companies;

(*v*) sale of air rights;

by which, property whether movable or immovable or any estate or interest in any property is transferred to, or vested in, any other person, *inter vivos* and which is not otherwise specifically provided for by Schedule I."

The legislative intent in including a decree or final order of a Civil Court for the purpose of the definition of "Conveyance" appears to be to prevent collusive litigation which is ultimately compromised and transfers are effected under the relevant consent decrees. The definition, however, has travelled beyond the legislative intent and has adversely affected the Court Sales for genuine recovery of the dues of the Banks and Financial Institutions pursuant to the suits filed by them for enforcement of their securities. By virtue of the aforesaid definition of "Conveyance" under the Bombay Stamp Act, the decrees for sale of the properties obtained in such suits will attract heavy Stamp Duty and frustrate the very purpose the suits filed by the Banks and Financial Institutions. It may be emphasised in this context that the mortgages pursuant to which the property is sold through the Courts are already subjected to stamp duty and, therefore, there is no case for taxing the Court sales pursuant to such mortgage again.

Stamp duty on conveyance

Under s. 29(*c*) of the Indian Stamp Act, in case of conveyance of property, the expense of providing the proper stamp shall be borne by the person drawing, making or executing such instrument.

The stamp duty payable on a deed of gift is the same as that on a conveyance.

'Lease' as defined in the Stamp Act

The term 'lease' has been defined in s. 2(16) of the Indian Stamp Act in the following manner:

'*Lease*' means a lease of immovable property, and includes also—

(*a*) a patta;

(*b*) a kabuliyat or other undertaking in writing, not being a counterpart of a lease, to cultivate, occupy or pay or deliver rent for, immovable property;

(*c*) any instrument by which tolls of any description are let;

(*d*) any writing on an application for a lease intended to signify that the application is granted;

NOTE: Exploring and prospecting licenses are not leases for purposes of the definition in s. 2, sub-section (16) of the Indian Stamp Act (II of 1899). A license does not become a lease, merely because a rental is reserved. These licenses are chargeable as agreements with a stamp duty of Rupees one and fifty paise under Article 5(*b*). (Government of India Order No. 1677 S.R., dated the 10th April 1902, to the Government of Madras, received with Bengal Government Order No. 330 T.-R., dated the 2nd May 1902).

Mortgage deed and stamp duty payable

The term mortgage deed has been defined in s. 2(17) of the Indian Stamp Act as follows:

"*Mortgage deed*. Mortgage deed includes every instrument whereby, for the purpose of securing money advanced, or to be advanced, by way of loan, or an existing or future debt, or the performance of an engagement, one person transfers, or creates to, or in favour of another, a right over or in respect of specified property."

The scale of stamp duty as per entries in clause 40 of Schedule 1A is payable.

Partition and stamp duty

An 'instrument of partition' has been defined in s. 2(15) of the said Act in the following manner:

"Instrument of partition" means any instrument whereby co-owners of any property divide or agree to divide such property in severalty,

"and includes—

(*i*) a final order for effecting a partition passed by any revenue authority or any Civil Court;

(*ii*) an award by an arbitrator directing a partition; and

(*iii*) when any partition is effected without executing any such instrument, any instrument signed by the co-owners and recording, whether by way of declaration of such partition or otherwise, the terms of such partition amongst the co-owners."

The scale of stamp duty on partition is given in clause 45 of Schedule 1A of the said Act as follows:

Description of instrument	Proper stamp duty
45. Partition. Instrument of [as defined by section 2(15)]	The same duty as a Bond (No. 15) for the amount of the value of the separated share or shares of the property. *N.B.:* The largest share remaining after the property is partitioned (if there are two or more shares of equal value and not smaller than any of the other shares than one of such equal shares) shall be deemed to be that from which the other shares are separated: Provided always that— (*a*) when an instrument of partition containing an agreement to divide property in severalty is executed and a partition is effected in pursuance of such agreement, the duty chargeable upon the instrument effecting such partition shall be reduced by the amount of duty paid in respect of the first instrument but shall not be less than one rupee; (*b*) where land is held on Revenue Settlement for a period not exceeding thirty years and paying the full assessment, the value for the purpose of duty shall be calculated at not more than five times the annual revenue; (*c*) where a final order for effecting a partition passed by any Revenue Authority or any Civil Court, or an award by an arbitrator directing a partition, is stamped with the stamp required for an instrument of partition and an instrument of partition in pursuance of such order or award is subsequently executed the duty on such instrument shall not exceed one rupee.

It is relevant to consider a few court cases, where guidelines were laid down for arriving at minimum price of land in the context of registration of instrument. The validity of such guidelines was in issue in the case of *Chamkaur Singh* v *State of Punjab*.[18] It was held that the provisions of s. 47A of the Indian Stamp Act 1899 make it manifestly clear that the registering officer as well as the Collector have to perform, if not a judicial, at least a *quasi-judicial* function in determining or estimating the price of the properties which is the subject-matter of a particular transaction as if the property is being sold in 'open market' on the date of execution of the instrument relating to such transfer. As per sub-sec. (1), while registering the instrument of transfer, the registering officer has to take an independent decision as it has to be founded on the 'reason to believe' that the property has been under-valued or that the ostensible consideration is not the real or genuine consideration. The guidelines laying down the floor or minimum prices of different kinds and quality of land on the basis of the situation or location for purposes of registration of instruments relating to transferring any property, completely take away the jurisdiction of the Sub-Registrar to reach any quasi-judicial decision with regard to valuation of the property. Guidelines which are for all practical purposes are in the form of a command would bind the Collector even more than the Sub-Registrar or registering officer. Such guidelines, the Court decided, run counter the mandate of law and are violative of s. 47A, and cannot be issued for controlling the quasi-judicial decision of a particular functionary or authority under a particular statute.

In the same vein, the Supreme Court decided in the case of *Jawjaee Nagnathan* v *Revenue Divisional Officer, Adilabad, A.P.*[19] that the Basic Valuation Register maintained by the registering authority for collection of stamp duty has no statutory foundation to determine market value. The provision of s. 47A of the Indian Stamp Act 1899, does not confer power to determine market value of an entire area, region or block and to maintain Basic Valuation Register for levy of stamp

18 AIR 1991 P&H 26.
19 (1994)4 SCC 595.

duty. Neither the Registrar nor the vendor is bound by it. Evidence of *bona fide* sales, the Court observed, between willing prudent vendor and prudent vendee of the lands acquired or situated nearabout the subject land possessing same or similar advantageous features would furnish the basis to determine market value. The Basic Valuation Register prepared and maintained for the purpose of collecting stamp duty has no statutory base or force and accordingly, it cannot form a foundation to determine the market value of property mentioned in the instrument brought for registration.

While any instruction, circular or guidelines cannot really be valid if it has the effect of conditioning the decision-making process of a statutory authority called upon to value property, the fact remains that valuation is after all a specialised stream of practice which demands expertise. So there is every reason to offer necessary training to the valuing personnel to make them equal to the task, or provide them with such materials, information or tools as would equip them to take an appropriate decision on valuation. The later decisions of the Supreme Court seem to have appreciated this aspect of the matter.

It was held in the case of *Prakashwati* v *Chief Controlling Revenue Authority, U.P.*[20] that s. 47A of the Stamp Act and the rules thereunder in U.P. provide to say that the minimum market value determinable was not the end of the matter of valuation and value could be determined at a figure higher than that, if warranted.

In *State of Punjab* v *Mohabir Singh,*[21] it was observed that guidelines provided by the State under s. 47A of the Indian Stamp Act 1899 as amended by Punjab Stamp Act 1982, would serve only as *prima facie* material available before the registering authority to alert him regarding the value but cannot inhibit the registering authority to exercise his quasi-judicial satisfaction of the true value of the property.

Anomalies following certain State Amendments

Certain State amendments and legislation in pursuance of the Indian Stamp Act have created anomalies and complications

20 (1996)4 SCC 657.
21 (1996)1 SCC 609.

in the field of stamp duty and valuation therefor. The Bombay Stamp Act after its amendment in 1985 is one such instance. The Article 25(*d*)(1)(D) of Schedule I to the Bombay Stamp Act provides that stamp duty shall be payable "On the true market value of the property which is the subject matter of the conveyance ... (1) if relating to a residential premises consisting of building or unit .... (D) by a member of such society in favour of another member (whether in consequence of transfer of its shares to another member or not)", at the rates provided in that article. But this new provision has come in conflict with the levy of stamp duty on transfer of flats occupied within co-operative housing societies. In this context, s. 41(*a*) of the Maharashtra Co-operative Societies Act 1960 provides that the provisions of s. 17 of the Indian Registration Act 1908 shall not apply to any instrument relating to share in a society, notwithstanding that the assets of the society consist in whole or in part of immovable property. This presupposes that in the case of transfer of shares in a co-operative society, along with the transfer of shares the interest of the transferor in the assets of the society also may get transferred. If that was not so, then there was no need to provide for this exemption.

When the Bombay Stamp (Amendment) Act 1985 was enacted the Maharashtra Co-operative Societies Act 1960 was already in force and the legislature was aware that in the case of a co-operative housing society, not only the shares in a co-operative society but also the right of occupancy gets transferred therewith. The Bombay High Court in the case of *Usha Arvind Dongre* v *Suresh Raghunath Kotwal,*[22] which decision involves the Maharashtra Co-operative Societies Act and Registration Act held as follows:

> "In the case of tenant co-partnership housing society the title to the flat remains in the society and is not affected by the transfer of share in the society. Only right to occupy the flat flows from the ownership of the share in such a co-operative society. The shares thereby do not become immovable property. Transfer of such shares does not require registration under section 17(1)(*b*) of the Registration Act. Even if the transfer of such share is considered as the

22 1990 Mah LJ 306.

transfer of interest in immovable property. Section 41 of the Maharashtra Co-operative Societies Act exempts the document affecting such transfer of share from the ambit of section 17(1)(*b*) of the Registration Act. An award which deals with transfer of shares in a flat in a tenant co-partnership society does not require registration under section 17(1)(*b*) of the Registration Act."

The decision of the Gujarat High Court in the case of *Mulshanker Kunverji Gor*,[23] on the identical provisions, supports this view. The question involved was also whether, for transferring the flat allotted to a member in a co-operative society, registration of the instrument of transfer was required. It was held that in the case of a tenant co-partnership society, the transfer of shares necessarily carries with it the transfer of member's interest in the immovable property allotted to him and such a transfer can be brought about without a registered instrument because s. 42(*a*) of the Gujarat Co-operative Societies Act 1961 carves out an exception for such purpose.

In the case of *G. Rajeshwaran* v *Shankar Darshan Co-operative Housing Society Ltd.*,[24] the Bombay High Court held that the society is not concerned whether or not the parties to the transaction have paid stamp duty on transfer of shares and flat in a co-operative society.

At best, if the society and the seller so insist, the purchaser should give an appropriate indemnity to them regarding the payment of stamp duty, if it is ultimately payable, and consequences for non-payment of stamp duty.

The matter may also be looked at from the angle of beneficial interpretation of statutes of fiscal nature in favour of rate-payers when two opinions are possible.

The Bombay Stamp Act falls in the realm of the fiscal statutes and it is a well-settled principle that in interpreting a fiscal statute, the beneficial construction rule should be applied according to which, where more than one interpretation of a provision is possible, the one which is more beneficial to

23 AIR 1980 Guj 62 (FB).
24 1986 CTJ 695 (Bom).

the tax-payer should be adopted. This proposition is supported by several decisions of the Supreme Court reported in AIR 1965 SC 1092; 77 ITR 192; 89 ITR 236; 105 ITR 179 and 89 ITR 251.

Looking at it from another angle we may find that since the immovable property in a co-operative housing society vests in the society, no title is transferred to the purchaser with the transfer of shares. Title continues to remain with the society. Right to occupy it and enjoy it is transferred by the transfer of his shares by one member to another. This expression does not and cannot embrace within its sweep any personal interest, independent of the society, which a member may have in the immovable property which he occupies.

In this way, the Bombay Stamp Act as amended in 1985 faces a legal challenge that remains to be resolved.

Let us now look into another anomaly that has emerged with regard to mortgages by deposit of title deed which did not so long attract any stamp duty.

Historically, equitable mortgage always remained outside the purview of Stamp Duty provisions. This was because the said mortgage is created pursuant to the provisions of s. 58(*f*) of the Transfer of Property Act 1882, in terms of which no instrument is required to be executed or registered for creation of such mortgage and mere deposit of title deeds with intent to create a security on the immovable property is enough. Initially, such mortgages were permitted to be created only in Presidency towns such as Calcutta, Madras and Bombay. However, by virtue of the notifications issued by almost all the States pursuant to the provisions contained in s. 58 *ibid*, equitable mortgage can now be freely created in all major town/cities throughout the country. This mortgage is looked upon as an expeditious mode of creation of security by the financial institutions and Banks because of its simplicity of form and cost-saving effect. This position existed in all the States until 1977. However, thereafter, in the States of Maharashtra, Gujarat and Madhya Pradesh this privilege came under an attack because these commercially important States amended Stamp laws and subjected this mortgage also to payment of Stamp Duty. This development is said to have badly affected the loan transactions of the Banks and financial institutions and thereby the industrial and economic development. The trend is likely to be followed by more and more States. It is also well settled that Stamp Duty is payable on the instrument and not on the transaction. It, therefore, follows that since there is no instrument, no Stamp Duty should be chargeable on the equitable mortgage. However, the amendments made in the Stamp Laws in the above States unreasonably treat the Memorandum of Entry or other writing recorded by the Banks and financial institutions in connection with equitable mortgage for future memory as an instrument creating the mortgage. The true nature of such Memorandum is a record of past transaction and it is not the instrument creating the mortgage itself. The Courts in India have accepted this position and the same is now well settled.

'Market value' as determinable under State Acts

A distortion in the concept of market value of property has been created in a few State amendments of the Indian Stamp Act. In the Act itself, a definition of market value for the purpose of Stamp Duty is given in s. 2(16B) which is inserted by the Indian Stamp (West Bengal Amendment) Act 1990 in the following words:

> "*Section 2(16B)*. "Market value" means, in relation to any property which is the subject-matter of an instrument, the price which such property would have fetched or would fetch if sold in open market on the date of execution of such instrument as determined in such manner and by such authority as may be prescribed by rules made under this Act or the consideration stated in the instrument, whichever is higher."

The above concept has been varied under different State Acts a few of which are given below.

The West Bengal version

In West Bengal, a set of rules under the title of the West Bengal Stamp (Prevention of Undervaluation of Instruments) Rules 1994 has been enforced in modification of s. 2(16B) on the question of market value. In r. 3 thereof, a specified manner of determination of market value is provided along with particulars of property to be furnished for the purpose, in the manner as follows:

Manner of determination of market value and furnishing of particulars relating to any property

(1) The market value within the meaning of clause (16B) of section 2 in relation to any land or any land with building shall, after taking into consideration the particulars referred to in sub-rule (2), be determined on the basis of the highest price for which sale of any land, or any land with building, of similar nature and area, in a comparable locality, has been negotiated and settled during the five consecutive years immediately preceding the date of execution of any instrument setting forth such market value, or on the basis of any court decision, information, report or record that may be available from any court or any officer or authority of the Central Government or the State Government or any local authority or local body, or on the basis of consideration stated in such instrument for the sale of such land or land with building, whichever is greater.

(2) Any person executing an instrument shall furnish to the Registering Officer, in addition to the particulars referred to in sub-sec. (1) and sub-sec. (2) of s. 27, such of the following particulars in respect of any property, which is the subject-matter of registration, as may be applicable to such property:

(*i*) Locational details—

(*a*) House/Holding No.

(*b*) Name of the Lane/Road/Street

(*c*) Ward No.

(*d*) PIN Code No.

(*e*) District

(*f*) Dag No.

(*g*) Khatian No.

(*h*) Plot No.

(*i*) J.L. No.

(*j*) Mouja

(*ii*) Name of the Municipal Corporation/ Municipality/Notified Area/Cantonment Area.

(*iii*) Area of land (in cottah/square metre).

(*iv*) Built-up area (in square metre).

(*v*) Vacant land area (in square metre).

(*vi*) No. of floors in the building and the carpet area (in square metre).

(*vii*) Existing nature of land.

(*viii*) Type of construction of the building (tin shed/tile shed/pucca with brick and cement/pucca with brick and lime/roof tiles/mosaic/marbles on floors and walls).

(*ix*) Brief description of the nature of sanitary/electrical/other fittings on the building/flat.

(*x*) Year of construction of the building/flat.

(*xi*) Renovation made, it any—

(*a*) year of renovation

(*b*) details of addition/alteration

(*xii*) Facilities available within one kilometre—

(*a*) railway station

(*b*) bus stop

(*c*) market place

(*d*) high school

(*e*) college

(*f*) hospital

(*g*) main road and width of such road

(*h*) city centre

(*xiii*) Purpose for which the building/flat/land is being used (residential/commercial/ industrial/otherwise) with details.

(*xiv*) Details of tenancy or any other feature affecting the value of the property.

(*xv*) Property tax paid with reference to tax records of the local authority concerned.

(*xvi*) Other locational factors, if any, that may be relevant to the determination of market value.

(*xvii*) Market value set forth in the instrument—

(*a*) market value (per square metre) of building area

(*b*) market value per cottah/square metre of land/vacant land

(*xviii*) Transferor—

(*a*) name

(*b*) full address

(*xix*) Transferee—

(*a*) name

(*b*) full address

(*xx*) Deed writer—

(*a*) name

(*b*) licence No.

(*xxi*) Advocate, if any—

(*a*) name

(*b*) address

(3) The particulars referred to in sub-rule (2) shall be specified in a statement in Form I in case the land with building is situated in an urban area, in Form II in case the land with building is situated in a rural area, in Form III in case the land is situated in an urban area, or in Form IV in case the land is situated in a rural area, and such statement specifying the particulars, referred to in that sub-rule shall be signed and verified by the person executing the instrument of conveyance, exchange, gift, partition or settlement and presenting it before a Registering Officer for registration.

(4) The statement signed and verified as required by sub-rule (3) shall be attached in duplicate to the instrument of conveyance, exchange, gift, partition or settlement which is, upon execution, presented before the Registering Officer for registration.

(5) If an instrument of conveyance, exchange, gift, partition or settlement relates to more than one item of property, the particulars referred to in sub-rule (2) shall be furnished by the person executing such instrument for each item of property separately in a statement in Form I, Form II, Form III or Form IV, as the case may be.

(6) If, in relation to any property which is the subject-matter of registration of any instrument of conveyance, exchange, gift, partition or settlement, the market value is not set forth therein, and if the facts and circumstances affecting the chargeability of such instrument with stamp duty and the particulars relating to such facts and circumstances are not fully and truly set forth and furnished in a statement referred to in sub-rule (3), filled in, signed and verified by the person executing the instrument in the manner referred to in sub-rule (4), the Registering Officer may refuse registration of such instrument after giving such person a reasonable opportunity of being head.

(7) On receipt of any instrument of conveyance, exchange, gift, partition or settlement in relation to a property together with the statement in Form I, Form II, Form III or Form IV, as the case may be, attached thereto, if the Registering Officer has reason to believe that the market value of the property has not been truly set forth in such instrument, he may make such enquiries and take into account such court decision, information, report or record from any court or any officer or authority of the Central Government or the State Government or any local authority or local body or any person having knowledge relating to market value of property of the like nature and situated in a comparable locality as he deems fit.

(8) On the basis of enquiries, court decision, information, report or records referred to in sub-rule (7), as the case may be, if the Registering Officer finds that the market value of the property is more than what has been set forth in the instrument of conveyance, exchange, gift, partition or settlement, he shall communicate in writing to the person by whom the stamp duty is payable under section 29 or to his authorised agent or authorised advocate what he believes to be the market value of such property.

(9) If the person by whom the stamp duty is payable under section 29 or his authorised agent or authorised advocate to whom the market value has been communicated under sub-rule (8) offers to pay the deficit amount of stamp duty, if any, he shall deposit into a Government Treasury under appropriate challan, obtainable at any office of the Registering Officer or any Government Treasury, after it is countersigned by the

Registering Officer concerned, or shall pay by a bank draft drawn on any agency bank in favour of the appropriate District Registrar, such deficit amount of stamp duty, and furnish the receipted challan or the bank draft, as the case may be, to the Registering Officer.

(10) The challan as aforesaid shall be filled up in quadruplicate and shall contain the name and address of the person on whose behalf stamp duty is deposited and the particulars of the instrument. On deposit of the amount, the duplicate copy of the receipted challan shall be retained by the Government Treasury, the triplicate copy shall be sent to the Registering Officer and the other two copies shall be returned to the depositor duly signed as proof of payment. The original copy of the receipted challan shall be furnished by the depositor to the Registering Officer.

(11) On receipt of the receipted challan or bank draft, as the case may be, as proof of payment of the deficit amount of stamp duty, the Registering Officer shall, within ten days from the date of receipt of the said challan, register the instrument and certify by recording therein that the proper stamp duty has been paid with which such instrument is chargeable.

(12) If the person by whom the stamp duty is payable under section 29 does not offer to pay the deficit amount of stamp duty with which the instrument for conveyance, gift, partition, exchange or settlement would, in the opinion of the Registering Officer, have been chargeable, the Registering Officer shall register such instrument and certify by recording therein that the instrument has been registered subject to determination on reference under sub-section (1) of section 47A of the market value of the property by the Collector and payment of such deficit amount of stamp duty as may be determined by the Collector.

While the information called for under the above rules are necessary for determination of value, the method of determination as prescribed in sub-rule (1) is confusing and misleading. It also departs from the basic principles that judicial decisions in the realm have evolved.

The Mumbai version

Under the Bombay Stamp (Determination of Market Value of Property) Rules 1984, the principles to be taken into consideration for determination of market value is provided in Rule 8, which lays down in case of non-agricultural land that the Collector of the district shall while determining the true market-value of property which is the subject matter of an instrument for transfer, take into consideration primarily the capitalised value of property and also the following factors, namely:

(*i*) the general value of non-agricultural land in the vicinity

(*ii*) facilities such as road, rail station, bus route, shop, market and the like available in vicinity of the land;

(*iii*) amenities like public offices, hospitals and educational institutions available in the vicinity of the land;

(*iv*) developmental activities including development of industries in the vicinity of the land;

(*v*) any factor mentioned in the instrument which is relevant for the purpose of determination of true market value;

(*vi*) any other factor which the Collector of the district thinks to have bearing on the valuation of non-agricultural land.

Similarly, in case of building the factors to be taken into consideration have been laid down as follows:

(*i*) the area of construction;

(*ii*) the FSI;

(*iii*) type and structure;

(*iv*) year of construction;

(*v*) kind of material used;

(*vi*) locality in which constructed;

(*vii*) rate of depreciation;

(*viii*) and any factor as at (*v*) above;

(*ix*) any other factor which the Collector of district thinks to have bearing on the valuation of building.

It would appear that the factors enumerated above are only illustrative and not exhaustive. The valuer has to exercise his own judgment to arrive at a valuation and ascertain for this purpose how much weightage shall be given to each factor.

(c) INCOME-TAX INCLUDING CAPITAL GAINS

The practice and procedure of valuation assume a typified character under the spell of a statute with definite purpose. Though the discipline of valuation has evolved certain generic characteristics with the basic approaches to value like market approach, income approach or cost approach, there has been departures and distortions with demands in answering to specific requirements of purposive legislations. The fiscal laws are more designed to earn revenue for the Government while the law of compulsory acquisition is interested in ensuring a check to undue drainage of public exchequer through compensation. The law of insurance looks at valuation only to provide indemnification while valuation for financial statement has the objective to paint a bright picture for the prospectus of the company. As for an individual, one would like his property to be depressed in value when the issue is imposition of property tax, but would certainly expect an appreciation in value if the contingency is mortgage for loan. Thus, a uniform pattern of valuation for all purposes has become illusory. On the other hand, valuation assumes a new complexion with each purpose or under spell of each special statute. But there is nevertheless a reference point for each variety of deviation. That is what makes a wide gamut of valuation studies.

In this topic, we shall be dealing with valuation as shaped under the Income-tax laws. The fiscal objectives of Income-tax laws have imparted new definitions and meanings to various concepts relating to valuation and some of them are rooted in the process of historical evolution in the arena of fiscal laws. The taxes on personal and corporate income constitute the major source of revenue for the Central Government in India but the fact remains that the tax net on incomes is yet to cover even one per cent of the entire population of the country. Concealment of income and evasion of tax have become a widely-known assumption on which public policy is framed. There have been periodic attempts to usher in changes. As far back is 1936, the Aiyer Committee reviewed the system in all aspects. After Independence as a major step, the Taxation Enquiry Commission (1953-54) went into the question of tax evasion and recommended several legal and procedural changes. In 1956 Nicholas Kaldor made a special study of the

Indian tax system, particularly with reference to personal and business taxation and the prevalence of tax evasion. The years 1957-1958 witnessed several amendments and new legislation based on Kaldor report.

The Direct Taxes Administration Enquiry Committee was appointed in 1958 to advise the Government on administrative organisation and procedures necessary for implementing the integrated scheme of taxation with due regard to the need for eliminating tax evasion and avoiding inconvenience to the public, and also made substantial contribution to the reorganisation of the legal and administrative set-up.

As tax evasion continued unabated, the Government of India appointed the Direct Taxes Administration Enquiry Committee under the Chairmanship of K.N. Wanchoo, Former Chief Justice of India on 2nd March 1970. The terms of reference of this Committee were as under:

(1) Recommend concrete and effective measure:

(*a*) to unearth black money and prevent its proliferation through further evasion;

(*b*) to check avoidance of tax through various legal devices, including the formation of trusts; and

(*c*) to reduce tax arrears.

(2) Examine various exemptions allowed by the tax laws with a view to their modification, curtailment, or withdrawal.

(3) Indicate the manner in which tax assessment and administration may be improved, for giving effect to all its recommendations.

The Committee was of the view that understatement of prices in sale deeds of immovable properties had become widespread method of tax evasion and a major source and channel for the generation and circulation of black money. The Committee felt that the evil had assumed such proportions that it called for a drastic remedy. The Committee, therefore, recommended that the Government should be empowered to acquire properties where the consideration was found to be understated in sale deed with a view to evading tax, on payment of the disclosed sale consideration and solatium of 15 per cent thereof in addition.

In the Final Report further recommendations were made to the effect that the Government should assume powers to acquire immovable properties in cases of understatement of cost of construction as well, and further it was recommended that the Land Acquisition Act 1894 might be amended to the effect that where an immovable property to be acquired under that Act was the subject-matter of transfer within one year preceding the notification under s. 4 of the Land Acquisition Act 1894, (now s. 11 of the Right to Fair Compensation and Transparency in Land Acquisition, Rehabilitation and Resettlement Act 2013) the sale consideration stated in the transfer deed relating to that property would be deemed to be the fair market value for the purposes of determining compensation under s. 23 of the Land Acquisition Act 1894 (now s. 28 of the Right to Fair Compensation and Transparency in Land Acquisition, Rehabilitation and Resettlement Act 2013). Thus, the Wanchoo Committee recommended that the provisions of the Land Acquisition Act should be tightened to curb the malady understatement of the value of the properties.

The Committee also referred to the system of flats on ownership basis where the transfers were not treated as transactions in immovable properties and were consequently not required to be registered under the Indian Registration Act 1908. The Committee was of the opinion that the evasion of tax through transactions in ownership flats could be checked only if there was all India legislation providing that such transactions should be treated as transactions in immovable properties.

One more Committee known as the Direct Tax Laws Committee was appointed by the Government of India in 1977 under the Chairmanship of Shri N.A. Palkhiwala. Subsequently, on the acceptance of the resignation of Shri N.A. Palkhiwala from the Committee, pursuant to his appointment as Indian Ambassador to the USA, Shri C.C. Chokshi, one of the members of the Committee, was appointed as its Chairman.

The Committee took note of the fact that the law relating to ceiling and regulation of urban land had been modified by the Urban Land Ceiling Act 1976 and also that s. 54E had been introduced in the Act which would go to reduce the temptation for understatement of the sale consideration in the deed with a view to evading or reducing the capital gains tax liability. The Committee also took note s. 52(2) of the Act which empowered the Income-tax Officer to assess the capital gain arising on the transfer of capital asset with reference to its fair market value where he was of the opinion that the consideration had been understated in the deed of sale to the extent of more than 15 per cent. Having regard to all these factors the Chokshi Committee recommended that Chapter XXA should be deleted.

Government introduced the Income-tax (Amendment) Bill on 24th April 1981 in the Lok Sabha. The Bill sought to extend the provisions of Chapter XXA relating to the acquisition of immovable properties to the following types of transactions which were hitherto beyond the scope of the acquisition proceedings:

(1) Transfer of flats or premises owned through the medium of co-operative societies and companies.

(2) Agreement of sale followed by performance as visualised in section 53A of the Transfer of Property Act.

(3) Long-term leases (viz., leases for a period of not less than 12 years).

The Finance Act 1986 has deleted Chapter XXA with effect from 1.10.1986 and replaced it by a new Chapter XXC providing for the purchase by the Central Government of immovable properties by way of pre-emptive right.

Valuation under Direct Tax laws

Under the Direct Tax laws valuations are required to be made under Income-tax Act, Wealth-tax Act and Gift-tax Act. For each of the said Acts there are separate guiding Rules, Schedules etc. The provisions for valuation of 'house properties' under the Income-tax Act are the main topics relevant for the purpose of this book on valuation.

Valuation provisions for income-tax

Under the Income-tax Act valuation of house properties are required mainly for four purposes:

I. *For assessing the annual value of house properties* for the purpose of levy of Income-tax thereon, here valuation means 'annual value' and not the saleable value of the property. The assessment of annual value of house property for determining rental income is similar as in municipal taxation. Annual value is determined for tenanted properties as well as for self-occupied properties on notional basis although no income is earned from self-occupied properties. The income and the process of determining the annual value are provided in ss. 22 and 23 of the Income-tax Act while s. 24 lists the deductions from income for the purpose of computation. The same are reproduced below:

22. Income from house property. The annual value of property consisting of any buildings or lands appurtenant thereto of which the assessee is the owner, other than such portions of such property as he may occupy for the purposes of any business or profession carried on by him the profits of which are chargeable to income-tax, shall be chargeable to income-tax under the head "Income from house property".

23. Annual value how determined. For the purposes of section 22, the annual value of any property shall be deemed to be—

(*a*) the sum for which the property might reasonably be expected to let from year to year; or

(*b*) where the property or any part of the property is let and the annual rent received or receivable by the owner in respect thereof is in excess of the sum referred to in clause (*a*), the amount so received or receivable; or

(*c*) where the property or any part of the property is let and was vacant during the whole or any part of the previous year and owing to such vacancy the actual rent received or receivable by the owner in respect thereof is less than the sum referred to in clause (*a*), the amount so received or receivable:

Provided that the taxes levied by any local authority in respect of the property shall be deducted (irrespective of the previous year in which the liability to pay such taxes was incurred by the owner according to the method of accounting regularly employed by him) in determining the annual value of the property of that previous year in which such taxes are actually paid by him.

Explanation. For the purposes of clause *(b)* or clause *(c)* of this sub-section, the amount of actual rent received or receivable by the owner shall not include, subject to such rules as may be made in this behalf, the amount of rent which the owner cannot realise.

(2) Where the property consists of a house or part of a house which—

(*a*) is in the occupation of the owner for the purposes of his own residence; or

(*b*) cannot actually be occupied by the owner by reason of the fact that owing to his employment, business or profession carried on at any other place, he has to reside at that other place in a building not belonging to him,

the annual value of such house or part of the house shall be taken to be *nil*.

(3) The provisions of sub-section (2) shall not apply if—

(*a*) the house or part of the house is actually let during the whole or any part of the previous year; or

(*b*) any other benefit therefrom is derived by the owner.

(4) Where the property referred to in sub-section (2) consists of more than one house—

(*a*) the provisions of that sub-section shall apply only in respect of one of such houses, which the assessee may, at his option, specify in this behalf;

(*b*) the annual value of the house or houses, other than the house in respect of which the assessee has exercised an option under clause (*a*), shall be determined under sub-section (1) as if such house or houses had been let.

Section 24. *Deductions from income from house property*. Income chargeable under the head "Income from house property" shall be computed after making the following deductions, namely:

(*a*) a sum equal to thirty per cent, of the annual value;

(*b*) where the property has been acquired, constructed, repaired, renewed or reconstructed with borrowed capital, the amount of any interest payable on such capital:

Provided that in respect of property referred to in sub-section (2) of section 23, the amount of deduction shall not exceed thirty thousand rupees:

Provided further that where the property referred to in the first proviso is acquired or constructed with capital borrowed on or after the 1st day of April, 1999, and such acquisition or construction is completed within three years from the end of the financial year in which capital was borrowed, the amount of deduction under this clause shall not exceed one lakh fifty thousand rupees.

Explanation. Where the property has been acquired or constructed with borrowed capital, the interest, if any, payable on such capital borrowed for the period prior to the previous year in which the property has been acquired or constructed, as reduced by any part thereof allowed as deduction under any other provision of this Act, shall be deducted under this clause in equal instalments for the said previous year and for each of the four immediately succeeding previous years:

Provided also that no deduction shall be made under the second proviso unless the assessee furnishes a certificate, from the person to whom any interest is payable on the capital borrowed, specifying the amount of interest payable by the assessee for the purpose of such acquisition or construction of the property, or, conversion of the whole or any part of the capital borrowed which remains to be repaid as a new loan.

Explanation. For the purposes of this proviso, the expression "new loan" means the whole or any part of a loan taken by the assessee subsequent to the capital borrowed, for the purpose of repayment of such capital.

II. *For determination of Capital Gains Tax*, capital gains means the gain arising out of transfer of capital assets which includes land and building unless it is stock in trade of any business. Transfer includes sale, exchange etc. In short, capital gain arises if sale price fetched from a transfer is more than the cost of acquisition. Section 45 of the Income-tax Act describes what is capital gains and how it accrues, while s. 47 lists the transactions not regarded as transfer. Section 48 gives the mode of computation. These are reproduced below:

45. *Capital gains.* (1) Any profits or gains arising from the transfer of a capital asset effected in the previous year shall, save as otherwise provided in sections 54, 54B, 54D, 54E, 54EA, 54EB 54F, 54G and 54H, be chargeable to income-tax under the head "Capital gains", and shall be deemed to be the income of the previous year in which the transfer took place.

(1A) Notwithstanding anything contained in sub-section (1), where any person receives at any time during any previous year any money or other assets under an insurance from an insurer on account of damage to, or destruction of, any capital asset, as a result of—

(i) flood, typhoon, hurricane, cyclone, earthquake or other convulsion of nature; or

(*ii*) riot or civil disturbance; or

(*iii*) accidental fire or explosion; or

(*iv*) action by an enemy or action taken in combating an enemy (whether with or without a declaration of war),

then, any profits or gains arising from receipt of such money or other assets shall be chargeable to income-tax under the head "Capital gains" and shall be deemed to be the income of such person of the previous year in which such money or other asset was received and for the purposes of section 48, value of any money or the fair market value of other assets on the date of such receipt shall be deemed to be the full value of the consideration received or accruing as a result of the transfer of such capital asset.

Explanation. For the purposes of this sub-section, the expression "insurer" shall have the meaning assigned to it in clause (9) of section 2 of the Insurance Act 1938 (4 of 1938).

(2) Notwithstanding anything contained in sub-section (1), the profits or gains arising from the transfer by way of conversion by the owner of a capital assets into, or its treatment by him as stock-in-trade of a business carried on by him shall be chargeable to income-tax as his income of the previous year in which such stock-in-trade is sold or otherwise transferred by him and, for the purposes of section 48, the fair market value of the asset on the date of such conversion or treatment shall be deemed to be the full value of the consideration received or accruing as a result of the transfer of the capital asset.

(2A) Where any person has had at any time during previous year any beneficial interest in any securities, then, any profits or gains arising from transfer made by the depository or participant of such beneficial interest in respect of securities shall be chargeable to income-tax as the income of the beneficial owner of the previous year in which such transfer took place and shall not be regarded as income of the depository who is deemed to be the registered owner of securities by virtue of sub-section (1) of section 10 of the Depositories Act, 1996, and for the purposes of:

(*i*) section 48, and

(*ii*) proviso to clause (42A) of section 2,

the cost of acquisition and the period of holding of any securities shall be determined on the basis of the first-in-first-out method.

Explanation. For the purposes of this sub-section, the expressions "beneficial owner", "depository" and "security" shall have the meanings respectively assigned to them in clauses (*a*), (*e*) and (*l*) of sub-section (1) of section 2 of the Depositories Act, 1996.

(3) The profits or gains arising from the transfer of a capital asset by a person to a firm or other association of persons or body of individuals (not being a company or a co-operative society) in which he is or becomes a partner or member, by way of capital contribution or otherwise, shall be chargeable to tax as his income of the previous year in which such transfer takes place and for the purposes of section 48, the amount recorded in the books of account of the firm, association or body as the value of the capital asset shall be deemed to be the full value of the consideration received or accruing as a result of the transfer of the capital asset.

(4) The profits or gains arising from the transfer of a capital asset by way of distribution of capital assets on the dissolution of a firm or other association of persons or body of individuals (not being a company or a co-operative society) or otherwise, shall be chargeable to tax as the income of the firm, association or body of the previous year in which the said transfer takes place and, for the purposes of section 48, the fair market value of the asset on the date of such transfer shall be deemed to be the full value of the consideration received or accruing as a result of the transfer.

(5) Notwithstanding anything contained in sub-section (1), where the capital gain arises from the transfer of a capital asset, being a transfer by way of compulsory acquisition under any law, or a transfer the consideration for which was determined or approved by the Central Government or the Reserve Bank of India, and the compensation or the consideration for such transfer is enhanced or further enhanced by any court, Tribunal or other authority, the capital gain shall be dealt with in the following manner, namely:—

(*a*) the capital gain computed with reference to the compensation awarded in the first instance or, as the case may be, the consideration determined or approved in the first instance by the Central Government or the Reserve Bank of India shall be chargeable as income under the head "Capital gains" of the previous year in which such compensation or part thereof, or such consideration or part thereof, was first received; and

(*b*) the amount by which the compensation or consideration is enhanced or further enhanced by the court, Tribunal or other authority shall be deemed to be income chargeable under the head "Capital gains" of the previous year in which such amount is received by the assessee;

(*c*) where in the assessment for any year, the capital gain arising from the transfer of a capital asset is computed by taking the compensation or consideration referred to in clause (*a*) or, as the case may be, enhanced compensation or consideration referred to in clause (*b*), and subsequently such compensation or consideration is reduced by any court, Tribunal or other authority, such assessed capital gain of that year shall be computed by taking the compensation or consideration as so reduced by such court, tribunal or other authority to be the full value of the consideration.

Explanation.—For the purposes of this sub-section,

(*i*) in relation to the amount referred to in clause (*b*), the cost of acquisition and the cost of improvement shall be taken to be *nil*;

(*ii*) the provisions of this sub-section shall apply also in a case where the transfer took place prior to the 1st day of April, 1988;

(*iii*) where by reason of the death of the person who made the transfer, or for any other reason, the enhanced compensation or consideration is received by any other person, the amount referred to in clause (*b*) shall be deemed to be the income, chargeable to tax under the head "Capital gains", of such other person.

(6) Notwithstanding anything contained in sub-section (1), the difference between the repurchase price of the units referred to in sub-section (2) of section 80CCB and the capital value of such units shall be deemed to be the capital gains arising to the assessee in the previous year in which such repurchase takes place or the plan referred to in that section is terminated and shall be taxed accordingly.

Explanation.—For the purposes of this sub-section, "capital value of such units" means any amount invested by the assessee in the units referred to in sub-section (2) of section 80CCB.

47. *Transactions not regarded as transfer.* Nothing contained in section 45 shall apply to the following transfers:

(*i*) any distribution of capital assets on the total or partial partition of a Hindu undivided family;

(*ii*) (***)

(*iii*) any transfer of a capital asset under a gift or will or an irrevocable trust;

Provided that this clause shall not apply to transfer under a gift or an irrevocable trust of a capital asset being shares, debentures or warrants allotted by a company directly or indirectly to its employees under any Employees' Stock Option Plan or Scheme of the company offered to such employees in accordance with the guidelines issued by the Central Government in this behalf;

(*iv*) any transfer of a capital asset by a company to its subsidiary company, if —

(*a*) the parent company or its nominees hold the whole of the share capital of the subsidiary company, and

(*b*) the subsidiary company is an Indian company;

(*v*) any transfer of a capital asset by a subsidiary company to the holding company, if—

(*a*) the whole of the share capital of the subsidiary company is held by the holding company, and

(*b*) the holding company is an Indian Company:

Provided that nothing contained in clause (*iv*) or clause (*v*) shall apply to the transfer of a capital asset made after the 29th day of February, 1988, as stock-in-trade;

(*vi*) any transfer, in a scheme of amalgamation, of a capital asset by the amalgamating company to the amalgamated company if the amalgamated company is an Indian company;

(*via*) any transfer, in a scheme of amalgamation, of a capital asset being a share or shares held in an Indian company, by the amalgamating foreign company to the amalgamated foreign company, if—

(*a*) at least twenty-five per cent, of the shareholders of the amalgamating foreign company continue to remain shareholders of the amalgamated foreign company, and

(*b*) such transfer does not attract tax on capital gains in the country, in which the amalgamating company is incorporated;

(*viaa*) any transfer, in a scheme of amalgamation of a banking company with a banking institution sanctioned and brought into force by the Central Government under sub-section (7) of section 45 of the Banking Regulation Act, 1949 (10 of 1949), of a capital asset by the banking company to the banking institution.

Explanation.—For the purposes of this clause,—

(*i*) "banking company" shall have the same meaning assigned to it in clause *(c)* of section 5 of the Banking Regulation Act, 1949 (10 of 1949);

(*ii*) "banking institution" shall have the same meaning assigned to it in sub-section (15) of section 45 of the Banking Regulation Act, 1949 (10 of 1949);

(*vib*) any transfer, in a demerger, of a capital asset by the demerged company to the resulting company, if the resulting company is an Indian company;

(*vic*) any transfer, in a demerger, of a capital asset, being a share or shares held in an Indian company, by the demerged foreign company to the resulting foreign company, if—

(*a*) the shareholders holding not less than three-fourths in value of the shares of the demerged foreign company continue to remain shareholders of the resulting foreign company; and

(*b*) such transfer does not attract tax on capital gains in the country, in which the demerged foreign company is incorporated:

Provided that the provisions of sections 391 to 394 of the Companies Act, 1956 (1 of 1956), shall not apply in case of demergers referred to in this clause;

(*vica*) any transfer in a business reorganisation, of a capital asset by the predecessor co-operative bank to the successor co-operative bank;

(*vicb*) any transfer by a shareholder, in a business reorganisation, of a capital asset being a share or shares held by him in the predecessor co-operative bank if the transfer is made in consideration of the allotment to him of any share or shares in the successor co-operative bank.

Explanation.—For the purposes of clauses *(vica)* and *(vicb)*, the expressions "business reorganisation", "predecessor co-operative bank" and "successor co-operative bank" shall have the meanings respectively assigned to them in section 44DB;

(*vid*) any transfer or issue of shares by the resulting company, in a scheme of demerger to the shareholders of the demerged company, if the transfer or issue is made in consideration of demerger of the undertaking;

(*vii*) any transfer by a shareholder, in a scheme of amalgamation, of a capital asset being a share or shares held by him in the amalgamating company, if—

(*a*) the transfer is made in consideration of the allotment to him of any share or shares in the amalgamated company except where the shareholder itself is the amalgamated company, and

(*b*) the amalgamated company is an Indian company;

(*viia*) any transfer of a capital asset, being bonds or Global Depository Receipts referred to in sub-section (1) of section 115AC, made outside India by a non-resident to another non-resident;

(*viib*) any transfer of a capital asset, being a Government Security carrying a periodic payment of interest, made outside India through an inter-mediary dealing in settlement of securities, by a non-resident to another non-resident.

Explanation. For the purposes of this clause, "Government Security" shall have the meaning assigned to it in clause (*b*) of section 2 of the Securities Contracts (Regulation) Act, 1956 (42 of 1956).

(*viii*) any transfer of agricultural land in India effected before the lst day of March, 1970;

(*ix*) any transfer of a capital asset, being any work of art, archaeological, scientific or art collection, book, manuscript, drawing, painting, photograph or print, to the Government or a University or the National Museum, National Art Gallery, National Archives or any such other public museum or institution as may be notified by the Central Government in the Official Gazette to be of national importance or to be of renown throughout any State or States.

Explanation. For the purposes of this clause, "University" means a University established or incorporated by or under a Central, State or Provincial Act and includes an institution declared under section 3 of the University Grants Commission Act, 1956 (3 of 1956), to be a University for the purposes of that Act;

(*x*) any transfer by way of conversion of bonds or debentures, debenture-stock or deposit certificates in any form, of a company into shares or debentures of that company;

(*xa*) any transfer by way of conversion of bonds referred to in clause *(a)* of sub-section (1) of section 115AC into shares or debentures of any company;

(*xi*) any transfer made on or before the 31st day of December, 1998, by a person (not being a company) of a capital asset being membership of a recognised stock exchange to a company in exchange of shares allotted by that company to the transferor.

Explanation.—For the purposes of this clause, the expression "membership of a recognised stock exchange" means the membership of a stock exchange in India which is recognised under the provisions of the Securities Contracts (Regulation) Act, 1956 (42 of 1956);

(*xii*) any transfer of a capital asset, being land of a sick industrial company, made under a scheme prepared and sanctioned under section 18 of the Sick Industrial Companies (Special Provisions) Act, 1985 (1 of 1986), where such sick industrial company is being managed by its workers' co-operative:

Provided that such transfer is made during the period commencing from the previous year in which the said company has become a sick industrial company under sub-section (1) of section 17 of that Act and ending with the previous year during which the entire net worth of such company becomes equal to or exceeds the accumulated losses.

Explanation.—For the purposes of this clause, "net worth" shall have the meaning assigned to it in clause *(ga)* of sub-section (1) of section 3 of the Sick Industrial Companies (Special Provisions) Act, 1985 (1 of 1986);

(*xiii*) any transfer of a capital asset or intangible asset by a firm to a company as a result of succession of the firm by a company in the business carried on by the firm, or any transfer of a capital asset to a company in the course of demutualisation or corporatisation of a recognised stock exchange in India as a result of which an association of persons or body of individuals is succeeded by such company:

Provided that—

(*a*) all the assets and liabilities of the firm or of the association of persons or body of individuals relating to the business immediately before the succession become the assets and liabilities of the company;

(*b*) all the partners of the firm immediately before the succession become the shareholders of the company in the same proportion in which their capital accounts stood in the books of the firm on the date of succession;

(*c*) the partners of the firm do not receive any consideration or benefit, directly or indirectly, in any form or manner, other than by way of allotment of shares in the company; and

(*d*) the aggregate of the shareholding in the company of the partners of the firm is not less than fifty per cent, of the total voting power in the company and their shareholding continues to be as such for a period of five years from the date of the succession;

(*e*) the demutualisation or corporatisation of a recognised stock exchange in India is carried out in accordance with a scheme for demutualisation or corporatisation which is approved by the Securities and Exchange Board of India established under section 3 of the Securities and Exchange Board of India Act, 1992 (15 of 1992);

(*xiiia*) any transfer of a capital asset being a membership right held by a member of a recognised stock exchange in India for acquisition of shares and trading or clearing rights acquired by such member in that recognised stock exchange in accordance with a scheme for demutualisation or corporatisation, which is approved by the Securities and Exchange Board of India established under section 3 of the Securities and Exchange Board of India Act, 1992 (15 of 1992);

(*xiiib*) *any* transfer of a capital asset or intangible asset by a private company or unlisted public company (hereafter in this clause referred to as the company) to a limited liability partnership or any transfer of a share or shares held in the company by a shareholder as a result of conversion, of the company into a limited liability partnership in accordance with the provisions of section 56 or section 57 of the Limited Liability Partnership Act, 2008 (6 of 2009):

Provided that—

(*a*) all the assets and liabilities of the company immediately before the conversion become the assets and liabilities of the limited liability partnership;

(*b*) all the shareholders of the company immediately before the conversion become the partners of the limited liability partnership and their capital contribution and profit sharing ratio in the limited liability partnership are in the same proportion as their shareholding in the company on the date of conversion;

(*c*) the shareholders of the company do not receive any consideration or benefit, directly or indirectly, in any form or manner, other than by way of share in profit and capital contribution in the limited liability partnership;

(*d*) the aggregate of the profit sharing ratio of the shareholders of the company in the limited liability partnership shall not be less than fifty per cent, at any time during the period of five years from the date of conversion;

(*e*) the total sales, turnover or gross receipts in the business of the company in any of the three previous years preceding the previous year in which the conversion takes place does not exceed sixty lakh rupees; and

(*f*) no amount is paid, either directly or indirectly, to any partner out of balance of accumulated profit standing in the accounts of the company on the date of conversion for a period of three years from the date of conversion.

Explanation. For the purposes of this clause, the expressions "private company" and "unlisted public company" shall have the meanings respectively assigned to them in the Limited Liability Partnership Act, 2008 (6 of 2009);

(*xiv*) where a sole proprietary concern is succeeded by a company in the business carried on by it as a result of which the sole proprietary concern sells or otherwise transfers any capital asset or intangible asset to the company:

Provided that—

(*a*) all the assets and liabilities of the sole proprietary concern relating to the business immediately before the succession become the assets and liabilities of the company;

(*b*) the shareholding of the sole proprietor in the company is not less than fifty per cent, of the total voting power in the company and his shareholding continues to remain as such for a period of five years from the date of the succession; and

(*c*) the sole proprietor does not receive any consideration or benefit, directly or indirectly, in any form or manner, other than by way of allotment of shares in the company;

(*xv*) any transfer in a scheme for lending of any securities under an agreement or arrangement, which the assessee has entered into with the borrower of such securities and which is subject to the guidelines issued by the Securities and Exchange Board of India, established under section 3 of the Securities and Exchange Board of India Act, 1992 (15 of 1992) or the Reserve Bank of India constituted under sub-section (1) of section 3 of the Reserve Bank of India Act, 1934 (2 of 1934), in this regard;

(*xvi*) any transfer of a capital asset in a transaction of reverse mortgage under a scheme made and notified by the Central Government.

48. *Mode of computation.* The income chargeable under the head "Capital gains" shall be computed, by deducting from the full value of the consideration received or accruing as a result of the transfer of the capital asset the following amounts, namely—

(*i*) expenditure incurred wholly and exclusively in connection with such transfer;

(*ii*) the cost of acquisition of the asset and the cost of any improvement thereto:

Provided that in the case of an assessee, who is non-resident, capital gains arising from the transfer of a capital asset being shares in, or debentures of, an Indian company shall be computed by converting the cost of acquisition, expenditure incurred wholly and exclusively in connection with such transfer and the full value of the consideration received or accruing as a result of the transfer of the capital asset into the same foreign currency as was initially utilised in the purchase of the shares or debentures, and the capital gains so computed in such foreign currency shall be reconverted into Indian currency, so, however, that the aforesaid manner of computation of capital gains shall be applicable in respect of capital gains accruing or arising from every reinvestment thereafter in, and sale of, shares in, or debentures of, an Indian company:

Provided further that where long-term capital gain arises from the transfer of a long-term capital asset, other than capital gain arising to a non-resident from the transfer of shares in, or debentures of, an Indian company referred to in the first proviso, the provisions of clause (*ii*) shall have effect as if for the words "cost of acquisition" and "cost of any improvement", the words "indexed cost of acquisition" and "indexed cost of any improvement" had respectively been substituted:

Provided also that nothing contained in the second proviso shall apply to the long-term capital gain arising from the transfer of a long-term capital asset being bond or debenture other than capital indexed bonds issued by the Government.

Provided also that where shares, debenturer or warrants referred to in the proviso to clause (*iii*) of section 47 are transferred under a gift or an irrevocable trust, the market value on the date of such transfer shall be deemed to be the full value of consideration received or accruing as a result of transfer for the purposes of this section:

Provided also that no deduction shall be allowed in computing the income chargeable under the head 'capital gains' in respect of any sum paid on account of securities transaction tax under Chapter VII of the Finance (No. 2) Act, 2004 (23 of 2004).

Explanation. For the purposes of this section,—

(*i*) "foreign currency" and "Indian currency" shall have the meanings respectively assigned to them in section 2 of the Foreign Exchange Management Act, 1999 (42 of 1999);

(*ii*) the conversion of Indian currency into foreign currency and the reconversion of foreign currency into Indian currency shall be at the rate of exchange prescribed in this behalf;

(*iii*) "indexed cost of acquisition" means an amount which bears to the cost of acquisition the same proportion as Cost Inflation Index for the year in which the asset is transferred bears to the Cost Inflation Index for the first year in which the asset was held by assessee or for the year beginning on the 1st day of April, 1981, whichever is later;

(*iv*) "indexed cost of any improvement" means an amount which bears to the cost of improvement the same proportion as Cost Inflation Index for the year in which the asset is transferred bears to the Cost Inflation Index for the year in which the improvement to the asset took place;

(v) "Cost Inflation Index" in relation to a previous year means such Index as the Central Government may, having regard to seventy-five per cent of average rise in the Consumer Price Index for urban non-manual employees for the immediately preceding previous year to such previous year, by notification in the Official Gazette, specify in this behalf.

III. *For determining the cost of construction and the value of land* this is required by the Income-tax Department for ascertaining whether the amount spent for purchasing land and for construction is out of taxed income and other legitimate sources.

IV. *For exercising the pre-emptive right of the Central Government* to purchase any immovable property where the seller intends to sell his property to any third party and the apparent consideration (price) is less than the fair market value of the property, here valuation (fair market value) of an immovable property is determined by the Income-tax Department to detect whether the transaction (i.e. sale and purchase of property) is being done at a price which is lower than the fair market value and to exercise the pre-emptive right of the Government to purchase the said immovable property at the same price which was agreed between the buyer and seller. This is comprised in Chapter XX-C of the Income-tax Act. The provision enabling pre-emption is contained in section 269UD(1) which is reproduced below:

> 269UD. *Order by appropriate authority for purchase by Central Government of immovable property.* (1) Subject to the provisions of sub-sections (1A) and (1B), the appropriate authority, after the receipt of the statement under sub-section (3) of section 269UC in respect of any immovable property, may, notwithstanding anything contained in any other law or any instrument or any agreement for the time being in force, make an order for the purchase by the Central Government of such immovable property at an amount equal to the amount of apparent consideration:
>
> Provided that no such order shall be made in respect of any immovable property after the expiration of a period of two months from the end of the month in which the statement referred to in section 269UC in respect of such property is received by the appropriate authority.

Provided further that where the statement referred to in section 269UC in respect of any immovable property is received by the appropriate authority on or after the 1st day of June, 1993, the provisions of the first proviso shall have effect as if for the words "two months", the words "three months" had been substituted:

Provided also that the period of limitation referred to in the second proviso shall be reckoned, where any defect as referred to in sub-section (4) of section 269UC has been intimated, with reference to the date of receipt of the rectified statement by the appropriate authority:

Provided also that in a case where the statement referred to in section 269UC in respect of the immovable property concerned is given to an appropriate authority, other than the appropriate authority having jurisdiction in accordance with the provisions of section 269UB to make the order referred to in this sub-section in relation to the immovable property concerned, the period of limitation referred to in the first and second provisos shall be reckoned with reference to the date of receipt of the statement by the appropriate authority having jurisdiction to make the order under this sub-section:

Provided also that the period of limitation referred to in the second proviso shall be reckoned, where any stay has been granted by any court against the passing of an order for the purchase of the immovable property under this chapter, with reference to the date of vacation of the said stay.

(1A) Before making an order under sub-section (1), the appropriate authority shall give a reasonable opportunity of being heard to the transferor, the person in occupation of the immovable property if the transferor is not in occupation of the property, the transferee and to every other person whom the appropriate authority knows to be interested in the property.

(1B) Every order made by the appropriate authority under sub-section (1) shall specify the grounds on which it is made.

(2) The appropriate authority shall cause a copy of its order under sub-section (1) in respect of any immovable property to be served on the transferor, the person in occupation of the immovable property if the transferor is not in occupation thereof, the transferee, and on every other person whom the appropriate authority knows to be interested in the property.

Annual value for assessing income from house property

Section 23(*a*) of the Income-tax Act 1961 lays down that the annual value of a property is the sum for which the property could reasonably be expected to let from year to year. What is, therefore, to be seen is the inherent capacity of the property to yield income from year to year. In determining such notional income, several factors have to be taken into consideration, such as actual realisation by way of licence fee, consideration or premium received by the owner, charges normally payable by the owner being borne by the tenant, the location of the property, use of the property, the capacity of the property to command income over a period of years etc.

Municipal valuation is one of the tests to be applied in determining the *bona fide* value of a property. The municipal authorities determine the valuation of a property for levy of property tax with reference to the gross annual rent for which the property could reasonably be expected to let from year to year. If the property is given on leave and licence basis, the municipal authorities take the licence-fee into consideration for fixing the municipal valuation. Therefore, unless the actual realisation by way of rent or licence-fee is higher than the municipal valuation, the annual value is ordinarily determined with reference to the municipal rateable value on the basis of which municipal taxes are levied.

In the majority of cases, however, annual value can be determined by taking into consideration the following four factors:

(*a*) rent payable by the tenant;

(*b*) municipal valuation of the property;

(*c*) fair rent of the property; and

(*d*) standard rent under the rent control law in force.

From the reasonable letting value determined in the manner indicated above, a deduction is to be made under the first proviso to s. 23(1) on account of taxes levied by a local authority or Corporation or Municipality to the extent borne by the owner of the property. Here unless payment is made during the year, no deduction is allowed.

The amount so arrived at is the Annual Value of a house property.

In the case of building comprising of one or more residential units let out for residential purpose, the construction of which is completed after 31.3.1982 but before 1.4.1992 a deduction, in respect of such units will be allowed from its annual value at the rate of ₹ 3,600 per residential unit or the annual value of such unit, whichever is less, for a period of five years from the date of completion of such building under the second proviso to s. 23(1). However if the erection of the property is completed after 1.4.1992 no deduction in this respect is allowable.

The annual value of a house or part of a house shall be taken to be 'nil' if—

(*i*) it is in the occupation of the owner for the purposes of his own residence, or

(*ii*) it is not actually let during any part of the previous year and no other benefit therefrom is derived by the owner. If it is let out during the part of the previous year and for remaining part of the period it is in the occupation of owner, then, annual value of the house will be reduced in the proportion in which the period of occupation by the owner bears to the whole year.

Where two or more than two houses are in the occupation of owner for the purposes of his residence, then the annual value shall be taken to be 'nil' only in respect of any one house of his choice. The annual value of the remaining house or houses used for self-occupation by the owner will be computed as if the said house/houses were let out.

It may be noted that, where the annual value of the house is taken to be 'nil', as discussed above, then no deductions under s. 24(1) shall be allowed.

Sub-section (2) of s. 23 provides that where the property consists of a house or part of a house which cannot actually be occupied by the owner by reason of the fact that owing to his employment, business or profession carried on at any other place, he has to reside at that other place in a building not belonging to him, the annual value of such house or part of that house shall be taken to be 'nil'.

Section 26 of the Income-tax Act states that where a house property is owned by two or more persons and their respective shares are determinate, such persons shall not be assessed in respect of such property as an association of persons but the share of each co-owner will be included in his total income.

Under s. 24 of the Income-tax Act, the income under the head "Income from house property" is to be computed after making the following deductions from the annual value determined under s. 23.

(*i*) A sum equal to thirty per cent of annual value.

(*ii*) Where the property has been acquired, constructed, repaired, renewed or reconstructed with borrowed capital, the amount of any interest payable on such capital.

(*iii*) The property referred to in section 23(2), the amount of deduction shall not exceed ₹ 30,000.

(*iv*) Where the property referred to in the first proviso is acquired or constructed with capital borrowed on or after 1.4.1999 and the acquisition or construction is completed within three years from the end of the financial year in which capital was borrowed the amount of deduction shall not exceed ₹ 1,50,000.

Recovery of irrecoverable rent allowed as a deduction earlier will be brought to tax in the year of recovery as income from house property. No deduction either under s. 23 or 24 will be allowed from the amount so brought to tax.

Capital gains

While discussing capital gains it may be mentioned that in some cases the actual price of the property are not mentioned in the deed of conveyance, instead some lower amount of consideration are mentioned so that Stamp Duty as well as Income-tax can be evaded. So Income-tax Department seeks to ascertain the actual valuation of the property as on the date of sale or transfer as because basically capital gains is the excess of (transfer) price of capital assets over its cost subject to some adjustments. Nowadays, many promoters or developers or owners make over possession of flats to the buyers without making any deed of conveyance and in this way they deprive the Government from Stamp Duty as well as Capital Gains Tax. Hence, tax laws have suitably been amended to include capital gains on sale of immovable property even in the cases where the possession of immovable property is given without registration of conveyance deed. Transfer of movable property is complete with delivery of possession. Transfer of immovable property, normally, is complete only when the conveyance deed is registered. However, for the purposes of capital gains, the transfer is treated as complete with delivery of possession. When agreement to sell/buy immovable property is entered into and such agreement is itself a subject-matter of transaction, the fiscal authorities treat it as a deal transacted.

Hence it is necessary to know for the purpose of capital gains valuation, the date of actual sale or transfer or handing over of possession. Similarly, it is required to ascertain the original cost of acquisition of the property or as because capital gain is basically the difference between the original cost and the sale price and some people try to hide the actual valuation in both the matters by showing higher original cost and lower sale price in order to reduce the capital gain. Sometimes the person who sells the property acquired it by way of gift or inheritance. In such cases the original cost of the transferor will be the cost of the previous owner from whom he got it by gift or inheritance. The original cost will be increased by Stamp Duty, brokerage, legal expenses, registration fees and cost of improvement of the property.

As per s. 55(2)(*b*)(*i*) of the Act, where the Capital Asset became the property of the assessee before 1.4.1981 or where the capital assets became the property of the assessee by succession, inheritance, or any other mode referred to in s. 49(1) of the Income-tax Act, he has the option of substituting the fair market value as on 1.4.1981 in place of the original cost.

Since as a result of inflation the price of everything is rising very fast, the capital gain becomes too high for long-term capital assets on account of inflation factor alone. To reduce this hardship the law has allowed the tax-payers to take advantage of the Cost Inflation Index published by the Central Government and thereby raise the cost of the assets. The Cost Inflation Index can be availed of from the financial year 1981-82 onwards. If any property was inherited before 1.4.1981 then the assessee can substitute the cost by the value of the asset as on 1.4.1981 with the help of any registered valuer and thereafter he can take advantage of Cost Inflation Index.

In exercise of the powers conferred by clause (*v*) of the Explanation of section 48 of the Income-tax Act 1961 (43 of 1961), the Central Government, having regard to seventy-five per cent of the average rise in the Consumer Price Index for urban non-manual employees, specified the Cost Inflation Index as mentioned in column (3) of the Table below for the financial year mentioned in the corresponding entry in column (2) of the said Table.

TABLE

Sl. No.	Financial Year	Cost Inflation Index
1.	1981-1982	100
2.	1982-1983	109
3.	1983-1984	116
4.	1984-1985	125
5.	1985-1986	133
6.	1986-1987	140
7.	1987-1988	150
8.	1988-1989	161
9.	1989-1990	172
10.	1990-1991	182
11.	1991-1992	199
12.	1992-1993	223
13.	1993-1994	244
14.	1994-1995	259
15.	1995-1996	281
16.	1996-1997	305
17.	1997-1998	330
18.	1998-1999	351
19.	1999-2000	389
20.	2001-2002	426
21.	2002-2003	447
22.	2003-2004	463
23.	2004-2005	480
24.	2005-2006	497
25.	2006-2007	519
26.	2007-2008	551
27.	2008-2009	582
28.	2009-2010	632
29.	2010-2011	711
30.	2011-2012	785
31.	2012-2013	852

Capital gains in phases

In section 48 of the Income-tax Act the mode of computation needs elaboration. In the section as it stands capital gains shall be deemed to be the net gain in real terms accruing to the transferor of a property on account of unearned increase reckoned from the date of acquisition of the property. It is true, the rise in price due to inflation does not fetch any real gain to the transferor inasmuch as the monetary gain computed on the basis of the sale price *vis-a-vis* the price at the time of the acquisition might be eaten up wholly be inflation. That is why the assessee has been given the benefit of computation on the basis of the indexed cost of acquisition as well as the indexed cost of improvement so that only the portion of his real gains comes within the purview of the tax net.

But confusion may arise when the nature of right or interest in the property as originally acquired is not exactly the same when the property was disposed of. For example, the assessee might have acquired a tenanted property to which he subsequently obtained vacant possession and was ultimately able to transfer it at a high price accounting for a big margin for the computation of capital gains and *vice versa*. How the prescribed mode of computation shall be applied in such cases?

The right to property should be viewed in the perspective of the entire bundle of rights that go to make up an ownership. Rights or interests carved out of ownership are not the same as ownership itself. When a tenanted property is acquired, the buyer gets only the right to receive the rent since possession remains with the tenants. But when he succeeds in evicting the tenant and obtains vacant possession, he adds another stick to the bundle of rights. The acquisition of such right is referable only to the date when it accrues to the owner. Thus for the purpose of capital gains an assessee may have two dates of acquisition, one for the acquiring lessor's right and another for the lessee's right both merging to make absolute ownership. The computation of capital gain has to be done accordingly.

With a view to ascertaining the fair market value of a capital asset, the concerned Assessing Officer may refer the valuation of the capital asset to Valuation Officer appointed by the Income-tax Department in the following cases:

(a) where the value of the assets as claimed by the assessee is in accordance with the estimate made by a registered valuer (who works in a private capacity under a licence issued by the Central Board of Direct Taxes) but the Assessing Officer is of the opinion that the value so claimed is less than its fair market value;

(b) where the Assessing Officer is of the opinion that the fair market value of the asset exceeds the value of the asset by more than ₹ 25,000 or 15 per cent of the value claimed by the assessee, whichever is less (rule 111AA); or

(c) where the Assessing Officer is of the opinion that having regard to nature of an asset and relevant circumstances, it is necessary to do so.

Purchase of immovable properties by the Central Government (Chapter XXC)

In certain cases of transfer, the Central Government may opt to purchase the immovable properties in exercise of a power of pre-emption. Chapter XXC of the Income-tax Act deals with the relevant provisions which have come into force in Delhi, Bombay, Calcutta, Madras, Bangalore, Ahmedabad, Chandigarh, Jaipur, Kanpur, Lucknow, Coimbatore, Madurai, Surat, Gurgaon, Faridabad, Baroda, Ghaziabad and Noida. According to s. 269UC of the Act no transfer of immovable property of value exceeding a certain amount shall be effected except after an agreement for transfer between transferor and transferee at least three months before the intended date of transfer. Such agreement shall be reduced in writing in the form of a statement in the prescribed form (Form No. 37-I) by each of the parties and shall be furnished to the Appropriate Authority within 15 days from the date of agreement. The Appropriate Authority, after giving an opportunity of being heard to the transferor and the transferee may make an order within 3 months from the end of the month of filing the Form No. 37-I before the Appropriate Authority. Such order may be for the purchase by the Central Government of such immovable property at an amount equal to the amount of apparent consideration as shown in the agreement and the statement in Form No. 37-I. The order of the Appropriate Authority shall be final and conclusive and shall not be called in question in any proceeding under the Income-tax Act.

This is a right of pre-emption vested in the Central Government basically to prevent any underhand transaction by the parties. Here the role of a valuer is considerable since it must be proved that the apparent consideration is but the fair market value of the property. The property should be valued correctly before fixation of price as because if the price is fixed at a lesser amount than the fair market value, there is always the chance of the property being vested in the Central Government at that lesser price.

The relevant provisions of Chapter XXC are as follows:

(1) Transfer of any immovable property of a value exceeding the prescribed amount is prohibited, except after entering into an agreement for transfer between the transferor and the transferee at least three months before the intended date of transfer. The prescribed amount of valuation with effect from 31.07.1995 is as follows:—

Name of cities where property is situated	Valuation
Bombay	Exceeding ₹ 75 lakhs
Calcutta	" " 25 "
Bangalore	" " 25 "
Delhi	" " 50 "
Madras	" " 25 "
Ahmedabad	" " 25 "
Pune	" " 25 "
Others	" " 20 "

(2) The agreement should be reduced in writing in the form of a prescribed statement and should be sent to the Appropriate Authority constituted by the Government.

(3) The 'Appropriate Authority' for this purpose would comprise of three persons — two of whom should be at least of the rank of a Commissioner of Income-tax, and the third should be of the rank of at least a Chief Engineer.

(4) The Appropriate Authority could pass an order for the purchase of the property within a period of two full calendar months, starting from the end of the month in which the

statement is filed and when such order is passed the property will vest in the Government free from all encumbrances. If no order is passed within this time limit, the transferor would be free to go ahead with his original intention.

(5) The consideration payable by the Government to the transferor will be equal to the consideration declared in the agreement of transfer and this should be paid within one complete calendar month from the month in which the property vested in the Government. If this time limit is not adhered to by the Government the order passed by the Appropriate Authority would stand abrogated.

(6) Once a statement in Form 37-I is filed the transferor and transferee cannot revoke or alter the agreement until an order is passed by the Appropriate Authority.

(7) The registering authorities are prohibited from registering any document which purports to transfer any immovable property exceeding the prescribed value.

Another feature of the provision of this chapter is that there is no requirement to give the parties an opportunity of being heard before passing the order. However, the Appropriate Authority must record the reasons as to why the property should be purchased.

As there was no provision of giving a hearing before pre-emptive purchase, on the question of natural justice, a number of writ petitions were filed challenging the validity of this Chapter XXC. Ultimately, the Supreme Court took up a test case and delivered the landmark judgment on 17.11.1992 in *C.B. Gautam* v *Union of India*,[25] upholding the validity of acquiring such immovable property but struck down certain items. The Supreme Court held that:—

(*i*) Chapter XXC is to be resorted to only in case where undervaluation is 15% or more.

(*ii*) Reasons recorded must be disclosed to the affected parties.

(*iii*) Opportunity must be given to the aggrieved parties to be heard before making the order for purchase.

25 (1993)199 ITR 530 (SC).

(*iv*) The provision of vesting "free from all encumbrances" is invalid. The possession of *bona fide* lessees and encumbrance-holders is not to be affected.

Subsequently, in the light of the Supreme Court observations referred to above, the provisions of Chapter XXC were amended with effect from 17.11.1992. A few provisions have been inserted in s. 269 which are briefly as follows:—

(*i*) The Appropriate Authority shall specify the reasons for acquisition.

(*ii*) When the property vests in the Central Government, it shall vest in accordance with the terms of the agreement for transfer. (The phrase "free from all encumbrances" has been deleted).

(*iii*) Where the Appropriate Authority after giving an opportunity of being heard to the interested persons feel that the encumbrance on the property is to defeat the provisions of this Chapter, it may declare such encumbrance as void. In such a case, the property would vest in the Central Government free from such encumbrances or other interests.

There have been a number of judicial decisions touching on various issues of valuation arising in the context of purchases by the Central Government in exercise of powers under Chapter XXC of the Income-tax Act. These are narrated below:

In *CIT* v *Ganesh Builders*,[1] it was observed that it is not the value which is given by either the Departmental Valuation Officer or the private valuer's report that binds the authorities. These reports merely constitute evidence. The authorities have to find out themselves by appreciating the evidence on records as to what is the fair market value.

In *CIT* v *Dr. V.K. Bhaskaran Nair*,[2] it was held:

"Admittedly, no attempt has been made by the competent Authority to produce the valuation officer before the Tribunal so that the Tribunal could hear him so as to assess the fairness or otherwise of the valuation made by the valuation officer. For what reason the valuation officer has

1 (1979)116 ITR 911 (Bom).
2 (1979)116 ITR 873 (Mad).

been kept out of the purview of the Tribunal is not clear. It, however, appears to us that the valuation officer was not placed before the Tribunal because he could not support his report. Apart from this inference, which we are legitimately entitled to draw in the circumstances of the case. We are satisfied that the Tribunal did weigh the pros and cons and came to the conclusion that the order of the Competent Authority was not sustainable."

In *CIT* v *Smt. Prem Kumari,*[3] it was observed:

"The opinion of experts/valuers is admissible as evidence but they are not binding on the Court or Tribunal, who will be entitled to judge the same itself and if it finds that the same is not reliable, it will be free to do so. The experts give evidence and do not decide the issue."

In *CIT* v *Radhey Mohan,*[4] it was held that in respect of property partly let out, rent capitalisation method is the appropriate method for valuating such property. Hypothetical rent of self-occupied portion can be determined by taking into consideration the rent payable by tenant or that prevailing in the locality. Rent capitalisation method is applicable even to buildings to which Rent Control Acts do not apply.

In *Guran Dass* v *CIT,*[5] the acquired property was put to auction. It was held that in case of auction sale by the Chandigarh Administration of the kind, the number of bidders could be very high and a bidder could make a very high bid since he did not have to pay the entire amount in the lump sum. He could, after paying 25% of the sale price, invest the balance amount in constructing upon the site and thereafter, the building may enable him to earn and pay the balance amount. Such would not be the case with a private sale for two reasons: (*i*) there would not be competition between the buyers as in the case of auction sale, and (*ii*) the buyers who could pay the sale price in lump sum could not be many and, therefore, the comparable plot sold in, in a private sale would fetch much less.

3 (1984)146 ITR 191 (All).
4 (1985)153 ITR 399 (P&H).
5 (1984)148 ITR 770 (P&H).

In *Blue Star Ltd.* v *I.A.C.*,[6] it was held that the value on the date of agreement to sale and not on the date of Registration thereof is relevant. The property was purchased on 21st March 1972 but the conveyance deed lodged for registration in June 1977. It was observed that there is no ground to conclude that value on that date was fair market value.

In *Bhartiya Udyog* v *Competent Authority*,[7] the intention of demolishing the existing building and rebuilding a new structure was considered entirely irrelevant in the matter of valuation for acquisition. It is well settled that the present use of the land is not the sole criteria for determining fair market value. Its potentiality can be taken into consideration, but, as observed by the Privy Council in *Vyricherla Narayana Gajapati Raju* v *Revenue Divisional Officer*,[8] it is the possibility of the land and not its realised potentialities that must be taken into consideration.

In *CIT* v *Prem Narain Tandon*,[9] the Appellate Tribunal held that the Competent Authority was not justified in discarding the capitalisation method of determining the market price of the house in dispute on the basis of its annual rental value. The Appellate Authority observed that since ¾th portion of the house was let out to a tenant on rent, the FMV of the property could be determined on its annual rental value. Since ¾th of the property was let out on a rent of ₹ 3,000 per annum, the Tribunal determined the rent of the entire property at ₹ 4,000 and after making an allowance to the extent of 25% towards outgoings, it determined the net rental value on the basis of ₹ 3,000 per annum. According to the High Court, there is no error in this approach of the tribunal.

In *Vimal Agarwal* v *Appropriate Authority*,[10] the case relates to transfer of a flat in Parishram Apartment, Palle Hill, Bandra, Bombay. It was held that the Appropriate Authority should compare the apparent consideration with the market value

6 (1984)150 ITR 356 (Bom).
7 (1979)120 ITR 128 (All).
8 AIR 1939 PC 98.
9 (1984)145 ITR 359 (All).
10 (1994)210 ITR 16 (Bom).

reflected in the most comparable instances, whether furnished by the authority or the aggrieved parties; more so, in cases where the application in Form 37-I has been filed and NOC issued. The sale instances should be meticulously scrutinised and then adjustment can be made for plus and minus factors *vis-a-vis* the property under consideration. The Appropriate Authority has to determine the figures of fair market value with reference to which it can be ascertained whether the apparent consideration was lower by 15% or more. That was not done in the instant case.

In *Shrichand Raheja* v *S.C. Prasad*,[11] the case relates to transfer of a property known as Modi Bungalow situated on Nepean Sea Road, Malabar Hills, Bombay for ₹ 19.25 crores. The total land area is 1823.56 sq. yds. In appeal by the transferee against the order of acquisition by the Appropriate Authority, the learned Judges of the Bombay High Court observed as under:—

> "It must be borne in mind that by the exercising writ jurisdiction, we are not sitting in appeal over the order passed by the Appropriate Authority. We are conscious that the exercise is only to ascertain whether the order is passed by relying upon extraneous or irrelevant material. It is not permissible to reassess the material and the order cannot be disturbed unless it is found that the order suffers from serious infirmity, bordering on perversity. In our judgment, the order does not suffer from any infirmity and the conclusion is not required to be disturbed in exercise of writ jurisdiction."

In *Om Shri Jigar Association* v *Union of India*,[12] it was held that the provisions of Chapter XXC are not applicable in a transaction where a public charitable trust registered under Bombay Public Trusts Act 1960 proposes to sell its property after taking permission from Charity Commissioner and inviting offers from public at large through advertisement in newspapers.

11 (1994)122 CTR 131 (Bom).
12 (1994)209 ITR 608 (Guj).

Cost of construction—determination and valuation

Cost of construction is the amount with the spending of which the property has been constructed by the owner. It is a process by which the value of expenditure incurred by the owner of a property in constructing the property is determined. The present market conditions, profitability and increase in the cost of materials used etc. are irrelevant considerations for the purpose of valuating cost of construction of a property. Under the scheme of Direct Taxes, Cost of Construction is valued under Income-tax Act for fixing the extent of unaccounted money utilised in constructing the property. The meaning of words 'Cost of Construction' is essentially different from the words 'fair market value'. Whereas the words 'fair market value' denote the value or the price a property can fetch, if sold in the open market on a given date in normal conditions, the words 'cost of construction' mean the value for which the property in question was actually constructed by its owner. Fair market value is the price for which on a given date a willing buyer is ready to buy a particular property and a willing seller is ready to sell. Fair market value fluctuates in accordance with market conditions.

Valuation by arriving at cost of construction of capital asset had been a major source of discordance between the department and the tax-payer in recent times. It is the general impression of the taxmen that construction of immovable property gives scope for *utilisation* of unaccounted money and this impression is not totally unfounded. Now the question arises how to evaluate the cost of construction. In the beginning. Assessing Officers themselves used to estimate the amount of cost of construction having regard to area, type of construction etc. but in view of increasing complications of technical nature, the Central Board of Direct Taxes had enlisted valuers for the purpose with necessary technical background and also laid down the scale of fees to be charged by them. These valuers were called approved valuers. In cases where an Assessing Officer was not satisfied with the correctness of the Valuation Report submitted by the tax-payer he used to obtain valuation from another approved valuer and the difference between the two valuers usually resulted in litigation and the case was sent by the Appellate Authorities to a third valuer for Arbitration and so on.

To narrow down the scope for difference between the tax-payers and the department on valuation of capital assets and to minimise the tax evasion on account of undervaluation and to get the accurate valuation at the stage of assessment itself, the whole valuation machinery was reorganised by Taxation Laws (Amendment) Act 1972 (No. 45 of 1972) which provides for appointment of Valuation Officers by the Government with statutory powers. This new set up of Valuation Officers appointed by the Central Government popularly know as 'Valuation Cell' has given a fresh cause for prolonged litigation instead of minimising the same as expected originally. The department refers the cases of valuation on cost of construction to the Valuation Officer under s. 55A of the Income-tax Act 1961 which is reproduced hereunder:

"55A. *Reference to valuation officer.* With a view to ascertaining the Fair Market Value of a capital asset for the purposes of this Chapter, the Assessing Officer may refer the valuation of the capital asset to a Valuation Officer:

(*a*) in a case where the value of the asset as claimed by the assessee is in accordance with the estimate made by a registered valuer, if the Assessing Officer is of opinion that the value so claimed is at variance with its fair market value;

(*b*) in any other case, if the Assessing Officer is of opinion—

(*i*) that the Fair Market Value of the asset exceeds the value of the asset as claimed by the assessee by more than such percentage of the value of the asset as so claimed or by more than such amount as may be prescribed in this behalf; or

(*ii*) that having regard to the nature of the asset and other relevant circumstances, it is necessary so to do,

and where any such reference is made, the provisions of sub-sections (2), (3), (4), (5) and (6) of section 16A, clauses (*ha*) and (*i*) of sub-section (1) and sub-sections (3A) and (4) of section 23, sub-section (5) of section 24, section 34AA, section 35 and section 37 of the Wealth-tax Act, 1957 shall, with the necessary modifications, apply in relation to such reference as they apply in relation to a reference made by the Assessing Officer under sub-section (1) of section 16A of that Act.

Explanation—In this section, "Valuation Officer" has the same meaning as in clause (*r*) of section 2 of the Wealth-tax Act, 1957."

The only other section under the Income-tax Act 1961 which authorises the reference to the Valuation Officer is s. 269L under Chapter XXA of the Act which authorises the reference of the valuation of Fair Market Value with regard to acquisition of immovable property in certain cases of transfer. Section 269L is reproduced hereunder:

"269L. *Assistance by Valuation Officers.* (1) The competent authority may—

(*a*) for the purpose of initiating proceedings for the acquisition of any immovable property under section 269C or for the purpose of making an order under section 269F in respect of any immovable property, require a Valuation Officer to determine the fair market value of such property and report the same to him;

(*b*) for the purpose of estimating the amount by which the compensation payable under sub-section (1) of section 269J in respect of any immovable property may be reduced or, as the case may be, increased under clause (*a*) or clause (*b*) of sub-section (2) of that section, require the Valuation Officer to make such estimate and report the same to him.

(2) The Valuation Officer to whom a reference is made under clause (*a*) or clause (*b*) of sub-section (1) shall, for the purpose of dealing with such reference, have all the powers that he has under section 38A of the Wealth-tax Act, 1957.

(3) If in an appeal under section 269G against the order for acquisition of any immovable property, the fair market value of such property is in dispute, the Appellate Tribunal shall, on a request being made in this behalf by the competent authority, give an opportunity of being heard to any Valuation Officer nominated for the purpose by the competent authority.

Explanation. In this section, "Valuation Officer" has the same meaning as in clause (*r*) of section 2 of the Wealth-tax Act, 1957".

There has been a number of judicial decisions on this sensitive issue. The Punjab and Haryana High Court in a case *Jindal Strips Limited* v *Income-tax Officer, Central Circle III, New Delhi*,[13] wherein the assessee has challenged the jurisdiction of the Income-tax Officer (now Assessing Officer)

13 (1979)116 ITR 825.

in referring the case of valuation of Cost of Construction of company's mill to the Departmental Valuation Officer, has held "that the contention of the petitioner that the scope of s. 55A, as evident from its terms, was confined to ascertainment of the fair market value of a capital asset which has been the subject-matter of transfer, since s. 55A occurs under Chapter IV in Part E—Capital gains, is correct. Consequently, the contention that s. 55A would not apply in the facts and circumstances of the case has to be accepted".

However the Hon'ble High Court upheld the reference as valid on a contention that 'section 133(6) of the Act provides that the Assessing Officer may require any person to furnish information in relation to such points or matters, or to furnish statements of accounts and affairs as will be useful for, or relevant to any proceeding under the Act. A decision made by the Valuation Officer and the proceedings are quasi-judicial in nature as held by Hon'ble Delhi High Court in *Wanger and Co.* v *Dist. Valuation Officer, New Delhi.*[14]

In *K. Hari Rao* v *Second Income-tax Officer*[15] Income-tax Appellate Tribunal, Madras Bench has held: "We have considered the rival submissions. It is common ground that the assessee had put up the building in question during the period January 1971 to October 1973. It is also common ground that a large part of the work was done during the first year relevant to the assessment year 1973-74, and the remaining work was done during the accounting year relevant to the assessment year under appeal. The assessee had claimed that he has maintained books of accounts showing the cost of construction and that further all the purposes effected by the assessee for the construction of the said building were fully supported. The assessee had shown the cost of construction at ₹ 1,41,033 as per books. Besides, the assessee had also produced before the Income-tax Officer a valuation report in support of the above cost from an approved valuer. The correctness of these facts is not challenged by the Revenue. The Income-tax Officer has not pointed out any flaw in the books of accounts maintained for the cost of construction. It is not the case of the Revenue that assessee has not recorded all the purchases

14 (1978)115 ITR 648.
15 (1979)8 TTJ 15.

of raw materials for the construction or understated or inflated the purchases. Further the Income-tax Officer has nothing to say about the valuation report furnished by the approved valuer of the assessee. In the assessment order the Income-tax Officer has straightaway proceeded to refer to the estimate made by the Valuation Cell of the department. The Income-tax Officer has taken the cost of construction as per the estimate made by the departmental valuer and had arrived at the difference as unexplained investment.

In the absence of any material to discredit the accounts maintained by the assessee for the cost of construction, which is admittedly supported by vouchers, we see no reason why an estimate at all should be made of the cost of construction. We have, therefore, no hesitation in accepting the cost of construction as admitted by the assessee. We direct that the amount added towards deficiency in the cost of construction as sustained by the Appellate Assistant Commissioner, be deleted."

In *ITO* v *Sethna Ice and Cold Storage*,[16] the Income-tax Appellate Tribunal, Ahmedabad Bench held that where accounts of cost of construction were maintained even to the minutest detail and all the items of expenditure are duly supported by the vouchers, the accounts would have to be accepted. In *Singhvi Woollen Industries* v *ITO*,[17] the Income-tax Appellate Tribunal, Jaipur Bench held: "Unless the accounts books containing actual cost of construction are rejected for cogent reasons, there is no justification for the Income-tax Officer for making the addition on account of cost of construction".

In *ITO* v *Sethna Ice and Cold Storage*[18] the Income-tax Appellate Tribunal, Ahmedabad Bench held that no addition could be made on the only ground that one schedule of rates showed the rates higher than the rates shown by the assessee in respect of some items and other schedule of rates showed the rates higher than the rates, shown by the assessee in respect of other items. There can be no basis for the addition

16 (1980)9 TTJ 537 (Ahmd).
17 (1980)10 TTJ 276.
18 (1980)9 TTJ 537.

unless the lower of the rates in the two different schedules for each and every item, if applied, would justify such addition. The assessee may be able to purchase or get work executed at less than the market rate for more than one reason.

In *ITO* v *Prakash Chand Surena*[19] the Income-tax Appellate Tribunal, Jaipur Bench held that when the house was constructed under owner's supervision, a deduction of about 10% for supervision is given while estimating the cost of construction. The weak points of construction can be stressed. It should be checked whether depreciation as provided in the table in Income-tax Rules 1962 have been allowed or not in case the building is old. In *Panyam Cements and Minerals Ind Ltd.* v *Addl CIT,*[20] it was held that roads in premises of Factory are buildings entitled to depreciation.

In *S. Amir Rahim L/R of late SA Rahim* v *ITO,*[1] the Income-tax Appellate Tribunal, Madras Bench in a case where assessee claimed that period of construction is spread over 3 years but Income-tax Officer took it at 2 years without any detailed enquiry and the assessee was unable to produce any proof of the actual period of construction, held that as the Income-tax Officer has taken no steps to gather any material to controvert the assessee's claim and therefore, the assessee's claim for distribution over 3 years has to be accepted.

(D) WEALTH-TAX ACT

The Wealth-tax Act is an act to provide for the levy of wealth-tax. It is on every person who is deemed to be an assessee under this Act. It came into force on the 1st day of April 1957. A mode of valuation of assets is provided in s. 7(1) of the Act read with Schedule III thereof. Prior to 1st April 1989, such valuation used to be determined under r. 1B of the Wealth-tax Rules on the basis of s. 7(1) as it stood at that time. But under the Direct Tax Laws (Amendment) Act 1989 the provision has been changed into the present one and the relevant provision of Schedule III read as under:

19 (1979)7 TTJ 29.
20 (1979)117 ITR 770 (AP).
1 (1981)11 TTJ 505 (Mad).

3. *Valuation of immovable property*. Subject to the provisions of rules 4, 5, 6, 7 and 8, for the purposes of sub-section (1) of section 7, the value of any immovable property, being a building or land appurtenant thereto, or part thereof, shall be the amount arrived at by multiplying the net maintainable rent by the figure 12.5:

Provided that in relation to any such property which is constructed on lease hold land, this rule shall have effect as if for the figure 12.5—

(*a*) where the unexpired period of the lease of such land is fifty years or more, the figure 10.0 had been substituted; and

(*b*) where the unexpired period of the lease of such land is less than fifty years, the figure 8.0 had been substituted:

Provided further that where such property is acquired or construction of which is completed after 31st March 1974, if the value so arrived at is lower than the cost of acquisition or the cost of construction, as increased, in either case, by the cost of any improvement to the property, the cost of acquisition or, as the case may be, the cost of construction, as so increased, shall be taken to be the value of the property under this rule:

Provided also that the provisions of the second proviso shall not apply for determining the value of one house belonging to the assessee, where such house is acquired or the construction whereof is completed after the 31st March 1974, and the house is exclusively used by the assessee for his own residential purposes throughout the period of twelve months immediately preceding the valuation date and the cost of acquisition or, as the case may be, the cost of construction, as increased, in either case, by the cost of any improvement to the house, does not exceed,—

(*a*) if the house is situate at Bombay, Calcutta, Delhi or Madras, fifty lakh rupees;

(*b*) if the house is situate at any other place, twenty-five lakh rupees:

Provided also that where more than one house belonging to the assessee is exclusively used by him for residential purposes, the provisions of the third proviso shall apply only in respect of one of such houses which the assessee may, at his option, specify in this behalf.

In *Commissioner of Wealth Tax* v *Vallabh Das*,[2] it has, however, been held that in valuing a house property for the

2 (2003)262 ITR 319 (Raj).

purposes of wealth tax by the rent capitalisation method, it is proper to take ten times the net annual rent of the property for determining its market value. The cases of *Commissioner of Income Tax* v *Smt. Vimalaben Bhagwandas Patel*[3] and *Aditya Narain Roy* v *Commissioner of Wealth Tax*[4] were followed.

4. *Net maintainable rent how to be computed.* For the purposes of rule 3, "net maintainable rent" in relation to an immovable property referred to in that rule, shall be the amount of gross maintainable rent as reduced by—

(*i*) the amount of taxes levied by any local authority in respect of the property; and

(*ii*) a sum equal to fifteen per cent of the gross maintainable rent.

5. *Gross maintainable rent how to be computed.* For the purposes of rule 4, "gross maintainable rent", in relation to any immovable property referred to in rule 3, means—

(*i*) where the property is let, the amount received or receivable by the owner as annual rent or the annual value assessed by the local authority in whose area the property is situated for the purposes of levy of property tax or any other tax on the basis of such assessment, whichever is higher;

(*ii*) where the property is not let, the amount of annual rent assessed by the local authority in whose area the property is situated for the purpose of levy of property tax or any other tax on the basis of such assessment, or, if there is no such assessment or the property is situated outside the area of any local authority the amount which the owner can reasonably be expected to receive as annual rent had such property been let.

Explanation.—In this rule,—

(1) "annual rent" means,—

(*a*) where the property is let throughout the year ending on the valuation date (hereinafter referred to as "previous year"), the actual rent received or receivable by the owner in respect of such year;

3 (1979)118 ITR 134 (Guj).

4 (1990)183 ITR 175 (Cal).

(*b*) where the property is let for only a part of the previous year, the amount which bears the same proportion to the amount of actual rent received or receivable by the owner for the period for which the property is let as the period of twelve months bears to the number of months (including part of a month) during which the property is let during the previous year:

Provided that in the following cases, such actual rent under sub-clauses (*a*) and (*b*) shall be increased in the manner specified below:—

(*i*) where the property is in the occupation of a tenant and taxes levied by any local authority in respect of the property are borne wholly or partly by the tenant, by the amount of the taxes so borne by the tenant;

(*ii*) where the property is in the occupation of a tenant and expenditure on repairs in respect of the property is borne by the tenant, by one-ninth of the actual rent;

(*iii*) where the owner has accepted any amount as deposit (not being advance payment towards rent for a period of three months or less), by the amount calculated at the rate of 15 per cent per annum on the amount of deposit outstanding from month to month, for the number of months (excluding part of a month) during which such deposit was held by the owner in the previous year, and if the owner is liable to pay interest on such deposit, the increase to be made under this clause shall be limited to the sum by which the amount calculated as aforesaid exceeds the interest actually paid;

(*iv*) where the owner has received any amount by way of premium or otherwise as consideration for leasing of the property or any modification of the terms of the lease, by the amount obtained by dividing the premium or other amount by the number of year of the period of the lease;

(*v*) where the owner derives any benefit or perquisite, whether convertible into money or not, as consideration for leasing of the property or any modification of the terms of the lease, by the value of such benefit or perquisite;

(2) "rent received or receivable" shall include all payments for the use of the property, by whatever name called, the value of all benefits or perquisites whether convertible into money or not, obtained from a tenant or occupier of the property and any sum paid by a tenant or occupier of the property in respect of any

obligation which, but for such payment, would have been payable by the owner.

6. *Adjustments to value arrived at under rule 3, for unbuilt area of plot of land.* Where the unbuilt area of the plot of land on which the property referred to in rule 3 is constructed exceeds the specified area, the value arrived at in accordance with the provisions of rule 3 shall be increased by an amount calculated in the following manner, namely:—

(*a*) where the difference between the unbuilt area and the specified area exceeds five per cent but does not exceed ten per cent of the aggregate area, by an amount equal to twenty per cent of such value;

(*b*) where the difference between the unbuilt area and the specified area exceeds ten per cent but does not exceed fifteen per cent of the aggregate area, by an amount equal to thirty per cent of such value;

(*c*) where the difference between the unbuilt area and the specified area exceeds fifteen per cent but does not exceed twenty per cent of the aggregate area, by an amount equal to forty per cent of such value.

Explanation.—For the purposes of this rule and rule 6,—

(*a*) "aggregate area", in relation to the plot of land on which the property is constructed, means the aggregate of the area on which the property is constructed and the unbuilt area;

(*b*) "specified area", in relation to the plot of land on which the property is constructed, means—

(*i*) where the property is situate at Bombay, Calcutta, Delhi or Madras, sixty per cent of the aggregate area;

(*ii*) where the property is situate at Agra, Ahmedabad, Allahabad, Amritsar, Bangalore, Bhopal, Cochin, Hyderabad, Indore, Jabalpur, Jamshedpur, Kanpur, Lucknow, Ludhiana, Madurai, Nagpur, Patna, Pune, Salem, Sholapur, Srinagar, Surat, Tiruchirappalli, Trivandrum, Vadodara (Baroda) or Varanasi (Benaras), sixty-five per cent of the aggregate area; and

(*iii*) where the property is situate at any other place, seventy per cent of the aggregate area:

Provided that where, under any law for the time being in force, the minimum area of the plot of land required to be kept as open space for the enjoyment of the property exceeds the specified area, such minimum area shall be deemed to be the specified area;

(*c*) "unbuilt area", in relation to the aggregate area of the plot of land on which the property is constructed, means that part of such aggregate area on which no building has been erected.

7. *Adjustment for unearned increase in the value of the land.* Where the property is constructed on land obtained on lease from the Government, a local authority or any authority referred to in clause (20A) of section 10 of the Income-tax Act, and the Government or any such authority is, under the terms of the lease, entitled to claim and recover specified part of the unearned increase in the value of the land at the time of the transfer of the property, the value of such property as determined under rule 3 shall be reduced by the amount so liable to be claimed and recovered or by an amount equal to fifty per cent of the value of the property as so determined, whichever is less, as if the property had been transferred on the valuation date.

Explanation.—For the purpose of this rule, "unearned increase" means the difference between the value of such land on the valuation date as determined by the Government or such authority for the purpose of calculating such increase and the amount of the premium paid or payable to the Government or such authority for the lease of the land.

8. *Rule 3 not to apply in certain cases.* Nothing contained in rule 3 shall apply,—

(*a*) where, having regard to the facts and circumstances of the case, the Assessing Officer, with the previous approval of the Deputy Commissioner, is of opinion that it is not practicable to apply the provisions of the said rule to such a case; or

(*b*) where the difference between the unbuilt area and the specified area exceeds twenty per cent of the aggregate area; or

(*c*) where the property is constructed on leasehold land and the lease expires within a period not exceeding fifteen years from the relevant valuation date and the deed of lease does not give an option to the lessee for the renewal of the lease,

and in any case referred to in clause (*a*) or clause (*b*) or clause (*c*), the value of the property shall be determined in the manner laid down in rule 20.

* * *

20. *Valuation of assets in other cases.* (1) The value of any asset, other than cash, being an asset which is not covered by rules 3 to 19, for the purposes of this Act, shall be estimated to be the price which, in the opinion of the Assessing Officer, it would fetch if sold in the open market on the valuation date.

(2) Notwithstanding anything contained in sub-rule (1), where the valuation of any asset referred to in that sub-rule is referred by the Assessing Officer to the Valuation Officer under section 16A, the value of such asset shall be estimated to be the price which, in the opinion of the Valuation Officer, it would fetch if sold in the open market on the valuation date.

(3) Where the value of any asset cannot be estimated under this rule because it is not saleable in the open market, the value shall be determined in accordance with such guidelines or principles as may be specified by the Board from time to time by general or special order.

21. *Restrictive covenants to be ignored in determining market value.* For the removal of doubts, it is hereby declared that the price or other consideration for which any property may be acquired by or transferred to any person under the terms of a deed of trust or through or under any restrictive covenant in any instrument of transfer shall be ignored for the purposes of determining under any provision of this Schedule, the price such property would fetch if sold in the open market on the valuation date.

This is a method of valuation specific to the purpose of determination of Wealth-tax and for nothing else. The fiscal reasons have prompted imposition of some elements of arbitrariness in the method of such valuation but in so far as these methods do also follow the recognised approaches to valuation, they may as well qualify for standards to be followed in a general way.

Other considerations in Wealth-tax

Valuation of property in case of Wealth-tax is required to be made on valuation date which is nothing but the last date of the previous year (accounting year) of the assessee which is presently 21st March of each year in all cases. A property may be self-occupied, let out, vacant or dispossessed being forcefully occupied by others or it may be litigated. Previously there was much controversies in determination of value of house properties for the purpose of Wealth-tax. The law was that the value of the property would be estimated at the price which, in the opinion of the Wealth-tax Officer would fetch if sold in open market on the valuation date. So the process of determination was vague and ambiguous because it had scope of various variation, e.g. opinion of Wealth-tax Officer, nature of open market price, etc. In this process same property had the scope of being valued by different people at different price. However as per s. 7 the value of any property shall be its value as on the valuation date determined in the manner laid down in Schedule III.

Section 7(1) deals with general principle and s. 7(2) deals with self-occupied house property. As per s. 7(2) the value of house property belonging to the assessee and exclusively used by him for residential purpose throughout the year may, at the opinion of the assessee, be taken to be the value determined in the manner laid down in Schedule III as on the valuation date (31st March) next following the date on which he became the owner of the house or the valuation as of 1.4.1971 if he is possessing the property from 1.4.1971 or any earlier date. This benefit of taking value as of 1.4.1971 is available for one house only used by the owner for his own residential use.

House would mean an independent residential unit. Where the house has been constructed by the assessee, he shall be deemed to have become the owner thereof on the date on which the construction of such house was completed. Schedule III, Part B deals with valuation of immovable property whereas Part F deals with valuation of life interest.

Reversionary interest

A question arose as to how the reversionary interest has to be computed and valued in a leasehold property that devolves on inheritance and becomes a subject matter for levy of wealth-tax. In *H. Md. Zaid* v *Commissioner of Wealth Tax*,[5] it has been held that, since the assessee and the other joint lessees were owners only of the superstructure and they had no reversionary interest in the land, there was no question of adding the value of any reversionary interest to the leasehold

5 (2002)258 ITR 560 (Mad).

property that devolved on the demise of the lessees. The valuation concerning the interest of the lessor in the land, as the reversionary interest is, becomes wholly irrelevant in assessing the value of the lessee's interest for wealth-tax purposes.

Purchasing power parity

In *Commissioner of Wealth Tax* v *R. Ramanathan Chettiar*,[6] the question so arose that, and as it often arises, in valuation for wealth tax purposes of assets that includes property situated outside the country as to whether the valuation process has to proceed according to the official rate exchange between the currencies of the concerned countries or the purchasing power parity arises for consideration. It has been held that there is nothing in s. 7(1) of the Wealth Tax Act 1957, dealing with the valuation of assets which indicates that only the remittable value of the asset in a foreign country has to be included in the net wealth although such value of money in legal currency would normally be that value which is equivalent at the official rate of exchange. However, it would be open to an assessee to prove that the official exchange rate does not reflect the realistic exchange value or it was not fixed with reference to the convertibility of the currency. In case the assessee fails to place acceptable evidence about the real exchange rate being different from the official rate of exchange, the rate to be adopted would be the official rate only. Accordingly, in the instant case the High Court upheld the Tribunal's decision to remit the matter to the Wealth Tax Officer for a decision afresh after determining the real exchange rate and the assessee was to adduce evidence on that aspect. The decision in *Abdul Rahman (S)* v *Commissioner of Wealth Tax*[7] was applied.

Date of valuation

Held in the case of *Commissioner of Wealth Tax* v *A.S. Ananth*,[8] that what is taxed under the Wealth Tax Act 1957, is the net wealth as on the valuation date. The transferability or otherwise of that wealth during that year is not of material significance. If an asset is required to be valued in the manner

6 (2001)248 ITR 315 (Mad).
7 (1979)117 ITR 570 (Mad).
8 (2003)261 ITR 763 (Mad).

provided in the statute, it has necessarily to be valued by adopting that mode and no other. If the statute does not provide for any deduction therefrom, no such deduction can be allowed.

Valuation as per Schedule III, Part B

According to Part B of Schedule III, there are five steps by which immovable property is to be valued.

Step No. 1 Process of finding out gross maintainable rent.

Step No. 2 Process of finding out net maintainable rent.

Step No. 3 Process of capitalisation of net maintainable rent.

Step No. 4 Process of addition of premium to the capitalised value determined under Step No. 3 if unbuilt area of the plot of land on which property is built exceeds the specified area.

Step No. 5 Process of deduction of unearned increment payment.

However the aforesaid rules of valuation are not applicable under the following three circumstances:

(*i*) If the Assessing Officer with the previous approval of Deputy Commissioner is of opinion that it is not practicable to apply the above-mentioned provisions to a particular case.

(*ii*) Where unbuilt area exceeds the specified area by more than 70% of the aggregate area.

(*iii*) Where the property is built on leasehold land and the lease expires within a period of 15 years from the relevant valuation date and there is no clause in the lease deed for further renewal of lease.

The steps stated above may be discussed here as follows:

Process of determining gross maintainable rent

(*a*) If the property is let out, then annual rent received/ receivable by the owner or annual value of the property as assessed by local authority, whichever is higher.

(*b*) If the property is not let out, annual rent assessed by the local authority. If the property is situated outside the jurisdiction of local authority then reasonable annual rent had the property been let.

(*c*) If the property is let and vacant for a part of the year, then the annual value is to be increased proportionately on the basis of rent as if the rent had been received for the full year.

(*d*) Annual value is to be increased in the following cases:

(*i*) If municipal tax or part of it is paid by the tenant then the same will be added to the rent.

(*ii*) If repair is borne by the tenant then 1/9th of the rent will be added up with the rent.

(*iii*) If advance has been taken from the tenant of more than 3 months' rent, then 15 per cent interest per annum calculated on monthly basis on advance outstanding will be added up with the rent. However this interest will be reduced by the amount of interest if any payable to the tenant.

(*iv*) Proportionate lease premium will be added with the rent.

(*v*) Money value of any other benefit given by the tenant will be added up with the rent.

Process of determining net maintainable rent

In order to find out net maintainable rent, *gross maintainable rent will be reduced by Municipal Tax* or tax levied by local authority for the property *and an amount of 15 per cent of gross maintainable rent.*

It has been decided in the case of *Commissioner of Wealth Tax* v *Pradip D. Kothari,*[9] that part of the rental value being attributable to the availability of the lift and electrical installations, the same had to be excluded while determining the assessable value of the building by the rental method, as the lifts and the electrical installations were not owned by the assessee.

Process of addition of premium

In case of Bombay, Calcutta, Delhi and Madras, if the building has been built up upon an area being less than 60 per cent of

9 (2002)253 ITR 154 (155) (Mad).

the total area of land leaving the scope of further construction upon the vacant land then the capitalised value will be increased by a premium as follows:

The excess of 'unbuilt area' over 'specified area'	Premium
Less than 5% of the 'aggregate area'	Nil
More than 5% but not more than 10% of the 'aggregate area'	20% of capitalised value
More than 10% but not more than 15% of the 'aggregate area'	30% of capitalised value
More than 15% but not more than 20% of the 'aggregate area'	40% of capitalised value
More than 20% of the 'aggregate area'	Rules given Part B of Schedule III are not applicable (*see* par 513.11 for Valuation)

The specified area of 60 per cent as stated above will be 65 per cent in case of Agra, Ahmedabad, Allahabad, Amritsar, Bangalore, Bhopal, Cochin, Hyderabad, Indore, Jabalpur, Jamshedpur, Kanpur, Lucknow, Ludhiana, Madurai, Nagpur, Patna, Pune, Salam, Solapur, Srinagar, Surat, Tiruchirapalli, Trivandrum, Valodara and Varanasi and it is 70% in case of other places.

Process of capitalisation of net maintainable rent

For capitalisation of net maintainable rent, it should be multiplied by 12.5. When property has been constructed on leasehold land then the multiplying factor will be 10 where unexpired period of lease is 50 years or more and 8 where unexpired period of lease is less than 50 years. If the property is acquired or constructed after 31.3.1974 and the real cost of acquisition and/or construction plus cost of improvement is more than the capitalised value as stated above then the capital value will be substituted by higher cost of construction etc.

However this rule of substitution will not apply in case of one self-occupied house property of the owner constructed after 31.3.1974 provided he has used it as such for the relevant full year and the actual cost of the building is less than 50 lakhs in case of Bombay, Calcutta, Delhi and Madras and 25 lakhs for any other place.

Process of deduction of unearned increment

Fifth step is to deduct the amount of earned increment payable. If in the case of property built on leasehold land any part of unearned increase in value is payable to the Government or any authority at the time of transfer of the property, the value of such property, as determined above will be reduced by the amount liable to be so paid if the property has been transferred on the valuation date of 50 per cent of the value of the property as so determined, whichever is less.

Valuation of life interest

1. For the purposes of sub-sec. (1) of s. 7, the value of the life interest of an assessee shall be arrived at by multiplying the average annual income that accrued to the assessee from the life interest by the fraction $\frac{1}{p+d}-1$, where 'p' represents the annual premium for a whole life insurance without profits on the life of the life tenant for unit sum assured as specified in the Appendix to these rules, and 'd' is equal to $\frac{1}{1+i}$, i being the rate of interest.

Explanation.—In this rule,—

(*a*) 'life tenant' means a person for the duration of whose life the life interest is to subsist;

(*b*) 'average annual income' means the average of the gross income derived by the assessee from the life interest during each year of the period ending on the valuation date, reduced by the average of the expenses incurred on the collection of such income in each of those years:

Provided that the amount of the reduction for such expenses shall, in no case, exceed five per cent of the average of the annual gross income:

Provided further that in case the income so derived is for a period exceeding three years, only that income derived during the three years ending on the valuation date shall be taken into account;

(*c*) the rate of interest shall be $^1/_2$ per cent per annum.

2. Notwithstanding anything contained in sub-rule (1),—

(*a*) the Assessing Officer may, if he is of the opinion that in the case of the life tenant, a life insurance company would not take the risk of insuring his life at the normal premium rates in force but would demand a higher premium, vary the valuation suitably;

(*b*) the value of the life interest so determined shall, in no case, exceed the value as on the valuation date as determined under this Schedule, of the corpus of the trust from which the life interest is derived.

Assets of business

If any land or building is the assets of business of any assessee and he maintains regular books of accounts and prepare Balance Sheet as on valuation date then depreciable building will be taken at the written down value (i.e. net after depreciation) and non-depreciable assets like land will be taken at book value. If the value of any asset determined according to the provisions of Schedule III exceed the value above by more than 20 per cent, then higher value shall be taken as value of that asset. The value of an asset not shown in Balance Sheet shall be determined as per Schedule III.

Valuation of goodwill of business

The goodwill of a business is an asset, which is intangible in character. Such goodwill may be self-generated by the business itself or might have been purchased for a price. The question arose in *B. Virdhagiri* v *Commissioner of Wealth Tax*,[10] how far goodwill stands covered for the purpose of valuation of assets of a business under r. 2C(*d*) of the Wealth Tax Rules 1957. Following the decision in the case of *Harshad Kumar Natvarlal Dalal* v *Commissioner of Wealth Tax*[11] the Madras High Court held in the above case that self-generated goodwill cannot be taken into account in such valuation as it is not

10 (2003)260 ITR 292 (Mad).

11 (1996)219 ITR 592 (Guj).

covered by r. 2C(*d*) of the Wealth Tax Rules 1957. In other words, goodwill, which is not purchased for a price, is not covered by the above Rule.

Valuation of business assets—unquoted shares

In *Commissioner of Wealth Tax* v *Arun K. Parikh*[12] the matter of valuation of assets (unquoted equity shares of private limited company) as per r. 1D of the Wealth Tax Rules 1957 arose for decision. Held, the r. 1D has to be followed in every case where unquoted equity shares of a company (other than an investment company or a managing agency company) have to be valued. In the same vein, in *Commissioner of Wealth Tax* v *Shilaben Family Trust*[13] held that in making valuation of unquoted equity shares, r. 1D is mandatory. Valuation must be done as per the provisions of r. 1D. The same decision was consistently upheld in the case of *Commissioner of Wealth Tax* v *Sita Ram Jindal*[14] and followed in *Commissioner of Wealth Tax* v *L.G. Balakrishnan*[15] and *Commissioner of Wealth Tax/ Commissioner of Income Tax* v *T.R. Khanna.*[16] The consensus view is that there being no other method prescribed in the Wealth Tax Rules 1957, r. 1D is mandatory to be followed. The decision in *Bharat Hari Singhania* v *Commissioner of Wealth Tax*[17] also reflected the same view.

Examples on Wealth-tax

EXAMPLE 80. **A residential building of ground and one upper floor at Calcutta is partly rented and partly owner occupied. Ground floor plinth area is 180 sq.mts. and two tenants pay total rent of ₹ 800 per month. First floor 180 sq.mts. is owner occupied and Net Rateable Value of 1st floor is ₹ 4,500. Total plot area is 850 sq.mts. and land is of freehold tenure. Property taxes by local authority is ₹ 2,700 half-yearly. Value the property for wealth-tax purpose.**

12 (2001)248 ITR 379 (Guj).
13 (2001)248 ITR 183 (SC).
14 (2001)248 ITR 111 (SC).
15 (2001)249 ITR 578 (Mad).
16 (2001)252 ITR 382 (Mad).
17 (1994)207 ITR 1 (SC).

SOLUTION:

Aggregate plot area		=	850 sq.mts.
Specified area for Calcutta is 60% of aggregate		=	510 sq.mts.
Built-up area (Ground floor)		=	180 sq.mts.
Unbuilt area	= 850 – 180	=	670 sq.mts.
Difference of unbuilt and specified area	= 670 – 510	=	160 sq.mts.
Percentage of aggregate	$= \frac{160 \times 100}{850}$	=	18.82%

As percentage difference is less than 20%, rule 3 of Schedule III is applicable.

(*i*) As per rule 5(*i*) maintainable rent of rented portion = ₹ 800 p.m.

(*ii*) As per rule 5(*ii*), maintainable rent of owner occupied portion will be rent assumed by local authority. In present case N.R.V. of 1st floor is ₹ 4,500.

This N.R.V. corresponds to annual Gross Rent

$= ₹\ 4{,}500 + \frac{1}{9} \times 4{,}500$ = ₹ 5,000

Gross Annual Maintainable Rent (G.M.R.) of the residential building having ground and first floors

= ₹ 800 × 12 + ₹ 5,000 = ₹ 14,600

Less: Outgoings (Rule 4)

Property tax ₹ 2,700 × 2 = ₹ 5,400

15% of G.M.R. of ₹ 14,600 = ₹ 2,190

= ₹ 7,590

Net Maintainable Rent = ₹ 14,600 – ₹ 7,590 = ₹ 7,010

As land is of freehold tenure, multiplier of 12.50 is adopted as per rule 3.

Value of property as per rule 3

= ₹ 7,010 × 12.50 = ₹ 87,625

As per cent difference is 18.82%, adjustment in value as per rule 6(c) is necessary (more than 15% and less than 20%) for unbuilt plot area.

Increase in value $= \frac{40}{100} \times 87{,}625$ = ₹ 35,050

Total value of property for Wealth-tax purpose as on 31.3.1997

= ₹ 87,625 + ₹ 35,050	= ₹	1,22,675
	Say ... ₹	1,23,000

EXAMPLE 81. An ownership flat was purchased in Mumbai in year 1976 for ₹ 4,50,000. Flat was rented for ₹ 3,500 per month. A sum of ₹ 1,00,000 was taken as interest free security deposit. Society maintenance bill is ₹ 2,500 per quarter of which ₹ 1,500 per quarter towards property taxes of local authority. Society land is of leasehold tenure with unexpired period of lease more than 50 years. Value the property for Wealth-tax purposes.

SOLUTION

As this is flat without land, percentage difference is less than zero (0) and less than 20%, rule 3, Schedule III is therefore applicable.

(A) Value of property as per 1st proviso of rule 3, Schedule III.

Gross Annual Maintainable Rent (vide rule 5) (GMR)			
= ₹ 3,500 × 12 + 15% of ₹ 1,00,000		= ₹	57,000
Less: Outgoings (rule 4)			
Property taxes ₹ 1,500 × 4	= ₹ 6,000		
15% of GMR of 57,000	= ₹ 8,550	= ₹	14,550
Net Maintainable Rent (NMR)		= ₹	42,450

As land is of leasehold tenure, multiplier of 10 is adopted as per Rule 3.

Value of property as per 1st proviso of rule 3

= ₹ 42,450 × 10	= ₹	4,24,500

(B) Value of property as per 2nd proviso of Rule 3.

As the property is purchased after 31-3-1974, 2nd proviso of r. 3 is required to be considered. Cost of acquisition in present case is ₹ 4,50,000. Value as per 1st proviso of r. 3 is ₹ 4,24,500. Hence as per 2nd proviso, higher of the two value is required to be taken as value for Wealth-tax purpose.

Value of the property for W.T. purpose is ₹ 4,50,000.

EXAMPLE 82. Assessee purchased freehold land in Ahmedabad in 1989 for ₹ 4,00,000 (area 2000 sq.mts.). A bungalow is built in 1990 at cost of ₹ 16,00,000 (area 800 sq.mts.). Ground floor plinth is 400 sq.mts. Bungalow is wholly owner occupied. N.R.V. of bungalow is ₹ 54,000. Property taxes are ₹ 16,200 per annum. Improvement in building is done in 1994 at ₹ 2,00,000. Value the property for wealth-tax purposes.

SOLUTION

Aggregate area of plot		=	2000 sq.mts.
Specified are 65% of 2000 sq.mts.		=	1300 sq.mts.
Built-up area		=	400 sq.mts.
Unbuilt	= 2000 − 400 sq.mts.	=	1600 sq.mts.
Difference of unbuilt and specified	= 1600 − 1300 sq.mts.	=	300 sq.mts.
Percentage difference	$= \frac{300 \times 100}{2000} = 15\%$		

As it is less than 20%, Rule 3, Schedule III is applicable.

Gross Annual Maintainable Rent (G.M.R.)			
$= ₹\ 54,000 + \frac{1}{9} \times ₹\ 54,000$		= ₹	60,000
Less: Outgoings:			
Taxes per annum	= ₹ 16,200		
15% of GMR	= ₹ 9,000	= ₹	25,200
Net Maintainable Rent (N.M.R.) (₹ 60,000 – 25,200)		= ₹	34,800
Value of bungalow as per 1st proviso			
= ₹ 34,800 × 12.5		= ₹	4,35,000

As the percentage difference is 15%, value has to be increased by 30% as provided in Rule 6(*b*).

Increase in value			
$= \frac{30}{100} \times 4,35,000$		= ₹	1,30,500
Value as per 1st proviso			
= ₹ 4,35,000 + ₹ 1,30,500		= ₹	5,65,500
		Say ... ₹	5,66,000
Value as per 2nd proviso:			
Cost of land		= ₹	4,00,000
Cost of building		= ₹	16,00,000
Cost of improvement		= ₹	2,00,000
Total		= ₹	22,00,000

As per 2nd proviso, higher of two is required to be adopted. Hence value of property as per 2nd proviso of r. 3 ought to be ₹ 22,00,000.

Value as per 3rd proviso:

However as per 3rd proviso of Rule 3 if property is in Ahmedabad and cost of acquisition is less than 25 lacs and house is owner occupied in previous year, value as per 1st proviso could be adopted ignoring value under 2nd proviso. In present case, total cost of acquisition is 22 lacs which is less than 25 lacs and hence 3rd proviso is applicable.

Value for Wealth-tax purpose should be therefore adopted at ₹ 5,66,000 only.

In this example if total cost of acquisition was ₹ 26 lacs instead of 22 lacs, value for Wealth-tax purpose would have been ₹ 26 lacs as per 2nd proviso and not ₹ 5.66 lacs as per 3rd proviso.

EXAMPLE 83. Two brothers jointly owned a bungalow at Gwalior. Area of plot 5000 sq.mts. Built-up area of bungalow is 400 sq.mts. at ground floor and 200 sq.mts. at 1st floor. Bungalow is built in 1970. N.R.V. of house is ₹ 30,000. Property taxes are ₹ 35,000 half yearly. per month. Value the property for Wealth-tax purpose for one of the brother for date 31.3.2000 if value of land in 2000 was ₹ 330 per sq.mtr. and cost of construction was ₹ 3,800 per sq.mts.

SOLUTION

Aggregate area of plot		= 5000 sq.mts.
Specified area 70%		= 3500 sq.mts.
Built-up area		= 400 sq.mts.
Unbuilt area	= 5000 – 400 sqmts.	= 4600 sq.mts.

Difference of unbuilt and specified area

= 4600 – 3500 sq.mts. = 1100 sq.mts.

Percentage difference $= \frac{1100 \times 100}{5000} = 22\%$

As percentage difference is more than 20% of aggregate area, rule 3 for statutory value is not applicable in this case. Value for W.T. purpose has to be worked out as per rule 20(1) of Schedule III on fair market value concept.

(A) Total land value in 2000 = 5000 sq.mts. @ ₹ 330 per sq.mt.

= ₹ 16,50,000

(B) Building value in 2000:

Replacement cost = (400 + 200)

as price cost = 600 at ₹ 3,800 per sq.mt. = ₹ 22,80,000

Depreciation for 30 years (D) :
(Straight-line Method)

$$D = \frac{\text{Age}\,(100 - S)}{\text{Life}}\% \text{ on Prime cost;}$$

S = Salvage = 10%; Life = 70 years = ₹ 8,79,396

$$D = \frac{30 \times 90}{70}\% = 38.5\%$$

Net present value of building in year 2000

= ₹ 22,80,000 – ₹ 8,79,396 = ₹ 14,00,604

(C) Total value of property:

= ₹ 16,50,000 + ₹ 14,00,604 = ₹ 30,50,604

Say ... ₹ 30,51,000

(D) The property is jointly owned by two brothers and hence value of co-owners undivided share will be ½ of the total value. In *J.N. Bose* v *CWT Calcutta High Court* allowed 10% discount in value for undivided nature of share.

Total value	= ₹	30,51,000
Less: 10% discount	= ₹	3,05,100
Net value	= ₹	27,45,900

Value of co-owner's share in property

$\frac{1}{2} \times 27{,}45{,}900$ = ₹ 13,72,950

Say ... ₹ 13,73,000

Hence value of one of the brother's share in property for Wealth-tax purpose = ₹ 13,73,000.

EXAMPLE 84. An Industrial Complex is situated at 6 k.m. distance from Surat. Total plot are is 20,000 sq.mts. Total built-up area of industrial and non-industrial structures is 3000 sq.mts. Garden area in plot is 2000 sq.mts. and internal road area is 2500 sq.mts. F.S.I. of area is 0.50. There is a Guest House admeasuring 100 sq.mts. in plot. Three residential buildings of ground floor with 300 sq.mts. area/building has total 12 flats of which 6 flats are occupied by executives drawing salary of more than 2 lacs. Value the property for Wealth-tax purpose as on 31.03.2000 if rate of industrial land in locality is ₹ 400 per sq.mt. and cost of construction for non-industrial structure is ₹ 4,000 per sq. mt. All structures are built in year 1986.

SOLUTION

As per provisions of s. 2(*ea*) and Explanation (*b*)(*ii*) of said section, following land does not constitute 'urban land' chargeable to Wealth-tax.

(*i*)	Land under industrial and non-industrial buildings	=	3,000 sq.mts.
(*ii*)	Surrounding appurtenant land for existing buildings for F.S.I. of 0.50	=	3,000 sq.mts.
(*iii*)	Garden land	=	2,000 sq.mts.
(*iv*)	Internal Road area	=	2,500 sq.mts.
	Total area	=	10,500 sq.mts.

(A) Urban land = Total plot less non-urban land

= 20,000 – 10,500 sq.mts. = 9,500 sq.mts.

Value of urban land = 9,500 sq.mts. @ ₹ 400 per sq.mt.

= ₹ 38,00,000 .... (1)

(B) Buildings

As per provisions of section 2(*ea*)(*i*) of W.T. Act, 'Assets' chargeable to Wealth-tax does not include industrial and godown structures but it includes Guest Houses and residential premises occupied by executives drawing salary of more than ₹ 2 lacs per year.

In present case, all industrial structures are therefore excluded from valuation and only Guest Houses and 6 flats are valued.

Value of Guest House

Replacement cost = 100 sq.mt @ ₹ 4,000 per sq.mt.

Prime cost = ₹ 4,00,000

Less: Depreciation for 14 years age on straight line method:

$$= \frac{\text{Age}\,(100-10)}{70}\%\text{ on Prime cost}$$

$$= \frac{14 \times 90}{70}\% = 18\% \qquad = ₹\ 72{,}000$$

Net value of Guest House in 2000

= ₹ 4,00,000 – ₹ 72,000 = ₹ 3,28,000

Land appurtenant to Guest House = 100 × 2

= 200 sq.mts.

Value of land pertaining to Guest House

= 200 sq.mts. at ₹ 400 per sq.mt. = ₹ 80,000

Total value of Guest House

= ₹ 3,28,000 + ₹ 80,000

= ₹ 4,08,240 ... (2)

Value of residential flats

Area of 3 buildings = 3 × 300 = 900 sq.mts. (12 flats)

Only 6 flats are taxable as per section 2(*ea*)(*i*)(1)

Built-up area of 6 flats = $\frac{1}{2}$ × 900 = 450 sq.mts.

Replacement cost = 450 sq.mts. @ ₹ 4,000 per sq.mt.

= ₹ 18,00,000

Less: Depreciation for 14 years

= $\frac{\text{Age}\,(100-10)}{70}$% on ₹ 18,00,000 = 18% = ₹ 3,24,000

Net value of 6 flats in 2000

= ₹ 18,00,000 – ₹ 3,24,000 = ₹ 14,76,000

Land appurtenant to 6 flats for 0.50 F.S.I.

= 450 × 2 = 900 sq.mts.

Value of land (6 flats) = 900 sq.mts. @ ₹ 400 per sq.mt.

= ₹ 3,60,000

Total value of 6 flats

= ₹ 14,76,000 + ₹ 3,60,000

= ₹ 18,36,000 ...... (3)

Total value of Assets chargeable to Wealth-tax as on 31.3.2000 works out as under:

(*i*)	Urban land as per (1)	= ₹	38,00,000
(*ii*)	Guest House as per (2)	= ₹	4,08,000
(*iii*)	Residential flats 6 Nos. as per (3)	= ₹	18,36,000
	Total	= ₹	60,44,000
		Say ... ₹	60,44,000

EXAMPLE 85. An assessee owns three shops in three different localities of Calcutta. Area of shop 1 is 80 sq.mts. purchased in 1998. Area of shop 2 is 30 sq.mts. and area of third shop is 120

sq.mts. He conducts the business in largest shop No. 3. Small shop 2 is given on rent of ₹ 1,500 p.m. Municipal taxes for the said shop are ₹ 150 p.m. He has taken interest free deposit of 3 lacs from the tenant. Shop No. 1 is lying vacant and not in use. Ruling rate of commercial premises in the locality in 1998 were ₹ 50,000 per sq.mt. (shop 1 area), ₹ 20,000 per sq.mt. (shop 2 area) and ₹ 80,000 per sq.mt. (shop 3 area). Value the property for Wealth-tax purpose as on 31.3.1998.

SOLUTION

As per section 2(*ea*)(*i*) of Wealth-tax Act, (vide Finance Act 1996 effective from 1.4.1997) commercial premises within limits of local authority and upto 25 kilometers from its limits are assets chargeable to Wealth-tax. As per provisions of section 2(*ea*)(*i*)(3) commercial premises occupied for purposes of profession or business are excluded from list of assets chargeable to tax.

In present case shop 3 is used for business and hence said asset is not chargeable to Wealth-tax. Shop 1 is vacant and shop 2 is rented and hence both are chargeable to Wealth-tax.

(*i*) Shop 1 is vacant and is recently purchased. As per 2nd proviso of rule 3 it is valued at purchase price.

Value of Shop 1:

80 sq.mts. @ ₹ 50,000 per sq.mt.	= ₹	40,00,000

(*ii*) Shop 2 is rented and hence valued as per 1st proviso of rule 3.

Rental income ₹ 1,500 × 12	=	₹ 18,000		
Increase in G.M.R. 15% of 3,00,000	=	₹ 45,000		
	=	₹ 63,000		
Gross Annual Maintainable Rent (GMR)			= ₹	63,000
Less: Outgoings.				
Property tax ₹ 150 × 12	=	₹ 1,800		
15% of ₹ 63,000	=	₹ 9,450	= ₹	11,250
Net Maintainable Rent (NMR)			= ₹	51,750

It is assumed that land is of freehold tenure.

Value of Shop 2:

₹ 51,750 × 12.5	= ₹	6,46,875
	Say... ₹	6,47,000

Total value of property for Wealth-tax purposes as on 31.3.1998

Shop No. 1 = ₹ 40,00,000

Shop No. 2 = ₹ 6,47,000

Shop No. 3 = Nil

Total value = ₹ 46,47,000

If shop 1 was purchased prior to 31.3.1974, value could be worked out as per Rateable value (Rent assumed by local authority).

Cost Inflation Index fixed for Capital Gains Tax

Accounting Year	C.I. Index
1981-1982	100
1982-1983	109
1983-1984	116
1984-1985	125
1985-1986	133
1986-1987	140
1987-1988	150
1988-1989	161
1989-1990	172
1990-1991	182
1991-1992	199
1992-1993	223
1993-1994	244
1994-1995	259
1995-1996	281
1996-1997	305
1997-1998	330
1998-1999	351
1999-2000	389
2001-2002	426
2002-2003	447
2003-2004	463
2004-2005	480
2005-2006	497
2006-2007	519
2007-2008	551

Accounting Year	C.I. Index
2008-2009	582
2009-2010	632
2010-2011	711
2011-2012	785
2012-2013	852
2013-2014	–
2014-2015	–

Examples on Capital Gains Tax

EXAMPLE 86. An assessee received a gift of a flat 700 sq.ft. in area from his uncle in May 1988. Uncle had purchased flat in June 1982 for ₹ 70,000. Assessee improved the flat in Sept./Oct. 1989 at the cost of ₹ 50,000. Flat was sold in Feb. 1997 for ₹ 12,60,000. Society transfer charges were ₹ 20,000 and brokerage charges were ₹ 10,000. Compute Capital Gain at 20% if Index for June 1982 is 109, Feb. 1997 = 305 and Sept. 1989 = 172.

SOLUTION

As per provision of section 49 of Income-tax Act, in case of Gift, cost of acquisition shall be cost to previous owner *i.e.* Donor.

(a) Cost of Acquisition June 1982 = ₹ 70,000

Indexed cost in 1997 $= ₹\,70{,}000 \times \dfrac{305}{109}$ = ₹ 1,95,872

(b) Cost of improvement in 1989 = ₹ 50,000

Indexed cost of improvement

$= ₹\,50{,}000 \times \dfrac{305}{172}$ = ₹ 88,662

Total sale price = ₹ 12,60,000

Less: Society transfer and brokerage vide 48(1)(*a*)(*i*) = 20,000 + 10,000 = ₹ 30,000

= ₹ 12,30,000

Less: Index cost of acquisition and indexed cost of improvement vide 48(1)(*a*)(*ii*) = 1,95,872 + 88,662 = ₹ 2,84,534

Net Capital Gains = ₹ 9,45,466

Capital Gains Tax at 20% = ₹ 1,89,093

EXAMPLE 87. An assessee purchased in 1966 land of 500 sq.mts. area with 200 sq.mts. building constructed on plot. Purchase was in 1966 and for price of ₹ 1,00,000. Said property was sold in February 1996 for a price of ₹ 15 lacs. Compute Capital Gains at 20% rate if land rate in 1981 was ₹ 200 per sq.mts. and building cost when new in 1981 was ₹ 1,000 per sq.mts. C.I. 1996 = 281.

SOLUTION

As cost of acquisition is before 1981, value as of 1.4.1981 is to be computed.

(a) Land value 1981:

500 sq.mts. @ ₹ 200 per sq.mts. = ₹ 1,00,000

(b) Building value 1981: Replacement cost as Prime cost 200 sq.mts. @ ₹ 1,000 per sq.mts. = ₹ 2,00,000

Less: Depreciation for 15 years with 60 years life (On Straight Line Method of Depreciation, acquiring salvage as 10%)

$$D = \frac{\text{Age}\,(100-10)}{60}\%\text{ on Prime cost}$$

$$= \frac{15 \times 90}{60}\% = 22.5\%$$ = ₹ 45,000

Net building cost

= ₹ 2,00,000 – ₹ 45,000 = ₹ 1,55,000

(c) Indexed cost of 1981

$$= (1{,}00{,}000 + 1{,}55{,}000) \times \frac{281}{100}$$ = ₹ 7,16,550

Net capital gains

= ₹ 15,00,000 – ₹ 7,16,550 = ₹ 7,83,450

Capital Gains Tax at 20%

= ₹ 7,83,450 × 0.20 = ₹ 1,56,690

EXAMPLE 88. An assessee sold property for 55 lacs in February 1996. Land was purchased in 1985 for 3 lacs. Ground floor building was constructed in 1988 for 5 lacs. First floor was constructed in 1991 for 7 lacs. After sale, the owner purchased a bungalow at Ahmedabad for ₹ 20 lacs. He also purchased Capital Bonds of ₹ 5 lacs. Brokerage charges paid was ₹ 82,000. Legal charges were

₹ 10,000. Compute Capital Gains Tax at 20%, if C.I. Index of 1985, 1988, 1991 and 1996 were 133, 161, 182 and 281 respectively.

SOLUTION

(a) Indexed cost of land

$$3,00,000 \times \frac{281}{133} = ₹ \quad 6,33,834$$

(b) Indexed cost of ground

floor $$5,00,000 \times \frac{281}{161} = ₹ \quad 8,72,670$$

(c) Indexed cost of 1st

floor $$7,00,000 \times \frac{281}{182} = ₹ \quad 10,80,769$$

Total indexed cost of Acquisition	= ₹	25,87,273
Sale price	= ₹	55,00,000
Less: Cost of legal charges and brokerage	= ₹	92,000
	= ₹	54,08,000
Less: Indexed cost of Acquisition	= ₹	25,87,273
Net Capital Gain	= ₹	28,20,727
Less: Bungalow cost at Ahmedabad	= ₹	20,00,000
Balance Capital Gain ...	= ₹	8,20,727
Less: Investment in Capital Bond	= ₹	5,00,000
Net Taxable Gain	= ₹	3,20,727
Capital Gains Tax at 20% = ₹ 3,20,727 × 0.20	= ₹	64,145

EXAMPLE 89. The assessee company purchased factory plot (area 1000 sq.mts.) in 1970 at cost of ₹ 50,000. 800 sq.mts. factory building was constructed on plot in 1974. Factory was sold in October 1994 for ₹ 40 lacs. Depreciation on building was claimed by company from 1974 to 1994. W.D.V. is ₹ 1,28,000. Land value in 1981 was ₹ 60 per sq.mt. Compute capital gain tax for company at 40%.

SOLUTION

As per provision of section 50 of I.T. Act, this factory building is depreciable asset and hence in capital gains only W.D. value is admissible as deduction [section 50(1)(*ii*)].

Land value 1981	= 1000 sq.mts. × 60	= ₹	60,000
Indexed land value	= ₹ 60,000 × $\frac{259}{100}$	= ₹	1,55,400
Total sale value		= ₹	40,00,000
Less: Indexed land value		= ₹	1,55,400
		= ₹	38,44,600
Less: W.D.V. of factory		= ₹	1,28,000
Net gain		= ₹	37,16,600
Capital Gains Tax at 40% of ₹ 37,16,600		= ₹	14,86,640

(E) CENTRAL EXCISE DUTY

Union excise duties are leviable under the provisions of the Central Excises and Salt Act 1944. This duty is functionally called the Basic Excise Duty. The excise tariff in this regard is enumerated in the Schedule to the Central Excise Tariff Act 1985. The Finance Acts passed by the Parliament of India may provide for the levy of what is called a Special Excise Duty as a percentage of the Basic Excise Duty. The power to levy excise duties is derived by the Government of India in pursuance Entry 84 of List I (Union List) of the Seventh Schedule of the Constitution of India, which provides for such levy on tobacco and other goods manufactured or produced in India including medicinal and toilet preparations containing alcohol or similar substances. This is an indirect tax on commodity manufacturer the revenue realisation of which is triggered by industrial growth within the country. The manufacture includes processing of goods whether as intermediate products, or marginally incomplete goods, or mere assembly of various components.

Valuation of excisable goods is a vital step for quantification of the duty payable in all cases, where an *ad valorem* duty is levied. In recent years, there is a marked tendency towards *ad valorem* levy as against specific duties. Hence the aspect of valuation has assumed importance. In arriving at the assessable value of the commodity, certain deductions are allowed viz., trade discount, amount of levy towards excise, sales tax and other taxes; all costs of packing except primary packing; value of accessories; after sale service charges, delivery charges etc. Corporate veil should not be a facade for tax evasion and hence inter-company dealings are left to scrutiny.

Valuation of excisable goods

The entire scheme of valuation of the excisable good where duties are leviable at *ad valorem* rates is contained in s. 4 of the Central Excises and Salt Act read with the Central Excise Valuation Rules 1975. The assessable value under s. 4 of the Act and the selling price would seldom be the same. This is because excise duty is a levy on manufacture and there might be some more components of costs related to the stage after the goods have been manufactured and cleared which are added to arrive at the actual selling price. In order to comprehensively provide what items of costs or expenses are includible and what are not includible in the assessable value, s. 4 provides for a set of wholesome principles. The manufacturer of excisable goods has the freedom to fix selling price of the manufactured goods. But, the Revenue also has powers to arrive at the assessable value from the selling price of the goods in order to ensure that there is no evasion of duty which is properly payable by an assessee.

The scheme of valuation of excisable goods where the goods are leviable with *ad valorem* rates of duties as per s. 4 of the Act read with the Central Excise Valuation Rules 1975, can be analysed under the following broad heads:—

(*i*) Where the manufacturer sells the goods at the normal price—section 4(1)(*a*).

(*ii*) Where the manufacturer adopts different normal prices for different classes of buyers—*proviso* (*i*) to section 4(1)(*a*).

(*iii*) Where the normal price of the excisable goods is statutorily fixed—*proviso* (*ii*) to section 4(1)(*a*).

(*iv*) Where the excisable goods are sold generally to or through a related person—*proviso* (*iii*) to section 4(1)(*a*).

(*v*) Where price of the excisable goods is not ascertainable for the reason that they are not sold or for any other reason—section 4(1)(*b*).

(*vi*) Where the price of excisable goods is not known at the time of removal but is known at any time nearest to the time of removal of such goods—Rule 4.

(*vii*) Where according to the Revenue the price charged is not the sole consideration for sale—Rule 5.

(*viii*) Where the manufacturer sells the goods directly in retail and not in wholesale—Rule 6(*a*).

(*ix*) Where the manufacturer sells the goods to related persons who in turn sell them in retail—Rule 6(*c*)(*i*).

(*x*) Where the manufacturer does not sell the goods but uses the goods for captive consumption in his factory—Rule 6(*b*).

(*xi*) Where the manufacturer sells the goods to related persons who use the goods for captive consumption—Rule 6(*c*)(*ii*).

(*xii*) Where the manufacturer sells the goods to a related person who in turn sells the goods to various classes of wholesale buyers—Rule 6(*c*)(*iii*).

(*xiii*) Where, if the value cannot be determined under the foregoing set of rules, the Revenue is empowered to make the best judgment/assessment—Rule 7.

Measure of duty and charge leviable

Section 4 underwent an amendment in 1973 with the result that from the 1st October 1975 the old s. 4 got substituted. The Supreme Court in its land-mark judgment in *Union of India* v *Bombay Tyre International*,[1] held that the new section was not in any way different from the old section. In both the sections the price charged by the manufacturer on a sale in the wholesale trade represents the measure. The value of the excisable article has to be computed with reference to the price charged by the manufacturer. The Supreme Court drew a parallel from the levy in municipal taxation where the tax levy is linked with annual value of land and building. Here annual valuation is only a mode of measuring value on the basis of which the charging of tax operates. The Supreme Court held:

> "it may be and is often so that the tax on circumstances and property is levied on the basis of income which the assessee receives from his profession, trade, calling or property. That is, however, not conclusive on the nature of

1 (1983)14 ELT 1896.

the tax. It is only as a matter of convenience the income is adopted as a yardstick or measure for assessing the tax. As pointed out in Re.—a reference under Government of Ireland Act (*supra*), the measure of the tax is not a true text of the nature of the tax. Therefore, while determining the nature of the tax, though the standard on which the tax is levied may be a relevant consideration, it is not a conclusive consideration."

Thus, the scheme of valuation under s. 4 making the sale price of the article as the basis of arriving at the assessable value of the excisable goods was held not to militate against the levy under the Act being contemplated as one on manufacture or production of goods. The Supreme Court explained the point at length in the following words:

"It will be noticed that the basic scheme for determination of the price in the new section 4 is characterised by the same dichotomy as that observable in the old section 4. It was not the intention of Parliament, when enacting the new section 4 to create a scheme materially different from that embodied in the superseded section 4. The object and purpose remained the same, and so did the central principle at the heart of the scheme. The new scheme was merely comprehensive and the language employed more precise and definite. As in the old section 4 the terms in which the value was defined, remained the price charged by the assessee in the course of wholesale trade for delivery at the time and place of removal. Under the new section 4 the phrase "place of removal" was defined by section 4(*b*) not merely as "the factory or any other.place or premises of production or manufacturer of the excisable goods" from where such good are removed but was extended to "a warehouse or any place or premises wherein the excisable goods have been permitted to be deposited without payment of duty" and the from where such goods are removed. The judicial construction of the provisions of the old section 4 had already declared that the price envisaged under clauses (*a*) and (*b*) of that section was the price charged by the manufacturer in a transaction at arms length. After referring to several cases, some of which have already been mentioned here earlier, this court pointed out in Voltas

Limited (*supra*) that "the wholesale cash price has to be ascertained only on the basis of transactions at arms length. If there is a special or favoured buyer to whom a specially low price is charged because of extra-commercial considerations, e.g., because he is a relative of the manufacturer, the price charged for those sales would not be the "whole sale cash price" for levying excise under section 4(*a*) of the Act. A sole distributor might or might not be a favoured buyer according as terms of the agreement with him are fair and reasonable and were arrived at on purely commercial basis."

That was also the view taken in *Atic Industries Ltd.*[2] The new s. 4 makes express provision in that behalf. Under the new s. 4 also, it is necessary to take the price charged by the manufacturer as one which is uneffected by any concessional or manipulative considerations, and therefore the "normal price" mentioned in the new s. 4(1)(*a*) speaks of a price "where the buyer is not the related person and the price is the sole consideration for the sale". The expression "related person" has been specifically defined in the new s. 4(4)(*c*), and transaction in which a "related person" is involved are covered by the third proviso of s. 4(1)(*a*).

Normal price as conceived under section 4(1)(a)

Section 4(1)(*a*) provides that the value of excisable goods for purposes of levy of duty at *ad valorem* rates shall be deemed to be the normal price of such goods. Normal price for this purpose contains the following essential features—

(*a*) It should be a price at which such goods are ordinarily sold by the assessee to a buyer. Goods captively consumed are excepted.

(*b*) Such a sale must be in the course of wholesale trade and not a sale in retail.

(*c*) The price should be for delivery at the time and place of removal and it should be known at the factory gate.

(*d*) The buyer should not be a related person or in other words, the transaction shall be at arm's length.

2 1978 ELT J 444 (SC); (1975)3 SCR 563.

(*e*) The price of the goods must be the sole consideration for sale. In other words, there shall not be a flow-back of consideration.

Goods captively consumed

According to Rule 6(*b*) of the Valuation Rules, assessable value in the case of excisable goods which are not sold by the assessee but are used or consumed by the assessee in the production or manufacture of other articles shall be determined on comparability basis. In such cases, the value shall be based—

(*i*) on the value of the *comparable goods* produced or manufactured by the assessee or by any other assessee provided that in determining the value, the proper officer shall make such adjustments as appear to him reasonable, taking into consideration all relevant factors and in particular, the difference if any, in the material characteristics of the goods to the assessed and of the comparable goods;

(*ii*) on the cost of production or manufacture including the profits, if any, which the assessee would have normally earned on the sale of such goods, if the value as under (*i*) above cannot be determined.

In *Gwalior Rayon Manufacturing & Weaving Company* v *Union of India*,[3] it was held that there was no inconsistency between the provisions of s. 4(1)(*b*) of the Act and r. 6(*b*)(*i*) of the Central Excise Valuation Rules inasmuch as the words 'nearest ascertainable equivalent' used in s. 4(1)(*b*) was not any different from the words 'comparable goods' used in r. 6(*b*)(*i*). On the issue as to whether 'comparable goods' should be construed to mean 'identical goods' the High Court held, "Instances may be available where the assessee himself or any other assessee manufactures identical goods in a different unit in the same locality and sells it. There appears to be no reason why identical goods manufactured in a different unit in the same locality or the nearest place available and sold by the assessee himself or any other assessee cannot be taken as 'comparable goods' and its value taken as the 'nearest ascertainable equivalent' of the value of the excisable goods in

3 1982 ELT 844 (MP).

accordance with s. 4(1)(*b*). In fact taking identical goods manufactured and sold at the nearest place available would be more reasonable and would reduce to the minimum the discretion available to the proper officer for equating the comparable goods with the excisable goods."

Assessable value where price is not known at the time and place of removal

Rule 4 of the Central Excise Valuation Rules 1975 provides that the value of the excisable goods shall be based on the value of such goods sold by the assessee for delivery at any time nearest to the time of the removal of the goods under assessment, subject if necessary to such adjustment on account of the difference in the dates of delivery of such goods and of the excisable goods under assessment as may appear reasonable to the proper officer. In *Collector of Central Excise, Madras* v *Madras Rubber Factory Limited*[4] the question of applicability of r. 4 arose. The Tribunal was considering in the case a direction from the Supreme Court (arising out of Special Leave Petition (Civil) Nos. 1409 10/77 10108/80 and C.A. Nos. 3/95/79 and 6811/83-*ACCE etc. etc.* v *Madras Rubber Factory Ltd. etc. etc.)* to decide the question whether the sales effected by MRF Ltd. at their depot were not retail sales, as contended by the Revenue and if they were retail sales, then what further deductions were permissible to MRF under r. 6(*a*) of the Central Excise Rules 1975. MRF had declared that there was no sale by them to a buyer in the course of wholesale trade for delivery at the time and place of removal and that, therefore, s. 4(1)(*a*) of the Act was inapplicable. MRF contended that the goods were sold by them in retail and that the prices shown in the price list were retail prices and that their case was covered by r. 6(*a*) of the Valuation Rules. MRF claimed appropriate deductions from these retail prices to arrive at the price at which they could sold such goods in the course of wholesale trade. The Appellate Collector of Central Excise, Madras, by his order dated 21.4.1980, held that:

(*a*) the department had not adduced any evidence to reject MRF's contention that the prices quoted by them were retail prices;

4 (1984)18 ELT 111 (Mad).

(*b*) the uniform prices at which the goods were delivered in MRF's depots were nothing but retail prices;

(*c*) consequently, the normal prices of the goods have to be determined under r. 6(*a*).

He directed the lower authorities to allow post-manufacturing expenses after verification and to fix the assessable value of the goods under r. 6(*a*). But the Central Government issued a notice dated 6.10.1980 to MRF calling upon them to show cause why the Appellate Collector's order dated 21.4.1980 should not be set aside.

MRF, by their reply contended that the Appellate Collector's order being based on the admitted material and the actual position that MRF's prices were retail prices, was proper, legal and correct. MRF reiterated that there were no sales at the factory gate, the prices at which the goods were sold to consumers and dealers were the same, the dealers' hands were not tied down by any conditions and that the dealers bought only one or two tyres at a time. Thus MRF depots were in retail trade and not in wholesale trade. The submissions made on behalf of the appellants (Revenue) *inter alia* includes:

"(a)(*i*) A sale to a dealer is a sale in wholesale. The quantity in a particular transaction is not necessarily relevant or conclusive of the character of the sale.

(*ii*) The definition of "wholesale trade" in section 4(4)(*e*) was an artificial one. The natural meaning was sale to a dealer for the purpose of re-sale in retail. However, the definition covered not only wholesale dealers but also industrial consumers, Government, local authorities, and other buyers, who or which purchase their requirements otherwise than in retail.

(*iii*) What, in effect, the MRF is asking is that their goods should be assessed on the basis of a value from which all post-manufacturing expenses and post-manufacturing profits are excluded.

(*iv*) Considering the totality of circumstances, MRF sales, leaving aside the 5% sales to Defence authorities, were in wholesale and not retail.

The Tribunal held that apart from Defence sales all sales are made through 42 depots of MRF, located at different place in the country. Removals to depots are on stock-transfer challans. There are no invoices covering these transactions and, therefore, no ex-factory sales are involved.

Sale to or through a related person

Proviso (*iii*) to s. 4 envisages a possibility where the assessee makes an arrangement by which the goods manufactured by him are generally not sold by him in the course of wholesale trade except to or through a related person. In such cases, the normal price of the goods sold by the assessee to or through such related person shall be deemed to be the price at which the goods are ordinarily sold by the related person in the course of wholesale trade at the time of removal, to dealers (not being related persons), or where such goods are not sold to such dealers, to dealers (being related persons) who sell such goods in retail. The idea is that revenue which is properly due to the Government should not get reduced or emaciated only by reason of the fact that the goods generally sold to related persons do not normally fetch the full value to the assessee.

(F) CUSTOMS DUTY

Ever since the adventuring explorers charted the maritime routes across the vast oceans, the traders found it profitable to exchange goods with merchandise carried in sea vessels from country to country. The rules of the land were not slow to impose a levy to extract a share out of the profits or license fees to permit such trade with a view to swelling the treasury. Sea customs duty thus evolved in ancient days. Before this era, trade through land routes with all its limitations as regards hazards of journey and carriage of bulk goods had continually developed amongst neighbouring nations quite behind the gaze of cognizability. The nations of the world at that time had no defined boundaries and might was the right. Ancient India's trade routes opened up since Alexander's invasion in the fourth century B.C. The Periplus of the Erythaean Sea, written between A.D. 70's and 80's gives an account of Greek ships landing in the port town of India at Barygaza (modern Broach or Bharuch). Trade had been taxed during the time of Chandragupta Maurya and Kautilya's *Arthashastra* gives an account as to how inter-State trade had to be regulated by export and import duties.

Kautilya's *Arthashastra* in its elaborate discourse prescribes that the officer-in-charge of commodities should cause the commodities which are produced in foreign countries to be invited by showing favour. To the sailors and carriers by caravan he should grant exemptions sustainable in future. No complaints against the foreign visitors shall be allowed in money matters, except those who belong to an association and their benefactors. Again, it shall be the duty of such designated officer to ascertain the quoted price and the intrinsic value of the commodity originating in the foreign country and the commodity to be bartered from the home country; and he should find out the profit after deducting the expenditure on duty, road cess, tax, transport charge, military cess, ferry charge, food expenses and escort expenses; he should also find out if profit can be earned by exporting goods or by the price of commodities in lieu of those to be bartered. Then with a quarter of the commodities left over he should promote trade by protected route. The *Arthashastra* also recommends him to establish contact with foreign chiefs, border chiefs, and the heads of cities and the countryside for gaining their favour. In case of danger, he should save precious goods or himself. If he does not reach his own lands he should trade only after clearing all the dues. On the water route he should find out charges for carriage and armed guards, provisions on the way, prices and quantities of commodities demanded, time for journey, safeguards against danger and the customs of the port.[5]

During the visit of Megasthenes at the Mauryan empire, trade routes provided a network throughout the country and even beyond where toll, carriage-cess, and transit duties were collected. From remote antiquity India thus had trade relations with other countries both by land and sea. The over land route ran through the Khyber Pass and across the Hindukush to a place called Balkh where the principal highways from Central Asia and China converged. Sea routes developed across the

5 Dr. P.C. Chunder's *Kautilya—Arthashastra* (1995) published by M.P. Birla Foundation, pp. 139-141.

Mediterranean and Black Sea. Sea going vessels generally kept close to the coast and made long voyage along the shores of India, Baluchistan, Persia and Arabia through the Red Sea to a head near. Suez. From this point merchandise were carried by land to Egypt on the West and other famous ports, like Tyre and Sidon on the North. The evidence of coins discovered bears the testimony to India's trade with Rome and the Western countries even in the Fourth Century A.D.

India's wealth attracted traders from abroad. The East India Company from Britain and France vied for the Indian market. So did the Dutch. Thus, with the gradual development of nation states, sea customs and land customs, as are now commonly understood, did evolve.

With the advent of the British rule in India, there came into being the Sea Customs Act 1878, containing provisions, such as, the power to fix tariff values and also the procedure to be adopted by the authorities where under-valuation of the goods by the importer is attempted. The provisions of the Sea Customs Act have been substantially amended by an Act of 1962 to bring it in tune with the GATT (General Agreement on Tariff and Trade).

With the growth of the modern means of transport, a bulk of the international trade is now carried on by aircarfts side by side with land and sea routes. The Land Customs Act was passed in 1924. Air Customs was covered by making some rules under the Indian Aircraft Act 1911. The Customs Act of 1962 consolidates the law on Sea Customs, Land Customs, as well as provisions for Air Customs. Most of the Customs Duties are *ad valorem*. Goods are therefore to be valued for levying the rates of assessment. Packaged goods have to be assessed on the basis of maximum retail price (MRP) declared on the package. For the rest, unless the Board has notified a tariff value, goods have to be valued as per the relevant statutory provisions as embodied in s. 14 of the Customs Act 1962 and Customs Valuation (Determination of Price of Imported Goods) Rules 1988. In particular, r. 4 of the said Rules lay down the "transaction value" which should normally be accepted for the purpose of imposition of Customs Duty.

The international scenario also changed by now. The GATT, that regulates the multilateral trade negotiations amongst the consenting nations came into existence after the World War II in 1947. After a number of changes it ultimately gave way to the World Trade Organisation (WTO), which came into being on 1st January 1995. A change not only in the name but also in the functional pattern of the multilateral trade negotiations having introduced in which the issues on customs valuation is an important component. The valuation systems in certain countries adopted arbitrarily leading to fictitious values of transacted goods having little nexus with the "real price" thereof has been attempted to be cured by the changes.

Indian law

Customs duty leviable on movables imported into the country has been in vogue for centuries in the coastal States. It was known in the earlier days as 'protection money' under the British regime in India, this was regulated by the Sea Customs Act of 1878. Later on, the same was replaced by the Customs Act of 1962 (52 of 1962) and the Rules thereunder known as the Customs Valuation Rules 1963. The earlier law on valuation considered the 'wholesale price' of the transacted goods for levy of customs duty. The same now abides by the 'transaction value' as conceived by Art. VII of the General Agreement on Tariffs and Trade (GATT) which ruled the roast in international trade at the relevant period. It means the price actually paid or payable for the goods when sale for export to the country of importation adjusted in accordance with the provisions of the Art. 8 thereof which lays down the principles of exclusion and inclusions for determination of customs value. The international scenario changed and on 1st January 1995, the GATT yielded place to WTO (World Trade Organisation) a change not only in name but also in its functional parameters. The Customs Co-operation Council born in Brussels in the year 1952 was entrusted with the task of application of the conventions relating to the valuation of goods for customs purposes. In the year 1955, the Customs Cooperation Council was rechristened as the World Customs Organisation (WCO).

A new system was introduced in the field of valuation of imported goods in India with the promulgation of the Customs Valuation (Imported Goods) Rules 1988. Custom duties are levied at such rates as may be specified under the Customs Tariff Act 1975 on the principles of 'transaction value' as enunciated under the Customs Valuation Rules 1988 which includes transaction value of identical goods, transaction value of similar goods. Deductive value and computed value as well as the residual method. The Rules enable the Government to levy both duties on imported goods as well as goods exported from India. Again, the levies serve the purpose of not only raising revenue but also the purposes aimed at realisation of economic and social objectives like discouraging import and stimulating exports of selected item of goods.

About the transaction values

Transaction value is provided in r. 4 of the Customs Valuation (Determination of Price of Imported Goods) Rules 1988 while r. 5 lays down the transaction value of identical goods. In the next stage, r. 6 gives the transaction value of similar goods. Rule 4(3)(*a*) is applicable in cases where the buyer and the seller are related by way of having belonged to the same organisations or being related as master and servant or father and son or similar relationship. But it would not be of any effect if such relationship did not influence the price. It is not intended to raise an adverse presumption about it. Such a probe will follow only when there are legitimate doubts about the acceptability of the price.

However, the rr. 4, 5, 6, 6A, 7, 7A and 8 are reproduced below verbatim:

4. *Transaction value.* (1) The transaction value of imported goods shall be the price actually paid or payable for the goods when sold for export to India, adjusted in accordance with the provisions of Rule 9 of these rules.

(2) The transaction value of imported goods under sub-rule (1) above shall be accepted:

Provided that—

(*a*) there are no restrictions as to the disposition or use of the goods by the buyer other than restrictions which—

(*i*) are imposed or required by law or by the public authorities in India; or

(*ii*) limit the geographical area in which the goods may be resold; or

(*iii*) do not substantially affect the value of the goods;

(*b*) the sale or price is not subject to some condition or consideration for which a value cannot be determined in respect of the goods being valued;

(*c*) no part of the proceeds of any subsequent resale, disposal or use of the goods by the buyer will accrue directly or indirectly to the seller, unless an appropriate adjustment can be made in accordance with the provisions of Rule 9 of these rules; and

(*d*) the buyer and seller are not related, or where the buyer and seller are related, that transaction value is acceptable for customs purposes under the provisions of sub-rule (3) below.

(3)(*a*) Where the buyer and seller are related, the transaction value shall be accepted provided that the examination of the circumstances of the sale of the imported goods indicate that the relationship did not influence the price.

(*b*) in a sale between related persons, the transaction value shall be accepted, whenever the importer demonstrates that the declared value of the goods being valued, closely approximates to one of the following values ascertained at or about the same time—

(*i*) the transaction value of identical goods, or of similar goods, in sales to unrelated buyers in India;

(*ii*) the deductive value for identical goods or similar goods;

(*iii*) the computed value for identical goods or similar goods;

Provided that in applying the values used for comparison, due account shall be taken of demonstrated difference in commercial levels, quantity levels, adjustments in accordance with the provisions of Rule 9 of these rules and cost incurred by the seller in sales in which he and the buyer are not related;

(*c*) substitute values shall not be established under the provisions of clause (*b*) of this sub-rule.

5. *Transaction value of identical goods.* (1)(*a*) Subject to the provisions of Rule 3 of these rules, the value ofimported goods shall be the transaction value of identical goods sold for export to India and imported at or about the same time as the goods being valued.

(*b*) In applying this rule, the transaction value of identical goods in a sale at the same commercial level and in substantially the same quantity as the goods being valued shall be used to determine the value of imported goods.

(*c*) Where no sale referred to in clause (*b*) of sub-rule (1) of this rule, is found, the transaction value of identical goods sold at a different commercial level or in different quantities or both, adjusted to take account of the difference attributable to commercial level or to the quantity or both, shall be used, provided that such adjustments shall be made on the basis of demonstrated evidence which clearly establishes the reasonableness and accuracy of the adjustments, whether such adjustment leads to an increase or decrease in the value.

(2) Where the costs and charges referred to in sub-rule (2) of Rule 9 of these rules are included in the transaction value of identical goods, an adjustment shall be made, if there are significant differences in such costs and charges between the goods being valued and the identical goods in question arising from differences in distances and means of transport.

(3) In applying this rule, if more than one transaction value of identical goods is found, the lowest such value shall be used to determine the value of imported goods.

6. *Transaction value of similar goods.* (1) Subject to the provisions of Rule 3 of these rules, the value of imported goods shall be the transaction value of similar goods sold for export to India and imported at or about the same time as the goods being valued.

(2) The provisions of clauses (*b*) and (*c*) of sub-rule (1), sub-rule (2) and sub-rule (3) of Rule 5 of these rules shall, *mutatis mutandis,* also apply in respect of similar goods.

6A. *Determination of value when transaction value is not available.* If the value of imported goods cannot be determined under the provisions of Rules 4, 5 and 6, the value shall be determined under the provisions of Rule 7 or, when the value cannot be determined under that rule, under Rule 7A:

Provided that at the request of the importer, and with the approval of the proper officer, the order of application of Rules 7 and 7A shall be reversed.

7. *Deductive value.* (1) Subject to the provisions of Rule 3 of these rules, if the goods being valued or identical or similar imported goods are sold in India, in the condition as imported at or about the time at which the declaration for determination of value is presented, the value of imported goods shall be based on the unit

price at which the imported goods or identical or similar imported goods are sold in the greatest aggregate quantity to persons who are not related to the sellers in India, subject to the following deductions:

(*i*) either the commission usually paid or agreed to be paid or the additions usually made for profits and general expenses in connection with sales in India of imported goods of the same class or kind;

(*ii*) the usual costs of transport and insurance and associated costs incurred within India;

(*iii*) the customs duties and other taxes payable in India by reason ofimportation or sale of the goods.

(2) If neither the imported goods nor identical nor similar imported goods are sold at or about the same time of importation of the goods being valued, the value of imported goods shall, subject otherwise to the provisions of sub-rule (1) of this rule, be based on the unit price at which the imported goods or identical or similar imported goods are sold in India, at the earliest date after importation but before the expiry of ninety days after such importation.

(3)(*a*) If neither the imported goods nor identical nor similar imported goods are sold in India in the condition as imported, then, the value shall be based on the unit price at which the imported goods, after further processing, are sold in the greatest aggregate quantity to persons who are not related to the seller in India.

(*b*) In such determination, due allowance shall be made for the value added by processing and the deductions provided for in items (*i*) to (*iii*) of sub-rule (1) of this rule.

7A. *Computed value.* Subject to the provisions of Rule 3, the value of imported goods shall be based on a computed value, which shall consist of the sum of—

(*a*) the cost or value of materials and fabrication or other processing employed in producing the imported goods;

(*b*) an amount for profit and general expenses equal to that usually reflected in sales of goods of the same class or kind as the goods being valued which are made by producers in the country of exportation for export to India;

(*c*) the cost or value of all other expenses under sub-rule (2) of Rule 9 of these rules.

8. *Residual method.* (1) Subject to the provisions of Rule 3 of these rules, where the value of imported goods cannot be determined under the provisions of any of the preceding rules, the value shall be determined using reasonable means consistent with the principles and general provisions of these rules and sub-section (1) of section 14 of the Customs Act, 1962 (52 of 1962) and on the basis of data available in India.

(2) No value shall be determined under the provisions of this rule on the basis of—

(*i*) the selling price in India of the goods produced in India;

(*ii*) a system which provides for the acceptance for customs purposes of the highest of the two alternative values;

(*iii*) the price of the goods on the domestic market of the country of exportation;

(*iiia*) the cost of production other than computed values which have been determined for identical or similar goods in accordance with the provisions of Rule 7A.

(*iv*) the price of the goods for the export to a country other than India;

(*v*) minimum customs values; or

(*vi*) arbitrary or fictitious values.

(G) COURT-FEES

The court-fees payable on property in litigation in India is governed by the Court-fees Act 1870 (VII of 1870). The different States have promulgated adaptation laws in the form of State Act on court-fees in exercise of powers given under the said Central Act VII of 1870.

Suits Valuation Act 1887 (7 of 1887) is a Central Act that prescribes the mode of valuing certain suits for the purpose of determining the jurisdiction of courts with respect thereto. It empowers the State Governments to make rules for determining the value of land for the purpose of jurisdiction in the suits (s. 3). The State Government shall, before making rules under s. 3 consult the High Court with respect thereto (s. 5). In s. 11 of the Act, procedure is laid down for raising objection in appeal or revision that a suit or appeal was not properly valued for jurisdictional purposes. Such objection has to be taken in the court of first instance at or before the hearing at which the issues were first framed and recorded, or in the lower appellate court in the Memorandum of Appeal, as the case may be.

The real estates and other properties are often required to be valued under provisions of the law on court-fees in order that the litigants pay for the cost of securing justice which, however, devolves ultimately on the party at fault as a general feature. The State Acts though passed by each individual State to suit its specific conditions are, however, similar in general pattern. Hence, we shall deal with one or two of such State enactments to bear out the relevance valuation has in the realm of court-fees.

Suits for recovery of possession of property

The Bombay Court-fees Act 1956 in its paragraph (*v*) to s. 6 lays down that the suits for the possession of land, houses and gardens have to be levied with court-fees according to the value of the subject-matter; and value shall be deemed to be, where the subject-matter is a house or garden, according to the market value of the house or garden. According to paragraph (*vi*) of the same section, in suits to enforce a right of pre-emption, the valuation process in respect of land, house or garden is the same.

In West Bengal, the West Bengal Court Fees Act 1970 came into force on the 26th of February 1970. In its Chapter III, computations of fees for various purposes are laid down. In accordance with the provisions of s. 7(*vi*), suit for recovery of possession of immovable property has to be valued according to the amount at which the relief sought is valued in the plaint. This is subject to the provision as to enquiry on valuation of suits by the court under s. 11, if the suit is wrongly valued, in which case revision may be done. In suits for the possession of land, building or garden, not being suits referred to in cl. (*vi*) above, the valuation is made under cl. (*v*) of s. 7 by computing net profits as fifteen times of that have arisen during that year next before the date of presenting the plaint, or the market value thereof, whichever is considered lower. It has been specifically held that the provision of cl. (*vi*) of s. 7 is always subject to the provision of s. 11 of the Act.[6] In a suit

6 *Smt. Nilima Bose* v *Santosh Kumar Ghosh* AIR 1997 Cal 202; (1997)2 CWN 152.

for declaration of title converted into that for recovery of possession by amendment of the plaint, court-fees at enhanced rate as fixed by the trial court is payable.[7]

Suits for partition

Paragraph (*vii*) of the Bombay Court-fees Act lays down the provision for levy of court-fees for partition claiming share in joint property. According to the same, in suits for partition and separate possession of a share of joint family property or of joint property, or to enforce a right to a share in any property on the ground that it is a joint family property or joint property whether or not the plaintiff is in actual or constructive possession of the property of which he claims to be a coparcener or co-owner, the amount of court-fees shall be computed according to the value of the share in respect of which the suit is instituted. Needless to say, valuation of the entire property and shares therein is essential to determine owelty money payable on partition.

According to the provision of cl. (*viii*) of s. 7 of the West Bengal Court Fees Act 1970, in suits for partition and separate possession of a share of joint property, if the plaintiff has been excluded from possession thereof or seeks to enforce a right to a share therein, court-fees are payable according to the market value of the share in respect of which the suit is instituted.

In the case of a partition, market value of the joint properties has to be determined at the time of partition. 'Market Value' has but one meaning, be it a case of acquisition or a case of partition. So, for the purpose of partition, the Valuer should adopt the same method and follow the same principles as he will have to do in the case of acquisition. In point of fact, it is often found that in partition deeds values of properties are fixed at the low side, namely, at figures lower than the market value. This is the reason why partition values do not, generally speaking, furnish good and reliable guides in determination of the market value of a property. The observations of the Calcutta High Court in the case of *Sushil Chandra Ghose* v *Satish Chandra Ghose* in A.O.D. No. 459 of 1928 (unreported) are pertinent on this point. The question that arose in that appeal was the valuation of the allotments made by the lower court

7 *Lina Sengupta* v *Sovarani Guha* AIR 1995 Cal 152.

in a suit for partition. It was contended by the Appellants that certain sales and a partition valuation contained in a partition award were wrongly excluded by the lower court. Their Lordships (Mukherjee & Guha, JJ.) rejected that contention holding that the sales were not of firm land and the title was defective. As for the partition valuation, Their Lordships observed that "the valuation was made not for ascertaining the real value but only to equalise the shares in a case of partition between the co-owners who must have been interested in keeping down the value to avoid payment of higher court-fees".

Specific performance

In suits for specific performance, the amount of court-fees is computed according to the amount or value of the property when the subject-matter is an award, as laid down in paragraph (*xi*)(*d*) of s. 6 of the Bombay Court-fees Act.

Under the West Bengal Court Fees Act 1970, in suits for specific performance, court-fees are payable according to the amount of the consideration in case of a contract of sale; according to the amount secured in case of a mortgage; according to the aggregate amount of the fine or premium, if any, and of the rent agreed during the first year of the term in case of a lease; and according to the amount or value of the disputed property in case of an award.

Probate and letters of administration

The valuation of property lies at the core of any application for Probate of a Will or Letters of Administration. The applicant has to estimate the value of the property of the deceased. Section 276 of the Indian Succession Act requires that a petition for probate shall *inter alia* give the amount of assets likely to come to the petitioner's hand. Under s. 29(1) of the Bombay Court-fees Act, no order entitling the petitioner to the grant of probate or letters of administration shall be made upon an application for such grant until the petitioner has filed in the court a valuation of the property in the prescribed form, and the court is satisfied that the requisite fee has been paid on such valuation. It was held by the Bombay High Court in *Madhusudan Dwarkadas Vora* v *Superintendent of Stamps*[8]

8 (1983)141 ITR 802.

that the petitioner for probate is obliged, by virtue of item 10 of Sch. I of the Bombay Court-fees Act 1959, to pay court-fees on the value of the property in respect of which the grant is sought. Where such property is a house, its value, i.e. the price it would fetch if sold in the open market, on the date of the death must be determined in the same manner as it would for the purpose of estate duty, that is to say, by an application of the principles laid down in rule 1BB of the W.T. Rules 1957, made under the W.T. Act 1957.

Rule 1BB is however not in application any more. Instead, Schedule III in pursuance of s. 7(1) of the W.T. Act has come into force with effect from 1st April 1989.

In West Bengal Court Fees Act 1970, adjudication on valuation in respect of Probates, Letters of Administration, and Certificates of Administration, is regulated in accordance with the provisions as laid down in Chapter IV of the Act. Accordance to s. 32 thereof, the petitioner has to file in the court a valuation of the property in the form set forth in Schedule III of the Act and the court has to satisfy itself that the requisite fee, as per Article No. 10 of Schedule I which prescribes the rate of imposition of court-fees on the value of property in such Probate of Letters of Administration, has been paid on such valuation.

Valuation—how determined

The point now arises how valuation of property, immovable or movable, is made for the purpose of levy of court-fees. Is there any scientific basis for the same? Has any method of valuation been prescribed? Is valuation done by persons having recognised expertise in the field? To these questions, the Court-fees Act do not provide any suitable answer. Section 19H of the Court-fees Act 1870 lays down the procedure to be adopted by the Collector if any property for probate is under-valued. There is hardly any professional expertise at the disposal of the Collector in our country to make a valuation in this behalf. In s. 8 of the Bombay Court-fees Act, it is provided that if the court is of opinion that the subject-matter of any suit has been wrongly valued or if an application is made to the court for the revision of any valuation made, the court may revise the valuation and determine the correct valuation and may hold such enquiry as it thinks fit for such purpose. The provision in the next s. 9(1) lays down how such enquiry shall be made. According to it, for the purpose of an enquiry under s. 8, the Court may depute, or issue a commission to, any suitable person to make such local or other investigation as may be necessary to report thereon to the Court. Such report and any evidence recorded by such person shall be evidence in the inquiry. The inquiry made by the Court for ascertaining valuation is deemed to be a judicial proceeding within the meaning of ss. 193 and 228 of the Indian Penal Code.

Now it remains to be established if a judicial process as traditionally followed is sufficient to arrive at a just and fair valuation. It is often said that 'Courts are final not because they are infallible, but they are infallible because they are final'. Thus, a system of rational valuation of property for levy of court-fees is long overdue in the in-house of the institution that decides the issues of valuation in their finality as precedence to be followed.

(H) GIFT-TAX

Valuation is required for the purpose of Gift-tax also. Gift is a voluntary transfer of asset without consideration. Under provisions of the Transfer of Property Act the donee must accept the gift during the lifetime of the donor or during the period the donor is still capable of making a gift. If the donee dies before such acceptance, the gift is void.

Under provisions of s. 6 of the Gift-tax Act 1958 the value of any property, other than cash, transferred by way of gift shall, for the purpose of the said Act, be its value as on the date on which the gift was made and shall be determined in the manner laid down in Schedule II. Where a person makes a gift which is not revocable for a specified period, the value of the property gifted shall be the capitalised value of the income from such property during the period for which the gift is not revocable.

The transfer of an immovable property way of gift can be effected only by a registered instrument. If the subject-matter of gift is a movable asset, registration is optional and transaction is complete by delivery of possession.

While the rates of gift-tax are provided in Schedule I, in rules for determining the value of property gifted are given in Schedule II as under:

SCHEDULE II

[*See* section 6(1)]

Rules for Determining the Value of Property Gifted

1. *Value of gifted property, how to be determined.* Subject to the provisions of rules 2 to 7, the value of any property, other than cash, transferred by way of gift shall, for the purposes of this Act, be determined in accordance with the provisions of Schedule III to the Wealth-tax Act, 1957 (27 of 1957) (hereinafter referred to as the Wealth-tax Act) which shall apply subject to the following modifications, namely:

In the said Schedule,—

(*a*) references by whatever form of words to the Wealth-tax Act shall be construed as references to this Act;

(*b*) in rule 5, the reference to the year ending on the valuation date shall be construed as a reference to the previous year as defined in this Act;

(*c*) save as provided in clause (*b*), references to the valuation date shall the construed as references to the date on which the gift was made;

(*d*) reference to section 7 of the Wealth-tax Act shall be construed as references to section 6 of this Act;

(*e*) references to section 16A of the Wealth-tax Act shall be construed as references to sub-section (6) of section 15 of this Act.

2. *Quoted shares and debentures of companies.* The value of an equity share or a preference share in any company or a debenture of any company which is a quoted share or a quoted debenture shall be taken as the value quoted in respect of such share or debenture on the date on which the gift was made or where there is no such quotation on such date, the quotation on the date closest to such date and immediately preceding such date.

Explanation.—The words and expressions used in this rule and rules 3 to 7 but not defined and defined in rule 2 of Schedule III to the Wealth-tax Act shall have the meanings respectively assigned to them in rule 2 of that Schedule.

3. Special provision for quoted shares of companies. Notwithstanding anything in rule 2, the value of an equity share in any company which is a quoted share may, at the option of the assessee or a company, be taken on the basis of the average of the value quoted on the 31st day of March immediately preceding the assessment year and the values quoted in respect of such share on the said dates in relation to each of the immediately preceding nine assessment years, or where there is no such quotation on any of the aforesaid dates, the quotation on the date closest to the said date and immediately preceding such date.

The fiscal provisions relating to gift have undergone further changes in recent time. The donee's acquisition in pursuance of a gift is now treated as his income liable to income-tax as per fiscal law in force. Thus the provisions relating to gift-tax have only a referential value for resolving any relevant question that may arise.

CHAPTER

22

Valuation for other Statutory and Non-Fiscal Purposes

(A) LAND ACQUISITION

The discipline of valuation has been nursed in our country in the cradle of compulsory acquisition of the real property. That is why judicial decisions in the realm of land acquisition under the Land Acquisition Act of 1894 which is now repealed and replaced by the Right to Fair Compensation and Transparency in Land Acquisition, Rehabilitation and Resettlement Act 2013, have again and again appeared in the different chapters of this book. All the approaches to value, such as, market approach, income approach or cost approach have been pressed into application while valuing real property in the context of land acquisition as already discussed in the relevant chapters of this book. But it must not be forgotten that the very fact of compulsory acquisition is itself a constraint in assessing an objective value of real property. Because in compulsory acquisition, the idea behind valuation is to arrive at just compensation for the property acquired and not valuation as such. But the fact remains that the judicial decisions in this field have immensely contributed in evolving the theory and practice of valuation. That is why appropriate decisions had to be quoted in every chapter of this book. It now remains to understand the basic concept behind compulsory acquisition in order to provide a proper perspective to the topic of valuation it handles.

The power of the eminent domain

The power of compulsory acquisition of real property is an inherent and necessary attribute of sovereignty in the Government of the country. In the early seventeenth century it was given the name "eminent domain" (*dominium eminens*) by Grotius, Puffendorf and other contemporary continental writers. The sovereign power was created for the common security and that alone will give a Government sufficient right and title to make use of the goods of the subject whenever necessity, in the public interest, so requires. In England, all land is in theory the property of the Crown, and with certain limitations this is also the case in India. The highest title known to the law in England is that of 'fee simple in possession free from restriction,' but even this is subject to the right of the Crown acting through Parliament to resume all private rights in the interests of the community. The King is deemed to have originally owned all the land in his realm, and it was customary in earlier centuries for him to reward meritorious services by grants of lands, and this was done to such a degree that in due course the majority of the lands passed into possession of Crown favourites. On the continent of Europe the same thing prevailed to a very large extent.

In the United States of America compulsory purchase is exercised under the powers given by the 'law of eminent domain.' Eminent domain is defined as being, the right or power of the State to appropriate private property to particular uses, for the purpose of promoting the public welfare. Municipal and other corporations have been given authority with certain restrictions to take private property, subject always to the payment of just compensation. The power of eminent domain is inherent in the Government and in the various States, by virtue of their sovereignty. It does not consist in any subordinate political division or public corporation, unless granted by the supreme Government, that is by the Congress. But the power, however, is vested in the legislature of the several States, by the general grant of the legislative powers contained in the Constitution. Whether the power of eminent domain shall be exercised for any particular purpose, and whether the exigencies of the occasion, require or justify its exercise, are questions which rest entirely with the legislature and it follows that the instrumentalities to be used is entirely a matter within the discretion of the legislature.

Municipal corporations, public companies and even private persons, are constantly having the powers conferred upon them. France, Germany, Italy and in fact all European countries have their own particular form of compulsory acquisition on the principle of eminent domain.

There still exists among jurists a difference of opinion as to the nature of the power of eminent domain. Some maintain it is a sort of reserved right, and others a super-estate or interest in all property, vested in the sovereign power. Thus the right to take private property for public use and the common weal, is a reserved right attached to every man's land, and paramount to his right of ownership. He holds his land subject to that right and has no ground for complaint of injustice, if it is lawfully used.

The true theory of the matter is that the legislature resume dominion over the property, and having resumed it, they either use it themselves or re-vest it in other individuals (such as public companies) or corporations, to be used by them in such manner, as to effect, directly, indirectly, or incidentally as the case may be, the public good intended.

Thus the correct view is that the power of compulsory purchase, is an inherent right which pertains to sovereignty as a necessary, constant and inextinguishable attribute.

It is interesting to distinguish between the burden of this right and the burden of taxation. Taxation exacts money, or services from individuals, as their shares of, or contribution to, any public burden. Compulsory exaction is, therefore, distinguishable from compulsory acquisition. Private property taken for public use is taken, not however, merely as the owner's share of contribution to a public burden, but as so much beyond his share, and compensation is therefore to be made for the property involved.

The theory of compensation

It is obvious that if the person deprived of his property was completely reinstated in a similar or better property, equally suitable to him, he would be fairly treated and would have no cause for complaint, provided his incidental expenses were also paid. But reinstatement is not always possible or convenient. Failing reinstatement the only equitable thing would be to pay such a sum in compensation as would result in the claimant not suffering any financial loss.

The general rule with regard to damages was wisely stated by Lord Blackburn in the English case of *Livingstone* v *Rawyards Coal Company*[1] as follows:

> "Where any injury is to be compensated by damages, in settling the sum of money to be given for reparation as damages, you should as nearly as possible get at that sum of money which will put the party who has been injured, or who has suffered, in the same position, as he would have been in if he had not sustained the wrong for which he is now getting his compensation or reparation." That is equity.

The Indian law of compulsory acquisition

In India, although the first general Land Acquisition Act was passed in 1857, its successor in title—The Land Acquisition Act 1894 and now the Right to Fair Compensation and Transparency in Land Acquisition, Rehabilitation and Resettlement Act 2013 may be looked upon as the source Act that gave rise to provisions for compulsory acquisition in a plethora of legislations in the field of planning, municipal Government, city improvement, Railway, etc.

The Land Acquisition Act of 1894 which is now repealed and replaced by the Right to Fair Compensation and Transparency in Land Acquisition, Rehabilitation and Resettlement Act 2013, did not allow of the value to an owner being taken as the basis for compensation in equity it should and it is for this reason, that reinstatement is not recognized.

Certain general principles of valuation apply in all cases of compulsory purchase under the Land Acquisition Act 1894 as amended now the Right to Fair Compensation and Transparency in Land Acquisition, Rehabilitation and Resettlement Act 2013 (w.e.f. 1.1.2014) may be briefly stated seriatim.

(1) Sale by the owner is compulsory. He is given no option.

1 5 App Case 250.

(2) Under the Act the compensation to the owner is not necessarily the value of the property to the owner himself, but is the Market Value of the property dealt with, in theory, in the most lucrative manner practically possible.

(3) Apart from the reservation made in the preceding item, the compensation is intended to cover all the loss suffered by the owner, apart from the value of the property taken. Such for instance as 'injurious affection' resulting from the 'taking', to his other lands, if any; or the depreciation in value of his remaining lands due to 'severance' as the result of the 'taking'.

(4) The Act does not allow of the taking of part only of a house or building without the consent of the owner, and if such action is attempted he may insist on the acquisition of the whole.

(5) No credit is allowed to be taken by the acquiring body in arriving at the compensation, for any betterment which may result from the carrying out of the works contemplated.

(6) The value of the property is to be as at the date of notification under s. 4 of the Land Acquisition Act now under s. 11 of the Right to Fair Compensation and Transparency in Land Acquisition, Rehabilitation and Resettlement Act 2013 (w.e.f. 1.1.2014).

Compensation from fundamental right to constitutional remedy

The provision for payment of compensation for acquisition of property was originally included in Article 31(2) of the Constitution of India. Such compensation was held to mean "a just equivalent of what the owner has been deprived of" in the leading case of *State of West Bengal* v *Bela Banerjee*.[2] But the Government of India wanted to reserve to itself the absolute right to assess the quantum of compensation payable. So an amendment was made to Article 31(2) of the Constitution in 1955 incorporating that "no such law shall be called in question in any Court on the ground that the compensation provided by law is not adequate." But that did not serve the purpose. In the *Bank Nationalisation* case,[3] the Supreme Court held that "Constitution guarantees right to compensation, that is,

2 1954 SCR 558; 1954 SCJ 95; AIR 1954 SC 170.
3 AIR 1970 SC 564; (1970)1 SCC 248; (1970)3 SCR 530.

the equivalent in money of the property compulsorily acquired." Thus, in effect, the adequacy of compensation virtually remained justiciable before the court of law. Then the Government of India came up with further amendment of the Constitution in the year 1971 by which the word "compensation" was struck off the statute book of Constitution and the amount payable to the person whose property was acquired was left to be determined in accordance with such principles as may be specified in the relevant law of acquisition. The aspect of determination of such amount was kept beyond the pale of challenge in any court. Then came the case of *Kesavananda Bharati* v *State of Kerala*.[4] It was held that the amount payable for the acquired property either fixed by the legislature or determined on the basis of the principles engrafted in the Law of Acquisition, cannot be wholly arbitrary or illusory, nor can an amount be fixed that virtually amounts to confiscation. So the question of justiciability still remained. The result was the drastic deletion of the entire Art. 31 by the 44th Amendment of the Constitution in 1978. In order to make the step foolproof, even Article 19(1)(*f*) providing for the fundamental right to property was also deleted. Instead, a new Art. 300A was inserted in Part XII of the Constitution providing that "no person shall be deprived of his property save by authority of law". In this way, what was originally a fundamental right to property and compensation was converted into a constitutional remedy under Art. 300A.

44th Amendment does not affect L.A. Act

The 44th Amendment came into effect on the 19th June 1979. There have been a number of cases in which the *vires* of s. 23(1) of the Land Acquisition Act of 1894 was challenged on the ground that it offends the changed provisions of the Constitution after amendment. Section 23(1) of the Land Acquisition Act 1894 and s. 28(1) of the Right to Fair Compensation and Transparency in Land Acquisition, Rehabilitation and Resettlement Act 2013, provide for the matters to be considered in determining compensation under the said Act. But it was held in *Kundan Lal* v *Union of India*[5]

4 AIR 1973 SC 1461; (1973)4 SCC 225.

5 AIR 1988 Del 627.

that s. 23(1) is not *ultra vires* of the second proviso to Art. 31A(1) of the Constitution. It was also held in the case of *Singareni Collieries Co. Ltd* v *V. Satyanarayana Murthy*[6] that s. 23(1) in so far as it directs that the compensation shall be determined taking into consideration the market value as on the date of publication of the notification cannot be held to be *ultra vires* of the second proviso to Art. 31A(1) of any other provision of the Constitution so as to declare it null and void.

The Land Acquisition Act is a pre-Constitution Act. The effect of the 44th Amendment of the Constitution has not thus shaken its validity so far as payment of compensation is concerned. On the other hand, the new Art. 300A of the Constitution has to buttressed it by ensuring that no person shall be deprived of his property except by authority of law.

For purposes of valuation, ss. 23 and 24 of the Land Acquisition Act 1894 provide the guiding principles. Both this sections are reproduced below:

> *23. Matters to be considered in determining compensation.* (1) In determining the amount of compensation to be awarded for land acquired under this Act, the court shall take into consideration—
>
> *first,* the market value of the land at the date of the publication of the notification under section 4, sub-section (1);
>
> *secondly,* the damage sustained by the person interested, by reason of the taking of any standing crops or trees which may be on the land at the time of the Collector's taking possession thereof;
>
> *thirdly,* the damage (if any) sustained by the person interested, at the time of the Collector's taking possession of the land, by reason of severing such land from his other land;
>
> *fourthly,* the damage (if any) sustained by the person interested, at the time of the Collector's taking possession of the land, by reason of the acquisition injuriously affecting his other property, movable or immovable, in any other manner, or his earnings;
>
> *fifthly,* if, in consequence of the acquisition of the land by the Collector, the person interested is compelled to

6 AIR 1984 NOC 271 (AP); 1984(1) Andh LT 108.

change his residence or place of business, the reasonable expenses (if any) incidental to such change; and

sixthly, the damage (if any) *bona fide* resulting from diminution of the profits of the land between the time of the publication of the declaration under section 6 and the time of the Collector's taking possession of the land.

(1A) In addition to the market value of the land, as above provided, the court shall in every case award an amount calculated at the rate of twelve per centum per annum on such market value for the period commencing on and from the date of publication of the notification under section 4, sub-section (1), in respect of such land to the date of the award of the Collector or the date of taking possession of the land, whichever is earlier.

Explanation.—In computing the period referred to in this sub-section, any period or periods during which the proceedings for the acquisition of the land were held up on account of any stay or injunction by the order of any court shall be excluded.

(2) In addition to the market value of the land, as above provided, the court shall in every case award a sum of thirty per centum on such market value, in consideration of the compulsory nature of the acquisition.

24. *Matters to be neglected in determining compensation.* But the court shall not take into consideration—

first, the degree of urgency which has led to the acquisition;

secondly, any disinclination of the person interested to part with the land acquired;

thirdly, any damage sustained by him which, if caused by a private person, would not render such person liable to a suit;

fourthly, any damage which is likely to be caused to the land acquired, after the date of the publication of the declaration under section 6, by or in consequence of the use to which it will be put;

fifthly, any increase to the value of the land acquired likely to accrue from the use to which it will be put when acquired;

sixthly, any increase to the value of the other land of the person interested likely to accrue from the use to which the land acquired will be put;

seventhly, any outlay or improvements on, or disposal of, the land acquired, commenced, made or effected without the sanction of the Collector after the date of the publication of the notification under section 4, sub-section (1); or

eighthly, any increase to the value of the land on account of its being put to any use which is forbidden by law or opposed to public policy.

The above ss. 23 & 24 of the Land Acquisition Act 1894 are replaced by ss. 28 and 69 of the Right to Fair Compensation and Transparency in Land Acquisition, Rehabilitation and Resettlement Act 2013 which are reproduced below:

28. *Parameters to be considered by Collector in determination of award.* In determining the amount of compensation to be awarded for land acquired under this Act, the Collector shall take into consideration—

firstly, the market value as determined under section 26 and the award amount in accordance with the First and Second Schedules;

secondly, the damage sustained by the person interested, by reason of the taking of any standing crops and trees which may be on the land at the time of the Collector's taking possession thereof;

thirdly, the damage (if any) sustained by the person interested, at the time of the Collector's taking possession of the land, by reason of severing such land from his other land;

fourthly, the damage (if any) sustained by the person interested, at the time of the Collector's taking possession of the land, by reason of the acquisition injuriously affecting his other property, movable or immovable, in any other manner, or his earnings;

fifthly, in consequence of the acquisition of the land by the Collector, the person interested is compelled to change his residence or place of business, the reasonable expenses (if any) incidental to such change;

sixthly, the damage (if any) *bona fide* resulting from diminution of the profits of the land between the time of the publication of the declaration under section 19 and the time of the Collector's taking possession of the land; and

seventhly, any other ground which may be in the interest of equity, justice and beneficial to the affected families.

69. *Determination of award by Authority.* (1) In determining the amount of compensation to be awarded for land acquired including the Rehabilitation and Resettlement entitlements, the Authority shall take into consideration whether the Collector has followed the parameters set out under section 26 to section 30 and the provisions under Chapter V of this Act.

(2) In addition to the market value of the land, as above provided, the Authority shall in every case award an amount calculated at the rate of twelve per cent per annum on such market value for the period commencing on and from the date of the publication of the preliminary notification under section 11 in respect of such land to the date of the award of the Collector or the date of taking possession of the land, whichever is earlier.

Explanation. In computing the period referred to in this sub-section, any period or periods during which the proceedings for the acquisition of the land were held up on account of any stay or injunction by the order of any Court shall be excluded.

(3) In addition to the market value of the land as above provided, the Authority shall in every case award a solatium of one hundred per cent over the total compensation amount.

Matters to be considered to determine compensation

Section 23 of the Land Acquisition Act 1894 now s. 28 of the new Act enumerates the matters to be taken into consideration for determining the amount of compensation whereas s. 24 thereof gives what shall not be considered for purpose. Section 23 (now s. 28) is not exhaustive as it does not prohibit other matters from being considered in special cases.[7]

Compensation has to be fixed as per market value on the date of s. 4 notification of the L.A. Act 1894,[8] and s. 28 of the new Act of 2013.

Factors to be taken into account indetermining compensation—

(*a*) Market value of the land at the date of publication of notification.

(*b*) Damage for severance of other lands.

7 *Government of Bombay* v *Century Spinning and Manufacturing Co.* AIR 1942 Bom 105; 200 IC 161; 44 Bom LR 57.

8 *Tehmina* v *M.R. Mistry* (1982)3 SCC 382.

(*c*) Injurious affection of other property in any other manner or his earnings.
(*d*) Expenses incurred for change of residence or place of business as a result of acquisition.
(*e*) Damage to standing crops or trees.
(*f*) *Bona fide* damages caused from diminution of profits of land from the date of declaration under section 6 and taking possession.
(*g*) Any other ground which may be in the interest of equity, justice and beneficial to the affected families.

In addition interest at 12% p.a. on market value from the date of notification to the date of award or taking possession whichever is earlier and *solatium* (as prescribed) of the market value.

Issues specific to compulsory acquisition on valuation matters

We have discussed elaborately in earlier chapters the cases under the Law of Acquisition of Land that throw light on the methods of valuation applicable in different situations. The aspect of determination of market value or potential value of real estate has been covered at length in the appropriate chapter on them. In this present topic, we shall look into certain matters that contain issues specific to land acquisition.

The compensation is to cover all loss to the owner apart from the question of the value of his property 'taken'. It can readily be understood that 'taking' of a certain portion of a man's lands may easily result in injury to his remaining lands. It has been held that the owner is entitled to be compensated for injury caused by the construction of the undertaking contemplated, as well as that caused by the 'working' for it has been held that the reason for the acquisition is to be considered in arriving at the damage likely to be caused. 'Severance' is another item. It is perfectly apparent that if a strip of land is taken, say for the purpose of a Railways, or a sewer, or a hydraulic pipeline, or any similar purpose that lands on either side in the same ownership at the land being acquired, might be, and in fact generally are reduced in value, due to this 'severance' from each other. This would properly form a claim for damages.

In the case of business premises there may be considerable disturbance of trade, or even the complete extinguishment of the business. This will be a subject for compensation.

In England under the Land Clauses Act all persons who are deprived of any interest in land to be purchased or taken or whose land or interest therein is injuriously affected by the execution of works by the undertakers are entitled to receive compensation for such loss as they may sustain. If a notice to treat for the purchase of the land is served, the moment of the service fixes the time when the interests of the various parties so served are to be determined for the purposes of compensation. Interests created after the service of the notice to treat, out of the interest in the land in respect of the purchase of which the notice was served, are not a subject of compensation, but a person having an interest may part with it, and the assignee or grantee then stands in his place as regards the right to compensation. Notices of intention to take land as distinguished from notices to treat are required to be given by some special Acts, and these in the absence of special provisions, have the same effect as notices to treat.[9] Land was compulsorily purchased (acquired) for a new trunk road including a small quantity from the grounds of the claimant's house. As per section 44 of the Land Compensation Act 1973 (U.K.), where land is acquired or taken from any person for the purpose of works which are to be situated partly on that land and partly elsewhere, compensation for "injurious affection" of land retained by that person shall be assessed by reference to the whole of the works and not only the part situated on the land acquired or taken from him. The claimant's loss of amenity by reason of noise, light and other injurious affection caused by traffic using new trunk road was not compensatable regardless of the depreciation in value caused to his house, in so far as the trouble arose on land *not* taken from him. Yet in so far it arose on land taken from him comprising a small fraction of land not easily identifiable, and not in the least meaningful after the road was built was compensatable.[10]

9 Halsbury's *Laws of England*, 3rd Ed., vol 10, para 7, p. 8.

10 *Edwards* v *Minister of Transport* [1964]2 QB 134.

The consideration of injurious affection finds inclusion in the fourth item of s. 23(1) of the Land Acquisition Act 1894 and fourth item of s. 28 of the Right to Fair Compensation and Transparency in Land Acquisition, Rehabilitation and Resettlement Act 2013. The Courts in India have given due weightage to this aspect. As decided in the case of *Jaspal Singh* v *Union of India*[11] for the purpose of calculating damages under clause "fourthly" under s. 23(1) (now s. 28 of the new Act) as a consequence of acquisition, if any damage is sustained by the claimant or interested person at the time of Collector's taking possession of the land injuriously affecting the other property, movable or immovable, in any other manner or his earnings from the property, the Collector is required to determine the compensation as is available on the date when the compensation is awarded. The mere fact that after the acquisition, the claimant or interested person has quickly rehabilitated himself or set up business once over, or could not start his business lately would not be a ground to increase the compensation for the loss of business as a component of determination of the compensation on "loss of profit".

Although there is no mention of *"reinstatement"* in s. 23(1) (now s. 28 of the new Act), the court in India have recognised this principle. In the case land was acquired for sewage depot which affected the use of the remaining unacquired land. The court awarded fifteen per cent solatium. In this case the person affected is not the party whose land is acquired. Indian law is slightly different and this position is not covered by any authority as decided in *G.K. Chowdhury* v *Secy. of State.*[12]

Injurious affection

You are the owner of a vacant parcel, zoned for apartments and of proper dimensions to acquire a building permit, and a portion is taken for a road expansion. The residual is not capable of receiving a building permit, as the new, smaller size does not conform to the minimum required under the zoning by-law. The value of the residual is not only reduced by the size of the portion taken, but is severely reduced by

11 (1997)2 SCC 640.
12 18 CLJ 244.

this change in use potential. This is a case of injurious affection and compensation is payable for the total value lost.

You are the owner of the above parcel, but in this situation, the residual can still be awarded a building permit and the taking is for an elevated approach to a major bridge. The three floors of any building would face a concrete wall and all views of the river are blocked. It is evident that the residual value is greatly diminished and compensation is payable.

It is not unusual for the first example to be called severance damage and the second to be referred to as injurious affection.

The valuation of the loss is often done on a before-and-after basis where the value of the original property is calculated as 'the before-value', the value of the land remaining in the owner's hands is calculated as 'the after-value' and the subtraction of the after-value from the before-value is said to quantify the amount of compensation payable.

A railway company blocked off an existing public road and diverted it round to a new bridge that they built, all being within the proper exercise of their statutory powers. The claimant's land lay on a portion of the old road now converted into a *cul-de-sac*. He succeeded in claiming for the depreciation caused to his land thereby.[13]

Compensation is payable to the claimant whose land was injuriously affected due to depreciation caused by the use of public works rather than construction by reason of what was done by the acquiring authority on land not taken from him such as mischief depreciating their land comprised an interference with some other right existing over the land taken. In a general way it tends to be construction works which disrupt servitudes and misuse of property which causes the more direct types of private nuisance.

When fumes from the defendant's premises damaged the plaintiff's property that was interference that affected the plaintiff's land directly likely to arise from the use of the defendant's land rather than works of construction upon it.[14]

13 *Chamberlain* v *West End of London and Crystal Palace Rly. Co.* [1863]2 B & S 617.

14 *Halsey* v *Esso Ltd.* [1961]2 All ER 145; [1961]1 WLR 683.

Acquisition of frontage certainly affects the potential use of the remaining land. The guidelines laid down for determining the quantum of damages for injurious affection are as follows:

(1) The question of injurious affection depends much upon the nature and shape of the remaining land and the possible use to which it can be put after acquisition as compared to its previous use.

(2) In case of a large area with frontage at different directions, a partial or total acquisition of frontage on one side may not result in injurious affection to the remaining land and the enhanced route of the acquired frontage would be sufficient to cover the damage. But if the unacquired portion is totally locked on all sides the unacquired portion has to be separately assessed. So, damages caused to the remaining portion are covered by the enhanced market rate of the frontage is not correct in all cases.

(3) If the whole area of the estate consists of several survey numbers are so compact to constitute a unity of estate and the loss of the frontage adversely affects the value of remaining compact portion, then damages should be calculated with reference to the whole estate. If only a portion of the estate is affected, then damages should be assessed with reference to the portion so affected. What is relevant in such cases is the "unity of the estate" and not ownership of a single person.

"Unity of estate" means compactness of the parcel of land and also the topographical and developmental interdependence of each of the component parts.

(4) It is better to evaluate the whole area at the depreciated rate. The difference between the value before depreciation and after depreciation would represent the damage caused by severance.

(5) The damages caused by loss of the frontage can be assessed at 5% of the market value unless in exceptional circumstances.[15]

Injurious affection is anticipated depreciation in value of land on compulsory acquisition of a particular land and which

15 *Udayan Girijaprasad* v *Spl. LAO, Ahmedabad* (1976)17 GLR 668.

will give a right to compensation in case the land affected is held with land taken. But it should be attributable to some act authorised by statutory authority of the acquiring body and not on unauthorised action of the body in which case there can be no right to compensation. In such cases, the owner can seek his remedy by a suit for damages or injunction as decided in *Imperial Gas Light & Coke Co.* v *Broad-beat.*[16]

Where only part of an owner's property is acquired he is entitled to compensation not only for the loss of the part taken but also for severance and other injury which may result to his other land and for all other losses he may suffer depreciation in value by reason of the fact that that can no longer be occupied and enjoyed as one compact holding due to separation. The method adopted in awarding compensation in such cases is to value unacquired portions at it stood before or after the acquisition and to award the depreciation in value as compensation for severance and injurious affection[17]

The following rules must be applied to test the validity of a claim for injurious affection by an owner on part of whose land has been taken.

(*a*) The injury or damage or loss must result from some act made in exercise of statutory powers of the acquiring authority.

(*b*) The injury must be such as would have been actionable but for statutory powers.

(*c*) The injury must be to land and not merely to a personal injury to trade.

(*d*) The injury must arise from the execution of works and not from user.

Lands injury are not held with lands taken if they are not otherwise connected by being held under the same title.[18]

Concept of 'injurious affection' as a generic term

'Injurious affection' is a generic term. It means the damage (if any) sustained by the person interested, at the time of the

16 (1859)7 HCL 600.

17 *State of Kerala* v *Krishna Udayan* 1984 Ker LT 617.

18 *Holditch* v *Canadian Northern Ontario Railway* [1916]1 AC 536.

Collector's taking possession of the land, by reason of the acquisition injuriously affecting his other property, movable or immovable, in any other manner, or his earnings. The injury may arise in any of the following manner:

(1) injurious affection when other lands of the owner acquired;
(2) injurious affection when no land of the person interested is acquired;
(3) infringement of privacy;
(4) loss of earnings or profits from trade;
(5) diminution in value of goodwill;
(6) prospective and retrospective damages;
(7) remote damages to person not interested;
(8) depreciation in value.

In *Hiralal* v *State of U.P.*,[1] in determining the amount to compensation to be awarded for the land acquired the court took into consideration various factors. In the first place, it took into consideration the market value of the land at the date of publication of the notice. In the second place, it had to take into consideration the damages if any, sustained by the person interested by reason of standing crop or trees which may be on the land at the time of taking of possession by the Collector. In the third place, damages, if any, sustained by the person interested by reason of severing such land from his other land. In the fourth place, damages, if any sustained by reason of acquisition affecting his other property movable or immovable in any other manner or his earnings. In the fifth place by taking into consideration consequences of the person interested being compelled to change his residence or place of business, the reasonable expenses and incidental to such change being incurred by him. In the sixth place, damages, if any, *bona fide* resulting from diminution of profit of the land between the time of publication of the declaration and the time of Collector's taking possession of the land and in the seventh place any other ground which may be in the interest of equity, justice and beneficial to the affected families. The

1 AIR 1994 NOC 147 (All).

method of calculating the amount of determination by capitalising net profits and the fair market value not exceeding twenty times is not at all recognised by the Act. The method of capitalising the actual or immediately prospective profits or the rent of a number of years' purchase should not be resorted to if there is evidence of comparable sales or other evidence of computation of the market value.

Damage claimed for injurious affection must have been sustained at the time of Collector's taking possession. The owner should be paid compensation for the value of the land acquired and also compensation for the injury caused to his other land not acquired. For construction of an overhead bridge over the acquired land, the owner lost his ferry income across the river, the injury to ferry income is compensable.[2]

Where the claimant's access to his land is injuriously affected by the lowering of the two roads constructed on the acquired land, compensation is payable to the claimant.[3]

The claimant owned certain land whereon he had a tubewell for irrigating his remaining land on the other side of the road. While the land in which there was the tubewell was not acquired, most of the land on the other side of the road was acquired resulting in the tubewell sunk being useless. So, the claimant was allowed enhanced compensation for the severance.[4]

RULE 1. Cost incurred in erecting a wall to give privacy against the gaze of passengers in trains on the railway for which the acquisition was made was allowed by court.[5]

RULE 2. Compensation is payable for injurious affection if an actionable nuisance caused by the construction of a sewage depot injuriously affects other lands of the owner.[6]

2 *Collector of Dinajpore* v *Girijanath Roy* ILR 25 Cal 346.

3 *M.E. Moola* v *Collector of Rangoon* AIR 1927 Rang 29; 68 IC 461.

4 *Radhey Shyam Gupta* v *State of Haryana* AIR 1982 P&H 57; (1982)84 PLR 743.

5 *Prasanna Kumar Dutta* v *Secretary of State* AIR 1934 Cal 525; ILR 61 Cal 254.

6 *Gurudas Kundu Chowdhury* v *Secretary of State* 22 IC 354; (1900)18 CLJ 244.

RULE 3. Whereby the acquisition of certain portion of the land the remaining land has been truncated into two small areas depriving one piece of the facility of access to the public road and practically rendering the other piece useless and of no utility to the claimant having no point of contact with the fire block, the claimant will be entitled to some amount of compensation on account of loss by severance.[7]

RULE 4. Actionable nuisance such as a railway so near to a Cotton Mill as to expose it to risk of fire and an additional burden for insurance or a sewage farm so situate as by smell and feeling actually to affect the standard of comfort or enjoyment and therefore the selling value of the land. User is otherwise actionable doing physical injury.[8]

"Injurious affection" resulting in damages to the owner's other properties are factors to be considered.[9]

The method adopted in awarding severance compensation is to value the unacquired portion of the owner's land as it stood before or after the acquisition and to award the depreciation in value as compensation for severance and injurious affection.[10]

Damages caused by severance to the land left out by injurious affection is the difference between the market value before the injury and the market value after injury.[11] The owner should be paid compensation for the injury caused to his other land not acquired.[12]

7 *Lal Seheb Nabin Chandra Bhani Deo* v *State of Orissa* AIR 1975 Ori 125.

8 *Secretary of State* v *Mohammad Ismail Khan* AIR 1927 All 246; ILR 49 All 353.

9 *Hooghly Mills Co.* v *Secretary of State* 8 IC 800; 12 CLJ 489.

10 *State of Kerala* v *Krishna Udayar* 1984 Ker LT 671.

11 *Special L.A.O., Mangalore* v *Piadale Fernandez* AIR 1977 Kant 28.

12 *Collector of Dinajpore* v *Girijanath Roy* ILR 25 Cal 346; *Rajeshwari Poddar (Smt.)* v *Sub-Collector, Berhampore* AIR 1964 Ori 12; *State of Bihar* v *Rameshwar Singh* AIR 1973 Pat 123.

When plea of injurious affection is not available

The claimant was held not injuriously affected for the lands retained and did not suffer damage as he was not required to spend any money for construction of boundary walls, culverts, bridges or roads.[13]

In the case, acquisition of land is only from one side and it cannot be said that the land left out is of such a nature that it cannot be utilised for any purpose. There is no division of lands comprised in the rest of the survey numbers. There is no data on record to find out the actual measurement of the pieces of land, but damages were granted at the rate of 2% of the market rate. There is no evidence on record justifying any additional award under the head of damages because of severance of the land.[14]

The defendant was going to construct an oil refinery after acquiring land adjoining houses of the plaintiff and the houses were dwarfed by the refinery. The plaintiff sued in nuisance and negligence seeking injunctions to restrain the refinery company which depreciated their houses by fumes, vibrations, noise, flames and fears of explosion. It was held that the defendants were not at fault, but must exercise powers without negligence, meaning reasonable regard for the interests of others. The absence of compensation clauses in the Act was intended not to interfere with private rights. Despite proof of nuisance, the plaintiff were denied legal redress.[15]

Severance

Severance is depreciation of land by virtue of its own inadequacy after being cut off from other land previously held by the owner. Thus severance is one kind of 'injurious affection'. Though closely related with each other, it is usual to regard the two terms as different. Injurious affection is a generic concept while severance is a leading species.

13 *Periyar and Pareekanni Rubbers Ltd.* v *State of Kerala* AIR 1990 SC 2192: (1991)4 SCC 195.

14 *Bhikhubhai Kedarbhai Patel* v *Deputy Collector, Modasa* AIR 1996 Guj 16.

15 *Allen* v *Gulf Oil Refining Co.* [1981] AC 101; [1981]1 All ER 353.

Severance compensation which is the subject-matter of clause thirdly of s. 23(1) of the Land Acquisition Act (now clause thirdly of s. 28 of the new Act of 2013) has a special significance. It is such severance which in the eye of law could be said to have damnified by reason of a compulsory acquisition that could be the subject-matter of the claim. In every such case damage has to be proved by acceptable evidence. Conspicuous evidence is necessary for a court to accept such a claim for severance compensation.[16]

When a portion of the land is acquired out of a large tract of land and a large portion of the land is left out there would be a diminution in the value of the land that is left out for which some compensation has to be allowed. The 5% allowed by the Judicial Commission is reasonable.[17]

The measure of damage by severance is the diminution in the value of the unacquired land. When a portion of a house is acquired rendering the rest of it useless, compensation is payable for the entire holding.[18]

Where due to acquisition, the unacquired area became completely inaccessible and a total loss, the diminution in value is 50% of the market value of the unacquired land by way of damages in addition to compensation of market value of acquired land.[19]

Where in consequence of acquisition the whole area and the street have greatly been improved, no compensation for severance can be claimed.[20] In estimating the damage for severance the actual and prospective use of the land must be considered.[1]

Where severance due to construction of a new railway line separated the residence of the manager of the company and the building and office from the garden and further compelled

16 *Binny Ltd.* v *L.A.O., Madras* (1978)2 MLJ 13; 91 LW 257.

17 *Tribeni Devi* v *Collector of Ranchi* AIR 1972 SC 1417; (1972)1 SCC 480; (1972)3 SCR 208.

18 *Saratchandra Bose* v *Secretary of State* 10 CWN 250.

19 *Narinder Kaur* v *State of Punjab* (1980)82 PLR 473.

20 *Karachi Municipality* v *Khatun Mal Hira Nand* 27 IC 326; 8 SLR 126.

1 *Secretary of State* v *F.E. Dinshaw* AIR 1933 Sind 21.

the coolies employed on either side to cross the line, the compensation has to include the market value of the land, the amount of standing charges, the increased cost of working the garden in consequence of severance of the garden as also the statutory allowance of 15%.[2]

A road constructed on the acquired land has split up the land of the claimant in two awkward small parts rendering them unsaleable. The court can determine the extent of injurious affection to evaluate just compensation without any expert opinion.[3]

Loss of earnings

Loss of earnings to be an injurious affection must be one in trade or other service carried on by the owner in the premises acquired. Where a coffee house is acquired where the practitioners in court frequently visited, the loss in income of that trade should also be added to the value of the land.[4]

Compensation for loss of the business or of the factory income is not the same thing as the compensation for the land and fixture of machineries. Income from business or factory is also the profit of labour, skill etc. Such loss of earnings does not come under the clause first of s. 23(1) (now clause first of s. 28 of the new Act of 2013) which compensates only the land, machinery etc., but would fall under the clause fourthly of the section.[5]

For the determination of compensation for loss of business on account of acquisition of poultry farm it was held that as the claimant remained in illegal possession and carried on his business, he did not suffer any loss. The court should take into account the damages, if any, sustained by the person interested at the time of the Collector's taking possession of the land for loss of his earnings which is the compensation for the loss of business as on the date of taking possession. So, the claimant is not entitled to get compensation for loss of

2 *Baraoora Tea Co.* v *Secretary of State* ILR 28 Cal 685.
3 *Amirbibi* v *Special L.A.O.* AIR 1981 Guj 219.
4 *Venkatachariar* v *Divisional Officer, Tinevelly* 1912 MWN 460; 14 IC 625.
5 *State of West Bengal* v *T.N. Gupta* AIR 1959 Cal 65.

business and the High Court erred in directing payment of compensation for one year @ Re. 1 per month per bird for 12,000 birds. However, since this amount was not questioned by the State, findings of the High Court was not disturbed.[6]

In acquisition of land there is no deprivation of right to livelihood in view of the provisions for payment of compensations solatium and interest, under the Land Acquisition Act now the Right to Fair Compensation and Transparency in Land Acquisition, Rehabilitation and Resettlement Act 2013.[7]

The case of a person interested in land such as a tenant may also be injuriously affected by reason of the acquisition of the land. The time which an oustee businessman may take in re-establishing his business depends upon a variety of circumstances which cannot be easily foreseen and a rough and ready measure has more often than not to be adopted for the determination of the amount of compensation. In the normal case the ends of justice will be amply met if six months income is awarded as compensation.[8]

A claimant who abandoned his business perforce as his site of business being acquired by the Government and restarted it at another place, was entitled to compensation on account of loss of earnings. In the case, he was allowed compensation for the loss of approach road to the kiln site constructed by him due to its becoming useless in consequence of the acquisition.[9]

A poultry farm will require at least one year to purchase or take on lease another suitable land, arrange for electricity, water, construction of necessary sheds, structures, godowns etc. The compensation has to be granted for loss of earnings for the period taken to restart the poultry business and receive income from the stock. It is held that the claimants are entitled to compensation equivalent to income for one year at the rate

6 *Ramesh Dutta* v *State of Punjab* (1996)10 SCC 160; AIR 1996 SC 2831.
7 *Chameli Singh* v *State of U.P.* AIR 1996 SC 1051.
8 *Collector of Bilaspur* v *Hans Raj* AIR 1961 P&H 25.
9 *Raghbir Singh* v *Union of India* AIR 1974 P&H 321.

of a rupee per bird per month. As the compensation for loss of earnings is also part of compensation, he is entitled to *solatium* and interest at the prescribed rate till the realisation of the enhanced compensation.[10] In another case, it was held that compensation cannot be awarded for loss of business caused by acquisition of shop.[11]

Where loss of business is caused by acquisition additional compensation in the form of six months income from business may be properly awarded. In the case compensation for the acquired huts and houses was also enhanced.[12]

If a person earns money by dint of his personal labour and skill that money is regarded as his earnings. But if he engages others to assist him then that expenditure is deducted to arrive at his gross income to ascertain his earnings. The word "earnings" has not been defined in the Act. It has been held that in assessing the amount of compensation for loss of the earnings of a businessman ousted from the business premises as a result of acquisition of the same, no deduction should be made on account of the assumed daily wages of the claimant. It has also been held in the case that he will be sufficiently compensated if he is awarded six months' income.[13]

Loss of goodwill

The goodwill which attaches to a particular house increases the value of that house. But there may be other kinds of goodwill attached to personal reputation, a thing personal to the man whose skill and whose name have acquired that goodwill. Any kind of goodwill which a compulsory purchase (acquisition) of commercial premises reduces or destroys will normally be the subject of disturbance compensation; yet if it pertains to the property rather than to the person, the loss may be attributable not to the dispossessed occupier but to a mortgagee or landlord or some other party entitled to a capital interest in the property. But in most cases the goodwill is

10 *Savitri Devi (Smt.)* v *State of Haryana* (1984)86 Punj LR 47; (1984)1 Land LR 245 (DB).
11 *State of M.P.* v *Abdul Karim* 1982 MPLJ 19.
12 *Ridhan Sao* alias *Ridhan Prasad* v *State of Bihar* 1970 BLJR 1248.
13 *Collector, Bilaspur* v *Janki Devi* AIR 1961 HP 42.

probably the occupier's alone and does not 'attach to' the property.[14]

Diminution of profit

The clause fourthly of s. 23(1) contemplates those cases in which on account of declaration of acquisition, there is diminution in the profits, e.g. in case of agricultural land when there is no cultivation and in case of building and tenanted lands when there is a falling off of tenants. Ordinarily no compensation is payable on account of delay between the date of the notification and the actual acquisition of land but when damage is actually sustained by reason of such delay, it should be awarded.[15]

Loss of profits is a proper item of compensation; but it must consist of profits which would have been made in the existing course of business. Future profits from a business operation not yet started are a different matter, so that if for example compulsory acquisition of land prevents it from being used for a prospective purpose the loss of profits expected to have accrued from the carrying out of that purpose is not a proper item of compensation for disturbance.[16]

Reinstatement

When the land was used for some particular purpose not of commercial nature, such as a public park, it is very difficult to estimate the loss. One method adopted is known as reinstatement, by which is meant that the amount of compensation to be awarded shall be assessed according to the cost of acquiring an equally convenient site and erecting an equally convenient premises. Thus, the cost of construction of water supply culverts was included on principle of reinstatement.[17]

Government acquired a piece of land for public purpose over which there was a municipal drain for discharge of water from the locality into the river. The land was valued by the court at the same rate as the adjoining land as the drain was

14 *Cooper* v *Metropolitan Board of Works* [1883]25 Ch D 472.
15 *Johnston* v *Secretary of State* 60 PR 191.
16 *Watson* v *Secretary of State* [1954]3 All ER 582; [1954]1 WLR 1477.
17 *Province of West Bengal* v *Raja of Jhargram* AIR 1955 Cal 392.

a shallow one. The Municipality claimed that two culverts over a new drain would have to be constructed in place of the drain acquired which was an important outfall and the costs of the construction of such culverts should be included within the compensation and the valuation of land made earlier being inadequate the compensation should be redetermined by taking the aid of the principle of reinstatement.[18]

Where a piece of land over which there was a municipal drain was acquired by the Government and compensation was paid at the rate of the value of the adjoining land. The municipality claimed a larger amount on the ground of expenditure in constructing a diversion drain. It was held, allowing the claim of the municipality, that the compensation awarded was inadequate in view of the principle of reinstatement, which is that an owner cannot be placed in a favourable position as he was in before the exercise of compulsory powers unless such a sum is assessed as will enable him to replace the premises lands taken, by premises or land which would be to him of the same value.[19]

> "There are some cases in which the income derived or probably to be derived from land would not constitute a fair basis in assessing the value to the owner and then the Principle of Reinstatement should be applied. This principle is that the owner cannot be placed in as favourable a position as he was in before the exercise of compulsory powers, unless such a sum is assessed as will enable him to replace the premises or lands which would be to him of the same value. It is not possible to give an exhaustive catalogue of all cases to which the Principle of Reinstatement is applicable. But we may instance clinics, hospitals, houses of exceptional character and business premises in which the business can only be carried on under special conditions or by means of special licences."[20]

It has been decided in the case of *State of Gujarat* v *Vakhatsinghji Vajesinghji Vaghela*[1] that awards have been given on the basis of reinstatement value which is assessed

18 *Chairman, Serampore Municipality* v *Secretary of State* AIR 1922 Cal 386.

19 *Baroda Prasad Dey* v *Secretary of State* 25 CWN 677; ILR 40 Cal 83.

20 *Compulsory Acquisition of Land,* 11th Ed., p. 696—Cripps Treatise.

1 AIR 1968 SC 1481.

according to the cost of acquiring an equally convenient land. For the purpose of the case, it is sufficient to say that this method should not be adopted where the market value deduced from the income derived from the lands would fairly compensate the owner and in no case reinstatement value be given unless reinstatement in some other place is *bona fide* intended. The High Court rejected the reinstatement method and adopted rightly the yield basis of valuation as the value of irrigation, bunds, tanks and wells are not what they cost but what they paid in annual income.

The doctrine of reinstatement value cannot be applied in determining the market value under s. 23(1) of the Land Acquisition Act 1894 and now s. 28 of the Right to Fair Compensation and Transparency in Land Acquisition, Rehabilitation and Resettlement Act 2013. There will always be a gap between the date of notification and the date of payment. To recompensate the loss, payment of interest under s. 28 (now s. 72 of the new Act of 2013), *solatium* under s. 23(2) (now s. 69(3) of the new Act of 2013) in appropriate cases after the Amendment Act 68 of 1984 has come into force, 12% p.a. of the additional amount under s. 23(1A) (s. 30(3) of the new Act of 2013) is provided for. It would, therefore, be illogical and unrealistic to apply the doctrine of reinstatement value in determination of the compensation under s. 23(1) of the Act of 1894.[2]

Depreciation compensation

Whereby the construction of works, there is a physical interference with any right, public or private, which the owners or occupiers of property are by law entitled to make use of in connection with such property apart from the use to which any particular owner or occupier might put it, there is a title to compensation if by reason of such interference, the property as a property is lessened in value. The injury must be actual injury to the land itself as by loosening the foundations of the building on it, obstructing its light, or its drains, making it inaccessible by lowering or raising the grounds immediately in front of it or by some such physical deterioration.[3]

2 *K. Posayya* v *Special Tehsildar* AIR 1995 SC 1641.

3 *Metropolitan Board of Works* v *McCarthy* [1874] LR 7 HL 243.

Depreciation depends upon and is deducted from factors such as the cost of the construction; the expected life-span, its salvage-value realisable at the end of the period of utility etc. Rate of depreciation is generally the prime cost less salvage-value divided by life-span.[4]

The claimants, a registered housing association, owned two blocks of flats with eight flats in each, which provided sheltered housing accommodation for elderly and disabled people and thus restricted to this use under planning permission. The claimants claimed compensation of £10,300 under the Land Compensation Act 1973, Part I (English Law) on the ground that their freehold reversionary interest in the property had been *depreciated* as a result of the physical factors of traffic noise from a newly opened bypass nearby. *Held* that the subject property was affected by noise from the bypass and had benefited, although to a lesser extent as it is now situated in a *cul-de-sac,* i.e. half. At the date of claim, the property was subject to fifteen secure tenancies whose rents did not show any depreciation effect from the bypass and that there were restrictions on the use of the flats and the claimants had limited interest (only reversionary interest) and thus limited power of disposal. Although the Lands Tribunal went on to concede that the value of sheltered housing or flats could be depreciated by traffic noise. The claim for compensation for depreciation caused by the use of public works was rejected.[5]

Calculations of damage are to be made on a "before and after" basis, i.e. the true depreciation is quantified by deducting the value of the remainder of the property, after severance and injurious affection, from its value before.

Depreciation in the value of land on account of acquisition causing severance of the acquired portion from the remaining portion is injury as per s. 23(1), clause fourthly which is corresponds to clause fourthly of s. 28 of the Right to Fair Compensation and Transparency in Land Acquisition, Rehabilitation and Resettlement Act 2013.[6] When an owner is

4 *Administrator General of West Bengal* v *Collector, Varanashi* AIR 1988 SC 943; (1988)2 SCC 150.

5 *Clwyd Alyn Housing Association* v *Wesh Office* [1996]71 P&CR 195.

6 *Rajeshwari Poddar (Smt.)* v *Sub-Collector, Berhampore* AIR 1964 Ori 12.

injuriously affected by the Railways acting in excess of its power but no land of the owner is acquired, he has no remedy under s. 23 of the Land Acquisition Act but the only remedy available to him is by suit.[7]

Loss of privacy as an actionable claim is a ground for compensation for injurious affection in India.[8]

In order to claim compensation for damages for injurious affection, the damage must have been sustained, whether on account of injurious affection of the other property or on account of loss of earnings at the time when the Collector took possession of the property acquired. The date relevant to the assessment under this clause is the date of the Collector taking possession of the property and not the date of publication of notification under s. 4 of the Act.[9]

Nowhere in the Right to Fair Compensation and Transparency in Land Acquisition, Rehabilitation and Resettlement Act 2013 or in the Land Acquisition Act 1894 or rules framed thereunder has any rule been laid down relating to the deduction on account of depreciation value on account of age of the building and also the amount required for repairs to keep the building in a fit condition. To arrive at the present value of the building, the proper course would be to find out the cost of constructing the building at the time of acquisition and deduct therefrom the depreciation value and repairing cost. In the process, the approximate number of years the building could be used with proper care and maintenance to be found out and then divide the total cost of maintenance by the number of years and deduct the quotient as depreciation for each year. In the case of first class building no depreciation is to be deducted for five years and then $^5/_6$% has to be deducted for every subsequent year. Due allowance has to be made for maintenance and repairs. In case of other class of buildings $^5/_6$% depreciation has to be deducted for each year.[10]

7 *Gurudas Kundu Chowdhury* v *Secretary of State* (1900)18 CLJ 244; 22 IC 354.

8 *Narain Chowdhury* v *Jadoo Nath Chowdhury* 5 CWN 1473; 11 WR 10.

9 *Ram Labhaya* v *State of Haryana* AIR 1984 P&H 427.

10 *Mytheen Kunju Abdulrehiman Kunju* v *State* AIR 1955 Trav-Co 110.

Disturbance compensation

If a person is compelled to change his residence or place of business by reason of the acquisition, reasonable transit expenses incidental to such change *viz.* transport charges incurred for the displacement and carrying the material due to displacement are required to be awarded, in addition to the compensation determined. But the mere fact that the claimant happened to secure alternative land at a far off place and that too said to be an insecure place, even if it is assumed to be so, cannot be a ground to contend that he is entitled to compensation under clause "fifthly" due to change of business and setting up of business in an insecure place. *Held,* it cannot be laid as a principle of law that loss of business till the claimant is resuscitated in his business in securing a place and the expenses incurred in that behalf also should always be a component of the determination of the compensation under s. 23(1) of the Land Acquisition Act 1894.[11]

Disturbance payments do not apply to agricultural land. If the farmer is a yearly tenant or a fixed-term leaseholder whose term has come to an end or will shortly do so, his security of tenure will not prevail against compulsory purchase (acquisition) but subsisting for compensation purposes when assessing the value of expropriated interests. A periodic tenancy is not terminated by notice to quit but is expropriated. In case of short-term tenant compensation comprises disturbance included in expropriation compensation. A tenant is entitled to a 'reorganisation of affairs' in addition to disturbance compensation. The acquiring authority has discretion to pay reasonable sums for 'removables and trade' loss to occupiers of farm. But disturbance compensation must not duplicate such items.

The claimants attempted to get 'disturbance compensation' to cover bank charges and loan interest (not a 'bridging loan') which they had incurred when building themselves a new factory. The claim was rejected, on the ground that such expenses are frequently incurred as part of the normal capital cost of obtaining a new asset: it is value for money.[12]

11 *Jaspal Singh* v *Union of India* (1997)2 SCC 640.

12 *Service Welding Ltd.* v *Tyne and Wear County Council* [1979]38 P&CR 352.

The cost of transferring to suitable new premises is precisely what 'equivalent reinstatement' is about. But the latter is almost always appropriate when the value of the land taken is practically restricted to a non-marketable, and thus usually a non-commercial, existing use; whereas adaptation is normally appropriate where the land taken has at the very least an appreciable market value in respect of an existing use which is commercial in nature. One form of disturbance that is incompatible with 'equivalent reinstatement' is the adaptation of new premises.[13]

The authority compulsorily purchased (acquired) the premises comprising the claimants' bottling department. The claimants put forward the cost of buying the new equipment less an estimated saving in operating costs. It was held in appeal that the purchase of a new and more expensive house was 'value for money', and thus not an item calling for 'disturbance compensation', seems *prima facie* to be relevant also to the purchase of new and more expensive bottling equipment, at any rate in regard to the capital cost as distinct from any loan charges incurred.[14]

Increased operating costs were put forward as a disturbance item. The Court of Appeal expressed the view that they may well be compensatable—but only if (*i*) they are incurred unavoidably, and (*ii*) no benefit is derived from them. The disturbance claim in regard to them failed in this case.[15]

The House of Lords held that an amount equivalent to any tax that would have been incurred must be deducted from the equivalent quantity of damages awarded in cases of compulsory purchase (acquisition) compensation.[16]

Business premises were compulsorily purchased (acquired) for the purpose of widening a bridge. A disturbance payment in respect of a temporary loss of profits was included in the

13 *Powner and Powner* v *Leeds Corporation* [1953]4 P&CR 167.

14 *Tamplins Brewery Ltd.* v *County Borough of Brighton* [1970]22 P&CR 746.

15 *Bibby (J) & Sons Ltd.* v *Merseyside County Council* [1980]39 P&CR 53.

16 *British Transport Commission* v *Gourley* [1955]3 All ER 796; [1956] AC 185.

compensation, which would have been subject to tax if actually earned. It was held that the estimated amount that would have been payable in tax ought to have been deducted from the compensation.[17] Removal costs included in the disturbance claim should be calculated with a deduction in respect of tax.[18]

In addition to actual market value of the house when sold with vacant possession, the freeholder is entitled to compensation for "disturbance" which is specifically preserved by s. 2(6) of the Act of 1919 and includes all damages directly consequent on the taking of the house under statutory powers. The freeholder gets compensation for having to move out her furniture and but in the new house. She gets compensation for having to alter the curtains and carpets and remake them to fit the new windows and floors. Take business premises where fixtures and fitting have to be removed or there is loss of business, through being turned out, or loss of goodwill. All that loss and expenses are the proper subjects of "compensation for disturbances" in addition to the open market value of the land.[19]

Compensation for disturbance is founded upon an expense or loss from being disturbed; this accrues of the trouble and expenses of new houses, transportation cost, loss of business and goodwill, stock depreciation, injury to fixtures, cost of temporary storage, fitting up in new premises, increase in rent, rates etc. and is limited to actual damage and cannot be too remote or speculative.[20]

Special circumstances

An old adage suggests "that you cannot jump until you find a place to stand". The place to stand may well be normal market value, for the owner is at least entitled to the amount that could be obtained in the open market for the interests held. To this may be added any special value in the hands of the owner

17 *West Suffolk County Council* v *W. Rought Ltd.* [1956]3 All ER 216; [1957] AC 403.

18 *Rosenberg & Son (Tinware) Ltd.* v *Manchester Corpn.* [1971]23 P&CR 68.

19 *Harvey* v *Crawley Development Corporation* [1957]1 All ER 504; [1957]1 QB 485.

20 *Roberts* v *Coventry Corporation* [1947]1 All ER 308.

in respect to a unique location for a special business pursuit, or because land or improvements have been tailored to a special use: certain rules or principles have been developed over the years:

(1) Value to owner does not include sentimental considerations as the prudent man is deemed to base his real property decisions upon pure business factors.

(2) It is the present value of future benefits that is to be valued.

(3) The owner is entitled to payment for any special value or characteristic of the land as it relates to him.

There may be circumstances besides those mentioned in first to fourthly clauses of s. 23(1) (now clauses first to fourthly of s. 28 of the Right to Fair Compensation and Transparency in Land Acquisition, Rehabilitation and Resettlement Act 2013 which may very well be taken into consideration in awarding compensation for the lands acquired. So, s. 23 is not exhaustive. It was held that though a claimant may not be entitled to compensation for the loss of earning of a prospective business on the site acquired under s. 23(1)(*first*) to (*fourthly*) of the Land Acquisition Act under the circumstances of the case, he was entitled to a compensation by way of a percentage return on the locked up capital over and above the value of the land and materials therein.[1]

Where the land to be valued possesses some unusual or unique feature as regards its position or its potentialities, the court determining the market value will have to ascertain as best as it can from the materials before it what a willing vendor might reasonably expect to obtain from a willing purchaser for the land in that particular position and with those potentialities. This was observed in the case of *Hit Karini Sabha* v *Jabbalpore Corporation*.[2]

It was held in the case of *Collector of Darrang* v *Phani Bhusan Bose*[3] that the owner is entitled to the value of the

1 *L.A.O.* v *Jamnabai* 47 Bom LR 893; *State of West Bengal* v *Arun Kumar Mitra* (1984)1 CLJ 220 (DB).
2 (1972)2 SCC 325.
3 AIR 1955 Assam 124 (DB).

property in its actual conditions at the time of expropriation notice with all its existing advantages and with all its future possibilities excluding such advantages as may arise on account of any scheme for the purpose of which the property is being acquired.

A person whose land has not been taken suffers damage for acquisition for construction of works of an adjoining part of the land under law and if his land thereby deteriorates in value or if any easement right appurtenant to the land is taken away by the authority, he should be paid reasonable compensation. If the authority substitutes a road for a waterway affecting the premises of the person having the waterway, that person can claim compensation whether the loss is a loss of easement, or prospect or privacy or any other amenity. In such case, the damage must arise from the execution of the works and not from their user or must arise from a physical interference with a public or private right incident to the affected land.[4]

As the acquired lands were very near to the city and possessed of potential value, compensation awarded by the Collector and confirmed by the High Court was enhanced by the Supreme Court. Claimants were held, entitled to solatium @ 15% and interest @ 6% under unamended ss. 23(2) and 28 of the Land Acquisition Act 1894 respectively.[5]

Though the acquired land was wasteland and situated in the outskirts of industrial city and possessed of potential value, courts below were right in taking into account the potential value of the land for determination of compensation. Sale instance in respect of land situated at a distance of 2 km. from the acquired land should be excluded. As the land possessed potential value *held* compensation should be @ ₹ 22 per sq. mtr. after deducting 1/3rd of the amount towards development charges and the claimants are also entitled to the statutory benefits on enhanced compensation.[6]

4 *Duke of Buccleuch* v *Metropolitan Board of Works* [1889]14 AC 153.

5 *Chintaman* v *State of Maharashtra* (1996)10 SCC 36; AIR 1997 SC 448.

6 *Gujarat Industrial Development Corporation* v *Narottambhai Morarbhai* (1996)11 SCC 159.

Claimants purchased agricultural land situated beyond municipal limits on uneven land near a moped factory but no sanction from Municipal Corporation or any competent authority was obtained by them to construct housing colony. The land was acquired for industrial purposes. The claimants did not produce their own sale deeds which would have furnished best material at the time of the determination of the market value. So, the land was to await sometime for development either for industrialisation or colonisation. They themselves had sold at Re. 0.50 per sq. ft. a small extent of land. *Held* as the lands were possessed of potential value, the compensation could be determined on the basis of the market value on square yards basis.[7]

In the case evidence on record shows that the acquired land is very close to railway station and is almost adjacent to highway. The land is very near to the river Ganga and, therefore, water is available in plenty all the year round. There is an Atomic Power Station situated just across the river Ganga. So, bulk of the power presumably, is available from the Power Station. The town with the railway station is the centre of chemical industries. All these facts show that the acquired land has potentiality for future development and this fact has to be kept in mind in determining market value.[8]

Sometimes it happens that the land to be valued possesses some unusual, unique features as regards it location and potentialities. When the Land Acquisition Officer does not take into account the potential value of the land acquired and values the land on the basis that it is an agricultural land, such award is nothing but arbitrary.[9]

(B) INSURANCE

Insurance is considered as a social device whereby a large group of individuals or an organisation through a system of equitable contributions called premium may reduce or eliminate certain measurable risks of economic loss.

7 *State of M.P.* v *Hari Shankar Goel* (1997)2 SCC 487.

8 *Tata Chemicals (Ltd.) Bombay* v *Sadhu Singh S/o Baljeet* AIR 1994 All 66.

9 *Saraswathi* v *Assistant Commissioner* AIR 1976 Kant 124.

It is a means of providing protection against financial loss in a great variety of situations. For example, life insurance helps replace income loss to a family if the wage earner dies. Health insurance helps pay medical bills. Fire insurance pays all or part of the damage if the house is destroyed by fire. Car insurance helps cover the cost of damages caused by accidents including the victim. Similarly unusual types of financial losses are covered in various countries through insurance. For example athletes, footballers, and dancers insure their legs against injury.

Insurance Policy is a contract of Indemnity, that is to say, a legal agreement wherein, in consideration of payment of premium by the insured, one party, that is the insurer, undertakes to indemnify the other party, that is the insured, any loss or damage caused by fire or other insured peril to specified property. In the event of loss, payment by the insurer is determined on the actual loss sustained by the insured and it is subject to the sum insured under the policy and the terms and conditions as laid down in the policy. Rights and duties of the contracting parties are also stated in the policy.

It is the business of the insurer to cover himself. It is for this purpose that he has to value the risk by considering the probabilities of loss. This is the process of ascertaining reasonable premium with reference to the liability that has to be met in the event of loss. It is the business of the actuaries to measure the risk which is often done on the basis of the information in the light of past experiences.

Insurance companies take advantage of the laws of probability. These laws enable an insurance mathematician called an actuary to determine the likelihood that an event would occur. Laws of probability are based on the laws of large numbers. For example, as the number of car insurance policy holders increases, the insurance company can use the law of probability to predict with greater accuracy the number of accidents the policy holders may come across.

The insurer calculates the premium according to the probable nature and the extent of risk for which the insured desires to be protected. The risk of loss is co-extensive with the value of insurable interest the insured has. The dimensions of the risk covered by an insurance contract is important to both the parties. The risk itself depends upon various elements of events insured against and on their happening sooner, later or never. In property insurance, the risk depends upon the nature of the property, its character, area, location, inherent defects and the exposure to outside dangers, title to the property and various other factors. In a marine contract, it may depend upon the nature of the voyage, routes generally adopted, winds and storms in the locality, danger of war, capture and seizure, piracy, mutiny of the crew and various other factors. Risk measurement is a highly specialised area and it has great importance in modern business as it reduces the impact of loss which any entrepreneur undergoes by having himself indemnified by a contract of insurance. It is in this context that risk has to be valued on actuarial principles.

Principle of indemnity

According to the principle of indemnity an insured should not profit by a claim but should be put in the same financial position as he was immediately before it happened. Personal accident policies can be an exception to the rule, as they have fixed sums insured. Policies that give "new for old" replacement covers could put the insured in a better position. Reinstatement of the sum insured should not be confused with reinstatement. Most contracts of indemnity usually state a sum insured. If a claim occurs, this sum insured is often diminished by the amount of the claim. Personal accident policies are not contracts for indemnity and it is, therefore, important that the insurer checks that the sums insured are commensurate with the insured's lifestyle.

But property insurance restores the insured to his original financial condition after suffering a loss. The idea is that the insured cannot profit by his misfortune.

Adequate insurance cover

For insurance purposes we are concerned with the cost of rebuilding in the event of total destruction and this may be more or less than the market price of the property. The importance of adequate insurance becomes obvious when a building is totally destroyed, but some property-owners tend to take the view that total destruction is so unlikely that they can safely insure for a lesser amount than the full cost of rebuilding. If a property is damaged by fire or some other peril and is found to be insured for less than the full rebuilding cost, the owner is deemed to be his own insurer for the deficiency in accordance with the stipulation that the policy is 'subject to average'. The insurance company can insist on allowance to be discounted for wear and tear which existed prior to the damage occurring. On the other hand, if full cover has been maintained such deductions are not normally made. Hence the need for adequate cover.

But it is again imprudent to overinsure to be on the safe side, as substantial premiums are involved. The object must be to insure for a figure which, whilst not excessive, may reasonably be expected to be adequate. Hence the requirement of just valuation for the purpose of insurance.

Insurable interest

It is necessary for the insured to have insurable interest in the insured property at the time of loss. To constitute insurable interest it must be an interest such that the risk would by its proximate effect cause damage to the assured, that is to say, cause him to incur a liability. The person seeking an insurance policy must establish some kind of interest in the life or property to be insured, in the absence of which, the insurance policy would amount to a wager and consequently void in nature.[10] The test for determining if there is any insurable interest is whether the insured will in case of damage to the life or property being insured, suffer pecuniary loss.[11] A person having a limited interest can also insure such interest. But such interest must exist at the time of happening of the event that gives rise to the claim.

Principle of reinstatement

Reinstatement value policy is an exception to the principle of indemnity. It is usually applicable to buildings, plant and machinery but not to stocks-in-trade or merchandise. Reinstatement value provisions contemplate that the basis upon which the amount payable under the policy is to be calculated, shall be the cost of replacing or reinstating on the

10 *Anctil* v *Manufacturers Life Insurance Company* [1899] AC 604 (PC).
11 *New India Insurance Company Limited* v *G.N. Sainani* (1997)6 SCC 383.

same site, property of the same kind or type but not superior to or more extensive than the insured property when new, subject to the work of reinstatement being completed within stipulated time-limit; and the condition of average would operate if at the time of reinstatement or replacement, the sum insured is inadequate. Also the insurance company shall not be liable for any payment in excess of the amount which would have been payable under the policy if the reinstatement clause had not been there, until expenditure has been incurred by the insured in replacing or reinstating the property destroyed or damaged.

Average clause

If the property hereby insured shall at the breaking out of any fire or at the commencement of any destruction of or damage to the property by any other peril hereby insured against, be collectively of greater value than the sum insured thereon, then the insured shall be considered as being his own insurer for the difference and shall bear a rateable proportion of the loss accordingly. Thus if the subject-matter is not adequately insured on the date of accident or damage, then the condition of average shall apply. In other words, if the property is underinsured insurance value being less than market value or reinstatement value as the case may be, then the claim gets reduced in that proportion.

On the other hand, if the property is overinsured, the insured gets only the actual value of what he has lost. Excess premium paid by insured due to excessive value estimation at the commencement of the policy shall be of no avail at the time of settlement of the claim. Insured will not be paid anything more than the actual worth of the asset in the market and actual replacement cost of asset under reinstatement value policy.

Principles of fire insurance

Generally, the insurance companies undertake either to replace the physical property destroyed or damaged by fire, riot, earthquake etc., or to pay the money equivalent of such replacement and reinstatement. The replacement cost is based upon the physical condition of the property at the time of the loss.

It should be borne in mind that Fire (including other risks) Insurance is not a valued policy, hence the insurer and insured are prohibited into entering an agreement as to the exact value of the subject-matter of the insurance at the commencement of insurance. Even if the valuation is done by an independent valuer, the Insurance Company or the insurer cannot bind itself to that valuation at the commencement of the Insurance. Only at the time of claim by the insured, the valuation aspect has to be considered. In other words, we can say that the sum insured under any policy of Indemnity including fire insurance policies is the insured's own estimate of the value of his property and it is the amount on which the premium is calculated. However, it is not the amount the insurer promises to pay either partly or fully in the event of the loss. Amount payable at the time of loss will be determined on the basis of the sum insured, the extent of the damage to the property of the insured and the type of policy taken to cover the risk.

The business of insurance

The amount of money paid by the insurance company to the policyholder when the contingency of payment takes place, is known as the benefit or the claim. The insurance company uses the premiums to invest in stocks, bonds, mortgages, Government securities and other income generating enterprises. The company pays the claim out of the premium it collects and also from the investment income the premiums earn. Insurance works because policyholders are willing to sacrifice a small loss by way of payment of premiums for the guarantee that they will be indemnified in case of a bigger loss and the policyholder may not ever have the opportunity to prefer a claim at all. A feeling of security gives the policyholders a relief, which is considered adequate for the payment of premium. Insurance company play vital role in the economy of a nation. It acts as a major financial institution for promotion of business and trade. In India, life insurance was nationalised in 1956 and in 1972 general insurance was nationalised as well, recently the business of insurance has been relaxed for private players in life insurance. The other types of insurances are privatised along with public undertakings operating in the field.

Good faith and other essential conditions

In addition to general law of contract, Insurance contract is also subject to certain special principles under the Common Law. They are:

(i) Utmost good faith.

(ii) Insurable interest.

(iii) Indemnity, subrogation and contribution.

In Insurance contracts, legal doctrine of 'utmost good faith' applies. This casts on the insured, the duty to disclose all material facts which has bearing on the Insurance. A breach of this duty may make the contract void or voidable depending upon the nature of the breach.

Insurable interest covers the rights of the insured over the insured property and rights to receive claim.

The third condition implies that the subject-matter of insurable item must exist when the contract is effected and it must be described adequately so that it can be identified in the event of loss.

Market value policy

Under this policy, the assets are insured at the market value, i.e. for its actual worth in the market at the relevant point of time. Hence it can be seen that as long as the property is insured for the market value, the insurer is adequately protected. This type of policy is available for all the types of fixed assets, i.e. buildings, plants and machineries, furniture and fixtures and electrical installations. Market value concept differs only in one respect from the reinstatement value basis and that is in regard to the depreciation due to various factors of the assets. Market value takes into account the physical depreciation of the asset which is ignored in the reinstatement value policy.

Doctrine of proximate cause

In every insurance, the insurer prescribes the list of peril against which the assets of the insured are covered and indemnity is offered by the insurer.

If the loss is attributed to the insured peril as the direct and unavoidable result of that peril so that a direct casual relationship is established, the insurers are liable for the loss.

However, if the loss is the direct and inevitable result of some other event which has either preceded the insured peril or followed it and if such an event or cause is not included in the policy or is excepted thereunder, the insurers are not liable to pay for the financial losses suffered by the insured.

Thus, liability of the insurer is determined in the light of the legal maxim or principle of "Proximate Cause", viz. the immediate and not the remote cause of damage or loss.

Every event is the effect of a cause. There may be succession of causes and effects for a loss or damage to the property. But the law does not look into the several causes of events in the infinite past. It concerns itself with identifying of the dominant, effective and proximate cause to the exclusion of all other causes which are too remote.

Thus loss which is not occasioned by the direct action of fire is not a loss by fire unless it is proximately caused by fire. On the other hand, under this very principle, a damage due to falling of wall of a burnt building is constructed as a damage due to fire as falling of wall is deemed to be an event proximately caused by the fire.

This principle applies equally to the exceptions. If the loss is proximately caused by an expected peril (risks not covered in policy) then there is no liability of the insurer to pay for the financial losses of the insured.

Valuation of insurance

Valuation is an excellent tool to determine from time to time or at a given specific time, the value of a specific asset insured for. Thus, valuation is an exercise, which is time-related and purpose-oriented. It becomes necessary for the insured to obtain a valuer's report from a competent professional and submit the same along with his proposal. An insurance policy for the valuation purpose can broadly be divided into two categories, namely—valued and unvalued policies. If the insurance policy is a valued policy, the amount recoverable by the assured is the agreed value. The taking of a valued policy is beneficial to the insurer where the loss is greater than the sum stated in the policy. It will be beneficial to the assured if the actual loss is less than the agreed valuation. The same principle applies to a partial loss in which case it is necessary to calculate the amount of actual depreciation and express the partial loss as a fraction of the actual value. The insurer will then be liable to pay that fraction of the agreed value.[12] If the policy contains to agreement on valuation the measure of indemnity is calculated with reference to the value at the date and place of loss.[13] The value may have increased during the currency of the policy and thus the assured may be able to recover more than he paid for it.

Under any insurance policy, risk is covered only for the value in the range of the policy. Only the value of those items specifically mentioned in the policy will be taken into account and not those items which are omitted in the descriptive workings of the policy. Moreover, under usual conditions, the insured person has to substantiate his claim by proving not only the existence of every article but the value of each. Thus the importance of an inventory and valuation for insurance is evident. It is also the condition of the insurance companies that the items insured will be insured for their full value; where it is found that they have been underinsured the company will invoke their average clause whereby the policyholder will be considered as being his own insurer for the difference and shall bear that proportion of the loss.

The process of valuation demands full information as to the nature, size and quality of the building and an understanding of other factors which may affect valuation including the cost of demolishing and clearing away what remains after a major calamity and thereafter rebuilding completely. Thus, factors like location, size, occupational use, type of construction, approximate age, amenities or services provided, neighbourhood,—all have to be recorded for being taken into consideration. The need for valuation arises before the loss as well as after the loss. Before the loss, the objective of valuation is to fix sound insurable value whereas after the loss, the objective is to establish the relevant facts and present then for arriving at sound conclusions.

Replacement cost survey—buildings

To arrive at the replacement cost of a building, a survey must be made and complete information obtained in detail, giving

12 *Compania Martima Astra SA* v *Archdale* [1954]2 Lloyds Rep 95.
13 *Wlcock* v *Thomson* [1949]2 KB 755.

the type of construction of said building. This involves such elements as the kind and thickness of walls, type of framing, kind of floors, kind of roof, and all interior and exterior fixtures, such as plumbing, heating, lighting, elevators, sprinklers, platforms, penthouses, entrances etc. From this information, a valuer can estimate how much it would cost to replace the structure using present day costs for materials and labour. The extent to which the valuer goes in obtaining accurate estimates of quantities and costs will depend on the purposes of the survey. In this respect, the operations will be practically the same as a Contractor's Method in estimating for bids. In some cases, it will be necessary to go into great detail and in others, approximate figures will suffice.

Another method used is to apply a proper appreciation factor to the original cost of the building. This method works well provided that the building is not of such age that technological factors tend to distort the picture.

Replacement cost survey—equipment

To obtain replacement cost on equipment, it is necessary to prepare a detailed survey. This involves listing each piece of equipment with sufficient information as to the manufacturer, type, model numbers, serial numbers, capacity, etc. Information must also be obtained on the installation costs of the equipment. Just as in the case of the building, the amount of detail necessary will depend on the purpose of the survey. In some case, the survey will include each foot of pipe or wire installed, but in other cases, only the major pieces of equipment will be detailed and the minor equipment estimated by buildings. It is then necessary to obtain from manufacturers or catalogues and price lists the costs of new equipment. While many problems may arise due to changes in types of equipment manufactured or manufacturers going out of business the valuer has to use his judgment to arrive at the appropriate replacement costs.

Valuation considerations in assessment of loss

There are several principles on the basis of which valuation is done in an insurance case. If there is a total loss the assured will be paid the value of the thing insured at the time of the loss. In case of partial loss the difference between the value of the damaged property before the loss and after the loss is assessed for payment as indemnity. The undamaged property before the loss is to be taken at the market value immediately before the loss occurred. The assured is not entitled to take the cost price or the cost of construction or manufacture as conclusive evidence of the value of the property at the time of loss. It may be a *prima facie* evidence but not a conclusive one as the assured may have paid more than that as its value and the market value may have fallen since then. Conversely, the property might have risen in value to which the insured is entitled if the agreed terms so permits.

If there is no market for the property before the loss the value will have to be measured in some other way. It is often difficult to decide the appropriate value of the property after the loss. There are different approaches towards the valuation of the property after the loss, viz., (*a*) the market value of the property in its damaged condition, or, (*b*) the value of the property before the loss *minus* the cost of repair. There are cases where the cost of repair exceeds the value of the property before the loss or greater than the cost of replacement. In such cases the general rule is that, (*a*) the cost of repair is allowed only in those cases where the insurer genuinely intends to repair, and, (*b*) such a course is not eccentric or absurd.

If an old house or an old article is destroyed or damaged and the insured replaces or repairs it he may end up with a house or article, which is considerably better than the old and the question arises whether he should make any allowance with the insurer to the extent that he is better off. The conventional view is to say if the undamaged value is taken as 100 and the repaired value is in excess of it, say 110, and the cost of repair is, then the damaged value being the difference between the repaired value and the cost of repair is 40, which should be deducted not against the repaired value but against the undamaged value that is 100, to assess the amount recoverable as compensation being (100-40) or 60.

The Insurance Act 1938

The statutory provisions that regulate the business of insurance in our country is the Insurance Act 1938 and rules framed thereunder. The following types of policies are generally available according to the practices that prevail:

(*i*) Fire policy on indemnity basis at market value based on Depreciated Replacement Cost which is called value at risk. The condition of average applies if under-insured. There are two kinds of fire policy, one of which covers act of God while the other does not unless extra premium is paid.

(*ii*) Reinstatement policy for total loss or partial loss: reinstatement has to be concluded within twelve months of loss with evidence of expenses incurred. Thus the policy is virtually for reimbursement.

(*iii*) Machinery Breakdown policy in which the ensured person gives a value at the time of proposal which is accepted for the time being. It is not an agreed value policy which is an essential feature in Marine Insurance. An active valuation exercise is called for in respect of the policy as the value is not agreed upon. The agreed value policy is issued only in respect of marine contract, antic motor-car or objects of art.

It has already been stated that the insurance industry in India was nationalised in 1956 and the Life Insurance Corporation of India was accorded the monopoly of the business. The general insurance business was also nationalised with also nationalised with effect from 1st January 1973 by an Act passed in 1972. But from 1991 onwards the Government of India introduced various reforms in the financial sector paving the way for liberalisation of the Indian economy and the entry of private players into the business of life insurance as well as general insurance became permissible. To regulate the realm, on the recommendations of the Malhotra Committee the Indian parliament passed the Insurance Regulatory and Development Act 1999 on 2nd December 1999 with the objective "to provide for the establishment of an Authority to protect the interests of the policy holders, to regulate, to promote, and ensure orderly growth of the insurance industry and to amend the Insurance Act 1938, the Life Insurance Corporation of India Act 1956, and the general Insurance Business (Nationalisation) Act 1972". The Act of 1999 established the Insurance Regulatory and Development Authority as a statutory body to regulate and promote the insurance industry in India and to protect the interests of policyholders. The Act also carried out a series of amendments to the Act of 1938 and conferred the powers of control of insurance on the Insurance Regulatory and Development Authority. Thus the Insurance Act of 1938 has become relevant again for sustained growth of the insurance industry.

(c) Merger, Amalgamation, Take-overs and Disinvestment of PSUs

The experiments with economic liberalisation in India was set in mid-1970's with relaxation in licensing system of engineering industries under the Industries (Development and Regulation) Act. The real opening up of the economy started with the statement of Industrial policy made on 24th June 1991 by the Government of India whereby it was, *inter alia*, declared that the blocks in the way of achieving fast industrial development would be removed by dismantling those regulatory system that created them. With the opening up of the economy, business enterprises are designed to be given freedom to expand, diversify, modernise the operations and set up new undertakings. Indian economic system, so far has been tethered to a regulated economy to meet the planned objectives of socialist pattern of economic development. It was thought that concentration of economic powers could be effectively counteracted by tightened regulations. But the benign breeze of globalisations that now sweeps from one end of the world to the other has ushered in a new era. Thus liberalisation, has come as an irreversible approach the Government has started relaxing various restrictions that were in-built in our legal system.

At present the following enactments and statutory regulations contain provisions relating to or affecting merger, amalgamation or take-over of corporate enterprises:

(1) Companies Act 2013

(2) Industries (Development & Regulation) Act 1951.

(3) Competition Act 2002.

(4) Foreign Exchange Management Act 1999.

(5) Sick Industrial Companies (Special Provisions) Act 1985.

(6) Income-tax Act 1961.

(7) Securities Contracts (Regulation) Act 1956.

(8) Securities and Exchange Board of India Act 1992.

(9) SEBI (Substantial Acquisition of Shares and Take-overs) Regulations 1997.

Preparation of financial statement

Valuation of assets—land, buildings, plants and machineries for the purpose of preparation of financial statement has assumed considerable significance in recent times. The prospectus of company has to be updated from time to time in order to reflect the financial gains, growth of turn-overs and modernisation so that it may permeate the boom in the capital market. Revolution of assets enable a company to come out of the shell of book value of assets based on historical costs and illusory picture of profit or loss arising out of it.

In the wake of globalisation, the industrial and trading scenario is undergoing a marked change by merger, amalgamation and take-over of enterprises. Competition for survival as well as ambitions.to build up industrial empires have propelled combination, consolidation and acquisition among the companies spread over all around the globe. There is a multitude of reasons for such moves. When two undertakings combine their resources and efforts they may produce better results through savings in operating costs. They can diversify the activities so as to avoid putting all the eggs in one basket. Procurement of supplies of raw materials, entry into new market zones, revamping of production facilities, availing of technical know-how, reinforcement of financial strength, attraction of superior managerial talents and general gains are the major impulses behind merger, amalgamation or take-overs. Deployment of surplus capital and looking for virgin areas for marketing have prompted developed countries to turn to the underdeveloped regions for new partners in enterprise. The inevitable impact in the field of valuation has been a spurt in the preparation of financial statements of companies.

In the matter of amalgamation it has been decided in In re, *Tata Oil Mills Co. Ltd.*[14] that when a scheme of valuation on the basis of valuation report in which the share exchange ratio between the amalgamating companies had been approved

14 (1994) Comp Cas 754 (Bom).

by an overwhelming majority of shareholders of the two companies, on the basis of the opinion of two reputed auditors who had reviewed the methodology in valuation and confirmed the ratio to be fair, the same should generally be relied upon and should not be interfered with by the court unless the valuation arrived at is shown to be grossly unfair. The *ratio decidendi* in *Piramal Spinning and Weaving Mill Ltd.*, in re (1980)50 Comp Cas 514 (Bom) was relied upon. The same principle has been adopted in a different context in In re, *SPS Pharma Ltd.* and In re, *Targof Pure Drugs Ltd.* (1997)88 Comp Cas 774 (AP).

In the same vein, the court had held in an earlier case of *Bank of Baroda* v *Mahindra Ugine Steel Co. Ltd.*[15] in the matter arising after nationalisation of the Bank of Boroda Ltd. as Bank of Boroda with effect from 19th July 1969 under an Ordinance. A scheme of amalgamation of the said Bank with MUS. Co. Ltd. under s. 391 of the Companies Act 1956 was approved by the court upon a meeting of the shareholders. The question of valuation and fixation of ratio of exchange came up as a dispute and it was submitted that the said questions are matters of commercial judgment and the court should not sit in judgment over it. Accordingly, the court refused to go deeper into the question of valuation in the absence of any opposition which satisfies the court that it must go into the question on the ground raised.

Valuation of assets and stock

The valuation of the assets and stock of the company is required to be made whenever there is a question of merger, amalgamation or take-over. The principles and methods of valuation in all such cases are more or less similar.

The method of valuation generally observed abide by any of the following:

(1) Assets value on going concern.

(2) Capitalisation of earnings basis.

(3) Market value of listed stock.

(4) Investment value.

15 (1976)46 Comp Cas 227 (Guj).

(5) Book value.

(6) Cost minus depreciation.

(7) Reproduction value.

(8) Replacement value.

Often a combination of methods is also tried to arrive at just valuation.

(1) GOING CONCERN VALUE consisting of tangible assets and intangibles like, goodwill has been discussed at length in an earlier chapter.

(2) CAPITALISED EARNINGS is arrived at with reference to a predetermined rate of return expected on an investment. The system involves the assessment of present worth of a series of future benefits or returns on investment.

(3) MARKET VALUE of the stock of shares of listed companies at the stock exchange is often taken as the basis of valuation of such companies. Such market value does not always reflect the real worth of the company because of speculative factors involved. Share market price usually reflects investors' anticipation as regards prospects of the company's ability to defray dividends, confidence in company's management, sustainability of earning capacity in the future, and relative advantage over other avenues of investment. To arrive at a fair value, it is expedient to track the trend over a sufficient period of time so that transient manoeuvres may not camouflage the real picture of a company.

(4) INVESTMENT VALUE is arrived at by taking into account the original investment together with the accrued interest thereon which is sought to be salvaged through merger or amalgamation.

(5) BOOK VALUE represents the total worth of the assets after depreciation but with periodic revaluation to capture the inflationary effect on assets. It is the audited written down money worth of the total tangible assets comprising both fixed assets and working capital.

(6) COST MINUS DEPRECIATION ignores intangible like goodwill and may serve a limited purpose.

(7) REPRODUCTION VALUE is based on assessing the current cost of duplicating the properties of constructing similar enterprise on the same design and material.

(8) REPLACEMENT VALUE is the estimate of the cost of the undertaking or enterprise with the same utility and capacity. It need not necessarily depend on the same design and technology so long as the productive efficiency is not impaired or lessened.

Issues relating to valuation have been dwelt upon elaborately in different chapters of this book. So far as preparation of financial statement is concerned, a few standard practices need particular mention. The owner-occupied assets have to be valued in accordance with their existing use and with due consideration of the expectation that the enterprise will continue in operation. The rationale for distinguishing assets in existing use from other assets in the valuation process is that a business cannot as a practical matter sell assets which are necessary to its operation and still be productive. The sale of such assets would be inconsistent with continuation of the business. The assets in existing use may have a potential value of much better return on market approach. But that is immaterial as the question of disposal does not arise at all. But the same cannot be said about assets which are surplus to the company's requirements. Since there is no compulsion to retain such surplus assets, those are to be valued on the basis of market value at their highest and best use.

Again, all investment assets one to be valued according to principles for determination of open market value. In determining the value of property in existing use, a distinction can be made between a specialised property and non-specialised property. All specialised owner-occupied property that are neither surplus nor for investment shall be valued on the basis of Depreciated Replacement Cost. The non-specialised property are, however, to be valued on the basis of market value for the existing use. When the assets include property with trading potential and commonly sold in the market as an operating package, those shall be reported in the financial statement separately from the land and buildings, or if the type of property is commonly sold as in inseparable combination with land and building, the same shall clearly be identified as such.

A question arose if premises held on leave and licence could be included as asset of a company in the matter of valuation for amalgamation purposes. It was held in In re *Tata Oil Mills Co. Ltd.* and In re, *Hindustan Lever Ltd.* (1994)81 Comp Cas 754 (Bom) that the premises held by TOMCO on leave and licence were not its assets and could not have been included in the valuation and there was no question of providing particulars thereof in the scheme of amalgamation.

Public sector undertakings

There is a strong case for revaluation of assets of the public sector undertakings particularly in the context of proposals for their disinvestment. In the process of valuation, all the principles in the preparation of financial statement are relevant. But it has to be borne in mind that the public sector undertakings are not uniform in character, nor have they the same role to perform. Some of the undertakings were brought into existence to create infrastructure for growth and development or act as catalyst to growth. In such cases, the benefit approach to valuation is the most appropriate strategy. The benefit approach has been outlined in an earlier chapter. The undertakings of highly specialised character may have to be valued on the basis of Depreciated Replacement Cost. The other undertakings producing generally capital goods or consumer goods or carrying on trading activities, are perhaps liable to be valued according to income approach or market approach according to circumstances demand.

(D) AUCTION RESERVE

Auction is one of the oldest mode of disposing of property, particularly chattels. An auction sale was recorded in the twenty-third chapter of the Book of Genesis, when Abraham bought the fields of Machpela from Ephron by giving his word in front of witnesses at the gates of the city. In U.K. until the end of the eighteenth century, very few public auctions were concerned with land and building; goods and chattels were their stock-in-trade. The word 'chattel' means a movable possession or any possession of a tangible property other than real estate or freehold. The legislative control of auction came in U.K. with the passing of the Auctions' (Bidding Agreements) Act in 1927. This was later strengthened by the Mock Auctions

Act 1961 and the Auctions' (Bidding Agreements) Act 1969 since there was a phenomenal increase in soles in auction market including that in real estates too. An inventory in an auction market now encompasses a wide range of property—carpet, chair, table, curtains, household linens, ornaments, glass, silver, paintings, electrical gadgets, furniture and fixture, books, porcelain and pottery, antiques and what not. Plots of land, buildings and estates add to this list.

Valuation is needed for the purpose of auction reserve. A valuer generally advises his client on what reserves to put on his goods which is earmarked for sale in auction. The object of placing a reserve upon an article is to prevent it being sold at a figure much below its fair value and yet on the other hand, the vendor is desirous of selling his article which demand that the figure must not be too high so as to prevent a sale.

To sell a property by auction, just as by other means of disposal, requires much research into evidence of value, as well as intuitive skills of the valuer. The auctioneer must also know what a property is likely to fetch in order to advise on the reserve. No prices are printed on the catalogue as is usual in a market sale in a departmental store, but an approximate reserve price has to be agreed between the vendor and auctioneer, as an indication for prospective buyers; and the vendor has to decide at what price, if any, he will sell, prior to the auction taking place. From the information, auction department usually prepares a guide price which may range from below the reserve to the 'sell-prior' figure. Advertising, mailing of lists and public relations constitute the major strategy for organising an auction with the prospect of attracting buyers.

The types of property that are considered suitable for bidding in an auction can be divided into two broad categories; those that will prove popular and will therefore generate competition in the auction room and realise a price in excess of expectation; and conversely those for which there is likely to be minimal demand and which therefore will benefit from the extensive marketing that only an auctioneer, with numerous lots in his catalogue, can employ. A private deal of sale with a fixed quoting price cannot do then well, as each prospective buyer is working to reach the set figure, rather than trying to arrive at the maximum price he is prepared to pay. It necessarily follows that any property which is likely to appeal to a specially motivated purchaser who, for whatever reason, is able to pay more than its market value, is eminently suitable for auction.

In this situation, the fixation of auction reserve involve a pre-auction marketing analysis, which forms the basis of valuation. This is a technique of valuation specific to auctioneering. It may take the form of 'test bidding' prior to auction or may simply be a question of ascertaining the amount of interest in a property. Once it is reasonably established that the property placed in auction will evoke popular enthusiasm, it may be expected that open competition will take over and biddings will take care of fetching a price well above the reserve.

If, on the other hand, a property has attracted little or no interest, the reserve should be fixed close to the expected realisation in order to avoid selling at too low a price. Sometimes, the property may fetch just a liquidation value and no more. The art of an auctioneer lies in fixing the reserve at a level which will encourage buyers who think they see a bargain at the same time satisfy vendors that their properties are reaching the maximum price possible under the circumstances. Auction sale of scraps in railway yards is an example of recovery of liquidation value which has been in practice in India for a long time. But the auction market is vitiated by a sort of cartel amongst the prospective bidders that would not allow the price to rise to its appropriate value. On the other extreme, antique or articles of historical significance or artistic fame can reach an astounding figure in auction, provided its possession enhances greatly the richness of a gallery or collection, or lends a status symbol to the richest few of the world. All depends how an interest is evoked in the market and how a potential interest is captured in the auction theatre. An estimate of it lies in the arena of the valuer's expertise.

The Supreme Court gave a momentous decision in *Anil Kumar Srivastava* v *State of U.P.*,[16] on the question as to how

16 (2004)8 SCC 671.

far valuation of property is reflected in the reserve price for auction. In doing so the Apex Court relied on the decision in *Duncan Industries Limited* v *State*[17] and referred to the discussions in *Mc Manus* v *Fortescue*;[18] where the Court of Appeals had held that in a sale by auction, subject to reserve, every offer/bid and its acceptance is conditional, that the public is informed by the fact that the sale is subject to a reserve, that the auctioneer has agreed to sell for the amount which the bidder is prepared to give only in case that amount is equal to or higher than the reserve, that the reserve puts a limit on the authority of the auctioneer, he cannot accept a price below the upset or reserve price, that he could refuse the hid which is below the upset price. Discussing on the subject, the Supreme Court observes that in the present case, the Board resolution prescribes the guidelines for fixing the reserve price. The concept of reserve price is not synonymous with "valuation of property". These two terms operate in different spheres. An invitation to tender is not an offer. It is an attempt to ascertain whether an offer can be obtained with margin see Pollock & Mulla, *Indian Contract & Specific Relief Acts*, 14th Ed., p. 42. However, notwithstanding the fixation of the upset price and notwithstanding the fact that a bidder has offered an amount higher that the reserve or upset price, the sale is still open to challenge on the ground that the property has not fetched the proper price and the sale be set aside, that the fixation of the reserve price does not affect the rights of the parties, that the sale has to commence at the higher price and in the absence of bidders, the price will have to be progressively brought down till it reaches the upset price, that the upset price is fixed to facilitate the conduct of the sale; that fixation of upset price does not preclude the claimant from adducing proof that the land is sold for a low price.

(E) MORTGAGE, LOAN & SECURITY

It is common that lending financial institutions including Banks, Life Insurance Corporation of India, Housing Finance Corporations etc. provide financing to be secured by specific

17 (2001)1 SCC 633.
18 [1907]2 KB 1; [1904-1907] All ER 707; 96 LT 444.

collateral fixed assets rather than the general credit of an individual or enterprise. Valuation of such fixed assets then become necessary to assess the worth of collateral securities. In some instances, the net worth of an enterprise is pledged as security without regard to specific assets. In such cases, the Going Concern Value, Liquidation Value, or other types of value has to be worked out with due regard to regulatory laws, special circumstances and secured party's requirements. A large percentage of corporate and private loans from and other financial institutions are secured by an interest in specific assets. A comprehensive understanding of such specific interests, structure of the loan arrangement, terms and conditions implied in agreements are necessary for the purpose of valuation. Phasing and timing for funding in the lending agreement are required to be linked with periodic market valuations over a development cycle. There is often time difference between the date of development completion and the effective date of valuation. The market charges have to be anticipated during the development period when the two do not coincide.

Methods of considerations in valuation

The methods, techniques and procedures relevant and applied in the determination of market value lead only to market value as commonly understood and expressed. Sales comparison or other methods of market comparison are structured in market value determination based on analysis of market data by reference to market-based estimates of costs and accumulated depreciation. The capitalised earnings method or the discounted cash flow method should also be based on market-determined cash flows and market-derived rates of return.

But those seeking security for financing, or trying to evaluate the status of that security will sometimes require valuation on a basis other than market value. Under such circumstances, the valuation exercise will include an estimation of market value as well as the extent to which a valuation based on non-market value may deviate from market value.

The following particular considerations are accordingly relevant in the valuation of property meant for securitisation:

(*i*) Investment property yielding income may have to be valued or part of a portfolio of properties. A distinction may have to be made between a leveraged and unleveraged overall property yields. Similarly, references to Internal Rate of Return (IRR) should set forth whether they are debt-leveraged or not.

(*ii*) When a property belonging to an owner is occupied by him for use, the property should be valued as if such property is vacant. The valuation method shall proceed on the basis of the highest and best use of such property.

(*iii*) Specialised properties with limited marketability shall be valued on the basis of Depreciated Replacement Cost in the absence of market data.

(*iv*) Property having trading potential like a hotel or cold storage have to be valued upon an assessment of the sustainable level of income derived from accounting data or projections, excluding any special goodwill apart from what an operator derives with average management and normal skill.

(*v*) Property not yielding an income but held for redevelopment or as sites for development with non-specialised buildings should be valued with due regard to existing value as well as potential value upon development as under controls of planning and developmental regulations.

(*vi*) Wasting assets like mines or quarries need to be valued with due regard to the duration and profile of the loan including interest and capital repayment schedule as they relate to the extraction programme of the wasting assets.

Valuation for mortgage purposes

A very common method of borrowing money is to take an advance on the security of land and buildings. The person who borrows the money is known as the Mortgagor and the lender is known as the Mortgagee. A valuer may frequently have to advise his client on the amount of money he should advance on the security of land and buildings, and he should, therefore, have no connection whatsoever with the Mortgagor since his valuation must be completely without bias on the side of the Mortgagor.

The owner is not selling his property, he is only borrowing money and pledging it as security. If he pays interest regularly, observes the covenants in the Mortgage Deed, and repays the principal on the due date, the property remains in his ownership.

The valuer should first make a valuation of the fair market value, excluding all items which are of a speculative nature, and he must take into account the income which is practically certain to be maintained. The best method is to make a valuation by the Rental Method, testing each item to see that not only is the amount fair but is likely to be maintained in the future. The security should be at least one per cent more than normally would be taken if valuing for compulsory purchase.

Before an advance can be made the valuer will have to work in conjunction with the Mortgagee's Solicitor. The title of the property to be mortgaged must be thoroughly investigated, the slightest defect in the title must be carefully examined, because if the Mortgagor fails to observe any of the covenants of the Mortgage Deed, there must not be any clog to bar a quick sale of the property so that the Mortgagee may realise his just and due demands.

If the mortgaged property includes buildings from which rent is derived, then one of the clauses in the Mortgage Deed should stipulate that the buildings must be insured. The valuer may have to advise on the value of the buildings and the method of valuation has been explained in earlier chapters.

It has been explained in the earlier chapters how various events can change the character of a district within a very short time; therefore, a prudent mortgagee will never advance the full value of the property and the amount advanced will usually be from one half to two-thirds the full value of the property. In order to see that the security is ample, the mortgagee should cause to be made periodic valuations of the mortgaged property. If this is done by the person who originally advised on the loan, then the work will be comparatively simple and can be done for a nominal fee. If the mortgagee allows the loan to be outstanding for several years, then these periodic valuations become absolutely necessary.

(F) Betterment Levy for Planning Regulations

Betterment is a general and comprehensive term, which, when applied to the public administration of landed property, refers to the enhancement in the value of private property, due to some action or undertaking carried out by a public or statutory body. It does not include any improvement in the value of property due to the personal action of the owner, and hence it is often referred to as "Unearned Increment". There has been a growing recognition by Legislatures, that this betterment is morally the property of the public authorities. It does not need any argument to establish that this unearned increment is purely due to the exertions of the public authorities either directly or indirectly. Until recent years the private individual has been putting this profit into his own pocket at the cost of the general tax-payers, and untold sums have in this way been lost to the public purse.

No work on the valuation of Real Property would be complete without a reference to the subject of "Betterment". It has been defined as a peculiar species of taxation, and had early legal sanction in an English Act passed in 1667 and re-enacted in 1670 to regulate the rebuilding of London after the Great Fire. The original idea of the legislature was to completely rebuild the City to a plan which was prepared by the great architect Wren who designed and built St. Paul's Cathedral. But in the end Government dallied so long with the discussion, that owners began to rebuild on their lands, and ultimately Parliament abandoned this scheme, and carried out a poor substitute which has resulted in a terrible handicap to the City ever since.

In 1691 the province of New York copied the English Act almost word for word, in so far as it could be made applicable to New York but it was not until over a century later that the New York courts recognized the principle. By 1875 sixteen States adopted the idea, which consisted in the levying of special assessments on all property which benefited as the result of the municipal expenditure upon developments of almost any character.

Where improvements result in increasing the value of adjacent land, it is becoming more and more the practice in all civilized countries to assess property-owners with the whole or part of the cost of such improvements, the levy being made in proportion to the benefit received.

The principle was first applied in England as far back as in 1427 when a certain Act provided for the apportioning, among the benefited land-owners, the cost of construction and repair of walks, ditches, gutters, sewers, bridges, causeways, and trenches which had been damaged by an inundation of the sea. It seems but just that those whose property is thus enhanced in value, and who receive peculiar benefits from the improvement, should contribute specially to defray its cost.

A more modern and important public Act in England which deals with the question of "Betterment" is the Public Health Act 1875, under which sanitary improvements carried out by a Local Authority should be considered as "Private Improvement Expenses" which could be met by a special Improvement Tax on the properties benefited thereby. Since then the principle of charging betterment has been adopted in U.K. in one form or another in various special Acts, e.g., the Metropolis (Prevention of Floods) Act 1879, the Manchester Corporation Act 1894, the London County Council (Tower Bridge Approach) Act 1895, the Light Railways Acts 1896, the Housing and Town Planning Acts 1909 (later revised as the Housing Act 1925 and the Town Planning Act 1925). In these Acts one or more of three forms or phases in which betterment is levied from private individuals are recognized:

(1) Set off.

(2) Betterment proper, and

(3) Recoupment.

(1) *Set off.* The amount of betterment accruing to an owner's remaining property, as a result of the undertaking or scheme is "set off" against the amount of compensation payable to him for any acquisition of his land. Under this method, if the betterment exceeds the amount of compensation the excess is lost to the public. It also implies that the betterment accruing to any other owner whose property is not acquired for the scheme, or who is not otherwise liable to be compensated, is also forgone.

(2) *Betterment proper.* Here the full betterment charges are levied from the owner, either as a lump sum or by instalments as a periodical tax. This pure form is in some Acts modified by being limited to the amount of 'actual expenditure' (or a proportion thereof) to which is directly attributed the betterment of the properties, e.g. as provided for in the Bombay Town Planning Act 1915.

(3) *Recoupment.* The third form of levying betterment charges is by an indirect method, generally known as the "recoupment" method. In this instead of charging the betterment to the owners, all the property which is expected to rise in value as the result of the undertaking, is acquired forthwith along with whatever is actually necessary for the carrying out of the scheme, and then after the scheme is executed the surplus land is sold. It has been the general experience that this method usually more than pays for the cost of acquisition plus the cost of construction under the scheme particularly when the area being acquired is a slum surrounded by a business district.

The necessity for encouraging private enterprise, by relieving the promoting bodies from enormous financial burdens, due to cost of acquisitions, has led to the inclusion of the betterment principle in all Acts authorizing constructive works or improvement schemes at the public cost.

The great schemes of slum clearance and arterial road construction in Paris associated with the name of Baron Haussman are earlier examples of the use of "recoupment". In Bombay the Improvement Trust did quite a number. The Betterment principle was applied in the city of Mumbai and State of Maharashtra in the following Acts in which betterment was levied on unearned increment:

(A) Bombay Town Planning Act 1915.

(B) City of Bombay Improvement Act 1898.

(C) Bombay District Municipal Act (11 of 1901).

(D) Bombay Cities Municipal Act 1925.

(E) Land Revenue Code (Bom. Act V of 1879).

Bombay Town Planning Act

Under this Act betterment is charged on owners of final plots included within a Town Planning Scheme, in proportion to the benefit derived by them, from the works under the Scheme, and the general effect of the scheme. The total amount recoverable must not exceed the cost of the scheme, and the levy is limited to a maximum of 50 per cent of the increment accruing in the value of the plot.

The calculation of the unearned increment in the case of Town Planning schemes is a highly technical matter, and must be made by trained valuers. It does not merely involve the finding out of the market value of the land under the existing circumstances, but also the market value on the assumption that the scheme has been completed.

Madras Town Planning Act

A great deal can be said in favour of the provisions of the Madras Town Planning Act which provides for the recovery of the betterment contribution by an annual charge, at a uniform rate, not exceeding 10 per cent of the betterment, for the number of years provided in the scheme, the aggregate recovery not exceeding 50 per cent of the total betterment. For the purpose of arriving at the amount of betterment, as at the date of publication of notification of the scheme, under s. 10 or s. 12, the lands are again valued on the 1st of April of every year, following that on which the Scheme comes into force, and the difference between these, and original valuation, is considered as the betterment of which a fixed percentage, not exceeding 10 per cent is levied. As in the Bombay Act the value of buildings or other works is not taken into account in these valuations.

Calcutta Improvement Act

Under the Calcutta Improvement Act 1911, if a scheme is framed, certain properties which are situated outside the limits of acquisition will be increased in value due to the operation of the scheme, the Board may declare that a betterment fee shall be payable by the owner of the land or any person having an interest therein.

The betterment fee shall be an amount equal to one-half of the increase in value of the land resulting from the execution of the scheme, estimated as if the land were clear of buildings, exceeds the value of the land prior to the execution of the scheme estimated in a like manner.

The method of estimating the amount of betterment fee is very simple. Two figures are required:

(1) The value of the land at the date of notification.

(2) The value of the land after the completion of the scheme.

The first value is generally found by sales and awards of the Collector and the value is for bare land only cleared of all buildings. The second value is based on sales of land which have taken place after the new roadways have been constructed. The difference between the two values is the increase resulting from the operations of the scheme, and the betterment fee payable is half of this amount.

West Bengal Apartment Ownership Act

The W.B. Apartment Ownership Act 1972 in its s. 10(1)(*g*) requires the value of the property to a whole and also of each flat or apartment to be ascertained for the purpose of declaration under s. 2 of the Act. The declaration with regard to value of apartment includes the percentage of undivided interest in the common areas and facilities appertaining to each apartment and its owner.

The same provision also prevails with regard to the flats or apartments together with such proportionate share in a multi-storied building, owned by a Co-operative Society under the W.B. Co-operative Societies Act 2006 which has been enforced only with effect from 18.1.2011. There is a separate chapter in the Act providing for special provisions for Housing Co-operative Societies which describes in s. 92(5) that a member of a co-operative housing society shall not be entitled to any interest or title beyond the right to use the common area and facilities and there are restrictions on letting and the property by the owner thereof in s. 93. This makes a difference in valuation of the flats belonging to an allottee-member of a co-operative housing society and an owner of apartment governed by the W.B. Apartment Ownership Act.

(G) ELECTRICITY ACT

There are a few statutes which require valuation to be made of assets for specified purpose. The modes of valuation prescribed in such statutes depart from the general principles but are relevant when a valuation exercise has to be undertaken for the purpose of the statute in question. One such statute is the Electricity Act 2003 (36 of 2003). It lays down a specific mode of valuation of assets when an undertaking belonging to a licensee (meaning a person licensed under the Act to supply energy), is sold in consequence of revocation of licence by the State Government in exercise of powers under sub-sec. (1) of s. 19 and the undertaking is purchased by a designated purchaser in pursuance of the provisions of s. 20 of the said Act.

The particular mode of determination of purchase price was laid down in s. 7A of the Electricity Act 1910 which is reproduced below:

> 7A. *Determination of purchase price.* (1) Where an undertaking of a licensee, not being a local authority, is sold under sub-section (1) of section 5, the purchase price of the undertaking shall be the market value of the undertaking at the time of purchase or where the undertaking has been delivered before the purchase under sub-section (3) of that section, at the time of the delivery of the undertaking and if there is any difference or dispute regarding such purchase price, the same shall be determined by arbitration.
>
> (2) The market value of an undertaking for the purpose of sub-section (1) shall be deemed to be the value of all lands, buildings, works, materials and plant of the licensee suitable to, and used by him, for the purpose of the undertaking, other than: (*i*) a generating station declared by the licence not to form part of the undertaking for the purpose of purchase, and (*ii*) service-lines or other capital works or any part thereof which have been constructed at the expense of consumers, due regard being had to the nature and condition for the time being of such land, buildings, works, materials and plant and the state of repair thereof and to the circumstance that they are in such position as to be ready for immediate working and to the suitability of the same for the purpose of the undertaking, but without any addition in respect of compulsory purchase or of goodwill or of any profits which may be or might have been made from the undertaking or of any similar consideration.
>
> (3) Where an undertaking of a licensee, being a local authority, is sold under sub-section (1) of section 5, the purchase price of the undertaking shall be such as the State Government, having regard to the market value of the undertaking at the date of delivery of the undertaking, may determine.

(4) Where an undertaking of a licensee is purchased under section 6, the purchase price shall be the value thereof as determined in accordance with the provisions of sub-sections (1) and (2):

Provided that there shall be added to such value such percentage, if any, not exceeding twenty per centum of that value as may be specified in the licence on account of compulsory purchase.

There were numbers of State Amendments to s. 7A applicable in Assam, Bihar, Gujarat, Haryana, Madhya Pradesh, Maharashtra, Uttar Pradesh and West Bengal which were required to be consulted whenever any matter of determination of price was arose in any of the above States.

CHAPTER

23

Non-Money Economy and Valuation

The discipline of valuation is built upon the notion of price and price is determined in market through the inter-play of the forces of demand and supply. Value and price are two different phenomena and the relationship between the two is established by a reasoned exercise termed estimation. Being linked with price, value is always expressed in monetary terms but the concept of value originates as a command of a commodity over other commodities in the process of transaction. Money acts only as the medium of exchange measuring the price of each item in transaction for comparison of relative value. In other words, we arrive at value in the barter sense as we lift the screen of pricing in monetary terms that lies in between the two sets of commodities transacted. As a matter of fact, we buy only consumable goods which has the power of satisfying want and thereby obtains utility. We do not consume money as such. But money is sought for as it is a liquid asset that can assume the shape and character of any commodity that commands utility on mere asking. That is how the focus of human concern has shifted from goods and services to money. But money is only subservient to value as it indexes the price which provides an essential tool to determine value. Price is the mechanism or device for translating into quantitative terms of currency the perceived value of a commodity to the consumer at a point of time. According to J.S. Mill: "Value is relative term, the value of a thing means the quantity of some other thing or things in general which it exchanges for."

Money and price

While money and price are inextricable of each other as because price can feed content to itself only in terms of money, the same cannot be said of value. The command of a commodity to purchase a specified quantity or quality of another commodity in exchange, may be called its purchasing power. The parity of purchasing power between two commodities may be resolved independent of money and price, although price measured by money is certainly an aid in the process. It is quite possible and it often happens that value is created or added to a commodity or services by non-monetary factors. But mankind's long interaction, association and experiences with the monetary system has made them oblivious of this aspect of valuation. In the meantime, commodities have multiplied in variety of assets; consumable and durable goods; tangible fixed assets like plant, machinery and equipment; real estate like land and buildings; intangible assets like goodwill, copyright, know-how and other intellectual property. Along with this trend, money has emerged in parallel lines as financial assets arrayed in an well-ordered series in near—money, credit cards, financial investments, as well as claims to various categories of debts, securitised or unsecured. The inter-twining of money or credit with goods and services,—existing, past or in future—has made people almost forgetful about the original value of commodities in a barter system and which is still continuing sheltered in a rudiment form in societies not fully marketised in the sense the Western world understands it.

Value-in-use

We have at the outset in this book referred to a distinction between VALUE-IN-USE and VALUE-IN-EXCHANGE. VALUE-IN-USE is essentially a non-market related term denoting the value that a specific property has for a specific use to a specific user, although such value may not be translated in monetary terms in the exchange market. If we look at the concept from a broader view we can identify a host of items satisfying human wants in the non-monetised sector of the economy and hence capable of being categorised as "assets" in the sense the term is understood in the valuation parlour. These items assume significance in the realm of valuation as because they have all the potentials of portage into the exchange economy with the growth of civilization and economic activities. Modern trend of investment seeks newer posture in the non-money economy after exhausting possibilities in the monetised sector. The division of labour paves the way and technology makes possible to create sophisticated markets for various kinds of services, which enrich the quality of life. Let us come to concrete illustrations. The parameters of quality of life outlined by the advanced countries generally include *per capita* intake of sufficient calorie as nutritional security, enjoyment of reasonable square meter of space for decent living, use of conventional electricity as energy base for maintaining a smooth living standard, consumption *per capita* of enough water, textile products, paper, plastic, etc.; use of individual car, or institutional health care or formal education facilities calculated in terms of provisions per thousand of population and the like. The environmental issues and 'carrying capacity' of the planet have posed a challenge if such prescribed quality of life standard can really be universalised or should it remain confined to a few privileged countries or privileged segments within a particular country. Again, satisfaction or happiness of life has not always been found resulting as *quid pro quo* to the adherence to prescribed standards. Alienation, suicide rate, divorce, drug-addiction alcoholism, crime, loneliness, frustration, etc. answer in a negative tone to rise in consumerism and consequent expansion of economic market by corroding the non-money economy.

Parameters of good quality of life

The parameters of good life came up for review in the sceptic quarters of futurists and thinkers. A pyrrhonian approach coins a new slogan that good life must after all seek a happy and contended existence on earth. The parameters thus attracted a fresh look and redefinition. In the revised perception, longevity together with healthy existence no doubt figure as the prime objective of man's earthly pursuits. Conducive to it, one must have gainful engagement during the working period of life and such engagement ought to bring a sense of fulfilment to the doer. In a nutshell, all these spell out the essence of good living, which, if universalised, may sustain the human civilization for rolling on an even track.

Relevance of non-money economy

It is in this context that non-money economy surfaces as a relevant consideration in the field of valuation. For a quality of life, it is immaterial whether the inputs come from monetised sector or from non-money economy. The traditional societies in the less-developed tribes or clans or developing countries carry a lot of economic activities in the womb of non-money economy and hence not treated as assets for valuation purposes in computation of national income. The processing of food in consumable form in many stages takes place within the household in a traditional society while the processed food in marketable form substitutes in a busy community—fruits are plucked and sized, fish scaled off and fried, meat cut into pieces and cooked, bread prepared in hand and baked, vegetables pieced and washed, milk skimmed and boiled in a traditional community by the mother herself. But in a high society of expanding markets populated by working people, these are available in the market fully processed with little to be done at home or ready in all respects in the hotels or restaurants or for home delivery in organised markets. The more busy the society is, the more it is taken as an advanced one; and more is the resultant division of labour for an expanding market. Concomitantly, value-addition takes place at every stage of processing and monetary valuation measures the contribution of each such stage at the consumption point of pricing. The potential valuation of activities within the household in a traditional society in its dietetic practices go unnoticed in the national income computation for having taken place behind the curtain. Similarly unaccounted are the labour of washing the lines or polishing the shoes within the household either by self-help or by the inmates. As soon as such washing or polishing takes place outside by hired labour or a machine bought from the market is made to perform the task, a market price for the service can be tagged.

The quality of life maintained in a traditional community is said to be the result of "bread labour". Such "bread labour" which essentially means supplying one's own needs by one's personal labour is not unique for traditional societies alone. The high price tag for manual labour has compelled a lot of economic activities in so-called an advanced economy being accomplished with personal labour rather than with hired labour. Even in an advanced society, a car-owner becomes his own chauffeur, a landlady becomes the cook and maid-servant for herself, a house-owner is its own painter and so on. A micro-economic analysis will reveal a huge area of such unaccounted activities having economic significance of value. For example, the father may be offering regular tuition to his son, the grandmother may be performing the task of baby-sitting, and the daughter may be entrusted with nursing and so on. As soon as those services are not available within the household, the activity enters into the formal market of the economy commanding valuation for the services rendered. The mother is replaced by a cook, father by a paid tutor, grandmother by a baby-sitter, and daughter by a paid nurse. The market in an expanding economy is replete with newer services for the changing society. Investment opportunities seek innovative ways of providing response to social needs in an ever-changing society and at the same time ensuring adequate return on investment. In this way, catering service, security service, courier service, telephonic booths, home nursing for the old etc. have made headway in the economic field. Valuation consideration necessarily creeps in. Today even the profession of surrogate motherhood has emerged as service on payment. Women have started shying motherhood to yield place to surrogate mothers hired at market rate. In Japan old people who miss the company of grandchildren in an atomized lonely families are known to hire the environ of the young kiddies' affection and tactile touch at heavy market rate. The trend is on and the non-money economy is the pasture of the future market. The economic horizon is ever-widening.

This vast area of non-money economy needs a "shadow valuation" so that the potential value of non-monetised economy does not go unaccounted. Again, the value-addition at each stage of performance in the non-monetised sector may find an "opportunity cost" for reckoning in order to reflect the real picture having meaningful reference to the acknowledged quality of life. As we have observed, it is immaterial from the view point of valuation whether the perceived quality of life is served in the formal sector of the economy or substantially in the non-monetised sector.

Services of voluntary organisations and potential value

From the micro-level analysis of the traditional households, we may turn to the macro-analysis of community-based activities performed by numerous voluntary organisations, which supplement the market-provided services. Such activities in the socio-economic front include extension work in the fields of health care, education to the poor, sanitation, rural development, women's empowerment, income-generation for the under-privileged, old age homes, orphanages and the like. The impact of all these services voluntarily provided no doubt can claim monetary value for appraisal of its contribution as against alternative market devices.

So long we have talked about goods and services in the non-money economy that can have 'realised value'. We may extend our research to areas of potential value, which lies in the non-money sector as because assets having value-in-use may nevertheless have potential value in the economic market of exchange. A scenic beauty in the deep untrodden mountain may have an exhilarating experience for an adventurous camper, but as soon as a network of communication brings it within the industry of tourism, the value-in-use reappears as having value-in-exchange too. Similarly, industrial research has made it possible for untapped natural forces to serve the cause of mankind in the formal sector of the economy. The telecommunication service is gradually abandoning the travel of messages and images through cables or wires laid for the purpose. Instead, free gift of nature like electromagnetic wave or satellite revolving in the gravitational field of nature is harnessed for service to mankind. Thus, the potential values of the free gifts of nature are gradually being converted into economic assets of realised value. The investments in scientific research and development concomitantly gain a momentum or leverage in valuation because of the enhanced potentiality it bears. The border-line between value-in-exchange and value-in-use is gradually becoming thin and shady. The capital-rich countries, thus, get a perpetual edge over others in a competitive international economy. In recent times, the overseas trunk call charges in telephone have shown a downward slope. The investments have been able to cut down a lot of expenses arising out of cable laying which is generally being replaced by movement along wireless devices using natural physical phenomenon of electromagnetic waves. The solar energy is coming more and more into use for heating, cooling and generation of non-conventional energy. Experiments in biotechnology have a tremendous potential for finding ways in our food chain by enriching the vegetational-yield as well as fodder for herbivorous animals as a stock of protein for human consumption.

Valuation approach in this way opens up a new window to peep into the non-monetised phenomenon around us. Since valuation is a process of estimating the worth of a commodity or service, it can ill-afford to ignore the potential contribution to the economy of these activities that stem from the non-monetary sector. A vast non-monetary sector awaits our concern as valuers. For example, in the tropical region, including countries like India, have the blessings of bright sunshine. But the solar energy remains yet to be harnessed for value-addition in diverse fields where it is relevant, whether in food chain or in non-conventional energy supply. The outlay on research in this field thus calls for an appraisal in a revised perspective. In the ultimate analysis, valuation as a discipline of study may provide a suitable technique for computation of the economic worth of assets that lie frozen in the non-money economy and also for estimating the probable realised value of various assets that silently yield contribution in the non-monetised sector of the economy.

Incidentally, it may be mentioned that in various countries including India, there is separate set of law that regulates the non-commercial organizations not meant for profit as distinct and different from laws applicable to companies or organization that are brought into existence for the commercial purpose of monetary gain. The non-commercial non-profit organizations are voluntary in character and generally known as non-governmental organizations or societies. Since they too own assets, deal with public fund and employ people, their income, accounts and functioning are subjected to regulatory control by the State. The Societies Registration Act of the State supplemented by the internal bye-laws of the society or organization provide the legal framework within which they operate. On the other hand, the companies for profit, private or public, having liabilities, limited or unlimited, are regulated and governed by an omnibus Central law called the Companies Act. We are not concerned in this paper with the valuation of assets owned by them. Nor are we concerned here with the assets owned by Government companies, although some of the Government-sponsored companies devote their assets exclusively for creating infrastructure not meant for profit, nor even for income. The norms for valuation of their assets are quite different. We exclude from our present valuation inquiry also the assets owned by the co-operative societies guide by different set of State laws as the co-operative societies do also exist for corporate profit and distribute dividends amongst the co-operative members.

In fine, the non-profit institutions mean those voluntary societies which are registered under the Societies Registration Act of the State Government and are guide by charitable or philanthropic purposes and even if they earn income from investment, projects, activities or commercial pursuits, no dividend or profit is distributed amongst its members or office-bearers; although in course of such activities or pursuits they may own property or assets including plant and machinery and employ hired personnel apparently in the same manner as any other commercial organizations.

Search for an appropriate approach to value

The next question is whether the non-profit activities, because of their charitable and philanthropic character, qualify for an approach to value different from others.

It is usual to categories assets for the purpose of valuation into three broad groups:

(1) Investment property having marketability.

(2) Non-investment property having marketability.

(3) Non-marketable non-investment property.

Valuation arises out of the three attributes of an asset.

- Utility;
- Scarcity;
- Marketability.

It is usually held that investment assets having marketability may be valued in accordance with both income capitalization method or sales comparison method since they possess all the attributes of utility, scarcity and marketability. The third category, i.e. non-marketable non-investment property known also as service property is valued in accordance with cost approach to valuation. As for example, schools, hospitals, temples, churches, city halls, etc. are neither investment property nor marketable ones. These are conveniently valued through estimating current construction cost and subtracting accrued depreciation and adding estimated land value thereto—an exercise which in substance is the cost approach to valuation.

Now a question arises if such an approach is sufficient to estimate the value of services rendered to the priority areas of the society which is often a void filled in by philanthropic or charitable non-governmental organizations piloted by followers of dedicated service not for profit but for social benefit. The assets held in the hands of such organizations are animated by a much greater purposeful use than one held for a mere commercial gain. If investment is the use and purpose of the asset, the income gives index for valuation. Why then should there not be an appropriate method of computing the total benefits arising out of such charitable venture? Take for example, a reformatory school or an orphanage run by a non-profit-making institution which converts liabilities of human resources into assets of social value. Had the same asset in terms of land, building and accessories been utilized as a commercial school, the income out of investment could have been an essential ingredient towards computation of value. When the same asset fulfils a priority need of the society and fills the void of a critical area, the series of benefits ensuing out of it assume a different character altogether. More so, when a missionary group of dedicated souls organized as a charitable institution pilots it with a sincere philanthropic motive. The co-efficient to the asset is changed and gives it a synergic value, as looked at from the societal end. It requires a close programming by the computer to quantify the burden relieved from the society in terms of social security expenses or together with other possibilities of employability of human resources in different vocations etc.

As the estranged children are given education or training in schools, it becomes necessary and to commute the economic and social value of their contribution as they pass out of the institution. An appropriate approach to valuation for computing the projected total benefit stream in a series at different stages is thus necessary for such cases for estimating the worth of it which may be quite different from the usual cost approach, income approach or market approach to value.

A valuer may look askance at the import of social element in valuation. But this is not uncommon. We know of economics of education which work out the value of investment in human capital in the field of education with reference to the return it provides to the community. We come across exercises to work out the benefit of inputs in health services by measuring the series of expected return to the community by a healthier manpower. Why should not there be an attempt to quantity the benefits or series of benefits of social services rendered by a new approach, i.e. the benefit approach to valuation? The only precaution that has to be taken is to identify the services and assets in the non-money economy that ought to be brought under the purview of valuation. Such benefit approach to valuation may apply also to the infra-structural projects of the Government like bridges across rivers, new townships, new thoroughfares, area development schemes, electricity provisions, etc. which are neither for profit nor for income but for aiding value-addition to existing resources. Now-a-days, valuation exercise is called for in privatisation of the same by schemes like 'Build-operate-Transfer (BOT) or Build-Operate-Own and Transfer (BOOT) and other variant forms of them. Valuation is also compulsive in making planning decisions in such matters as an internal exercise not covered by the traditional cost-benefit analysis. A highway scheme may give results for centuries in a series of benefits. So also a river bridge, which develops both sides of a city across the river centuries after centuries cities like Budapest, London, New York, Hong Kong, Paris or Kolkata has grown up in this way. A computerised system of assessing the growth potential at different stages in time may provide the 'Benefit Approach' as a new approach value in such cases.

CHAPTER

24

The Construction & Application and Use of Life Tables

A valuer may be called upon to value a property which is subject to a Life Interest of a person or persons, and it is for this reason that a thorough knowledge of the Mortality Tables, the Expectation of Life Tables, and the Year's Purchase for Life Tables should be had by the valuer.

A Life Interest may be of two kinds:

(1) *Tenant for life.* In this case the Tenant for Life is in the same position as a freeholder, except that he only owns the property for the duration of his or her life. The person is not bound by any repairing covenants like a tenant holding under a lease, and for the duration of his or her life the person has an absolute right in the property. The Tenant for Life cannot sell the property, because after his or her death the property will pass to the reversioner or remainder-man. The Tenant for Life may sell his or her interest in the property, but the purchaser's interest will only be for the duration of the life of the vendor.

(2) *Lessee for life.* In this case the Lessee for Life holds the property under a lease for the duration of his or her life, subject to the payment of rent and the observance of any other clause in the lease. In valuing the interest of a "Lease for Life" the first item will be for the Profit Rental to be ascertained in the same way as has been explained in the valuation of leasehold interests. The capitalisation of the Profit Rental will be done

at the ordinary leasehold rates per cent, instead of the lower percentages which will be applicable for a "Tenant for Life".

The tables will give at a glance the year's purchase at a given rate per cent and according to the age of the party. These tables have been compiled from—

Expectation of Life

MALES

Age	Carlisle Table	England and Wales Census by Census					
	1779-87	1881	1891	1901	1911	1921	1931
0	38.7	43.4	43.2	45.9	51.6	55.5	58.7
5	51.2	52.0	51.8	54.1	57.2	58.8	60.1
10	48.8	48.6	48.1	50.1	53.1	54.7	55.8
15	45.0	44.4	43.7	45.7	48.6	50.2	51.2
20	41.5	40.3	39.5	41.5	44.2	45.8	46.8
25	37.9	36.5	35.6	37.4	40.0	41.6	42.6
35	31.0	29.1	28.0	29.5	31.7	33.3	33.9
45	24.5	22.4	21.1	22.3	23.9	25.3	25.5
55	17.6	16.0	15.0	15.9	16.9	17.8	17.9
65	11.8	10.5	9.7	10.4	11.0	11.4	11.3
75	7.0	6.1	5.7	6.1	6.4	6.6	6.4
85	4.1	3.3	3.1	3.4	3.6	3.7	3.5

FEMALES

Age	Carlisle Table	England and Wales Census by Census					
	1779-87	1881	1891	1901	1911	1921	1931
0	38.7	46.6	46.7	49.8	55.4	59.5	62.9
5	51.2	54.0	54.1	56.7	59.9	61.7	63.2
10	48.8	50.6	50.4	52.9	55.9	57.5	58.9
15	45.0	46.4	46.0	48.5	51.4	53.1	54.3
20	41.5	42.4	41.9	44.3	47.1	48.7	49.9
25	37.9	38.6	37.9	40.1	42.8	44.5	45.6
35	31.0	31.4	30.3	32.0	34.4	36.1	36.9
45	24.5	24.4	23.2	24.5	26.3	27.8	28.3
55	17.6	17.5	16.3	17.5	18.9	19.9	20.2
65	11.8	11.5	10.6	11.4	12.4	12.9	13.1
75	7.0	6.7	6.2	6.8	7.3	7.5	7.5
85	4.1	3.6	3.4	3.7	4.1	4.1	4.0

Mortality Tables

The object of Mortality Tables is to ascertain the rates of Mortality prevailing amongst the community in order that forecasts may be made for the future. The first known tables were compiled by De Wit, the Grand Pensionary of Holland, who in the 17th century prepared life annuity tables in which the interest element was correctly used. The best two known tables are the Northampton and the Carlisle Tables.

The Northampton Tables were compiled by Dr. Richard Price from data recorded in the Parish registers at Northampton in 1780. The number of selected lives according to the tables was 11,650 and each year is shown the number of persons still living until after 97 years all were dead. Northampton at this time was not a very healthy neighbourhood, and although these tables were used fairly extensively at the time, in later years they were generally discarded in favour of the Carlisle Tables.

The Carlisle Tables were compiled by Mr. Joshua Milne from the abridged bills of Mortality of Carlisle for the nine years 1779—87 by Dr. Heysham. The population of two parishes in Carlisle, St. Mary and St. Cuthberts, were also tabulated in January 1780, and December 1787, in groups of ages, and for years afterwards these Mortality Tables, when compiled, were extensively used and are still being used today.

In England and Wales since the Census of 1841 it has been the custom to review the mortality experience of each successive census and the latest tables that have been compiled from these figures are the English Life Tables.

The Carlisle Tables do not show any distinction between males and females and a comparison of the Expectation of Life taken from the Carlisle Tables with the Expectation of Life in England and Wales taken from Whitakers Almanac Census by Census is of interest.

From a perusal of these tables it will be seen that very little change has taken place from the age of 45 and upwards, whereas the Expectation of Life for an infant has been advanced 20 years. The reason is not far to seek. In the United Kingdom considerable advances have been made in Child Welfare, and throughout that country many prenatal and maternity clinics have been opened and many Child Welfare Committees throughout the country have been established. This has had the result of considerably lessening the mortality amongst the young inhabitants.

The death rate amongst infants and children in India is one of the highest in the world and it would be absurd to capitalise incomes receivable by young persons based on the English Life Tables. There are no up-to-date tables published for Indian lives, and the best guide will be to take the Carlisle Tables until such times as tables are published for this country. The Carlisle Tables will undoubtedly give slightly higher values than if actual tables based on Indian lives were available, but if any person is to derive any slight benefit from an estate, it is only equitable that this should go to the life estate-holder in preference to the reversioner.

It must be distinctly understood that the Expectation of Life Tables does not show the years a person will live, but the number of years that the average person may be expected to live. This again is not absolute because a person aged 75 has an expectation of 7 years, and at 80 years, when 5 years have passed, he still has an expectation of a 5.51 years, and again at 85 after a further 5 years have passed, he still has an expectation 4.12 years. The Carlisle Tables of Mortality show how many people out of the 10,000 selected lives attain different ages and it is from these tables that the probability of a person living another year can be calculated.

In making calculations of the value of a life interest it would appear at first sight that the mean Expectation of Life Tables would be all that is required. This, of course, is wrong. To capitalise an income you cannot multiply the amount by the assumed average number of years a person will live, because there is always the probability that he may die before he reaches his next birthday. The present value of ₹ 1 per annum (or Year's Purchase) for a single life according to the Carlisle Table of Mortality is set out in Parry's book pages 178 to 181, and the following is the method adopted for the compilation of these tables.

Year's purchase—single life

The figure of year's purchase will be made up of a series of sums of ₹ 1 each receivable at the ends of successive years, and continued to be so received until, according to the Mortality Tables adopted, the life ceases to exist. These figures of present value are known as contingent values, since they are contingent on the person living long enough to receive it. For instance, if you were calculating the present value of an income of ₹ 1 per annum receivable for the lifetime of a man aged 102. The Present Value of ₹ 1 receivable in 1 year at, say, 4% = .9615. From the tables you will see that 5 people attain the age of 102 and only 3 of them celebrate their 103rd birthday; therefore, the first year's income value would be .9615 multiplied by $^3/_5$ or .6 being the probability fraction that the man will survive another year. For the next year you take the Present Value of ₹ 1 in 2 years' time = .9245 and multiply this by the probability fraction that the man will survive another year. From the tables it will be seen that one person celebrated his 104th birthday; therefore, the fraction is $^1/_5$ or 0.2.

The following example shows clearly the process necessary for calculation of the Year's Purchase:

EXAMPLE 90. What is the Year's Purchase for a Single Life according to the Carlisle Mortality Tables at 5 per cent for a person aged 95?

1. Present value to a person aged 95 years of the right to receive ₹ 1 one year hence, provided he lives one year:

   P.V. of ₹ 1 in one year @ 5% = .952381

   No. of persons alive at age of 95 according to Carlisle Mortality Tables 30

   No. of persons surviving until age of 96 23

   Probability of person aged 95 living to age 96 ... ... $\frac{23}{30}$ = .766666

   Contingent Value. (P.V. of ₹ 1 in 1 year × by probability fraction) ... .730158

2. P.V. to person aged 95 yrs. of right to receive ₹ 1 two years hence, provided he lives 2 years:

   P.V. of ₹ 1 in 2 years @ 5% = .9070295

Probability of person aged 95 living to age 97 = .6

Contingent Value = .544218

3. P.V. to person aged 95 of right to receive ₹ 1, 3 years hence, provided he lives 3 years.

   P.V. of ₹ 1 in 3 years @ 5% = .8638375

   Probability of person aged 95 living to age 98 = .4666666

Contingent Value = .403124

4. P.V. to person aged 95 of right to receive ₹ 1, 4 years hence, provided he lives 4 years.

   P.V. of ₹ 1 in 4 years @ 5% = .8227025

   Probability of person aged 95 living to age 99 = .3666666

Contingent Value = .301658

5. P.V. to person aged 95 of right to receive ₹ 1, 5 years hence, provided he lives 6 years.

   P.V. of ₹ 1 in 5 years @ 5% = .7835262

   Probability of person aged 95 living to age 100 = .3

Contingent Value = .235057

6. P.V. to person aged 95 of right to receive ₹ 1, 6 years hence, provided he lives 6 years.

   P.V. of ₹ 1 in 6 years @ 5% = .7462154

   Probability of person aged 95 living to age 101 = .2333333

Contingent Value = .174117

7. P.V. to person aged 95 of right to receive ₹ 1, 7 years hence, provided he lives 7 years.

   P.V. of ₹ 1 in 7 years @ 5% = .7106813

Probability of person aged 95 living to age 102	= .1666666	
Contingent Value	=	.118447
8. P.V. to person aged 95 of right to receive ₹ 1, 8 years hence, provided he lives 8 years.		
P.V. of ₹ 1 in 8 years @ 5%	= .6768394	
Probability of person aged 95 living to age 103	= .1	
Contingent Value	=	.067684
9. P.V. to person aged 95 of right to receive ₹ 1, 9 years hence, provided he lives 9 years.		
P.V. of ₹ 1 in 9 years @ 5%	= .6446089	
Probability of person aged 95 living to age 104	= .0333333	
Contingent Value	=	.021487
10. P.V. to person aged 95 of right to receive ₹ 1, 10 years hence, provided he lives 10 years.		
P.V. of ₹ 1 in 10 years @ 5%	= .6139133	
Probability of person aged 95 living to age 105	= *Nil*	
Contingent Value	=	.000000
Y.P. for life aged 95 according to the Carlisle Mortality Tables at 5%	=	2.595950

YEAR'S PURCHASE FOR THE JOINT CONTINUATION OF TWO OR MORE LIVES

These tables are very little used, but in order to show how to calculate the longer of two lives and for those who may have to deal with a case involving the interest of this nature, the following is the method adopted for ascertainment of year's purchase:

"Add together the contingent values of a series of sums of ₹ 1 each receivable at the end of successive years continued to be so received until, according to the Mortality Tables, the elder person ceases to exist."

The following examples will make this clear:

EXAMPLE 91. What is the Year's Purchase for the joint continuation of 2 lives aged 75 and 101 using the Carlisle Mortality Tables and $3^1/_2$%?

Probability of person aged 75 living to age 76	Probability of person aged 101 living to age 102	Present value of ₹ 1 in one year	Contingent Present Value of ₹ 1
(1) = $\frac{1515}{1675}$	$\times \frac{5}{7} \times$	.9661836 =	.624208
(2) = $\frac{1359}{1675}$	$\times \frac{3}{7} \times$	.9335107 =	.324599
(3) = $\frac{1213}{1675}$	$\times \frac{1}{7} \times$	.9019427 =	.093310
(4) = $\frac{1081}{1675}$	$\times \frac{0}{7} \times$	.8714422 =	.000000
		Year's Purchase =	1.042117

If the valuer was required to ascertain the Year's Purchase for the joint continuation of 3 lives, he would simply multiply the contingent Present Values by the probability of the 3rd person living another year.

YEAR'S PURCHASE FOR THE LONGER OF 2 LIVES

The ascertainment of the Year's Purchase for the longer of two lives has frequently to be found by a valuer and the following is the correct formula:

> "Add together the Year's Purchase for each single life and subtract the year's Purchase for the joint continuation of the two lives."

The method of ascertaining the Year's Purchase for a single life and for the joint continuation of two lives has been explained. The figures, taken from Parry's Table for the example, are as follows:

EXAMPLE 92. What is the Year's Purchase for the longer of two lives aged 40 and 65 according to the Carlisle Mortality Tables? 3 per cent table to be used.

SOLUTION

Y.P. single life aged 40 @ 3%.	Carlisle Tables	=	17.142
Y.P. single life aged 65 @ 3%.	Carlisle Tables	=	8.917
	Total	=	26.059

Y.P. joint continuation of 2 lives aged 40 and 65 @ 3%.
Carlisle Table = 8.006

Y.P. longer of two lives aged 40 and 65 @ 3%.
Carlisle Tables = 18.053

YEAR'S PURCHASE FOR THE LONGEST OF 3 LIVES

The ascertainment of the Year's Purchase for the longest of three lives is found by the following formula:

> "Add together the Year's Purchase for each single life and for the joint continuation of the three lives and subtract from this sum the total of the Year's Purchase for the joint continuation of each pair of lives."

EXAMPLE 93. What is the Year's Purchase for the longest of three lives aged 40, 60 and 102 according to the Carlisle Mortality Tables and at 4 per cent?

SOLUTION

Three Single Lives—

Y.P. single life aged 40 @ 4%.	Carlisle Tables	=	15.074
Y.P. single life aged 60 @ 4%.	Carlisle Tables	=	9.663
Y.P. single life aged 102 @ 4%.	Carlisle Tables	=	.762
			25.499

Joint Continuation of three lives—

(1) $\frac{5009}{5075} \times \frac{3521}{3643} \times \frac{3}{5} \times .9615385 = .5503$

(2) $\frac{4940}{5075} \times \frac{3395}{3643} \times \frac{1}{5} \times .9245562 = .1677$

(3) $\frac{4869}{5075} \times \frac{3268}{3643} \times \frac{0}{5} \times .8889964 = .0000$

= .718

Total of the Y.P. for the 3 Single Lives and the Joint Continuation of the three lives = 26.217

Joint Continuation of each pair of lives—

Aged 40 and 60 @ 4%. Pages 186 = 8.5530

$= \frac{5009}{5075} \times \frac{3}{5} \times .9615385 = .5694$

$$= \frac{4940}{5075} \times \frac{1}{5} \times .9245562 \quad = \quad .1800$$

$$= \frac{4869}{5075} \times \frac{0}{5} \times .8889964 \quad = \quad .0000$$

$$= \quad .7494$$

Aged 60 *and* 102—

$$= \frac{3521}{3643} \times \frac{3}{5} \times .9615385 \quad = \quad .5576$$

$$= \frac{3395}{3643} \times \frac{1}{5} \times .9245562 \quad = \quad .1723$$

$$= \frac{3268}{3643} \times \frac{0}{5} \times .8889964 \quad = \quad .0000$$

$$= \quad .7299$$

Y.P. for joint continuation of each pair of lives = 10.0323

Y.P. for the longest of 3 lives aged 40, 60 and 102 = 16.1847

The calculation for the longest of 3 lives is of a very speculative nature since so much depends on the state of health of the life holders and therefore one decimal place is all that is required. The answer to this example would therefore be *16.2 year's purchase*.

This method of calculating the Year's Purchase for the longest of three lives, whilst being as near accurate as statistics can prove, the calculation would be very laborious if the three lives were of tender years, and Parry Tables page 198 give an easier formula which will give an answer approximately correct:

Let *X, Y, Z* represent the three ages (*X* being the youngest and *Z* the eldest).

Let *W* be that age at which the Year's Purchase for a single life is the same as the Year's Purchase for the joint continuation of two lives *Y* and *Z*.

Rule—Add together the Year's Purchase for the longer of two lives aged (*X* and *Y*) and (*X* and *Z*) respectively and subtract from this sum the Year's Purchase for the longer of two lives aged (*X* and *W*).

EXAMPLE 94. What is the Year's Purchase for the longest of three lives aged 20, 30 and 40 using the $4\frac{1}{2}$ per cent Carlisle Tables?

SOLUTION

Y.P. $4^1/_2$% longer of two lives aged 20 and 30	=	18.935
Y.P. $4^1/_2$% longer of two lives aged 20 and 40	=	18.473
		37.408
Y.P. joint continuation of lives aged 30 and 40 @ $4^1/_2$%	=	12.224
Y.P. single life $4^1/_2$% age 50	=	12.239
∴ W = 50 years.		
Y.P. $4^1/_2$% longer of two lives aged 20 and 50	=	18.019
Y.P. longest of 3 lives aged 20, 30 and 40 @ $4^1/_2$%	=	19.389

APPLICATION OF LIFE TABLES

The following are few examples of the valuation of life interests which are likely to be met with in a valuer's practice:

EXAMPLE 95. What is the present value to a person aged 50 of the right to receive ₹ 10,000 in 10 years' time providing he lives 10 years, using the Carlisle Mortality Tables at 6 per cent?

SOLUTION

Sum to receive in 10 years' time = ₹ 10,000

P.V. of ₹ 1 receivable in 10 yrs @ 6% = .5583948

Multiply by probability of person person aged 50 living to age 60 = 3643 / 4397

= .46264

Present Value ... = ₹ 4,626

EXAMPLE 96. What is the present value of a net income of ₹ 5,000 per annum received from freehold secured ground rents, receivable during the lifetime of a person aged 50, according to the Carlisle Mortality Tables?

SOLUTION

Net Income	= ₹	5,000
Y.P. single life aged 50 @ $4^1/_2$%	=	12.239
Present Value	= ₹	61,195

EXAMPLE 97. What is the Reversioner's Interest in the property described in Example 96?

SOLUTION

Net Income		= ₹	5,000
Y.P. @ $4^1/_2$% perpetuity	= 22.222		
Y.P. single life aged 50 @ $4^1/_2$%	= 12.239		
Y.P. @ $4^1/_2$% perpetuity after death of person aged 50		=	2.983
Present Value of Reversioner's Interest		= ₹	49,915

EXAMPLE 98. What is the present value of a reversion to a leasehold property producing a net income of ₹ 10,000 per annum. The lease has a life of 50 years but at present is held by a person aged 55 years?

SOLUTION

The property being between ₹ 1 and 2 lakhs in value the security would be $6^1/_2$ per cent. For leasehold and 1 per cent. But as this is a very speculative reversion add another $^1/_2$ per cent.

Net Income		= ₹	10,000
Y.P. 50 years @ 8%	= 12.233		
Y.P. single life aged 55 @ 8%	= 8.179		
Y.P. for Reversion to remainder of 50 years lease after death of a person now aged 55 according to Carlisle Table at 8%	= 4.054		
Value of Reversion		= ₹	40,540

EXAMPLE 99. What is the present value to the heir of a person aged 60 who has just purchased the life interest held by a person aged 25 in a property producing a net income of ₹ 10,000 per annum? Use the Carlisle 8 per cent tables.

SOLUTION

Net Income		= ₹	10,000
Y.P. single life aged 25 @ 8%	= 10.762		
Y.P. single life aged 60 @ 8%	= 7.245		

Y.P. for the Reversion to an income during the life of a person aged 25 after the death of a person aged 60 according to Carlisle Table at 6%	=	3.517
Value of Reversion	= ₹	35,170

EXAMPLE 100. Mr. *X* aged 70 has a life interest in a leasehold property having 5 years' unexpired life and producing a net income of ₹ 10,000 per annum. Mr. *Y* has a reversionary interest in Mr. *X*'s Estate. What is the present value of *Y*'s interest?

SOLUTION

Net Income		= ₹	10,000
Y.P. 5 years @ 10%	= 3.791		
Y.P. single life aged 70 @ 10%	= 4.918		
Remainder man's interest		=	Nil
Value of Remainder		= ₹	0

This answer is worked out on the assumption that Mr. *X* is unlikely to die during the remainder of the unexpired portion of the lease, but there is no certainty that the man aged 70 will live to the age of 75, therefore, there is a chance that Mr. *Y* may succeed to the estate. Most valuers would make a spot valuation of Mr. *Y*'s chances based on his personal knowledge of Mr. *X* and Mr. *Y* and in this case he might say that *Y*'s value may be estimated at ½ Y.P.

The true value can, however, be calculated and the following calculation is the method to adopt:

Year's Purchase for a term of 5 years contingent on prior death of man aged 70 on Carlisle Tables at 10

Year of instalment of income	P.V. of ₹ 1 if certain of receipt	Age at date of instalment & age today	Contingent PV. of ₹ 1 to lifeholder	Contingent P.V. of ₹ 1 to remainderman
(1) .909	$\frac{71}{70}$	$\frac{2277}{2401} \times .909$	$.909 - \left(\frac{2277}{2401} \times .909\right)$	= .047
(2) .826	$\frac{72}{70}$	$\frac{2143}{2401} \times .826$	$.826 - \left(\frac{2143}{2401} \times .826\right)$	= .089

Year of instalment of income	P.V. of ₹ 1 if certain of receipt	Age at date of instalment & age today	Contingent PV. of ₹ 1 to lifeholder	Contingent P.V. of ₹ 1 to remainderman
(3) .751	$\frac{73}{70}$	$\frac{1997}{2401} \times .751$	$.751-\left(\frac{1997}{2401}\times.751\right)$	= .126
(4) .683	$\frac{74}{70}$	$\frac{1841}{2401} \times .683$	$.683-\left(\frac{1841}{2401}\times.683\right)$	= .159
(5) .621	$\frac{75}{70}$	$\frac{1675}{2401} \times .621$	$.621-\left(\frac{1675}{2401}\times.621\right)$	= .188

Y.P. for reversion to temporary income lasting 5 years but not received until the death of the lifeholder aged 70, Carlisle Tables 10 per cent	=		.609
Net Income	=	₹	10,000
Y.P. as above			.609
Reversionary value of Mr. *Y*	=	₹	6,090

This answer must be considered much more accurate than the approximation of 1/2 Y.P. which is equivalent to ₹ 5,000.

EXAMPLE 101. What is the value of a Net Income of ₹ 1,000 per annum receivable so long as two people aged 40 and 60 remain alive according to the Carlisle Mortality Tables at 6 per cent?

SOLUTION

Net Income	= ₹	1,000
Y.P. Joint continuation of 2 lives aged 40 and 60 at 6%	=	7.436
Present Value	= ₹	7,436

EXAMPLE 102. What is the Reversionary value of the property described in Example 101?

SOLUTION

Net Income		= ₹	1,000
Y.P. for perpetuity at 6%	... 16.667		
Y.P. Joint continuation of 2 lives aged 40 and 60 @ 6%	... 7.436		
Y.P. for Reversion		=	9.231
Present Value of Reversion		= ₹	9,231

EXAMPLE 103. What premium should the lifeholders mentioned in Example 101 pay, if their interest is extended to the longer of two lives?

SOLUTION

Net Income		= ₹ 1,000
Y.P. longer of 2 lives and aged 40 and 60 at 6%	... 12.870	
Y.P. Joint continuation of 2 lives aged 40 and 60 @ 6%	... 7.436	
Year's Purchase for Premium		= 5.434
		= ₹ 5,434

EXAMPLE 104. What is the value of a Net Income of ₹ 1,000 per annum receivable for the longer of two lives aged 40 and 60 in accordance with the Carlisle Mortality Tables at 6 per cent?

SOLUTION

Net Income	= ₹ 1,000
Y.P. for longer of 2 lives aged 40 and 60 at 6%	= 12.870
Present Value	= ₹ 12,870

EXAMPLE 105. What is the Reversionary Value of the property mentioned Example 104?

SOLUTION

Net Income		= ₹ 1,000
Y.P. for perpetuity @ 6%	= 16.667	
Y.P. for longer of 2 lives aged 40 and 60 at 6%	= 12.870	
Y.P. for perpetuity at 6% deferred for the longer of 2 lives aged 40 and 60		= 3.797
Reversionary Value		= ₹ 3,797

EXAMPLE 106. What premium should a tenant for life aged 55 pay to the reversioner for extending his life interest in a net income of ₹ 1,000 per annum so that it may include his son's life now aged 25 according to the Carlisle Mortality Tables at 6 per cent?

SOLUTION

Net Income			= ₹	1,000
U.P. longer of 2 lives aged 25 and 55 @ 6%	=	14.190		
Y.P. single life aged 55 @ 6%	=	9.524		
Year's Purchase			=	4.666
Premium			= ₹	4,666

EXAMPLE 107. Find the total interest of two life tenants and their separate interests in a net income of ₹ 2,000 per annum. The tenants are aged 30 and 50. They hold as joint tenants, eight annas share each, for the longer of two lives. Six per cent interest is required.

SOLUTION

Total Interest—

Net Income	= ₹	2,000		
Y.P. longer of 2 lives aged 30 and 50 at 6% Carlisle Tables	=	14.097		
Value of Combined interest of the two tenants *A* and *B*			= ₹	28,194

A's Interest—

Net Income, half of total Income	= ₹	1,000		
Y.P. single life aged 30 @ 6% Carlisle Tables	=	13.020	= ₹	13,020
A's Reversion to *B*'s Income of ₹ 1,000 Y.P. longer of 2 lives aged 30 and 50 @ 6%	=	14.097		
Y.P. single life aged 50 @ 6%	=	10.631		
Y.P. for *A*'s Reversion	=	3.466	= ₹	3,466
Value of *A*'s Interest			= ₹	16,486

B's Interest—

Net Income, half of total Income	= ₹	1,000		
Y.P. single life aged 50 @ 6%	=	10.631	= ₹	10,631
B's Reversion to *B*'s Income of ₹ 1,000 Y.P. longer of 2 lives aged 30 and 50 @ 6%	=	14.097		
Y.P. single life aged 30 @ 6%	=	13.020		

Y.P. for *B*'s Reversion	=	1.077	= ₹ 1,077
Value of *B*'s Interest			= ₹ 11,708

EXAMPLE 108. What is the present value of a Net Income of ₹ 1,000 per annum held for the longest of 3 lives aged 20, 30 and 40; Interest required is $4^1/_2$ per cent?

SOLUTION

Net Income	= ₹	1,000
Y.P. longest of 3 lives aged 20, 30 and 40, Carlisle Table @ $4^1/_2$%	=	19.389
Present Value		= ₹ 19,389

EXAMPLE 109. What is the Reversionary Value of the income mentioned in Example 108?

SOLUTION

Net Income		= ₹ 1,000
Y.P. @ $4^1/_2$% in perpetuity	= 22.222	
Y.P. longest of 3 lives aged 20, 30 and 40, @ $4^1/_2$%	= 19.389	
Y.P. for Reversion	= 2.833	
Value of Reversion		= ₹ 2,833

EXAMPLE 110. A net income of ₹ 1,000 per annum is held by 2 persons aged 30 and 40 for the longer of their two lives. They wish to add another life at present aged 20. What premium should they pay. Interest required is $4^1/_2$ per cent?

SOLUTION

Net Income		= ₹ 1,000
Y.P. longer of 3 lives aged 20, 30 and 40 @ $4^1/_2$%	= 19.389	
Y.P. longer of 2 lives aged 30 and 40 @ $4^1/_2$%	= 17.692	
Y.P. for premium	= 1.697	
Premium		= ₹ 1,697

ANNUITIES

A valuer may have to advise a client on the cost of purchasing an annuity. He will naturally consult the leading Insurance Companies before finally committing himself but he can with very little trouble ascertain the approximate amount required from the Carlisle Tables. The best guide he can have is to take the Carlisle Tables for a single life loaded 20 per cent. Three of the leading Insurance Companies were asked to quote for the purchase of an annuity for a man aged 74. The figures quoted represented 6.01, 6.55 and 7.23 Year's Purchase. At that time $3\frac{1}{2}$ per cent G.P. Notes were yielding about 4 per cent and the following example will show the method of ascertaining the purchase price:

EXAMPLE 111. What would be the approximate cost of purchasing an Annuity of ₹ 2,500 per annum for a man aged 74?

SOLUTION

Annuity Required		= ₹ 2,500
Y.P. single life aged 74 @ 4%, Carlisle Tables	= 5.458	
Add 20% for Insurance risks and profits	= 1.092	
Year's Purchase	= 6.55	
Purchase Price of Annuity		= ₹ 16,375

SINGLE PREMIUM FOR LIFE ASSURANCE

A person may be the owner of a property which is subject to a life interest and he may now wish to invest a sum which will accumulate to the amount required after the death of the tenant for life. The rule for ascertainment of the Year's Purchase is—

> "Find the Year's Purchase for the reversion to a perpetuity after the given life and divide the result by the Year's Purchase for perpetuity *plus one.*"

EXAMPLE 112. What sum should be invested now so that it will accumulate to ₹ 1 after the death of a person aged 60? Use Carlisle 4 per cent tables.

SOLUTION

Y.P. for Perpetuity @ 4%		25.000
Y.P. single life aged 60 @ 4% ...		9.663
Y.P. Perpetuity @ 4% after death of person aged 60		15.337

Single Premium $= 15.337 \div (25.000 + 1)$

$$= \frac{15.337}{26}$$

$$= 0.58988$$

EXAMPLE 113. A man recently purchased the life interest in a property of a man aged 60 for ₹ 10,000. What sum should be invested now so that he may recover his capital after the death of the lifeholder?

SOLUTION

Amount to be redeemed	= ₹	10,000
Single premium to secure ₹ 1 after death of man aged 60 @ 6%.	=	0.58988
Amount to be invested now	= ₹	5,899

Instead of investing a single premium a man may wish to pay an annual premium. The rule for ascertainment of the premium is:

"Divide the Single Premium for an assurance of ₹ 1 on the life by the Year's Purchase for the *life plus one.*"

EXAMPLE 114. What annual sum should be paid at the beginning of each year to secure ₹ 1 after the death of a person aged 60 according to the Carlisle 4% tables?

SOLUTION

Single Premium	= 0.58988
Year's Purchase single life aged 60 @ 4%	= 9.663

Annual Premium $= 0.58988 \div (9.663 + 1)$

$$= \frac{0.58988}{10.663}$$

$$= 0.05532$$

EXAMPLE 115. A man recently purchased the life interest in a property of a man aged 60 for ₹ 10,000. What annual sum should he now pay to secure the recovery of his capital after the death of the tenant for life?

SOLUTION

Amount to be redeemed	= ₹	10,000
Annual premium to secure ₹ 1 after death of person aged 60 @ 4%. (See Example 114)	=	0.05532
Annual Premium	= ₹	553

Conversion Table

1 Acre	=	4,840	sq yds	=	4046.724	sq m
1 Hectare	=	10,000	sq m	=	2.4711	acres
1 sq km	=	100	hectares	=	0.3861	sq mile
1 sq cm	=	100	sq mm	=	0.1550	sq inch
1 sq metre	=	10,000	sq cm	=	1.1960	sq yds
1 sq mile	=	640	acres	=	259.0	hectares
1 sq yard	=	9	sq ft	=	0.8361	sq m
1 sq inch	=	6.4516	sq cm			
1 inch	=	25.4	mm	=	2.54	cm
1 ft	=	12	inches	=	0.3048	m
1 yard	=	3	feet	=	0.9144	m
1 mile	=	1760	yards	=	1.6093	km
1 mm	=	0.0394	inch			
1 cm	=	10	mm	=	0.3937	inch
1 metre	=	1,000	mm	=	1.0936	yds
1 km	=	1,000	m	=	0.6214	mile

Land Measure in West Bengal

45	Square feet	...	= 1 Chittack
16	Chittacks or 720 square feet or 80 square yards	...	= 1 Kottah
20	Kottahs	...	= 1 Bigha
1	Acre	...	= 3 Bighas (approx.)
			= 60.5 Kottahs (approx.)
1	Satak (Decimal)	= 0.01 Acre	= 0.605 Kottah
		= 435.6 sq ft	= 40.468 sq m
1	Kottah	= 66.888 Sq m	= 1.653 Satak (approx.)

Valuation Tables

Present Value of Re. 1 per annum	(Single Rate)
Present Value of Re. 1 per annum	(Dual Rate)
Present Value of Re. 1	
Annual Sinking Fund	
Present Value of Re. 1 per annum	(Single Life)
Mortality and Mean Expectàtion of Life	(Carlisle Tables)

PRESENT VALUE OF RE. 1 PER ANNUM
OR
YEAR'S PURCHASE

Yrs.	3%	$3^1/_2$%	4%	$4^1/_2$%	5%	$5^1/_2$%	Yrs.
1.	.971	.966	.962	.957	.952	:948	1.
2.	1.913	1.900	1.886	1.873	1.859	1.846	2.
3.	2.829	2.802	2.775	2.740	2.723	2.698	3.
4.	3.717	3.673	3.630	3.588	3.546	3.505	4.
5.	4.580	4.515	4.452	4.390	4.329	4.270	5.
6.	5.417	5.329	5.242	5.158	5.076	4.996	6.
7.	6.230	6.115	6.002	5.893	5.786	5.683	7.
8.	7.020	6.874	6.733	6.596	6.463	6.335	8.
9.	7.786	7.608	7.435	7.269	7.108	6.952	9.
10.	8.530	8.317	8.111	7.013	7.722	7.538	10.
11.	9.253	9.002	8.760	8.529	8.306	8.093	11.
12.	9.954	9.663	9.385	9.119	8.863	8.619	12.
13.	10.635	10.303	9.986	9.683	9.394	9.117	13.
14.	11.296	10.921	10.563	10.223	9.899	9.590	14.
15.	11.938	11.517	11.118	10.740	10.380	10.038	15.
16.	12.561	12.094	11.652	11.234	10.838	10.462	16.
17.	13.166	12.651	12.166	11.707	11.274	10.865	17.
18.	13.754	13.190	12.659	12.160	11.690	11.246	18.
19.	14.324	13.710	13.134	12.593	12.085	11.608	19.
20.	14.877	14.212	13.590	13.008	12.462	11.950	20.
21.	15.415	14.698	14.029	13.405	12.821	12.275	21.
22.	15.937	15.167	14.451	13.784	13.163	12.583	22.
23.	16.444	15.620	14.857	14.148	13.489	12.875	23.
24.	16.936	16.058	15.247	14.495	13.799	13.152	24.
25.	17.413	16.482	15.622	14.828	14.094	13.414	25.
26.	17.877	16.890	15.983	15.147	14.375	13.662	26.
27.	18.327	17.285	16.330	15.451	14.643	13.898	27.
28.	18.764	17.667	16.663	15.743	14.898	14.121	28.
29.	19.188	18.036	16.984	16.022	15.141	14.333	29.
30.	19.600	18.392	17.292	16.289	15.372	14.534	30.
31.	20.000	18.736	17.588	16.544	15.593	14.724	31.
32.	20.389	19.069	17.874	16.789	15.803	14.904	32.
33.	20.766	19.390	18.148	17.023	16.003	15.075	33.
34.	21.132	19.701	18.411	17.247	16.193	15.237	34.
35.	21.487	20.001	18.665	17.461	16.374	15.391	35.
36.	21.832	20.290	18.908	17.666	16.547	15.536	36.
37.	22.167	20.571	19.143	17.862	16.711	15.674	37.
38.	22.492	20.841	19.368	18.050	16.868	15.805	38.
39.	22.808	21.102	19.584	18.230	17.017	15.929	39.
40.	23.115	21.355	19.793	18.402	17.159	16.046	40.
41.	23.412	21.599	19.993	18.566	17.294	16.157	41.
42.	23.701	21.835	20.186	18.724	17.423	16.263	42.
43.	23.982	22.063	20.371	18.874	17.546	16.363	43.
44.	24.254	22.283	20.549	19.018	17.663	16.458	44.
45.	24.519	22.495	20.720	19.156	17.774	16.548	45.
46.	24.775	22.701	20.885	19.288	17.880	16.633	46.
47.	25.025	22.899	21.048	19.415	17.981	16.714	47.
48.	25.267	23.091	21.195	19.536	17.077	16.790	48.
49.	25.502	23.277	21.341	19.651	18.169	16.863	49.
50.	25.730	23.456	21.482	19.762	18.256	16.932	50.

PRESENT VALUE OF RE. 1 PER ANNUM

Yrs.	3%	3½%	4%	4½%	5%	5½%	Yrs.
51.	25.951	23.629	21.617	19.868	18.339	16.997	51.
52.	26.166	23.796	21.748	19.969	18.418	17.058	52.
53.	26.375	23.957	21.873	20.066	18.493	17.147	53.
54.	26.578	24.113	21.993	20.159	18.565	17.173	54.
55.	26.774	24.264	22.109	20.248	18.633	17.225	55.
56.	26.965	24.410	22.220	20.333	18.699	17.275	56.
57.	27.151	24.550	22.327	20.414	18.761	17.322	57.
58.	27.331	24.686	22.430	20.492	18.820	17.367	58.
59.	27.506	24.818	22.528	20.567	18.876	17.410	59.
60.	27.676	24.945	22.623	20.638	18.929	17.450	60.
61.	27.840	25.067	22.715	20.706	18.980	17.488	61.
62.	28.000	25.186	22.803	20.772	19.029	17.524	62.
63.	28.156	25.300	22.887	20.834	19.075	17.558	63.
64.	28.306	25.411	22.969	20.894	19.119	17.591	64.
65.	28.453	25.518	23.047	20.951	19.161	17.622	65.
66.	28.595	25.621	23.122	21.005	19.201	17.651	66.
67.	28.733	25.721	23.194	21.058	19.239	17.679	67.
68.	28.867	25.817	23.264	21.108	19.275	17.705	68.
69.	28.997	25.910	23.330	21.156	19.310	17.730	69.
70.	29.123	26.000	23.395	21.202	19.343	17.753	70.
71.	29.246	26.087	23.456	21.246	19.374	17.776	71.
72.	29.365	26.171	23.516	21.288	19.404	17.797	72.
73.	29.481	26.253	23.573	21.328	19.432	17.817	73.
74.	29.593	26.331	23.628	21.367	19.459	17.836	74.
75.	29.702	26.407	23.680	21.404	19.485	17.854	75.
76.	29.808	26.480	23.731	21.439	19.509	17.871	76.
77.	29.910	26.551	23.780	21.473	19.533	17.887	77.
78.	30.010	26.619	23.827	21.505	19.555	17.903	78.
79.	30.107	26.685	23.872	21.536	19.576	17.917	79.
80.	30.201	26.749	23.915	21.565	19.596	17.931	80.
81.	30.292	26.810	23.957	21.594	19.616	17.944	81.
82.	30.381	26.870	23.997	21.621	19.634	17.956	82.
83.	30.467	26.928	24.036	21.647	19.651	17.968	83.
84.	30.550	26.983	24.073	21.671	19.668	17.979	84.
85.	30.631	27.037	24.109	21.695	19.684	17.990	85.
86.	30.710	27.089	24.143	21.718	19.699	18.000	86.
87.	30.786	27.139	24.176	21.740	19.713	18.009	87.
88.	30.860	27.187	24.207	21.760	19.727	18.018	88.
89.	30.932	27.234	24.238	21.780	19.740	18.027	89.
90.	31.002	27.279	24.267	21.799	19.752	18.035	90.
91.	31.070	27.323	24.295	21.817	19.764	18.043	91.
92.	31.136	27.365	24.323	21.835	19.775	18.050	92.
93.	31.200	27.406	24.349	21.852	19.786	18.057	93.
94.	31.262	17.445	24.374	21.868	19.796	18.063	94.
95.	31.323	27.484	24.398	21.883	19.806	18.069	95.
96.	31.381	27.520	24.421	21.897	19.815	18.075	96.
97.	31.438	27.556	24.443	21.911	19.824	18.081	97.
98.	31.493	27.590	24.465	21.925	19.832	18.086	98.
99.	31.547	27.623	24.485	21.938	19.840	18.091	99.
100.	31.599	27.655	24.505	21.950	19.848	18.096	100.
PERP	33.333	28.571	25.000	22.222	20.000	18.182	PERP.

PRESENT VALUE OF RE. 1 PER ANNUM
OR
YEAR'S PURCHASE

Yrs.	6%	$6^1/_2$%	7%	$7^1/_2$%	8%	10%	Yrs.
1.	.913	.939	.935	.930	.926	.909	1.
2.	1.833	1.821	1.808	1.796	1.783	1.736	2.
3.	2.673	2.648	2.624	2.601	2.577	2.487	3.
4.	3.465	3.426	3.387	3.349	3.312	3.170	4.
5.	4.212	4.156	4.100	4.046	3.993	3.791	5.
6.	4.917	4.841	4.767	4.694	4.623	4.355	6.
7.	5.582	5.485	5.389	5.297	5.206	4.868	7.
8.	6.210	6.089	5.971	5.857	5.747	5.336	8.
9.	6.802	6.656	6.515	6.379	6.247	5.759	9.
10.	7.360	7.189	7.024	6.864	6.710	6.145	10.
11.	7.887	7.689	7.499	7.315	7.139	6.495	11.
12.	8.384	8.159	7.943	7.735	7.536	6.814	12.
13.	8.853	8.600	8.358	8.126	7.904	7.103	13.
14.	9.295	9.014	8.745	8.489	8.244	7.367	14.
15.	9.712	9.403	9.108	8.827	8.559	7.606	15.
16.	10.106	9.768	9.447	9.142	8.851	7.824	16.
17.	10.477	10.111	9.763	9.434	9.122	8.022	17.
18.	10.828	10.432	10.059	9.706	9.372	8.201	18.
19.	11.158	10.735	10.336	9.959	9.604	8.365	19.
20.	11.470	11.019	10.594	10.194	9.818	8.514	20.
21.	11.764	11.285	10.836	10.413	10.017	8.649	21.
22.	12.042	11.535	11.061	10.617	10.201	8.772	22.
23.	12.303	11.770	11.272	10.807	10.371	8.883	23.
24.	12.550	11.991	11.469	10.983	10.529	8.985	24.
25.	12.783	12.198	11.654	11.147	10.675	9.077	25.
26.	13.003	12.392	11.826	11.299	10.810	9.161	26.
27.	13.211	12.575	11.987	11.441	10.935	9.237	27.
28.	13.406	12.746	12.137	11.573	11.051	9.307	28.
29.	13.591	12.907	12.278	11.696	11.158	9.370	29.
30.	13.765	13.059	12.409	11.810	11.258	9.427	30.
31.	13.929	13.201	12.532	11.917	11.350	9.479	31.
32.	14.084	13.334	12.647	12.015	11.435	9.526	32.
33.	14.230	13.459	12.754	12.107	11.514	9.509	33.
34.	14.368	13.577	12.854	12.193	11.587	9.609	34.
35.	14.498	13.687	12.948	12.273	11.655	9.644	35.
36.	14.621	13.791	13.035	12.347	11.717	9.677	36.
37.	14.737	13.888	13.117	12.415	11.775	9.706	37.
38.	14.846	13.979	13.193	12.479	11.829	9.733	38.
39.	14.949	14.065	13.265	12.539	11.879	9.757	39.
40.	15.046	14.146	13.332	12.594	11.925	9.779	40.
41.	15.138	14.221	13.394	12.646	11.967	9.799	41.
42.	15.225	14.292	13.452	12.694	12.007	9.817	42.
43.	15.306	14.359	13.507	12.739	12.043	9.834	43.
44.	15.383	14.421	13.558	12.780	12.077	9.819	44.
45.	15.456	14.480	13.606	12.819	12.108	9.863	45.
46.	15.524	14.535	13.650	12.855	12.137	9.875	46.
47.	15.589	14.587	13.692	12.883	12.164	9.887	47.
48.	15.650	14.636	13.730	12.919	12.189	9.897	48.
49.	15.708	14.682	13.767	12.948	12.212	9.906	49.
50.	15.762	14.725	13.801	12.975	12.233	9.915	50.

PRESENT VALUE OF RE. 1 PER ANNUM

Yrs.	6%	$6^1/_2$%	7%	$7^1/_2$%	8%	10%	Yrs.
51.	15.813	14.765	13.832	13.000	12.253	9.923	51.
52.	15.861	14.803	13.862	13.023	12.272	9.930	52.
53.	15.907	14.838	13.890	13.045	12.288	9.936	53.
54.	15.950	14.872	13.916	13.065	12.304	9.942	54.
55.	15.991	14.903	13.940	13.084	12.319	9.947	55.
56.	16.029	14.932	13.963	13.101	12.332	9.952	56.
57.	16.065	14.960	13.984	13.117	12.344	9.956	57.
58.	16.099	14.986	14.003	13.132	12.356	9.900	58.
59.	16.131	15.010	14.022	13.146	12.367	9.964	59.
60.	16.161	15.033	14.039	13.159	12.377	9.967	60.
61.	19.190	15.054	14.055	13.172	12.386	9.970	61.
62.	16.217	15.075	14.070	13.183	12.394	9.973	62.
63.	16.242	15.094	14.084	13.193	12.402	9.975	63.
64.	16.266	15.111	14.098	13.203	12.409	9.978	64.
65.	16.289	15.128	14.110	13.212	12.416	9.980	65.
66.	16.310	15.144	14.121	13.221	12.422	9.981	66.
67.	16.331	15.158	14.132	13.228	12.428	9.983	67.
68.	16.350	15.172	14.142	13.236	12.433	9.985	68.
69.	16.368	15.185	14.152	13.243	12.438	9.986	69.
70.	16.385	15.197	14.160	13.249	12.443	9.987	70.
71.	16.401	15.209	14.169	13.255	12.447	9.988	71.
72.	16.416	15.219	14.176	13.260	12.451	9.990	72.
73.	16.430	15.230	14.183	13.265	12.455	9.990	73.
74.	16.443	15.239	14.190	13.270	12.458	9.991	74.
75.	16.456	15.248	14.196	13.275	12.461	9.992	75.
76.	16.468	15.256	14.202	13.279	12.464	9.993	76.
77.	16.479	15.264	14.208	13.282	12.467	9.994	77.
78.	16.490	15.271	14.213	13.286	12.469	9.994	78.
79.	16.500	15.278	14.218	13.289	12.471	9.995	79.
80.	16.509	15.285	14.222	13.292	12.474	9.995	80.
81.	16.518	15.291	14.226	13.295	12.475	9.996	81.
82.	16.526	15.297	14.230	13.298	12.477	9.996	82.
83.	16.534	15.302	14.234	13.300	12.479	9.996	83.
84.	16.542	15.307	14.237	13.303	12.481	9.997	84.
85.	16.549	15.312	14.240	13.305	12.482	9.997	85.
86.	16.556	15.316	14.243	13.307	12.483	9.997	86.
87.	16.562	15.320	14.246	13.309	12.485	9.997	87.
88.	16.568	15.324	14.249	13.310	12.486	9.998	88.
89.	16.573	15.328	14.251	13.312	12.487	9.998	89.
90.	16.579	15.331	14.253	13.313	12.488	9.998	90.
91.	16.584	15.335	14.255	13.315	12.489	9.998	91.
92.	16.588	15.338	14.257	13.316	12.489	9.998	92.
93.	16.593	15.341	14.259	13.317	12.490	9.999	93.
94.	16.597	15.343	14.261	13.318	12.491	9.999	94.
95.	16.601	15.346	14.263	13.319	12.492	9.999	95.
96.	16.605	15.348	14.264	13.320	12.492	9.999	96.
97.	16.608	15.350	14.266	13.321	12.493	9.999	97.
98.	16.611	15.352	14.267	13.322	12.493	9.999	98.
99.	16.615	15.354	14.268	13.323	12.494	9.999	99.
100.	16.618	15.356	12.269	13.324	12.494	9.999	100.
PERP.	16.667	15.385	14.286	13.333	12.500	10.000	PERP.

PRESENT VALUE OF RE. 1 PER ANNUM
ALLOWING FOR REDEMPTION OF CAPITAL AT 3 PER CENT

Yrs.	INTEREST REQUIRED ON CAPITAL						Yrs.
	5%	5½%	6%	6½%	7%	8%	
1.	.952	.948	.943	.939	.935	.926	1.
2.	1.843	1.826	1.810	1.793	1.777	1.746	2.
3.	2.677	2.642	2.607	2.574	2.541	2.478	3.
4.	3.460	3.401	3.344	3.289	3.236	3.135	4.
5.	4.195	4.109	4.027	3.947	3.871	3.726	5.
6.	4.888	4.771	4.660	4.554	4.452	4.263	6.
7.	5.540	5.391	5.249	5.115	4.987	4.750	7.
8.	6.155	5.972	5.799	5.635	5.481	5.196	8.
9.	6.737	6.517	6.312	6.119	5.937	5.604	9.
10.	7.287	7.031	6.792	6.569	6.360	5.980	10.
11.	7.808	7.514	7.242	6.989	6.753	6.326	11.
12.	8.301	7.971	7.665	7.382	7.119	6.646	12.
13.	8.770	8.401	8.063	7.750	7.461	6.943	13.
14.	9.214	8.809	8.437	8.095	7.781	7.219	14.
15.	9.637	9.194	8.790	8.420	8.080	7.476	15.
16.	10.039	9.559	9.123	8.725	8.360	7.715	16.
17.	10.422	9.906	9.438	9.013	8.624	7.939	17.
18.	10.786	10.235	9.736	9.284	8.872	8.149	18.
19.	11.134	10.547	10.019	9.541	9.106	8.346	19.
20.	11.466	10.844	10.286	9.783	9.327	8.531	20.
21.	11.782	11.127	10.541	10.013	9.535	8.705	21.
22.	12.085	11.396	10.782	10.230	9.733	8.869	22.
23.	12.374	11.653	11.012	10.437	9.919	9.024	23.
24.	12.651	11.898	11.230	10.633	10.096	9.170	24.
25.	12.915	12.132	11.438	10.819	10.264	9.309	25.
26.	13.169	12.355	11.636	10.996	10.423	9.439	26.
27.	13.411	12.568	11.825	11.165	10.575	9.564	27.
28.	13.644	12.772	12.006	11.326	10.719	9.681	28.
29.	13.867	12.968	12.178	11.479	10.856	9.793	29.
30.	14.081	13.155	12.343	11.625	10.987	9.899	30.
31.	14.286	13.334	12.500	11.765	11.111	10.000	31.
32.	14.483	13.505	12.651	11.898	11.230	10.096	32.
33.	14.672	13.669	12.795	12.026	11.344	10.183	33.
34.	14.854	13.827	12.933	12.147	11.452	10.275	34.
35.	15.029	13.978	13.065	12.264	11.555	10.358	35.
36.	15.197	14.124	13.192	12.376	11.654	10.438	36.
37.	15.358	14.263	13.314	12.483	11.749	10.514	37.
38.	15.514	14.397	13.430	12.585	12.840	10.587	38.
39.	15.663	14.526	13.542	12.683	11.927	10.656	39.
40.	15.807	14.649	13.650	12.777	12.010	10.722	40.
41.	15.946	14.768	13.753	12.868	12.090	10.786	41.
42.	16.079	14.883	13.852	12.955	12.167	10.847	42.
43.	16.208	14.993	13.947	13.038	12.240	10.905	43.
44.	16.332	15.099	14.039	13.118	12.311	10.901	44.
45.	16.451	15.201	14.127	13.195	12.379	11.015	45.
46.	16.567	15.299	14.212	13.269	12.444	11.067	46.
47.	16.678	15.394	14.294	13.340	12.506	11.116	47.
48.	16.785	15.485	14.372	13.409	12.566	11.163	48.
49.	16.888	15.573	14.448	13.475	12.624	11.209	49.
50.	16.988	15.658	14.521	13.538	12.680	11.253	50.

PRESENT VALUE OF RE. 1 PER ANNUM

	INTEREST REQUIRED ON CAPITAL						
Yrs.	5%	$5^{1}/_{2}$%	6%	$6^{1}/_{2}$%	7%	8%	Yrs.
51.	17.084	15.740	14.591	13.599	12.733	11.295	51.
52.	17.177	15.818	14.659	13.658	12.785	11.336	52.
53.	17.267	15.895	14.724	13.715	12.835	11.375	53.
54.	17.353	15.968	14.787	13.769	12.882	11.412	54.
55.	17.437	16.039	14.848	13.822	12.928	11.448	55.
56.	17.518	16.107	14.907	13.873	12.973	11.483	56.
57.	17.596	16.173	14.963	13.922	13.016	11.517	57.
58.	17.671	16.237	15.018	13.969	13.057	11.540	58.
59.	17.744	16.298	15.070	14.014	13.097	11.580	59.
60.	17.815	16.358	15.121	14.058	13.135	11.610	60.
61.	17.883	16.415	15.170	14.101	13.172	11.639	61.
62.	17.949	16.471	15.217	14.142	13.208	11.667	62.
63.	18.013	16.524	15.263	14.181	13.242	11.694	63.
64.	18.074	16.576	15.307	14.219	13.275	11.720	64.
65.	18.134	16.626	15.350	14.256	13.307	11.745	65.
66.	18.191	16.675	15.391	14.292	13.338	11.769	66.
67.	18.247	16.722	15.431	14.326	13.368	11.792	67.
68.	18.301	16.767	15.570	14.359	13.397	11.815	68.
69.	18.353	16.811	15.507	14.391	13.425	11.836	69.
70.	18.404	16.853	15.543	14.422	13.452	11.857	70.
71.	18.453	16.894	15.578	14.452	13.478	11.878	71.
72.	18.500	16.934	15.612	14.481	13.504	11.897	72.
73.	18.546	16.972	15.644	14.509	13.528	11.916	73.
74.	18.590	17.009	15.676	14.537	13.552	11.934	74.
75.	18.633	17.045	15.706	14.563	13.574	11.952	75.
76.	18.675	17.080	15.736	14.588	13.596	11.969	76.
77.	18.715	17.114	15.765	14.613	13.618	11.986	77.
78.	18.754	17.146	15.792	14.637	13.638	12.002	78.
79.	18.792	17.178	15.819	14.660	13.656	12.017	79.
80.	18.828	17.208	15.845	14.682	13.678	12.032	80.
81.	18.864	17.238	15.870	14.703	13.696	12.046	81.
82.	18.898	17.266	15.894	14.724	13.714	12.060	82.
83.	18.931	17.294	15.918	14.744	13.732	12.074	83.
84.	18.963	17.321	15.941	14.764	13.749	12.087	84.
85.	18.995	17.347	15.963	14.783	13.765	12.100	85.
86.	19.025	17.372	15.984	14.801	13.781	12.112	86.
87.	19.054	17.397	16.005	14.819	13.797	12.124	87.
88.	19.083	17.420	16.025	14.836	13.811	12.135	88.
89.	19.110	17.443	16.044	14.853	13.826	12.146	89.
90.	19.137	17.466	16.063	14.869	13.840	12.157	90.
91.	19.163	17.487	16.081	14.884	13.853	12.168	91.
92.	19.188	17.508	16.099	14.899	13.866	12.178	92.
93.	19.212	17.528	16.116	14.914	13.879	12.188	93.
94.	19.235	17.548	16.132	14.928	13.891	12.197	94.
95.	19.258	17.567	16.148	14.942	13,903	12.206	95.
96.	19.280	17.585	16.164	14.955	13.915	12.215	96.
97.	19.302	17.603	16.179	14.968	13.926	12.224	97.
98.	19.323	17.620	16.194	14.981	13.937	12.232	98.
99.	19.343	17.637	16.208	14.993	13.947	12.240	99.
100.	19.362	17.653	16.221	15.004	13.957	12.248	100.
PERP.	20.000	18.182	16.667	15.385	14.285	12.500	PERP.

PRESENT VALUE OF RE. 1 PER ANNUM

Yrs.	3%	3½%	4%	4½%	5%	Yrs.
1.	.97087	.96619	.96154	.95694	.95238	1.
2.	.94260	.93351	.92456	.91573	.90703	2.
3.	.91514	.90194	.88900	.87630	.86384	3.
4.	.88849	.87144	.85480	.83856	.82270	4.
5.	.86261	.84197	.82193	.80245	.78353	5.
6.	.83748	.81350	.79031	.76790	.74622	6.
7.	.81309	.78599	.75992	.73483	.71068	7.
8.	.78941	.75941	.73069	.70319	.67684	8.
9.	.76642	.73373	.70259	.67290	.64461	9.
10.	.74409	.70892	.67556	.64393	.61391	10.
11.	.72242	.68495	.64958	.61620	.58468	11.
12.	.70138	.66178	.62460	.58966	.55684	12.
13.	.63095	.63940	.60057	.56427	.53032	13.
14.	.66112	.61778	.57748	.53997	.50507	14.
15.	.64186	.59689	.55526	.51672	.48102	15.
16.	.62317	.57671	.53391	.49447	.45811	16.
17.	.60502	.55720	.51337	.47318	.43630	17.
18.	.58739	.53836	.49363	.45280	.41552	18.
19.	.57029	.52016	.47464	.43330	.39573	19.
20.	.55368	.50257	.45639	.41464	.37689	20.
21.	.53755	.48557	.43883	.39679	.35894	21.
22.	.52189	.46915	.42196	.37970	.34185	22.
23.	.50669	.45329	.40573	.36335	.32557	23.
24.	.49193	.43796	.39012	.34770	.31007	24.
25.	.47761	.42315	.37512	.33273	.29530	25.
26.	.46369	.40884	.36069	.31840	.28124	26.
27.	.45019	.39501	.34682	.30469	.26785	27.
28.	.43703	.38165	.33348	.29157	.25509	28.
29.	.42435	.36875	.32065	.27901	.24295	29.
30.	.41199	.35628	.30832	.26700	.23138	30.
31.	.39999	.34423	.29646	.25550	.22036	31.
32.	.38834	.33259	.28506	.24450	.20987	32.
33.	.37703	.32134	.27409	.23397	.19987	33.
34.	.36604	.31048	.26355	.22390	.19035	34.
35.	.35538	.29998	.25342	.21425	.18129	35.
36.	.34503	.28983	.24367	.20503	.17266	36.
37.	.33498	.28003	.23430	.19620	.16444	37.
38.	.32523	.27056	.22529	.18775	.15661	38.
39.	.31575	.26141	.21662	.17967	.14915	39.
40.	.30656	.25257	.20829	.17193	.14205	40.
41.	.29763	.24403	.20028	.16453	.13528	41.
42.	.28896	.23578	.19257	.15744	.12884	42.
43.	.28054	.22781	.18517	.15066	.12270	43.
44.	.27237	.22010	.17805	.14417	.11636	44.
45.	.26444	.21266	.17120	.13796	.11130	45.
46.	.25674	.20547	.16461	.13202	.10600	46.
47.	.24926	.19852	.15828	.12634	.10095	47.
48.	.24200	.19181	.15219	.12090	.09614	48.
49.	.23495	.18532	.14634	.11569	.09156	49.
50.	.22811	.17905	.14071	.11071	.08720	50.

PRESENT VALUE OF RE. 1 PER ANNUM

Yrs.	3%	$3^1/_2$%	4%	$4^1/_2$%	5%	Yrs.
51.	.22146	.17300	.13530	.10594	.08305	51.
52.	.21501	.16715	.13010	.10138	.07910	52.
53.	.20875	.16150	.12509	.09701	.07533	53.
54.	.20267	.15603	.12028	.09284	.07174	54.
55.	.19677	.15076	.11566	.08884	.06833	55.
56.	.19104	.14566	.11121	.08501	.06507	56.
57.	.18547	.14073	.10693	.08135	.06197	57.
58.	.18007	.13598	.10282	.07785	.05902	58.
59.	.17483	.13138	.09886	.07450	.05621	59.
60.	.16973	.12693	.09506	.07129	.05354	60.
61.	.16479	.12264	.09140	.06822	.05099	61.
62.	.15999	.11849	.08789	.06528	.04856	62.
63.	.15533	.11449	.08451	.06247	.04625	63.
64.	.15081	.11062	.08126	.05978	.04404	64.
65.	.14641	.10688	.07813	.05721	.04195	65.
66.	.14215	.10326	.07513	.05474	.03995	66.
67.	.13801	.09977	.07224	.05239	.03805	67.
68.	.13399	.09640	.06946	.05013	.03623	68.
69.	.13009	.09314	.06679	.04797	.03451	69.
70.	.12630	.08999	.06422	.04590	.03287	70.
71.	.12262	.08694	.06175	.04393	.03130	71.
72.	.11905	.08400	.05937	.04204	.02981	72.
73.	.11558	.08116	.05709	.04023	.02839	73.
74.	.11221	.07842	.05489	.03849	.02704	74.
75.	.10895	.07577	.05278	.03684	.02575	75.
76.	.10577	.07320	.05075	.03525	.02453	76.
77.	.10269	.07073	.04880	.03373	.02336	77.
78.	.09970	.06834	.04692	.03228	.02225	78.
79.	.09680	.06603	.04512	.03089	.02119	79.
80.	.09398	.06379	.04338	.02956	.02018	80.
81.	.09124	.00164	.04172	.02829	.01922	81.
82.	.08858	.05955	.04011	.02707	.01830	82.
83.	.08600	.05754	.03857	.02590	.01743	83.
84.	.08350	.05559	.03709	.02479	.01664	84.
85.	.08107	.05371	.03566	.02372	.01581	85.
86.	.07870	.05190	.03429	.02270	.01506	86.
87.	.07641	.05014	.03297	.02172	.01434	87.
88.	.07419	.04844	.03170	.02079	.01366	88.
89.	.07203	.04681	.03048	.01989	.01301	89.
90.	.06993	.04522	.02931	.01903	.01239	90.
91.	.06789	.04369	.02818	.01821	.01180	91.
92.	.06591	.04222	.02710	.01743	.01124	92.
93.	.06399	.04079	.02606	.01668	.01070	93.
94.	.06213	.03941	.02505	.01596	.01019	94.
95.	.06032	.03808	.02409	.01527	.00971	95.
96.	.05856	.03679	.02316	.01462	.00924	96.
97.	.05686	.03555	.02227	.01399	.00880	97.
98.	.05520	.03434	.02142	.01338	.00838	98.
99.	.05359	.03318	.02050	.01881	.00798	99.
100.	.05203	.03206	.01980	.01226	.00760	100.

PRESENT VALUE OF RE. 1 PER ANNUM

Yrs.	5½%	6%	6½%	7%	8%	Yrs.
1.	.94787	.94340	.93897	.93458	.92593	1.
2.	.89845	.89000	.88166	.87344	.85754	2.
3.	85161	.83962	.82785	.81630	.79383	3.
4.	.80722	.79209	.77732	.76290	.73503	4.
5.	.76513	.74726	.72988	.71299	.68058	5.
6.	.72525	.70496	.68533	.66634	.63017	6.
7.	.68744	.66506	.64351	.62275	.58349	7.
8.	.65160	.62741	.60423	.58201	.54027	8.
9.	.61763	.59190	.56735	.54393	.50025	9.
10.	.58543	.55839	.53273	.50835	.46319	10.
11.	.55491	.52676	.50021	.47509	.42888	11.
12.	.52598	.49697	.46968	.44401	.39711	12.
13.	.49856	.46884	.44102	.41496	.36770	13.
14.	.47257	.44230	.41410	.38782	.34046	14.
15.	.44793	.41727	.38883	.36245	.31524	15.
16.	.42458	.39365	.36510	.33873	.29189	16.
17.	.40245	.37136	.34281	.31657	.27027	17.
18.	.38147	.35034	.32189	.29586	.25025	18.
19.	.31658	.33051	.30224	.27651	.23171	19.
20.	.34273	.31180	.28380	.25842	.21455	20.
21.	.32486	.29416	.26648	.24151	.19866	21.
22.	.30793	.27751	.25021	.22571	.18394	22.
23.	.29087	.26180	.23494	.21095	.17032	23.
24.	.27666	.24698	.22060	.19715	.15770	24.
25.	.26223	.23300	.20714	.18425	.14602	25.
26.	.24856	.21981	.19450	.17220	.13520	26.
27.	.23560	.20737	.18263	.16093	.12519	27.
28.	.22332	.19563	.17148	.15040	.11591	28.
29.	.21168	.18456	.16101	.14056	.10733	29.
30.	.20064	.17411	.15119	.13137	.09938	30.
31.	.19018	.16425	.14196	.12277	.09202	31.
32.	.18027	.15496	.13329	.11474	.08520	32.
33.	.17087	.14619	.12516	.10723	.07889	33.
34.	.16196	.13791	.11752	.10022	.07305	34.
35.	.15352	.13011	.11035	.09366	.06763	35.
36.	.14552	.12274	.10361	.08754	.06262	36.
37.	.13793	.11579	.09729	.08181	.05799	37.
38.	.13074	.10924	.09135	.07646	.05369	38.
39.	.12392	.10306	.08578	.07145	.04971	39.
40.	.11746	.09722	.08054	.06678	.04603	40.
41.	.11134	.09172	.07563	.06241	.04262	41.
42.	.10553	.08653	.07101	.05833	.03946	42.
43.	.10003	.08163	.06668	.05451	.03654	43.
44.	.09482	.07701	.06261	.05095	.03383	44.
45.	.08988	.07265	.05879	.04761	.03133	45.
46.	.08519	.06854	.05520	.04450	.02901	46.
47.	.08075	.06466	.05183	.04159	.02686	47.
48.	.07654	.06100	.04867	.03887	.02487	48.
49.	.07255	.05755	.04570	.03632	.02303	49.
50.	.06877	.05429	.04291	.03395	.02132	50.

PRESENT VALUE OF RE. 1 PER ANNUM

Yrs.	$5^1/_2$%	6%	$6^1/_2$%	7%	8%	Yrs.
51.	.06518	.05122	.04029	.03173	.01974	51.
52.	.06178	.04832	.03783	.02965	.01828	52.
53.	.05856	.04558	.03552	.02771	.01693	53.
54.	.05551	.04300	.03335	.02590	.01567	54.
55.	.05268	.04057	.03132	.02420	.01451	55.
56.	.04987	.03827	.02941	.02262	.01344	56.
57.	.04727	.03610	.02761	.02114	.01244	57.
58.	.04481	.03406	.02593	.01976	.01152	58.
59.	.04247	.03213	.02434	.01847	.01067	59.
60.	.04026	.03031	.02286	.01726	.00988	60.
61.	.03816	.02860	.02146	.01613	.00914	61.
62.	.03617	.02698	.02015	.01507	.00874	62.
63.	.03428	.02545	.01892	.01409	.00784	63.
64.	.03250	.02401	.01777	.01317	.00726	64.
65.	.03089	.02265	.01668	.01230	.00672	65.
66.	.02920	.02137	.01566	.01150	.00622	66.
67.	.02767	.02016	.01471	.01075	.00576	67.
68.	.02623	.01902	.01381	.01004	.00534	68.
69.	.02486	.01794	.01297	.00939	.00494	69.
70.	.02357	.01693	.01218	.00877	.00457	70.
71.	.02234	.01597	.01143	.00820	.00424	71.
72.	.02117	.01507	.01074	.00766	.00392	72.
73.	.02007	.01421	.01008	.00716	.00363	73.
74.	.01902	.01341	.00947	.00669	.00336	74.
75.	.01803	.01265	.00889	.00625	.00311	75.
76.	.01709	.01193	.00835	.00585	.00288	76.
77.	.01620	.01126	.00784	.00546	.00267	77.
78.	.01536	.01062	.00736	.00511	.00247	78.
79.	.01456	.01002	.00691	.00477	.00229	79.
80.	.01380	.00945	.00649	.00446	.00212	80.
81.	.01308	.00892	.00609	.00417	.00196	81.
82.	.01240	.00841	.00572	.00390	.00182	82.
83.	.01175	.00794	.00537	.00364	.00168	83.
84.	.01114	.00749	.00504	.00340	.00156	84.
85.	.01056	.00706	.00473	.00318	.00144	85.
86.	.01001	.00666	.00445	.00297	.00134	86.
87.	.00948	.00629	.00417	.00278	.00124	87.
88.	.00899	.00593	.00392	.00260	.00114	88.
89.	.00852	.00559	.00368	.00243	.00106	89.
90.	.00808	.00528	.00346	.00227	.00098	90.
91.	.00766	.00498	.00324	.00212	.00091	91.
92.	.00726	.00470	.00305	.00198	.00084	92.
93.	.00688	.00443	.00286	.00185	.00078	93.
94.	.00652	.00418	.00269	.00173	.00072	94.
95.	.00618	.00394	.00252	.00162	.00067	95.
96.	.00586	.00372	.00237	.00151	.00062	96.
97.	.00555	.00351	.00222	.00141	.00057	97.
98.	.00526	.00331	.00209	.00132	.00053	98.
99.	.00499	.00312	.00196	.00123	.00049	99.
100.	.00473	.00295	.00184	.00115	.00045	100.

ANNUAL SINKING FUND

Yrs.	2%	$2^1/_2$%	3%	$3^1/_2$%	Yrs.
1.	1.00000	1.00000	1.00000	1.00000	1.
2.	.49505	.49383	.49261	.49140	2.
3.	.32675	.32514	.32353	.32193	3.
4.	.24262	.24082	.23903	.23725	4.
5.	.19216	.19025	.18835	.18648	5.
6.	.15853	.15655	.15460	.15267	6.
7.	.13451	.13250	.13051	.12854	7.
8.	.11651	.11447	.11246	.11048	8.
9.	.10252	.10046	.09843	.09645	9.
10.	.09133	.08926	.08723	.08524	10.
11.	.08218	.08011	.07808	.07609	11.
12.	.07456	.07249	.07046	.06848	12.
13.	.06812	.06605	.06403	.06206	13.
14.	.06260	.06054	.05853	.05657	14.
15.	.05783	.05577	.05377	.05183	15.
16.	.05365	.05160	.04961	.04768	16.
17.	.04997	.04793	.04595	.04404	17.
18.	.04670	.04467	.04271	.04082	18.
19.	.04378	.04176	.03981	.03794	19.
20.	.04116	.03915	.03722	.03536	20.
21.	.03878	.03679	.03487	.03304	21.
22.	.03663	.03465	.03275	.03093	22.
23.	.03467	.03270	.03081	.02902	23.
24.	.03287	.03091	.02905	.02727	24.
25.	.03122	.02928	.02743	.02567	25.
26.	.02970	.02777	.02594	.02421	26.
27.	.02829	.02638	.02456	.02285	27.
28.	.02699	.02509	.02329	.02160	28.
29.	.02578	.02389	.02211	.02045	29.
30.	.02465	.02278	.02102	.01937	30.
31.	.02360	.02174	.02000	.01837	31.
32.	.02261	.02077	.01905	.01744	32.
33.	.02169	.01986	.01816	.01657	33.
34.	.02082	.01901	.01732	.01576	34.
35.	.02000	.01821	.01654	.01500	35.
36.	.01923	.01745	.01580	.01428	36.
37.	.01851	.01674	.01511	.01361	37.
38.	.01782	.01607	.01446	.01298	38.
39.	.01717	.01544	.01384	.01239	39.
40.	.01656	.01484	.01326	.01183	40.
41.	.01597	.01427	.01271	.01130	41.
42.	.01542	.01373	.01219	.01080	42.
43.	.01489	.01322	.01170	.01033	43.
44.	.01439	.01273	.01123	.00988	44.
45.	.01391	.01227	.01079	.000945	45.
46.	.01345	.01183	.01036	.00905	46.
47.	.01302	.01141	.00996	.00867	47.
48.	.01260	.01101	.00958	.00831	48.
49.	.01220	.01062	.00921	.00796	49.
50.	.01182	.01026	.00887	.00763	50.

ANNUAL SINKING FUND

Yrs.	2%	$2^1/_2$%	3%	$3^1/_2$%	Yrs.
51.	.01146	.00991	.00853	.00732	51.
52.	.01111	.00957	.00822	.00702	52.
53.	.01077	.00925	.00791	.00674	53.
54.	.01045	.00895	.00763	.00647	54.
55.	.01014	.00865	.00735	.00621	55.
56.	.00985	.00837	.00708	.00597	56.
57.	.00956	.00810	.00683	.00573	57.
58.	.00929	.00784	.00659	.00551	58.
59.	.00902	.00759	.00636	.00529	59.
60.	.00877	.00735	.00613	.00509	60.
61.	.00852	.00712	.00592	.00489	61.
62.	.00829	.00690	.00571	.00470	62.
63.	.00806	.00669	.00552	.00453	63.
64.	.00784	.00648	.00533	.00435	64.
65.	.00763	.00628	.00515	.00419	65.
66.	.00742	.00609	.00497	.00403	66.
67.	.00722	.00591	.00480	.00388	67.
68.	.00703	.00573	.00464	.00373	68.
69.	.00685	.00556	.00449	.00359	69.
70.	.00667	.00540	.00434	.00346	70.
71.	.00649	.00524	.00419	.00333	71.
72.	.00633	.00508	.00405	.00321	72.
73.	.00616	.00494	.00392	.00309	73.
74.	.00601	.00479	.00379	.00298	74.
75.	.00586	.00465	.00367	.00287	75.
76.	.00571	.00452	.00355	.00276	76.
77.	.00556	.00439	.00343	.00266	77.
78.	.00543	.00426	.00332	.00257	78.
79.	.00529	.00414	.00322	.00247	79.
80.	.00516	.00403	.00311	.00238	80.
81.	.00503	.00391	.00301	.00230	81.
82.	.00491	.00380	.00292	.00222	82.
83.	.00479	.00370	.00282	.00214	83.
84.	.00468	.00359	.00273	.00206	84.
85.	.00456	.00349	.00265	.00199	85.
86.	.00445	.00340	.00256	.00192	86.
87.	.00435	.00330	.00248	.00185	87.
88.	.00424	.00321	.00240	.00178	88.
89.	.00414	.00312	.00233	.00172	89.
90.	.00405	.00304	.00226	.00166	90.
91.	.00395	.00296	.00219	.00160	91.
92.	.00386	.00287	.00212	.00154	92.
93.	.00377	.00280	.00205	.00149	93.
94.	.00368	.00272	.00199	.00144	94.
95.	.00360	.00265	.00193	.00139	95.
96.	.00351	.00258	.00187	.00134	96.
97.	.00343	.00251	.00181	.00129	97.
98.	.00335	.00244	.00175	.00124	98.
99.	.00328	.00238	.00170	.00120	99.
100.	.00320	.00231	.00169	.00116	100.

PRESENT VALUE OF RE. 1 PER ANNUM
SINGLE LIFE—CARLISLE TABLES

Age	3%	4%	5%	6%	7%	8%	Age
0.	17.320	14.282	12.083	10.439	9.177	8.178	0.
1.	20.084	16.555	13.995	12.078	10.605	9.439	1.
2.	21.500	17.726	14.983	12.925	11.342	10.088	2.
3.	22.683	18.715	15.824	13.652	11.978	10.651	3.
4.	23.285	19.231	16.271	14.042	12.322	10.957	4.
5.	23.693	19.592	16.590	14.325	12.574	11.184	5.
6.	23.846	19.745	16.735	14.460	12.698	11.298	6.
7.	23.867	19.790	16.790	14.518	12.756	11.354	7.
8.	23.801	19.764	16.786	14.526	12.770	11.371	8.
9.	23.677	19.691	16.742	14.500	12.754	11.362	9.
10.	23.512	19.583	16.669	14.448	12.717	11.334	10.
11.	23.327	19.459	16.581	14.384	12.669	11.296	11.
12.	23.143	19.335	16.494	14.321	12.621	11.259	12.
13.	22.957	19.209	16.406	14.257	12.572	11.221	13.
14.	22.769	19.082	16.316	14.191	12.522	11.182	14.
15.	22.582	18.955	16.227	14.126	12.473	11.144	15.
16.	22.404	18.836	16.144	14.067	12.429	11.111	16.
17.	22.232	18.721	16.066	14.012	12.389	11.081	17.
18.	22.059	18.607	15.987	13.956	12.348	11.051	18.
19.	21.880	18.486	15.904	13.897	12.305	11.019	19.
20.	21.695	18.362	15.817	13.835	12.259	10.985	20.
21.	21.505	18.232	15.726	13.769	12.210	10.948	21.
22.	21.305	18.094	15.628	13.697	12.156	10.906	22.
23.	21.099	17.950	15.525	13.621	12.098	10.861	23.
24.	20.886	17.801	15.417	13.541	12.037	10.813	24.
25.	20.666	17.645	15.303	13.456	11.972	10.762	25.
26.	20.443	17.486	15.187	13.368	11.904	10.709	26.
27.	20.213	17.320	15.065	13.275	11.832	10.652	27.
28.	19.982	17.154	14.942	13.182	11.759	10.594	28.
29.	19.762	16.997	14.827	13.096	11.693	10.542	29.
30.	19.557	16.852	14.723	13.020	11.636	10.498	30.
31.	19.349	16.705	14.617	12.942	11.578	10.454	31.
32.	19.135	16.552	14.506	12.860	11.516	10.407	32.
33.	18.911	16.391	14.387	12.771	11.448	10.355	33.
34.	18.676	16.219	14.260	12.675	11.374	10.297	34.
35.	18.434	16.041	14.127	12.573	11.295	10.235	35.
36.	18.183	15.856	13.987	12.465	11.211	10.168	36.
37.	17.929	15.666	13.846	12.354	11.124	10.098	37.
38.	17.669	15.471	13.695	12.239	11.033	10.026	38.
39.	17.405	15.272	13.542	12.120	10.939	9.950	39.
40.	17.142	15.074	13.390	12.002	10.845	9.875	40.
41.	16.889	14.883	13.245	11.890	10.757	9.805	41.
42.	16.639	14.695	13.101	11.779	10.671	9.737	42.
43.	16.388	14.505	12.957	11.668	10.585	9.669	43.
44.	16.130	14.309	12.806	11.551	10.494	9.597	44.
45.	15.863	14.105	12.648	11.428	10.397	9.520	45.
46.	15.584	13.889	12.480	11.296	10.292	9.436	46.
47.	15.293	13.662	12.301	11.154	10.178	9.344	47.
48.	14.986	13.419	12.107	10.998	10.052	9.241	48.
49.	14.653	13.153	11.892	10.283	9.908	9.121	49.
50.	14.302	12.869	11.660	10.631	9.749	8.987	50.
51.	13.932	12.566	11.410	10.422	9.573	8.838	51.
52.	13.558	12.258	11.154	10.208	9.392	8.684	52.

PRESENT VALUE OF RE. 1 PER ANNUM
SINGLE LIFE—CARLISLE TABLES

Age	3%	4%	5%	6%	7%	8%	Age
53.	13.180	11.945	10.892	9.988	9.205	8.523	53.
54.	12.798	11.627	10.624	9.761	9.011	8.356	54.
55.	12.409	11.300	10.347	9.524	8.807	8.179	55.
56.	12.014	10.966	10.063	9.280	8.595	7.995	56.
57.	11.614	10.626	9.771	9.027	8.375	7.802	57.
58.	11.218	10.286	9.478	8.772	8.153	7.606	58.
59.	10.841	9.963	9.199	8.529	7.940	7.418	59.
60.	10.491	9.663	8.940	8.304	7.743	7.245	60.
61.	10.181	9.398	8.712	8.108	7.572	7.095	61.
62.	9.875	9.137	8.487	7.913	7.403	6.947	62.
63.	9.567	8.872	8.258	7.714	7.229	6.795	63.
64.	9.246	8.593	8.016	7.502	7.042	6.630	64.
65.	8.917	8.307	7.765	7.281	6.847	6.457	65.
66.	8.578	8.010	7.503	7.049	6.641	6.272	66.
67.	8.228	7.700	7.227	6.802	6.421	6.065	67.
68.	7.868	7.380	6.941	6.546	6.189	5.866	68.
69.	7.499	7.049	6.643	6.277	5.945	5.643	69.
70.	7.123	6.709	6.336	5.998	5.690	5.410	70.
71.	6.736	6.358	6.015	5.704	5.420	5.160	71.
72.	6.372	6.025	5.711	5.424	5.162	4.922	72.
73.	6.043	5.725	5.435	5.170	4.927	4.704	73.
74.	5.752	5.458	5.190	4.944	4.719	4.511	74.
75.	5.512	5.239	4.989	4.760	4.549	4.355	75.
76.	5.277	5.024	4.792	4.579	4.382	4.200	76.
77.	5.059	4.825	4.609	4.410	4.227	4.056	77.
78.	4.838	4.622	4.422	4.238	4.067	3.908	78.
79.	4.592	4.393	4.210	4.040	3.883	3.736	79.
80.	4.365	4.183	4.015	3.858	3.713	3.577	80.
81.	4.119	3.953	3.799	3.656	3.523	3.398	81.
82.	3.898	3.746	3.606	3.474	3.352	3.237	82.
83.	3.672	3.534	3.406	3.286	3.174	3.069	83.
84.	3.454	3.329	3.211	3.102	2.999	2.903	84.
85.	3.229	3.115	3.009	2.909	2.815	2.727	85.
86.	3.033	2.928	2.830	2.739	2.652	2.571	86.
87.	2.873	2.776	2.685	2.599	2.519	2.443	87.
88.	2.776	2.683	2.597	2.515	2.439	2.366	88.
89.	2.665	2.577	2.495	2.417	2.344	2.276	89.
90.	2.499	2.416	2.339	2.266	2.198	2.133	90.
91.	2.481	2.398	2.321	2.248	2.180	2.115	91.
92.	2.577	2.492	2.412	2.337	2.266	2.198	92.
93.	2.687	2.600	2.516	2.440	2.367	2.297	93.
94.	2.736	2.650	2.569	2.492	2.419	2.350	94.
95.	2.757	2.674	2.596	2.522	2.451	2.383	95.
96.	2.704	2.628	2.555	2.486	2.420	2.358	96.
97.	2.550	2.492	2.428	2.368	2.309	2.253	97.
98.	2.388	2.332	2.278	2.227	2.177	2.129	98.
99.	2.131	2.087	2.045	2.004	1.964	1.926	99.
100.	1.683	1.653	1.624	1.596	1.569	1.543	100.
101.	1.228	1.210	1.192	1.175	1.159	1.142	101.
102.	0.771	0.762	0.753	0.744	0.735	0.727	102.
103.	0.324	0.321	0.317	0.314	0.312	0.309	103.
104. & Over	0.000	0.000	0.000	0.000	0.000	0.000	104. & Over

CARLISLE TABLES
MORTALITY AND MEAN EXPECTATION OF LIFE

Age	Number who attain the given age	Mean expectation (Years)	Age	Number who attain the given age	Mean expectation (Years)
0	10000	38.72	53	4211	18.97
1	6797	51.24	58	3842	15.54
1	8461	44.67	54	4143	18.27
2	7779	47.55	55	4073	17.58
3	7274	49.81	56	4000	16.89
4	6998	50.76	57	3924	16.21
6	6676	51.16	59	3749	14.92
7	6594	50.79	60	3643	14.34
8	6536	50.24	61	3521	13.82
9	6493	49.57	62	3395	13.31
10	6460	48.82	63	3268	12.81
11	6431	48.04	64	3143	12.30
12	6400	47.27	65	3018	11.79
13	6368	46.50	66	2894	11.27
14	6335	45.74	67	2771	10.75
15	6300	44.99	68	2648	10.23
16	6261	44.27	69	2525	9.70
17	6219	43.57	70	2401	9.17
18	6176	42.87	71	2277	8.65
19	6133	42.16	72	2143	8.16
20	6090	41.46	73	1997	7.72
21	6047	40.75	74	1841	7.33
22	6005	40.03	75	1675	7.00
23	5963	39.31	76	1515	6.69
24	5921	38.58	77	1359	6.40
25	5879	37.86	78	1213	6.11
26	5836	37.13	79	1081	5.80
27	5793	36.40	80	953	5.51
28	5748	35.68	81	837	5.20
29	5698	34.99	82	725	4.93
30	5642	34.34	83	623	4.65
31	5585	33.68	84	529	4.39
32	5528	33.02	85	445	4.12
33	5472	32.36	86	367	3.90
34	5417	31.68	87	296	3.71
35	5362	31.00	88	232	3.59
36	5307	30.32	89	181	3.47
37	5251	29.63	90	142	3.28
38	5194	28.95	91	105	3.26
39	5136	28.17	92	75	3.37
40	5075	27.61	93	54	3.48
41	5009	26.97	94	40	3.52
42	4940	26.33	95	30	3.53
43	4869	25.71	96	23	3.46
44	4798	25.08	97	18	3.28
45	4727	24.45	98	14	3.07
46	4657	23.81	99	11	2.77
47	4588	23.16	100	9	2.28
48	4521	22.50	101	7	1.79
49	4458	21.81	102	5	1.30
50	4397	21.11	103	3	0.83
51	4338	20.39	104	1	0.50
52	4276	19.68	105	0	0.00

Index